Phil Edmonston

LEMON-AID
2007|08
USED CARS
and MINIVANS

W9-AJW-561

Phil Edmonston
LEMON-AID
2007|08
USED CARS and MINIVANS

Copyright © 2007 Les Editions Edmonston

Published in Canada by Fitzhenry and Whiteside Limited, 195 Allstate Parkway, Markham, Ontario L3R 4T8

All rights reserved. No part of this book may be reproduced in any manner without the express written consent of the publisher, except in the case of brief excerpts in critical reviews and articles. All inquiries should be addressed to:

www.fitzhenry.ca   godwit@fitzhenry.ca

1 3 5 7 9 10 8 6 4 2

Library and Archives Canada has catalogued this publication as follows:

Edmonston, Louis-Philippe, 1944–
Lemon-aid used cars and minivans / Phil Edmonston.

Annual.
2003–
Imprint varies.
Continues: Lemon-aid used cars, ISSN 1485-1121.
ISSN 1701-6908
ISBN 978-1-55455-039-5 (2007/2008 edition)

1. Used cars—Purchasing—Periodicals. 2. Vans—Purchasing--Periodicals.
I. Title.

TL162.E3398   629.222'2'05   C2002-900797-6

Fitzhenry & Whiteside acknowledges with thanks the Canada Council for the Arts, and the Ontario Arts Council for their support of our publishing program. We acknowledge the financial support of the Government of Canada through the Book Publishing Industry Development Program (BPIDP) for our publishing activities.

Printed in Canada by Webcom
Packaged by Colborne Communications, Toronto
Publications manager: Greg Ioannou
Project co-ordinator: Andrea Battiston
Layout and production: Jack Steiner
Editing: Jenny Govier, Andrea Douglas, Andrea Battiston, Greg Ioannou
Illustrations: Rachel Rosen
Design: Ingrid Paulson

CONTENTS

Appendix II

LEMON-PROOFING AND COST-CUTTING...... 583

Appendix III

INTERNET SLEUTHING 593

KEY DOCUMENTS

Lemon-Aid is a feisty owner's manual that has no equal anywhere. We don't want you stuck with a lemon, or to wind up paying for repairs that are the automaker's fault and are covered by secret "goodwill" warranties. That's why we are the only book that includes many hard-to-find, confidential, and little-known documents that automakers don't want you to see.

In short, we know you can't win what you can't prove.

The following charts, documents, and service bulletins are included in this index so that you can stand your ground and be treated fairly. Photocopy and circulate whichever document will prove helpful in your dealings with automakers, dealers, service managers, insurance companies, or government agencies. Remember, most of the hundreds of summarized service bulletins outline repairs or replacements that should be done for free.

Introduction

BEATING THE SYSTEM

Part One

DEALERS AND DOLLARS

Part Two

JUSTICE AND INJUSTICE

Part Three

1970–2006 WINNERS AND LOSERS

SMALL CARS

Appendix III

INTERNET SLEUTHING

Introduction
BEATING THE SYSTEM

Say NO to New

A decade ago, says Toronto automobile analyst Dennis DesRosiers, the average cost of a new car was equal to 20 weeks' gross income for a typical Canadian worker. Now, that figure is up to 31 weeks. Partly as a result, sales of new cars and light trucks totalled 1.2 million in 1995, lower than at any time since 1983. The affordability issue is one reason why sales of used cars are booming.

TOM FENNELL
MACLEAN'S
MARCH 18, 1996

Millionaires Know Best

Thirty-seven percent of millionaires buy used cars, which is one reason why they're so well off.

DWIGHT R. LEE AND RICHARD B. MCKENZIE
GETTING RICH IN AMERICA

Forget trusts, RRSPs, offshore tax shelters, Prime Minister Harper's "green" car rebates, or brown-bagging your lunch. Save money the easy way by not spending it on a new car or minivan in the first place—a smart choice made by 58.8 percent of Canadian car buyers in 2006.

Lemon-Aid Used Cars and Minivans 2007–08 reveals how buying a used car or minivan will put over $20,000 in your pocket, right now.

This windfall represents over half of the average $30,000 purchase price. It's made up of interest savings, cheaper insurance costs, no $1,500 freight charge, more than $1,500 in GST tax savings if bought privately, and no $500 dealer "administrative" fee.

And there has never been a better time to buy used.

Cars and minivans are cheaper and safer than ever because recently announced federal government new-car rebates and Chrysler's new owners, Cerberus, are driving all prices down; there is an abundant supply of post-2002 off-lease and off-fleet vehicles; crashworthiness scores are at an all-time high; a wide variety of standard safety features have been added; and quality has improved markedly during the past five years among both American and South Korean makes.

More Than a Car Guide

Lemon-Aid Used Cars and Minivans 2007–08 is more than a guide to the best and worst vehicles sold over the past 36 years. It's a practical owner's manual that lists real prices, shows which repairs are covered by secret warranties, and uses confidential manufacturer service bulletins and government logs of owner complaints to predict which safety- and performance-related problems you are likely to experience with each model.

That's why *Lemon-Aid* is such a popular annual guide: It kicks automakers in their tailpipes as it exposes the industry's lies, obfuscations, and deceptions to even out the playing field. Sure, this book is 600 pages long, but we need that much space to keep service managers honest by publishing the actual confidential service bulletins that give you free "goodwill" repairs. *Lemon-Aid* is a uniquely Canadian consumers' guide that's been a bestseller for over 36 years because it pulls no punches in disclosing what's a fair price, which cars and minivans are good buys and which should be avoided, which post-warranty repairs are the automakers' responsibility, and how you can spot sales and repair scams.

Secret Warranties

Car owners are fed up with cars that don't shift properly, overheat from faulty engine head gaskets, or require constant brake caliper and rotor replacements. Adding further to their misery, they often find out, after shelling out thousands of dollars, that secret "goodwill" warranties could have paid for their engine, transmission, and other repairs.

Who gets these free repairs?

They're mainly readers who use internal service bulletins from *Lemon-Aid* to prove that a failure is factory-related and, ipso facto, the manufacturer's responsibility. Carefully peruse all the bulletins concerning free repairs found throughout this book. Does one apply to your car? Or your neighbours' cars? Take copies to the dealer, but don't be shocked if the service manager and automaker lie through their teeth, denying these bulletins' existence—until you threaten to file in small claims court, that is.

Honda, Lexus, and Toyota Transmissions

Many Toyota and Lexus models, as well as Honda's venerable Civic and Odyssey, have serious automatic transmission flaws. To their credit, these automakers usually repair the problem for free under a "goodwill" policy, no questions asked.

2001–04 HONDA CIVIC DOESN'T MOVE IN DRIVE

BULLETIN NO.: 04-036   DATE: JULY 13, 2004

SYMPTOM: The vehicle cannot move when you select Drive. The MIL comes on ('01–03 models) or the D indicator blinks ('04 models) with A/T DTC P0730 (shift control system) set.
PROBABLE CAUSE: Excessive wear in the 2nd clutch.
VEHICLES AFFECTED: 2001–04 Civic 2-door and 4-door with A/T. **CORRECTIVE ACTION:** Replace the A/T. Use the Honda Interface Module (HIM) to update the PCM software ('01–03 models only).

Nevertheless, for the past five years, Toyota has had a delayed transmission engagement and engine surging defect on many models that is both hazardous and annoying. Toyota has tried numerous software and hardware fixes, yet the problem continues to occur.

TOYOTA ENGINE CONTROLS—A/T DOWNSHIFT LAG/GEAR HUNTING

BULLETIN NO.: TC005-05   DATE: JUNE 21, 2005

ECM CALIBRATION: SHIFT FEELING ENHANCEMENT
2004–05 Camry
To improve the transmission shift feeling during specific operating modes, the Engine Control Module (SAE term: Powertrain Control Module/PCM) calibration has been revised. These improvements include:
• Reduced downshift lag when accelerating at speeds from 10 to 20 mph [16–32 km/h].
• Less gear hunting when driving on/off accelerator pedal at 20 to 30 mph [32–48 km/h] (for example: during heavy rush-hour traffic).
• Improved response rate during heavy acceleration from a stop.

For a full listing of bulletins and copies of bulletins that may be helpful to you, look in each car model's rating in Part Three, or check the Key Documents list.

Using a manufacturer's own bulletins to prove you're right won't win you friends in Detroit, Stuttgart, or Tokyo. I'll never forget the time, three decades ago, when Ford's goons threw me out of Toronto's auto show after I published Ford's internal bulletins and demanded that the company extend its secret American rust repair warranty to Canadians. Three years later, the company relented and paid out almost $3 million in refunds to members of the Rusty Ford Association, a group organized by the Automobile Protection Association—and I had founded both groups.

Lemon-Aid isn't just about fallen American and Japanese car quality. European automakers let their owners down, too. Their products aren't half as good as their hype; they do well only because they spend millions of dollars on a fawning North American motoring press corps and market their vehicles to insecure social climbers with more money than brains. Want to know why Germans prefer Lexus to Mercedes-Benz? Go to Part Three, or surf the websites recommended in Appendix III.

Independent Information

Lemon-Aid's goal for over 36 years has been to keep auto ownership costs low, to promote safe and reliable vehicles, and to make automakers and dealers more honest and accountable—even as they hire lawyers and PR flacks to plead that peeling paint is caused by bird poo and rotten-egg exhaust smells can be cured with a tune-up. This guide continues a tradition of publicizing abusive auto industry practices and providing hard-to-get information that may save your life, or at least protect your wallet.

Lemon-Aid's information is biased in favour of its Canadian sources—particularly reports from owners who buy and drive these vehicles—not travel-junket-junkie, free-car-mongering car columnists. We have over two dozen provincial correspondents scattered throughout Canada. Our database also includes U.S. sources and is refined throughout the year with information gathered from owner complaints, automaker whistle-blowers, lawsuits and judgments, confidential Technical Service Bulletins (TSBs), and independent garages.

We combine test results with owner feedback to provide a critical comparison of the many cars and minivans sold during the past three decades. If improvements and additional safety features don't justify the higher costs of newer models (and most don't), then we say so. Safer, more reliable, and often cheaper alternatives are given for each vehicle, and reliability and crashworthiness ratings are shown for each model year.

Paying a fair price is crucial now that rebates, low-percentage new-car financing, and subsidized 3- and 5-year leases have driven used prices to new lows. Fully loaded off-lease vehicles and used rentals have the potential to be veritable bargains—but only if you know what to buy and how to use depreciation timing to your advantage (Ford Crown Vic, yes; front-drive Cadillacs, no; recent Hyundai and Kia models, yes; Saturn, no; Honda Odyssey, yes; Nissan Quest and some Toyota Siennas, no).

Finally, for frugal readers, this year's guide includes a helpful appendix that rates the best vehicles starting at $1,000; tips on reaching the 10-year/250,000 km mark without spending a fortune; a list of the perils posed by used hybrids; and reasons why diesel-equipped vehicles are risky buys.

As always, *Lemon-Aid*'s around 600 pages give you current information and exact duplicates of troubleshooting service bulletins. With these tools, you won't pay for factory mistakes, and defects can be diagnosed quickly and correctly by cheaper independent repair agencies.

Lemon-Aid makes you a smart shopper and a smart driver. By knowing what to buy, how much to pay, and which repairs should be free, your dollar will go much further and servicing disputes will be kept to a minimum.

Phil Edmonston
May 2007

Part One
DEALERS AND DOLLARS

Pay to Save?

People want economy and they will pay any price to get it.

LEE IACOCCA

NEW YORK TIMES

OCTOBER 13, 1974

Used Cars Are Big Business

Dealers make more money selling used vehicles than they make selling new cars. Used-vehicle prices are more easily manipulated (there's no such thing as a "manufacturer's suggested retail price"), and used-car purchasers are often more docile than new-car shoppers (they are less informed about their choices and more in need of immediate transportation). About 20–23 percent of consumers replace their vehicle each year, with over one-third buying another vehicle from a private owner and almost two-thirds buying through a dealer.

Even rental agencies are in the used-car business.

Dealers get their vehicles from fleets, lessees, wholesalers, trade-ins, and private sales. Chrysler, GM, and Ford dealers generally have an abundance of "young" used vehicles for sale, while dealers selling import brands are chronically short of product because owners keep these vehicles three to four years longer. Interestingly, the majority of private sales comprise vehicles six years or older, while independent used car dealers get most of their profit from selling vehicles that are six to 10 years old or are nearly new.

There are 19.3 million cars on Canada's roads, and they're all used. The transformation from new to used occurs as soon as the sales contract is signed. This creates a huge pool of less expensive used vehicles for buyers to choose from.

What Canadians buy, however, is quite different from what Americans choose. For example, we are more conservative in the types and sizes of vehicles we buy, with 51 percent of Canadians opting for small cars. Minivans are also more popular north of the border, and they don't carry the soccer mom stigma fuelling American crossover wagon sales. Canadians also don't care if a car hails from Oakville, Ontario, or Oaxaca, Mexico, as long as it's cheap and reliable. Finally, we're reluctant to trade in a vehicle that suits our needs just because it's old. In fact, almost 51 percent of Canadians keep cars and trucks nine years or more, 50 percent of the vehicles purchased 15 years ago are still on the road today, and one-quarter of light trucks are still on the road after 20 years of operation, according to Toronto-based auto consultant Dennis DesRosiers.

The Honda Civic is Canada's favourite small car, but the popularity of the better-equipped Accord has softened new and used Civic prices by about $500. In the States, it's the larger Toyota Camry that rules the small car roost. Downsized SUVs—such as the Subaru Forester, the Honda CR-V, and the Toyota RAV4—make up almost half of our small car market, but only account for one-quarter of the sales south of the border. As far as minivans go, we believe that less is more and, therefore, favour small imports over Detroit's truck-based rear-drives.

Car owners are driving more than ever, despite higher fuel prices. The used-fleet mileage has almost doubled within the past 30 years. Back in the '70s, the average car racked up 160,000 km before it was dropped off at the junkyard. In the '90s, the average car reached 240,000 km before it was recycled. Nowadays, new models are expected to see 300,000 km before they're discarded.

And most cars and minivans are more reliable than ever before (with a few Detroit exceptions). One Canadian Automobile Association (CAA) ownership survey revealed that less than 10 percent of Canadians who owned cars five years old or younger got rid of them because of reliability problems or high maintenance costs.

Far more common reasons for selling a car five years old or younger were as follows: 43 percent were sold because the lease had expired, 30 percent of owners said they just wanted a change, and 21 percent felt the vehicle no longer met their requirements. Only 22 percent of survey participants who owned vehicles six to 10 years old got rid of them due to reliability problems.

There are lots of reasons why it's a great time to buy a used car or minivan—as long as you stay away from some of the rotten products. Fortunately, there's not as much late-'70s and early-'80s junk out there as there once was, and vehicles are now safer and come loaded with extra convenience and performance features. Additionally, there's a lot of cheap product to choose from as dealers cut prices in response to pressure from the zero percent interest programs and unrealistically high residual values used to keep new-car monthly payments small.

Even Chrysler's little Neon went from a dim bulb to a bright light, beginning with the 2000 model year.

But dealers aren't giving anything away. Popular, fuel-efficient, 3-year-old small cars are selling at a bit less than two-thirds of their original price and aren't likely to depreciate much over the next few years, although federal green rebates are softening used prices by a few hundred dollars. Smart shoppers are buying downsized vehicles or going to the South Koreans to keep costs manageable. Rather than getting a Ford Focus or Buick LeSabre, buyers are opting for family sedans, crossover wagons like the Mazda5, and small cars from Daewoo, Hyundai, and Kia.

But lower fuel consumption and cheaper prices aren't the only factors to consider. Vehicle quality and dependability are equally important. Sure, you can prance around telling your friends how you "stole" that used GM Venture/Montana or Ford Windstar/Freestar—until you have to spend $3,500 for engine or transmission work (or both, in GM's case). Granted, some of the junk is fairly well known, and vehicles are safer now; however, many Detroit models are loaded with non-essential convenience and performance features that fail around the fifth year of ownership. Chief among these are navigation systems, adaptive cruise control, ABS brakes, and sunroofs.

Luxury Lemons

But let's not just pick on Ford, GM, and Chrysler. European automakers make their share of lemons as well. For example, J.D. Power and Associates has consistently ranked Mercedes' quality as worse than average.

If, however, you have been a steady reader of *Lemon-Aid* over the past 36 years, you've been wary of Mercedes' poor quality for almost a decade and probably saved money buying a Lincoln Town Car or Toyota Avalon instead. BMW owners have proven to be some of the most satisfied with their cars' overall dependability when compared with most other European makes, including Audi, Volkswagen, and Volvo.

Lincoln's front-drive Continental (a failure-prone Taurus in disguise), and Mercedes' unreliable entry-level cars and SUVs are proof positive that there's absolutely no correlation between safe, dependable transportation and the amount of money a vehicle costs. In fact, almost the opposite conclusion could be reached with front-drive Ford and GM luxury cars. Rear-drive Lincolns and Cadillacs, however, have always performed well after many years. Recent Chrysler luxury rear-drives like the 300 and Magnum have turned in a mixed performance and have been on the market for a relatively short time. In general, Japanese luxury cars that originally retailed from $25,000 to $35,000 and have been on the market for a few years are far better buys used than most luxury cars costing twice as much. Again, J.D. Power and *Consumer Reports* confirm this fact.

Three Decades of Success and Failure

Smart buys

Acura—Integra
Chrysler—Avenger, Colt, recent Neons, Sebring, and Stealth
Ford—Crown Victoria, Escort, Grand Marquis, Mustang, and Probe
GM—Astro, Aveo, Camaro, Firebird, and Safari
Honda—Accord, Civic, CR-V, and Odyssey
Hyundai—Accent, Elantra, and Tiburon
Lincoln—the Mark series and Town Car
Mazda—323, 626, Mazda3, Mazda5, Mazda6, Miata, MX-6, and Protegé
Nissan—510, Axxess, and Sentra
Suzuki—Aerio and Swift
Toyota—Avalon, Camry, Corolla, Cressida, Echo, Sienna, and Tercel

Dumb buys

Chrysler—Concorde, Horizon, Intrepid, LHS, all minivans, early Neons, New Yorker, Omni, Shadow, Sprinter, and Sundance
Daewoo—all models
Ford—Aerostar, Contour, Focus, Mystique, Sable, Taurus, Tempo, Topaz, and Windstar/Freestar
GM—Astre, Catera, Cimarron, Corvette, Fiero, Firenza, J-body cars, Lumina/Montana/Trans Sport/Venture, Vega, and X-body cars
Hyundai—Excel, Pony, early Sonatas, and Stellar
Infiniti—G20
Jaguar—all models
Kia—all models up to 2005
Lada—all models
Lexus—ES series
Lincoln—Continental front-drive
Mercedes-Benz—190, C-Class, and M series
Merkur—all models
Nissan—240Z, 250Z, 260Z, Altima, B210, Maxima, and Quest
Saab—all models
Saturn—all models
Suzuki—Samurai and X-90
VW—Eurovan, Passat, Rabbit, and all diesels

Note in the list above how frequently so-called premium luxury brands have fallen out of favour and have been orphaned by shoppers, then abandoned by the automakers themselves, leaving early purchasers with unreliable cars that can't be properly serviced.

Also, keep in mind that many Honda, Toyota, and Nissan vehicles have had a resurgence of engine and transmission problems, in addition to an apparent overall decline in reliability. For example, Nissan engineers have been working overtime during the past few years to correct Altima, Maxima, Quest, and Titan glitches. As they capture more of the market share, it seems the Asian automakers are coasting on their earlier reputations and cutting quality, thereby committing the same mistake Detroit did years ago. Nevertheless, they are still far ahead of the American automakers in terms of quality control and publicly disclosing "good-will" extended warranties.

Barbarians at Chrysler's Gates

Chrysler is finished. Head office administrators, dealers, and suppliers are running for the hills while flashing that "I'm all right, Jack" smile. They know Chrysler's new owner doesn't know beans about running an auto company and that the true target of the purchase is money-making Chrysler Financial.

This May, DaimlerChrysler sold the Chrysler Group for $7.4 billion in a desperate move to unload the $36 billion lemon it purchased just nine years ago. The buyer, Cerberus Capital Management, is a private equity firm fronted by George W. Bush's former Secretary of the Treasury, John Snow, and George H.W. Bush's Vice President (and noted English grammarian), Dan Quayle (Dan, can you spell "vulture investor"?).

This sale will cut the ranks of the dealer body by a quarter, drive new and used car prices down, stifle new vehicle development, and likely lead to the company's Jeep and minivan divisions being spun-off to China.

These changes will have some positive and some negative effects for auto owners everywhere.

All new and used vehicle prices will plummet as Chrysler dealers unload their stockpile of unsold cars and trucks at fire-sale prices so they can close their dealerships with a few loonies in their pockets. Chrysler's giveaway prices will spark a brutal price war that will further destabilize Ford and GM and force Asian automakers to cut their prices as well.

All of this price-cutting will make cars and trucks at least 15–20 percent cheaper than they are now. However, servicing will become more problematic as the dealers and parts supply dry up, and trade-in values will decline because no one will want a vehicle that's not backed by a legitimate automaker or an ironclad warranty.

Vehicle quality will worsen; warranty disputes will be legion; supplier, dealer, and customer lawsuits will be pandemic; and Cerberus will fade away, leaving union workers, dealers, suppliers, and customers holding the bag.

The last act of this fiasco and subterfuge will have Canadian Auto Workers president Buzz Hargrove asking for federal bailout funds, all the while repeating ad nauseam "I got the best deal I could" to angry CAW members left holding the bag, while former DaimlerChrysler CEO Jürgen Schrempp walks away from the deal hold a different bag—one stuffed with cash from the money he'll earn off the Cerberus deal (estimated at $100 million plus).

Jeep's four-door Wrangler is a bestseller that will easily survive Chrysler's suicide.

So what's a smart consumer strategy?

First, hold onto your Jeep or your Chrysler minivan, or buy one if the price is tempting; values should stay relatively stable, and servicing won't be much of a problem due to the large number of independent garages that can fix these vehicles using the tons of available generic parts. However, recent-model trucks; vehicles equipped with diesel engines; the Crossfire, with its mixture of Chrysler and Mercedes parts; and the new Sebring and Caliber will likely have serious servicing problems. Keep away, sell what you have, or scout out a resourceful and competent independent repair facility.

As far as warranty disputes go, it's unclear what Cerberus' liability will be. Of course, selling dealers can be named as co-defendants, but if the dealer shuts down, you may be left without any recourse. Small claims court, with its quick case turnover and high claimant threshold, is your best bet for getting compensation before all assets disappear.

Dangerous Junk

There is presently a lot of hand-wringing over Chrysler's takeover by Cerberus and the possible auctioning off or bankruptcy of Ford and General Motors. Frankly, I have little sympathy for these automakers. Their wounds are self-inflicted. And they were warned repeatedly over the past three decades, by *Lemon-Aid* and by independent journalists, that the dangerous junk they were selling and their cheapskate warranty handouts would lead to their downfall.

I've spent more than 36 years battling automakers and dealers who lie through their teeth as they try to convince customers, financial analysts, and journalists that their vehicles are well made and that the "few" defects reported are caused mainly by the proverbial nut behind the wheel, poor maintenance, or abusive driving. That's why the auto industry has such a lousy reputation—car owners know better. The average Canadian either has personally experienced the lying, cheating, and stealing that's so rampant at all levels of the automotive manufacturing and marketing processes, or knows someone who has.

Chrysler Automatic Transmissions

For almost two decades, practically all models in Chrysler's lineup have had disposable automatic transmissions. What adds insult to injury, though, is that Chrysler regularly stiffs its customers with transmission repair bills that average about $3,000—about a third of what the average vehicle is worth. Since this is far less than what a new car or minivan would cost, most owners pay the bill and hop onto the transmission merry-go-round, replacing the same transmission at regular intervals. Go ahead, ask any transmission shop.

Ford Diesels and Firestone Tires

Ford is even worse. After years of stonewalling and rejecting owner refund claims for faulty 6.0L diesel engines found on most of its trucks, the automaker now says the engines were crap and refuses to pay International Engine Group for the defective diesels. In retaliation, International has halted shipments of the new 6.4L diesel destined for the 2007 pickups, many of which have already been ordered by Ford customers. Ironic, isn't it? Ford is now doing to International what many angry owners of Powerstroke 6.0L diesel-equipped trucks threatened to do to Ford. And, as in the Ford Explorer/Firestone Tire debacle, neither company will ever admit guilt, or simply apologize to owners, for their shoddy product.

Tire blowouts are especially deadly with SUVs and pickups because these vehicles have a high tendency to roll over.

Firestone wasn't an aberration; it was a microcosm of what goes on throughout the industry. When the tires started shredding in other countries and injuries and deaths started to mount, Ford used a secret warranty program to pay off Explorer owners in South America and the Middle East. When the media discovered the cover-up, Ford lied to both customers and officials, saying either that the company wasn't aware of the tire failures or that it was all Firestone's fault. Both excuses were shot down in subsequent probes carried out in Saudi Arabia and Venezuela.

The Venezuelan federal Institute for the Defense and Education of the Consumer and the User (INDECU) recommended in September 2000 that both Firestone and Ford face criminal charges for their roles in creating and using defective tires that have led to at least 47 deaths in that country since 1998.

General Motors Engine Intake Manifold Gaskets

Afflicting most of GM's lineup since 1994, intake manifold gasket failures cause engine oil or coolant leaks and can cost from $1,000 to $5,000 to repair if the engine is overheated. Following *Lemon-Aid*'s prodding a few years ago, Ford of Canada made public its secret warranty to repair faulty engine intake manifolds on vehicles going back to 1996 and re-opened its compensation program applicable to Ford and Lincoln V8 engines. Although that second extended warranty has expired, owners who threaten small claims court litigation are still getting some money back because Ford's admission of liability through its own press release permits judges to award additional refunds.

Unlike Ford, General Motors won't admit anything publicly, even though its own service bulletins candidly admit that most of the intake manifold gaskets are poorly designed, and independent gasket suppliers like Federal-Mogul confirm the fact (see bulletin below).

GM's stubborn refusal to accept blame and pay owner claims has produced one of the largest class actions ever brought against an automaker in Canada. Seeking $1.2 billion (CDN) in damages, the lawsuit was filed in Toronto on June 20, 2006, by Stevensons LLP on behalf of an estimated 400,000 owners of 1995 through 2004 model year vehicles equipped with 3.1, 3.4, 3.8, or 4.3L engines. (Stevensons LLP: Colin Stevenson 416-599-7900 and Harvin Pitch, Counsel, 416-865-5310; Borden Ladner Gervais LLP: Robert Bell 416-367-6160 and Paulette Pommells 416-367-6631; Koskie Minsky LLP: Kirk Baert 416-595-2117, Jonathan Ptak 416-595-2149, and David Rosenfeld 416-595-2700; *Kenneth David Stewart v. General Motors of Canada Limited and General Motors Corporation*, Ontario Superior Court of Justice, Court File No. 06-CV-310082PDI, June 20, 2006, Amended Statement of Claim.)

The above-cited Canadian action includes an important affidavit from Clemente Alejandro Mesa, engineer and expert witness for the plaintiffs against General Motors in a similar American class action: *Michael Amico, David Paolini, and Mark Glover v. General Motors Corporation*, Superior Court of the State of Arizona in and for the County of Maricopa, Case No. CV2004-092816 (Johnson Rasmussen Robinson & Allen PLC, Mesa, Arizona, 480-964-1421; Levy, Ram & Olson LLP, San Francisco, California, 415-433-4949).

Expert witness Mesa's report makes the following conclusions:

> 15. GM engineering modified the basic nylon and silicone gasket construction and related engine assembly procedures several times from 1997 to 2005 in unsuccessful attempts to address the increasing failure rated. The modifications included the addition of compression limiters, various silicone formulations and virgin nylon for the carrier. The gasket carrier was eventually changed

GM'S REDESIGNED ENGINE INTAKE MANIFOLD AND GASKETS

BULLETIN NO.: 04-06-01-017   DATE: MAY 26, 2004

NEW UPPER INTAKE MANIFOLD AND GASKET KITS

1995–1997 Buick Riviera; 1995–2004 Buick Park Avenue; 1996–2004 Buick Regal; 1997–2004 Buick LeSabre; 1998–1999 Chevrolet Lumina; 1998–2004 Chevrolet Monte Carlo; 2000–2004 Chevrolet Impala; 1995–1996 Oldsmobile Ninety-Eight; 1995–1999 Oldsmobile Eighty-Eight; 1998–1999 Oldsmobile Intrigue; 1995–2004 Pontiac Bonneville; and 1997–2003 Pontiac Grand Prix. All with 3.8L V6 engines.

OVERVIEW: New upper intake manifold and gasket kits have been released. These new kits will provide the dealer with the ability to get exactly what is necessary for a correct repair. **In addition some of the gaskets have been updated to a more robust design.** Please reference the part numbers when ordering from GMSPO.

to metal, and the sealing to an edge-bonded bead. Timing for this introduction of the several gasket part numbers is not available, but is believed to have taken place in 2005. GMAMICO0000014656-61 dated August 6, 2002 (Exhibit L).

. . .

18. By 2002, high warranty repair rates and service issues mounted with a high cost to GM, which perhaps was doubled that for customers out of warranty. Service and OE parts availability appear to have been under stress at GM dealers for the increasing number of gasket repairs and short service parts supply, although aftermarket parts seem to have been readily available from several manufacturers for post-warranty repairs. GMAMICO0000014658, dated uncertain, believed August 6, 2002 (Exhibit W).

This cheap engine gasket may bankrupt GM.

19. It appears GM attempted to keep what GM engineering had learned about the gasket failures from its customers. A GM Service Know-How VHS tape dated July 2000 labeled "Understanding Radiator Cap and Cooling System Contamination Issues" (Exhibit X) states that better-maintained fleet vehicles do not exhibit the same level of cooling system contamination and brings up retail customer inadequate maintenance of the coolant level, in fact contradicted by internal GM document GMAMICO0000050423 (Exhibit Y).

20. Federal-Mogul document FM-004114 dated 10/25/2004 (Exhibit Z) states, "GM has contacted us and complained about our press release for the intake gaskets. They claim they don't have a problem and our press release will cause them problems concerning the lawsuits. I was asked to supply some basic information on our testing."

Conclusions

21. In my expert opinion, the design of the GM lower manifold gasket was fundamentally flawed with all iterations of its design intended to address its deficiencies failing to provide acceptable service life. The gasket design deficiencies presented an unreasonable risk of gasket and even engine failures to customers that purchased GMC vehicles equipped with engines using this gasket design, along with the associated risk and expense, something a reasonable GMC customer would not have been aware of.

22. There is no technical reason why GM could not have adopted a more robust gasket design with more appropriate materials, as adopted by other original equipment manufacturers, both domestic and foreign, as well as aftermarket producers, for example by using a stamped metal carrier with over-molded beads of sealing materials more suitable for the fluids.

Four Decades of Deception and Defects

Think of bad cars of the '60s, and the Ralph Nader–targeted Chevrolet Corvair comes to mind. Yet by the time Nader's bestselling book *Unsafe at Any Speed* came out in 1965, the car's handling had been substantially improved. No, what killed the Corvair were GM's lies, cover-ups, and their stalking of Nader, who was a scheduled witness at upcoming Senate hearings on auto safety in February 1967.

"The requirement of a just social order," Nader told the senators, "is that responsibility shall lie where the power of decision rests. But the law has never caught up with the development of the large corporate unit. Deliberate acts emanate from the sprawling and indeterminable shelter of the corporate organization. Too often responsibility for an act is not imputable to those whose decision enables it to be set in motion."

Following Nader's testimony, GM President James M. Roche reluctantly admitted, after many denials, that his company—without his knowledge—had hired a private eye to peer into Nader's personal life by questioning over 50 of his friends and colleagues. Roche apologized twice to the Senate Committee and Nader and gave this assurance: "It will not be our policy in the future to undertake investigation of those who speak or write critically of our products."

GM then agreed to a $425,000 out of court settlement of Nader's lawsuit against the company for invasion of privacy. That money was subsequently used to finance many of Nader's non-profit public-interest groups, including the Center for Auto Safety, an organization that effectively forces automakers to correct safety defects and cease fraudulent activities.

The GM–Nader debacle is nothing new. Automakers have always been hostile to the most simple safety improvements. For example, GM President Frederic G. Donner told Congress in 1965 that turn signals and seat belts ought to remain optional features and not be required under federal regulations.

Dishonest practices, poor quality control, and a reckless disregard for public safety have always been a part of the automobile industry. When I founded the Automobile Protection Association in Montreal in the fall of 1969, American Motors was giving out free television sets with its new cars, and the TVs lasted longer than the Eagle (Ford gave free Dell computers to 2005 Focus buyers). Volkswagen had a monopoly on hazardous and poorly heated Beetles and, later, self-starting Rabbits. Ford was churning out disintegrating cars and trucks, and denying that it had a secret "J-67" warranty to cover rust repairs. Firestone was dragged, kicking and screaming, into announcing the recall of 11 million tires for catastrophic tread separation in the late '70s, and Chrysler's entire product line was rain-challenged—stalling and leaking in wet weather because of faulty ballast resistors, distributor caps, and rotors and misaligned body panels.

Japanese and European cars imported into Canada during the '70s were unreliable rustbuckets, yet they got a toehold in the North American car market because the Big Three's products were worse—and they still are. Seizing the opportunity, foreign automakers smartened up within a remarkably short period of time. They quickly began building reliable and durable cars and trucks, and offering them fully loaded and reasonably priced.

Meanwhile, American automakers continued pumping out dangerous and unreliable junk throughout the '90s—including GM's Chevy Vega, Firenza, and Fiero, as well as early Saturns, Cavaliers, Sunbirds, and the Lumina/Trans Sport minivan; Chrysler's Omni, Horizon, Dynasty, Imperial, Concorde, Neon, and post-'90 minivans; and Ford's Pinto, Bobcat, Tempo, Topaz, Taurus, Sable, Contour, Mystique (Mistake?), Merkur, Bronco, Explorer, and Windstar. Not surprisingly, sales continued to nosedive.

Then, in the early '90s, Detroit got a second chance to prove itself. The minivan carved out a popular new marketing niche, and American SUVs such as the Ford Explorer were piling up profits. But, as Micheline Maynard makes crystal clear in *The End of Detroit* (Doubleday, 2004), the American auto industry's arrogance disconnected its products from reality, and by focusing mainly on high-profit trucks and SUVs, Detroit abandoned average car buyers to the Japanese and the South Koreans:

> Foreign companies like Toyota and Honda solidified their dominance in family and economy cars, gained market share in high-margin luxury cars, and, in an ironic twist, soon stormed in with their own sophisticatedly engineered and marketed SUVs, pickups, and minivans. Detroit, suffering from a "good enough" syndrome and wedded to ineffective marketing gimmicks like rebates and zero-percent financing, failed to give consumers what they really wanted: reliability, the latest technology, and good design at a reasonable cost.

American automakers lost the knack for making quality machines three decades ago when they became more interested in the deal than the product. Suppliers of high-quality components were often rewarded with increased demands for price cuts and sudden changes in specifications. Quality dropped, and owner loyalty shifted to Asian automakers who used identical suppliers but treated them better.

Today, the Big Three's quality control is still way below average when compared with Japanese and South Korean automakers. Where the gap is particularly noticeable is in engine, automatic transmission, airbag, and anti-lock brake reliability, as well as fit and finish.

You can reduce your risk of buying a lemon by getting a used vehicle rated as "Recommended" in this guide—one that has some of the original warranty still in effect. This protects you from some of the costly defects that are bound to crop up shortly after your purchase. The warranty allows you to make one final inspection before it expires and requires both the dealer and the automaker to compensate you for all warrantable defects found at that time, even though they may not be fixed until after the warranty expires.

Why Canadians Buy Used

We buy used vehicles simply because new cars are too expensive. According to the Royal Bank of Canada (RBC), the average Canadian's take-home income hasn't kept pace with the rising costs of purchasing and owning a new vehicle. Read on to learn five more reasons why Canadians prefer to buy used vehicles from one another.

1. Less Initial Cash Outlay, Slower Vehicle Depreciation, "Secret" Warranty Repair Refunds, and Better and Cheaper Parts Availability

New-vehicle prices have moderated somewhat over the past few years, but they're still quite high—Dennis DesRosiers pegs the cost of an average new vehicle at over $31,200. Insurance is another wallet buster, costing about $2,500 a year for young drivers. And once you add financing costs, maintenance, taxes, and a host of other expenses, CAA calculates the yearly outlay for a medium-sized car at over $8,252, or 36.7 cents/km; trucks or SUVs may run you about 10 cents/km more. For a comprehensive, though depressing, comparative analysis (cars versus trucks, minivans, SUVs, etc.) of all the costs involved over one- to 10-year periods, access Alberta's consumer information website at *www.agric.gov.ab.ca/app24/costcalculators/ vehicle/getvechimpls.jsp.*

Used vehicles aren't sold with $900–$1,600 transport fees or $495 "administration" charges, either. And you can legally avoid paying some sales tax when you buy privately. That's right: You'll pay at least 10 percent less than the dealer's price and you may avoid the federal Goods and Services Tax (GST) that applies in some provinces to dealer sales only.

Depreciation savings

If someone were to ask you to invest in stocks or bonds guaranteed to be worth less than half their initial purchase value after three to four years, you'd probably head for the door.

But this is exactly the trap you're falling into when you buy a new vehicle that will likely lose 60 percent of its value after three years of use (minivans and other specialty vehicles, like sport-utilities and trucks, depreciate more slowly). Here's how that would work out in Ontario:

COST OF A NEW VEHICLE	
Purchase (2003 Honda Accord EX)	$28,000
Federal GST (7 percent)	$1,960
Provincial tax (8 percent)	$2,240
Total price	**$32,200**

When you buy used, the situation is altogether different. That same vehicle can be purchased four years later, in good condition and with much of the manufacturer's warranty remaining, for less than half its original cost. Look at what happens to the price:

COST OF A USED VEHICLE

Purchase price (2003 Honda Accord EX, four years old, 80,000 km)	$14,000
No GST (if sold privately)	—
Provincial tax (8 percent)	$1,120
Total price	**$15,120**

In this example, the Accord buyer saves $14,000 on the selling price, $1,960 in federal taxes, and $1,120 in provincial taxes, and gets a reliable, guaranteed set of wheels. Furthermore, the depreciation hit will be negligible in the ensuing years.

Secret warranty refunds

Almost all automakers use secret "goodwill" warranties to cover factory-related defects long after the original warranty has expired. This creates a huge fleet of used vehicles eligible for free repairs.

We're not talking about merely a few months' extension on small items. In fact, some free repairs—like those related to Mercedes engine sludge and GM diesel engines—are authorized up to 10 years or more as part of "goodwill" programs. Still, most secret warranty extensions hover around the 5- to 7-year mark and seldom cover vehicles exceeding 160,000 km (100,000 mi.). This benchmark includes engine and transmission defects affecting Detroit's Big Three, Honda, Hyundai, Lexus, and Toyota. Ford's 1995–98 Windstars carry a little-known 10-year warranty extension covering front coil spring breakage and free tire replacement if a tire is punctured.

NHTSA CAMPAIGN ID NUMBER: 01I007000

DEFECT SUMMARY: This is not a safety defect in accordance with the safety act. However, it is deemed a safety improvement campaign by the agency. Vehicle description: 1995–1998 Ford Windstar Minivans. The front coil springs could potentially fracture due to corrosion.
CONSEQUENCE SUMMARY: Some tires have deflated due to contact with a broken spring.
CORRECTIVE SUMMARY: Ford is extending the warranty for front coil spring replacement to a total of 10 years of service from the warranty start date, with unlimited mileage. This coverage is automatically transferred to subsequent owners at no charge. If either front coil spring fractures during the coverage period noted above, the dealer will replace both springs at no charge to the owner.

Knowing which free repairs apply to your car will cut maintenance costs dramatically.

Incidentally, automakers and dealers claim that there are no secret warranties, since they are all published in service bulletins. Although this is technically correct, have you ever tried to get a copy of a service bulletin? Or—if you did manage to get a copy—did the dealer or automaker say the benefits are applicable only in the States? Oh yeah!

Parts

Used parts can have a surprisingly long lifespan. Generally, a new gasoline-powered car or minivan can be expected to run with few problems for at least 200,000–300,000 km (125,000–200,000 mi.) in its lifetime, and a diesel-powered vehicle can easily double those figures. Some repairs will crop up at regular intervals, and, along with preventive maintenance, your yearly running costs should average about $800. Buttressing the argument that vehicles get cheaper to operate the longer you keep them, the U.S. Department of Transportation (DOT) points out that the average vehicle requires one or more major repairs after every five years of use. Once these repairs are done, however, the vehicle can then be run relatively trouble-free for another five years or more, as long as the environment isn't too hostile. In fact, the farther west you go in Canada, the longer owners keep their vehicles—an average of 10 years or more in some provinces.

Time is on your side in other ways, too. Three years after a model's launching, the replacement-parts market usually catches up to consumer demand. Dealers stock larger inventories, and parts wholesalers and independent parts manufacturers expand their output.

Used replacement parts are unquestionably easier to come by after this three-year point through bargaining with local garages, carefully searching auto wreckers' yards, or looking on the Internet. And a reconditioned or used part usually costs one-third to one-half the price of a new part. There's generally no difference in the quality of reconditioned mechanical components, and they're often guaranteed for as long as, or longer than, new ones. In fact, some savvy shoppers use the ratings in Part Three of this guide to see which parts have a short life and then buy those parts from retailers who give lifetime warranties on their brakes, exhaust systems, tires, batteries, etc.

Buying from discount outlets or independent garages, or ordering through mail-order houses, can save you big bucks (30–35 percent) on the cost of new parts and another 15 percent on labour when compared with dealer charges. Costco is another good source of savings realized through independent retailers. The retailer sells competitively priced replacement tires and offers free rotation, balancing, and other inspections during the life of the tire.

Body parts are a different story. Although car company repair parts cost 60 percent more than certified generic aftermarket parts, buyers would be wise to buy only original equipment manufacturer (OEM) parts supplied by automakers in order to get body panels that fit well, protect better in collisions, and have maximum rust resistance, says *Consumer Reports* magazine in its February 1999 study. Insurance appraisers often substitute cheaper, lower-quality aftermarket body parts in collision repairs, but *Consumer Reports* found that 71 percent of those policyholders who requested OEM parts got them with little or no hassle. It suggests that consumers complain to their provincial Superintendent of Insurance if OEM parts aren't provided. Ontario car owners have filed a class action lawsuit against that province's major insurers, alleging that making repairs with non-OEM parts is an unsafe practice and that it violates insureds' rights.

With some European models, you can count on a lot of aggravation and expense caused by the unacceptably slow distribution of parts and the high markup. Because these companies have a quasi-monopoly on replacement parts, there are few independent suppliers you can turn to for help. And junkyards, the last-chance repository for inexpensive car parts, are unlikely to carry foreign parts for vehicles that are more than three years old or are manufactured in small numbers.

Finding parts for Japanese and domestic cars and vans is no problem because of the large number of vehicles produced, the presence of hundreds of independent suppliers, the ease with which relatively simple parts can be interchanged from one model to another, and the large reservoir of used parts stocked by junkyards.

2. Insurance Costs Less

The price you pay for insurance can vary significantly, not only between insurance companies but also within the same company, over time. But one thing does remain constant: The insurance for used vehicles is a lot cheaper than new-car coverage, and through careful comparison shopping, insurance premium payouts can be substantially reduced.

This is especially important with young shoppers buying their first used car, as Pete Whittington writes from Waterloo, Ontario:

I bought *Lemon-Aid Used Cars and Minivans* about two weeks before purchasing my first car. It gave me important tips on "what to look for" and "how to negotiate." I felt more comfortable with my decisions and was able to shave a few thousand dollars off the purchase price. However, when I finally agreed to buy the car, I was at a loss as to what came next—but at least the hard part was done. I knew I needed licence plates and insurance but wasn't sure if I was responsible for that, or the dealer. I consulted my parents and friends and found out that I needed to arrange to have insurance in place before my car could be registered with the [MTO].

I got some Internet insurance quotes (about $2,000 a year) and then called my parents' insurance company (who insured me when I drove my parents' cars) and they wanted double what the online quotes offered! Essentially it boiled down to when I received my full G licence, as opposed to my G2. (Ontario has a graduated licensing program.) Because I waited to take my G test, as far as my parents' insurance company was concerned I had only had my license for three years, not seven (i.e., starting when I got my G2). I called the company (RBC Insurance) who gave me the cheaper online quote and they recognized my pre-G2 time and credited me with a seven year clean record. I then asked them to fax all the insurance info to the dealer to complete the registration process. Remember, the fax is only valid for 30 days or basically until the permanent "pink" card comes in the mail and be prepared to pay up front for two months worth of insurance.

The registration process cost me $45 because of when my birthday was in the year, so expect to pay upwards of $100 to get registered if your birthday has just past. This price is in addition to the negotiated price—so don't be shocked, it isn't really a hidden fee, every year near your birthday you will have to re-register your car (the little stickers you see on licence plates).

The dealer also paid for the car's mandatory safety inspection.

Beware of "captive" brokers

Although the cost of insurance premiums for used cars is often one-third to one-half the cost of the premiums you would pay for a new vehicle, using the Internet to find the lowest auto insurance quote and accepting a large deductible are critical to keeping premiums low.

The Consumers' Association of Canada's (CAC) national study on auto insurance rates, released July 19, 2005, found that consumers in Ontario paid 45 percent more for their auto insurance than B.C. drivers did. The average auto insurance rate in Ontario was $2,383, while in B.C., it was $1,324.

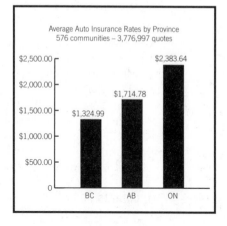

Average Auto Insurance Rates by Province
576 communities – 3,776,997 quotes

These extraordinarily high rates were charged throughout Ontario. In cities such as Thunder Bay, Sault Ste. Marie, Sudbury, Windsor, Guelph, London, Kingston, and Ottawa, consumers are most definitely paying. The CAC blamed the high costs on Ontario insurance brokers who, they say, may actually be fronts for a handful of affiliated insurers to offer non-competitive rates.

Investigators say a pattern that drives up prices has emerged among so-called independent brokers. With almost one hundred auto insurance companies operating in Ontario, a typical broker may sell policies from one or two insurance companies only. "Many of these brokerage firms have financial ties to insurance companies, which limits real consumer choice," said Bruce Cran, president of the Ottawa-based association.

Use InsuranceHotline.com

One effective agency that tracks the lowest premiums is *InsuranceHotline.com*. It has created a watchdog service to alert drivers to the changes in their insurance rates. For $20 per year, the agency will automatically rerun members' profiles to ensure that they always know which insurer has the lowest rate from its database of 30 insurance companies (representing over 80 percent of the written premiums in Canada).

Surprisingly, some of the vehicles with the poorest reliability, durability, and fuel economy ratings, such as GM's Hummer, have good insurance rates. Additionally, if you are ticketed or have one accident, your premiums can almost quadruple. When rates for a 2006 Hummer and a 2006 Honda Civic were calculated, the Civic driver only saved $49 compared to the Hummer premium. But add a police ticket and accident to the equation, and the Civic owner could pay over $2,500 more (see chart below).

INSURANCE PREMIUMS COMPARISON

MODEL	NO CLAIMS		ONE TICKET & ONE ACCIDENT	
	LOW	HIGH	LOW	HIGH
Hummer	$1,651	$3,138	$2,812	$8,769
Honda Civic	$1,602	$3,125	$2,812	$11,271

Here are some other *InsuranceHotline.com* findings:

- A family car under $35,000 can cost more to insure than one over $35,000.
- SUVs under $35,000 don't always cost more to insure than a family car or a small luxury model.
- Luxury cars mean luxury premiums, costing on average about $500 more annually to insure than family cars, SUVs, muscle cars, or hybrids.
- Hybrids' fuel savings can be wiped out by higher-cost insurance premiums that rival what you would pay to insure a muscle car.

3. Defects Can't Hide

You can easily avoid any nasty surprises by having your choice of used vehicle checked out before your purchase by an independent mechanic (for $85–$100). This examination protects you against any hidden defects the vehicle may have. It's also a tremendous negotiating tool, since you can use the cost of any needed repairs to bargain down the purchase price.

It's easier to get permission to have the vehicle inspected if you promise to give the seller a copy of the inspection report should you decide not to buy it. If you still can't get permission to have the vehicle inspected elsewhere, walk away from the deal, no matter how tempting the selling price. The seller is obviously trying to put something over on you. Ignore the standard excuses that the vehicle isn't insured, that the licence plates have expired, or that the vehicle has a dead battery.

4. You Know the Vehicle's History

Smart customers will want answers to the following questions before signing a contract: What did it first sell for, and what is its present insured value? Who serviced it? Has it had accident repairs? Are parts easily available? How much of the original warranty or repair warranties are left? Does the vehicle have a history of costly performance-related defects? What free repairs are available through "goodwill" warranty extensions? (See "Secret Warranties/Internal Bulletins/Service Tips" in Part Three.)

5. Cheap and Easy Lawsuits

Lawyers win, regardless of whether you win or lose. And you're likely to lose more than you'll ever get back using the traditional court system in a used-car dispute.

But, if you're just a bit creative, you'll discover there are many federal and provincial consumer-protection laws that go far beyond whatever protection may be offered by the standard new-vehicle warranty. Furthermore, buyers of used vehicles don't usually have to conform to any arbitrary rules or service guidelines to get this protection.

Let's say you do get stuck with a vehicle that's unreliable, has undisclosed accident damage, or doesn't perform as promised. Most small claims courts have a jurisdiction limit of $3,000–$10,000 (Alberta, B.C., and Ontario now have a $25,000 ceiling—more than enough for most car purchases), which should cover the cost of repairs or compensate you if the vehicle is taken back. That way, any dispute between buyer and seller can be settled within a few months, without lawyers or excessive court costs. Furthermore, you're not likely to face a battery of lawyers standing in for the automaker and dealer in front of a stern-faced judge. You may not even have to face a judge at all, since many cases are settled through court-imposed mediators at a pretrial meeting usually scheduled a month or two after filing.

Be Wary of Auto Quality Rankings

There are two major surveyors of automobile quality: J.D. Power and Associates, a private American automobile consulting organization, and Consumers Union, an American non-profit consumer organization that publishes *Consumer Reports* magazine.

J.D. Power

Each year, J.D. Power and Associates publishes the results of two important surveys, measuring both vehicle quality and owners' customer service satisfaction. Interestingly, these two polls often contradict each other. For example, its Vehicle Dependability Index (VDI) places Saturn near the bottom of the list; however,

Saturn placed sixth from the top in the Customer Service Index (CSI). This leads one to conclude that the car isn't very reliable, but service is given with a smile!

J.D. Power does have influence in the auto industry. Its criticism of Nissan's 2004 Quest minivan had that company's engineers working overtime fixing or replacing faulty sliding doors, power window switches, interior reading lights, second-row seat levers, and airbag sensors after the firm's 2004 Initial Quality Study rated the Quest last among minivans in consumer perceptions of quality during the first 100 days of ownership. Nissan's full-sized Titan pickup and full-sized Armada SUV also placed last in their categories for other problems.

Another revealing, though lesser-known, report is J.D. Power's annual Customer Retention Study, which measures the percentage of owners who remain loyal to a particular automaker. Since poor build quality or inadequate servicing are factors that may lead to owners taking their business elsewhere, this study provides an early warning that an automaker is struggling to keep its customers. In the 2005 study, here is how the owner-retention rate fluctuated among major automakers:

2005 OWNER RETENTION RATE (J.D. POWER)

COMPANY	2003	2005	COMPANY	2003	2005
Hyundai	55.1	53.1	Chevrolet	54.1	48.5
Ford	53.8	47.6	Toyota	52.7	56.5
Mercedes-Benz	49.4	45.3	Lexus	48.2	51.6
Honda	46.9	52.5	Subaru	44.7	54.2
BMW	37.9	43.5	Nissan	35.5	43.3

Consumer Reports

Consumer groups and non-profit auto associations such as the Automobile Protection Association (APA) and Car Help Canada (see Appendix III) are your best bets for the most unbiased auto ratings for Canadians. They're not perfect, though, so it's a good idea to consult both groups to look for ratings that match.

Consumer Reports (CR) is an American publication that once had a tenuous affiliation with the Consumers' Association of Canada (CAC) before they had a falling out several decades ago. CR's ratings, extrapolated from Consumers Union's annual U.S. member survey, don't quite mirror the Canadian experience. Components that are particularly vulnerable to our harsh climate usually don't perform as well as the CR reliability ratings indicate, and poor servicing caused by a weak Canadian dealer body can make some service-dependent vehicles a nightmare to own here, whereas the American experience may be less problematic.

Based on over a million American and Canadian member responses, CR lists used vehicles that, according to owner reports, are significantly better or worse than the industry average. Statisticians agree that CR's sampling method leaves some room for error, but, with a few notable exceptions, the ratings are fair, conservative, and consistent guidelines for buying a reliable new vehicle. I have only three criticisms of the ratings, the first being that many Asian models aren't as harshly scrutinized as their American counterparts. Secondly, older vehicles are excluded from *CR*'s ratings. Lastly, many of the ratings regarding the frequency of repairs of certain components aren't specific enough.

Lemon-Aid *disagrees with* Consumer Reports

I have a lot of respect for *Consumer Reports*, having been an elected member of its Board over 30 years ago. I know they do a very good job picking the best and worst vehicles each year. In fact, *CR* and *Lemon-Aid* ratings are often in agreement. Where they differ is in *Lemon-Aid*'s greater reliance upon National Highway Traffic Safety Administration (NHTSA) safety complaints, service bulletin admissions of defects, and owner complaints received through the Internet (rather than from *CR*'s subscriber base, which may simply attract owners singing from the same hymnal).

My main criticism of the auto ratings are that many Asian models, like Toyota and Honda, are not as harshly scrutinized as American models, yet service bulletins and extended "goodwill" warranties have shown for years that they also have serious engine, transmission, brake, and electrical problems. *Consumer Reports* confirms this anomaly in its April 2006 edition, where it admits that Asian vehicle quality improvement has "slowed" since 2002.

Two other annoyances: older vehicles (pre-1998) are excluded from *CR*'s detailed ratings, just as statistics show that owners are keeping their vehicles for a decade or longer. Furthermore, many of the ratings about the frequency of repairs of certain components aren't specific enough. For example, instead of just mentioning problems with the engine or the fuel or electrical systems, ratings should be specific about which components are likely to fail. Is it the engine intake manifold and fuel pumps that are failure-prone, is it the injectors that clog up, or is it the battery that suddenly dies?

In looking over *CR*'s best new- and used-vehicle picks for 2003 through 2005 models, there are a number of "Recommended" vehicles that defy all logic.

Foremost is the Ford Windstar, followed by the Saturn Vue. It is inconceivable that *CR* isn't aware of the multiplicity of powertrain, body, and suspension failures affecting these vehicles. Then there's the assorted Chrysler lineup. Now, you'd have to live on another planet not to know that Chryslers are afflicted with chronic automatic transmission, ball joint, body, brake, and AC defects. And, in fact, *Consumer Reports*' "Frequency of Repair" tables give out plenty of black marks to the aforementioned models and components—in the very same edition where these vehicles are praised. I'll admit that car ratings are part science and part art, but in this case I'll have to assume that sloppy research and editing failed to pick up on the contradictions.

CR did a better job with its 2005–06 ratings. But, once again, Ford tripped them up. This time they gave a Recommended rating to the Focus, one of the worst Fords ever built. Ironically, CR pulled its rating the very next day when NHTSA government crash tests showed the Focus to be dangerously vulnerable to side impacts.

The publication got another black eye when it botched a study released in January 2007 that said 10 out of 12 infant car safety seats provided inadequate protection in side impacts at speeds of 56–61 km/h. NHTSA checked CR's findings and discovered that the side-impact speeds actually exceeded 112 km/h. *Consumer Reports* blamed its mistake on a "series of misjudgments" and "miscommunication with an outside lab."

After five years, a Honda Civic Hybrid will save you $406 over a gasoline-powered Civic.

Sometimes simple math errors can skew *Consumer Reports'* car ratings. Take, for example, its recent analysis of hybrid driving costs. The magazine admitted that errors in calculating depreciation caused it to mistakenly conclude that not a single gas-electric hybrid would save owners money, compared with regular gasoline versions of the same vehicles driven for five years. When the math was corrected, it showed that Toyota Prius and Honda Civic Hybrid owners would save $317 and $406 respectively, compared with owners of their gas-only counterparts. And, although owners of other hybrids like the Honda Accord, Ford Escape, Toyota Highlander, and Lexus RX 400h would end up spending $1,883 to $5,508 more, those amounts were far less than what CR originally estimated: $3,700 more for a buyer of a 2006 Honda Civic Hybrid compared with a gas-only Civic EX, to $13,300 for the person who buys a Lexus RX 400h Hybrid versus a Lexus RX 330.

Choosing a Safe, Reliable, and "Green" Vehicle

Looking through Part Three and reading through the above-noted websites and magazines can help you find good, reliable used-car buys. Finding a safe car is a bit more difficult, though, since few used-car guides want to get into that kind of discussion.

The best indicator of a car's overall safety is NHTSA's front, side, and rollover crashworthiness ratings, applicable to most vehicles made over the past several decades and sold in North America. You will then want to compare NHTSA scores with ratings from the Insurance Institute for Highway Safety (IIHS), which crashes vehicles at a higher speed and at an offset angle, more common in collisions than the head-on scenario. Results from these two bodies are posted for each model rated in Part Three. However, there are many other national and international testing agencies that you may consult, and they can be found at *www.crashtest.com/*

netindex.htm. This site shows the results of early crash tests of cars that were sold in Australia, Europe, and Japan that are just now coming onto the North American market. Take the Mercedes Smart Car as an example: nowhere in Mercedes' or Chrysler's sales brochures did I see a reference to the Smart's "Acceptable" frontal crash test rating.

SMART CAR CRASHWORTHINESS 1999–2006			
Euro NCAP (front)	**3**	Weight class	**1**
Euro NCAP (side)	**5**	Overall rating	**3**

Note: The European New Car Assessment Program (Euro NCAP) is a consortium of European Union agencies that conducts tests and assesses the safety performance of individual car models sold in Europe. Ratings are on a numbered scale where **5** is good and **1** is bad (see pages 130–132 for more information).

Of course, no one expects to be in a collision, but NHTSA estimates that every vehicle will be in two accidents of varying severity during its lifetime. So why not put the averages on your side?

Most Environmentally Friendly Vehicles

Consider these important points when making your used-car choice:

- The 19.3 million cars and light-duty trucks on Canada's roads today are responsible for 12 percent of the nation's greenhouse gas emissions.
- Nationwide, 5,000 deaths per year are attributed to smog pollutants, which alone cost the Ontario economy $9.9 billion in health care costs and business losses, according to the Ontario Medical Association.
- By purchasing a used vehicle, you are already doing a lot for the environment by not adding to the vehicle population. Nevertheless, in choosing a fuel-efficient, safe small car, you are also protecting your life and your wallet.

Here are *Lemon-Aid*'s picks of the top 15 most environmentally friendly, reliable, and cheap used cars and minivans.

Chrysler Neon—Year 2000 and later models are dirt-cheap, peppy, and fuel-frugal
GM Aveo—An inexpensive upgraded Daewoo that sips gas
Honda Civic—Not the cheapest, but likely the most reliable
Honda Odyssey—Better engineered than the Toyota Sienna; price haggling discouraged, however
Hyundai Accent—Rapid depreciation and not-so-rapid acceleration
Hyundai Elantra/Tiburon—Reliable and carries an excellent warranty; horsepower may be a lie
Mazda5—A mini-minivan that carries six passengers and burns fuel like a compact car
Nissan Sentra—Reasonably priced, reliable, and stylish
Suzuki Aerio, Accent, and Swift—Cheap, cheap, and cheap; an urban dweller

GM's Aveo (shown here) has been surprisingly trouble-free, considering its Daewoo DNA.

Toyota Corolla—A more spacious and comfortable (though not as reliable) Echo

Toyota Echo—Economical, bland, and reliable

Toyota Tercel—The best of the Toyota triad; a motoring Energizer bunny

Toyota Yaris—Not as refined as a Honda Fit or Nissan Versa

Note: In spite of the federal government's $2,000 rebates for fuel-frugal cars, we don't recommend gas-electric engine hybrids such as the Toyota Prius and Honda Insight (no longer sold) or Civic Hybrid. Their fuel economy can be 40 percent worse than the automakers' reports, their long-term reliability is unknown, battery replacement cost may be $7,000, their retail prices are almost double what an Echo would cost, and the resale value for a 2001 Prius that originally sold for $29,990 (Cdn.) is a disappointing $10,000. Hmmm…let's see: $10,000 minus $7,000 for a battery pack… Hello, Car Heaven?

Green Car Rebates and Penalties

Prime Minister Harper's 2007 budget gives rebates of up to $2,000 to purchasers of new fuel-efficient cars (an estimated 21 vehicles, mostly hybrids), and levies maximum penalties of $4,000 on the purchase of gas-guzzlers (about 100 vehicles; pickups are exempted). Essentially, it's a $160-million political gift (over two years) to the Japanese automakers from a government desperate to put on a "green" veneer in time for the next federal election. It won't really change Canadian car buying habits that already favour small cars. However, the rebates and penalties will likely cut prices on used compact and subcompact cars by about 5 percent, and will probably increase prices on used large cars, vans, and SUVs by almost 10 percent.

Passenger cars with a combined fuel-economy rating of 6.5 L/100 km or less according to manufacturer-submitted tests (they wouldn't lie, would they?), approved by Transport Canada and published by Natural Resources Canada, will be eligible for the rebate. So will minivans, sport-utility vehicles, and other light trucks with a combined rating of 8.3 L/100 km or less. Rebates will start at $1,000, with $500 added for each half-litre/100 km until the $2,000 maximum is reached. Here are some of the vehicles most likely to be affected:

REBATE-ELIGIBLE CARS

$2,000 REBATE	$1,500 REBATE	$1,000 REBATE		
Ford Escape HEV	Ford Escape HEV	Chrysler Compass	GM Impala Flex-Fuel Vehicle	Saturn VUE Hybrid
Honda Civic Hybrid	4×4	Chrysler Patriot	GM Monte Carlo	Toyota Corolla
Toyota Prius Hybrid	Nissan Altima Hybrid	Chrysler Sebring Flex-Fuel Vehicle	Flex-Fuel Vehicle	Toyota Highlander 4×4 Hybrid
	Toyota Camry Hybrid		Lexus RX 400h 4×4	Toyota Yaris
			Mini Cooper M6	

A handful of Canadian provinces offer similar rebates on fuel-efficient vehicles, allowing eligible owners to dip into both federal and provincial programs. To find out more about provincial rebate programs, go to Transport Canada's website (*www.tc.gc.ca/programs/environment/ecotransport/ecoauto.htm*) and click on the Prince Edward Island, Quebec, Ontario, Manitoba, and British Columbia rebate sites at the bottom of the page.

The penalty on gas guzzlers applies only to about 5 percent of passenger vehicles sold in Canada, and pickup trucks are exempt from the provisions. Nevertheless, producers of large cars, SUVs, and vans, like Ford, DaimlerChrysler, and General Motors, will be especially hard hit by these green penalties, and CAW President Buzz Hargrove will once again have his hand out for government money to save Ontario autoworker jobs.

LEVY-ELIGIBLE VEHICLES
13.0–13.9 L/100 km: $1,000
14.0–14.9 L/100 km: $2,000
15.0–15.9 L/100 km: $3,000
16.0 L/100 km or more: $4,000

One final thought. Fewer vehicles are likely to be eligible for green rebates as the U. S. Environmental Protection Agency and Transport Canada continue to revise fuel-economy figures downward later this year to reflect "real" driving conditions. For example:

- City ratings will drop by an average of 12 percent. The fuel economy estimates of hybrid vehicles and other vehicles designed for high fuel economy (read ethanol) might drop up to 30 percent of their existing rating.
- Highway ratings will drop by an average of 8 percent while hybrids and other specialized fuel economy vehicles (read ethanol) might be reduced by up to 25 percent.

Fuel-economy fantasies

Consumer Reports has discovered what we have known for the past several decades: The mileage promised on car stickers is grossly inflated, sometimes by as much as 40 percent. *CR* says that hybrids alone account for fuel consumption discrepancies that average 12.0 L/100 km (19 mpg) worse than the city-driving rating given by the U.S. Environmental Protection Agency and Transport Canada.

But Chrysler, Ford, GM, Honda, Lexus, and Toyota don't tell the average buyer that their so-called fuel-frugal hybrid, ethanol-friendly, and diesel-powered vehicles are simply high-tech, feel-good PR machines. Not only are the costs of running vehicles equipped with special engines and alternate fuels much higher than advertised, but poor reliability and higher servicing costs also give these green vehicles a decidedly lemony flavour.

Yet most public environmental protection groups and government agencies, seconded by the major automobile clubs, genuflect whenever the hybrid, ethanol, or diesel alternative is proposed.

Once again, we have to be wary of the lies. Toyota, for example, seldom mentions the fact that its hybrid battery packs can cost $4,000–$6,000 (U.S.) to replace, or that *Automotive News, Car and Driver,* and Edmunds have also found that diesel and hybrid fuel consumption figures can be 30–40 percent more than advertised.

What about ethanol? After all, the federal Conservative government committed $2 billion in incentives for ethanol, made from wheat and corn, and for biodiesel in its 2007 budget. The Canadian Renewable Fuels Association says ethanol is "good for the environment," a position echoed by the Manitoba and Saskatchewan governments, which emphasize that ethanol "burns cleaner" than gasoline.

Hogwash! Environment Canada's own unpublished research says ethanol "burns no cleaner than gasoline."

Scientists at Environment Canada studied four vehicles of recent makes, testing their emissions in a range of driving conditions and temperatures. "Looking at tailpipe emissions, from a greenhouse gas perspective, there really isn't much difference between ethanol and gasoline," said Greg Rideout, head of Environment Canada's toxic emissions research.

The study found no statistical difference between the greenhouse gas emissions of regular unleaded fuel and 10 percent ethanol blended fuel. Although the study found a reduction in carbon monoxide, a pollutant that forms smog, emissions of some other gases, such as hydrocarbons, actually increased under certain conditions.

This scoop was broadcast by CBC on March 30, 2007—barely a week after the Budget was approved (*www.cbc.ca/canada/manitoba/story/2007/03/30/ethanol-emissions.html?ref=rss#skip300x250*).

Other drawbacks of ethanol: it's hard to find (only two outlets in all of Canada), it eats fuel line and gas tank components, it performs poorly in cold climates, and it gives you 25–30 percent less fuel economy than gasoline.

Smart drivers should continue to ignore automaker gas-saving hype, hunker down, and keep their paid-for, reliable, gas-guzzling used vehicles, because the depreciation savings will more than offset the increased cost of fuel.

Courts blast fuel-economy lies

It had to happen. Car owners, panicked over soaring fuel prices, are being scammed by retailers with bogus gas-saving devices and additives, while salespeople and automakers lie about the fuel economy of the vehicles they sell.

Fortunately, Canadian courts are cracking down on lying dealers who use false gas consumption figures to sell their cars. Ontario's revised *Consumer Protection Act, 2002* (*www.e-laws.gov.on.ca/DBLaws/Statutes/English/02c30_e.htm*), for example, lets consumers cancel a contract within one year of entering into the agreement if a dealer makes a false, misleading, deceptive, or unconscionable representation. This includes false fuel-economy claims.

Dealers cannot make the excuse that they were fooled or that they were simply providing data supplied by the manufacturer. The law clearly states that both parties are jointly liable, and therefore the dealer is *presumed* to know the history, quality, and true performance of what is sold.

Fuel economy misrepresentation can lead to a contract's cancellation if the dealer gives a higher-than-actual figure, even if they claim it was an innocent misrepresentation, according to the precedent-setting decision in *Sidney v. 1011067 Ontario Inc. (c.o.b. Southside Motors)*. In *Sidney,* the buyer was awarded $11,424.51 plus pre-judgment interest because of a false representation made by the defendant regarding fuel efficiency. The plaintiff claimed that the defendant advised him that the vehicle could run 800–900 km per tank of fuel when in fact the maximum distance was only 500 km per tank.

This consumer victory is particularly important as fuel prices soar and everyone from automakers to sellers of ineffective gas-saving gadgets make outlandishly false fuel-economy claims.

When and Where to Buy

When to Buy

In the fall, dealer stocks of quality trade-ins and off-lease returns are at their highest level, and private sellers are moderately active. Prices are higher, but a greater choice of vehicles is available. In winter, prices decline substantially, and dealers and private sellers are generally easier to bargain with because buyers are scarce and weather conditions don't present their wares in the best light. In spring and summer, prices go up a bit as private sellers become more active and increased new-car rebates bring in more trade-ins.

Private Sellers

Private sellers are your best source for a cheap and reliable used vehicle because you're on an equal bargaining level with a vendor who isn't trying to profit from your inexperience. A good private sale price would be about 5 percent *more* than the rock-bottom wholesale price, or approximately 20 percent *less* than the retail price advertised by local dealers. You can find estimated wholesale and retail prices in Part Three.

Remember, no seller, be it a dealer or a private party, expects to get his or her asking price. As with price reductions on home listings, a 10–20 percent reduction on the advertised price is common with private sellers. Dealers usually won't cut more than 10 percent off their advertised price.

Your *Lemon-Aid* guide has levelled the playing field for the consumer when it comes to shopping for new or used vehicles. *Lemon-Aid* has also helped us consumers get the inside edge on how to protect ourselves from car manufacturers, secret warranties, goodwill service, etc.

I recently used your publication to help me in my decision to purchase a 1999 Toyota Tercel. Your *Lemon-Aid* guide also helped me avoid paying an "administration fee." I just walked out of the dealer's showroom. They must have thought I was crazy.

I didn't even have time to take my shoes off when my wife called me and said the Toyota dealership was on the telephone. She had no idea what had happened.

Suffice it to say, this wise consumer didn't pay an "administration fee" so someone could have dinner on me. If there is value in something, I will pay it. If not, this customer walks. Here's to many years of carefree driving with my Toyota.

Just an off note. After 17 years of working for General Motors I thought I knew it all about vehicles, making deals, problems, defects, warranties, etc.

Was I wrong. You can never know it all. Keep publishing *Lemon-Aid* and I will keep reading it.

I'm a long-time GM employee who bought his first foreign-made vehicle with the help of Phil Edmonston. Patriotism is one thing, but blowing your hard-earned money for junk is another, just so you can wave the flag.

SINCERELY,
L.C.

Buying Without Fear and Loathing

No matter from whom you're buying a used vehicle, there are a few rules you should follow to get the best deal.

First, have a good idea of what you want and the price you're willing to pay. If you have a pre-approved line of credit, that will keep the number crunching and extra fees to a minimum. Finally, be resolute and polite, but make it clear that you are a serious buyer and won't participate in any "showroom shakedowns."

Here's a successful real-world technique used by Kurt Binnie, a frequent *Lemon-Aid* tipster:

> 1) Wireless, hand-held VIN [vehicle information number] searches
>
> Imagine the surprise of the used-car salesman when I pulled out my BlackBerry and did a VIN search right in front of him using Carfax. Threw him right off balance. Carfax results for Ontario vehicles give a good indication, but not the complete MTO [Ministry of Transportation, Ontario] history. I bought the UVIP [Used Vehicle Information Package]…before closing the deal. For the car I ended up buying, I didn't even tell the sales staff that I was running the VIN while I was there. I was able to see it wasn't an auction vehicle or a write-off. This technique should work with pretty much any WAP [Wireless Application Protocol] enabled phone.
>
> 2) Buying a problem used car without the problems
>
> A previous car I owned was a 1994 Mazda 626 4cyl manual tranny…. There are a myriad of complaints at the NHTSA as well as in Mazda discussion forums about this. Same thing goes for the 2.5 V6. Resale values on that car were really low, so armed with the proper knowledge of what components to avoid, a consumer can get a low-cost, relatively reliable vehicle that has taken a resale value hit. I never had any major issues with the 4-cylinder manual and have never found any major issues except for the distributors on '93, '94 models.

Kurt's letter goes on to describe how he avoids negotiations with sales staff and managers. He figures out the price he's willing to pay beforehand, using a combination of book values and the prices listed at *www.autotrader.ca*. He then test-drives the vehicle, runs the VIN through his BlackBerry, and then makes a point-blank, one-time offer to the dealer. He has also found that used-car staff often have no knowledge about the vehicles on their lots beyond their asking price, and make no distinction between cars manufactured early or late in the model year. An alert buyer could get a car built in August 2002 for the same price as one from September 2001, since they're both used 2002 cars.

Kurt runs a car blog dedicated to preventing people from buying the wrong car, where he also describes how to fix common failures (such as Subaru's clutch shudder) on most vehicles. He answers most questions via email. Although Kurt's not a mechanic, he's quite resourceful. If he doesn't have the answer, he knows where to get it. His website address is *www.onthehoist.com*.

Primary Precautions

As a buyer, you should get a printed sales agreement, even if it's just handwritten, that includes a clause stating that there are no outstanding traffic violations or liens against the vehicle. It doesn't make a great deal of difference whether the car will be purchased "as is" or certified under provincial regulation. A vehicle sold as safety certified can still turn into a lemon or be dangerous to drive. The certification process can be sabotaged if a minimal number of components are checked, the mechanic is incompetent, or the instruments are poorly calibrated. "Certified" is not the same as having a warranty to protect you from engine seizure or transmission failure. It means only that the vehicle met the minimum safety standards on the day it was tested.

Make sure the vehicle is lien-free and has not been damaged in a flood or written off after an accident. Flood damage can be hard to see, but it impairs ABS, power steering, and airbag functioning (making deployment 10 times slower).

Canada has become a haven for rebuilt U.S. wrecks. Write-offs are also shipped from provinces where there are stringent disclosure regulations to provinces where there are lax rules or no rules at all.

If you suspect your vehicle is a rebuilt wreck from the States, or was once a taxi, there's a useful Canadian search agency called CarProof that can quickly give you a complete history of any vehicle within a day.

CarProof (www.carproof.com)

Operating out of London, Ontario, CarProof's services cost $29.95, $44.95, or $59.95, plus GST, per report, depending on which package you choose. For your $30 plus, you can get the following:

- **Section 1:** VIN decode and complete vehicle description.
- **Section 2:** Report summary, which highlights the data found in the complete report.
- **Section 3:** Cross-Canada current vehicle registration update, which includes vehicle warning tags applied by any provincial or territorial Ministry of Transportation, such as Normal, Salvage, Rebuilt, Non-repairable, and Stolen. This section includes registration-effective dates and odometer data, if available.
- **Section 4:** Cross-Canada lien search, which reports any enforceable lien registered against the VIN in all 13 provinces and territories.
- **Section 5:** United States and Canadian vehicle history details. CarProof provides these details through a live connection to Experian Automotive. This section includes all data that would be provided in Experian's AutoCheck report, plus other insurance and registration history provided by CarProof's other data suppliers.
- **Section 6:** New import/export section. Data in this section comes from Transport Canada's Registrar of Imported Vehicles (RIV) as well as from the U.S. Department of Transportation. This section reports whether a vehicle has been legally imported into either country as a used vehicle.
- **Section 7:** Odometer history, which reports any odometer records found in Canada or the United States in chronological order.

- **Section 8:** Third-party history, which includes information about aftermarket anti-theft system installations, independent inspections, and other maintenance records.
- **Section 9:** Canadian insurance history. This section provides insurance coverage information and claims histories from the private insurance industry across Canada.

Information requests can be completed overnight online. Contact the company through its website, or if you prefer to talk, call 519-675-1415.

In most provinces, you can do a lien and registration search yourself, but it's hardly worth the effort considering the low cost and comprehensive nature of CarProof's services.

If a lien does exist, you should contact the creditor(s) listed to find out whether any debts have been paid. If a debt is outstanding, you should arrange with the vendor to pay the creditor the outstanding balance, or agree that you can put the purchase price in a trust account to pay the lender. If the debt is larger than the purchase price of the car, it's up to you to decide whether you wish to complete the deal. If the seller agrees to clear the title personally, make sure that you receive a written relinquishment of title from the creditor before transferring any money to the seller. Make sure the title doesn't show an "R" for restored, since this indicates that the vehicle was written off as a total loss and may not have been properly repaired.

Even if all documents are in order, ask the seller to show you the vehicle's original sales contract and a few repair bills in order to ascertain how well it was maintained. The bills will show you if the odometer was turned back and will also indicate which repairs are still guaranteed. If none of these can be found, run (don't walk!) away. If the contract shows that the car was financed, verify that the loan was paid. If you're still not sure that the vehicle is free of liens, ask your bank or credit union manager to check for you. If no clear answer is forthcoming, look for something else.

Don't Pay Too Much

Used prices for large and mid-sized passenger cars have dropped because new prices have been slashed due to huge inventories and soaring fuel prices, but this drop hasn't occurred yet with small cars and minivans. Their prices on the used-car market are relatively stable and are expected to stay that way through the summer as fuel costs settle down.

But prices won't stay steady for long. In early fall, we'll see a brutal discount war spearheaded by Chrysler, as its new Cerberus owners begin milking their new company for capital. Looking for immediate cash, they'll cut the size of the dealer body and slash new car, truck, and minivan prices. Ford and GM will reluctantly follow suit, Hyundai and Kia will adjust their prices easily, and the Japanese will do likewise.

As prices for new vehicles fall, used-car sellers will lower their prices even more to attract customers who might consider buying new. In effect, we are moving into "perfect storm" conditions, where the buyer will be king and dealerships will be turned into flea markets.

If you'd like to save even more when buying used, consider these tips:

- Buy an older vehicle. Choose one that's five years old or more and has a good reliability and durability record. Buy extra protection with an extended warranty. The money you save from the extra years' depreciation and lower insurance premiums will more than make up for the extra warranty cost.
- Look for off-lease vehicles sold privately by owners who want more than what their dealer is offering. If you can't find what you're looking for in the local classified ads, put in your own ad asking for lessees to contact you if they're not satisfied with their dealer's offer.
- Buy a vehicle that's depreciated more than average simply because of its bland styling, unpopular colour (dark blue, white, and champagne are out; silver is in), lack of high-performance features, or discontinuation.
- Buy a cheaper twin or re-badged model like a fully loaded Camry instead of a Lexus ES, a Toyota Matrix in lieu of a Pontiac Vibe, or a Plymouth Voyager instead of a Dodge Caravan.

Price Guides

The best way to determine the price range for a particular model is to read the *Lemon-Aid* values found in Part Three. From there, you may wish to get a free second opinion by accessing Vehicle Market Research International's (VMR) Canadian Used Car Prices at *www.vmrcanada.com*. It is one of the few free sources listing wholesale and retail values for used cars in Canada. The site even includes a handy calculator that adjusts a vehicle's value according to model, mileage, and options.

Black Book and *Red Book* price guides, found in most libraries, banks, and credit unions, can also be helpful. But accessing their information for free on the Internet takes a little insider knowledge. To access the *Canadian Black Book* values, simply copy the following URL into your web browser: *www.canadianblackbook.com/prv/ auth.cfm?token=AB04DC39ZKL01*.

Now, if you want to use the *Canadian Red Book Vehicle Valuation Guide*, which seems more attuned to Quebec and Ontario sales, you can order single copies of their used car and light truck wholesale and retail price guide for $16.95 at *www. canadianredbook.com/default2.asp* (an annual subscription costs $95, plus PST). There are no restrictions as to who may subscribe.

You may also go to *Auto Trader* magazine's website at *www.autotrader.ca* to see at what prices other Canadians are trying to sell your vehicle.

Don't be surprised to find that many national price guides have an Eastern Ontario and Quebec price bias. They often list unrealistically low prices compared with what you'll actually see in the eastern and western provinces and in rural areas, where good used cars are often sold for outrageously high prices or simply passed down through the family for an average of eight to 10 years. Other price guides may list prices that are much higher than those found in your region. Consequently, use whichever price guide lists the highest value when selling your trade-in or negotiating a write-off value with an insurer. When buying, use the guide with the lowest values as your bargaining tool.

Repossessed Vehicles

Repossessed vehicles frequently come from bankrupt small businesses or sub-prime borrowers who failed to make their finance payments. They are usually found at auctions, but finance companies and banks sometimes sell them as well. Canadian courts have held that financial institutions are legally responsible for defects found in what they sell, so don't be at all surprised by the disclosure paperwork that will be shoved under your nose. Also, as with rental car company transactions, the combination of these companies' deep pockets and their abhorrence of bad publicity means you'll likely get your money back if you make a bad buy. The biggest problem with repossessed vans, sport-utilities, and pickups in particular is that they were likely abused or neglected by their financially troubled owners. Although you rarely get to test-drive or closely examine these vehicles, a local dealer may be able to produce a vehicle maintenance history by running the VIN through their manufacturer's database.

Rental and Leased Vehicles

Next to buying privately, the second-best choice for getting a good used vehicle is a rental company or leasing agency. Due to a slumping economy, Budget, Hertz, Avis, and National are selling, at cut-rate prices, vehicles that have one to two years of service and approximately 80,000–100,000 km on the odometer. These rental companies will gladly provide a vehicle's complete history and allow an independent inspection by a qualified mechanic of the buyer's choice, as well as arrange for competitive financing.

Rental vehicles are generally well maintained, sell for a few thousand dollars more than privately sold vehicles, and come with strong guarantees, like Budget's 30-day money-back guarantee at some of its retail outlets (including three in B.C.). Rental car companies also usually settle customer complaints without much hassle so as not to tarnish their images with rental customers.

Rental agencies tend to keep their stock of cars on the outskirts of town near the airport (particularly in Alberta and B.C.) and advertise in the local papers. Sales are held year-round as inventory is replenished. Late summer and early fall are usually the best times to see a wide selection because the new rentals arrive during this time period.

Vehicles that have just come off a 3- or 5-year lease are much more competitively priced than rentals, generally have less mileage, and are usually as well maintained. You're also likely to get a better price if you buy directly from the lessee, rather than going through the dealership or an independent agency. But remember that you won't have the dealer's leverage to extract post-warranty "goodwill" repairs from the automaker.

New-Car Dealers

New-car dealerships aren't bad places to pick up good used cars or minivans. Prices are 15–20 percent higher than those for vehicles sold privately, but rebates and zero percent financing plans can trim used values dramatically. Plus, dealers are insured against selling stolen vehicles or vehicles with finance or other liens owing. They also usually allow prospective buyers to have the vehicle inspected by an independent garage, offer a much wider choice of models, and have their own repair facilities to do warranty work. Also, if there's a possibility of getting post-warranty "goodwill" compensation from the manufacturer, your dealer can provide additional leverage, particularly if the dealership is a franchisee for the model you have purchased. Finally, if things do go terribly wrong, dealers have deeper pockets than private sellers, so there's a better chance of winning a court judgment.

"Certified" vehicles

The word certified doesn't mean much. Ideally, it tells us the vehicle has undergone some reconditioning that was monitored by the manufacturer. Of course, some dealers don't do anything but slap a "certified" sticker on the car and inflate the selling price. Sometimes, an auto association will certify a vehicle that has been inspected and has had the designated defects corrected. In Alberta, the Alberta Motor Association (AMA) will perform a vehicle inspection at a dealer's request. On each occasion, the AMA gives a written report to the dealer that identifies potential and actual problems, required repairs, and serious defects.

Used-car leasing

It's not a good idea to lease either new or used vehicles. It has been touted as a method of making the high cost of vehicle ownership more affordable, but don't you believe it. Leasing is generally costlier than an outright purchase, and, for most people, the pitfalls far outweigh any advantages. If you must lease, do so for the shortest time possible and make sure the lease is close-ended (meaning that you walk away from the vehicle when the lease period ends). Also, make sure there's a maximum mileage allowance of at least 25,000 km per year and that the charge per excess kilometre is no higher than 8–10 cents.

Used-Car Dealers

Used-car dealers usually sell their vehicles for a bit less than what new-car dealers charge. However, their vehicles may be worth a lot less because they don't get the first pick of top-quality trade-ins. Many independent urban dealerships are marginal operations that can't invest much money in reconditioning their vehicles, which are often collected from auctions and new-car dealers reluctant to sell the vehicles to their own customers. And used-car dealers don't always have repair facilities to honour the warranties they do provide. Often, their credit terms are easier (but more expensive) than those offered by franchised new-car dealers.

That said, used-car dealers operating in small towns are an entirely different breed. These small, often family-run businesses recondition and resell cars and trucks that usually come from within their communities. Routine servicing is usually done in-house, and more complicated repairs are subcontracted out to specialized garages nearby. On one hand, these small outlets survive by word-of-mouth advertising and wouldn't last long if they didn't deal fairly with local townsfolk. On the other hand, their prices will likely be higher than elsewhere due to the better quality of their used vehicles and the cost of reconditioning and repairing what they sell under warranty.

Auctions

First of all, make sure it's a legitimate auction. Many are fronts for used-car lots where sleazy dealers put fake ads in complicit newspapers, pretending to hold auctions that are no more than weekend selling sprees.

Furthermore, you'll need lots of patience, smarts, and luck to pick up anything worthwhile. Government auctions—places where the mythical $50 Jeeps are sold—are fun to attend but highly overrated as places to find bargains. Look at the odds against you: It's impossible to determine the condition of the vehicles put up for bid, prices can go way out of control, and auction employees, professional sellers, their relatives, and their friends usually pick over the good stuff long before you ever see it.

To attend commercial auctions is to swim with the piranhas. They are frequented by "ringers" who bid up the prices, and by professional dealers who pick up cheap, worn-out vehicles unloaded by new-car dealers and independents. There are no guarantees, cash is required, and quality is apt to be as low as the price. Remember, too, that auction purchases are subject to provincial and federal sales taxes, the auction's sales commission (3–5 percent), and, in some cases, an administrative fee of $25–$50.

If you are interested in shopping at an auto auction, remember that certain days are reserved for dealers only, so call ahead. You'll find the vehicles locked in a compound, but you should have ample opportunity to inspect them and, in some cases, take a short drive around the property before the auction begins.

The Internet

The Internet is the worst place to buy a used car. You don't know the seller and you know even less about the car. It's easy for an individual to sell a car they don't own, and it's even easier to create a virtual dealership, with photos of a huge inventory and a modern showroom, when the operation is likely made up of one guy working out of his basement.

Rating systems are unreliable too. Ratings from "happy customers" may be nothing but ploys—fictitious postings created by the seller to give out five-star ratings and the appearance that the company is honest and reliable.

If you must use the Internet, get the seller's full name and a copy of their driver's licence, plus lots of references. Then go see the vehicle, take a road test, and have a mechanic verify if the car is roadworthy and able to pass a safety inspection.

Although you take an even bigger risk buying out of province or in the States, there are a few precautions you can take to protect yourself. First off, compare shipping fees with a Canadian automobile transporter like Hansen's (*www.lhf.com/ebay*), and put your money into an escrow account until the vehicle is delivered in satisfactory condition.

If the car is located in the United States, print out the tips found on eBay's website at *pages.ebay.ca/ebaymotors/explained/checklist/howtobuyUS.html*. The website takes you through each step in detail and will tell you if the car is admissible in Canada and what are the likely modification requirements. If it needs modification, you should check with a mechanic for an estimate. You will also need to get a recall clearance letter from the dealer or automaker in order to pass federal inspection. Additional information can be obtained by calling the Registrar of Imported Vehicles (RIV) at 1-888-848-8240, or by visiting their website at *www.riv.ca*.

Canadian car sales websites

- *AMVOQ.ca*—Quebec used car classifieds
- *AutoHunter.ca*—Alberta used car classifieds
- *Autonet.ca*—New and used cars and trucks, new car dealers, new car prices, and reviews
- *Autotrader.ca*—Used car classifieds from all across Canada
- *BuySell.com*—Classifieds from all across Canada
- *eBay.ca*—The premiere site for used cars located anywhere in the world
- *Samarins.com/dealers*—New and used car dealers in the Toronto area; *www.samarins.com/links.html* is a valuable compendium of other helpful links for Canadians
- *UsedCarsOntario.com*—Used car classifieds for major cities in Ontario, with links and articles

U.S. car sales websites

- *Autotrader.com*—New and used car classifieds
- *Cars.com*—Ditto, except for an Advanced Search option
- *CarsDirect.com*—One of the largest car buying sites
- *eBay.com*—Similar to the Canadian site

- *Edmunds.com*—Lots of price quotes and articles
- *TheBigLot.com*—Another large car buying site

Financing Choices

You shouldn't spend more than 30 percent of your annual gross income on the purchase of a new or used vehicle. By keeping the initial cost low, there is less risk to you, and you may be able to pay mostly in cash. This can be an effective bargaining tool to use with private sellers, but dealers are less impressed by cash sales because they lose their kickback from the finance companies.

Credit Unions

A credit union is the best place to borrow money for a used car at competitive interest rates (expect around 8.75 percent) and with easy repayment terms. You'll have to join the credit union or have an account with it before the loan is approved. You'll also probably have to come up with a larger down payment relative to what other lending institutions require.

In addition to giving you reasonable loan rates, credit unions help car buyers in other ways. Toronto's Alterna Savings (*www.metrocu.com/Personal/Services/AutoAdvisoryServices*), for example, has a CarFacts Centre, which provides free, objective advice on car shopping, purchasing, financing, and leasing. Their Automotive Advisors provide free consultations in person or by phone.

Banks

Banks are less leery of financing used cars than they once were, and they generally charge rates that are competitive with what dealers offer. As of April 2007, the interest rates provided by Canadian financial institutions on a 3-year, $15,000 car loan were as follows:

INTEREST RATES FOR A $15,000 CAR LOAN	
Bank of Montreal	7.60 %
Bank of Nova Scotia	6.75 %
Caisses Desjardins	8.59 %
CIBC	7.75 %
Ontario Civil Service Credit Union	6.00 %
Royal Bank	8.35 %
TD Canada Trust	8.50 %
Source: Canoe.ca.	

In your quest for a bank loan, keep in mind that the loan officer will be impressed by a prepared budget and sound references, particularly if you seek out a loan before choosing a vehicle. If you haven't got a loan, it wouldn't hurt to buy from the local dealer, since banks like to encourage businesses in their area.

The Internet also offers help for people who need an auto loan and want quick approval but don't want to face a banker. Used-car buyers can post a loan application on a bank's website, such as TD Canada Trust's 6- and 7-Year Auto Loan (*www. tdcanadatrust.com/lending/autoloan.jsp*), even if they don't have an account. Scotiabank offers a great Personal Lending website with resources for students as well as car buyers (*www.scotiabank.com/cda/content/0,1608,CID513_LIDen,00.html*); however, you have to contact a branch to apply for a loan.

Dealers

Dealer financing isn't the rip-off it once was, but still be watchful for all the expensive little extras the dealer may try to pencil into the contract, because, believe it or not, dealers make far more of a profit on used-car sales than on new-car deals. Don't write them off for financing, though—they can finance your purchase at rates that compete with those of banks and finance companies because they agree to take back the vehicle if the creditor defaults on the loan (Mitsubishi is adrift in red ink because of its sub-prime loans to dead-beat drivers). Some dealers mislead their customers into thinking they can get financing at rates far below the prime rate. Actually, the dealer jacks up the base price of the vehicle to compensate for the lower interest charges.

Dealer Scams

Most dealer sales scams are so obvious, they're laughable. But like the Nigerian "lost fortune" email scams, enough stupid people get sucked in to make these dealer deceptions profitable.

One of the more common tricks is to not identify the previous owner because the vehicle either was used commercially, was problem-prone, or had been written off as a total loss after an accident. It's also not uncommon to discover that the mileage has been turned back, particularly if the vehicle was part of a company's fleet. Your best defence? Demand the name of the vehicle's previous owner and then run a VIN check through CarProof as a prerequisite to purchasing it.

It would be impossible to list all the dishonest tricks employed in used-vehicle sales. As soon as the public is alerted to one scheme, crooked sellers use other, more elaborate frauds. Nevertheless, under industry-financed provincial compensation funds, buyers can get substantial refunds if defrauded by a dealer.

Here are some of the more common fraudulent practices you're likely to encounter.

Evading Sales Tax by Trimming the Price

Here's where your own greed will do you in. In a tactic used almost exclusively by small, independent dealers and some private sellers, the buyer is told that he or she can pay less sales tax by listing a lower selling price on the contract. But what if the vehicle turns out to be a lemon, or the sales agent has falsified the model year or mileage? The hapless buyer is offered a refund on the fictitious purchase price indicated on the contract. If the buyer wanted to take the dealer to court, it's quite unlikely that he or she would get any more than the contract price. Moreover, both the buyer and dealer could be prosecuted for making a false declaration to avoid paying sales tax.

Phony Private Sales ("Curbsiders")

Individual transactions account for about three times as many used-vehicle sales as dealer sales, and crooked dealers get in on the action by posing as private sellers. Called "curbsiders," these scammers lure unsuspecting buyers through lower prices, cheat the federal government out of the GST, and routinely violate provincial registration and consumer protection regulations. Bob Beattie, executive director of the Used Car Dealers Association of Ontario, *www.ucda.org*, once estimated that about 20 percent of so-called private sellers in Ontario are actually curbsiders. Dealers in large cities like Toronto, Calgary, and Vancouver believe curbsiders sell half of the cars advertised in the local papers. This scam is easy to detect if the seller can't produce the original sales contract or show repair bills made out over a long period of time in his or her own name. You can usually identify a car dealer in the want ads section of the newspaper—just check to see if the same telephone number is repeated in many different ads. Sometimes you can trip up a curbsider by requesting information on the phone, without identifying the specific vehicle. If the seller asks you which car you are considering, you know you're dealing with a curbsider.

Legitimate car dealers claim to deplore the dishonesty of curbsider crooks, yet they are their chief suppliers. Dealership sales managers, auto auction employees, and newspaper classified ad sellers all know the names, addresses, and phone numbers of these thieves but don't act on the information. Newspapers want the ad dollars, auctions want the action, and dealers want someplace they can unload their wrecked, rust-cankered, and odometer-tricked junkers with impunity. Talk about hypocrisy, eh?

Curbsiders are particularly active in Western Canada, importing vehicles from other provinces where they were sold by dealers, wreckers, insurance companies, and junkyards (after having been written off as total losses). They then place private classified ads in B.C. and Alberta papers, sell their stock, and then import more. Writes one Vancouver *Lemon-Aid* reader frustrated by the complicity of the provincial government and local papers in this rip-off:

> The story is the lack of sensitivity by the newspapers who turn a blind eye and let consumers get ripped off…. The newspapers are making money, ICBC [Insurance Corporation of British Columbia] is making money, the cops acknowledge wide-scale dumping on the West Coast…. Governments have no willpower to take on organized fraud.

Buyers taken in by these scam artists should sue both the seller and the newspaper that carried the original classified ad in small claims court. When just a few cases are won in court and the paper's competitors play up the story, the practice will cease.

"Free-Exchange" Privilege

Dealers get a lot of sales mileage out of this deceptive offer. The dealer offers to exchange any defective vehicle for any other vehicle in stock. What really happens, though, is that the dealer won't have anything else selling for the same price and so will demand a cash bonus for the exchange—or you may get the dubious privilege of exchanging one lemon for another.

"Money-Back" Guarantee

Once again, the purchaser feels safe in buying a used car with this kind of guarantee. After all, what could be more honest than a money-back guarantee? Dealers using this technique often charge exorbitant handling charges, rental fees, or mechanical repair costs to the customer who's bought one of these vehicles and then returned it.

"50/50" Guarantee

This can be a trap. Essentially, the dealer will pay half of the repair costs over a limited period of time. It's a fair offer if an independent garage does the repairs. If not, the dealer can always inflate the repair costs to double their actual worth and then write up a bill for that amount (a scam sometimes used in "goodwill" settlements). The buyer winds up paying the full price of repairs that would probably have been much cheaper at an independent garage. The best kind of used-vehicle warranty is 100 percent with full coverage for a fixed term, even if that term is relatively short.

"As Is" and "No Warranty"

Neither phrase means much.

Remember, every vehicle carries a provincial legal warranty protecting you from misrepresentation and the premature failure of key mechanical or body components. Nevertheless, sellers often write "as is" or "no warranty" in the contract in the hope of dissuading buyers from pressing legitimate claims.

Generally, when "as is" has been written into the contract or bill of sale, it usually means that you're aware of mechanical defects, you're prepared to accept the responsibility for any damage or injuries caused by the vehicle, and you're agreeing to pay all repair costs. However, the courts have held that the "as is" clause is not a blank cheque to cheat buyers, and must be interpreted in light of the seller's true intent. Was there an attempt to deceive the buyer by including this clause? Did the buyer really know what the "as is" clause could do to his or her future legal rights? It's also been held that the courts may consider oral representations ("parole evidence") as an expressed warranty, even though they were never written into the formal contract. So, if a seller makes claims as to the fine quality of the used vehicle, these claims can be used as evidence. Courts generally ignore "as is" clauses when the vehicle has been intentionally misrepresented, when the dealer is the seller, or when the defects are so serious that the seller is presumed to have known of their existence. Private sellers are usually given more latitude than dealers or their agents.

Odometer Fraud

Who says crime doesn't pay? It most certainly does if you turn back odometers for a living in Canada.

Carfax (*www.carfax.com*) estimates that each year close to 90,000 vehicles with tampered odometers reach the Canadian marketplace—at a cost to Canadians of more than $3.56 million. This is about double the incidents one would expect based on a 2002 U.S. National Highway Traffic Safety Administration study that pegs odometer fraud at 450,000 vehicles annually. NHTSA estimates that half of the cars with reset odometers are relatively new high-mileage rental cars or fleet vehicles.

Obviously, gangs of odometer scammers ply their trade in Canada because it seems as if no one cares what they do, and the average resale value of a doctored car can be boosted by thousands of dollars, or 10 cents profit for each mile erased from the odometer. Moreover, electronic digital odometers make tampering child's play for anyone with a laptop computer, or anyone who has sufficient skill to simply replace the dashboard's instrument panel.

Think: When was the last time you heard of a dealership being charged with odometer fraud? Probably a long time ago, if at all. And what is the punishment for those dealers convicted of defrauding buyers? Not jail time or loss of their franchises. More than likely, it'll be just a small fine.

The RCMP hate odometer-tampering complaints because rolling back a vehicle's odometer is a common crime that's hard to prove and gobbles up law enforcement man-hours. In theory, these fraud artists face $100,000 fines and two years in jail under the Federal Weights and Measures Act, the Canadian Criminal Code, and provincial consumer-protection statutes. However, in practice, few odometer tampering cases make it to court because the intent to defraud is so difficult to prove against mechanics who claim they only fixed the odometer, a practice allowed under Canadian federal and provincial laws.

Misrepresentation

Used vehicles can be misrepresented in a variety of ways. A used airport commuter minivan may be represented as having been used by a Sunday school class. A mechanically defective sports car that's been rebuilt after several major accidents may have plastic filler in the body panels to muffle the rattles or hide the rust damage, heavy oil in the motor to stifle the clanks, and cheap retread tires to eliminate the thumps. Your best protection against these dirty tricks is to have the vehicle's quality completely verified by an independent mechanic before completing the sale. Of course, you can still cancel the sale if you learn of the misrepresentation only after taking the vehicle home, but your chances of successfully doing so dwindle as time passes.

> I'm finding it difficult finding a reasonably priced used car in the Toronto area. Many of the ads for private sales here turn out to be dealers or mechanics selling cars pretending to be private persons. Also, the prices are ridiculously inflated. Your books are a great read and have made me at least slow down and ask questions. For example, I almost got caught in a lease the other day and pulled out at the last minute. All this advertising had me believe there would be zero down, zero delivery, etc. until I found out there would be a $350 lease acquisition fee and a $250 admin. fee and all kinds of other charges, some legitimate such as licensing. However, my zero down turned into a whopping $1,200! I'm just now getting into your leasing section....

Private Scams

A lot of space in this guide has been used to describe how used-car dealers and scam artists cheat uninformed buyers. Of course, private individuals can be dishonest, too. In either case, protect yourself at the outset by keeping your deposit small and by getting as much information as possible about the vehicle you're considering. Then, after a test drive, you may sign a written agreement to purchase the vehicle and give a deposit of sufficient value to cover the seller's advertising costs, subject to cancellation if the automobile fails its inspection. After you've taken these precautions, watch out for the following private sellers' tricks.

Vehicles That Are Stolen or Have Finance Owing

Many used vehicles are sold privately without free title because the original auto loan was never repaid. You can avoid being cheated by asking for proof of purchase and payment from a private seller. Be especially wary of any individual who offers to sell a used vehicle for an incredibly low price. Check the sales contract to determine who granted the original loan, and call the lender to see if it's been repaid. Place a call to the provincial Ministry of Transportation to ascertain whether the car is registered in the seller's name. Find out if a finance company is named as beneficiary on the auto insurance policy. Finally, contact the original dealer to determine whether there are any outstanding claims.

In Ontario, all private sellers must purchase a Used Vehicle Information Package at one of 300 provincial Driver and Vehicle Licence Issuing Offices, or online at *www.mto.gov.on.ca/english/dandv/vehicle/used.htm*. This package, which costs $20, contains the vehicle's registration history in Ontario; the vehicle's lien information (i.e., if there are any liens registered on the vehicle); the fair market value on which the minimum tax payable will apply; and other information such as consumer tips, vehicle safety standards inspection guidelines, retail sales tax information, and forms for bills of sale.

In other provinces, buyers don't have easy access to this information. Generally, you have to contact the provincial office that registers property and pay a small fee for a computer printout that may or may not be accurate. You'll be asked for the current owner's name and the car's VIN, which is usually found on the driver's side of the dashboard.

There are two high-tech ways to get the goods on a dishonest seller. First, have a dealer of that particular model run a vehicle history check through the automaker's online network. This will tell you who the previous owners and dealers were, what warranty and recall repairs were carried out, and what other free repair programs may still apply. Second, you can use CarProof (*www.carproof.com*) to carry out a background check.

Wrong Registration

Make sure the seller's vehicle has been properly registered with provincial transport authorities; if it isn't, it may be stolen, or you could be dealing with a curbsider.

Summary: Buying the Best for Less

You can get a reliable used car or minivan at a reasonable price—it just takes some patience and homework. Avoid potential headaches by becoming thoroughly familiar with your legal rights, as outlined in Part Two, and by buying a vehicle recommended in Part Three. The following is a summary of the steps to take to keep your level of risk to a minimum.

1. Keep your present vehicle at least eight to 10 years. Don't get panicked over high fuel costs—depreciation is a greater threat to your pocketbook.
2. Sell to a dealer if the reduction in GST and PST on your next purchase is greater than the potential profit of selling privately.
3. Sell privately if you can get at least 15 percent more than what the dealer offered.
4. Buy from a private party, rental car outlet, or dealer (in that order).
5. Use an auto broker to save time and money, but pay a set fee, not a commission.
6. Buy only a *Lemon-Aid* recommended 3- or 5-year-old vehicle with some original warranty left that can be transferred.
7. Carefully inspect front-drive vehicles that have reached their fifth year. Pay particular attention to the engine intake manifold and head gasket, CV joints, steering box, and brakes. Make sure the spare tire and tire jack haven't been removed.
8. Buy a full-sized, rear-drive delivery van and then add the convenience features that you would like (seats, sound system, etc.) instead of opting for a more expensive, smaller, less powerful minivan.
9. Don't buy an extended warranty for a particular model year unless it's recommended in *Lemon-Aid*.
10. Have repairs done by independent garages offering lifetime warranties.

11. Install used or reconditioned parts; demand that original parts be used for accident repairs.
12. Keep all the previous owner's repair bills to facilitate warranty claims and to let mechanics know what's already been replaced or repaired.
13. Upon delivery, adjust mirrors to reduce blind spots and adjust head restraints to prevent your head from snapping back in the event of a collision. On airbag-equipped vehicles, move the seat backward more than half its travel distance and sit at least a foot away from the airbag housing.
14. Ensure that the side airbags include head protection.
15. Make sure that both the dealer and automaker have your name in their computers as the new owner of record. Ask for a copy of your vehicle's history, which is stored in the same computer. Get a $25 Internet download or data disc of all your vehicle's service bulletins from ALLDATA (see Appendix III). This will keep you current as to the latest secret warranties, recalls, and troubleshooting tips for correcting factory screw-ups.

Part Two
JUSTICE AND INJUSTICE

Butts and Ears

Businesses and politicians hear better through their rears than their ears.

SAUL ALINSKY

GRASSROOTS HUMAN RIGHTS ADVOCATE

Regulatory Agencies

In youth they are vigorous, aggressive, evangelistic and even intolerant. Later they become mellow; and in old age after some 10 or 15 years they become, with some exceptions, either an arm of the industry they are regulating or senile.

JOHN KENNETH GALBRAITH

CANADIAN ECONOMIST

THE GREAT CRASH

When Good Cars Turn Bad

Used cars can turn out to be bad buys for two reasons: Either they were misrepresented, or they are afflicted with defects that make them unreliable or dangerous to drive. Misrepresentation is relatively easy to prove; you simply have to show the vehicle doesn't conform to the oral or written sales representations made before or during the time of purchase. These representations include sales brochures and newspaper, radio, and television ads.

Private sales can easily be cancelled if the mileage has been turned back, if accident damage hasn't been disclosed, or if the seller is really a dealer in disguise. Even descriptive phrases like "well-maintained," "driven by a woman" (is this meant to be a positive or negative feature?), or "excellent condition" can get the seller into trouble if misrepresentation is alleged.

Defects are usually confirmed by an independent garage examination that shows that either the deficiencies are premature, factory-related, or not maintenance-related, or that they were hidden at the time of purchase. It doesn't matter if the vehicle was sold new or used. In fact, most of the small claims court victories against Ford relating to defective engines and transmissions were won by owners of used Windstars, Tauruses, and Sables who sued both the seller and the automaker.

Nipping that Lemon in the Bud

Here is 37 years' worth of information on strategy, tactics, negotiation tools, and jurisprudence you may cite to hang tough and get an out-of-court settlement, or to win your case without spending a fortune on lawyers and research.

Used-car and minivan defects are covered by two warranties: the *expressed* warranty, which has a fixed time limit, and the *implied*, or *legal*, warranty, the application of which is entirely up to a judge's discretion.

Expressed warranties

The expressed warranty given by the seller is often full of empty promises, and it allows the dealer and manufacturer to act as judge and jury when deciding whether a vehicle was misrepresented or is afflicted by defects they'll pay to correct. Rarely does it provide a money-back guarantee.

Some of the more familiar lame excuses used in denying expressed warranty claims are "You abused the car," "It was poorly maintained," "It's normal wear and tear," "It's rusting from the outside, not the inside," and "It passed the safety inspection." Ironically, the expressed warranty sometimes says there is no warranty at all or that the vehicle is sold "as is." Fortunately, courts often throw out these exclusions by upholding two legal concepts:

- The vehicle must be fit for the purpose for which it was purchased.
- The vehicle must be of merchantable quality when sold.

USED CAR EXPRESSED WARRANTY EXCLUSIONS

FOR ANY DAMAGE AND/OR BREAKDOWN RESULTING FROM FREEZING, RUST OR CORROSION, WATER OR FLOOD, ACTS OF GOD, SALT, ENVIRONMENTAL DAMAGE, CHEMICALS, CONTAMINATION OF FLUIDS, FUELS, COOLANTS OR LUBRICANTS.

FOR ANY BREAKDOWN CAUSED BY MISUSE, ABUSE, NEGLIGENCE, LACK OF NORMAL MAINTENANCE, OR IMPROPER SERVICING OR REPAIRS SUBSEQUENT TO PURCHASE. FOR ANY BREAKDOWN CAUSED BY CONTAMINANTS RESULTING FROM YOUR FAILURE TO PERFORM RECOMMENDED MAINTENANCE SERVICES, OR FAILURE TO MAINTAIN PROPER LEVELS OF LUBRICANTS AND/OR COOLANTS, OR FAILURE TO PROTECT YOUR VEHICLE FROM FURTHER DAMAGE WHEN A BREAKDOWN HAS OCCURRED OR FAILURE TO HAVE YOUR VEHICLE TOWED TO THE SERVICE FACILITY WHEN CONTINUED OPERATION MAY RESULT IN FURTHER DAMAGE. CONTINUED OPERATION INCLUDES YOUR FAILURE TO OBSERVE WARNING LIGHTS, GAUGES, OR ANY OTHER SIGNS OF OVERHEATING OR COMPONENT FAILURE, SUCH AS FLUID LEAKAGE, SLIPPING, KNOCKING, OR SMOKING, AND NOT PROTECTING YOUR VEHICLE BY CONTINUING TO DRIVE CREATING DAMAGE BEYOND THE INITIAL FAILURE.

FOR ANY REPAIR OR REPLACEMENT OF ANY COVERED PART IF A BREAKDOWN HAS NOT OCCURRED OR IF THE WEAR ON THAT PART HAS NOT EXCEEDED THE FIELD TOLERANCES ALLOWED BY THE MANUFACTURER.

FOR LOSS OF USE, TIME, PROFIT, INCONVENIENCE, OR ANY OTHER CONSEQUENTIAL LOSS AND ANY CONSEQUENTIAL DAMAGE TO A NON-COVERED PART THAT RESULTS FROM A BREAKDOWN.

WHEN THE RESPONSIBILITY FOR THE REPAIR IS COVERED BY A MANUFACTURER AND/OR DEALER CUSTOMER ASSISTANCE PROGRAM

FOR ANY PRE-EXISTING CONDITION KNOWN TO YOU OR FOR ANY BREAKDOWN OCCURRING BEFORE COVERAGE TAKES EFFECT OR PRIOR TO THE CONTRACT PURCHASE DATE.

Not surprisingly, sellers use the expressed warranty to reject claims, while smart plaintiffs ignore the expressed warranty and argue for a refund under the implied warranty instead.

Implied warranties

The implied warranty ("of fitness") is your ace in the hole. As clearly stated in the under-reported Saskatchewan decision *Maureen Frank v. General Motors of Canada Limited* (see page 99), in which the judge declared that paint discoloration and peeling shouldn't occur within 11 years of the purchase of the vehicle, the implied warranty is an important legal principle. It is solidly supported by a large body of federal and provincial laws, regulations, and jurisprudence, and it protects you primarily from hidden defects that may be either dealer- or factory-related. But the concept also includes misrepresentation and a host of other scams.

This warranty also holds dealers to a higher standard of conduct than private sellers since, unlike private sellers, they are presumed to be aware of the defects present in the vehicles they sell. That way, they can't just pass the ball to the automaker or previous owner and walk away from the dispute.

Dealers are also expected to disclose defects that have been repaired. For instance, in British Columbia, provincial law (the *Motor Dealer Act*) says that a dealer must disclose damages that cost more than $2,000 to fix. This is a good law to cite in other jurisdictions.

In spite of all your precautions, there's still a 10 percent chance you'll buy a lemon, says Runzheimer International. It confirms that one out of every 10 vehicles produced by the Detroit Big Three is likely to be a lemon (a figure also used by GM VP Bob Lutz). This number would have likely been much higher if Ford Focus and Windstar, Chrysler Caravan, and GM Saturn owners had also been polled.

Why the implied warranty is so effective

- It establishes the concept of reasonable durability (see "How Long Should a Part or Repair Last"), meaning that parts are expected to last for a reasonable period of time, as stated in jurisprudence, judged by independent mechanics, or expressed in extended warranties given by the automaker in the past (7–10 years/160,000 km for engines and transmissions).
- It covers the entire vehicle and can be applied for whatever period of time the judge decides.
- It can order that the vehicle be taken back, or a major repair cost be refunded.

> I wanted to let you and your readers know that the information you publish about Ford's paint failure problem is invaluable. Having read through your "how-to guide" on addressing this issue, I filed suit against Ford for the "latent" paint defect. The day prior to our court date, I received a settlement offer by phone for 75 percent of what I was initially asking for.

- It can order that plaintiffs be given compensation for supplementary transportation, inconvenience, mental distress, missed work, screwed-up vacations, insurance paid while the vehicle was in the repair shop, repairs done by other repairers, and exemplary, or punitive, damages in cases where the seller was a real weasel.
- It is often used by small claims court judges to give refunds to plaintiffs "in equity" (out of fairness), rather than through a strict interpretation of contract law.

How Long Should a Part or Repair Last?

How do you know when a part or service hasn't lasted as long as it should and whether you should seek a full or partial refund? Sure, you have a gut feeling based on the use of the vehicle, the way you maintained it, and the extent of work that was carried out. But you'll need more than emotion to win compensation from garages and automakers.

You can definitely get a refund if a repair or part lasts beyond its guarantee but not as long as is generally expected. You'll have to show what the auto industry considers to be "reasonable durability," however.

This isn't all that difficult if you use the following benchmarks that automakers, mechanics, and the courts have recognized over the years:

REASONABLE PART DURABILITY

ACCESSORIES

Air conditioner	7 years
Cruise control	5 years/100,000 km
Power doors, windows	5 years
Radio	5 years

BODY

Paint (peeling)	7–11 years
Rust (perforations)	7–11 years
Rust (surface)	5 years
Water/wind/air leaks	5 years

BRAKE SYSTEM

Brake drum	120,000 km
Brake drum linings	35,000 km
Brake rotor	60,000 km
Brake calipers/pads	30,000 km
Master cylinder	100,000 km
Wheel cylinder	80,000 km

ENGINE AND DRIVETRAIN

CV joint	6 years/160,000 km
Differential	7 years/160,000 km
Engine (diesel)	15 years/350,000 km
Engine (gas)	7 years/160,000 km
Motor	7 years/112,000 km
Radiator	4 years/80,000 km
Transfer case	7 years/160,000 km
Transmission (auto.)	7 years/160,000 km
Transmission (man.)	10 years/250,000 km
Transmission oil cooler	5 years/100,000 km

EXHAUST SYSTEM

Catalytic converter	5 years/100,000 km or more
Muffler	2 years/40,000 km
Tailpipe	3 years/60,000 km

IGNITION SYSTEM		STEERING AND SUSPENSION	
Cable set	60,000 km	Alignment	1 year/20,000 km
Electronic module	5 years/80,000 km	Ball joints	10 years/160,000 km
Retiming	20,000 km	Coil springs	10 years/160,000 km
Spark plugs	20,000 km	Power steering	5 years/80,000 km
Tune-up	20,000 km	Shock absorber	2 years/40,000 km
		Struts	5 years/80,000 km
SAFETY COMPONENTS		Tires (radial)	5 years/80,000 km
Airbags	life of vehicle	Wheel bearing	3 years/60,000 km
ABS brakes	7 years/160,000 km		
ABS computer	10 years/160,000 km	**VISIBILITY**	
Seatbelts	life of vehicle	Halogen/fog lights	3 years
		Sealed beam	2 years
		Windshield wiper	5 years

Much of the above table's guidelines are extrapolated from the terms of automaker payouts to dissatisfied customers within the past three decades, and from Chrysler's original 7-year powertrain warranty, applicable from 1991 to 1995 and then reapplied in 2001. Other sources for this table are:

- Ford and GM transmission warranties, which are outlined in their secret warranties
- Ford, GM, and Toyota engine "goodwill" programs, which are laid out in their internal service bulletins
- Court judgments where judges have given their own guidelines as to what constitutes reasonable durability

Airbags

Airbags usually carry a lifetime warranty. Chrysler confirmed as much in its replacement program for 1999 minivan airbags (go to the NHTSA website at *www-odi.nhtsa.dot.gov/cars/problems/recalls/recallsearch.cfm* and search for Campaign ID Number 04V480000). The admission on the following page can serve as a handy benchmark as to how long one can expect these components to last.

Any personal injuries or interior damages caused by airbag deployment are covered by your accident insurance policy. However, if the airbag fails to deploy, or there is a sudden deployment for no apparent reason, the automaker and the dealer should be held jointly responsible for all injuries and damages caused by the failure.

Inadvertent deployment may occur after passing over a bump in the road or slamming the car door, or, in some Chrysler minivans, simply by putting the key in the ignition. This happens more often than you might imagine, judging by the

NHTSA CAMPAIGN ID NUMBER: 04V480000

Make: DODGE Model: CARAVAN Year: 1999 Manufacturer: DAIMLERCHRYSLER CORPORATION
NHTSA CAMPAIGN ID Number: 04V480000 Mfg's Report Date: OCT 05, 2004 Component:
AIRBAGS Potential Number Of Units Affected: 955,344

SUMMARY: On certain minivans, the driver's airbag may become disabled due to a failure of the
clockspring, which is located in the hub of the steering wheel.

CONSEQUENCE: This condition will manifest itself through illumination of the airbag warning
lamp, and could eventually result in a driver's airbag open circuit if the part is not replaced in
a reasonable amount of time.

REMEDY: Dealers will replace the clockspring assembly on all covered vehicles with 70,000
miles [112,650 km] or less. For those vehicles with more than 70,000 miles [112,650 km],
DaimlerChrysler will offer an extended lifetime warranty, under which it will replace the
clockspring at no charge if it fails. DaimlerChrysler will also reimburse owners who have paid
to have the clock spring replaced on their vehicles. The recall began on October 12, 2004.
Owners should contact DaimlerChrysler at 1-800-853-1403.

NOTES: DaimlerChrysler Recall No. D17. Customers can contact the National Highway Traffic
Safety Administration's auto safety hotline at 1-888-dash-2-dot (1-888-327-4236).

hundreds of recalls and thousands of complaints recorded on NHTSA's website.

Your car's data recorder (see page 88) can be used to prove that the airbag, brakes, or throttle control failed prior to an accident. Simply hook a computer up and then download the data from your vehicle's "black box." This will likely lead to a more generous settlement from the two parties and will prevent your insurance premiums from being jacked up.

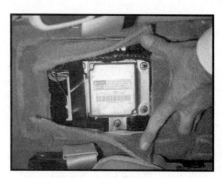

Emissions Components

Car companies have got themselves into hot water repeatedly over the years for refusing to replace emissions parts free of charge. These parts are covered by the emissions warranty. The warranty was set up by automakers with the approval of the U.S. Environmental Protection Agency (EPA), which also monitors the warranty. Canada has approved the same warranty, but leaves enforcement up to the States and the courts. Ford and Chrysler have both been fined by the EPA for violating the warranty's provisions, and have entered into consent agreements to respect owner warranty rights (see "Emissions Control Warranties" on page 63).

Use the manufacturer's emissions warranty as your primary guideline for the expected durability of high-tech electronic and mechanical pollution-control components, such as powertrain control modules (PCMs) and catalytic converters. Look first at your owner's manual for an indication of which parts on your vehicle are covered. If you don't come up with much information, ask the auto manufacturer for a list of specific components covered by the emissions warranty. If you're stonewalled, ask your local Member of Parliament to get the info from Transport Canada or Environment Canada and invest $25 (U.S.) in an ALLDATA service bulletin subscription (1982–2006 models). Or you can avoid the ALLDATA fee by accessing bulletin numbers and titles at *www.alldata.com/recalls*, or NHTSA's free service bulletin summary at *www-odi.nhtsa.dot.gov/cars/problems/tsb* (search for the complete bulletin by its number or by the car model and year).

Getting Action

Before we go any further, let's get one thing straight: A telephone call usually won't get you much action from a corporation. Automakers and their dealers want to make money, not give it back. Customer service advisors are paid to *apply* the warranty policy; don't expect them to *make* policy due to your claim's extenuating circumstances.

To get action, you have to kick your claim upstairs, where the company representatives have more power. This can usually be accomplished by sending your claim to the legal affairs department (typically found in Ontario). It should be a registered letter, fax, or email—something that creates a paper trail and gets attention. What's more, that letter must contain the threat that you will use the implied warranty against the defendant and cite convincing jurisprudence to win your small claims court action in the same region where that business operates.

On the following pages are two sample complaint letters that show you the type of ammunition you'll need in order to invoke the implied warranty to get a refund for a bad car or ineffective repairs.

Legal "Secrets" that Work for You

Send a claim letter to both the seller (if they're a dealer) and the automaker to let them work out together how much they will refund to you. Make sure you keep plenty of copies of the complaint and indicate how you can most easily be reached.

Unfair sales contracts can be cancelled by a judge, even though they were never intended to be fair—lawyers spend countless hours making sure their corporate clients are well protected with ironclad standard-form contracts. Judges look upon these agreements, called "contracts of adhesion," with a great deal of skepticism. They know these loan documents, insurance contracts, and automobile leases grant consumers little or no bargaining power. So when a dispute arises over terms or language, provincial consumer protection statutes require that judges interpret these contracts in the way most favourable to the consumer. Simply put, ignorance can be a good defence.

USED VEHICLE COMPLAINT LETTER/FAX/EMAIL

WITHOUT PREJUDICE

Date: _____
Name: _____

Please be advised that I am dissatisfied with my used vehicle, a (state model), for the following reasons:

1. _____

2. _____

3. _____

4. _____

5. _____

In compliance with the provincial consumer protection laws and the "implied warranty" set down by the Supreme Court of Canada in *Donoghue v. Stevenson, Wharton v. GM*, and *Sharman v. Ford Canada*, I hereby request that these defects be repaired without charge. This vehicle has not been reasonably durable and is, therefore, not as represented to me.

Should you fail to repair these defects in a satisfactory manner and within a reasonable period of time, I shall get an estimate of the repairs from an independent source and claim them in court, without further delay. I also reserve my right to claim up to $1 million for punitive damages, pursuant to the Supreme Court of Canada's February 22, 2002, ruling in *Whiten v. Pilot*.

I have dealt with your company because of its honesty, competence, and sincere regard for its clients. I am sure that my case is the exception and not the rule.

A positive response within the next five (5) days would be appreciated.

(signed with telephone number, fax number, or email address)

Judges in civil courts in common-law provinces have considerable latitude in allowing hearsay evidence if it's introduced properly. But it is essential that printed evidence and/or witnesses (relatives are not excluded) be available to confirm that a false representation actually occurred, that a part is failure-prone, or that its replacement is covered by a secret warranty or internal service bulletin alert. If you can't find an independent expert, introduce this evidence through the auto-maker reps and dealership service personnel who have to be at the trial anyhow. They know all about the service bulletins and extended warranty programs cited in *Lemon-Aid* and will probably contradict each other, particularly if they are excluded from the courtroom prior to testifying. Incidentally, you may wish to

SECRET WARRANTY CLAIM LETTER/FAX/EMAIL

WITHOUT PREJUDICE

Date: _____
Name: _____

Please be advised that I am dissatisfied with my vehicle, a _____, bought from
you on _____.

It has had the following recurring problems that I believe are factory-related defects, as
confirmed by internal service bulletins sent to dealers, and are covered by your "goodwill"
policies:

1. _____

2. _____

3. _____

If your "goodwill" program has ended, I ask that my claim be accepted nevertheless,
inasmuch as I was never informed of your policy while it was in effect and should not be
penalized for not knowing it existed.

I hereby formally put you on notice under federal and provincial consumer protection
statutes that your refusal to apply this extended warranty coverage in my case would be
an unfair warranty practice within the purview of the above-cited laws.

Your actions also violate the "implied warranty" set down by the Supreme Court of
Canada (*Donoghue v. Stevenson* and *Longpre v. St. Jacques Automobile*) and repeatedly
reaffirmed by provincial consumer protection laws (*Lowe v. Chrysler, Dufour v. Ford du
Canada*, and *Frank v. GM*).

I have enclosed several estimates (my bill) showing that this problem is factory related
and will (has) cost $_____ to correct. I would appreciate your refunding me
the estimated (paid) amount, failing which, I reserve the right to have the repair done
elsewhere and claim reimbursement in court without further delay. I also reserve the
right to claim up to $1 million for punitive damages, pursuant to the Supreme Court of
Canada's February 22, 2002, ruling in *Whiten v. Pilot*.

A positive response within the next five (5) days would be appreciated.

(signed with telephone number, fax number, or email address) have the court clerk send a subpoena requiring the deposition of the documents you intend to cite, all warranty extensions relevant to your problem, and other lawsuits filed against the company for similar failures. This will make the fur fly in Oshawa, Oakville, and Windsor, and will likely lead to an out-of-court settlement. Sometimes, the service manager or company representative will make key admissions if questioned closely by you, a court mediator, or the trial judge. Here are some questions to ask: Is this a common problem? Do you recognize this service bulletin? Is there a case-by-case "goodwill" plan covering this repair?

Automakers often blame owners for having pushed their vehicle beyond its limits. Therefore, when you seek to set aside the contract or get repair work reimbursed, it's essential that you get an independent mechanic or your co-workers to prove the vehicle was well maintained and driven prudently.

When asking for a refund, keep in mind the "reasonable diligence" rule that requires that a suit be filed within a reasonable amount of time after the purchase, which usually means less than a year. Because many factory-related deficiencies take years to appear, the courts have ruled that the reasonable diligence clock starts clicking only after the defect is confirmed to be manufacturer- or dealer-related (powertrain, paint, etc.). For powertrain components like engines and transmissions, this allows you to make a claim for up to seven years after the vehicle was originally put into service, regardless of whether it was bought new or used. Body failures like paint delamination (see *Frank v. GM*) are reimbursable for up to 11 years. If there have been negotiations with the dealer or the automaker, or if either the dealer or the automaker has been promising to correct the defects for some time or has carried out repeated unsuccessful repairs, the deadline for filing the lawsuit can be extended.

Yes, you can claim for hotel and travel costs or compensation for general inconvenience. Fortunately, when legal action is threatened—usually through small claims court—automakers quickly up their out-of-court offer to include most of the owner's expenses because they know the courts will be far more generous. For example, a British Columbia court's decision gave $2,257 for hotel and travel costs, and then capped it off with a $5,000 award for "inconvenience and loss of enjoyment of their luxury vehicle," to a motorist who was fed up with his lemon Cadillac (see *Wharton v. Tom Harris Chevrolet Oldsmobile Cadillac Ltd. and General Motors of Canada Limited*; B.C. Supreme Court, Vancouver, 1999/12/02; Docket C982104). In the *Sharman v. Ford* case (see page 116), the judge gave the plaintiff $7,500 for "mental distress" caused by the fear that his children would fall out of his 2000 Windstar equipped with a faulty sliding door.

As of March 19, 2005, the Supreme Court of Canada confirmed that car owners can ask for punitive, or exemplary, damages when they feel the seller's or the automaker's conduct has been so outrageously bad that the court should protect society by awarding a sum of money large enough to dissuade others from engaging in similar immoral, unethical conduct. I call this the "weasel-whacker" law. In *Prebushewski v. Dodge City Auto (1985) Ltd. and Chrysler Canada Ltd.* (2001 SKQB

537; QB1215/99JCS), the plaintiff got $25,000 in a judgment handed down December 6, 2001, in Saskatoon. The award followed testimony from Chrysler's expert witness that the company was aware of many cases where daytime running lights shorted and caused 1996 Ram pickups to catch fire. The plaintiff's truck had burned to the ground and Chrysler refused the owner's claim, saying it had fulfilled its expressed warranty obligations, in spite of its knowledge that fires were commonplace. The plaintiff sued on the grounds that there was an implied warranty that the vehicle would be safe. Justice Rothery gave this stinging rebuke in his judgment against Chrysler and its dealer:

> Not only did Chrysler know about the problems of the defective daytime running light modules, it did not advise the plaintiff of this. It simply chose to ignore the plaintiff's requests for compensation and told her to seek recovery from her insurance company. Chrysler had replaced thousands of these modules since 1988. But it had also made a business decision to neither advise its customers of the problem nor to recall the vehicles to replace the modules. While the cost would have been about $250 to replace each module, there were at least one million customers. Chrysler was not prepared to spend $250 million, even though it knew what the defective module might do.
>
> Counsel for the defendants argues that this matter had to be resolved by litigation because the plaintiff and the defendants simply had a difference of opinion on whether the plaintiff should be compensated by the defendants. Had the defendants some dispute as to the cause of the fire, that may have been sufficient to prove that they had not willfully violated this part of the *Act*. They did not. They knew about the defective daytime running light module. They did nothing to replace the burned truck for the plaintiff. They offered the plaintiff no compensation for her loss. Counsel's position that the definition of the return of the purchase price is an arguable point is not sufficient to negate the defendants' violation of this part of the *Act*. I find the violation of the defendants to be willful. Thus, I find that exemplary damages are appropriate on the facts of this case.
>
> In this case, the quantum ought to be sufficiently high as to correct the defendants' behaviour. In particular, Chrysler's corporate policy to place profits ahead of the potential danger to its customers' safety and personal property must be punished. And when such corporate policy includes a refusal to comply with the provisions of the *Act* and a refusal to provide any relief to the plaintiff, I find an award of $25,000 for exemplary damages to be appropriate. I therefore order Chrysler and Dodge City to pay: Damages in the sum of $41,969.83; Exemplary damages in the sum of $25,000; Party and party costs.

Warranty Rights

The manufacturer's or dealer's warranty is a written legal promise that a vehicle will be reasonably reliable, subject to certain conditions. Regardless of the number of subsequent owners, this promise remains in force as long as the warranty's original time/kilometre limits haven't expired. Tires aren't usually covered by car manufacturers' warranties and are warranted instead by the tiremaker on a pro-rated basis. This isn't such a good deal, because the manufacturer is making a profit by charging you the full list price. If you were to buy the same replacement tire from a discount store, you'd likely pay less, without the pro-rated rebate.

But consumers have gained additional rights following Bridgestone/Firestone's massive recall in 2001 of its defective ATX II and Wilderness tires. Because of the confusion and chaos surrounding Firestone's handling of the recall, Ford's 575 Canadian dealers stepped into the breach and replaced the tires with any equivalent tires they had in stock, no questions asked. This is an important precedent that tears down the traditional wall separating tire manufacturers from automakers in product liability claims. In essence, whoever sells the product can now be held liable for damages. In the future, Canadian consumers will have an easier time holding the dealer, the automaker, and the tire manufacturer liable, not just for recalled products but for any defect that affects the safety or reasonable durability of that product.

This is particularly true now that the Supreme Court of Canada (*Winnipeg Condominium v. Bird Construction* [1995] 1 S.C.R. 85) has ruled that defendants are liable in negligence for any designs that result in a risk to the public's safety or health. In doing so, the Supreme Court reversed a long-standing policy and provided the public with a new cause of action that had not existed before in Canada.

Other Warranties

In the U.S., safety restraints such as airbags and safety belts have warranty coverage extended for the lifetime of the vehicle, following an informal agreement made between automakers and the National Highway Traffic Safety Administration. In Canada, however, some automakers have tried to dodge this responsibility, alleging that they are separate entities, their vehicles are different, and no U.S. agreement or service bulletin can bind them. That distinction is both disingenuous and dishonest and wouldn't likely hold up in small claims court—probably the reason why most automakers relent when threatened with legal action.

Aftermarket products and services—such as gas-saving gadgets, rustproofing, and paint protectors—can render the manufacturer's warranty invalid, so make sure you're in the clear before purchasing any optional equipment or services from an independent supplier.

How fairly a warranty is applied is more important than how long it remains in effect. Once you know the normal wear rate for a mechanical component or body part, you can demand proportional compensation when you get less than normal durability—no matter what the original warranty says. Some dealers tell customers that they need to have original equipment parts installed in order to maintain their warranty. A variation on this theme requires that the selling dealer does routine servicing—including tune-ups and oil changes (with a certain brand of oil)—or the warranty is invalidated. Nothing could be further from the truth. Canadian law stipulates that whoever issues a warranty cannot make that warranty conditional on the use of any specific brand of motor oil, oil filter, or any other component, unless it's provided to the customer free of charge.

Sometimes dealers will do all sorts of minor repairs that don't correct the problem, and then after the warranty runs out, they'll tell you that major repairs are needed. You can avoid this nasty surprise by repeatedly bringing your vehicle to the dealership before the warranty ends. During each visit, insist that a written work order include the specific nature of the problem, as you see it, and a statement that this is the second, third, or fourth time the same problem has been brought to the dealer's attention. Write this down yourself, if need be. This allows you to show a pattern of non-performance by the dealer during the warranty period and establishes that the problem is both serious and chronic. When the warranty expires, you have the legal right to demand that it be extended on those items consistently reappearing on your handful of work orders. *Lowe v. Fairview Chrysler* (see page 112) is an excellent judgment that reinforces this important principle. In another lawsuit, *François Chong v. Marine Drive Imported Cars Ltd. and Honda Canada Inc.* (see page 111), a Honda owner forced Honda to fix his engine six times—until they got it right.

A retired GM service manager suggested another effective tactic to use when you're not sure that a dealer's warranty "repairs" will actually correct the problem for a reasonable period of time after the warranty expires. Here's what he says you should do:

> When you pick up the vehicle after the warranty repair has been done, hand the service manager a note to be put in your file that says you appreciate the warranty repair, however, you intend to return and ask for further warranty coverage if the problem reappears before a reasonable amount of time has elapsed—even if the original warranty has expired. A copy of the same note should be sent to the automaker.... Keep your copy of the note in the glove compartment as cheap insurance against paying for a repair that wasn't fixed correctly the first time.

Extra-Cost Warranties

Supplementary warranties providing extended coverage may be sold by the manufacturer, the dealer, or an independent third party and are automatically transferred when the vehicle is sold. They cost between $1,500 and $2,000 and should be purchased only if the vehicle you're buying is off its original warranty, if it has a reputation for being unreliable or expensive to service (see Part Three), or if you're reluctant to use the small claims courts when factory-related trouble arises. Don't let the dealer pressure you into deciding right away.

Generally, you can purchase an extended warranty any time during the period in which the manufacturer's warranty is in effect or, in some cases, shortly after buying the vehicle from a used-car dealer. An automaker's supplementary warranty is the best choice, but it will likely cost about a third more than warranties sold by independents. And in some parts of the country, notably B.C., dealers have a quasi-monopoly on selling warranties, with little competition from the independents.

Dealers love to sell extended warranties, whether you need them or not, because dealer markup represents up to 60 percent of the warranty's cost. Out of the remaining 40 percent comes the sponsor's administration costs and profit margin, calculated at another 15 percent. What's left to pay for repairs is a paltry 25 percent of the original amount. The only reason that automakers and independent warranty companies haven't been busted for this Ponzi scheme is that only half of the car buyers who purchase extended service contracts actually use them.

It's often difficult to collect on supplementary warranties because independent companies frequently go out of business or limit the warranty's coverage through subsequent mailings. Provincial laws cover both situations. If the bankrupt warranty company's insurance policy won't cover your claim, take the dealer to small claims court and ask for repair costs and the refund of the original warranty payment. Your argument for holding the dealer responsible is a simple one: By accepting a commission to act as an agent of the defunct company, the dealer took on the obligations of the company as well. As for limiting the coverage after you have bought the warranty policy, this is illegal, and it allows you to sue both the dealer and the warranty company for a refund of both the warranty and the repair costs.

Emissions Control Warranties

These little-publicized warranties can save you big bucks if major engine or exhaust components fail prematurely. They come with all new vehicles and cover major components of the emissions control system for up to 8 years/130,000 km, no matter how many times the vehicle is sold. Unfortunately, although owner's manuals vaguely mention the emissions warranty, most don't specify which parts are covered. The U.S. Environmental Protection Agency has intervened on several occasions with hefty fines against Chrysler and Ford and ruled that all major motor and fuel-system components are covered. These include fuel metering, ignition spark advance, restart, evaporative emissions, positive crankcase ventilation, engine electronics (computer modules), and catalytic converters, as well as hoses, clamps, brackets, pipes, gaskets, belts, seals, and connectors. Here are Ford's guidelines as to what the emissions warranty covers and for how long, as approved by the federal government in a recent warranty brochure (the full version can be found at *www.fordvehicles.com/assets/pdf/2007warranty.pdf*):

FORD'S EMISSIONS WARRANTY COVERAGE

EMISSIONS DEFECT WARRANTY COVERAGE

During the warranty coverage period, Ford Motor Company warrants that:

- your vehicle or engine is designed, built, and equipped to meet—at the time it is sold—the emissions regulations of the U.S. Environmental Protection Agency (EPA).
- your vehicle or engine is free from defects in factory-supplied materials or workmanship that could prevent it from conforming with applicable EPA regulations.
- you will not be charged for diagnosis, repair, replacement, or adjustment of defective emissions-related parts listed under What is Covered?

The warranty coverage period for:

- Passenger cars, light duty trucks (vehicles with a GVWR of 8,500 pounds [3,900 kg] or less
    - 8 years or 80,000 miles [129,000 km] (whichever occurs first) for catalytic converter, onboard emissions diagnostic device, natural gas vehicle (NGV) module (Bi-fuel/CNG), electronic emission control unit, and transmission control module;
    - 3 years or 36,000 miles [58,000 km] (whichever occurs first) for all other covered parts.
- Heavy duty vehicles (vehicles with a gross vehicle weight over 8,500 pounds [3,900 kg])
    - 5 years or 100,000 miles [161,000 km] (whichever occurs first) for covered diesel engine parts;
    - 5 years or 50,000 miles [80,500 km] (whichever occurs first) for all other covered parts.

See WHAT IS COVERED for list of covered parts.

EMISSIONS PERFORMANCE WARRANTY COVERAGE

Under Emissions Performance Warranty Coverage, Ford Motor Company will repair, replace, or adjust—with no charge for labor, diagnosis, or parts—any emissions control device or system, if you meet all of the following conditions:

- You have maintained and operated your vehicle according to the instructions on proper care in the Owner Guide, the Scheduled Maintenance Guide, and this booklet.
- Your vehicle fails to conform, during the warranty coverage period, to the applicable national EPA standards, as determined by an EPA approved inspection and maintenance program.
- You are subject to a penalty or sanction under local, state, or federal law because your vehicle has failed to conform to the emissions standards. (A penalty or sanction can include being denied the right to use your vehicle.)
- Your vehicle has not been tampered with, misused, or abused.

The warranty coverage period for:

- Passenger cars, light duty trucks (vehicles with a GVWR of 8,500 pounds [3,900 kg] or less)
    - 8 years or 80,000 miles [129,000 km] (whichever occurs first) for catalytic converter, onboard emissions diagnostic device, natural gas vehicle (NGV) module (Bi-fuel/CNG), electronic emission control unit, and transmission control module;
    - 2 years or 24,000 miles [39,000 km] (whichever occurs first) for all other covered parts.
- Heavy duty vehicles (vehicles with a gross vehicle weight over 8,500 pounds [3,900 kg])
    - 5 years or 100,000 miles [161,000 km] (whichever occurs first) for covered diesel engine parts;
    - 5 years or 50,000 miles [80,500 km] (whichever occurs first) for all other covered parts.

See WHAT IS COVERED for list of covered parts.

WHAT IS COVERED?

These parts are covered by both the Emissions Defect Warranty and the Emissions Performance Warranty.

LIST OF PARTS COVERED BY EMISSIONS WARRANTIES FOR CARS, LIGHT DUTY TRUCKS AND HEAVY DUTY VEHICLES

- Air Flow Sensor
- Air/Fuel Feedback Control System and Sensors
- Air Induction System
- Altitude Compensation System
- Catalytic Converter
- Cold Start Enrichment System
- Cold Start Fuel Injector[1]
- Controls for Deceleration
- Electronic Ignition System
- Electronic Engine Control Sensors and Switches
- Electronic Engine Control Unit (ECU)
- Emissions Labels
- Evaporative Emission Control System
- Exhaust Gas Recirculation (EGR) System

- Exhaust Heat Control Valve
- Exhaust Manifold
- Exhaust Pipe (Manifold to Catalyst)
- Fuel Filler Cap and Neck Restrictor
- Fuel Injection System
- Fuel Injector Supply Manifold
- Fuel Sensor[1]
- Fuel Tank (non diesel only)
- Fuel Tank Pressure Control Valve[1]
- High Voltage Battery (HEV)
- Idle Air Bypass Valve
- Ignition Coil and/or Control Module
- Intake Manifold
- Intercooler Assembly— Engine Charger

- Malfunction Indicator Lamp (MIL)/On-Board Diagnostic (OBD) System
- NGV module (Bi-fuel/CNG)
- PCV System and Oil Filler Cap
- Secondary Air Injection System
- Spark Control Components
- Spark Plugs and Ignition Wires
- Supercharger Assembly
- Synchronizer Assembly
- Thermostat
- Throttle Body Assembly (MFI)
- Transmission Control Module (TCM)
- Turbocharger Assembly
- Vacuum Distribution System

[1] Flex Fuel vehicle only

LIST OF PARTS COVERED FOR 5 YEARS OR 100,000 MILES [161.000 KM] (WHICHEVER OCCURS FIRST) BY EMISSIONS WARRANTIES FOR DIESEL ENGINES

- Air Flow Sensor
- Air Induction System
- Catalytic Converter
- Cold Start Enrichment System
- Electronic Engine Control Sensors and Switches
- Electronic Engine Control Unit (ECU)
- Emissions Labels

- Exhaust Gas Recirculation (EGR) System
- Exhaust Manifold
- Fuel Injection System
- Fuel Injector Supply Manifold
- Intake Manifold
- Intercooler Assembly— Engine Charger

- Malfunction Indicator Lamp (MIL)/On-Board Diagnostic (OBD) System
- PCV System and Oil Filler Cap
- Supercharger Assembly
- Throttle Body Assembly (MFI)
- Turbocharger Assembly

IMPORTANT INFORMATION ABOUT PARTS

Also covered by the two emissions warranties are all emissions-related bulbs, hoses, clamps, brackets, tubes, gaskets, seals, belts, connectors, non diesel fuel lines, and wiring harnesses that are used with components on the list of parts, above.

Unlike the United States, Canada has no governmentally defined list of parts that must be covered. Nevertheless, Environment Canada and the Canadian Vehicle Manufacturers' Association (CVMA) do have a Memorandum of Understanding that says emissions warranties will be identical on both sides of the border (*www.ec.gc.ca/CEPARegistry/participation/LEV_MOU_E.pdf*).

MEMORANDUM OF UNDERSTANDING

1. New light-duty vehicles and light-duty trucks sold or offered for sale in Canada by the motor vehicle manufacturers will be equipped with the same emissions control, and monitoring equipment, as the equivalent U.S. Federal models and designed to meet applicable U.S. Federal emission standards.

2. The motor vehicle manufacturers will continue their voluntary practice of warranting all exhaust and evaporative emissions components on light-duty vehicles and light-duty trucks referenced in paragraph 1 and sold in Canada for which similar warranties are offered in the U.S., except to the extent that emission control and monitoring components may be affected by Canadian fuel composition or other relevant Canadian conditions.

Many of the confidential technical service bulletins listed in Part Three show parts failures that are covered under the emissions warranty, even though motorists are routinely charged for their replacement. The following example, applicable to Ford's 2002–05 Tauruses and Sables, shows that the automaker will pay for fuel gauge repairs under the emissions warranty. Applying the same principles to other automakers' fuel gauges should be a breeze.

FORD FUEL GAUGE DOES NOT READ FULL AFTER FILLING TANK
BULLETIN NO.: 04-14-14   **DATE: MAY 2002**

FORD TAURUS, SABLE

ISSUE: Some 2002–05 Taurus/Sable vehicles may exhibit a fuel gauge which indicates the tank is only 7/8 full after filling the fuel tank. This may be due to the calibration of the fuel level indication unit.

ACTION: To service, remove the fuel delivery module and replace the fuel level indication unit. DO NOT REPLACE THE ENTIRE FUEL DELIVERY MODULE FOR THIS CONDITION.

WARRANTY STATUS: Eligible under provisions of new vehicle limited warranty coverage and **emissions warranty coverage**.

OPERATION	DESCRIPTION	TIME
041414A	Replace Fuel Gauge tank unit (includes time to remove tank, drain and refill)	1.3hrs

---

Make sure to get your emissions system checked out thoroughly by a dealer or an independent garage before the emissions warranty expires and before having the vehicle inspected by provincial emissions inspectors. In addition to ensuring you pass provincial tests, this precaution could save you up to $1,000 if both your catalytic converter and other emissions components are faulty.

Furthermore, go to the NHTSA website (*www-odi.nhtsa.dot.gov/cars/problems/recalls/recallsearch.cfm*) to look for service bulletins acknowledging that a problem exists or emissions warranties that have been extended through manufacturer recall settlements with the federal government. Then ask that your vehicle's component be covered by a similar extended warranty.

DaimlerChrysler, for example, has announced that it is extending its warranty to 10 years on catalytic converters found in 1996–2001 Cherokees, Grand Cherokees, Wranglers, Dakota trucks, and Ram vans, wagons, and pickup trucks. The investigation disclosed that a significant percentage of these vehicles experience excessive deterioration or failure of the catalytic converter—a device installed in the exhaust system to control emissions and reduce pollutants.

As a result of a design defect, the internal components of the converter move around excessively, causing the device's ceramic core to break up. Most owners experience a rattling noise from the underside of their vehicle as the catalytic converter deteriorates. Government investigators also discovered that the OBD ("check engine" light) system installed on certain 1996–98 vehicles may malfunction, leaving some owners unaware of the problem with the catalytic converter.

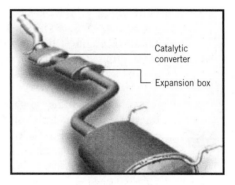

Catalytic converter

Expansion box

Under the settlement, DaimlerChrysler agreed to notify Jeep, Ram, and Dakota owners that the catalytic converter warranty on their vehicle is being extended to 10 years/193,000 km (120,000 mi.). All of these vehicles will also be covered for at least one year without mileage limitation and for two years if the vehicle fails an emissions inspection due to a factory-installed defective catalytic converter.

DaimlerChrysler says it will send notices warning owners of the potential catalytic converter failure and reminding them that their original catalytic converters are still covered by the original 8-year/130,000 km (80,000 mi.) warranty. Some owners will also receive a recall notice for repair of the defective OBD system on their vehicles. For those recalled vehicles, the catalytic converter will be inspected and repaired if found to be defective.

DaimlerChrysler has also promised to establish procedures to reimburse customers who own vehicles covered by the settlement's extended warranty or recall provisions and who paid out of their own pockets for the repair or replacement of a defective factory-installed catalytic converter.

Despite DaimlerChrysler's promises, *Lemon-Aid* predicts many owners will never learn of this free replacement—adding another secret warranty to the hopper.

Few vehicle owners know that secret warranties exist. Automakers are reluctant to make these free repair programs public because they feel that doing so would weaken confidence in their product and increase their legal liability. The closest they come to an admission is sending a "goodwill policy," "product improvement program," or "special policy" technical service bulletin (TSB) to dealers or first owners of record. Consequently, the only motorists who find out about these policies are the original owners who haven't changed their addresses or leased their vehicles. The other motorists who get compensated for repairs are the ones who read *Lemon-Aid* each year, staple TSBs to their work orders, and yell the loudest.

Remember, vehicles on their second owners and repairs done by independent garages are included in these secret warranty programs. Large, costly repairs, such as blown engines, burned transmissions, and peeling paint, are often covered. Even mundane little repairs, which can still cost you a hundred bucks or more, are frequently included in these programs.

If you have a TSB but you're still refused compensation, keep in mind that secret warranties are an admission of manufacturing negligence. Try to compromise with a pro rata adjustment from the manufacturer. If polite negotiations fail, challenge the refusal in court on the grounds that you should not be penalized for failing to make a reimbursement claim under a secret warranty you never knew existed!

Here are a few examples of secret warranties that may save you thousands of dollars. More extensive listings are found in Part Three's model ratings.

Acura

2001–03 3.2 CL; 1999–2003 TL; 2004–05 TSX

Problem: Breakage of the rear stabilizer bar link. **Warranty coverage:** Honda will replace both stabilizer bar links under a "goodwill" warranty extension that was confirmed in TSB #05-015, issued June 24, 2005.

2004–05 TL

Problem: Defective Bridgestone Turanza EL42 tires wear out prematurely. **Warranty coverage:** This "goodwill" warranty extension was confirmed in the December 24, 2005, TSB #05-076, whether owners bought their vehicle new or used. The company will also reimburse owners who already paid for the tire replacement.

Acura/Honda

1999–2003 Acura CL and TL; Honda Accord, Prelude, and Odyssey models

Problem: Defective automatic transmission and torque converter. **Warranty coverage:** This "goodwill" warranty extension was confirmed in the August 4,

2003, edition of *Automotive News*. Honda will fix or replace the transmission free of charge up to 7 years/160,000 km (100,000 mi.) whether owners bought their vehicle new or used. The company will also reimburse owners who already paid for the repair.

Audi

2002–06 S4 and A6 equipped with 2.7L turbocharged V6 engines

Problem: Defective auxiliary coolant pump leaks coolant from the pump body. When the pump fails, the coolant light will come on, warning that continued driving could cause serious engine damage. **Warranty coverage:** VW will install a Repair Kit free of charge up to 7 years/160,000 km. See TSB #05-05, published October 28, 2005.

Audi, Chrysler, Mercedes-Benz, Saab, Toyota, and VW

1997–2004 Audi A4; 1999–2002 Chrysler models equipped with a 2.7L V6; 1998–2002 Mercedes-Benz vehicles; 1998–2003 Saab 9-3 and 9-5 models; 1997–2002 Toyota and Lexus vehicles with 2.2L 4-cylinder or 3.0L V6 engines; and 1997–2004 VW Passat

Problem: Engine sludge. **Warranty coverage:** Varies; usually 7–10 years/ 160,000 km. Automakers can't automatically deny this free repair because you don't have proof of all of your oil changes, unless they can show that the sludge was caused by a missed oil change (which, according to independent mechanics, is impossible to do). Remember, the warranty has been extended to fix a factory-related problem that occurs despite regular oil changes. That's why it's the automaker's responsibility.

Service bulletins, press releases, and dealer memos are all admissions of responsibility. From there, the legal doctrine of "the balance of probabilities" applies. To wit, a defect definitely causes engine sludge, while a missed oil change may cause engine sludge. Therefore, it is more probable that the defect caused the sludge.

> My 2000 Intrepid with a 2.7L engine just recently had complete engine failure. I spent $1,200 on engine repairs. Of course Chrysler told me afterwards that they were completely unaware of this problem.
>
> After looking on the Internet I have become aware that this is a very common defect and that Chrysler is hiding from the problem. My question: Why is there not more being done to alert consumers about the Chrysler product and the total disrespect being shown to customers by Chrysler? There are many Chrysler vehicles on the road with this engine and Chrysler continues to sell this engine in the new 300 and Charger. Chrysler should be made to pay for this fraudulent business behavior.

Once the sludge condition is diagnosed, the dealer and automobile manufacturer are jointly liable for all corrective repairs plus additional damages for your inconvenience, your loss of use or the cost of a loaner vehicle, and the cost to replace the oil. The automaker's owner notification letter may not have gone out to Canadian owners, since it is not required by any Canadian recall or by statute. If a letter goes out, it is usually sent only to first owners of record. And in the case of Chrysler's engine, as the above-cited reader reports, no customer notification letters have been sent to anyone.

Some automakers say owners must use a special, more expensive oil to prevent sludge. This after-sale stipulation is illegal and can also provide owners with a reason to ask for damages, or even a refund, since it wasn't disclosed at the time of sale. All of the letter restrictions and decisions made by the dealer and the manufacturer can easily be appealed to the small claims court, where the sludge letter is powerful proof of the automaker's negligence.

Audi and VW

2001–03 cars equipped with 1.8L engines, including the Audi TT and A4; and the VW Golf/GTI, Jetta, New Beetle, and Passat (also the Passat W8 engine; all VWs equipped with the 2.8L VR6; and the Audi 3.0L V6 engine)

Problem: Defective ignition coils. When these coils fail, the vehicle suddenly stalls and won't start. **Warranty coverage:** VW will fix every single car by replacing the coils whether they are broken or not. There is no mileage or time limit on this warranty extension.

Chrysler, Ford, General Motors, and Asian Automakers

All years, all models

Problem: Faulty automatic transmissions that self-destruct, shift erratically, gear down to "limp mode," are slow to shift in or out of Reverse, or are noisy. **Warranty**

coverage: If you have the assistance of your dealer's service manager, or some internal service bulletin that confirms the automatic transmission may be defective (such as the bulletins that follow), expect an offer of 50–75 percent (about $2,500) if you threaten to sue in small claims court. Acura, Honda, Hyundai, Lexus, and Toyota coverage varies between seven and eight years.

I've just been told that I need my fourth transmission on my '96 Town & Country minivan with 132,000 miles [212,000 km] on it. I've driven many cars well past that mileage with only *one* transmission. The dealer asked Chrysler, who said they would not help me. My appeals to Chrysler's customer service department yielded me the same result.... Chrysler split some of the costs with me on the previous rebuilt replacements.

CBC TV's *Marketplace* recently presented a series on "Underdogs," or people who have successfully taken on Chrysler and other companies for customer service problems. Review the program at *www.cbc.ca/consumers/market/files/services/underdogs*.

CHRYSLER TRANSMISSION DELAYED ENGAGEMENT

BULLETIN NO.: 21-004-05   DATE: JANUARY 22, 2005

OVERVIEW: This bulletin involves replacing the front pump assembly in the transmission and checking the Transmission Control Module (TCM) for the latest software revision level.

2004 (CS) Pacifica

2002 – 2004 (JR) Sebring Convertible/Sebring Sedan/Stratus Sedan

2003 (KJ) Liberty

2003 (KJ) Cherokee (International Markets)

2002 2004 (LH) 300M/Concorde/Intrepid

2002 2003 (PL) Neon

2002 2003 (PT) PT Cruiser

2002 2003 (RG) Chrysler Voyager (International Markets)

2002 2003 (RS) Town & Country/Caravan/Voyager

2003 (TJ) Wrangler

GM TRANSMISSION FLUID LEAKS

BULLETIN NO.: 04-07-30-028   DATE: JUNE 15, 2004

TRANSMISSION LEAKS FROM REVERSE SERVO COVER (REPLACE REVERSE SERVO COVER AND SEAL)

2004 and Prior Cars and Light Duty Trucks (Automatic Transmission 4T65-E)

CONDITION: Some customers may comment on a fluid leak under the vehicle.

CAUSE: A possible cause of a transmission fluid leak usually only during cold ambient temperatres below –6.7°C (20°F) may be the reverse servo cover/seal. The reverse servo cover seal may shrink in cold ambient tempertures causing a transmission fluid leak.

All years, all models

Problem: Premature wearout of brake pads, calipers, and rotors. Produces excessive vibration, noise, and pulling to one side when braking. **Warranty coverage:** *Calipers and pads:* "Goodwill" settlements confirm that brake calipers and pads that fail to last 2 years/40,000 km will be replaced for 50 percent of the repair cost; components not lasting 1 year/20,000 km will be replaced for free. *Rotors:* If they last less than 3 years/60,000 km, they will be replaced at half price; replacement is free up to 2 years/40,000 km.

All years, all models

Problem: A nauseating rotten-egg smell permeates the interior. **Warranty coverage:** At first, owners are told they need a tune-up. Then they are told to

switch fuels and to wait a few months for the problem to correct itself. When this fails, the catalytic converter will likely be replaced and the power control module recalibrated. Toyota has been particularly hard hit by this stink.

Chrysler, Ford, General Motors, and Honda

All years, all models

Problem: Faulty paint jobs that cause paint to turn white and peel off in horizontal panels. **Warranty coverage:** Automakers will offer a free paint job or partial compensation for up to six years (no mileage limitation). Thereafter, most manufacturers will offer 50–75 percent refunds on the small claims courthouse's front steps.

In *Maureen Frank v. General Motors of Canada Limited,* the Saskatchewan small claims court judge ruled that paint finishes should last for 11 years, and three other Canadian small claims judgments have extended the benchmark to seven years, to second owners, and to pickups.

Although the automakers' attempts to blame paint delamination on the sun, acid rain, tree sap, bird droppings, and owners' lack of care appear comical at first, professional car washers are not laughing. The International Carwash Association advises its members to inform drivers that the paint defect is due to a poor factory paint job—not the soap or brushes used in car washes (see *www.carwash.com/article.asp?IndexID=6633551*, halfway down the page).

The International Carwash Association issued an alert that many General Motors vehicles and light-duty trucks from 1988 through 1992 may demonstrate a peeling paint condition called delamination.

Joe Ward, ICA director of engineering, said the condition consists of colorcoat paint peeling from the electrocoat primer.

Ward said it is caused by prolonged exposure to ultraviolet sunlight and humidity and usually occurs on horizontal surfaces, such as the hood, roof and deck lid.

General Motors has identified this condition and has issued Technical Service Bulletin 23-10-54, which describes the cause of the problem and the recommended repair procedure, the ICA said.

Chrysler, Ford, General Motors, and Hyundai

1994–2004 engine head gasket and intake manifold failures; 1998–99 Hyundai Accent

Problem: Between 60,000–100,000 km, the engine may overheat, lose power, burn extra fuel, or possibly self-destruct. Under the best of circumstances, the repair will take a day and cost about $800–$1,000. **Warranty coverage:** If you have the assistance of your dealer's service manager, expect a first offer of 50 percent up to 5 years/100,000 km (about $1,500, if other parts are damaged).

Ford

Ford's 6- and 8-cylinder engines are covered up to 7 years/160,000 km through various warranty extensions and class action settlements. If you threaten to go to small claims court, cite the *Dufour* or *Reid* Windstar judgments (see page 106) or the most recent Ford settlement at *www.fordmanifoldsettlement.com/faq.html*. In March 1999, Ford issued Owner Notification Program 97M91 informing its dealers that "fatigue cracks may develop in some of the composite [plastic] intake manifolds used on the 4.6L SOHC engines installed in the affected cars. This condition may result in engine coolant leakage which, if not detected or ignored, will cause engine overheating. Complete loss of coolant may result in engine damage or engine failure." Under that Owner Notification Program, Ford extended the warranty on this part to seven years with no mileage limitation.

General Motors

GM isn't as easy to deal with as Ford. The company has never admitted the intake manifold gasket problem exists, except in some obscure service bulletins, listed below. Additionally, GM's faulty intake manifold gaskets afflict a huge number of models, notably the 3.1L, 3.4L, and 3.8L V6 engines used since 1996. GM obviously doesn't want to lose hundreds of millions of dollars by extending the warranty to cover almost all of its production within most of a decade. Nevertheless, a GM service manager whistleblower told *Lemon-Aid* that the weak intake manifold is a "time bomb" that may cause extensive engine damage within a short period of time:

One problem that I do not see mentioned on your website involves late 1990s full-sized GM cars (LeSabre, Delta 88, Bonneville) with the 3.8L (VIN K) engine. GM has released a TSB regarding a poorly designed intake manifold that actually melts from EGR heat. Their cure is to replace the upper and lower intake manifold at a cost of approximately $1,000 to the consumer.

What the TSB does not reveal is that by the time most consumers are aware that there is a problem, irreversible engine damage has occurred. This is because when the intake fails, coolant leaks internally into the crankcase, therefore contaminating engine oil. The only way to know that this is happening is to check the oil on a daily basis. Once enough coolant is lost, the vehicle overheats and by that time, there are several quarts of coolant in the oil (and a wiped out engine).

I know of many defects on various cars, but this one bothers me the most, as the consumers have no way to protect themselves. Most of these folks (the LeSabre and Delta 88 crowd, who are mostly elderly) are driving around in mechanical time bombs.

Elderly or not, the owners of these cars are not all meekly paying for engine repairs caused by factory-related goofs and penny pinching. Many people are demanding that GM pay for its mistake up to 7 years/160,000 km (see the sample complaint letters on pages 57–58). When this demand is sent by registered letter, fax, or email to the company's Legal Affairs Department in Oshawa, Ontario, a "goodwill" offer is usually made to partially cover the repair.

I just wanted to let you know that after contacting you back in January regarding our 2001 Chevy Venture head gasket problem, I have just received my judgment through the Canadian Arbitration Program.

I used the sample complaint letter as well as the judgment you have posted in the *Ford Canada v. Dufour* court case. This combined with an avalanche of similar Chevy Venture complaints that are posted on the Internet helped us to win a $1,700 reimbursement of the $2,200 we were looking for.

There are a handful of Canadian class actions filed against GM over the automaker's faulty intake manifold gaskets. The largest and most recent of these is *Stewart v. GM*. It claims an estimated $1.2 billion in damages for owners of defective 1996–2004 GM cars and minivans (see *www.gmcanadianclassaction.ca*).

Lemon-Aid knows of only one GM intake manifold claim that has been litigated, and it was a winner (see *www.lemonaidcars.com* under "Regional Reports from Ontario"). There has also been a notable Canadian Motor Vehicle Arbitration Plan (CAMVAP) victory concerning 3.4L engines (see "Jo Ann's 1999 Oldsmobile Silhouette—A Victory Story!" below), and a class action lawsuit over GM's 3.8L engine was filed in New Jersey in August 2004 (see *www.sheller.com/Practice. asp?PracticeID=143*):

This consumer class action was filed on August 18, 2004 in the Superior Court of New Jersey. The Complaint alleges that the Defendants, General Motors, manufactured, marketed and sold numerous vehicles with a defective 3.8 liter V6 engine. The Complaint states that the K engine is prone to coolant leakage, which leads to overheating, continual coolant replacement and ultimately engine failure. Symptoms include a milky substance on the oil dipstick or oil fill cap, a strong and unpleasant odor while operating the vehicle, and coolant puddles beneath the vehicle when parked.

Additionally, the Complaint discusses General Motors response to the problem, termed "Customer Satisfaction Program Engine Coolant Leak #03034." The Complaint alleges that the repair is only a temporary remedy and is designed to hide the problem until after the consumer's warranty has expired.

The Complaint lists owners and lessees of Buick Park Avenue, Buick Regal, Chevrolet Impala, Chevrolet Monte Carlo, Pontiac Bonneville and Pontiac Grand Prix from the model year 2000, 2001, and 2003 as those affected by the defective K Engine and to be included in the Class.

The law firm of Post Kirby Noonan & Sweat LLP has also filed a similar class action lawsuit in Sacramento, California, against General Motors Corporation, regarding defective engines. The complaint alleges that these engine defects involve excessive coolant leakage around the plastic-based intake manifold plenum, caused by deformation of the plastic-based material from ambient engine heat. The complaint further alleges that the defect produces, among other things, a precipitous drop in the coolant level, a milky white substance on the oil dipstick or oil fill cap, an unpleasant coolant odour during operation, and puddles of coolant below the vehicle when parked. The complaint also alleges that vehicle owners report that engine temperatures run unreasonably high with consequent damage to engine components, and occasionally the seizing of the engine, and that the leaking coolant also sometimes mixes with the motor oil, causing problems with combustion and performance. The vehicles involved, again, include the 2000 through 2003 Buick LeSabre, Park Avenue, and Regal; Chevrolet Impala, Monte Carlo, and Malibu; and Pontiac Bonneville and Grand Prix models.

Keep in mind that Ford's V8 engine secret warranty resulted in a formal retroactive warranty extension only after Ford settled a class action in the States that was similar to the GM lawsuit cited above. So, when GM settles these American class actions, Canadians can expect to receive similar compensation. In the meantime, nothing stops owners from going to small claims court now, inasmuch as the settlement may not occur before another year passes.

Jo Ann's 1999 Oldsmobile Silhouette—A Victory Story!

I am the original owner of a 1999 Oldsmobile, Silhouette minivan. Before any major problems occurred, the van would leave small fluid leaks on the garage floor. At 91,000 km it was finally obvious that the lower intake manifold gasket was leaking and was repaired for $976.00. At 113,000 km the camshaft split in two and at that time the engine had to be replaced. Cost for the engine replacement was $6,600.00.

My mechanic felt that the intake manifold gasket had been leaking internally before it was finally detected and the mixing of the antifreeze and oil directly resulted in the seizing of the bearings, which caused the camshaft to split.

I contacted the dealership where I purchased the vehicle as well as the local GM dealership and received no help whatsoever. The dealerships denied knowing of any problem with the intake manifold gasket leaks or the possibility of the camshaft splitting. I then contacted General Motors' head office in Oshawa, Ontario, and was told that they would not accept any responsibility for the problem and that they were not aware of any gasket defect.

The local GM dealership suggested I approach CAMVAP, which is an arbitration company that is funded by car manufacturers. They were extremely supportive and sent me an information package detailing the steps to be completed before attempting arbitration.

GM head office said I could have my repairs/engine replacement done by my own mechanic but a GM dealership would have to assess the damage and confirm what the problem was. After the van was evaluated by the dealership my mechanic installed a new engine.

I gathered all receipts for routine maintenance, intake manifold gasket and engine replacement repairs and proceeded with arbitration through CAMVAP. The hearing was held at a local hotel and there was a GM representative, an arbitrator, my mechanic and myself in attendance.

We were able to provide enough evidence from my mechanic's testimony and copies of other testimonials off the internet to support my claim.

The arbitrator's decision was sent to me within two weeks and ruled in my favour. General Motors had to compensate me for the total cost of the gasket and engine replacement. Even though the van was considerably over the recognized warranty the arbitrator believed that the gasket was defective from the time of purchase and was directly related to the engine failure.

The only options I had were to proceed with arbitration or go to small claims court. There is no fee for arbitration but you can only try one method…. If arbitration fails, you cannot then go to small claims.

Apparently the new engine has the same type of gasket as the original one, and I am just waiting for the same problems to occur. In the meantime I am currently looking for a new vehicle and definitely not a GM with a 3.4 L engine.

GM bulletins: A "smoking gun"

Numerous GM service bulletins confirm a pattern of engine intake manifold gasket defects, which have been covered by a 6-year/100,000 km secret warranty since 1996. Owners who have successfully dealt with the company's customer reps in Oshawa have communicated these time and mileage parameters to *Lemon-Aid*.

The first incriminating GM internal service bulletin, below, admits to poor-quality engine intake manifolds. Note that this defect has existed over 10 model years. Imagine how many owners have paid thousands of dollars to fix this problem, which GM admits here is clearly its own fault.

GM ENGINE OIL OR COOLANT LEAK

BULLETIN NO.: 03-06-01-010A   DATE: APRIL 2003

ENGINE OIL OR COOLANT LEAK (INSTALL NEW INTAKE MANIFOLD GASKET)

2000–03 Buick Century; 2002–03 Buick Rendezvous; 1996 Chevrolet Lumina APV; 1997–2003 Chevrolet Venture; 1999–2001 Chevrolet Lumina; 1999–2003 Chevrolet Malibu, Monte Carlo; 2000–03 Chevrolet Impala; 1996–2003 Oldsmobile Silhouette; 1999 Oldsmobile Cutlass; 1999–2003 Oldsmobile Alero; 1996–99 Pontiac Trans Sport; 1999–2003 Pontiac Grand Am; 2000–03 Pontiac Grand Prix, Montana
2001–03 Pontiac Aztek with 3.1L or 3.4L V6 engine (VINs J, E–RPOs LGB, LA1)

CONDITION: Some owners may comment on an apparent oil or coolant leak. Additionally, the comments may range from spots on the driveway to having to add fluids.
CAUSE: Intake manifold may be leaking allowing coolant, oil or both to leak from the engine.
CORRECTION: Install a new-design intake manifold gasket. The material used in the gasket has been changed in order to improve the sealing qualities of the gasket. When replacing the gasket, the intake manifold bolts must also be replaced and torqued to a revised specification. The new bolts will come with a pre-applied threadlocker on them.

In the second service bulletin (on following page), GM admits to having a special "voluntary" program to refund engine repair costs. Although referred to by GM as a recall, this free repair isn't under Transport Canada's jurisdiction and isn't part of the safety recall process, which usually has an 8-year repair period with notification sent out by the automaker. It is important to note that GM takes responsibility for this engine failure, specifically includes Canadian owners in retroactive payouts to independent repair agencies, and promises to offer courtesy transportation.

All of the above benefits should be cited whenever an extended or "goodwill" warranty is offered by any automaker or whenever a claim is filed in small claims court.

The third GM bulletin (see page 79) lists several of the symptoms indicating an intake manifold gasket failure and describes under what conditions a more thorough repair should be undertaken. The nuts are also listed as having been upgraded for better retention—another liability admission by GM.

GM CUSTOMER SATISFACTION PROGRAM ENGINE COOLANT LEAK

PROGRAM NO.: 03034   DATE: JULY 7, 2003

All 2000–02 and certain 2003 Chevrolet Impala, Monte Carlo; Pontiac Grand Prix, Bonneville; and Buick Regal, LeSabre, Park Avenue equipped with 3.8L V6 engine.

THIS RECALL IS IN EFFECT UNTIL JULY 31, 2005.

CONDITION: General Motors has decided that all 2000–02 and certain 2003 Chevrolet Impala, Monte Carlo; Pontiac Grand Prix, Bonneville; and Buick Regal, LeSabre, Park Avenue model vehicles equipped with 3.8L (RPO L36–VIN Code K) engines, may have a condition in which engine coolant may leak at the upper intake manifold throttle body gasket, or at the upper intake manifold to lower intake manifold gasket. This condition may result in a low engine coolant level and higher engine operating temperatures.

CORRECTION: Dealers are to replace the three throttle body fastener nuts and add cooling system sealant to the radiator tank.

VEHICLES: Involved are all 2000–02 Chevrolet Impala, Monte Carlo; Pontiac Grand Prix, Bonneville; and Buick Regal, LeSabre, Park Avenue model vehicles equipped with 3.8L (RPO L36–VIN Code K) engines

CUSTOMER REIMBURSEMENT FOR CANADA

All customer requests for reimbursement of previously paid coolant leaks that were repaired by replacing the upper intake manifold/gasket, throttle body nuts or throttle body gasket are to be submitted by July 31, 2004. All reasonable customer paid receipts should be considered for reimbursement. The amount to be reimbursed will be limited to the amount the repair would have cost if completed by an authorized General Motors dealer.

Dealers are to ensure that these customers understand that shuttle service or some other form of courtesy transportation is available and will be provided at no charge. Dealers should refer to the General Motors Service Policies and Procedures Manual for Courtesy Transportation guidelines.

GENERAL MOTORS PRODUCT PROGRAM CUSTOMER REIMBURSEMENT PROCEDURE

If you have paid to have this condition corrected by replacing the upper intake manifold/gasket, throttle body nuts, or throttle body gasket before August 8, 2003, you may be eligible to receive reimbursement. Requests for reimbursement may include parts, labor, fees and taxes. Reimbursement may be limited to the amount the repair would have cost if completed by an authorized General Motors dealer. Your claim will be acted upon within 60 days of receipt. Letters will be sent to known owners of record located within areas covered by the US National Traffic and Motor Vehicle Safety Act. For owners outside these areas, dealers should notify customers using the attached suggested dealer letter.

In the fourth and most recent bulletin (see page 79), GM says that its revised intake manifold gasket is more "robust" and adds 2004 models to the afflicted-models list. This is another admission of liability under the implied warranty statutes.

Note: Internet references to Ford and GM engine head gasket and intake manifold defects, their causes and fixes, and various lawsuits can be found simply by typing

GM LOSS OF COOLANT, MILKY COLORED OIL

BULLETIN NO.: 03-06-01-016   DATE: MAY 21, 2003

2000–03 LeSabre, ParkAvenue, Regal; 2000–03 Chevrolet Impala, Monte Carlo; 2000–03 Bonneville; 2000–03 Grand Prix with 3.8L V6 Engine.

CONDITION: Some owners may comment on a loss of coolant, coolant odor, having to add coolant or a milky substance on either the oil dipstick or oil fill cap. Additionally, owners may indicate that there are signs of coolant loss left on the ground where the vehicle is normally parked.

CAUSE: Condition may be due to coolant leaking past intermediate intake or throttle body gaskets.

CORRECTION: The upper intake manifold should not be replaced for a coolant leak condition, unless a rare instance of physical damage is found. Even if the throttle body surface shows a slight warpage, the upper intake should not be replaced unless a drivability concern is noted or a relevant engine DTC, such as a code for an unmetered air leak, is set and the upper intake manifold can clearly be shown as the cause of the concern.

Thoroughly check for any external leaks. If no external leaks are found, then replace the intermediate intake manifold gasket and the throttle body gasket. When changing the throttle body gasket, the nuts that retain the throttle body should be replaced with a new design that improves torque retention. Medium strength thread locker should be applied to the studs before installing the new nuts.

GM REDESIGNED UPPER INTAKE MANIFOLD AND GASKETS

BULLETIN NO.: 04-06-01-017   DATE: MAY 26, 2004

1995–97 Riviera; 1995–2004 Park Avenue; 1996–2004 Regal; 1997–2004 LeSabre; 1998–99 Lumina; 1998–2004 Monte Carlo; 2000–04 Impala;
1995–96 Ninety-Eight; 1995–99 Eighty-Eight; 1998–99 Intrigue;
1995–2004 Bonneville; 1997–2003 Grand Prix with 3.8L V6 engine

New upper intake manifold and gasket kits have been released. These new kits will provide the dealer with the ability to get exactly what is necessary for a correct repair. In addition some of the gaskets have been updated to a more robust design.

"GM intake manifold class action" or "Ford intake manifold class action" into a search engine such as Google.

Chrysler

1998–2000 Caravan, Grand Caravan, Voyager, Grand Voyager, and Town & Country

Problem: Defective airbag clock springs cause multiple failures of the electrical system governing other components. **Warranty coverage:** Lifetime coverage up to 110,000 km (70,000 miles).

CHRYSLER RECALL—CLOCK SPRING REPLACEMENT/WARRANTY EXTENSION
DATE: OCTOBER 2004

DEALER SERVICE INSTRUCTIONS FOR SAFETY RECALL D17—CLOCKSPRING/LIFETIME WARRANTY

1998–2000 Caravan, Grand Caravan, Voyager, Grand Voyager, and Town & Country

IMPORTANT: The clockspring on about 1,290,000 of the above vehicles may lose the electrical connection to the steering wheel mounted electrical components. This could cause the driver's airbag, horn, speed control and/or steering wheel mounted radio controls (if equipped) to be inoperative. An inoperative driver's airbag will not deploy, which can result in increased injury to the driver in a frontal crash.

REPAIR: Vehicles with a failed clockspring or vehicles with 70,000 miles [112,000 km] or LESS, must have the clockspring assembly replaced. Vehcles involved in this recall have a lifetime warranty on the clockspring assembly.

Ford

1992–2004 Aerostar, Focus, Sable, Taurus, and Windstar

Problem: Defective front coil springs may suddenly break, puncturing the front tire and leading to loss of steering control. **Warranty coverage:** Under a "Safety Improvement Campaign" negotiated with NHTSA, Ford will replace *broken* coil springs at no charge up to 10 years/unlimited mileage. The company initially said that it wouldn't replace the springs until they had broken—if you survived to submit a claim, that is—but it relented when threatened with a lawsuit. Since then, customer complaints have trailed off. 1997–98 models that are registered in rust-belt states or Canada have been recalled for the installation of a protective shield (called a "spring catcher bracket" in the Canadian recall) to prevent a broken spring from shredding the front tire.

1996–2004 F-Series trucks, SUVs, and Windstar vans

Problem: Sudden steering loss due to the premature wear and separation of the steering tie rod ends. **Warranty coverage:** Presently Ford is advising owners to have their vehicles inspected regularly. If pressed, the dealer will replace the component for free up to 5 years/100,000 km.

Ford/Lincoln

1996–2001 Crown Victoria, Mercury Grand Marquis, and Lincoln Town Car; 1997 Mercury Cougar, Ford Thunderbird, and Ford Mustang; 1998–2001 Mustang; and 2002 Ford Explorer

Problem: Intake manifolds may crack at the coolant crossover, resulting in V8 engine coolant leakage. **Warranty coverage:** For over a decade, *Lemon-Aid* has chided Ford for stonewalling engine intake manifold complaints and hiding the existence of a secret warranty slush fund. And then late last year, after some prodding by *Lemon-Aid*, Ford formally granted free engine intake manifold repairs and an extended warranty to Canadian owners. Ford agreed to reimburse money paid for the repair and also to provide a free 7-year retroactive warranty with unlimited mileage. Owners report getting their refund cheques directly from their dealers, a move that speeds up the refund program considerably.

> In mid-January 2006, Ford refunded me 100% ($1,400) for the intake manifold repair carried out on my 1997 Mercury Grand Marquis in October of 2002. The odometer reading at the time of the repair was 144,700 km. Current reading is around 202,500 km.
>
> GREG

1998–2000 Crown Victoria and Lincoln Town Car fleet vehicles

Problem: Rear-suspension upper-control arm brackets may crack and allow the bracket to separate from the frame. This will cause a clunking noise, and the rear suspension will feel loose. **Warranty coverage:** Owner Notification Program (ONP) #00B60 will pay for the repair of the crack and the installation of a reinforcement bracket. Affected owners who drive non-fleet cars should demand a refund, using the threat of a small claims court action for leverage.

GM

2003–05 Corvette; 2004–05 Cadillac XLR

Problem: Faulty fuel gauge reads empty when there actually is fuel in the tank. **Warranty coverage:** GM will replace the left fuel tank level sensor for free up to 5 years/100,000 km.

2005–06 Corvette

Problem: Roof delaminates and separates from the frame. **Warranty coverage:** GM will repair or replace for free the affected roofs.

CUSTOMER SATISFACTION PROGRAM 05112D

Customer Satisfaction Program 05112D addresses all 2005 Corvettes and 2006 through VIN 31106. If a customer has a concern and the VIN is within these break points the bulletin can be used to correct the condition even though the VIN is not listed in VIS. If the VIN is not listed in VIS dealers should use labor operation B2308 and use the time that is supplied in bulletin 05112D.

Roofs that are partially delaminated or debonded can be repaired using the procedure outlined in Bulletin 05112D. When the roof remains attached on one of the four sides it can be repaired and the vehicle placed back into service. Bulletin 05112D outlines this is as a temporary repair until a replacement roof can be obtained. Once a roof is properly repaired with the foam process, tests indicate the roof will not separate from the frame.

2000–03 Buick LeSabre; 2002–06 Buick Rendezvous; 2000–05 Cadillac DeVille; 2003–06 Cadillac CTS; 2004–06 Cadillac SRX; 2005–06 Cadillac STS; 2006 Cadillac DTS; 1997–2002 Venture, Trans Sport/Montana, and Silhouette; 2001–03 Oldsmobile Aurora; 2000–03 Pontiac Bonneville

Problem: Roof paint delamination, peeling and rust perforation; hood paint blistering. **Warranty coverage:** GM will replace, repair, or repaint the roof for free up to 6 years/100,000 km.

GM BLISTERING, BUBBLING PAINT

BULLETIN NO.: 01-08-51-004　　　　　　　DATE: OCTOBER 2001

PREMATURE ALUMINUM HOOD CORROSION/ BLISTERING (REFINISH)

1997–2001 Trans Sport (export only); 1997–2001 Venture; 1997–2001 Silhouette; 1997–98 Trans Sport; 1999–2001 Pontiac Montana

Some vehicles may have the appearance of blistering or bubbling paint on the top of the hood or under the hood.

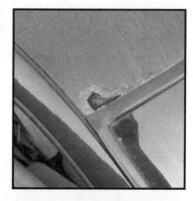

GM FRONT/REAR ROOF RUST PERFORATION

BULLETIN NO.: 02-08-67-006B　　　　　　　DATE: MARCH 2003

ROOF PERFORATION (REPLACE ROOF)

1997–2003 Chevrolet Venture; 1997–2003 Oldsmobile Silhouette; 1997–2003 Pontiac TranSport/Montana

IMPORTANT: Implementation of this service bulletin by "GM of Canada" dealers requires prior District Service Manager approval.

CONDITION: Some customers may comment that there is rust forming around the front or rear portion of the roof.

CAUSE: During production, the E-coating (ELPO primer) may have been missed in concealed areas of the front or rear portions of the outer roof panel.

2001 Alero

Problem: Transmission bearing failure. **Warranty coverage:** Customer Satisfaction Campaign for 4T40-E transaxle converter bearing failure inspection/ replacement (TSB #01031; Date: April, 2001; NHTSA Item Number: SB619400).

2002–03 Alero, Cavalier, Grand Am, Malibu, and Sunfire

Problem: Transmission shifts erratically, slips, or won't shift due to defective driven sprocket support assembly. **Warranty coverage:** GM will replace the component free of charge up to seven years (TSB #03-07-30-012B; Date: August 22, 2005).

2005 Cobalt and Pursuit

Problem: Inaccurate fuel gauge. **Warranty coverage:** GM will recalibrate the electronic control module (ECM) free of charge (TSB #05-08-49-002A; Date: January 28, 2005).

2001 DeVille

Problem: Engine crankshaft pulley failure. **Warranty coverage:** Customer Satisfaction Campaign allows for a rebuilt crankshaft or engine replacement (TSB #01012; Date: February, 2001; NHTSA Item Number: SB619207).

2003–06 Saturn Ion

Problem: No crank; no start. **Warranty coverage:** Owners will be offered free replacement of the body control module, and ignition if necessary (TSB #04-08-45-005C5; Date: December 14, 2005).

2004–05 Saturn Ion Red Line

Problem: Engine camshaft-position sensor housing seal failure may cause an oil leak and engine damage. **Warranty coverage:** This Customer Satisfaction Campaign allows for the free replacement of the component without any mileage or prior ownership limitations (TSB #05522; Date: May 6, 2005).

2001–02 Grand Prix, Impala, Monte Carlo, and Regal

Problem: Defective catalytic converters may cause vehicle to lose power or the dash warning light to come on. **Warranty coverage:** The converter warranty is extended to 10 years. Owners will also be reimbursed for previous converter/OBD system repairs or replacements.

2003–06 Vibe

Problem: Rear hatch rust. **Warranty coverage:** GM will refinish, at no charge, the affected hatch area (TSB #05-08-51-002A; Date: December 2, 2005).

Honda

2003–04 Civic

Problem: Inaccurate fuel gauge reading. **Warranty coverage:** Honda believes the problem occurs due to incorrect software and will replace the gauge assembly free of charge under a "goodwill" program, whether owners bought their vehicles new or used (TSB #05-002; Date: March 4, 2005).

1996–2000 Civic and 1997–99 CR-V

Problem: Harsh-shifting automatic transmission and torque converter. **Warranty coverage:** Honda will fix or replace the transmission free of charge up to 7 years/160,000 km under a "goodwill" program whether owners bought their vehicle new or used.

1998–2003 Honda Accord, Odyssey, and Pilot models equipped with 6-cylinder engines

Problem: Defective aluminum engine block. **Warranty coverage:** Repair or replace engine under a "goodwill" program.

2003–04 Honda Accords equipped with 6-cylinder engines

Problem: When turning, either a clunking is heard from the steering or looseness is felt in the steering wheel. **Warranty coverage:** Under a "goodwill" program, Honda will replace the tie-rod ball joints and perform an alignment, free of charge (TSB #05-013; Date: March 25, 2005).

1999–2003 Odyssey and Pilot

Problem: EGR valve contamination or EGR port clogging may cause engine surging or stalling. **Warranty coverage:** Honda will install a new EGR valve and a valve kit under a "goodwill" program applicable up to 8 years/160,000 km (TSB #05-026; Date: July 20, 2005).

Hyundai

1999–2002 Elantra; 1999–2003 Tiburon

Problem: The exhaust manifold may crack, causing the engine to overheat. **Warranty coverage:** Hyundai will inspect and replace any defective exhaust manifold free of charge up to 7 years/160,000 km under Campaign V04, initiated in March 2005.

Mazda

2002–03 MPV

Problem: A faulty fan control module may cause fan failure or battery drain. **Warranty coverage:** Mazda will replace the fan control module for free.

2004 RX-8

Problem: Vehicle stalls and is impossible to start. **Warranty coverage:** Under Mazda Service Program 04, the automaker will correct the problem free of charge. (Memo to dealers was sent out February 2005.)

Mercedes-Benz

1998–2001 (all models)

Problem: Defective engine harmonic-balancer pulley may cause excessive vibration. **Warranty coverage:** Dealers will inspect and replace for free.

Toyota

1997–2002 Toyota and Lexus vehicles with 2.2L 4-cylinder or 3.0L V6 engines

Problem: Sludge buildup may require the engine to be rebuilt. **Warranty coverage:** Toyota will repair or replace the engine at no charge up to 8 years/160,000 km (100,000 mi.) whether you bought the vehicle new or used. Toyota has said owners will not be forced to show oil change receipts. But some dealers, apparently, haven't got the word:

> The service manager quietly told me that there was a "flaw" in the engine but would not elaborate. When I asked if there was a flaw why wouldn't Toyota warranty it, I was told, "If you can't prove you did the oil change there is no use taking it to Toyota."

> In May 2002 we received the letter mentioned in [your book], and we took our 1998 Sienna into the dealer (after spending three weeks talking to them and producing all the oil change records except the missing one). The engine could not be rebuilt—it had to be replaced. The cost was $5,017.22, finally covered by this goodwill warranty.

VW

1998–2002 Beetles and 1999–2002 Golfs, GTIs, and Jettas—850,000 vehicles are affected

Problem: If the window clamp malfunctions, it prevents the window from being raised or lowered. **Warranty coverage:** The new clamp and the work to install it will be free of charge under this special warranty.

Free Recall Repairs

Vehicles are recalled for one of two reasons: Either they are potentially unsafe or they don't conform to federal pollution control regulations. Whatever the reason, recalls are a great way to get free repairs—if you know which ones apply to you and you have the patience of Job.

Auto recalls are on the rise in Canada, despite automakers' claims that build quality has improved. Transport Canada says auto recalls rose 44 percent to 3.77 million vehicles in 2004 (approximately one in six vehicles on the road).

In North America, almost a half billion unsafe vehicles have been recalled by automakers for the free correction of safety-related defects since American recall legislation was passed in 1966 (a weaker Canadian law was enacted in 1971). During that time, about one-third of the recalled vehicles never made it back to the dealership for repairs because owners were never informed, didn't consider the defect to be that hazardous, or gave up waiting for corrective parts.

Subsequent American legislation targets automakers who drag their feet in making recall repairs. Owners on both sides of the border may wish to cite the following NHTSA guidelines for support:

> **DEALER RECALL RESPONSIBILITY—FOR U.S. AND IPC (U.S. STATES, TERRITORIES, AND POSSESSIONS)**
>
> The U.S. *National Traffic and Motor Vehicle Safety Act* provides that each vehicle that is subject to a recall must be adequately repaired within a reasonable time after the customer has tendered it for repair. A failure to repair within 60 days after tender of a vehicle is *prima facie* evidence of failure to repair within a reasonable time. If the condition is not adequately repaired within a reasonable time, the customer may be entitled to an identical or reasonably equivalent vehicle at no charge or to a refund of the purchase price less a reasonable allowance for depreciation. To avoid having to provide these burdensome remedies, every effort must be made to promptly schedule an appointment with each customer and to repair their vehicle as soon as possible.
>
> GM Bulletin No.: 00064C, issued September 2002

If you've moved or bought a used vehicle, it's smart to pay a visit to your local dealer, give him your address, and get a report card on which recalls, warranties, and free-service campaigns apply to your vehicle. Simply give the service advisor the vehicle identification number (VIN)—found on your insurance card, or on your dash just below the windshield on the driver's side—and have the number run through the automaker's computer system. Ask for a computer printout of the vehicle's history (have it faxed to you, if you're so equipped) and make sure you're listed in the automaker's computer as the new owner. This ensures that you'll receive notices of warranty extensions and emissions and safety recalls.

Regional Recalls

Don't let any dealer refuse you recall repairs because of where you live.

In order to cut recall costs, many automakers try to limit a recall to vehicles in a certain designated region. This practice doesn't make sense, since cars are mobile and an unsafe, rust-cankered steering unit can be found anywhere—not just in certain rust-belt provinces or American states.

In 2001, Ford attempted to limit to five American states its recall of faulty Firestone tires. Public ridicule of the company's proposal led to an extension of the recall throughout North America.

In July 2004, Ford announced a regional recall to install protective spring shields on almost one million 1999, 2000, and 2001 model year Taurus and Sable sedans to correct defective front springs that can break and puncture a tire. As it did for Windstars and Aerostars recalled earlier for the same problem, Ford says it will send recall letters only to owners whose vehicles are registered in high-corrosion areas, or where salt is used on roads.

Wherever you live or drive, don't expect to be welcomed with open arms when your vehicle develops a safety- or emissions-related problem that's not yet part of a recall campaign. Automakers and dealers generally take a restrictive view of what constitutes a safety or emissions defect and frequently charge for repairs that should be free under federal safety or emissions legislation. To counter this tendency, look at the following list of typical defects that are clearly safety related. If you experience similar problems, insist that the automaker fix the problem at no expense to yourself, including a car rental:

- Airbag malfunctions
- Corrosion affecting safe operation
- Disconnected or stuck accelerators
- Electrical shorts
- Faulty windshield wipers
- Fuel leaks
- Problems with original axles, drive shafts, seats, seat recliners, or defrosters
- Seat belt problems
- Stalling or sudden acceleration
- Sudden steering or brake loss
- Suspension failures
- Trailer coupling failures

In the U.S., recall campaigns force automakers to pay the entire cost of fixing a vehicle's safety-related defect for any vehicle purchased up to eight years before the recall's announcement. A reasonable period beyond that time is usually a slam dunk in small claims court. Recalls may be voluntary or ordered by the U.S. Department of Transportation. Canadian regulation has an added twist: Transport Canada can only order automakers to notify owners that their vehicles may be unsafe; it can't force them to correct the problem. Fortunately, most U.S.-ordered recalls are carried out in Canada, and when Transport Canada makes a defect determination on its own, automakers generally comply with an owner notification letter.

Voluntary recall campaigns, frequently called Special Service or Safety Improvement Campaigns, are a real problem, though. The government doesn't monitor the notification of owners; dealers and automakers routinely deny there's a recall, thereby dissuading most claimants; and the company's so-called fix, not authorized by any governing body, may not correct the hazard at all. Also, the voluntary recall may leave out many of the affected models or unreasonably exclude certain owners.

Safety Defect Information

If you wish to report a safety defect or want recall info, you may access Transport Canada's website at *www.tc.gc.ca/roadsafety/recalls/search_e.asp*. You can get recall information in French or English, as well as general information relating to road safety and importing a vehicle into Canada. Web surfers can now access the recall database for 1970–2004 model vehicles but, unlike NHTSA's website, owner complaints aren't listed, defect investigations aren't disclosed, voluntary warranty extensions (secret warranties) aren't shown, and service bulletin summaries aren't provided. You can also call Transport Canada at 1-800-333-0510 (toll-free within Canada) or 613-993-9851 (within the Ottawa region or outside Canada) to get additional information.

If you're not happy with Ottawa's treatment of your recall inquiry, try NHTSA's website. It's more complete than Transport Canada's (NHTSA's database is updated daily and covers vehicles built since 1952). You can search the database for your vehicle or tires at *www.nhtsa.dot.gov/cars/problems*. You'll get immediate access to four essential database categories applicable to your vehicle and model year: the latest recalls, current and closed safety investigations, defects reported by other owners, and a brief summary of TSBs.

NHTSA's fax-back service provides the same info through a local line that can be accessed from Canada—although long-distance charges will apply (most calls take 5–10 minutes to complete). The following local numbers get you into the automatic response service quickly and can be reached 24 hours a day: 202-366-0123, and 202-366-7800 for the hearing impaired.

"Black Box" Data Recorders

If your car has an airbag, it's probably spying on you. And if you get into an accident caused by a mechanical malfunction, you will be glad that it does.

Event data recorders (EDRs) the size of a VCR tape have been hidden near the engine, under the seat, or in the centre consoles of about 30 million airbag-equipped Ford and GM vehicles since the early '90s. Presently, about 30 percent of all domestic and imported cars carry them. To find out if your car or truck carries an EDR, read your owner's manual, contact the regional office of your car's manufacturer, or go to *www.harristechnical.com/downloads/cdrlist.pdf*.

The data recorders operate in a similar fashion to flight data recorders used in airplanes: They record data during the last five seconds before impact, including the force of the collision, the airbag's performance, when the brakes were applied, engine and vehicle speed, gas pedal position, and whether the driver was wearing a seat belt.

Who, what, where?

In the past, automakers have systematically hidden their collected data from government and insurance researchers, citing concerns for drivers' privacy. This argument, however, has been roundly rejected by law enforcement agencies, the courts, and car owners who need the independent information to prove negligence or simply to keep track of how and where their vehicles are driven. Car owners, rental agencies, and fleet administrators are also using EDR data to pin legal liability on automakers for accidents caused by the failure of safety components, such as airbags that don't deploy when they should (or that do deploy when they shouldn't) and anti-lock brakes that don't brake.

One handy portable tool for downloading EDR data to any PC is made by the Vetronix Corporation and sells for $2,500 (U.S.). It's presently marketed to accident reconstructionists, safety researchers, law enforcement agencies, and insurance companies as a tool to assess culpability in criminal and civil trials. Car owners who wish to dispute criminal charges, oppose their insurer's decision as to fault, or hold an automaker responsible for a safety device's failure (airbags, seat belts, or brakes) will find this data invaluable—if the data hasn't been wiped clean by the dealer!

A tool for parents

One of the scariest days for parents is when their teenager passes the driver's exam. Today there are cell phones, flip-down DVD players, satellites, radios, and other entertainment options to distract even the most seasoned drivers. Teenagers just learning the rules of the road are especially susceptible to these distractions, and even more so when other teens are in the car.

It's now possible to electronically monitor your teenage driver's driving habits and the places he or she visits with a device called the Road Safety RS-1000 On-Board Computer (see *www.roadsafety.com/teen.php*). It is a relatively inexpensive device that plugs into the data recorder and sets off an audible alarm when the driver exceeds a preset speed limit. The device also uses an accelerometer, similar to those used in automotive testing, to measure vehicle G-forces that are created by aggressive driving. As G-forces become excessive, an audible warning immediately tells the driver to back off. The only way to avoid hearing the audible warning (and feeling the embarrassment when friends are in the vehicle) is to drive safely.

The RS-1000 black box tells you how and when your teen was driving on a second-by-second basis. If you say, "I don't want you speeding on the freeway," and your teen does it anyway, you will know it. If curfew is at midnight and your darling gets home at 1:00 a.m., you will know it. The data is always accessible: Just pop the memory card out of the RS-1000 black box and plug it into your family's computer to display the reports and graphs.

Electronic monitors are a constant reminder to teens that driving is a privilege that can be taken away if they don't drive safely. No more "he said, she said"!

The RS-1000 can be bought through Road Safety International's website. Devices cost $295 (U.S.). For 1996 and newer vehicles, anyone can install the system by simply plugging the on-board computer into the vehicle's OBD-II connector. The device will also work in 1995 and older vehicles, but it will require hard-wire installation by a qualified automotive technician. For more information, contact the company at *rsi@roadsafety.com* or 805-498-9444.

Another useful monitoring gadget is the CarChipE/X (see *www.davisnet.com/drive/products/drive_product.asp?pnum=08221*). It costs $179 (U.S.) and can be used with any PC using Windows 98SE and above.

The CarChipE/X holds 300 hours worth of driving data (the Road Safety RS-1000 stores about a month's worth). The CarChipE/X has a USB port that connects to your computer. To download the data, you'll need to remove the device from the vehicle (Road Safety RS-1000 uses a removable memory card with a USB port). Both devices are fairly tamper-proof. If turned off or removed, that action will show up in their data logs.

Lower insurance rates

Aviva Canada (*www.avivacanada.com/autograph*), an automobile insurance company operating primarily in Ontario, says its Autograph program will give customers up to 25 percent off their premiums if the monitoring device they attach to their EDR system proves they are safe drivers.

Once connected, the Autograph device records specific information about a vehicle's use, including speed, distance driven, and time of the day. This information remains in the device until you choose to download it to your computer. The company then reviews the data and adjusts your premium accordingly. Drivers are given a standard 5 percent discount for agreeing to be part of the program.

Safety benefits

EDRs are not simply good tools for collecting safety data; they have also had a positive effect on accident prevention. A 1992 study by the European Union, cited by the Canada Safety Council, found that EDRs reduced the collision rate by 28 percent and costs by 40 percent in police fleets where drivers knew that they were being monitored.

The recorders are particularly helpful in getting compensation for accident victims, prompting automaker recalls, and punishing dangerous drivers—even those who happen to be U.S. Congressmen. In January 2004, South Dakota Congressman Bill Janklow was convicted of manslaughter for speeding through a stop sign—his EDR readout proved he was driving faster than the speed limit, although slower than police had estimated.

In October 2003, Montreal police won their first dangerous driving conviction using EDR data (*R. v. Gauthier*; 2003/05/27 QC C.Q. Dossier: 500-01-013375-016; *www.canlii.org/qc/jug/qccq/2003/2003qccq17860.html*). In June 2003, Edwin Matos of Pembroke Pines, Florida, was sentenced to 30 years in prison for killing two teenage girls after crashing into their car at more than 160 km/h (100 mph). The recorder's speed data convicted him. Two months earlier, an Illinois police officer received a $10 million (U.S.) settlement after data showed the driver of a hearse was negligent. The hearse driver claimed that just prior to the collision he lost consciousness from a diabetes attack; however, the EDR showed he had actually accelerated and braked in the moments before slamming into the officer's patrol car. In July 2002, New Brunswick prosecutors sent a dangerous driver to jail for two years based on his car's EDR data (*R. v. Daley*; 2003 NBQB 20; Docket(s): S/CR/7/02; *www.canlii.org/nb/cas/nbqb/2002/2003nbqb20.html*). GM was forced to recall more than 850,000 Cavaliers and Sunfires when its own data recorders showed that the cars' airbags often deployed inadvertently. Incidentally, California is the only jurisdiction where EDR data cannot be downloaded unless the car owner agrees or a court order is issued.

A chronological list of dozens of Canadian and American court cases related to automotive Event Data Recorders has been prepared by Harris Technical Services (traffic accident reconstructionists) and is available at *www.harristechnical.com*.

Three Steps to a Settlement

Step 1: Can We Talk?

Not likely. You can try phoning the seller or automaker, but don't expect to get much out of the call. Private sellers won't want to talk with you, and dealer customer service agents will tell you the vehicle was sold "as is." They simply apply the dealership's policy, knowing that 90 percent of complainers will drop their claims after venting their anger.

Still, try to work things out by contacting someone higher up who can change the policy to satisfy your request. In your attempt to reach a settlement, ask only for what is fair and don't try to make anyone look bad.

Speak in a calm, polite manner and try to avoid polarizing the issue. Talk about co-operating to solve the problem. Let a compromise emerge—don't come in with a rigid set of demands. Don't insist on getting the settlement offer in writing, but make sure that you're accompanied by a friend or relative who can confirm the offer in court if it isn't honoured. Be prepared to act upon the offer without delay so your hesitancy won't be blamed if the seller or automaker withdraws it.

Service manager help

Service managers have more power than you may realize. They make the first determination of what work is covered under warranty or through post-warranty "goodwill" programs, and they are directly responsible to the dealer and manufacturer for that decision (dealers hate manufacturer audits that force them to pay back questionable warranty decisions). Service managers are paid both to save the dealer and automaker money and to mollify irate clients—almost an impossible balancing act. Nevertheless, when a service manager agrees to extend warranty coverage, it's because you've raised solid issues that neither the dealer nor the automaker can ignore. All the more reason to present your argument in a confident, forthright manner with your vehicle's service history and *Lemon-Aid's* "Reasonable Part Durability" table on hand. Also, bring as many technical service bulletins and owner complaint printouts as you can find from NHTSA's website and similar sources. It's not important that they apply directly to your problem; they establish parameters for giving out after-warranty assistance, or "goodwill."

Don't use your salesperson as a runner, since the sales staff are generally quite distant from the service staff and usually have less pull than you do. If the service manager can't or won't set things right, your next step is to convene a mini-summit with the service manager, the dealership principal, and the automaker's service rep, if he represents that make. Regional service representatives are technicians who are regularly sent out by the manufacturer to help dealers with technical problems. By getting the automaker involved, you can often get an agreement where the seller and the automaker pay two-thirds of the repair cost, even though the vehicle was bought used.

Independent dealers and dealers who sell a brand of vehicle used that they don't sell new will give you less latitude. You have to make the case that the vehicle's defects were present at the time of purchase or should have been apparent to the seller, or that the vehicle doesn't conform to the representations made when it was purchased. Emphasize that you intend to use the courts if necessary to obtain a refund—most sellers would rather settle than risk a lawsuit with all the attendant publicity. An independent estimate of the vehicle's defects and repair costs is essential if you want to convince the seller that you're serious in your claim and that you stand a good chance of winning your case in court. Come prepared with an estimated cost of repairs to challenge the dealer who agrees to pay half the repair costs and then jacks up the price 100 percent so that you wind up paying the whole shot.

Step 2: Create a Paper Trail

If you haven't sent a written claim letter, fax, or email, you really haven't complained—or at least, that's the auto industry's mindset. If your vehicle was misrepresented, has major defects, or wasn't properly repaired under warranty, the first thing you should do is give the seller a written summary of the outstanding problems and stipulate a time period within which the seller can fix the vehicle or refund your money. Follow the format of the sample complaint letters prepared for you in this section (see pages 57–58).

Remember, you can ask for compensation for repairs that have been done or need to be done, insurance costs while the vehicle is being repaired, towing charges, supplementary transportation costs such as taxis and rented cars, and damages for inconvenience. If no satisfactory offer is made, ask for mediation, arbitration, or a formal hearing in your provincial small claims court. Make the manufacturer a party to the lawsuit, especially if the emissions warranty, a secret warranty extension, a safety-recall campaign, or extensive chassis rusting is involved.

Step 3: Try Mediation and Arbitration

If the formality of a courtroom puts you off, or you're not sure that your claim is all that solid and don't want to pay legal costs to find out, consider using mediation or arbitration. These services are sponsored by the Better Business Bureau (BBB), the Automobile Protection Association (APA), the Canadian Automobile Association (CAA), and by many small claims courts where compulsory mediation is a prerequisite to going to trial.

Getting Outside Help

Don't lose your case because of poor preparation. Ask government or independent consumer protection agencies to evaluate how well you've prepared before going to your first hearing. Also, use the Internet to ferret out additional facts and gather support (*www.lemonaidcars.com* and its links are good places to start).

Pressure Tactics

You can put additional pressure on a seller or garage, and have fun at the same time, by putting a lemon sign on your car and parking it in front of the dealer or garage, by creating a "lemon" website, or by forming a self-help group. Angry Chrysler and Ford owners, for example, have received sizeable settlements in Canada by forming their own Chrysler Lemon Owners Group (CLOG) and Ford Lemon Owners Group (FLOG).

Use your website to gather data from others who may have experienced a problem similar to your own. As with placing a newspaper ad, this can help you set the foundation for a meeting with the automaker, or even for a class action, and it pressures the dealer or manufacturer to settle. Websites are often the subject of news stories, so the media may pick up on yours.

Here's some more advice from this consumer advocate with hundreds of pickets and mass demonstrations under his belt from the past 40 years: Keep a sense of humour, and never break off the negotiations.

Finally, don't be scared off by threats that it's illegal to criticize a product or company. Unions, environmentalists, and consumer groups do it regularly (it's called informational picketing), and the Supreme Court of Canada in *R. v. Guinard* reaffirmed this right in February 2002. In that judgment, an insured posted a sign on his barn claiming the Commerce Insurance Company was unfairly refusing his claim. The municipality of Saint-Hyacinthe, Quebec, told him to take the sign down. He refused, maintaining that he had the right to state his opinion. The Supreme Court agreed.

This judgment means that consumer protests, signs, and websites that criticize the actions of corporations or government cannot be shut up or taken down simply because they say unpleasant things. However, what you say must be true, and your intent must be to inform, without malice.

Winning Claim Strategies

Safety Failures

Incidents of sudden acceleration and chronic stalling are quite common. However, they are very difficult to diagnose, and individual cases can be treated very differently by federal safety agencies. Sudden acceleration is considered to be a safety-related problem—stalling isn't. Never mind that a vehicle's sudden loss of power on a busy highway puts everyone's lives at risk (as is the case with 2001–05 Toyota and Lexus models). The same problem exists with engine and transmission powertrain failures, which are only occasionally considered to be safety-related. ABS and airbag failures are universally considered to be life-threatening defects. If your vehicle manifests any of these conditions, here's what you need to do:

1. Get independent witnesses to confirm that the problem exists. This includes verification by an independent mechanic, passenger testimony, downloaded data from your vehicle's data recorder, and lots of Internet browsing using *www.lemonaidcars.com* and a search engine like Google as your primary tools. Notify the dealer or manufacturer by fax, email, or registered letter that you consider the problem to be a factory-induced, safety-related defect. Make sure you address your correspondence to the manufacturer's product liability or legal affairs department. At the dealership's service bay, make sure that every work order clearly states the problem as well as the number of previous attempts to fix it. (You should end up with a few complaint letters and a handful of work orders confirming that this is an ongoing deficiency.) If the dealer won't give you a copy of the work order because the work is a warranty claim, ask for a copy of the order number "in case your estate wishes to file a claim, pursuant to an accident." (This will get the service manager's attention.) Leaving a paper trail is crucial for any claim you may have later on, because it shows your concern and persistence and clearly indicates that the dealer and manufacturer had ample time to correct the defect.

2. Note on the work order that you expect the problem to be diagnosed and corrected under the emissions warranty or a "goodwill" program. It also wouldn't hurt to add the phrase on the work order or in your claim letters that "any deaths, injuries, or damage caused by the defect will be the dealer's and manufacturer's responsibility" since this work order (or letter, fax, or email) constitutes you putting them on formal notice.

3. If the dealer does the necessary repairs at little or no cost to you, send a follow-up confirmation saying that you appreciate the assistance. Also, emphasize that you'll be back if the problem reappears, even if the warranty has expired, because the repair renews your warranty rights applicable to that defect. In other words, the warranty clock is set back to its original position. You won't likely get a copy of the repair bill, because dealers don't like to admit that there was a serious defect present. Keep in mind, however, that you can get your complete vehicle file from the dealer and manufacturer by issuing a subpoena, which costs about $75 (refundable), if the case goes to small claims or a higher court. This request has produced many out-of-court settlements

when the internal documents show extensive work was carried out to correct the problem.

4. If the problem persists, send a letter, fax, or email to the dealer and manufacturer saying so, look for ALLDATA service bulletins to confirm that your vehicle's defects are factory related, and call Transport Canada or NHTSA, or log onto NHTSA's website, to report the failure. Also, contact the Center for Auto Safety in Washington, D.C., at 202-328-7700 or *www.autosafety.org* for a lawyer referral and an information sheet covering the problem.

5. Now come two crucial questions: Should you repair the defect now or later, and should you use the dealer or an independent? Generally, it's smart to use an independent garage if you know the dealer isn't pushing for free corrective repairs from the manufacturer, if weeks or months have passed without any resolution of your claim, if the dealer keeps claiming that it's a maintenance item, or if you know an independent mechanic who will give you a detailed work order showing the defect is factory related and not a result of poor maintenance. Don't mention that a court case may ensue, since this will scare the dickens out of your only independent witness. A bonus of using an independent garage is that the repair charges will be about half of what a dealer would demand. Incidentally, if the automaker later denies warranty "goodwill" because you used an independent repairer, use the argument that the defect's safety implications required emergency repairs to be carried out by whoever could see you first.

6. Dashboard-mounted warning lights usually come on prior to airbags suddenly deploying, ABS brakes failing, or engine glitches causing the vehicle to stall out. (Sudden acceleration, however, usually occurs without warning.) Automakers consider these lights to be critical safety warnings and generally advise drivers to immediately have the vehicle serviced to correct the problem (advice that can be found in the owner's manual) when any of the above lights come on. This bolsters the argument that your life was threatened, emergency repairs were required, and your request for another vehicle or a complete refund isn't out of line.

7. Sudden acceleration can have multiple causes, isn't easy to duplicate, and is often blamed on the driver mistaking the accelerator for the brakes or failing to perform proper maintenance. Yet NHTSA data shows that factory-related defects are often the culprit. For example, 1997–2004 Lexus ES 300/330s and Toyota Camrys may have a faulty transmission that may cause engine surging. So how do you satisfy the burden of proof showing that the problem exists and is the automaker's responsibility? Use the legal doctrine called "the balance of probabilities" by eliminating all of the possible dodges the dealer or manufacturer may employ. Show that proper maintenance has been carried out, that you're a safe driver, and that the incident occurs frequently and without warning.

8. If any of the above defects causes an accident, the airbag fails to deploy, or you're injured by its deployment, ask your insurance company to have the vehicle towed to a neutral location and clearly state that neither the dealer nor the automaker should touch the vehicle until your insurance company and Transport Canada have completed their investigation. Also, get as many

witnesses as possible and immediately go to the hospital for a check-up, even if you're feeling okay. You may be injured and not know it because the adrenalin coursing through your veins is masking your injuries. A hospital exam will easily confirm that your injuries are related to the accident, which is essential in court or for future settlement negotiations.

9. Peruse NHTSA's online accident database to find reports of other accidents caused by the same failure.

10. Don't let your insurance company settle the case if you're sure the accident was caused by a mechanical failure. Even if an engineering analysis fails to directly implicate the manufacturer or dealer, you can always plead the aforementioned balance of probabilities. If the insurance company settles, your insurance premiums will probably be increased.

Paint and Body Defects

The following tips on making a successful claim apply mainly to paint defects, water and air leaks, and subpar fit and finish, but you can use the same strategy for any other vehicle defect that you believe is the automaker's or dealer's responsibility. If you're not sure whether the problem is a factory-related deficiency or a maintenance item, have it checked out by an independent garage or get a technical service bulletin summary for your vehicle. The summary may include specific bulletins relating to the diagnosis, correction, and ordering of upgraded parts needed to fix your problem.

1. If you know that your vehicle's paint problem is factory related, take your vehicle to the dealer and ask for a written, signed estimate. When you're handed the estimate, ask if the paint job can be covered by some "goodwill" assistance. (Ford's euphemism for this secret warranty is "Owner Notification Program" or "Owner Dialogue Program," GM's term is "Special Policy," and Chrysler simply calls it an "Owner Satisfaction Notice." Don't use the term "secret warranty" yet; you'll just make everyone angry and evasive.)

2. Your request will probably be met with a refusal, an offer to repaint the vehicle for half the cost, or (if you're lucky) an agreement to repaint the vehicle free of charge. If you accept the half-cost offer, make sure that it's based on the original estimate you have in hand, since some dealers jack up their estimates so that your 50 percent is really 100 percent of the true cost.

3. If the dealer or automaker has already refused your claim and the repair hasn't been done yet, get an additional estimate from an independent garage that shows the problem is factory related.

4. If the repair has yet to be done, mail or fax a registered claim to the automaker (and send a copy to the dealer), claiming the average of both estimates. If the repair has been done at your expense, mail or fax a registered claim with a copy of your bill.

5. If you don't receive a satisfactory response within a week, deposit a copy of the estimate or paid bill and claim letter/fax before the small claims court and await a trial date. This means that the automaker/dealer will have to appear, no lawyer is required, and costs should be minimal (under $100). Usually, an

informal pretrial mediation hearing with the two parties and a court clerk will be scheduled within a few months, followed by a trial a few weeks later (the time varies among different regions). Most cases are settled at the mediation stage. You can help your case by collecting photographs, maintenance work orders, previous work orders dealing with your problem, and technical service bulletins, and by speaking to an independent expert (the garage or body shop that did the estimate or repair is best, but you can also use a local teacher who teaches automotive repair). Remember, service bulletins can be helpful, but they aren't critical to a successful claim.

Other situations

- If the vehicle has just been repainted or repaired but the dealer says that "goodwill" coverage was denied by the automaker, pay for the repair with a certified cheque and write "under protest" on the cheque. Remember, though, if the dealer does the repair, you won't have an independent expert who can affirm that the problem was factory related or that it was a result of premature wearout. Plus, the dealer can say that you or the environment caused the paint problem. In these cases, technical service bulletins can make or break your case.
- If the dealer or automaker offers a partial repair or refund, take it. Then sue for the rest. Remember, if a partial repair has been done under warranty, it counts as an admission of responsibility, no matter what "goodwill" euphemism is used. Also, the repaired component or body panel should be just as durable as if it were new. Hence, the clock starts ticking from the time of the repair until you reach the original warranty parameter—again, no matter what the dealer's repair warranty limit says.

Very seldom do automakers contest these paint claims before small claims court, instead opting to settle once the court claim is bounced from their customer relations people to their legal affairs department. At that time, you'll probably be offered an out-of-court settlement for 50 to 75 percent of your claim.

Stand fast, and make reference to the service bulletins you intend to subpoena in order to publicly contest in court the unfair nature of this "secret warranty" program (automakers' lawyers cringe at the idea of trying to explain why consumers aren't made aware of these bulletins). One hundred percent restitution will probably follow.

Four good examples of favourable paint judgments are *Shields v. General Motors of Canada, Bentley v. Dave Wheaton Pontiac Buick GMC Ltd. and General Motors of Canada, Maureen Frank v. General Motors of Canada Limited,* and the most recent, *Dunlop v. Ford of Canada.*

Dunlop v. Ford of Canada (No. 58475/04; Ontario Superior Court of Justice, Richmond Hill Small Claims Court; January 5, 2005; Deputy Judge M. J. Winer). The owner of a 1996 Lincoln Town car purchased used in 1999 for $27,000 was awarded $4,091.64. Judge Winer cited the *Shields* decision (see below) and gave the following reasons for finding Ford of Canada liable:

> Evidence was given by the Plaintiff's witness, Terry Bonar, an experienced paint auto technician. He gave evidence that the [paint] delamination may be both a manufacturing defect and can be caused or speeded up by atmospheric conditions. He also says that [the paint on] a car like this should last ten to 15 years, [or even for] the life of the vehicle...
>
> It is my view that the presence of ultraviolet light is an environmental condition to which the vehicle is subject. If it cannot withstand this environmental condition, it is defective in my view.

Paint delamination is a common defect that automakers often blame on everything from bird droppings to ultraviolet light. DaimlerChrysler usually settles out of court, while Ford and General Motors often blame the environment or simply say the warranty has expired. The courts haven't been very receptive to these kinds of excuses.

Shields v. General Motors of Canada (No. 1398/96; Ontario Court, General Division; Oshawa Small Claims Court, 33 King Street West, Oshawa, Ontario, L1H 1A1; July 24, 1997; Robert Zochodne, Deputy Judge). The owner of a 1991 Pontiac Grand Prix purchased the vehicle used with over 100,000 km on its odometer. Beginning in 1995, the paint began to bubble and flake and eventually peeled off. Deputy Judge Robert Zochodne awarded the plaintiff $1,205.72 and struck down every one of GM's environmental/acid rain/UV rays arguments. Here are the other important aspects of this 12-page judgment that GM did not appeal:

1. The judge admitted many of the technical service bulletins referred to in *Lemon-Aid* as proof of GM's negligence.
2. Although the vehicle already had 156,000 km on it when the case went to court, GM still offered to pay for 50 percent of the paint repairs if the plaintiff dropped his suit.
3. Deputy Judge Zochodne ruled that the failure to protect the paint from the damaging effects of UV rays is akin to engineering a car that won't start in cold weather. In essence, vehicles must be built to withstand the rigours of the environment.
4. Here's an interesting twist: The original warranty covered defects that were present at the time it was in effect. The judge, taking statements found in the GM technical service bulletins, ruled that the UV problem was factory related, existed during the warranty period, and represented a latent defect that appeared once the warranty expired.
5. The subsequent purchaser was not prevented from making the warranty claim,

even though the warranty had long since expired from a time and mileage standpoint and he was the second owner.

Bentley v. Dave Wheaton Pontiac Buick GMC Ltd. and General Motors of Canada (Victoria Registry No. 24779; British Columbia Small Claims Court; December 1, 1998; Judge Higinbotham). This small claims judgment builds upon the Ontario *Shields v. General Motors of Canada* decision and cites other jurisprudence as to how long paint should last on a car. If you're wondering why Ford and Chrysler haven't been hit by similar judgments, remember that they usually settle out of court.

Maureen Frank v. General Motors of Canada Limited (No. SC#12 (2001); Saskatchewan Provincial Court; Saskatoon, Saskatchewan; October 17, 2001; Provincial Court Judge H.G. Dirauf).

On June 23, 1997, the Plaintiff bought a 1996 Chevrolet Corsica from a General Motors dealership. At the time, the odometer showed 33,172 km. The vehicle still had some factory warranty. The car had been a lease car and had no previous accidents.

During June of 2000, the Plaintiff noticed that some of the paint was peeling off from the car and she took it to a General Motors dealership in Saskatoon and to the General Motors dealership in North Battleford where she purchased the car. While there were some discussions with the GM dealership about the peeling paint, nothing came of it and the Plaintiff now brings this action claiming the cost of a new paint job.

During 1999, the Plaintiff was involved in a minor collision causing damage to the left rear door. This damage was repaired. During this repair, some scratches to the left front door previously done by vandals were also repaired.

The Plaintiff's witness, Frank Nemeth, is a qualified auto body repairman with some 26 years of experience. He testified that the peeling paint was a factory defect and that it was necessary to completely strip the car and repaint it. He diagnosed the cause of the peeling paint as a separation of the primer surface or colour coat from the electrocoat primer. In his opinion no primer surfacer was applied at all. He testified that once the peeling starts, it will continue. He has seen this problem on General Motors vehicles. The defect is called delamination.

Mr. Nemeth stated that a paint job should last at least 10 years. In my opinion most people in Saskatchewan grow up with cars and are familiar with cars. I think it is common knowledge that the original paint on cars normally lasts in excess of 15 years and that rust becomes a problem before the paint fails. In any event, paint peeling off, as it did on the Plaintiff's vehicle, is not common. I find that the paint on a new car put on by the factory should last at least 15 years.

It is clear from the evidence of Frank Nemeth (independent body shop manager) that the delamination is a factory defect. His evidence was not seriously challenged. I find that the factory paint should not suffer a delamination defect for at least 15 years and that this factory defect breached the warranty that the paint was of acceptable quality and was durable for a reasonable period of time.

There will be judgment for the Plaintiff in the amount of $3,412.38 plus costs of $81.29.

Some of the important aspects of the *Frank* judgment are as follows:

1. The judge accepted that the automaker was responsible, even though the car had been bought used. The subsequent purchaser was not prevented from making the warranty claim, even though the warranty had long since expired from a time and mileage standpoint.
2. The judge stressed that the provincial warranty can kick in any time an automaker's warranty has expired or isn't applied.
3. By awarding full compensation to the plaintiff, the judge rejected the argument that there was a significant "betterment," or improvement, added to the car that would warrant reducing the amount of the award.
4. The judge decided that the paint delamination was a factory defect.
5. The judge also concluded that without this factory defect, a paint job should last up to 15 years.
6. GM offered to pay $700 of the paint repairs if the plaintiff dropped the suit; the judge awarded five times that amount.
7. Maureen Frank won this case despite having to confront GM lawyer Ken Ready, who had considerable experience defending GM in this type of lawsuit.

Other paint and rust cases

Whittaker v. Ford Motor Company (1979) (24 O.R. (2d), 344). A new Ford developed serious corrosion problems in spite of having been rustproofed by the dealer. The court ruled that the dealer, not Ford, was liable for the damage for having sold the rustproofing product at the time of purchase. This is an important judgment to use when a rustproofer or paint protector goes out of business or refuses to pay a claim, since the decision holds the dealer jointly responsible.

Martin v. Honda Canada Inc. (March 17, 1986; Ontario Small Claims Court; Scarborough; Judge Sigurdson). The original owner of a 1981 Honda Civic sought compensation for the premature "bubbling, pitting, [and] cracking of the paint and rusting of the Civic after five years of ownership." Judge Sigurdson agreed with the owner and ordered Honda to pay $1,163.95.

Thauberger v. Simon Fraser Sales and Mazda Motors (3 B.C.L.R., 193). This Mazda owner sued for damages caused by the premature rusting of his 1977 Mazda GLC. The court awarded him $1,000. Thauberger had previously sued General Motors for a prematurely rusted Blazer truck and was also awarded $1,000 in the same court. Both judges ruled that the defects could not be excluded from the automaker's expressed warranty or from the implied warranty granted by British Columbia's *Sale of Goods Act*.

See also:

- *Danson v. Chateau Ford (1976) C.P.* (Quebec Small Claims Court; No. 32-00001898-757; Judge Lande)
- *Doyle v. Vital Automotive Systems* (May 16, 1977; Ontario Small Claims Court; Toronto; Judge Turner)
- *Lacroix v. Ford* (April 1980; Ontario Small Claims Court; Toronto; Judge Tierney)
- *Marinovich v. Riverside Chrysler* (April 1, 1987; District Court of Ontario; No. 1030/85; Judge Stortini)

Using the Courts

Sue as a Last Resort

If the seller you've been negotiating with agrees to make things right, give him or her a deadline and then have an independent garage check the repairs. If no offer is made within 10 working days, file suit in court. Make the manufacturer a party to the lawsuit only if the original, unexpired warranty was transferred to you; if your claim falls under the emissions warranty, a TSB, a secret warranty extension, or a safety recall campaign; or if there is extensive chassis rusting due to poor engineering.

Choosing the Right Court

You must decide what remedy to pursue; that is, whether you want a partial refund or a cancellation of the sale. To determine the refund amount, add the estimated cost of repairing existing mechanical defects to the cost of prior repairs. Don't exaggerate your losses or claim for repairs that are considered routine maintenance. A suit for cancellation of sale involves practical problems. The court requires that the vehicle be "tendered," or taken back to the seller, at the time the lawsuit is filed. This means that you are without transportation for as long as the case continues, unless you purchase another vehicle in the interim. If you lose the case, you must then take back the old vehicle and pay storage fees. You could go from having no vehicle to having two, one of which is a clunker.

Generally, if the cost of repairs or the sales contract amount falls within the small claims court limit (discussed later), file the case there to keep costs to a minimum and to get a speedy hearing. Small claims court judgments aren't easily appealed, lawyers aren't necessary, filing fees are minimal (about $125), and cases are usually heard within a few months.

Watch what you ask for. If you claim more than the small claims court limit, you'll have to go to a higher court—where costs quickly add up and delays of a few years or more are commonplace.

Small Claims Courts

Crooked automakers scurry away from small claims courts like cockroaches from bug spray, not because the courts can issue million-dollar judgments or force litigants to spend millions in legal fees (they can't), but because they can award sizeable sums to plaintiffs and make jurisprudence that other judges on the same bench are likely to follow.

For example, in *Dawe v. Courtesy Chrysler* (Dartmouth Nova Scotia Small Claims Court; SCCH #206825; July 30, 2004) Judge Patrick L Casey, Q.C., rendered an impressive 21-page decision citing key automobile product liability cases over the past 80 years. He awarded $5,037 to the owner of a new 2001 Cummins-equipped Ram pickup that wandered all over the road; lost power, or jerked and bucked; shifted erratically; lost braking ability; bottomed out when passing over bumps; allowed water to leak into the cab; produced a burnt-wire and oil smell in the interior as the lights would dim; and produced a rear-end whine and wind noise around the doors and under the dash. Dawe had sold the vehicle and reduced his claim to meet the small claims threshold.

There are small claims courts in most counties of every province, and you can either make a claim in the county where the problem happened or in the county where the defendant lives and conducts business. Simply go to the small claims court office and ask for a claim form. Instructions on how to fill it out accompany the form. Remember, you must identify the defendant correctly, and this may require some help from the court clerk or a law student because some automakers name local attorneys to handle suits (look for other recent lawsuits naming the same party). Crooks often change their company's name to escape liability; for example, it would be impossible to sue Joe's Garage (1999) if your contract is with Joe's Garage Inc. (1984).

At this point, it wouldn't hurt to hire a lawyer or a paralegal for a brief walk-through of small claims procedures to ensure that you've prepared your case properly and that you know what objections will likely be raised by the other side. If you'd like a lawyer to do all the work for you, there are a number of law firms around the country that specialize in small claims litigation. "Small claims" doesn't mean small legal fees, however. In Toronto, some law offices charge a flat fee of $1,000 for the basic small claims lawsuit and trial.

Remember that you're entitled to bring to court any evidence relevant to your case, including written documents such as a bill of sale or receipt, contract, or letter. If your car has developed severe rust problems, bring a photograph (signed and dated by the photographer) to court. You may also have witnesses testify, but it's important to discuss witness testimony prior to the court date. If a witness can't attend the court date, he or she can write a report and sign it for representation in court. This situation usually applies to an expert witness, such as an independent mechanic who has evaluated your car's problems.

If you lose your case in spite of all your preparation and research, some small claims court statutes allow cases to be retried, at a nominal cost, in exceptional circumstances. If a new witness has come forward, additional evidence has been discovered, or key documents that were previously not available have become accessible, apply for a retrial. In Ontario, this little-known provision is Rule 18.4 (1).B.

Alan MacDonald, a *Lemon-Aid* reader who won his case in small claims court, gives the following tips on beating Ford:

> I want to thank you for the advice you provided in my dealings with the Ford Motor Company of Canada, Limited, and Highbury Ford Sales Limited regarding my 1994 Ford Taurus wagon and the problems with the automatic transmission (Taurus and Windstar transmissions are identical). I also wish to apologize for not sending you a copy of this judgment earlier that may be beneficial to your readers. (*MacDonald v. Highbury Ford Sales Limited,* Ontario Superior Court of Justice in the Small Claims Court London, June 6, 2000, Court File #0001/00, Judge J. D. Searle).
>
> In 1999 after only 105,000 km the automatic transmission went. I took the car to Highbury Ford to have it repaired. We paid $2,070 to have the transmission fixed, but protested and felt the transmission failed prematurely. We contacted Ford, but to no avail: their reply was we were out of warranty period. The transmission was so poorly repaired (and we went back to Highbury Ford several times) that we had to go to Mr. Transmission to have the transmission fixed again nine months later at a further $1,906.02.
>
> It is at that point that I contacted you, and I was surprised, and somewhat speechless (which you noticed) when you personally called me to provide advice and encouragement. I am very grateful for your call. My observations with going through small claims court involved the following: I filed in January of 2000, the trial took place on June 1 and the judgment was issued June 6.
>
> At pretrial, a representative of Ford (Ann Sroda) and a representative from Highbury Ford were present. I came with one binder for each of the defendants, the court, and one for myself (each binder was about 3 inches thick—containing your reports on Ford Taurus automatic transmissions, ALLDATA Service Bulletins, [and extracts from the following websites:] Taurus Transmissions Victims (Bradley website), Center for Auto Safety...Read This Before Buying a Taurus...and the Ford Vent Page....
>
> The representative from Ford asked a lot of questions (I think she was trying to find out if I had read the contents of the information I was relying on). The Ford representative then offered a 50 percent settlement based on the initial transmission work done at Highbury Ford. The release allowed me to still sue Highbury Ford with regards to the necessity of going to Mr. Transmission because of the faulty repair done by the dealer. Highbury Ford displayed no interest in settling the case, and so I had to go to court.

For court, I prepared by issuing a summons to the manager at Mr. Transmission, who did the second transmission repair, as an expert witness. I was advised that unless you produce an expert witness you won't win in a car repair case in small claims court. Next, I went to the law school library in London and received a great deal of assistance in researching cases pertinent to car repairs. I was told that judgments in your home province (in my case, Ontario) were binding on the court; that cases outside of the home province could be considered, but not binding, on the judge.

The cases I used for trial involved *Pelleray v. Heritage Ford Sales Ltd.*, Ontario Small Claims Court (Scarborough) SC7688/91 March 22, 1993; *Phillips et al. v. Ford Motor Co. of Canada Ltd. et al*, Ontario Reports 1970, 15th January 1970; *Gregorio v. Intrans-Corp.*, Ontario Court of Appeal, May 19, 1994; *Collier v. MacMaster's Auto Sales*, New Brunswick Court of Queen's Bench, April 26, 1991; *Sigurdson v. Hillcrest Service & Acklands (1977)*, Saskatchewan Queen's Bench; *White v. Sweetland*, Newfoundland District Court, Judicial Centre of Gander, November 8, 1978; *Raiches Steel Works v. J. Clark & Son*, New Brunswick Supreme Court, March 7, 1977; *Mudge v. Corner Brook Garage Ltd.*, Newfoundland Supreme Court, July 17, 1975; *Sylvain v. Carroseries d'Automobiles Guy Inc. (1981)*, C.P. 333, Judge Page; and *Gagnon v. Ford Motor Company of Canada, Limited et Marineau Automobile Co. Ltée. (1974)*, C.S. 422–423.

In court, I had prepared the case, as indicated above, and had my expert witness and two other witnesses who had driven the vehicle (my wife and my 18-year-old son). As you can see by the judgment, we won our case and I was awarded $1,756.52, including prejudgment interest and costs.

Key Court Decisions

The following Canadian and U.S. lawsuits and judgments cover typical problems that are likely to arise. Use them as leverage when negotiating a settlement or as a reference should your claim go to trial. Legal principles applying to Canadian and American law are similar; Quebec court decisions, however, may be based on legal principles that don't apply outside of that province. Nevertheless, you can find a comprehensive listing of Canadian decisions from small claims courts all the way to the Supreme Court of Canada at *www.legalresearch.org/docs/internet3.html* or *www.canlii.org*.

You can find additional court judgments in the legal reference section of your city's main public library or at a nearby university law library. Ask the librarian for help in choosing the legal phrases that best describe your claim. LexisNexis (*www. lexis-nexis.com*) and FindLaw (*www.findlaw.com*) are two useful Internet sites for legal research. Their main drawback, though, is that you may need to subscribe or use a lawyer's subscription to access jurisprudence and other areas of the sites.

Some of the small claims court cases cited in *Lemon-Aid* may not be reported. If that happens, contact the office of the presiding judge named in the decision and ask his or her assistant to send you a copy of the judgment. If the judge or assistant aren't available, ask for the court clerk of that jurisdiction to search for the case file and date referenced in *Lemon-Aid*.

An excellent reference book that will give you plenty of tips on filing, pleading, and collecting your judgment is Judge Marvin Zuker's *Ontario Small Claims Court Practice 2007* (Carswell, 2006). Judge Zuker's book is easily understood by non-lawyers and uses court decisions from across Canada to help you plead your case successfully in almost any Canadian court.

Product Liability

Almost three decades ago, in *Kravitz v. GM*, the Supreme Court of Canada clearly affirmed that automakers and their dealers are jointly liable for the replacement or repair of a vehicle if independent testimony shows that it is afflicted with factory-related defects that compromise its safety or performance. The existence of a secret warranty extension or technical service bulletin also helps prove that the vehicle's problems are the automaker's responsibility. For example, in *Lowe v. Fairview Chrysler* (see page 112), technical service bulletins were instrumental in showing an Ontario small claims court judge that Chrysler's history of automatic transmission failures went back to 1989.

In addition to replacing or repairing the vehicle, an automaker can also be held responsible for any damages arising from the defect. This means that loss of wages, supplementary transportation costs, and damages for personal inconvenience can be awarded. However, in the States, product liability damage awards often exceed millions of dollars, while Canadian courts are far less generous.

Implied Warranty

Reasonable durability

This is that powerful "other" warranty that they never tell you about. It applies during and after the expiration of the manufacturer's or dealer's expressed or written warranty and requires that a part or repair will last a reasonable period of time. What is reasonable depends in a large part on benchmarks used in the industry, the price of the vehicle, and how it was driven and maintained. Look at the reasonable durability table on pages 53–54 for some guidelines as to what you should expect. Judges usually apply the implied or legal warranty when the manufacturer's expressed warranty has expired and the vehicle's manufacturing defects remain uncorrected.

Chevrier v. General Motors Du Canada, (October 18, 2006; Quebec Small Claims Court; Joliette District (Repentigny) No. 730-32-004876-046; Justice Georges Massol). Judgment can be obtained at *www.canlii.org/fr/qc/qccq/doc/2006/ 2006qccq15312/2006qccq15312.pdf.*

The plaintiff leased and then bought a 2000 Montana minivan. At 71,000 km the automatic transmission failed and two GM dealers estimated the repairs to be between $2,200 and $2,500. They refused warranty coverage because the warranty had expired after the third year of ownership or 60,000 km of use. The owner repaired the transmission at an independent garage for $1,869 and kept the old parts, which GM refused to examine.

A small claims court lawsuit was filed and Judge Massol gave the following reasons for ruling against GM's two arguments that 1. There was no warning that a claim would be filed; and 2. All warranties had expired:

- GM filed a voluminous record of jurisprudence in its favour relative to other lawsuits rejected because they were filed without prior notice, but Judge Massol reasoned that GM could not plead a "failure to notify" because the owner went to several dealers, who were essentially agents of the manufacturer.
- He also reasoned that the expiration of GM's written warranty does not nullify the legal warranty set out in articles 38 and 39 of the *Consumer Protection Act*. The legal warranty requires that all products be "reasonably durable," which did not appear to be the case with the plaintiff's vehicle, given the low mileage and number of years of use.

GM was ordered to pay the entire repair costs, plus interest, plus the $90 filing fee.

Dufour v. Ford Canada Ltd. (April 10, 2001; Quebec Small Claims Court; Hull; No. 550-32-008335-009; Justice P. Chevalier). Ford was forced to reimburse the cost of engine head gasket repairs carried out on a 1996 Windstar 3.8L engine—a vehicle not covered by the automaker's Owner Notification Program, which cut off assistance after the '95 model year.

Schaffler v. Ford Motor Company Limited and Embrun Ford Sales Ltd. (Ontario Superior Court of Justice; L'Orignal Small Claims Court; Court File No. 59-2003; July 22, 2003; Justice Gerald Langlois). The plaintiff bought a used 1995 Windstar in 1998. Its engine head gasket was repaired for free three years later, under Ford's 7-year extended warranty. In 2002, at 109,600 km, the head gasket failed again, seriously damaging the engine. Ford refused a second repair. Justice Langlois ruled that Ford's warranty extension bulletin listed signs and symptoms of the covered defect that were identical to the problems written on the second work order ("persistent and/or chronic engine overheating; heavy white smoke evident from the exhaust tailpipe; flashing 'low coolant' instrument panel light even after coolant refill; and constant loss of engine coolant"). Judge Langlois concluded that "the problem was brought to the attention of the dealer well within the warranty period; the dealer was negligent." The plaintiff was awarded $4,941 plus 5 percent interest. This judgment included $1,070 for two months' car rental.

John R. Reid and Laurie M. McCall v. Ford Motor Company of Canada (Superior Court of Justice; Ottawa Small Claims Court; Claim No: #02-SC-077344; July 11, 2003; Justice Tiernay). A 1996 Windstar, bought used in 1997, experienced engine head gasket failure in October 2001 at 159,000 km. Judge Tiernay awarded the plaintiffs $4,145 for the following reason:

COUR DU QUÉBEC
Division petites créances

QUÉBEC
DISTRICT DE HULL

NO: 550-32-008335-009

Hull, le 10 avril 2001

SOUS LA PRESIDENCE DE:
L'HONORABLE PIERRE
CHEVALIER
Juge de la Cour du Québec

BASTIEN DUFOUR

Partie requérante,
-c.-

FORD DU CANADA LTÉE, 7800,
route Transcanadienne à Pointe-
Claire (Québec) H9H 1C6

Partie intimée

JUGEMENT

Les parties essentielles de la requête se lisent comme suit :

I am hereby claiming from Ford Canada expenses and collateral expenses incurred for the repair of the 3.8 litter engine of a Ford Windstar GL 1996, VIN 2FMDA5147TBA95586.

The said engine had to have the head gasket and thermostat replaced on 02 June 2000, after a total of 118,892 kms indicated on the vehicle odometer. This repair was deemed necessary by my hometown Ford dealership (Mont-Bleu Ford in Gatineau, Que.) after I observed inadequate performance of the interior heating system and abnormal engine coolant temperature indications, and after a leak down test performed by the Mont-Bleu Ford dealership.

I consider such a defect to be abnormal as components such as an engine should have a life expectancy of at least 160,000 kms of 7 years without major repairs such as head gasket repair or replacement.

2

I have enclosed a copy of my bill showing that this problem is factory related and has cost $1364.35 to correct; this amount includes the cost for the engine head gasket repair and appropriate provincial and federal sales taxes

L'ensemble de la preuve satisfait le Tribunal par prépondérance de preuve que la détérioration impliquée est survenue prématurément par rapport à un bien identique et que cette détérioration n'est pas due à un défaut d'entretien.

L'article 1729 C.c.Q. stipule qu'en cas de vente par un vendeur professionnel, l'existence d'un vice au moment de la vente est présumée, lorsque la détérioration du bien survient prématurément par rapport à des biens identiques. De plus, les intimés n'ont pas repoussé la présomption en établissant que le défaut serait dû à une mauvaise utilisation du bien par l'acheteur. Selon l'art. 1730, le fabricant est soumis à cette même garantie.

Vu les articles 1729 et 1730 du Code civile du Québec, le Tribunal fait droit à la réclamation et condamne la partie intimée à payer à la partie requérante la somme de 1 364,35 $ avec intérêts au taux légal de 5% depuis la requête, soit le 19 septembre 2000 et les frais de 72 $.

PIERRE CHEVALIER
Juge de la Cour du Québec

A Technical Service Bulletin dated June 28, 1999, was circulated to Ford dealers. It dealt specifically with "undetermined loss of coolant" and "engine oil contaminated with coolant" in the 1996–98 Windstar and five other models of Ford vehicles. I conclude that Ford owed a duty of care to the Plaintiff to equip this vehicle with a cylinder head gasket of sufficient sturdiness and durability that would function trouble-free for at least seven years, given normal driving and proper maintenance conditions. I find that Ford is answerable in damages for the consequences of its negligence.

Dawe v. Courtesy Chrysler (Dartmouth Nova Scotia Small Claims Court; SCCH #206825; July 30, 2004; Judge Patrick L Casey, Q.C.). "Small claims" doesn't necessarily mean small judgments. This recent 21-page, unreported Nova Scotia small claims court decision is impressive in its clarity and thoroughness. It applies *Donoghue, Kravitz, Davis, et al.* in awarding a 2001 Dodge Ram owner over $5,000 in damages. Anyone with engine, transmission, and suspension problems or water leaking into the interior will find this judgment particularly useful.

Fissel v. Ideal Auto Sales Ltd. (1991) (91 Sask. R. 266). Shortly after the vehicle was purchased, the car's motor seized and the dealer refused to replace it, even though the car was returned on several occasions. The court ruled that the dealer had breached the statutory warranties in sections 11 (4) and (7) of the *Consumer*

Products Warranties Act. The purchasers were entitled to cancel the sale and recover the full purchase price.

Friskin v. Chevrolet Oldsmobile (72 D.L.R. (3d), 289). A Manitoba used-car buyer asked that his contract be cancelled because of his car's chronic stalling problem. The garage owner did his best to correct it. Despite the seller's good intentions, the *Manitoba Consumer Protection Act* allowed for cancellation.

Graves v. C&R Motors Ltd. (April 8, 1980; British Columbia County Court; Judge Skipp). The plaintiff bought a used car on the condition that certain deficiencies be remedied. They never were, and he was promised a refund, but it never arrived. The plaintiff brought suit, claiming that the dealer's deceptive activities violated the provincial *Trade Practices Act*. The court agreed, concluding that a deceptive act that occurs before, during, or after the transaction can lead to the cancellation of the contract.

Hachey v. Galbraith Equipment Company (1991) (33 M.V.R. (2d) 242). The plaintiff bought a used truck from the dealer to haul gravel. Shortly thereafter, the steering failed. The plaintiff's suit was successful because expert testimony showed that the truck wasn't roadworthy. The dealer was found liable for damages for being in breach of the implied condition of fitness for the purpose for which the truck was purchased, as set out in section 15 (a) of the New Brunswick *Sale of Goods Act*.

Henzel v. Brussels Motors (1973) (1 O.R., 339 (C.C.)). The dealer sold a used car, brandishing a copy of the mechanical fitness certificate as proof that the car was in good shape. The plaintiff was awarded his money back because the court held the certificate to be a warranty that was breached by the car's subsequent defects.

Johnston v. Bodasing Corporation Limited (February 23, 1983; Ontario County Court; Bruce; No. 15/11/83; Judge McKay). The plaintiff bought a used 1979 Buick Riviera that was represented as being "reliable" for $8,500. Two weeks after purchase, the motor self-destructed. Judge McKay awarded the plaintiff $2,318 as compensation to fix the Riviera's defects. One feature of this particular decision is that the trial judge found that the *Sale of Goods Act* applied, notwithstanding the fact that the vendor used a standard contract that said there were no warranties or representations. The judge also accepted the decision in *Kendal v. Lillico (1969)* (2 Appeal Cases, 31), which indicates that the *Sale of Goods Act* covers not only defects that the seller ought to have detected, but also latent defects that even his or her utmost skill and judgment could not have detected. This places a very heavy onus on the vendor, and it should prove useful in actions of this type in other common-law provinces with laws similar to Ontario's *Sale of Goods Act*.

Kelly v. Mack Canada (53 D.L.R. (4th), 476). Kelly bought two trucks from Mack Sales. The first, a used White Freightliner tractor and trailer, was purchased for $29,742. It cost him over $12,000 in repairs during the first five months, and another $9,000 was estimated for future engine repairs. Mack Sales convinced Kelly to trade in the old truck for a new Mack truck. Kelly did this, but shortly thereafter, the new truck had similar problems. Kelly sued for the return of all his money, arguing that the two transactions were really one. The Ontario Court of Appeal agreed and awarded Kelly a complete refund. It stated: "There was such a congeries of defects that there had been a breach of the implied conditions set out in the *Sale of Goods Act*."

Although Mack Sales argued that the contract contained a clause excluding any implied warranties, the court determined that the breach was of such magnitude that the dealer could not rely upon that clause. The dealer then argued that since the client used the trucks, the depreciation of both should be taken into account in reducing the award. This was refused on the grounds that the plaintiff never had the product he bargained for, and in no way did he profit from the transaction. The court also awarded Kelly compensation for loss of income while the trucks were being repaired as well as the interest on all of the money tied up in both transactions from the time of purchase until final judgment.

General Motors Products of Canada Ltd. v. Kravitz, (1979) (1 S.C.R. 790). The court said the seller's warranty of quality was an accessory to the property and was transferred with it on successive sales. Accordingly, subsequent buyers could invoke the contractual warranty of quality against the manufacturer, even though they did not contract directly with it. This precedent was then codified in articles 1434, 1442, and 1730 of Quebec's Civil Code.

Morrison v. Hillside Motors (1973) Ltd. (1981; 35 Nfld. & P.E.I.R. 361). A used car advertised to be in A-1 condition and carrying a 50/50 warranty developed a number of problems. The court decided that the purchaser should be partially compensated because of the ad's claim. In deciding how much compensation to award, the presiding judge considered the warranty's wording, the amount paid for the vehicle, the model year of the vehicle, the vehicle's average life, the type of defect that occurred, and the length of time the purchaser had use of the vehicle before its defects became evident. Although this judgment was rendered in Newfoundland, judges throughout Canada have used a similar approach for more than a decade.

Neilson v. Maclin Motors (71 D.L.R. (3d), 744). The plaintiff bought a used truck on the strength of the seller's allegations that the motor had been rebuilt and that it had 210 hp. The engine failed. The judge awarded damages and cancelled the contract because the motor had not been rebuilt, it did not have 210 hp, and the transmission was defective.

Parent v. Le Grand Trianon and Ford Credit (1982) (C.P., 194; Judge Bertrand Gagnon). Nineteen months after paying $3,300 for a used 1974 LTD, the plaintiff sued the Ford dealer for his money back because the car was prematurely rusted out. The dealer replied that rust was normal, there was no warranty, and the claim was too late. The court held that the garage was still responsible. The plaintiff was awarded $1,500 for the cost of rust repairs.

"As is" clauses

Since 1907, Canadian courts have ruled that a seller can't exclude the implied warranty as to fitness by including such phrases as "there are no other warranties or guarantees, promises, or agreements than those contained herein." See *Sawyer-Massey Co. v. Thibault* (1907), 5 W.L.R. 241.

Adams v. J&D's Used Cars Ltd. (1983) (26 Sask. R. 40 Q.B.). Shortly after purchase, the car's engine and transmission failed. The court ruled that the inclusion of "as is" in the sales contract had no legal effect. The dealer breached the implied warranty set out in Saskatchewan's *Consumer Products Warranties Act.* The sale was cancelled and all monies were refunded.

Leasing

Ford Motor Credit v. Bothwell (December 3, 1979; Ontario County Court; Middlesex; No. 9226-T; Judge Macnab). The defendant leased a 1977 Ford truck that had frequent engine problems, characterized by stalling and hard starting. After complaining for one year and driving 35,000 km (22,000 mi.), the defendant cancelled the lease. Ford Credit sued for the money owing on the lease. Judge Macnab cancelled the lease and ordered Ford Credit to repay 70 percent of the amount paid during the leasing period. Ford Credit was also ordered to refund repair costs, even though the corporation claimed that it should not be held responsible for Ford's failure to honour its warranty.

Salvador v. Setay Motors/Queenstown Chev-Olds (Hamilton Small Claims Court; Case No.1621/95). The plaintiff was awarded $2,000, plus costs, from Queenstown Leasing. The court found that the company should have tried harder to sell the leased vehicle, and at a higher price, when the "open lease" expired.

Incidentally, in 2004, about 3,700 dealers in 39 American states paid from $3,500 to $8,000 each to settle an investigation of allegations that they and Ford Motor Credit Co. had overcharged customers who had terminated leases early.

Schryvers v. Richport Ford Sales (May 18, 1993; B.C.S.C.; No. C917060; Justice Tysoe). The court awarded $17,578.47, plus costs, to a couple who paid thousands of dollars more in unfair and hidden leasing charges than if they had simply purchased their Ford Explorer and Escort. The court found that this price difference constituted a deceptive, unconscionable act or practice, in contravention of the *Trade Practices Act*, R.S.B.C. 1979, c. 406.

Judge Tysoe concluded that the total of the general damages awarded to the Schryvers for both vehicles would be $11,578.47. He then proceeded to give the following reasons for awarding an additional $6,000 in punitive damages:

> Little wonder Richport Ford had a contest for the salesperson who could persuade the most customers to acquire their vehicles by way of a lease transaction. I consider

the actions of Richport Ford to be sufficiently flagrant and high handed to warrant an award of punitive damages.

There must be a disincentive to suppliers in respect of intentionally deceptive trade practices. If no punitive damages are awarded for intentional violations of the legislation, suppliers will continue to conduct their businesses in a manner that involves deceptive trade practices because they will have nothing to lose. In this case I believe that the appropriate amount of punitive damages is the extra profit Richport Ford endeavoured to make as a result of its deceptive acts. I therefore award punitive damages against Richport Ford in the amount of $6,000.

See also:

- *Barber v. Inland Truck Sales* (11 D.L.R. (3rd), No. 469)
- *Canadian-Dominion Leasing v. Suburban Super Drug Ltd. (1966)* (56 D.L.R. (2nd), No. 43)
- *Neilson v. Atlantic Rentals Ltd. (1974)* (8 N.B.R. (2d), No. 594)
- *Volvo Canada v. Fox* (December 13, 1979; New Brunswick Court of Queen's Bench; No. 1698/77/C; Judge Stevenson)
- *Western Tractor v. Dyck* (7 D.L.R. (3rd), No. 535)

Repairs: Faulty Diagnosis

Davies v. Alberta Motor Association (August 13, 1991; Alberta Provincial Court; Civil Division; No. P9090106097; Judge Moore). The plaintiff had the AMA's Vehicle Inspection Service check out a used 1985 Nissan Pulsar NX prior to buying it. The car passed with flying colours. A month later, the clutch was replaced and numerous electrical problems ensued. At that time, another garage discovered that the car had been involved in a major accident, had a bent frame and a leaking radiator, and was unsafe to drive. The court awarded the plaintiff $1,578.40 plus three years' interest. The judge held that the AMA set itself out as an expert and should have spotted the car's defects. The AMA's defence—that it was not responsible for errors—was thrown out. The court held that a disclaimer clause could not protect the association from a fundamental breach of contract.

Secret Warranties

It's common practice for manufacturers to secretly extend their warranties to cover components with a high failure rate. Customers who complain vigorously get extended warranty compensation in the form of "goodwill" adjustments.

François Chong v. Marine Drive Imported Cars Ltd. and Honda Canada Inc. (May 17, 1994; British Columbia Provincial Small Claims Court; No. 92-06760; Judge C.L. Bagnall). Mr. Chong was the first owner of a 1983 Honda Accord with 134,000 km on the odometer. He had six engine camshafts replaced—four under Honda "goodwill" programs, one where he paid part of the repairs, and one via this small claims court judgment.

In his ruling, Judge Bagnall agreed with Chong and ordered Honda and the dealer to each pay half of the $835.81 repair bill for the following reasons:

> The defendants assert that the warranty, which was part of the contract for purchase of the car, encompassed the entirety of their obligation to the claimant, and that it expired in February 1985. The replacements of the camshaft after that date were paid for wholly or in part by Honda as a "goodwill gesture." The time has come for these gestures to cease, according to the witness for Honda. As well, he pointed out to me that the most recent replacement of the camshaft was paid for by Honda and that, therefore, the work would not be covered by Honda's usual warranty of 12 months from date of repair. Mr. Wall, who testified for Honda, told me there was no question that this situation with Mr. Chong's engine was an unusual state of affairs. He said that a camshaft properly maintained can last anywhere from 24,000 to 500,000 km. He could not offer any suggestion as to why the car keeps having this problem.

> The claimant has convinced me that the problems he is having with rapid breakdown of camshafts in his car is due to a defect, which was present in the engine at the time that he purchased the car. The problem first arose during the warranty period and in my view has never been properly identified nor repaired.

Automatic Transmission Failures (Chrysler)

Lowe v. Fairview Chrysler-Dodge Limited and Chrysler Canada Limited (May 14, 1996; Ontario Court; General Division; Burlington Small Claims Court; No. 1224/95). This judgment, in the plaintiff's favour, raises important legal principles relative to Chrysler:

- Technical dealer service bulletins are admissible in court to prove that a problem exists and that certain parts should be checked out.
- If a problem is reported prior to a warranty's expiration, warranty coverage for the problematic component(s) is automatically carried over after the warranty ends.
- It's not up to the car owner to tell the dealer/automaker what the specific problem is.
- Repairs carried out by an independent garage can be refunded if the dealer/automaker unfairly refuses to apply the warranty.
- The dealer/automaker cannot dispute the cost of the independent repair if they fail to cross-examine the independent repairer.
- Auto owners can ask for and win compensation for their inconvenience, which in this judgment amounted to $150.

Court awards quickly add up. Although the plaintiff was given $1,985.94, with the addition of court costs and prejudgment interest, plus costs of inconvenience fixed at $150, the final award amounted to $2,266.04.

Tire Failures: Premature Wear

Blackwood v. Ford Motor Company of Canada Ltd., 2006, Docket: PO690101722, Registry: Canmore, Date: 20061208, Provincial Court of Alberta, Civil Division, judgment rendered by the Honourable J. Shriar. This four-page judgment gives important guidelines as to how a plaintiff can successfully claim a refund for a defective tire.

The plaintiff bought a new 2005 Ford Focus. After 10 months and 22,000 kilometres, his dealer said all four tires needed replacement at a cost of $560.68. Both the dealer and Ford refused to cover the expense under the 3-year/60,000 km manufacturer's tire warranty, alleging that the wear was "normal wear and tear." Judge Shriar disagreed and awarded the plaintiff the full cost of the replacement tires, plus the filing fee and costs related to the registered mail and corporate records address check. An additional $100 was awarded for court costs, plus interest on the total amount from the date of the filing.

False Advertising

Misrepresentation

Goldie v. Golden Ears Motors (1980) Ltd (Port Coquitlam; June 27, 2000; British Columbia Small Claims Court; Case No. CO8287; Justice Warren). In a well written eight-page judgment, the court awarded plaintiff Goldie $5,000 for engine repairs on a 1990 Ford F-150 pickup in addition to $236 court costs. The dealer was found to have misrepresented the mileage and sold a used vehicle that didn't meet Section 8.01 of the provincial *Motor Vehicle Act Regulations* due to its unsafe tires and defective exhaust and headlights.

In rejecting the seller's defence that he disclosed all information "to the best of his knowledge and belief" as stipulated in the sales contract, Justice Warren stated,

> The words "to the best of your knowledge and belief" do not allow someone to be willfully blind to defects or to provide incorrect information. I find as a fact that the business made no effort to fulfill its duty to comply with the requirements of this form.... The defendant has been reckless in its actions. More likely, it has actively deceived the claimant into entering into this contract. I find the conduct of the defendant has been reprehensible throughout the dealings with the claimant.

This judgment closes a loophole that sellers have used to justify their misrepresentation, and it allows for cancellation of the sale and damages if the vehicle doesn't meet highway safety regulations.

MacDonald v. Equilease Co. Ltd. (January 18, 1979; Ontario Supreme Court; Judge O'Driscoll). The plaintiff leased a truck that was misrepresented as having an axle stronger than it really was. The court awarded the plaintiff damages for repairs and set aside the lease.

Seich v. Festival Ford Sales Ltd. (1978) (6 Alta. L.R. (2nd), No. 262). The plaintiff bought a used truck from the defendant after being assured that it had a new motor and transmission. It didn't, and the court awarded the plaintiff $6,400.

Used car sold as new (demonstrator)

Bilodeau v. Sud Auto (Quebec Court of Appeal; No. 09-000751-73; Judge Tremblay). This appeals court cancelled the contract and held that a car can't be sold as new or as a demonstrator if it has ever been rented, leased, sold, or titled to anyone other than the dealer.

Rourke v. Gilmore (January 16, 1928; as found in *Ontario Weekly Notes*, vol. XXXIII, p. 292). Before discovering that his new car was really used, the plaintiff drove it for over a year. For this reason, the contract couldn't be cancelled. However, the appeals court instead awarded damages for $500, which was quite a sum in 1928!

Vehicle not as ordered

Whether you're buying a new or used vehicle, the seller can't misrepresent the vehicle. Anything that varies from what one would commonly expect or from the seller's representation must be disclosed prior to signing the contract. Typical misrepresentation scenarios include odometer turn-backs, undisclosed accident damage, used or leased cars being sold as new, new vehicles that are the wrong colour and the wrong model year, or vehicles that lack promised options or standard features.

Chenel v. Bel Automobile (1981) Inc. (August 27, 1976; Quebec Superior Court; Quebec City; Judge Desmeules). The plaintiff didn't receive his new Ford truck with the Jacob brakes essential for transporting sand in hilly regions. The court awarded the plaintiff $27,000, representing the purchase price of the vehicle less the money he earned while using the truck.

Lasky v. Royal City Chrysler Plymouth (February 18, 1987; Ontario High Court of Justice; 59 O.R. (2nd), No. 323). The plaintiff bought a 4-cylinder 1983 Dodge 600 that was represented by the salesman as being a 6-cylinder model. After putting 40,000 km on the vehicle over a 22-month period, the buyer was given her money back, without interest, under the provincial *Business Practices Act*.

Punitive Damages

Punitive damages (also known as exemplary damages) allow the plaintiff to get compensation that exceeds his or her losses as a deterrent to those who carry out dishonest or negligent practices. These kinds of judgments have been quite common in the U.S. for almost 50 years and sometimes reach hundreds of millions of dollars.

Punitive damages are rarely awarded in Canadian courts and are almost never used against automakers. When they are given out, it's usually for sums less than $100,000. During the past five years, though, our courts have cracked down on business abuses and awarded plaintiffs amounts varying from $5,000 to $1 million.

- In February 2002, the Supreme Court of Canada let stand an unprecedented million-dollar award against what it called "the insurer from hell." In *Whiten v. Pilot Insurance Co.*, the couple's home burned down and the insurer refused to pay the claim. The jury was so outraged that it ordered the company to pay $345,000 for the loss, plus $320,000 for legal costs and $1 million in punitive damages, making it the largest punitive damage award in Canadian history. The Supreme Court refused to overturn the jury's decision. This judgment scares the dickens out of insurers, who fear that they face huge punitive damage awards if they don't pay promptly.
- In May 2005, the Supreme Court of Canada once again re-affirmed the use of punitive damages in *Prebushewski v. Dodge City Auto (1985) Ltd. and Chrysler Canada Ltd.* (2001 SKQB 537; Q.B. No. 1215). The Court backed the Saskatchewan court's $25,000 punitive damage award against Chrysler, rendered on December 6, 2001, in Saskatoon, which cited egregious violations of provincial consumer protection statutes (see "Legal 'Secrets' that Work for You"). It took almost four years for a final judgment to be rendered in Ottawa. It followed testimony from Chrysler's expert witness that the company was aware of many cases where daytime running lights shorted and caused 1996 Ram pickups to catch fire. The plaintiff's truck had burned to the ground and Chrysler had refused the owner's claim, in spite of its knowledge that fires were commonplace. Angered by Chrysler's stonewalling, Justice Rothery rendered a stinging judgment, the text of which can be found on page 60. The Supreme Court of Canada's confirmation of the judgment can be found at *scc. lexum.umontreal.ca/en/2005/2005scc28/2005scc28.html*.

- *Vlchek v. Koshel* (1988) (44 C.C.L.T. 314; B.C.S.C., No. B842974). The plaintiff was seriously injured when she was thrown from a Honda all-terrain cycle on which she had been riding as a passenger. The Court allowed for punitive damages because the manufacturer was well aware of the injuries likely to be caused by the cycle. Specifically, the Court ruled that there is no firm and inflexible principle of law stipulating that punitive or exemplary damages must be denied unless the defendant's acts are specifically directed against the plaintiff. The Court may apply punitive damages "where the defendant's conduct has been indiscriminate of focus, but reckless or malicious in its character. Intent to injure the plaintiff need not be present, so long as intent to do the injurious act can be shown."

See also:

- *Granek v. Reiter* (Ontario Court, General Division; No. 35/741)
- *Morrison v. Sharp* (Ontario Court, General Division; No. 43/548)
- *Schryvers v. Richport Ford Sales* (May 18, 1993; B.C.S.C., No. C917060; Judge Tysoe)
- *Varleg v. Angeloni* (B.C.S.C., No. 41/301)

Mental distress

Canadian courts have become more generous in awarding plaintiffs money for mental distress experienced when defects aren't repaired properly under warranty. In *Sharman v. Formula Ford Sales Limited, Ford Credit Limited, and Ford Motor Company of Canada Limited,* Justice Shepard of the Ontario Superior Court in Oakville awarded the owner of a 2000 Windstar $7,500 for mental distress resulting from the breach of the implied warranty of fitness, plus $7,207 for breach of contract and breach of warranty. The Windstar's sliding door wasn't secure and leaked air and water after many attempts to repair it. Interestingly, the judge cited the *Wharton* decision as support for his award for mental distress:

> The plaintiff and his family have had three years of aggravation, inconvenience, worry, and concern about their safety and that of their children. Generally speaking, our contract law did not allow for compensation for what may be mental distress, but that may be changing. I am indebted to counsel for providing me with the decision of the British Columbia Court of Appeal in *Wharton v. Tom Harris Chevrolet Oldsmobile Cadillac Ltd.,* [2002] B.C.J. No. 233, 2002 BCCA 78. This decision was recently followed in *T'avra v. Victoria Ford Alliance Ltd.,* [2003] B, CJ No. 1957.

> In *Wharton,* the purchaser of a Cadillac Eldorado claimed damages against the dealer because the car's sound system emitted an annoying buzzing noise and the purchaser had to return the car to the dealer for repair numerous times over two and a half years. The trial court awarded damages of $2,257.17 for breach of warranty with respect to the sound system, and $5,000 in non-pecuniary damages for loss of enjoyment of their luxury vehicle and for inconvenience, for a total award of $7,257.17. The Court of Appeal upheld the decision of the trial judge and Levine J.A. spent considerable

time reviewing the law, but in particular the law relating to damages for breach of implied warranty of fitness: "The principles applicable to an award of damages for mental distress resulting from a breach of contract were thoroughly and helpfully analyzed in the recent judgment of the House of Lords in *Farley v. Skinner,* [2001] 3 W.L.R. 899, [2001] H.L.J. No. 49, affirming and clarifying the decision of the English Court of Appeal in *Watts v. Morrow,* [1991] I W.L.R. 142 1. Both of those cases concerned a claim by a buyer of a house against a surveyor who failed to report matters concerning the house as required by the contract. In *Watts,* the surveyor was negligent in failing to report defects in the house, and non-pecuniary damages of $6,750 were awarded to each of the owners for the inconvenience and discomfort experienced by them during repairs. In *Farley,* the surveyor was negligent in failing to discover, as he specifically undertook to do, that the property was adversely affected by aircraft noise. The House of Lords upheld the trial judge's award of non-pecuniary damages of $610,000, reversing the Court of Appeal, principally on the grounds that the object of the contract was to provide 'pleasure, relaxation, peace of mind, or freedom from molestation' and also because the plaintiff had suffered physical discomfort and inconvenience from the aircraft noise."

. . .

The reasons for judgment in *Farley* provide a summary and survey of the law as it has developed, in England, to date. They are helpful in analyzing and summarizing the principles derived from *Watts,* which are, in my view, applicable to the case at bar. In summary they are (borrowing the language from both *Watts* and *Farley*):

(a) A contract-breaker is not in general liable for any distress, frustration, anxiety, displeasure, vexation, tension, or aggravation which the breach of contract may cause to the innocent party.

(b) The rule is not absolute. Where a major or important part of the contract is to give pleasure, relaxation or peace of mind, damages will be awarded if the fruit of the contract is not provided or if the contrary result is instead procured.

(c) In cases not falling within the "peace of mind" category, damages are recoverable for inconvenience and discomfort caused by the breach and the mental suffering directly related to the inconvenience and discomfort. However, the cause of the inconvenience or discomfort must be a sensory experience as opposed to mere disappointment that the contract has been broken. If those effects are foreseeably suffered during a period when defects are repaired, they create damages even though the cost of repairs are not recoverable as such.

Application of Law to the Facts of This Case

In the *Wharton* case, the respondent contracted for a "luxury" vehicle for pleasure use. It included a sound system that the appellant's service manager described as "high end." The respondent's husband described the purchase of the car in this way:

"[W]e bought a luxury car that was supposed to give us a luxury ride and be a quiet vehicle, and we had nothing but difficulty with it from the very day it was delivered with this problem that nobody seemed to be able to fix.... So basically we had a luxury product that gave us no luxury for the whole time that we had it."

It is clear that an important object of the contract was to obtain a vehicle that was luxurious and a pleasure to operate. Furthermore, the buzzing noise was the cause of physical, in the sense of sensory, discomfort to the respondent and her husband. The trial judge found it inhibited listening to the sound system and was irritating in normal conversation. The respondent and her husband also bore the physical inconvenience of taking the vehicle to the appellant on numerous occasions for repairs. The inconvenience and discomfort was, in my view, reasonably foreseeable, if the defect in the sound system had been known at the date of the contract. The fact that it was not then known is, of course, irrelevant.

The award of damages for breach of the implied warranty of fitness satisfies both exceptions from the general rule that damages are not awarded for mental distress for breach of contract, set out in *Watts* as amplified in *Farley*.

The justice continued and said at para. 63 "...awards for mental distress arising from a breach of contract should be restrained and modest."

The court upheld the trial judge's award of $5,000 in *Wharton* where the issue was a buzzing in the sound system.

In my view, a defect in manufacture which goes to the safety of the vehicle deserves a modest increase. I would assess the plaintiff's damage for mental distress resulting from the breach of the implied warranty of fitness at $7,500.

Judgment to issue in favour of the plaintiff against the defendants, except Ford Credit, on a joint and several basis for $14,707, plus interest and costs....

Provincial business practices acts and consumer protection statutes prohibit false, misleading, or deceptive representations, and allow for punitive damages should the unfair practice toward the consumer amount to an unconscionable representation (see *Canadian Encyclopedic Digest* (3d) s. 76, pp. 140–45). "Unconscionable" is defined as "where the consumer is not reasonably able to protect his or her interest because of physical infirmity, ignorance, illiteracy, or inability to understand the language of an agreement or similar factors." This concept has been successfully used in consumer, environmental, and labour law.

- Exemplary damages are justified where compensatory damages are insufficient to deter and punish. See *Walker et al. v. CFTO Ltd. et al. (1978)* (59 O.R. (2nd), No. 104; Ontario Court of Appeal).
- Exemplary damages can be awarded in cases where the defendant's conduct was "cavalier." See *Ronald Elwyn Lister Ltd. et al. v. Dayton Tire Canada Ltd. (1985)* (52 O.R. (2nd), No. 89; Ontario Court of Appeal).
- The primary purpose of exemplary damages is to prevent the defendant and all others from doing similar wrongs. See *Fleming v. Spracklin (1921)*.

- Disregard of the public's interest, lack of preventive measures, and a callous attitude all merit exemplary damages. See *Coughlin v. Kuntz (1989)* (2 C.C.L.T. (2nd); B.C.C.A.).
- Punitive damages can be awarded for mental distress. See *Ribeiro v. Canadian Imperial Bank of Commerce (1992)* (Ontario Reports 13 3rd) and *Brown v. Waterloo Regional Board of Commissioners of Police (1992)* (37 O.R. 2nd).

In the States, punitive damage awards have been particularly generous. Whenever business complains of an "unrestrained judiciary," it trots out a 20-year-old case where an Alabama plaintiff won a multi-million dollar award because his new BMW had been repainted before he bought it and the seller didn't tell him so.

The case was *BMW of North America, Inc. v. Gore* (517 U.S. 559; 116 S. Ct. 1589; 1996). In this case, the Supreme Court cut the damages award and established standards for jury awards of punitive damages. Nevertheless, million-dollar awards continue to be quite common. In the following example, an Oregon dealer learned that a $1 million punitive damages award was not excessive under *Gore* and under Oregon law.

The Oregon Supreme Court determined that the standard it set forth in *Oberg v. Honda Motor Company* (888 P.2d 8; 1996), on remand from the Supreme Court, survived the Supreme Court's subsequent ruling in *Gore*. The court held that the jury's $1 million punitive damages award, 87 times larger than the plaintiff's compensatory damages in *Parrott v. Carr Chevrolet, Inc.* (2001 Ore. LEXIS; 1 January 11, 2001), wasn't excessive. In that case, Mark Parrott sued Carr Chevrolet, Inc. over a used 1983 Chevrolet Suburban under Oregon's *Unlawful Trade Practices Act*. The jury awarded Parrott $11,496 in compensatory damages and $1 million in punitive damages because the dealer failed to disclose collision damage to a new car buyer.

See also:

- *Grabinski v. Blue Springs Ford Sales, Inc.* (U.S. App. LEXIS 2073; 8th Cir. W.D. MO; February 16, 2000)

Part Three
1970–2006
Winners and Losers

Your Mileage *Will* Vary

If you simply guess how many miles per gallon of fuel your vehicle gets, you might do about as well as the Environmental Protection Agency has over the last couple of decades.

Last month, the EPA announced the first major revision in its fuel economy testing procedures since 1986, aiming to create more realistic mileage comparisons among vehicles.

The EPA acknowledges that fuel economy estimates may drop by as much as 30%, an explicit admission that its prior practices were far off the mark.

RALPH VARTABEDIAN
LOS ANGELES TIMES
JANUARY 10, 2007

All Cars Have Defects

No matter if you buy American or Japanese, new or used, you are taking on someone else's problems: the dealer and automakers', or the previous owners'. Fortunately, used cars don't easily hide their factory-related defects, and crashworthiness has likely been tested and re-tested by a handful of different agencies.

Knowing What's Important

Primarily, you buy used to save money and to have reliable transportation for 10 to 15 years. A good used car or minivan should cost you no more than one-third to one-half of its original selling price ($5,000–$10,000) and should be between three and five years old. A "new" used car must meet your everyday driving needs and have high crashworthiness and reliability scores. Annual maintenance should cost no

USED-CAR OLYMPICS

STYLISH	RELIABLE	GOOD REAR-DRIVES
GOOD PERFORMERS	DURABLE	BAD FRONT-DRIVES
SUFFER FROM ELECTRICAL SHORTS	OVERPRICED	POOR QUALITY

No automaker can be trusted; even the Japanese have their lemons.

more than the CAA-surveyed average of $800, and the depreciation rate should have levelled off. Parts and servicing costs shouldn't be excessive, as CBC TV's *Marketplace* found to be the case at some dealerships, and servicing shouldn't be given with a shrug or a snarl.

Fuel economy isn't all that important when you are buying used, since all of your other savings should easily compensate for the extra fuel costs. We don't recommend electric and gasoline engine hybrids found in some vehicles because their fuel economy can be 40 percent worse than the automakers' reports; their long-term reliability is unknown; their battery-replacement costs are estimated to run as high as $8,000 (U.S.); their expensive electric motors are predicted to have a high failure rate due to corrosion; their retail prices are incredibly high; and their potential resale values are no better than similar vehicles equipped with conventional engines. For example, a 2001 Toyota Prius that originally sold for $29,990 is now valued at a disappointing $10,000 (and we're only one year away from the expiration of that battery pack warranty). Compare that to the price of a fully equipped 2001 Camry CE V6, which sells for about $1,000 more—with no battery worries.

Depreciation Bargains

We now know that cars are not all born with equal attributes, and that they age (depreciate) at different rates, as well. When buying new, you want a reliable model that depreciates slowly; when buying used, you want a car that has lost much of its value but is still dependable and inexpensive to maintain.

Vehicles that hold their value well after four years won't be bargains now, but they will still have considerable equity in them should you have to sell due to a cash emergency. And, yes, models that depreciate slowly are usually seen as being more dependable vehicles that hold up better in the long run.

During the past decade, rebates, cut-rate financing, subsidized leasing, and poor quality reputations have depressed the residual values of the Detroit Big Three's cars and trucks. According to the Automotive Lease Guide (ALG), *www.alg.com*, 3-year-old Detroit-made vehicles that come off lease keep 37–48 percent of their sticker values after three years.

It's interesting to note that Kia's products retain their value almost as well as vehicles sold by Pontiac, Buick, or Mercury. Also, cars made by Hyundai, Kia's owner, depreciate at the same rate as GM's pricier Saturn models.

Duelling Quality Ratings

Lemon-Aid has been giving honest, independent, and dependable auto ratings for more than 35 years by following these simple rules:

- Ratings should be used primarily as a comparative database when the low-ranked or recommended models reappear in different driving tests and owner surveys. The best rating approach is to combine a driving test with an owner's survey of past models (only *Consumer Reports* does this).

- The responses must come from a large owner pool (1.2 million responses from *Consumer Reports* subscribers, for example). Anecdotal responses should then be cross-referenced, updated, and given depth and specificity through NHTSA's safety complaint prism. Responses must again be cross-referenced through automaker internal service bulletins to determine the extent of the defect over a specific model and model-year range and to alert owners to problems likely to occur.
- Rankings should be predicated upon important characteristics measured over a significant period of time, unlike Car of the Year contests, owner-perceived values, or J.D. Power–surveyed problems after only three months of ownership.
- Ratings must come from unimpeachable sources. There should be no conflicts of interest due to ties with advertisers or consultants and no results gathered from self-serving tests done under ideal conditions.
- Tested cars must be bought, not borrowed, and serviced, not pampered as part of a journalists' fleet lent out for ranking purposes. Also, all automakers need to be judged equally (Toyota at one time did not accept weekend car journalist "roundup" tests as valid and refused to lend its vehicles to the events; thus, they were penalized). Automakers must not be members of the ranking body.
- Beware of self-administered fuel economy ratings used by automakers in complicity with the federal government. *Automotive News* recently added its name to the list of skeptics when it found that Honda and Toyota hybrids get 20–40 percent less real-world gas mileage than advertised. The car industry publication discovered that hybrids need to be driven in a particular way in order to be fuel efficient; are penalized by short trips and use of air conditioning more than ordinary cars; and are affected by colder climates, resulting in increased fuel consumption way beyond what the ratings figures indicate. The U.S. federal Environmental Protection Agency (EPA) has admitted its fuel economy calculations were overestimated and has set up a web site at *www.fueleconomy. gov* that contains recalculated figures for 1985–2007 model-year vehicles that will leave you scratching your head.

NATURAL RESOURCES CANADA'S HONDA CIVIC FUEL ECONOMY ESTIMATE

Make/Model	Eng Size/Number of Cylinders	Transmission/ Number of Gears	Fuel		Consumption L/100 km		CO_2 kg per year
			$/year	L/year	City	Hwy	
Honda Civic	1.7/4	E4E	$966	1,393	8.0	5.7	3,343

Source: *oee.nrcan.gc.ca/transportation/tools/fuelratings/ratings-search.cfm?attr=8*

Definitions of Terms

We rate vehicles on a scale of one to five stars, with five stars being our top ranking. Models are designated as "Recommended," "Above Average," "Average," "Below Average," or "Not Recommended," with the most recent year's rating indicated by the number of stars beside the vehicle's name.

Recommended

Don't believe for one moment that the more you spend, the better the vehicle. For example, most Hondas are as good as Acuras, which cost thousands of dollars more for luxury cachet. The same is true when you compare Toyota and Lexus. Even more surprising, some luxury makes, such as Jaguar, are "pseudo-luxe," because they are merely dressed-up ordinary Fords sold at a luxury-car price. The extra money only buys you more features of dubious value and newer, unproven technology, such as rear-mounted video cameras and failure-prone electronic gadgetry.

In fact, the simplest choice is often the best buy. Chrysler's Sebring and PT Cruiser, GM's Camaro and Firebird, and Hyundai's Elantra and Tiburon get positive ratings because they are easy to find, fairly reliable, and reasonably priced—not the case with many overpriced Hondas and Toyotas.

Recommended vehicles don't need optional, extra-cost ($1,000–$2,000) extended warranties, either. Usually, but not always, an extended warranty is advised for those model years that aren't rated Recommended. But don't buy too much warranty. For example, if the vehicle has a history of powertrain problems, buy the cheaper powertrain warranty only—not the bumper-to-bumper product. Also, invest in only enough extra warranty to get you through the critical fifth year of ownership. When shopping for an extended warranty, don't be surprised to discover that dealers have the market practically sewn up. You can bargain the price down by getting competing dealers to bid against each other; contact them by fax or through their websites. Be wary of extended-warranty companies that aren't backed by the major automakers.

Above Average/Average

Vehicles that are given an Above Average or Average rating are good second choices if a Recommended vehicle isn't your first choice, isn't available, or isn't within budget.

Below Average/Not Recommended

A Below Average vehicle will likely be troublesome; however, its low price and reasonably priced servicing may make it an acceptable buy. Vehicles given a Not Recommended rating are best avoided altogether, no matter how low the price. They may be attractively styled and loaded with convenience features (like Ford and GM front-drive minivans, for example), but they're likely to suffer from so many durability and performance problems that you will never stop paying for them. Sometimes, however, a Not Recommended model will improve over several model years and garner a better rating (as the Chrysler Sebring and GM Astro and Safari minivans have done).

Incidentally, for those owners who wonder how I can stop recommending model years I once recommended, let me be clear: As vehicles age, their ratings change to reflect new information from owners and from service bulletins relating to durability and the automaker's warranty performance. For example, Nissan's Quest, Toyota's Sienna, and Ford's Escort have been downgraded because new service bulletins and additional owner complaints show some disturbing trends in dependability and servicing performance. Unlike Enron and Nortel stock analysts, I warn shoppers of changes via subsequent editions of *Lemon-Aid* and updates to my website, *www.lemonaidcars.com*.

I do more than simply write about failure-prone cars: Throughout the year, I try to get refunds for buyers who have made the wrong choice. I lobby automakers to compensate out-of-warranty owners, either through formal warranty extension programs or on a case-by-case basis. I also publish little-known lawsuits, judgments, and settlements in *Lemon-Aid* to help car owners win their cases or get a fair settlement without my personal assistance.

Some enterprising readers of *Lemon-Aid* use the Not Recommended rating as a buying opportunity. Dave Ingram, a friend and well-known B.C. broadcaster and tax/immigration specialist for CENTA Inc., has used my Not Recommended list as a shopping list for cheap vehicles: He buys them at depressed prices and refurbishes them, using garages that offer lifetime warranties on major components that I rate as weak. He's done that with several used Cadillacs and Jeeps and seems happy with his system. Personally, I don't think he would have done so well without the complicity of his independent garage contacts in North Vancouver, such as the mechanics at Fountain Tire.

Reliability data is compiled from a number of sources, including confidential technical service bulletins; owner complaints sent to me each year by *Lemon-Aid* readers; owners' comments posted on the Internet; and survey reports and tests done by auto associations, consumer groups, and government organizations. Some auto columnists feel this isn't a scientific sampling, and they're quite right. Nevertheless, the results have been mostly on the mark over the past three decades.

Not all vehicles sold since the '70s are profiled; those that are new to the market or relatively rare may receive only an abbreviated mention until sufficient owner or service bulletin information becomes available. Best and worst buys for each model category (e.g., "Small Cars" or "Medium Cars") are listed in a summary at the beginning of each rating section. Also, don't forget to look up the cheap alternatives profiled in Appendix I.

Strengths and Weaknesses

Every automaker has quality shortcomings, and many vehicles have serious electrical system glitches that require a trip to The Source, rather than to a dealer's service bay. This isn't so surprising if you consider that today's automobile has more computer power than the Apollo 11 spacecraft that took humans to the moon in 1969.

With the Detroit Big Three, engine head gasket and automatic transmission failures are omnipresent; South Korean vehicles have weak transmissions; and Japanese makes are mostly noted for their electrical system, brake, door, and window glitches, though engine and transmission failures have been appearing more frequently, especially with Toyota and Lexus models built during the past five years. Finally, the European automakers are in a high-tech bind: Electronic demons constantly bedevil Audi, BMW, Jaguar, Land Rover, Mercedes, Saab, Volvo, and VW products, making them unreliable and costly to service; plus, their vehicles are so complicated to understand, diagnose, and service that many mechanics simply throw up their hands in dismay.

Unlike other auto guides, *Lemon-Aid* knows where automotive skeletons are buried and pinpoints potential parts failures, explains why those parts fail, and advises you as to your chances of getting a repair refund. We also give parts numbers for upgraded parts (why replace poor-quality brake pads with the same brand, for example?) and offer troubleshooting tips direct from the automakers' bulletins, so that your mechanic won't replace parts unrelated to your troubles before coming upon the defective component that is actually responsible.

Parts supply can be a real problem. It's a myth that automakers have to keep a supply of parts sufficient to service what they sell, as any buyer of a Cadillac Catera, a front-drive Lincoln Continental, or a Ford Tempo/Topaz will quickly tell you. Additionally, apart from *Lemon-Aid,* there's no consumer database that warns prospective purchasers as to which models are "parts-challenged."

The "Secret Warranties/Internal Bulletins/Service Tips" sections and vehicle profile tables show a vehicle's overall reliability and safety, providing details as to which specific model years pose the most risk and why. This helps you to direct an independent mechanic to check out the likely trouble spots before you make your purchase.

Vehicle History

This section outlines a vehicle's differences between model years, including major redesigns and other modifications.

Safety Summary

Ongoing safety investigations, safety-related complaints, and safety probes make up this section. National Highway Traffic Safety Administration (NHTSA) complaints are summarized by model year, even though they aren't all safety related. The summary will help you spot a defect trend (like cracked Ford and GM engine intake manifolds and faulty fuel gauges) before a recall or bulletin is issued. You can also prove that a part failure is widespread and factory related and use that information for free "goodwill" repairs or in litigation involving accident damage, injuries, or death. NHTSA records indicate that ABS and airbag failures represent the most frequent complaints from car and van owners. Other common safety-related failures concern sudden acceleration, a vehicle rolling away with the transmission in Park, minivan sliding doors either not opening when they should or opening when they shouldn't, and power-assisted windows injuring or even killing children (see *www.kidsandcars.org*).

Earlier this year a Calgary mother left her two-year-old daughter in an idling SUV to run a quick errand. The child was strangled by the power-assisted window. A passerby extricated her from the window and left to call the police. The mother returned and saw what she thought was the child asleep in the rear seat. Almost an hour later, she realized her daughter was dead. Safety researchers know of at least eight other incidents in North America. Yet parents assume the window will retract automatically if a hand or neck is caught in its path.

If *Lemon-Aid* doesn't list a problem you have experienced, go to the NHTSA website's database at *www.nhtsa.dot.gov/cars/problems* for an update. Your vehicle may be currently under investigation or may have been recalled since this year's guide was published.

Automotive News says an estimated 72 percent of the 25 million vehicles recalled in 2005 were fixed, which is an improvement over the earlier 65-percent fix rate. *Lemon-Aid* doesn't list most recalls because there are so many, and the info can be easily obtained from either NHTSA or Transport Canada, by telephone or on their websites. Furthermore, most dealers willingly give out recall info when they run a vehicle history search through their computers, since they hope to snag the extra repair dollars. Just make sure you ask the dealer to also check for a "customer satisfaction program," a "service policy," a "goodwill" warranty extension, or a free emissions warranty service.

Secret Warranties/Internal Bulletins/Service Tips

It's not enough to know which parts on your vehicle are likely to fail. You should also know which repairs will be done for free by the dealer and automaker, even though you aren't the original owner and the manufacturer's warranty has long since expired.

Welcome to the hidden world of secret warranties, found in confidential technical service bulletins or gleaned from owners' feedback.

Over the years, I've grown tired of having service managers deny that service bulletins exist to correct factory-related defects free of charge. That's why I pore over thousands of bulletins each year and summarize or reproduce in *Lemon-Aid* the important ones for each model year, along with improved parts numbers. These bulletins target defects related to safety, emissions, and performance that service managers would have you believe either don't exist or are your responsibility to fix. If you photocopy the applicable service bulletin included in *Lemon-Aid*, you'll have a better chance of getting the dealer or automaker to cover all or part of the repair costs. Bulletins taken from *Lemon-Aid* have also been instrumental in helping claimants win in small claims court mediation and trials (remember, judges like to have the bulletins validated by an independent mechanic or the dealer/automaker witness you are suing).

Service bulletins listed in *Lemon-Aid* cover repairs that may be eligible for expressed or implied warranty coverage in one or more of the following five categories (although the description of the repairs is not always specific):

- Emissions expressed warranty (5–8 years/80,000–130,000 km)
- Safety component expressed warranty (this covers seat belts, ABS, and airbags and usually lasts from eight years to the lifetime of the vehicle)
- Body expressed warranty (paint: 6 years; rust perforations: 7 years)
- Secret implied warranty (coverage varies from 5–10 years)
- Factory defect/implied legal warranty (depends on mileage, use, and repair cost; may be as high as 11 years, according to GM paint delamination jurisprudence)

Use these bulletins to get free repairs—even if the vehicle has changed hands several times—and to alert an independent mechanic about defects to look for. They're also great tools for getting compensation from automakers and dealer service managers after the warranty has expired, since they prove that a failure is factory-related and, therefore, not part of routine maintenance or caused by a caustic environmental substance such as bird droppings or acid rain. In small claims court, the argument that bird droppings caused a paint problem usually loses credibility when only certain models or certain years are shown to be affected, pointing the finger at the paint process and quality.

Automakers' "bird-poop" defence doesn't explain why birds apparently defecate only on certain model vehicles (Chrysler Caravans, Ford's Taurus and Sable, GM minivans, etc.). Nevertheless, the implied warranty requires that all automakers use the same durability standard or disclose at the time of sale that their vehicles aren't "bird-proofed."

The diagnostic shortcuts and lists of upgraded parts found in many service bulletins make them invaluable in helping mechanics and do-it-yourselfers to troubleshoot problems inexpensively and replace the correct part the first time. Auto owners can also use the TSBs listed here to verify that a repair was diagnosed correctly, that the correct upgraded replacement part was used, and that the labour costs were fair.

Each annual edition of *Lemon-Aid* begins lists of safety-related failures, crashworthiness scores, service bulletins, and prices at a later model year. If your vehicle, perhaps a 1996 model, isn't included in this year's guide (which provides detailed information on 1997–2005 models), consult an earlier edition.

Getting your own bulletins

Summaries of service bulletins relating to 1982–2006 vehicles can be obtained for free from the ALLDATA or NHTSA websites (listed in Appendix III, "Internet Sleuthing"), but they are worded so cryptically that you really need the bulletins themselves. If you have a vehicle that's off warranty, you should get copies of the hundreds of pages of bulletins applicable to your model year, listing factory-related defects and diagnostic shortcuts. These bulletins can be ordered and downloaded from the Internet through ALLDATA for $25 (U.S.). Or you can get the bulletin title for free from ALLDATA and search for it on the Internet through a search engine such as Google. BMW, Acura, and Honda owners are excluded.

Vehicle Profile Tables

These tables cover the various aspects of vehicle ownership at a glance. Included for each model year are the vehicle's original selling price (the manufacturer's suggested retail price, or MSRP), the wholesale and retail prices you can expect to pay, reliability ratings (specific defective parts are listed in the "Strengths and Weaknesses" section), and details on crashworthiness.

Prices

Dealer profit margins on used cars vary considerably—giving lots of room to negotiate a fair price if you take the time to find out what the vehicle is really worth. Three prices are given for each model year: the vehicle's selling price when new, as suggested by the manufacturer; its maximum used price (▲), which is often the starting price with dealers; and its lowest used price (▼), more commonly found with private sellers.

The original selling price is given as a reality check for greedy sellers who inflate prices on some vehicles (mostly Japanese imports, minivans, and sport-utilities) in order to get back some of the money they overpaid in the first place. This happens particularly often in the Prairie provinces and British Columbia.

Used prices are based on sales recorded as of April 2007. Prices are for the lowest-priced standard model that is in good condition with a maximum of 20,000 km for each calendar year. Watch for price differences reflecting each model's equipment upgrades, designated by a numerical or alphabetical abbreviation. For example, L, LX, and LXT usually mean more standard features are included, progressively, in each model. Numerical progression usually relates to engine size.

Prices reflect the auto markets in Quebec and Ontario, where the majority of used-vehicle transactions take place. Residents of Eastern Canada should add

10 percent, and Western Canadians should add at least 15–20 percent to the listed price. Why the higher costs? Less competition, combined with inflated new-vehicle prices in these regions. Don't be too disheartened, though; you'll recoup some of what you overpaid down the road when you sell the vehicle.

Why are *Lemon-Aid*'s prices sometimes lower than the prices found in dealer guides such as the *Red Book*? The answer is simple: Much like a homeowner selling a house, dealers inflate their prices so that you can bargain the price down and wind up convinced that you made a great deal.

I use newspaper classified ads from Quebec, Ontario, and B.C., as well as auction reports, to calculate my used-car values. I then check these figures against the *Red Book* and *Black Book*. I don't start with the *Red Book*'s retail or wholesale figures because their prices are inflated about 10 percent for wholesale/private sales and almost 20 percent for retail/dealer sales (compare the two and you'll see what I mean). I then project what the value will be by mid-model year, and that lowers my prices further. I'll almost always fall way under the *Red Book*'s value, but not far under the *Black Book*'s prices.

I include a top and bottom price to give the buyer some margin for negotiation as well as to account for the regional differences in prices, the sudden popularity of certain models or vehicle classes, and the generally depreciated value of used vehicles.

Most new cars depreciate 50–60 percent during the first three years of ownership, despite the fact that good-quality used cars are in high demand. On the other hand, some minivans and most vans, pickups, and sport-utilities lose barely 40 percent of their value, even after four years of ownership.

Since no evaluation method is foolproof, check dealer prices with local private classified ads and then add the option values listed below to come up with a fairly representative offer. Don't forget to bargain the price down further if the odometer shows a cumulative reading of more than 20,000 km per calendar year. Interestingly, the value of anti-lock brakes in trade-ins plummeted during the last few years as they became a standard feature on many entry-level vehicles.

It will be easier for you to match the lower used prices if you buy privately. Dealers rarely sell much below the maximum prices; they claim that they need the full price to cover the costs of reconditioning and paying future warranty claims. If you can come within 5–10 percent of this guide's price, you'll have done well.

In the table on the following page, take note that some options—such as paint protector, rustproofing, and tinted windows—have little worth on the resale market, though they may make your vehicle easier to sell.

VALUE OF OPTIONS BY MODEL YEAR

OPTION	1997	1998	1999	2000	2001	2002	2003	2004	2005
Air conditioning	$200	$300	$300	$400	$500	$600	$700	$800	$950
AM/FM radio & CD player	100	100	100	150	175	200	300	500	600
Anti-lock brakes	0	50	100	125	150	175	300	300	400
Automatic transmission	150	200	250	275	300	400	500	700	800
Cruise control	0	50	50	75	100	125	225	300	350
Electric six-way seat	0	50	100	125	150	175	200	400	450
Leather upholstery	50	100	200	225	325	400	500	800	900
Level control (suspension)	0	50	75	100	125	150	250	350	450
Paint protector	50	50	50	50	50	50	50	50	50
Power antenna	0	0	0	0	0	75	75	75	75
Power door locks	0	50	100	125	150	175	200	250	250
Power windows	0	50	100	125	150	175	225	250	250
Rustproofing	0	0	0	0	25	25	50	50	50
Stability control	0	50	100	125	150	175	225	275	300
Sunroof	0	50	50	75	125	150	300	500	500
T-top roof	150	200	300	400	500	700	800	1,000	1,000
Tilt steering	0	50	50	75	75	100	175	250	200
Tinted windows	0	0	0	0	25	50	50	50	50
Tires (Firestone)	-100	-100	-100	-100	-100	-150	-150	-150	-150
Traction control	50	100	125	150	175	275	400	500	500
Wire wheels/locks	50	75	100	125	150	175	275	300	350

Reliability

The older a vehicle gets (at 5–7 years), the greater the chance that major components, such as the engine and transmission, will fail as the result of high mileage and environmental wear and tear. Surprisingly, a host of other expensive-to-repair failures are just as likely to occur in new vehicles as in older ones. The air conditioning, electronic computer modules, electrical systems, and brakes are the most troublesome components, manifesting problems early in a vehicle's life. Other deficiencies that will appear early, due to sloppy manufacturing and harsh environments, include failure-prone body hardware (trim, finish, locks, doors, and windows), susceptibility to water leakage or wind noise, and peeling and/or discoloured paint. The following legend shows a vehicle's relative degree of overall reliability; the numbers lighten as the rating becomes more positive.

1	**2**	**3**	**4**	**5**
Unacceptable	Below Average	Average	Above Average	Excellent

Crashworthiness

Some of the main factors weighed in the safety ratings are a model's crashworthiness, its front and rear visibility, and the availability of safety features such as seat belt pretensioners, de-powered airbags, airbag disablers, adjustable brake and accelerator pedals, integrated child safety seats, effective head restraints, and assisted stability and traction control.

Front and side crash protection figures are taken from NHTSA's New Car Assessment Program. For the front crash test, vehicles are crashed into a fixed barrier, head-on, at 57 km/h (35 mph). NHTSA uses star rankings to show the likelihood, expressed as a percentage, of the belted occupants being seriously injured—the higher the number, the greater the protection.

NHTSA COLLISION RATINGS: CHANCE OF SERIOUS INJURY

	FRONT	SIDE
5	10% or less	5% or less
4	11% to 20%	6% to 10%
3	21% to 35%	11% to 20%
2	36% to 45%	21% to 25%
1	46% or greater	26% or greater

Note: Two numbers indicate either driver or passenger injury risk (D/P) or front/rear occupant injury risk (F/R).

NHTSA's side crash test represents an intersection-type collision with a 1,368 kg (3,015 lb.) barrier moving at 62 km/h (38.5 mph) into a standing vehicle. The moving barrier is covered with material that has give in order to replicate the front of a car.

The Insurance Institute for Highway Safety (IIHS) rates vehicles' frontal offset, side, and head-restraint/rear crash protection as "Good," "Acceptable," "Marginal," or "Poor." Head restraints may be rated for both front- and rear-seat occupants.

In the Institute's 64 km/h (40 mph) frontal offset test, 40 percent of the total width of each vehicle strikes a barrier on the driver's side. The barrier's deformable face is made of aluminum honeycomb, which makes the forces in the test similar to those involved in a frontal offset crash between two vehicles of the same weight, each going just less than 64 km/h.

IIHS's 50 km/h (31 mph) side-impact test is carried out at a slower speed than NHTSA's test; however, the barrier uses a front end that is shaped to simulate the typical front end of a pickup or SUV, which is deemed to give truer results. The Institute also includes the degree of frontal-impact head injury in its ratings.

During the past three years, IIHS has twice tested head-restraint effectiveness in rear impacts. The latest test results were announced last April. Twenty-two current car models were rated Good for rear crash protection, but 53 other cars were rated Marginal or Poor. Among the winners are systems in use in all Volvos; Audi A4, A6, and S4; Ford Five Hundred/Mercury Montego; Nissan Sentra and Versa; Saab 9-3; and Subaru Impreza and Legacy/Outback. Seat/head restraints in 12 other car models were rated Acceptable.

IIHS believes auto manufacturers are paying greater attention to safe seat/head-restraint design, and this is reflected in better ratings for some cars, compared with ratings the Institute published in 2004. For example, seat/head restraints in the Audi A4 and S4, Honda Civic, Hyundai Sonata, Kia Optima, and Nissan Sentra improved from Poor to Good. Seat/head restraints in the Mercedes E-Class and

Subaru Legacy/Outback improved from Acceptable to Good. And improving to Acceptable are seat/head restraints in the BMW 3 Series, Ford Focus, Hyundai Elantra, Lexus IS, and Mercedes C-Class.

While many automakers are making improvements, a few are going in the wrong direction. Seat/head restraints in the Chrysler 300, Kia Amanti, and Nissan Altima earned Marginal ratings this time, compared with Acceptable ratings for their earlier designs, which were tested in 2004. Furthermore, a disappointingly large number of other models were rated Poor. They included the Acura TSX, BMW 5 Series, Buick LaCrosse (Allure in Canada) and Lucerne, Cadillac CTS and DTS, Chevrolet Aveo, Honda Accord and Fit, Hyundai Accent, Infiniti M35, Jaguar X-Type, Kia Rio, Mitsubishi Galant, Pontiac Grand Prix, Toyota Avalon and Corolla, and Suzuki Forenza and Reno.

A vehicle's rollover resistance rating is an estimate of its risk of rolling over in a single-vehicle crash, not a prediction of the likelihood of a crash. As the chart indicates,

NHTSA ROLLOVER RATINGS: CHANCE OF TIPPING OVER

ROLLOVER RISK

5	Less than 10%
4	Between 10% and 20%
3	Between 20% and 30%
2	Between 30% and 40%
1	Greater than 40%

NHTSA DRIVER SIDE-IMPACT PROTECTION (2006–07 DODGE GRAND CARAVAN WITHOUT SIDE AIRBAGS)

Save vehicles	Vehicle	Frontal Star Rating » based on risk of head & chest injury		Side Star Rating » based on risk of chest injury		Rollover Rating	
		Driver	Passenger	Front Seat	Rear Seat	2 wheel drive	4 wheel drive
☐	2006 Dodge Grand Caravan (Van)	★★★★★	★★★★★	★★★★★	★★★★★	★★★★	
☐	2007 Dodge Grand Caravan (Van)	★★★★★	★★★★★	★★★★★	★★★★★	★★★★	

IIHS DRIVER SIDE-IMPACT PROTECTION (2006–07 DODGE GRAND CARAVAN WITHOUT SIDE AIRBAGS)

OVERALL EVALUATION: P

	Injury measures			Head protection	Structure/safety cage
	Head/neck	Torso	Pelvis/leg		
Driver	A	P	G	P	A
Rear passenger	G	G	G	M	

Note: **P** = Poor; **M** = Marginal; **A** = Acceptable; **G** = Good

NHTSA gives Grand Caravans far more generous occupant protection ratings than IIHS due to different crash speeds and the use of a different barrier. It's not surprising car manufacturers prefer to cite the NHTSA scores.

the lowest-rated vehicles (one star) are at least four times more likely to roll over than the highest-rated vehicles (five stars) when involved in a single-vehicle crash.

Too many stars

After comparing crash tests performed by IIHS with NHTSA's government tests, the Government Accountability Office (GAO) admitted in 2005 what *Lemon-Aid* and safety groups have been saying for close to a decade: Government-run crash tests are outdated and should be revised for the 2008 model year. Specifically, GAO concluded that NHTSA's system, which uses one to five stars to rate vehicles for rollover and front- and side-impact dangers, now gives too many vehicles a top ranking. For example, among 2007 model-year vehicles tested, 68 percent were given the top five-star rating for occupant protection in a frontal collision. Another 30 percent got four stars. No model got one or two stars.

Safest used cars

Just as with quality, purchase price is no indication of how well a car will protect occupants in a collision. To be included in the list that follows, a vehicle must be fairly cheap, have two frontal crash test ratings and two side crash test ratings, and have earned four- and five-star ratings across the board. In addition, any vehicle meeting our pricing criteria and having five-star ratings across the board, as well as vehicles with three five-star ratings and one four-star rating, were also guaranteed a spot on the list.

Ford—Escape, Mustang
Honda—Accord, Civic, Element
Hyundai—Accent, Elantra
Kia—Sportage
Mazda—Mazda3, Tribute
Mitsubishi—Galant
Nissan—Frontier, Sentra
Suzuki—Aerio
Toyota—Corolla, Echo

"Fender-bender" wallet busters

Crashworthiness is usually defined as how well occupants are protected in different kinds of accidents at various speeds. However, it can also describe the measure of damage sustained by a vehicle in low-speed "fender-bender" collisions. In the IIHS fender-bender chart on the following page, note how the 1981 Ford Escort sustained only $469 in damages, while the 2007 Nissan Maxima required $9,051 in repairs.

Convertible crashworthiness

Surprisingly, crash test results released by IIHS this year show that a number of relatively cheap convertibles are good, crashworthy buys, especially used.

BUMPER PERFORMANCE IN LOW-SPEED CRASH TESTS: VEHICLE REPAIR COSTS

	FRONT FULL	FRONT CORNER	REAR FULL	REAR CORNER	TOTAL DAMAGE
Mitsubishi Galant	$2,929	$1,138	$1,048	$1,162	$4,277
Toyota Camry	$ 936	$1,467	$1,480	$1,028	$4,911
Mazda6	$ 978	$1,384	$1,202	$1,397	$4,961
Ford Fusion	$1,620	$ 991	$1,298	$1,121	$5,030
Volvo S40	$2,252	$1,306	$ 802	$1,240	$5,600
Kia Optima	$1,730	$1,534	$1,715	$ 756	$5,735
Saturn Aura	$1,032	$1,152	$3,191	$ 999	$6,374
Nissan Altima	$ 945	$ 969	$3,114	$1,431	$6,459
Chevrolet Malibu	$1,268	$1,610	$2,542	$1,226	$6,646
Subaru Legacy	$3,911	$1,287	$1,122	$1,128	$7,448
Chrysler Sebring	$1,084	$2,061	$3,210	$1,099	$7,454
Hyundai Sonata	$4,312	$1,349	$ 739	$1,165	$7,565
Honda Accord	$3,469	$1,169	$2,767	$ 605	$8,010
Volkswagen Passat	$4,594	$1,544	$ 982	$1,139	$8,259
Pontiac G6	$4,588	$1,183	$1,638	$1,510	$8,919
Volkswagen Jetta	$2,598	$1,223	$3,375	$1,824	$9,020
Nissan Maxima	$4,535	$1,732	$1,787	$ 997	$9,051
1981 Ford Escort	$ 86	$ 0	$ 383	$ 0	$ 469

Note: Sonata repair costs reflect reduced parts pricing, effective January 2007.

Remember, these vehicles were crashed at only 5–10 km/h (3–6 mph)—a brisk walk or run.

The results also show that a vehicle's cost has no relation to occupant crash protection.

For example, BMW's 3 Series ($55,800) got the second-lowest score of "Marginal" in side-impact tests, while a number of top performers cost considerably less than the top-rated Audi A4 ($53,520) and Volvo C70 ($36,000), are more easily serviced, and are just as reliable. The Chrysler Sebring ($36,000), Ford Mustang ($27,999), and Toyota Solara ($36,500) have posted good crash ratings during the past few years and can be purchased used for a third to a half of their original price. Smart buyers will shop these models. For the full list of convertibles tested in 2007, enter "convertible crash tests" into a search engine such as Google.

SMALL CARS

Ottawa's Incompetence: The Crude Reality

For instance, under the old rating, a 2007 Honda Civic Hybrid was listed at 49 miles per U.S. gallon [4.8 L/100 km] in city driving and 51 miles per gallon [4.6 L/100 km] on the highway. The new figures are more than 10 per cent lower at 40 mpg city and 45 mpg on the highway [5.9/5.2 L/100 km]. Canadian fuel consumption ratings list the same car at 60 miles per Imperial gallon [4.7 L/100 km] in the city and 66 [4.3 L/100 km] on the highway. Imperial gallons are 20 per cent bigger than U.S. gallons—but that still leaves the Canadian rating higher than the old American one.

Similarly, U.S. numbers for the Pontiac G6 drop from 23 mpg in the city and 33 mpg on the highway [10.2/7.1 L/100 km] to 20 mpg in the city and 30 on the highway [11.7/7.8 L/100 km]—a drop of about 10 per cent. In Canada, the same car is listed at 28 mpg in the city and 43 on the highway [10.1/6.6 L/100 km]—higher than the old American rating.

Transport Canada says it's studying the new American system to see if it can be adapted for Canadian driving conditions.

CBC NEWS

www.cbc.ca/news/background/your-car

MARCH 15, 2007

WHY DREAD A HYBRID?

$8,000 (U.S.) BATTERY PACK

BATTERY DISPOSAL?

ELECTROCUTION DURING ACCIDENTS

FUEL SAVINGS OFF BY 40%

DEALER-ONLY SERVICE

EXPENSIVE

50% DEPRECIATION AFTER 3 YEARS

HIGH INSURANCE RATES

$30,000 FOR A PRIUS

A BETTER IDEA: A 2002 HONDA CIVIC ($9,000)...LEAVES $21,000 FOR FUEL!

It's a no-brainer that your first line of defence against sky-high fuel prices isn't buying a Toyota Prius or Honda Insight hybrid. What you want instead is a cheap, small, crashworthy, reliable, and easy-to-repair used car. And, in the bargain, you'll be following the "reduce, reuse, and recycle" environmentalist creed.

Indeed, fuel-frugal 4-cylinder compact cars are primarily for city dwellers who want good fuel economy in the city/highway range of 9.3/5.9 L/100 km (30/48 mpg), easy manoeuvrability in urban areas, a relatively low retail price, and modest depreciation. In exchange, owners must accept a cramped interior that may carry only two passengers in comfort, an engine that can take eons to merge with traffic or pass other cars, and insufficient luggage capacity (hatchbacks, however, make the best use of what room there is). As well, engine and road noise are fairly excessive.

In response to these shortcomings, many cars in this class, such as the Honda Civic and Toyota Tercel, have been replaced during the past decade by much larger iterations that rival the size of Honda's early Accord and Toyota's Camry. This upsizing makes room for new "micro" small cars introduced in 2006 that vary in size between Mercedes-Benz's Smart Car and BMW's Mini Cooper.

Safety is a mixed bag, however.

One of the more alarming characteristics of a small car's highway performance is its extreme vulnerability to strong lateral winds, which may make the car difficult to keep on course. On the other hand, crashworthiness is not necessarily compromised by the small size. In fact, evidence suggests that lighter-weight vehicles can be made to be as safe as heavier ones.

In the October 17, 2005, edition of *Automotive News*, Robert Hall, professor emeritus of operations management at Indiana University, said the following:

> In the last 40 years, auto-racing speeds have increased, yet deaths have decreased significantly while the weights of the vehicles have gone down progressively. Why? Crushable fronts that absorb impact, "tubs" that shelter drivers after the entire car has disintegrated, a relocation of the front axle and, yes, crash bags. In this case, lighter is markedly safer.

Granted, the small size of some small, mass-produced vehicles may compromise their crash safety, but not necessarily. Many newer small cars incorporate a body structure that deflects crash forces away from occupants, making these cars more crashworthy than some larger vehicles. The Smart Car is a good example: It offers acceptable, though not impressive, crashworthiness through a well-designed restraint system and the use of a stiff chassis design that minimizes intrusion.

Smart Car publicity brochures don't herald the car's modest "Acceptable" European crash scores. Actually, the Honda Civic and Hyundai Accent are much safer.

The Smart Car sandwiches its powerplant under the floor—this raises the passenger compartment above the impact area in a collision with another passenger car. The powertrain is mounted on a sliding rack to diminish the force of a collision (see *Popular Science*, January 1998, page 82).

"Bargain" Prices

During the past several years, automakers have added features to their small cars that have subsequently driven down the prices of less refined models. Recent examples of this trend are General Motor's Cavalier and Sunfire, two recent "orphans" that were replaced by the 2005 Cobalt and Pursuit, a European Opel variant; and the Dodge Neon, dropped in favour of the 2007 Caliber. In both cases, the older cars are fairly reliable and can be picked up at fire-sale prices. Furthermore, Ottawa's $2,000 rebates to owners of new fuel-efficient small cars will also spill over into the used market and keep prices low as sellers of used cars compete with lower-priced new offerings.

The 2002 Chevrolet Cavalier.

Recommended

Honda Civic, del Sol (1992–2006)
Hyundai Elantra (2001–06)
Mazda Protegé (1999–2003)
Suzuki Aerio (2003–06)

Suzuki Esteem (1996–2002)
Suzuki Swift and Swift+ (2002–06)
Toyota Echo (2000–05)

Above Average

Acura CSX (2006)*
Daewoo/General Motors Aveo,
    Wave (2006)
Honda Civic, del Sol (1972–91)
Hyundai Accent (2001–06)
Hyundai Elantra (1996–2000)
Mazda3 (2004–06)

Mazda5 (2006)*
Mazda 323, Protegé (1991–98)
Mitsubishi Lancer (2005–06)*
Nissan Sentra (1995–2006)
Subaru Forester (2006)
Suzuki Swift and Swift+ (1995–2001)
Toyota Yaris (2006)*

Average

BMW Mini Cooper (2002–06)*
Daewoo/General Motors Aveo, Wave
    (2004–05)
DaimlerChrysler Neon, SX 2.0, SRT-4
    (2003–06)
Ford Focus (2004–06)
General Motors Cavalier,
    Sunfire (2003–2005)

General Motors Cobalt, Pursuit (2005–06)*
Hyundai Accent (1995–2000)
Hyundai Elantra (1994–95)
Kia Rio (2005–06)
Mazda 323, Protegé (1985–90)
Nissan Sentra (1988–94)
Subaru Forester (1994–2005)
Subaru Impreza (1997–2006)

Subaru Legacy, Outback (1997–2006)
Toyota Corolla (1985–2006)

Toyota/General Motors Matrix/Vibe (2003–06)
Volkswagen Cabrio, Golf, Jetta (1999–2006)

Below Average

Daewoo/General Motors Optra
 (2004–2006)
DaimlerChrysler Neon (2000–02)
Ford Escort, ZX2 (1997–2000)
General Motors Cavalier,
 Sunfire (1999–2002)
General Motors L-series (2000–05)
General Motors S-series (1998–2002)

General Motors Ion (2003–06)
Hyundai Elantra (1991–93)
Mercedes-Benz Smart Fortwo (2005–06)*
Subaru Impreza (1994–96)
Subaru Legacy, Outback (1989–96)
Subaru WRX (2002–06)
Volkswagen Cabrio, Golf, Jetta (1993–98)

Not Recommended

Daewoo Lanos, Nubira, Leganza
 (2000–02)
DaimlerChrysler Neon (1995–99)
Ford Escort (1981–96)
Ford Focus (2000–03)
General Motors Cavalier,
 Sunfire (Sunbird) (1984–98)
General Motors S-series (1992–97)

Honda Civic Hybrid (2003–06)
Honda Insight (2001–06)
Kia Rio (2001–04)
Nissan Sentra (1983–87)
Volkswagen Cabrio, Golf, Jetta (1985–92)
Volkswagen diesel versions (all years)

*See Appendix I.

Daewoo

Not Recommended

South Korean automaker Daewoo marketed three cars in Canada from 2000 to 2002: the Lanos subcompact, the Nubira compact sedan and wagon, and the Leganza luxury sedan. All of these cars are rated Not Recommended because Daewoo sold its car division to GM, and neither company will service these models, let alone respect their original warranties. By the way, Daewoo depreciation is mind-boggling: An entry-level, $13,395 2002 Lanos is now barely worth $2,500, and the top-of-the-line 2002 Leganza CDX that originally sold for $25,495 now sells for about $5,500.

Daewoo/General Motors

Daewoo skipped the 2003 model year in Canada and brought out three models under the GM banner as 2004 models. Chevrolet dealers sell the entry-level Aveo (a Lanos spin-off); the Optra, a compact based on the Daewoo Lacetti; and the Epica, a mid-sized vehicle based on Daewoo's Magnos. Suzuki sells the subcompact Swift+, based on the Kalos, and the Verona for GM.

AVEO, LANOS, WAVE ★★★★

RATING: Above Average (2006); Average (2004–05); Below Average, a subpar car (2000–02). An economical small car that has improved markedly since General Motors bought Daewoo. Best used as a bare-bones urban runabout. Although it is identical to Chevrolet's Aveo and the Suzuki Swift+, the Pontiac Wave is not sold in the U.S. **"Real" city/highway fuel economy:** 8.8/6.1 L/100 km. Owners report fuel savings may undershoot this estimate by about 10 percent. **Maintenance/Repair costs:** Average. **Parts:** Easily found and relatively inexpensive. **Extended warranty:** Not needed, judging by the handful of complaints registered with NHTSA. **Best alternatives:** Other cars worth considering are the Dodge Neon (post-'99); GM Firefly, Metro, Cavalier, or Sunfire (2000 or later); Honda Civic; Hyundai Accent; Mazda3 or Mazda Protegé; Suzuki Aerio, Esteem, or Swift+; and Toyota Echo, Tercel, Yaris, or Corolla. **Online help:** *www-odi.nhtsa.dot.gov/cars/problems/complain; www.autosafety.org/autodefects.html.*

Strengths and Weaknesses

First launched by Daewoo as the Lanos, this nondescript, cheaply made small South Korean car had practically no redeeming values, much like Kia's pre-2005 models. After a year's absence (2003), the car returned under GM's aegis as the Chevrolet Aveo and Pontiac Wave. Although they are nicely restyled and use better-quality components, both cars carry an underpowered 103-hp 1.6L 4-cylinder engine mated with a 5-speed manual or a 4-speed automatic. Overall, the powertrain and performance lack the refinement found with many other bantamweights anchoring the compact-car division. The engine is particularly noisy and strains going uphill with its maximum four-passenger load. Four *small* passengers. Around town, though, the car is peppy and nimble.

The 2004 Aveo's $6,500 price tag is very reasonable for a four-door that originally sold for $13,595. It beats by a couple of thousand dollars the price for a two-door Toyota Echo that's comparatively priced new but depreciates more slowly. Don't fret, however, if you pay a few thousand dollars extra for a better-performing and more reliable Honda, Mazda, or Toyota—the difference means nothing when spread out over a number of years, and it will likely be refunded through a higher resale price.

Lanos owners complain of an unending series of powertrain failures, serious fit and finish deficiencies, and electrical short circuits. These problems have moderated with the 2004 and later versions built under General Motors' supervision. Most Aveo glitches concern the automatic transmission shifting erratically, continuing electrical system shorts, infrequent stalling, brake malfunctions, excessive suspension noise (see bulletin, below, where GM admits liability), and premature tire wear. Fit and finish is about average, although owners report the occasional water leak and a plethora of squeaks, grunts, and rattles.

VEHICLE HISTORY: 2000—Debut of the Lanos. **2001**—No ABS, and the SE hatchback and SX four-door sedan are dropped. A gussied-up sport hatchback was launched, and power steering was offered as an option on the entry-level S model. Rumours of Daewoo's impending bankruptcy crippled its car sales. **2002**—Daewoo *does* go bankrupt. After Ford dithers for almost a year, GM buys Daewoo's assets and dumps the dealers, who finally got a few crumbs in an out-of-court settlement. **2003**—Skipped a model year. **2004**—Aveo was launched in early 2004 with a slightly longer sedan, the same puny engine, optional ABS, and no side airbags. **2005**—Additional models launched, and features like standard air conditioning were offered on some models. **2006**—Standard front side airbags and larger optional wheels. Many GM-imposed quality improvements mirror Hyundai's successful efforts to address similar Kia deficiencies during that fateful 2005 model year.

Safety Summary

2004—Stalling. • Brake failures. • Premature brake pad/rotor wearout. **2004–05**—Transmission won't go into Reverse. • Excessive on-road vibration felt in the front end and steering. • Early wiper replacement. **2005**—Sudden acceleration. • Airbags fail to deploy:

> The driver stated that in a front end collision the airbags did not deploy. Vehicle was travelling about 50 mph [80 km/h] and went under a truck. Most of the impact was to the hood, rooftop, and windshield. The steering wheel was completely damaged. There was no substantial damage to the bumper. The driver sustained the following injuries: the nose was fractured, left eyeball went out of orbit, and the cheekbone was crushed. The manufacturer stated all three sensors have to be hit simultaneously for the airbags to deploy.

• Repeated brake failure when car is put into Reverse. • Accelerator and brake pedal are mounted too close to each other. • Poor-quality windshield wipers.

Secret Warranties/Internal Bulletins/Service Tips

2004—Engine runs poorly when first started:

ENGINE—INTERMITTENT MISFIRE DURING WARM-UP

BULLETIN NO.: 05-06-04-003　　　　　　　　　　　　　　　**DATE: JANUARY 6, 2005**

INTERMITTENT ENGINE MISFIRE/HESITATION DURING VEHICLE WARM UP (REPLACE INTAKE AND EXHAUST VALVES)

2004 Chevrolet Aveo, Optra

CONDITION: Some customers may comment on intermittent engine misfire and/or hesitation during the vehicle warmup period.

CAUSE: This condition may be caused due to poor side contact on the valve seat. Because of this, compression pressure of some cylinders will leak from the intake or exhaust valve contact area during engine warm up.

CORRECTION: Replace the intake and exhaust valves.

• GM will replace the differential pinion gear washer free of charge under a special service campaign:

CAMPAIGN—DIFFERENTIAL PINION GEAR WASHER

BULLETIN NO.: 04064　　　　　　　　　　　　　　　　**DATE: AUGUST 10, 2004**

CUSTOMER SATISFACTION—DIFFERENTIAL PINION GEAR WASHERS

2004 Chevrolet Aveo

CONDITION: GMDAT has decided that certain 2004 Chevrolet Aveo model vehicles were built with pinion gear washers that do not meet engineering specifications. The suspect washer can become damaged due to stress and be ejected from the differential assembly. Dealers are to replace the differential pinion gear washers.

• Erratic transmission shifting may need a new channel plate gasket or the valve body bolt to be retightened, says TSB #04-07-30-033, published August 4, 2004. •
Poor AC performance:

A/C—POOR HEATING PERFORMANCE

BULLETIN NO.: 04-01-37-003A　　　　　　　　　　　　**DATE: JUNE 14, 2004**

POOR HEATING PERFORMANCE/INSUFFICIENT HEAT DURING LOW AMBIENT TEMPERATURES (CHECK COOLANT CONCENTRATION, DRAIN SPECIFIED AMOUNT OF COOLANT AND REFILL WITH WATER)

MODELS: 2004 Aveo and Optra

ATTENTION: This bulletin is intended for vehicles sold only in Canada.

• **2004–06**—Remedy for a noisy suspension:

NOISY SUSPENSION

BULLETIN NO.: 06-03-08-004　　　　　　　　　　　　　　　　　　**DATE: MAY 16, 2006**

CRUNCH, SQUAWK, OR GRIND NOISE FROM FRONT SUSPENSION WHILE DRIVING OVER BUMPS AT LOW SPEED (REPLACE FRONT STABILIZER BAR BUSHINGS)

2004–06 Chevrolet Aveo; 2004–06 Pontiac Wave

Some customers may comment on a crunch, squawk, or grind noise from the front suspension when driving over bumps at low speed. This condition may be more apparent in cold weather and is likely caused by friction between the stabilizer bar and the bushing.

AVEO, LANOS, WAVE PROFILE

	2000	2001	2002	2004	2005
Cost Price ($)					
Aveo	—	—	—	13,480	13,595
Aveo5	—	—	—	13,820	14,785
Lanos	12,750	12,900	13,395	—	—
Wave	—	—	—	—	13,595
Wave5	—	—	—	—	13,935
Used Values ($)					
Aveo ▲	—	—	—	6,000	7,000
Aveo ▼	—	—	—	5,000	6,500
Aveo5 ▲	—	—	—	6,300	7,200
Aveo5 ▼	—	—	—	5,400	6,700
Lanos ▲	900	1,200	2,000	—	—
Lanos ▼	700	1,000	1,500	—	—
Wave ▲	—	—	—	—	7,400
Wave ▼	—	—	—	—	6,700
Wave5 ▲	—	—	—	—	7,700
Wave5 ▼	—	—	—	—	7,200
Reliability	1	1	1	3	3
Crash Safety (F)	—	—	—	5	5
Side	—	—	—	3	3
Rollover Resistance	—	—	—	4	4

OPTRA ★ ★

RATING: Below Average (2004–06). A bit larger Daewoo *cum* Chevrolet, the Optra isn't versatile or reliable enough to compete against the Honda Civic, Mazda3, Hyundai Elantra, Kia Spectra, or Toyota Corolla, Echo, or Yaris. **"Real" city/ highway fuel economy:** 11.0/7.1 L/100 km. Owners report fuel savings may undershoot this estimate by at least 15 percent. **Maintenance/Repair costs:**

Average. **Parts:** Often in short supply. **Extended warranty:** Not needed, due to the few complaints recorded. **Best alternatives:** Other cars worth considering are the Honda Civic and Toyota Echo, Tercel, or Corolla. **Online help:** *www-odi. nhtsa.dot.gov/cars/problems/complain*; *www.autosafety.org/autodefects.html*.

Strengths and Weaknesses

Known in the U.S. as the Suzuki Forenza, the 2004 Optra was sold in Canada for almost $3,000 more than the same model year Aveo ($16,190). Presently, a 2004 Optra or Optra5 hatchback is worth between $6,500 and $7,500.

The Optra/Forenza is a reasonably equipped compact sedan that carries a puny 119-hp 2.0L 4-cylinder engine that has only 16 more horses than the entry-level Aveo. Standard features include a four-wheel independent MacPherson strut suspension, an AM/FM/CD stereo and four speakers, front power windows, power door locks, variable intermittent wipers, folding rear seats, a tachometer, a tilt steering wheel, 15-inch tires and wheels, and a driver's seat that is height-adjustable and includes a lumbar adjustment. The car has a nicely finished interior, but seating is comfortable for up to four passengers only.

Owner complaints have centred primarily upon loss of power and stalling, gear hunting, excessive body vibrations, premature brake wear, grinding when brakes are applied, electrical malfunctions, poor fit and finish, inadequate AC cooling, and excessive gas consumption.

U.S. government crash tests awarded the 2004–06 Optra/Forenza a four-star rating for occupant protection in frontal collisions; three stars for side collision protection; and four stars for rollover avoidance.

Safety Summary

2004—Airbag failed to deploy. • Passenger-side wheel sheared off. • Chronic stalling and hard starts. • Premature tire wear; vehicle easily hydroplanes. **2005**—Back wheel sheared off. • Sudden loss off power. • Erratic transmission shifting. • Passenger-side airbag is disabled when an average-sized passenger is seated. • Driver-side seat belt suddenly unlatches. • Wipers operate too slowly. **2006**—Sudden acceleration. • Jerky transmission shifts. • Hard starts:

> I purchased a 4 door 2006 Suzuki Forenza and on the next morning just a day after I purchased my car I put the key in the ignition and the car would not start. I tried again and the car started to shake like it was having a seizure. I let it sit for about 5 minutes before it started. When I told the dealership of what happen[ed] I was told it's a new car and I just had to break it in. Every morning the car would not start after sitting over night.

2004—Door frame paint peeling. **2004–05**—Rough idle and stalling. • Excessive rear brake noise. • Door lock falls into door. **2004–06**—Steering rubbing and growling.

DaimlerChrysler

NEON, SX 2.0, SRT-4 ★ ★ ★

RATING: Average (2003–06); Below Average (2000–02); Not Recommended (1995–99). A low-quality, fuel-thirsty small car that has improved a bit during the last three years. 1995–99 models eat engine head gaskets for breakfast and wallets for lunch. **"Real" city/highway fuel economy:** Owners report extremely poor fuel economy in the 19.0/18.0 L/100 km range. **Maintenance/Repair costs:** Higher than average. **Parts:** Easily found and relatively inexpensive. However, Chrysler is particularly slow in distributing parts needed for safety recall campaigns; waits of several months are commonplace. **Extended warranty:** A good idea for the powertrain if the base warranty has expired. **Best alternatives:** Other cars worth considering are the GM Firefly, Metro, Cavalier, or Sunfire (2000 or later); Honda Civic; Hyundai Accent; Mazda Protegé; Suzuki Esteem; and Toyota Echo, Tercel, or Corolla. **Online help:** *www.neons.org, www.srtforums. com, www.carsurvey.org/model_Dodge_Neon.html, www.geocities.com/norman_neon, www.allpar.com/fix/secret-warranties.html*, and *www.autosafety.org/autodefects.html*.

Strengths and Weaknesses

A small, noisy car with big quality problems in its first-generation models, the Neon does offer a spacious interior and responsive steering and handling. Nevertheless, it's seriously handicapped by an antiquated, feeble, and fuel-thirsty 3-speed automatic gearbox; a DOHC 4-cylinder 150-hp powerplant that has to be pushed hard to do as well as the SOHC 132-hp engine; and a mushy base suspension.

The 2003 Neon was renamed the SX 2.0 in Canada. It is roomy and reasonably powered for urban use, and recent refinements have given it a softer, quieter ride while enhancing the car's handling and powertrain performance.

Chrysler has tried to make its low-end cars more appealing and more profitable by adding high-performance features that quickly lose their value as the vehicle ages. For example, the $26,950 2004 SRT-4, equipped with a turbocharged 215-hp 2.4L 4-cylinder engine hooked to a manual 4-speed transmission, now sells for $13,000.

Reliability has never been the Neon's strong suit, primarily because of major powertrain defects characterized by 4-cylinder engine head gasket failures and an abruptly shifting, unreliable transmission. The air conditioning system often requires expensive servicing following condenser and compressor failures, and there's a multitude of electrical shorts, lots of interior noise and water leaks, uneven fit and finish, and poor-quality trim items that break or fall off easily. The Neon's finish is not as good as that of most other subcompacts.

Year 2003–05 models continue to have some engine and transmission glitches, but they are less serious than the failures reported on previous models. Engine stalling is a recurrent problem mostly caused by poorly calibrated computer modules (an 8-year/130,000 km emissions warranty item).

Owners of these newer models also say that when the car is passing through puddles, water is ingested into the engine though the air intake port (Chrysler will replace the engine when threatened with court action); the automatic transmission shudders when shifting; the AC fails to cool the vehicle adequately; they experience no-starts because of early starter rust-out; there's constant brake squeaking; and the engine noticeably loses power when windows are lowered, the sunroof is opened, or the AC is engaged. They also complain of overall poor fuel economy.

VEHICLE HISTORY: The Neon remained basically unchanged until the '99 models got de-powered airbags. **2000**—A second-generation redesign improved powertrain quality a bit and added interior room and trunk space. The manual transmission and stereo were also upgraded, traction control was offered, and redesigned doors reduced wind noise and water leaks. **2002**—An upgraded automatic transmission (some reliability problems remain, though). **2003**—Neons were renamed SX 2.0 and given new steering wheels, front and rear fascias, and engine mounts to smooth out engine roughness. A taller Fifth gear for the manual transmission was also added. **2004**—High-performance versions got a small 15-hp power boost and a limited-slip differential. An optional 4-speed automatic transmission was made available. **2005**—The SRT-4 got a specially tuned sport suspension, improved brakes, and sport seats.

Safety Summary

All models/years—Fires. • "Inappropriate" airbag deployment or failure to deploy. • Sudden acceleration. • Chronic stalling. • No-start because of rusted-out starter. • Throttle system failures. • Faulty cruise control. • Steering loss. • Steering locks up when it rains. • Chronic transmission failures and slippage. • Transmission suddenly downshifts to First gear when accelerating at 90 km/h. • ABS brake failures. • Defective brake master cylinder. • Premature front brake pad/rotor wearout. • Excessive vibration. • Small horn buttons are hard to find in an emergency. • Trunk lid or hood may fall. • Headlight switch is a "hide-and-go-seek" affair. • Axle shafts may suddenly collapse. **All models: 1995–99**—Chronic engine head gasket failures. • Engine camshaft seal leaks oil • Engine motor mount failures. **1995–2000**—NHTSA probe of seat belt latch. **1998**—Driver-side window exploded in warm weather. • Front right wheel bolt fell out, causing wheel to bend. • Engine surging and stalling. • Engine loses speed rapidly when going uphill. • Excessive engine carbon buildup. • Timing belt broke, causing extensive engine damage. • Partial steering hang-up when making a right turn. **1999**—Vehicle suddenly jumps out of gear. • In rainy weather, vehicle makes a loud noise, sometimes stalls, or loses steering power. • Defective ignition-switch fuse causes sudden shutdown. **2000**—Almost 400 safety complaints indicate that the 2000 refinements haven't improved overall reliability or safety. Main problem areas: airbag, automatic transmission, power steering, tire, and brake failures; engine fires; premature brake rotor and pad wear, signalled by excessive vibrations and squealing when brakes are applied; steering lock-ups; stalling and stumbling; interior/exterior light dimming; seat belts failing to retract; and an inoperative horn. • Snapping noises from the front suspension may be caused by loose front cross-member mounting bolts. • An upgraded right-side motor mount may reduce steering-wheel or chassis shaking. **2000–01**—Poor engine idle. **2001**—Engine stalling and stumbling and airbags failing to deploy are the most frequent problems reported. • Other incidents include electrical shorts (lights and gauges), Eagle low-profile tire blowouts, engine damage caused by water ingested through the air intake system, loss of steering, weak trunk lid springs, and an annoying reflection in the front windshield. **2002**—Stalling because of water ingestion into engine when it rains. • Transmission slips between First and Second gear. • Vehicle pulls when cruising or upon acceleration and tends to wobble side to side at low speeds. • Excessive steering-wheel vibration makes it hard to maintain control. • Brakes fail to "catch" when first applied. • Airbag light stays lit. • Tailpipe melted part of the rear bumper. **2003**—Engine manifold failure. • Burnt spark plug wires (especially with #4 plug). • Poor braking. • Power-steering failure. • Tire blew because rim peeled off. • Suspension bottoms out when passing over a dip in the road. **2004**—Seat belts failed to lock during a collision. • Unoccupied passenger seat flew off its track during a collision. • Vehicle jerks continually due to faulty throttle body. • Electrical system suddenly shuts down. • Hard to shift manual transmission into First gear. • Rusted, prematurely worn brake rotors. **2005**—Radio caught on fire. • Airbags failed to deploy. • Sudden acceleration. • Manual transmission self-destructed:

> I was driving on the freeway for several miles and got off an off ramp. I continued to drive throughout the city and had come to a four way stop. I proceeded to go an[d] accelerated in 1st gear and then put the car into 2nd gear. While in the 2nd gear, the engine came to an abrupt stop and sparks flew all over the street. The clutch had ejected itself out of the transmission causing massive damage to the engine bay and chassis.

• CV joint failure. • Brake pedal goes to the floor without effect. • Radiator hose and clamp leaks fluid.

Secret Warranties/Internal Bulletins/Service Tips

All models/years: Paint delamination, peeling, or fading. **All models: 1995–99**—A new multi-layer steel engine head gasket provided superior sealing characteristics, which constitutes an admission that the previous head gaskets were poorly designed. • Oil leakage at the cam position sensor is often mistaken for an engine head gasket failure. Chrysler says the cam seal should always be replaced when the head gasket is changed. • Smooth-road steering wheel vibration is likely caused by a faulty bushing. **1995–2000**—Tips on eliminating a steering-column clunk or rattle. **1996–99**—Troubleshooting a sunroof that makes a ratcheting noise when engaged. **1998**—AC compressor lock-up at low mileage. • Sag, hesitation, harsh AC operation, and flickering headlights. • Popping noise when passing over bumps or making turns. • Vehicle overheats, or radiator fan runs continuously. **1998–99**—How to fix a water leak in the left side of the trunk. **1999–2000**—Low mileage AC lock-up. **2000**—Erratic engine performance may be fixed by recalibrating the PCM (powertrain control module). • Delayed automatic transmission engagement, likely caused by a faulty front pump. • Harsh AC engagement and clunk noise. • Front-door water leaks. • Rear-door glass won't roll down all the way. • High window-cranking effort or slow power-window operation. • Blower motor noise or vibration. • Deck-lid rattle and water/dust intrusion past the deck-lid seal. • Difficulty moving front seats forward. • Water enters the horn assembly. **2000–01**—Poor performance of AC and engine. • Remedy for AC honking. • Rattling wheel covers. **2000–05**—Headlight water condensation. • TSB #M19-07-05 admits that a clicking noise heard when turning may be due to a misaligned or defective steering assembly. A similar clicking may emanate from the drivetrain:

FRONT HUB/HALF SHAFT POP/CLICK SOUND

BULLETIN NO.: 03-006-04   **DATE: SEPTEMBER 15, 2004**

OVERVIEW: This bulletin involves installing a rubber gasket to the face of the half shaft that mounts to the hub bearing.

MODELS: 2000–05 Neon and 2001–04 PT Cruiser

SYMPTOM/CONDITION: Vehicle may exhibit a popping/clicking/snapping/ticking sound from the front hub/half shaft area during acceleration after Drive to Reverse or Reverse to Drive shifts. The sound may also be present while turning and accelerating from a stop.

2001—AC expansion valve noise. • Engine hesitation. • Front-seat rattling. • No-start problem in cold weather. • Rear window may not go all the way down. **2002**—Poor engine and AC performance caused by miscalibrated or faulty computer modules. • Low-speed power-steering moan. • If the odometer reading is inaccurate, dealer will reprogram instrument cluster module free of charge under Customer Satisfaction Program #93. **2002–03**—Delayed shifts may require the installation of a new automatic transmission front pump assembly (see bulletin on following page).

A/T—DELAYED GEAR ENGAGEMENT/POSSIBLE DTC'S

BULLETIN NO.: 21-004-05   **DATE: JANUARY 22, 2005**

TRANSMISSION DELAYED ENGAGEMENT

This bulletin supersedes technical service bulletin 21-007-04, dated May 11, 2004, which should be removed from your files. All revisions are highlighted with **asterisks** and includes, additional model years.

OVERVIEW: This bulletin involves replacing the front pump assembly in the transmission and checking the Transmission Control Module (TCM) for the latest software revision level.

2004 Pacifica; 2002–04 Sebring/Stratus; 2003 Liberty; 2002–04; 300M/Concorde/Intrepid; 2002–03 Neon; 2002–03 PT Cruiser; 2002–03 Town & Country/Caravan/Voyager; 2003 Wrangler

SYMPTOM/CONDITION: Vehicle operator may experience a delayed or temporary loss of transmission engagement after initial start up. The condition follows an extended soak (several hours) and may be accompanied by a harsh 4–3 downshift.

2003—Water leaks onto the right front-seat floor. • Hard starting requires the reflashing of the PCM. **2003–04**—TSB #09-007-04 says an engine snapping sound is Chrysler's fault and can be remedied by chamfering the bore radius on cam bearing caps through L5 and R2 through R5:

IRREGULAR SNAPPING SOUND

BULLETIN NO.: 09-007-04   **DATE: MARCH 2, 2004**

IRREGULAR ENGINE SNAPPING SOUND

This bulletin involves chamfering the bore radius on cam bearing caps through L5 and R2 through R5.

2001–04 Sebring/Stratus; PT Cruiser; 2001–04 Chrysler Caravan, Voyager, and Town & Country; 2003–04 Neon and Jeep Wrangler.

NOTE: This bulletin applies to vehicles equipped with a 2.0L, 2.4L DOHC or 2.4L Turbo engine.

SYMPTOM/CONDITION: The sound may be noticed when the engine is idling in park between idle rpm and 1400 rpm at normal operating temperature. The sound is on the upper end of the engine (cylinder head) towards the front of the engine or passenger side (right side). The sound is irregular, not periodic or harmonious. The frequency of the sound will increase with RPM. The sound is more of a higher pitch snapping noise not a low metallic knock.

• Misaligned exhaust tips. **2004**—Hard starts, acceleration stumble. • Intermittent loss of audio. • Poor idle (see bulletin on following page). **2005**—Rough, shuddering 1–2 upshift. • Engine runs poorly.

This bulletin involves replacing the affected spark plug, ignition wire and/or reprogramming the Powertrain Control Module with new software.

2004 Sebring/Stratus; Liberty/Cherokee; Neon; 2004–05 PT Cruiser; 2004–05 Caravan, Voyager and Town & Country

NEON, SX 2.0, SRT-4 PROFILE

	1997	1998	1999	2000	2001	2002	2003	2004	2005
Cost Price ($)									
Base	14,750	15,350	15,215	17,995	18,375	18,505	—	—	—
Sport/SX 2.0	16,900	17,500	—	—	—	—	14,995	15,195	15,605
SRT-4	—	—	—	—	—	—	—	26,950	27,380
Used Values ($)									
Base ▲	1,500	2,000	2,500	3,000	3,500	5,500	—	—	—
Base ▼	1,000	1,500	2,000	2,500	3,000	4,000		—	—
Sport/SX 2.0 ▲	2,000	2,500	—	—	—	—	5,500	7,000	8,500
Sport/SX 2.0 ▼	1,500	2,000	—	—	—	—	5,000	6,000	7,500
SRT-4 ▲	—	—	—	—	—	—	—	14,500	17,000
SRT-4 ▼	—	—	—	—	—	—	—	13,000	16,000
Reliability	1	1	1	1	2	2	3	3	3
Crash Safety (F)	4	3	3	—	4	4	4	4	4
Side	—	2	2	—	3	3	3	3	3
Side (IIHS)	—	—	—	1	1	1	1	1	1
Offset	1	1	1	2	2	2	2	2	2
Head Restraints (F)	1	—	2	1	1	1	1	1	1
Rollover Resistance	—	—	—	—	4	4	4	4	4

Ford

RATING: Below Average (1997–2000); Not Recommended (1981–96). The Escort has become a risky buy, mainly because of its many powertrain deficiencies and Ford's lack of parts and servicing support in Canada. **"Real" city/highway fuel economy:** Fuel consumption with a manual transmission is an impressive 7.7 L/100 km in the city and 5.7 L/100 km on the highway. Owners report fuel savings with the automatic gearbox are about 10 percent less than that estimated by Natural Resources Canada (city 9.4 L/100 km (30 mpg); hwy 6.9 L/100 km (41 mpg)). **Maintenance/Repair costs:** Higher than average. Repairs can be done by independents or by Ford or Mazda dealers. **Parts:** Expensive, and getting harder to find. **Extended warranty:** You will need a bumper-to-bumper extended warranty, which will add at least $1,500 to the price—wiping out the attraction of a low price tag. **Best alternatives:** Consider the wagon version: It's easy to load, quite versatile, offers a raised rear roof that augments rear-passenger headroom, and has child-seat tether anchors that don't intrude into the baggage area. Other choices include the GM Firefly or Metro; Honda Civic; Hyundai Accent; Mazda Protegé; Suzuki Esteem or Aerio; and Toyota Tercel, Echo, or Corolla. **Online help:** *www.tgrigsby.com/views/ford.htm* (The Anti-Ford Page) and *www.autosafety.org/autodefects.html*.

Strengths and Weaknesses

These front-drive small cars are usually reasonably priced and economical to operate, and they provide a comfortable, though jittery, ride and adequate front seating for two adults. However, they have a Dr. Jekyll and Mr. Hyde disposition, depending on which model year you buy.

From 1982 to 1990, these subcompacts were dull performers with uninspiring interiors. Worse, they had a nasty reputation for being totally unreliable and expensive to repair. Models from 1991 to 1996 are more reliable, but performance with the 88-hp engine is mediocre at best when equipped with an automatic tranny. This performance deficit was corrected with the 1997 model's larger 2.0L SPI, single-cam, 2-valve/cylinder engine, which provided lots more power (110 hp versus 88 hp) than did the previous engine.

VEHICLE HISTORY: 1991—The 1991 model's changeover to more reliable Mazda components gave it a longer wheelbase, making for a more comfortable ride and a slightly roomier interior. **1994**—ABS added to the GT, and all models got a driver-side airbag. Motorized seat belts harassed front passengers. **1995**—Dual airbags were installed, and motorized seat belts remained (ugh). **1997**—Better steering, ride, and handling, plus a bigger and more-powerful 2.0L engine. A wagon variant joined the four-door sedan. Other highlights include fresh styling, dual airbags, a new 110-hp 2.0L 4-cylinder engine, a standard 5-speed manual transmission and optional 4-speed automatic, and optional ABS with rear discs. **1998**—Debut of a sporty Escort ZX2 coupe in the States (a year later in Canada). **2000**—Wagons axed, and the ZX2 coupe got a firmer suspension and a 130-hp engine.

Owner complaints relating to the 1991–96 model years primarily concern annoying seat belts; airbag, fuel-tank, coil-spring, and tie-rod failures; automatic transmission and engine breakdowns (premature timing-belt replacement at around 90,000 km); and cooling system, brake, electrical, air conditioning, fuel-pump, and ignition system failures. Quality control and reliability improved a bit with the 1997 and 1998 models, but many of the earlier powertrain deficiencies remained.

The 1999 and 2000 models continue to experience lots of engine and transmission failures, steering vibration, and electrical, fuel, and brake system problems (excessive wear of front brake pads and rotors at around 10,000 km).

> My car has had 4 transmissions before 40,000 miles [64,000 km] and now at 102,000 miles [164,000 km] I'm having to put a new motor in. This car has had excellent care and maintenance and [there is] no reason for this.

Safety Summary

All models: 1995–2000—An incredibly high number of safety-related complaints were recorded for these years, and the problems return continually. • No airbag deployment. • Inadvertent airbag deployment. • Airbag-induced injuries. • Electrical and engine wiring fires. • Brake failures and premature rotor and pad replacement. • Snapped front and rear coil springs damage tire. • Sudden tie-rod failure leading to steering loss. • Automatic transmission that slips, jumps out of gear, leaks, or fails early. • Unanticipated acceleration. • Seat belt malfunctions. • Horn blows inadvertently, won't blow, or is hard to access. • Faulty door locks. **1998**—Faulty fuel pump/pressure regulator, CV joints, and wheel bearings. • Delayed shifts. • Steering lock-up. **1999**—Chronic surging and stalling. • Headlight socket melts. • Hood flies open. • Poor structural integrity (broken welds and distorted sheet metal). • Suspension and alignment problems. • Poor defrosting. **2000**—Chronic stalling. • Vehicle suddenly jumps forward or rearward when the accelerator is only slightly depressed. • Slips in and out of gear when coming to a stop. • Transmission coolant line clamp comes apart. • Delayed transmission engagement, or slippage. • Power-steering loss caused by snapped serpentine belt. • Brake pedal slowly creeps to the floor when applied. • Shock absorber rubbed against tire, causing a blowout. • Sunroof shattered while vehicle was parked. • Windshield suddenly shattered. • Seat belts jam in the retracted position. • Intermittent failure of the power door locks and windows.

Secret Warranties/Internal Bulletins/Service Tips

All models/years: Radio whining or buzzing noise can be eliminated by following the service tips found in TSB #01-7-3. • Repeated heater core failures have also been a frequent problem, covered in TSB #01-15-6. • Paint delamination, peeling, or fading. **All models: 1994–98**—Tips on eliminating wind noise around doors are given in TSB #97-15-1. **1997–99**—Positive crankcase ventilation (PCV) system may freeze, resulting in a serious oil leak through the dipstick tube. • A front brake grinding noise, pulling or drag, and uneven brake pad wear are all signs of corrosion affecting the caliper slide pins. • Tips on silencing a variety of squeaks and rattles. • No restart in cold weather, the cooling fan not shutting off, or the battery going dead all signal the need to change the integrated relay control module. **1998**—Erratic fuel gauge operation or slow fill-ups may be corrected by installing a slosh module fuel gauge kit. **1999**—Tips on reducing noise, vibration, and harshness. **2000**—Delayed transmission engagement; MIL (malfunction indicator light) comes on. • Troubleshooting intake manifold air leaks. • Exhaust system buzzing or rattling (a problem for over a decade). • Fuel fill nozzle clicks off too soon when fuelling up. • Remedy for a burning oil smell. • Troubleshooting poor engine performance at idle and excessive gas consumption. • Remedies for an engine that won't start or shut down properly. • Engine oil leak at the oil pan, front cover, or the front and rear crankshaft oil seal. • Vehicle may not start in freezing weather because of moisture freezing in the fuel-pump relay. • Fuel delivery malfunctions. • Eliminating a high idle condition when starting or decelerating. • Light to moderate rear axle whine. • Front-seat cushion sagging. • Diagnostic tips to eliminate wind noise around doors. • Revise hood seal to reduce wind whistle. • AC goes into defrost mode when vehicle goes uphill.

ESCORT, ZX2 PROFILE

	1994	1995	1996	1997	1998	1999	2000
Cost Price ($)							
Base/LX	12,195	12,995	13,595	14,595	14,895	14,895	—
GT	13,995	14,295	15,295	—	—	—	—
ZX2	—	—	—	—	—	15,895	17,995
Used Values ($)							
Base/LX ▲	800	1,000	1,300	1,700	2,000	2,500	—
Base/LX ▼	600	900	1,100	1,400	1,800	2,000	—
GT ▲	1,100	1,400	1,700	—	—	—	—
GT ▼	900	1,300	1,500	—	—	—	—
ZX2 ▲	—	—	—	—	—	3,000	3,500
ZX2 ▼	—	—	—	—	—	2,500	2,500
Reliability	2	2	2	2	2	3	3
Crash Safety (F)	5	4	4	4	3	3	3
Side	—	—	—	—	3	3	3
Offset	—	—	—	3	3	3	3
Head Restraints	—	1	—	1	—	1	—

All ratings on a numbered scale where 5 is good and 1 is bad. See pages 130–132 for a more detailed description.

RATING: Average (2004–06); Not Recommended (2000–03). Poor engineering? Consider this: Some Focus models can't be driven through puddles because the low-mounted air intake hose ingests water into the engine ($5,000 repair). And then Ford blames the owner for driving through puddles! Chronic stalling is also a major problem, and Ford's secret warranty for earlier models doesn't cover afflicted 2002s and 2003s. **"Real" city/highway fuel economy:** 8.6/6.1 L/100 km with the manual transmission; 9.0/6.7 L/100 km with an automatic. *SVT:* 11.3/7.8 L/100 km, but owners say the automatic transmission cuts fuel economy by over 20 percent from this figure. **Maintenance/Repair costs:** Predicted to be higher than average once the warranty expires. **Parts:** Expensive and sometimes hard to find, especially if they are part of a recall campaign. **Extended warranty:** Having a bumper-to-bumper warranty, or a rich uncle, is a prerequisite to owning a 2000–03 Focus. **Best alternatives:** GM Firefly, Metro, Cavalier, or Sunfire; Honda Civic (it's softer-riding, quieter, and has a smoother-running engine); Hyundai Accent; Mazda Protegé; Suzuki Esteem or Swift; and Toyota Corolla, Echo, or Tercel. **Online help:** *www.autosafety.org/article.php?scid=37&did=841* and *www.tgrigsby.com/views/stories.htm* (The Anti-Ford Page).

Strengths and Weaknesses

Hailed as Europe's 1999 Car of the Year (yikes; that should be your first warning sign), Ford's sleek 2000 Focus came to North America shortly thereafter as a premium small car. The Escort's base engine, a 110-hp 2.0L 4-cylinder, was carried over to the Focus LX and SE, while the 130-hp twin-cam 2.0L (also used on the Escort ZX2 coupe) became the standard powerplant on the ZTS and ZX3 and optional on the SE.

VEHICLE HISTORY: 2002—Debut of a high-performance, 170-hp SVT Focus with sport suspension and 17-inch wheels, and the ZX5, a four-door hatchback that looks like a shortened version of the Focus wagon. **2003**—A standard 5-year warranty came on the scene (but it should be at least seven years). **2004**—No more anti-skid system, and a 145-hp 2.3L 4-cylinder is added.

Unlike competitors' small 4-cylinder "econo-engines," the 130-hp 2.0L powerplant is barely sufficient for highway cruising, where passing and merging require a bit more power. The Focus isn't a quiet car, either. Constant engine buzz and some hard shifting with the automatic gearbox accompany any decent speed. Brakes add to the Focus' symphony of sound by emitting a grinding noise when applied, and the front suspension creaks when the car is put through its paces. There is some vibration felt when driving over smooth highways, and uneven terrain causes the car to bounce about.

This small car does handle well in city traffic, thanks to its tight turning radius and nimble steering. The small back-corner windows are also handy for keeping the rear visibility unobstructed. The car's unusually tall roofline gives ample headroom and allows for a higher, more upright riding position than you'll see with traditional small cars. Front and rear legroom is impressive as well, as long as the front passengers don't push their seats too far back.

After all these positives, keep in mind that this is one of the most unreliable cars that Ford has built in recent memory. Powertrain, fuel, electrical, and brake system failures are commonplace. Service bulletins are replete with special instructions telling dealers how to practically rebuild the car to make it tolerably driveable. Powertrain problems include chronic stalling (covered up to 10 years by a secret warranty); excessive vibration; poor engine and transmission performance; and 2003 SVT flywheel, pressure plate, and clutch assembly failures. Other problems are as follows: premature rotor and brake pad wear and squeaking; failure-prone ignition switch won't turn, locks up, and eats keys (unlocking costs $300); seat-back bar digs into driver's back; power-window failures; excessive engine, brake, steering-column, suspension, and wheel noise; trunk latch sticks or suddenly opens; trunk leaks water; AC leaks coolant; driver's door won't open from the inside; fuel-door lid broke in half; hood latch broke off when closing hood; right rear-door moulding fell off; and interior panels fit poorly.

A threat to your wallet is annoying, but a threat to your genitalia is really scary:

> The 2004 Focus cigarette lighter after being pushed in and getting hot popped out of the holder and landed either on the occupant's lap or on the carpeting. When this was shown to the rental company, and a demonstration was done, the lighter burned the representative's legs. This was a Budget rental vehicle.

Safety Summary

All models: 2000—Rear-door latch failures on wagons. **2000–01**—Ford admits to chronic stalling and extends engine computer warranty to 10 years (see "Secret Warranties/Internal Bulletins/Service Tips," below). **2000–02**—NHTSA continues to investigate complaints of chronic stalling (see *www.autosafety.org/ EA02-022-OpeningMemo.pdf*), while Ford attempts different fixes outlined in confidential service bulletins. • Chronic stalling complaints with loss of brakes and steering continue unabated, believed to be caused by faulty fuel pump. • Airbag deploys either for no apparent reason or after the vehicle hits a pothole. • Differential fluid leaks on brake components (right side), causing brake loss. • Defective speed control causes sudden acceleration in spite of corrective recall. • Other sudden acceleration incidents ascribed to faulty power control module (PCM) and driver's shoe being caught under the plastic console. • Sudden acceleration in Reverse. • Collapse of tie-rod and axle, leading to loss of control. • Defective axle wheel bearing. • Sudden pull to the left when turning left. • Clutch pedal spring pops out, injuring driver. • Pedal fell on floorboard. • Transmission slippage and failure. • Inaccurate fuel gauge (sender and fuel pump replaced). • AC condensation drips on accelerator pedal. • Exhaust fumes enter passenger compartment. • Smoking electrical wiring in dash. • Under-hood fire ignited after

AC engaged. • Driver-side seat belt won't deploy. • Emergency brake often fails to engage because button on handle stays depressed. • Vehicle was cruising at 110 km/h when gas pedal fell off its mounting. • Frayed accelerator throttle cable snapped; cable also kinks, causing hesitation, acceleration, and surging. • Stabilizer bar suddenly broke. • Car left in Park rolled downhill. • Rear end is very unstable in snow, feels wobbly under normal conditions, and throws rear passengers about. • Sudden, unintended acceleration, and then engine cuts out. • Engine shuts down while cruising on the highway. • New engine needed after roadway rainwater ingested into engine because of low air intake valve. • Transmission hard to shift into Second and Reverse in cold weather. • Fuel-tank leak due to cracked filler pipe. • No brakes. • No steering. • Steering wheel locks while driving. • Broken rack and pinion. • Tie-rod suddenly broke off. • Front and rear wheels buckle. • Collapsed front wheel:

> My father owns this vehicle, but he bought it for me for safety reasons. I am a 16-year-old female. Travelling at normal highway speed on a dry, two-lane highway with no traffic at night, my 2002 Ford Focus lost control due to the front control arm fracturing. My right front tire ended up totally unattached to the control arm and only staying attached to the vehicle by the hold of the tie-rod. My vehicle swerved into the median and into the oncoming traffic (thankfully no traffic was around).

• Rear hatch opens on its own. • Faulty rear wheel bearings cause wheel to wobble and wander. • Original Firestone tires wear out prematurely. • Child-restraint bracket puts dents in the rear seat. • Dash lights flicker, then quit. **2002–03**—Airbags failed to deploy. • Sudden brake loss. • Windshield cracks or shatters for no reason. **2003**—Chronic stalling. • Reports of severe back trauma from seat-back failure in rear-enders. • Transmission and axle failures. • Excessive vibration. • Trunk latch suddenly releases. • Sunlight washes out speedometer reading. **2004**—Car fire believed to be caused by faulty fuel-line connection. • Sudden acceleration. • Cruise control self-activates, causing vehicle to surge suddenly. • Hood flew up, shattering windshield while car was cruising on the highway. • Automatic transmission, bearings, and throttle body replaced during first year. • Total brake failure and frequent rotor, pad, and caliper replacements:

> Brakes failed on our 2004 Ford Focus ZX5 4-door hatchback as my wife went to stop at a stop sign leaving our development and was broadsided by a truck. This resulted in a total loss of vehicle and injuries sustained to my wife.

•

> Three months after buying a 2004 Ford Focus LX, the brakes and calipers had to be replaced. Approximately, three months later again. Then again five months later. My rotors were destroyed. Every time I have complained that this shouldn't have happened and the dealership acted as if everything would be ok. I was in a small accident during this time because my brakes completely gave out. I was the only person involved in this accident. My front bumper is messed up because of this. All of these parts have been replaced every time!! I have spent over 400.00 dollars in

rentals while my car was being fixed. I'm sick of having to constantly have the same problem corrected. I don't know what else to do. My friend drives a Focus and had the same problems. Hers was returned immediately when she found out how many times it happened to me. I can't return my vehicle until damages are fixed, which I don't feel is my problem. I would never recommend this car, and try not to drive it in fear I'm going to hurt myself or another person.

• Chronic stalling and surging continues to be a problem:

Contact owns a 2004 Ford Focus. While driving on the highway the car shut down without warning. No particular speed or circumstance. This incident happened several times on interstate. While going 70 to 75 mph [110–120 km/h], the car shut down, no battery, no lights, and it was very hard to steer. It happened at stop signs or at speeds of 35 to 45 mph [56–72 km/h]. After putting vehicle in park then in neutral or park it will start back up. Vehicle was taken back to dealership 3 times in the last 3 weeks. Mechanic recalibrated the automatic transmission control module (PCM), and was told it would be okay. Took it off the dealership and within 10 miles [16 km] incident started happening again. Flight recorder was installed on October 6, 2005. Was told to push a button every time the vehicle shut off, but the problem was that there was no electricity going to anything to make the flight recorder show the problem.

• Automatic transmission self-destructed:

Vehicle has stalled/sputtered while driving or idling. I took the vehicle to the dealer on 3 separate occasions and each time they said something different was wrong. The dealer replaced the idle air control valve, cleaned out the entire fuel tank, replaced the fuel pump and filter and has now replaced the transmission.

• Bent steering tie-rod makes vehicle wander all over the road. • Wheel bearing failure. • No-start because ignition cylinder seized:

I drove and parked the 2004 Ford Focus about 40 mins from my home. About 2 hours later, I went to get in my car and the steering wheel was locked. I inserted the key and it would not turn. Several people tried jiggling the steering wheel, stepping on the brake all to no avail. I called AAA and Ford Roadside and was told by both that it would need to be towed and that they could do nothing at this time (Sat. evening/ Sun. morning of Columbus Day weekend).

I have researched the Internet and found this is a common problem in the Ford Focus dating back to the 2000 model and yet Ford has done nothing to correct the problem. This could be a dangerous problem for a mother with children if she were to travel at night and when returning to the car could not start her engine. It is not covered by insurance for repair or under warranty if expired and it is a manufacturing defect on the part of Ford.

• Goodyear Eagle RSA tires make vehicle difficult to control in winter weather. • Tire feathering. • Water entry destroys the horn. • Snow kills the windshield-wiper motor:

> Windshield wiper motor goes if it gets clogged up with a small amount of snow. The way the car is designed when you brush the car off from snow, some of it lodges into an area that is hard to get the snow out of, when wipers are turned on the motor does not work. Had this replaced approx. 4 or 5 months ago, and now it has happened again. I was told by the Ford service dept. this has happened to other Focus owners. I have owned many different cars of varying makes and models and this is the first time I have ever had this problem, it is definitely a design flaw. Some type of guard needs to be installed to protect it from snow and ice.

Secret Warranties/Internal Bulletins/Service Tips

All models: 2000—Ford Campaign No. 03M02 allows for the free replacement of fractured front coil springs up to 10 years or 240,000 km (150,000 mi.). • Under Special Service Instruction 00204, Ford will reprogram the powertrain computer module to correct poor engine performance on vehicles equipped with a manual transmission. • ONP 99B21 will replace the fuel pulse damper free of charge and ONP 99B22 will pay the costs associated with replacing the side engine mount. • Vehicles equipped with a manual transmission will have their clutch master cylinder and pedal return spring replaced, free of charge, under ONP 00B59. **2000–01**—Chronic stalling fix. Reuters News Service reported on November 20, 2003, that a faulty fuel delivery module linked to chronic engine stalling would be replaced free of charge by Ford up to 10 years, without any mileage limitation (Campaign No. 03N01). Ford spokesman Glenn Ray told Reuters, "It's a product improvement program. There is nothing fundamentally wrong with the quality of the fuel delivery module. It doesn't fail instantaneously or suddenly." • Replace rear wheel bearings through December 31, 2003, regardless of mileage, under Ford Campaign No. 01B85. **2000–02**—Low power and stalling. • AC evaporator case/cowl leaks water into the interior. • AC fluttering noise. • Whistling from the heater plenum. • Repeated heater core failure. **2000–03**—Troubleshooting rear-end water leaks. **2000–04**—Remedy for front suspension creak, crunch, grinding, or rattle. **2000–05**—Getting a little wet, are you? The bulletin at right looks at some of the reasons why. **2001**—Difficult to shift out of Park. • 2.0L Zetec engines may hesitate, surge, or idle roughly in cold weather. • Intermittent stalling, hesitation, or lack of power. • Engine may produce higher-than-normal idle speed or run

---

WATER LEAKS TO VEHICLE INTERIOR
BULLETIN NO.: 05-13-3   DATE: JULY 11, 2005

WATER LEAKS/A/C CONDENSATION LEAKS AT FRONT FLOOR AREA
2000–05 Focus

ISSUE: Some 2000–05 Focus vehicles may exhibit a difficult to diagnose or difficult to repair water leak or AC system condensation leak condition in the front floor area. This may be caused by sealer skips, loose grommets, mis-positioned seals or condensation leaking from the A/C evaporator case.

ACTION: Determine if the concern is an A/C condensation leak or a water leak and repair as necessary. Some common water leak locations and repair recommendations are listed in this article to help reduce repair time and increase repair effectiveness.

EXHAUST SYSTEM—CATALYTIC CONVERTER BRACKET BROKEN

BULLETIN NO.: 05-14-12   **DATE: JULY 25, 2005**

CATALYTIC CONVERTER MOUNTING BRACKET BROKEN

2002–04 Focus

ISSUE: Some 2002–04 Focus SVT vehicles may exhibit a broken or cracked catalytic converter mounting bracket.

ACTION: Replace the catalytic converter mounting bracket.

BRAKES—REAR DRUM BRAKE SQUEALING UPON APPLICATION

BULLETIN NO.: 05-10-5   **DATE: MAY 30, 2005**

REAR BRAKE SQUEAL

2000–05 Focus

ISSUE: Some 2000–05 Focus vehicles (excluding vehicles equipped with rear disc brakes) may exhibit a squealing noise from the rear drum brakes during stopping. This may be caused by a resonance traveling through the rear drum brake backing plates.

ACTION: Install damping weights to the rear (under vehicle side) of the rear drum brake backing plates.

roughly at idle. • Slight engine vibration at idle. • Troubleshooting the Check Engine light. • Power-steering pump pulley may squeak or chirp upon start-up. • Ignition key may be difficult to turn in cylinder. • Seat seams may split. **2002–03**—Hard starts and poor driveability may be caused by an incorrect PCM calibration. **2002–04**—Broken catalytic converter brackets will be replaced free of charge (see bulletin at left). **2002–05**—Service tips for manual-transmission-equipped vehicles that won't shift into Fifth gear. • TSB #04-15-2 says erratic windshield wiper operation is a Ford defect caused by a faulty wiper relay. • Ford makes a similar admission in the brake bulletin at left. **2003–05**—If the door locks lock or unlock when they shouldn't, try the following inexpensive remedy before investing in costly repairs (see bulletin below). **2004**—Loss of power, hesitation, or misfire after a cold start. • Runs rough in wet weather. • Harsh transmission engagement. • Premature clutch wear. • Transmission clunking or rattling. • Grinding when shifting into Third gear. • Gear rattle from the transaxle at idle. • Inoperative speed-control system. • Intermittent no-starts; odometer may show all dashes. • Customer Satisfaction Program #04B16 will pay for the correction of faulty front-seat heater element pads. • Diagonal wear or cupping of the rear tires. • Engine belt squeal.

POWER DOOR LOCKS CYCLING/SELF-LOCKING

BULLETIN NO.: 05-10-21   **DATE: MAY 30, 2005**

POWER DOOR LOCKS CYCLING OR SELF LOCKING

2003–05 Focus

Note if the vehicle is equipped with the autolock function refer to the owner guide or workshop manual for autolock operation information before continuing with this TSB. Automatic locking is normal under certain circumstances and service may not be required.

ACTION: Inspect and clean the door latch connectors. Pack the door latch connectors with dielectric grease. Refer to the following Service Procedure.

	2000	2001	2002	2003	2004	2005
Cost Price ($)						
LX	14,995	16,015	15,970	16,275	16,475	—
ZX3	16,697	16,690	17,390	17,550	17,775	17,555
Wagon SE	17,695	17,271	18,995	19,165	19,375	19,565
Used Values ($)						
LX ▲	3,000	4,500	6,000	7,000	9,000	—
LX ▼	2,500	3,500	5,000	6,000	7,500	—
ZX3 ▲	4,000	5,500	7,000	7,500	9,500	11,500
ZX3 ▼	3,000	4,000	6,000	6,500	8,000	10,000
Wagon SE ▲	4,200	5,000	6,500	8,000	9,800	11,600
Wagon SE ▼	3,200	4,500	5,500	7,000	8,500	10,100
Reliability	1	1	1	1	2	3
Crash Safety (F)						
2d	4	4	4	4	4	4
4d	4	4	5	5	5	5
Wagon	—	—	5	5	5	—
Side						
2d	4	4	4	4	4	4
4d	3	3	3	3	4	3
Side (IIHS)	1	1	1	1	1	1
Offset	5	5	5	5	5	5
Head Restraints	—	2	2	2	2	2
Rollover Resistance	—	—	4	4	4	4

General Motors

CAVALIER, SUNFIRE ★ ★ ★

RATING: Average (2003–05); Below Average (1999–2002); Not Recommended (1984–98). GM's best small cars, which isn't saying much. Side crashworthiness is unacceptably poor. Engine, transmission, and brake repair bills will run you bankrupt if you get a pre-1999 model. Try to get a 2003 or later version with a 4-speed automatic transmission because it will be a bit more reliable, have reduced engine noise, and make for more responsive performance. The base Sunbird changed its name to Sunfire in 1995; it shares the Cavalier's basic design. The Cavalier Z24 convertible was replaced by the LS in 1995. **"Real" city/highway fuel economy:** 9.8/6.6 L/100 km. Owners say automatic-transmission-equipped cars get about 15 percent less fuel economy than the above figure shows. **Maintenance/Repair costs:** Average. Repairs aren't dealer-dependent;

however, ABS troubleshooting is a real head-scratcher. **Parts:** Reasonably priced and often available for much less from independent suppliers. **Extended warranty:** Not essential. You should balance the cost of an engine head gasket ($800–$1,000) with that of an extended warranty, which will likely cost twice as much. **Best alternatives:** Honda Civic; Hyundai Accent or Elantra; Mazda Protegé or Mazda3; Nissan Sentra; Suzuki Aerio, Esteem, or Swift; and Toyota Corolla, Echo, or Tercel. Also take a look at the slightly more upscale Hyundai Elantra or Tiburon. **Online help:** *www.autosafety.org/article.php?did=41&scid=46* and *www.autooninfo.net/RelPerChevroletCharts.htm.*

Strengths and Weaknesses

These twins are two of the lowest-priced small cars to come equipped with standard ABS and dual airbags (1995–2003). In fact, GM claims it lost $1,000 on every one it sold. They are attractively styled (especially the Pontiac Sunfire), come with lots of interior room, and offer a nicely tuned suspension. The ride and handling have also improved markedly since 1999, with power rack-and-pinion steering, a longer wheelbase, and a wider track. The Sunfire is identical to the Cavalier, except for its more rakish look. The Cavalier Z24 and Sunfire are performance versions, equipped with a more refined form of the less-than-reliable Quad 4 2.4L DOHC 16-valve, 4-cylinder powerplant.

VEHICLE HISTORY: 1995—Wider and taller than previous models; standard dual airbags and ABS; a stiffer structure; and an improved suspension. **1996**—LS sedan and convertible were given standard traction control, and the Z24 picked up a new dual-camshaft 2.2L engine. **1998**—The base engine lost five horses. **1999**—2.4L twin-cam engine and front brake lining upgrades. **2000**—A slightly restyled front and rear end; an improved storage area; standard AC and PASSLOCK security system; upgraded standard ABS; and a smoother-shifting 5-speed manual transmission. **2003**—Restyled and lengthened; a new 140-hp 2.2L engine; a stiffer suspension; larger wheels and rear brakes; three-point centre seat belts; optional front side airbags; and ABS. **2004**—ABS is no longer standard on base models; CD player reads MP3-formatted discs.

Snappy road performance (with the correct engine and transmission hookup) has been marred by abysmally poor powertrain reliability. The early 2.0L versions are lacklustre performers—overwhelmed by the demands of passing and merging. On top of that, major reliability weaknesses afflict many mechanical and body components through the 1998 model year, where engine, transmission, electronic module, and brake failures are particularly common. Specifically, owners report that engine blocks crack, cylinder heads leak, and the turbocharged version frequently needs expensive repairs.

For 1990–94 versions, the Cavalier's base 2.2L 4-cylinder and optional 3.1L engines replaced the failure-prone 2.0L and 2.8L powerplants. Unfortunately, the newer engines also have a checkered reputation, highlighted by reports of chronic head gasket failures afflicting the 4-cylinder powerplant. Air conditioning and hood latch failures, seat belt defects, and a plethora of body deficiencies are also commonplace. Door bottoms and wheel housings are particularly vulnerable to rust perforation. Premature paint peeling and cracking, discoloration, and surface rust have been constant problems.

Since 1999, these vehicles have become a bit more reliable and durable. Nevertheless, owners are still plagued by troublesome engines (watch for blue exhaust smoke or excessive oil burning), faulty brakes, airbags that continue to malfunction and injure occupants, chronic stalling, and transmission and fuel-pump failures. The Getrag manual gearbox isn't very reliable, nor is it easily repaired, and faulty computer modules, fuel injections, and cooling systems cause stalling and a shaky idle. The power steering may lead or pull, and the steering rack tends to deteriorate quickly, usually requiring replacement some time shortly after 80,000 km. The front MacPherson struts also wear out rapidly, as do the rear shock absorbers. Many owners complain of rapid front brake wear and warped brake discs after a year or so.

Fit and finish quality is still quite variable, often leading to poor paint application, inside and outside body panel gaps, lots of exposed screw heads, and trunk and rear window water leaks, giving the car a mildew smell. Paint delamination is chronic:

> I have a 2004 Chevy Cavalier, which has been in no accidents and is very well taken care of. The paint on this car, and other cars like it, is peeling and chipping all over the place for no reason. The door edges, bumpers, hood, and fender all have chips of paint missing or about to fall off. The clear coat on the car is also very bad and is scratched very easily and washing the car sometimes does more bad than good.

Safety Summary

All models/years: Engine head gasket and intake manifold failures. • Transmission slippage or breakdown. • Owners report complete brake failure and lock-up, extended stopping distances, ABS that self-activates, premature rotor warpage and pad wear, and a grinding and knocking noise when braking. • Airbags fail to deploy or deploy accidentally. • Sudden acceleration or stalling. • Weak door hinges. • Inoperative horn. **All models: 1999–2001**—Engine fires. • Leaking fuel tank. • Plastic fuel tank is easily punctured. • Right wheel axle twisted off vehicle. • Chronic hesitation, stalling, and surging. • Clutch will not disengage, causing sudden acceleration. • Brake failure caused by leaking master cylinder fluid. • ABS locked up, causing vehicle to go into a skid. • Seat belt failed to retract. • Transmission wouldn't go into Reverse, transmission failed to engage upon start-up, automatic transmission locks up in Second gear, and vehicle rolled away even though parked with parking brake engaged. • When vehicle is in Drive with foot on the brake, it lurches forward, stalls, and produces a crashing sound. • During highway driving, the vehicle suddenly accelerated without steering control. • Rear leaf spring U-bolts broke, causing entire rear end to drop. • Front right side of the vehicle collapsed because of wheel bolts shearing off, causing the wheel to detach completely. • Springs are too weak, causing poor stability and control. • Floor mat impedes clutch pedal travel. • Sudden brake cable breakage while driving, brake grinding noise, and early warping of the front and rear brakes. • When driving with door locked, door came ajar. • Hood flew up while driving. **2002**—Reverse tail light bulb exploded, causing light assembly to catch on fire. • Considerable fuel spillage when refuelling. • Left rear axle fell off. • Plastic bumper fell off while driving. • Headlights often go out. **2003**—Tire jack collapsed. • Transmission allows vehicle to roll backward when parked. • Inoperative fuel gauge. • Stalling caused by defective fuel pump. • Burnt electrical wires and light sockets. • Excessive driver-side mirror vibration. **2004**—Fire ignited in engine compartment. • Strong fuel odour in the interior. • Stuck accelerator pedal. • Engine surging, sudden acceleration, and hard starts due to defective computer module. • Frequent transmission clutch assembly and flywheel failures. • Windshield wiper motor malfunctions. • Sun visor slips down while driving. • Trunk-lid bolts sheared off. **2005**—Automatic transmission failure. • A faulty master cylinder may be the cause of sudden brake loss. • Steering column froze while vehicle was underway. • Driver's seat is not well anchored; it moves constantly. • To access the accelerator pedal, some drivers have to move their seat uncomfortably close to the steering wheel. • Premature rusting of the door hinges.

Secret Warranties/Internal Bulletins/Service Tips

All models/years: Paint delamination, peeling, or fading. • Plastic wheel nut covers tend to fall off, says TSB #01-03-10-009. **All models: 1985–2000**—Snow may intrude into the rear brake drum assembly and interfere with braking, says TSB #00-05-24-001, April 2000. GM will install upgraded backing plates to prevent snow intrusion from freezing the brake shoes to the drums. Bargain down the installation cost since it is GM's fault in the first place. **1995–98**—Install a drain path in convertibles to prevent water from collecting in the rear footwell area. **1995–2003**—Engine head gasket failures that include overheating, loss of coolant, coolant odour, coolant leaks around the cylinder head, and white smoke from the exhaust. Sometimes the heater won't work, or a film (from the coolant) will be deposited on the inside glass surfaces. If the coolant leaks inside the engine, it can cause severe engine damage from overheating. GM "goodwill" covers head gasket problems for 7 years/160,000 km (100,000 mi.), whichever comes first. Remember, if you have an engine head gasket failure on a GM vehicle, or your engine isn't included in the above-noted programs, don't despair. Simply use the same benchmarks for your own vehicle to threaten small claims action on those grounds. Make sure to cite TSB #98054A, "Campaign: Cylinder Head Gasket Failure, Coolant Leakage," published September 1998. Incidentally, some *Lemon-Aid* readers say inexpensive sealers can plug minor head gasket leaks. • Automatic transmission delay and surging (flare). **1996–2002**—Coolant leakage from the water pump weep hole will be plugged by installing a free coolant collector, says TSB #01-06-02-012. **1997–2004**—A clunk noise from the front of the vehicle when turning may be fixed by simply lubricating the intermediate shaft, says TSB #01-02-32-001G. **1998**—A delayed, slow, or non-existent 2–3 upshift may require a new transmission case cover or assembly. • A 2.2L cold-engine hesitation, sag, or stall may be corrected by recalibrating the power control module (PCM). **1998–2004**—TSB #03-08-67-009A says a binding sunroof likely needs a new sunroof motor. **1999–2000**—No Third and Fourth gear may require a new direct clutch piston assembly. **1999–2002**—Problems opening the fuel-filler door can be fixed by installing a free fuel-filler pocket, says TSB #01-08-65-001. **2000–02**—Harsh transmission shifts accompanied by the Service Engine Soon warning light are caused by a short in the input speed sensor wiring, says TSB #00-06-04037A. • A wet road sizzle noise coming from the rear of the vehicle requires the installation of wheelhouse liners, says TSB #01-08-58-005. • Inaccurate fuel gauge readings can be corrected for free by installing a new fuel-tank sender sensor kit under Customer Satisfaction Campaign #00101. **2000–03**—Troubleshooting engine problems. **2000–05**—A damp trunk carpet means you may have to replace the pressure relief valve. **2001–02**—If the vehicle fails to crank or start, the battery cable connection may be at fault. **2001–05**—TSB #01-07-30-030A says there are four likely causes for harsh 1–2 upshifts. None of them are the owner's fault. **2002**—ABS light comes on when transmission is placed in Second or Fourth gear. • 4-speed automatic transmission fluid leakage. • Faulty automatic transmission converter pump. • Customer Satisfaction Campaign inspection for transaxle converter bearing failure is detailed in TSB #01031. • Inaccurate fuel gauge readings. **2002–04**—A slipping automatic transmission may need a new driven sprocket support assembly, says TSB #03-07-30-012A. • Stuck in Second or slipping in Fourth gear: Owner should repair conduit, splice/reposition conduit, or inspect/reinstall evaporation emission vent solenoid or replace, if necessary, per TSB #03-07-30-036. • Power steering may cut out in cold weather. **2002–05**—A suspension rattle, creak, or pop when turning could mean that the two front stabilizer bar brackets need replacing (TSB #02-03-08-008B). Dealers and GM will usually absorb half the repair cost up to 5 years/80,000 km. **2003**—Troubleshooting erratic shifting:

A/T—SHIFT FLARE/SES LAMP ON/DTC'S SET

BULLETIN NO.: 03-07-30-021   **DATE: MAY 2003**

NEUTRAL FLARE AND/OR RPM FLARE WHILE IN DRIVE, NO 1–2 UPSHIFT, SERVICE ENGINE SOON (SES) LIGHT ILLUMINATED, DIAGNOSTIC TROUBLE CODES (DTCS) P1810, DTC P1815 SET (REPLACE TRANSMISSION FLUID PRESSURE (TFP) MANUAL VALVE POSITION SWITCH)

1995–2003 Chevrolet Cavalier; 1997–2003 Chevrolet Malibu; 1999–2003 Oldsmobile Alero; 1995–2003 Pontiac Sunfire; 1998–2003 Pontiac Grand Am with 4T40E Transmission (RPO MN4) or 4T45E Transmission (RPO MN5)

SYMPTOMS: Some customers may comment on a neutral flare and/or rpm increase while in Drive or no 1–2 upshift and/or the Service Engine Soon (SES) telltale may be illuminated. On 1995–2002 model vehicles, the Powertrain Control Module (PCM) may set a DTC P1810 while on 2003 model vehicles, the PCM may set a DTC P1815. The cause may be the transmission fluid pressure (TFP) switch (also known as the pressure switch manifold [PSM]). It will be referred to as the TFP switch in this bulletin.

• Correcting transmissions that won't shift, or shift erratically (replace driven sprocket support assembly). **2003–04**—TSB #03-01-38-012A recommends that the AC system components be repositioned to cure an under-hood rattle or growl. • Troubleshooting AC problems, per TSB #03-01-38-005A. **2004**—Automatic transmission fluid leak caused by faulty reverse servo cover and seal. **2004–05**—Excessive oil consumption is corrected through the replacement of the engine intake manifold gasket or cam cover:

EXCESSIVE OIL CONSUMPTION/BLUE SMOKE ON ACCELERATION

BULLETIN NO.: 05-06-01-003A   DATE: MAY 25, 2005

EXCESSIVE OIL CONSUMPTION, BLUE SMOKE ON ACCELERATION (INSPECT INTAKE MANIFOLD AND/OR CAM COVER, REPLACE IF NECESSARY)

2004 Alero; 2004–05 Cavalier, Classic, Grand Am, Malibu, Saturn L-Series, ION, VUE, Sunfire; 2005 Cobalt and Pursuit (Canada Only)

ATTENTION: This bulletin covers any vehicle with the Ecotec 2.2L L61 engine built during calender year 2004.

CONDITION: Some customers may comment on excessive oil consumption or blue smoke on acceleration. Excessive oil consumption, not due to leaks, is the use of 0.9L (1 qt) or more of engine oil within 3,200 km (2,000 mi).

CAUSE: Incorrect sizing of the PCV orifice and/or misalignment of the oil baffle in the cam cover may allow higher than desired amounts of oil into the combustion chamber.

IMPORTANT: If the following information in this bulletin does not resolve the concern, refer to Oil Consumption Diagnosis in the appropriate Service Information (SI) procedures. Inspect the cam cover for heat stake marks and inspect the intake manifold for PCV orifice size. Replace either, as necessary, based on inspection.

2005—Water leaks onto driver-side floor.

CAVALIER, SUNFIRE PROFILE

	1997	1998	1999	2000	2001	2002	2003	2004	2005
Cost Price ($)									
Cavalier	14,390	14,765	15,365	15,765	14,260	15,100	15,785	16,125	16,230
Z24	19,000	19,295	20,035	20,515	21,165	22,475	21,550	22,125	22,230
Z24 Conv./LS	24,285	25,880	26,450	27,200	—	—	—	—	—
Sunfire GT	21,100	21,150	21,300	21,420	21,940	21,950	20,385	19,445	19,550
Used Values ($)									
Cavalier ▲	1,500	2,000	2,500	3,000	3,500	4,000	5,000	6,500	8,500
Cavalier ▼	1,100	1,700	2,200	2,500	3,000	3,500	4,000	5,500	7,000
Z24 ▲	3,000	4,000	4,500	5,500	6,500	8,000	9,000	11,000	13,000
Z24 ▼	3,500	3,000	4,000	4,500	5,000	7,000	8,000	10,000	11,500
Z24 Conv./LS ▲	4,000	4,500	5,500	6,000	—	—	—	—	—
Z24 Conv./LS ▼	3,500	4,000	5,000	5,500	—	—	—	—	—
Sunfire GT ▲	2,000	2,500	3,000	3,500	4,500	6,000	8,000	9,000	11,000
Sunfire GT ▼	1,700	2,000	2,500	3,000	3,500	5,000	6,500	8,000	9,500

Reliability	2	2	3	3	3	3	3	3	3
Crash Safety (F)									
Cavalier 2d	—	3	3	3	3	3	4	4	4
Cavalier 4d	3	4	4	4	4	4	4	4	4
Side									
Cavalier 2d	—	1	1	1	1	1	1	1	1
Cavalier 4d	—	1	1	1	1	1	1	1	1
Offset	1	1	1	1	1	1	1	1	
Rollover Resistance	—	—	—	—	4	4	4	4	4

Note: NHTSA says the Sunfire's safety ratings should be identical to the Cavalier's scores.

S-SERIES, L-SERIES, ION ★ ★

RATING: *S-series coupe:* Below Average (1998–2002); Not Recommended (1992–97). *L-series:* Below Average (2000–05). *Ion:* Below Average (2003–06). Saturn is a microcosm of all that is wrong with GM. It has lost billions of dollars, and Saturn models are late to market, bland, and inappropriate. Quality control is the pits, especially as it relates to powertrain dependability. Japanese and South Korean competitors have been proven to offer far better quality at a competitive cost. Even GM's less pretentious models, like the Cavalier and Sunfire or the minuscule Metro and Firefly, offer better quality and value for your money. As bizarre as it may seem, the Saturn division has a better reputation than do the cars it sells. **"Real" city/ highway fuel economy:** 9.4/6.2 L/100 km for the SL's 1.9L engine, and 10.2/6.8 L/100 km for the Ion's. Owners report that the automatic transmission burns almost 20 percent more fuel than the above figure indicates. **Maintenance/ Repair costs:** Average; repairs aren't dealer-dependent, unless you're seeking some Saturn "goodwill" refunds or have continuously variable transmission (CVT) glitches. **Parts:** Higher-than-average costs. CVT parts are often back-ordered, and they're hellacious to troubleshoot. **Extended warranty:** Don't go anywhere near a used Saturn unless you're armed to the teeth with a comprehensive extended warranty. **Best alternatives:** The Honda Civic LX, Hyundai Elantra, and Toyota Corolla perform much better and are more reliable. **Online help:** *www.geocities. com/saturn_hate/index.html* (The Saturn Hate Page), *www.geocities.com/lafire000* (Saturn Sucks), *www.koenigland.com/saturn*, and *www.saturnfans.com.*

Strengths and Weaknesses

S-series: This entry-level model is far from high-tech and remained virtually unchanged until it was replaced by the 2003 Ion. The base model provides a comfortable driving position, adequate instrumentation and controls, unobstructed visibility, good braking, dent-resistant body panels, and better-than-average crashworthiness scores. But, balancing these advantages, buyers have to contend with excessive engine noise, limited rear seatroom, glitch-prone anti-lock brakes and traction control, the coupe's third-door window that doesn't roll down, and serious factory-related deficiencies.

L-series: In an attempt to save money by adapting a European car to the American market, Saturn brought out the LS sedan and LW wagon, derivatives of GM's Opel Vectra. Some major differences, however, include a lengthened body, a standard ignition theft-deterrent system, a re-engineered chassis to give a more comfortable ride, and the use of a homegrown 137-hp 2.2L 4-banger constructed with aluminum components (remember the Vega?). Other components lifted directly from the European parts bin are the Opel's 3.0L V6 engine, a manual transmission from Saab, and German-made braking systems.

The more expensive L-series models provide a more comfortable driving position and a roomy interior with a full range of convenience features, instruments, and controls. The 2002 L-series got standard head curtain airbags, ABS brakes, four-wheel disc brakes on all but the base model, and traction control. The V6 powertrain matchup, firm ride, impressive high-speed stability, and impressive braking all point to the L-series' European heritage. Additionally, there's better soundproofing and lots of storage areas, including a large, accessible trunk.

Ion: A larger, more comfortable, and more powerful vehicle than its S-series predecessor, the Ion is powered by a 140-hp 2.2L 4-cylinder engine and gives buyers the choice of either a four-door coupe or sedan. Other features include power steering, a CVT automatic transmission, speed-sensitive windshield wipers, split folding rear seatbacks, and plastic body side panels.

The Ion's deficiencies mirror those of the S-series coupe it replaced and its L-series big brother. The only added wrinkle is the CVT transmission, which, despite an extended warranty following widespread quality complaints, is destined for the trash heap. In the meantime, Ion and Vue SUV owners are likely to face long servicing waits and mind-boggling depreciation.

VEHICLE HISTORY: *Coupe:* **1992**—Returns with upgrades to reduce engine noise and vibration. **1993**—A standard driver-side airbag. **1994**—A recalibrated transmission. **1995**—A standard passenger-side airbag, 15 more horses for the base engine, and minor styling changes. **1996**—An upgraded 4-speed automatic. **1999**—An innovative third half-door on the driver's side. **2000**—Front seats were given more travel. **2003**—Ion replaced the coupe. *L-series:* **2002**—Standard curtain side airbags. **2003**—A restyled front end, and four-wheel disc brakes. **2004**—Standard ABS and traction control; the 5-speed manual transmission is no more. *Ion:* **2003**—Ion arrives with a fuel-efficient continuously variable transmission (CVT), used since the late 1800s in milling machines and lathes, and in widespread use overseas by Japanese and European automakers. After first extending the warranty in 2003, Saturn dropped the CVT in its 2005 models because of quality problems. **2004**—Upgraded interior materials, and a high-performance Red Line model sporting a 205-hp 4-cylinder engine and sundry other performance features. **2005**—CVT transmission dropped and 5-speed automatic is replaced by a 4-speed automatic. Suspension and steering have also been upgraded.

Improved seating for the Ion-1 and Ion-2 versions. **2006**—The Ion-1 sedan is dropped and the Ion-3 gets a 170-hp 4-cylinder engine.

Saturns have exhibited a plethora of serious body and mechanical problems, which GM has masked by generously applying its base warranty to vehicles owned by original buyers. Owners of used Saturns are treated like they're from another planet, however, and frequently complain that they had to pay dearly for GM's powertrain and body mistakes. Servicing quality has been spotty, too, and will likely become more problematic as GM takes the division off life-support in an effort to make it profitable—which to most observers is a lost cause.

The loud, coarse standard single-cam engine gives barely adequate acceleration times with the manual transmission. This time is increased with the 4-speed automatic gearbox, which robs the engine of what little power it produces. Other generic problems affecting all model years are rough running, stalling, hard starting, and very poor gas mileage.

GM has been upfront in admitting its vehicles' failures; for example, it extended its "goodwill" warranty to six years on 1994–96 Saturns that overheat and blow their engine head gaskets. Nevertheless, in some cases the engine repair lasts for only a little while, as other powertrain problems soon appear.

How ironic that a company once ranked number one in dealer service by J.D. Power and Associates in its 2002 Customer Service Index Study can't assume its responsibilities when the original warranty expires.

Technical service bulletins and other owner complaints indicate that a variety of major quality problems are likely to crop up throughout all model years. These include self-destructing engines; chronically malfunctioning automatic transmissions; failure-prone brake, ignition, fuel, and electrical systems (are flickering, dimming lights your cup of tea?); alternator and AC compressor failures; a host of body defects, led by paint delamination, rattles, and wind and water leaks; poorly welded exhaust systems; and failure-prone Firestone tires (mostly the Affinity brand).

Safety Summary

All models/years: Reports of stuck accelerators. • Airbag failed to deploy. • Seat belt failed to restrain driver in collision. • Hard starts, surging and chronic stalling. • Gear lever slips out of gear and is hard to put into Reverse. • Manual transmission jumps out of Third and Fifth gears. • Frequent brake failures. • Brake rotor warpage and frequent pad replacement. • Sudden head gasket failure causes other engine components to self-destruct. • Loss of steering control. • Poor horn and radio performance. *SC1:* **2000–01**—Brake pedal makes a loud popping noise or drops to the floor without warning. *SC2:* **2000–01**—Seat belt tightens on any sudden movement, however slight. • The small, recessed horn buttons make it hard to find and activate the horn without looking down. **2002**—Ineffective, noisy brakes. *SL:* **2000–01**—Steering wheel came apart while driving. *SL1:* **2000–01**—Defrosting system doesn't work properly, causing moisture damage and poor visibility. **2002**—Seat belt suddenly unlatched when vehicle was rear-ended. Engine makes a ticking noise and then suddenly stalls in traffic. • In a rear-ender, seat lever released, causing seatback to suddenly recline. • Unable to shift to a lower gear when going downhill. • Inaccurate fuel gauge. *SL2:* **2000–01**—Sudden acceleration. • Seat belts are hard to engage. • When driving at night, one sees multiple lights when looking through the rear-view mirror at the vehicle in back, as well as the reflection of the defroster lights. • During rainy weather, rear windshield view is distorted or wavy. **2002**—Faulty throttle position sensor (TPS) causes vehicle to maintain speed when braking. *SW2:* **2000–01**—Automatic transmission slippage caused collision. • Film collects on interior of windshield. *L-series:* **2000–01**—Transmission can't be shifted into a Forward gear. • Location of power-seat button allows it to be accidentally activated, causing seat to suddenly recline. • Power door locks short out. **2000–02**—Inoperative rear-door glass confirmed by TSB #02-T27. • Electrical short causes all lights and gauges to suddenly come on. • Seat belt won't lock up at sudden stops. **2002**—Headlights and interior lights go out, flicker, or dim intermittently when foot is taken off accelerator or when clutch or cooling fan is engaged. • Tire rims broke off. • Door handles don't fall back into place after being used. **2003**—Prematurely worn brake pads and rotors. • Headlight dimming and flickering:

> A tractor trailer was passing me on the interstate. Just as his trailer was approximately 2/3 past me, my lights dimmed out on my car by themselves. The driver of the tractor trailer thought I had flashed my headlights at him, to let him know he had cleared my car and was safe to come into my lane, which was not the case. This made the drivers behind me and the tractor trailer in all 3 lanes slam on their brakes. The truck driver almost lost control of his rig trying to keep from hitting me when he realized that he did not have clearance as my lights "suggested" to him that he had.

Ion: **2003**—Transmission gear slippage creates a highway hazard:

> My 2003 Saturn Ion Quad 3's transmission slips constantly. A tech from Spring Hill says this is normal. Trying to turn left in front of oncoming traffic is a nightmare. The rear quarter panel is cracked and being replaced. The rear bumper is being painted because of scratches from the trunk rubbing. The front bumper is being painted because of runs in the paint. None of the body panels seem to match up. They're attempting to fix a popping noise in the front end. They're replacing the [driver-side glass] because it is severely scratched. It sometimes runs rough at first crank.

• Steering knuckle sheared off. • Steering lock-up. • Chronic turn signal failures; turn signal won't work if cigarette lighter is being used. • Key sticks in ignition. • Seat belt anchor bolt broke. • Seat belt retractor fell apart. **2004**—Accelerator pedal fell off. • CVT transmission causes sudden deceleration. • Multiple transmission replacements. • Engine replacement. • Doors don't close fully. • Water leaking into the trunk caused serious electrical shorts (lights, etc.). • Electronic assisted steering almost caused fatalities. • Fuel-filler pipe spits back fuel when refuelling. • Saturn cell phone charger can short circuit lights, etc., until more robust resistors and capacitors are installed. • Firestone tire-tread separation. • Steering failures:

> Steering failure during static and very slow turning exercises. This is a consistent problem with the vehicle. We teach new drivers and re-train elderly drivers and this is a major issue for a training vehicle. The dealer has confirmed the problem. The dealer has no cure. I think a manufacturer has a responsibility to provide a vehicle that can safely be operated upon a roadway regardless of static steering or slow steering.

• Vehicle suddenly went out of control; airbags failed to deploy:

> The vehicle was involved in a front end collision on June 10, 2005. The vehicle moved across the other side of the road and was hit by two other trucks. These were more of a side impact. It was hit head on by a semi truck; the driver was ejected from the vehicle and her husband was killed. [The contact]…has filed a complaint with the manufacturer. Both occupants were wearing their seat belts. [The contact's] daughter flew out from under the seat belt of the vehicle; she was the one driving. They were going the speed limit, and the roadway was wet. On the police report they listed it as hydroplane. None of the air bags deployed. There was no warning light on prior to the crash. The police report stated that she had done nothing wrong.

• Headlights create a shadow on the road, and they flicker or go out. • Headlight glazing. • Constant dash light dimming. • Manual shifter knob falls off:

> I have a 2004 Saturn Ion Red Line with a manual transmission (only transmission offered). I was shifting from First to Second gear, in traffic, and the entire shift knob assembly came off in my hand. The knob fell to the driver's side floor, causing me to look down. I was able to stop the vehicle in time to avoid the car in front of me. The vehicle is then difficult to shift, and the pull up for reverse feature was very difficult. There are a number of complaints on *www.saturnfans.com*. The "fix" is to epoxy the knob back onto the shifter bar as it is a press fit design (no mechanical lock or fasteners).

• Brake failures. • Unsafe safety belts:

> The consumer experienced a problem with the rear driver side seat belt. While driving down the road the child in the rear left seat complained that the seat belt harnessing the child was too tight around his/her neck. The driver had to call 911 to have the seat belt cut away from the child's neck and throat.

2005—Electrical fire ignited near the battery. • Transmission sticks in gear or suddenly pops out of gear. • Complete loss of braking:

I was driving my 2005 Saturn Ion-2 and the brakes totally failed when I depressed the clutch on my 5 speed transmission. After taking it in for service the mechanic told me that the slave cylinder was leaking and allowed air into the brake system because the brakes and clutch have a shared hydraulic fluid reservoir. I couldn't downshift because the clutch failed and I couldn't brake because the brakes failed. The warning system failed because there was still some fluid in the shared reservoir. The warning light goes on when the system is out of fluid not when it is running low. Scary stuff.... I could have been killed or killed others. Lucky for me I was not going highway speeds and/or on a busy street. I was able to use the emergency brake to stop.

• Defective rear brake rotors and drums (drums will warp if car isn't driven for several weeks). • Shifter knob fell off; shifter shaft replaced. • Dash gauges fail suddenly. • Door panels crack. • Driver's window fell into the door. • Water leaks into headlights.

Secret Warranties/Internal Bulletins/Service Tips

All models/years: Reprogramming of the power control module (PCM) and engine control module (ECM) now have equal coverage under the emission warranty up to 8 years/130,000 km (80,000 mi.), per TSB #04-1-08, published June 2004. **All models: 1991–2001**—GM admits in TSB #01-T-07 that a cracked engine-coolant temperature sensor may be the culprit behind hard starts, poor engine performance, engine overheating, and leaking or low coolant. **1996–2001**—Water leaks into headliner are likely caused by a faulty sunroof or plugged drain hole grommets. **1996–2004**—A rotten-egg odour coming from the exhaust is likely the result of a malfunctioning catalytic converter, which you can have replaced free of charge under GM's emissions warranty. **1998**—Dozens of bulletins target a plethora of rattles, whistles, pops, clicks, and knocking and grinding noises. • Sunroof, footwell, and trunk water leaks are also common problems, addressed in a variety of service bulletins. • Excessive vehicle vibration. • Loss of AC vent airflow. • Reducing AC odours. • Power steering pump drive shaft seal leak. • Intermittent no-start. • Transaxle whine in Second gear. • Rear brake noise and pulsation countermeasures. **1999**—Harsh shifting. • Steering-column popping. • Rattle, pop, or clicking noise from front of vehicle. • AC noise (hissing). • Clunking noise in front side door when windows are operated. • Troubleshooting chronic short circuits. • Water leak onto headliner and/or left footwell area and rear luggage compartment. • Excessive vibration at cruising speed. **1999–2002**—GM says in TSB #01-T-35 that it may replace the windshield washer pump seal and affected nozzle if the spray pattern is unacceptable. **2000**—In a March 2000 Customer Satisfaction Campaign letter (No. 00-C-09) sent to dealers, GM admits that the Saturn 2.2L 4-cylinder engines "were produced with internal engine components that may fail prematurely. The most likely symptom you may experience is an engine miss accompanied by an engine noise." GM says it will replace the engine at no charge without mileage or time limitations, in addition to providing a loaner vehicle or paying rental costs. **2000–01**—Delayed, harsh engagement into Reverse or Drive, erratic shifting between First and Second gear, or no Second or Third gears. • AC odours on start-up. • Steering-wheel shake or vibration at highway speeds. • Inoperative power windows and sunroof. **2000–02**—If the engine produces a whistling noise, GM suggests you replace the engine intake manifold gasket in TSB #02-T-22. Of course, this should be a free repair, under #J025-1. • GM has a quick fix for headliner sagging at rear of sunroof opening. • Water leaks into the interior will be fixed under warranty, says TSB #00-T-41A. **2002**—Transmission fluid leakage is likely from a faulty transaxle temperature sensor. *L-series, Ion:* **2003–04**—Engine coolant leakage into oil:

LOSS OF COOLANT/NO EXTERNAL LEAKS EVIDENT

BULLETIN NO.: 03-06-123-001   DATE: NOVEMBER 2003

SLIGHT LOSS OF COOLANT OR LOW COOLANT LIGHT COMING ON WITH NO SIGNS OF EXTERNAL LEAKS (PERFORM SERVICE PROCEDURE IN THIS BULLETIN)

2003–04 Saturn VUE and ION; 2004 L300 Vehicles with 2.2L Engine (VINs D, F–RPO L61)

Some customers may comment that the low coolant light is coming on and/or the coolant level is low with no external leaks visible. Low coolant may be accompanied by one of the following when the engine is cold:

• Engine difficult to start; misfiring; or white smoke, or coolant odour from the tailpipe.

This condition may be caused by porosity in the aluminum of the cylinder head casting and require a new cylinder head or cylinder block.

L-series: **2000–01**—No Third and Fourth gear (replace direct clutch piston assembly). • Steering-wheel shake or vibration at highway speeds. • Front doors re-lock after being unlocked with key. • Rattle from behind the right-hand side of the instrument panel. • Wind whistle from the front-door glass area and from the outside rear-view mirror. • Inoperative rear-door glass. **2000–02**—A free revised intake manifold gasket will cure engine whistle. • Troubleshooting the most common water leaks into the interior. • Headliner sagging. • Misaligned rear bumper. **2000–03**—Poor AC automatic temperature control performance. **2000–04**—Blue smoke at a V6 engine's start-up can mean you need to replace the engine valve guides or cylinder head, per TSB #04-06-01-010. Obviously, this bulletin and implied warranty statutes mean GM has to assume the cost of this repair up to 7 years/160,000 km. • A defective or contaminated fuel sender is the likely cause of inaccurate fuel readings. (see TSB #03-08-49-022). **2002**—Inadequate horn performance. *Ion:* **2003–04**—Intermittent no-starts may be caused by solidified grease in the ignition switch; a new switch must be installed at Saturn's expense (after all, it's their grease). • All Saturn Ion and Vue vehicles produced since the summer of 2002 and equipped with a continuously variable transmission (CVT) have extended warranty coverage on the transmission up to 5 years/120,000 km (75,000 mi.). • Low-speed grinding noise or hesitation requires the installation of a new transaxle control module (TCM) or its recalibration, says TSB #03-07-30-051. • Automatic transmission delay and surging requires the replacement of the control-valve body and recalibration of the ECM (TSB #03-07-30-052). • Clutch chatters and won't release. • No movement in Drive may require a new VT25E transaxle assembly, per TSB #04-07-30-024. • If you're lucky, the TCM may only need to be reprogrammed to cure upshift delays, harsh downshifts, or erratic gear engagement. • Coolant leak from water-pump plug; upgraded water pump. • Fuel-system buzzing or growling from rear of vehicle. • A squeak, rattle, pop, or clunk from the front of vehicle can be silenced by replacing the front stabilizer shaft insulators, says TSB #04-03-08-003A. • Water leaks into the interior. • Rear-door cracking. • Noisy sunroof. • Faulty blower motor. **2003–06**—Premature or irregular tire wear; Saturn will correct the problem and install new tires free of charge:

ALIGNMENT—PREMATURE/IRREGULAR TIRE WEAR

BULLETIN NO.: 05-03-07-001B   **DATE: JULY 27, 2005**

PREMATURE AND/OR IRREGULAR TIRE WEAR (SET FRONT SUM TOE AND ROTATE TIRES AS NECESSARY)

2003–06 Saturn ION Vehicles

CONDITION: Some customers may comment on premature and/or irregular tire wear on the inside edge of the tire.

CAUSE: This condition may be caused by a negative front total toe (sum toe) that is outside of wheel alignment specifications.

CORRECTION: Verify the concern and adjust the front total toe as necessary to the new preferred setting of (+ 0320°+/- 0.20°) for tire wear issues. Refer to the service procedure in this bulletin.

CLAIM INFORMATION: Canadian Retailers: To receive credit for this repair during the warranty coverage period, submit a claim through the normal procedures for E2000 (Toe, Front—Adjust) or E2020 (Wheel Alignment—Check and/or Adjust).

NOTE: Refer to Home Office Letter 1997-070 for guidelines on usage of E2000 and E2020. If the tire replacement is necessary due to the inside edge of the tire being worn to the wear indicators, refer to bulletin 01-03-10-003B for tire handling procedures.

2003–07—Saturn will replace the instrument-panel cluster lens if it is cloudy, scratched, cracked, or broken. • Remedy for incomplete rear window defogging. • Your key ring can kill you (see first bulletin on following page). **2004**—Loss of engine coolant (see bulletin on previous page). **2004–05**—Poor engine performance (see second bulletin on following page).

ACCIDENTAL ENGINE SHUT-OFF

BULLETIN NO.: 05-02-35-007A　　　　　　　　　　　　　　**DATE: OCTOBER 25, 2006**

INADVERTENT TURNING OF KEY CYLINDER, LOSS OF ELECTRICAL SYSTEM AND NO DTCS

2003–07 Saturn ION; 2005–06 Pontiac Pursuit (Canada Only); 2005–07 Chevrolet Cobalt; 2006–07 Chevrolet HHR and Pontiac Solstice; 2007 Pontiac G5 and Saturn Sky

There is potential for the driver to inadvertently turn off the ignition due to low ignition key cylinder torque/effort. The concern is more likely to occur if the driver is short and has a large and/or heavy key chain. In these cases, this condition was documented and the driver's knee would contact the key chain while the vehicle was turning and the steering column was adjusted all the way down. This is more likely to happen to a person who is short, as they will have the seat positioned closer to the steering column. In cases that fit this profile, question the customer thoroughly to determine if this may be the cause. The customer should be advised of this potential and should take steps to prevent it such as removing unessential items from their key chain.

Engineering has come up with an insert for the key ring so that it goes from a "slot" design to a hole design. As a result, the key ring cannot move up and down in the slot any longer it can only rotate on the hole. In addition, the previous key ring has been replaced with a smaller, 13 mm (0.5 in) design. This will result in the keys not hanging as low as in the past.

Oh, I get it... It's the customer's fault.

LOW ENGINE POWER/HESITATION/STUMBLE

BULLETIN NO.: 05-06-02-003　　　　　　　　　　　　　　**DATE: MARCH 21, 2005**

ENGINE LACKS POWER, HESITATES, AND/OR STUMBLES ON HARD ACCELERATION AND/OR LOSES SOME POWER AFTER HIGH RPM CRUISING IN HIGH TEMPERATURES (INSPECT COOLANT CHARGE PUMP ELECTRICAL CONNECTOR TERMINAL LOCATION, ADJUST IF NEEDED)

2004–05 Saturn ION Red Line Vehicles with the 2.0L Engine

CONDITION: Some customers may comment that the engine lacks power, hesitates, and/or stumbles on hard acceleration and/or loses some power after extended high speed (high revolutions per minute [RPM]) cruising in high ambient temperatures.

CAUSE: The condition may be caused by a wiring variation in the coolant charge pump wire connector that may reduce coolant flow from the pump.

CORRECTION: Inspect the coolant pump/air cooler charger electrical connector for correct wire terminal location, and adjust if necessary.

• Free engine-position sensor housing seal replacement:

CPS HOUSING SEAL REPLACEMENT (CANADA)

05522 CAMSHAFT POSITION SENSOR HOUSING SEAL REPLACEMENT (CANADA)
2004–05 ION Red Line Vehicles with Supercharged 2.0L 4-Cylinder Engines

CONDITION: Saturn has learned that certain 2004 and 2005 model year Saturn ION Red Line vehicles equipped with supercharged 2.0L 4-cylinder (LSJ) engines have a condition where the camshaft position sensor housing seal may fail prematurely, resulting in an engine oil leak. Engine damage could occur if the oil level is significantly low.
CORRECTION: To correct this condition, Saturn retailers will install a new camshaft position sensor housing seal that has been re-designed to improve seal life.

S-SERIES, L-SERIES, ION PROFILE

	1997	1998	1999	2000	2001	2002	2003	2004	2005
Cost Price ($)									
SL	13,948	14,188	13,488	13,588	14,358	14,245	—	—	—
SC	16,028	16,418	16,618	16,743	16,763	16,765	—	—	—
LS/L100	—	—	—	19,255	20,065	21,125	—	—	—
LW/LW200	—	—	—	24,400	25,235	23,325	25,355	—	—
L300	—	—	—	—	—	—	—	23,030	24,995
Ion	—	—	—	—	—	—	15,495	14,775	14,935
Used Values ($)									
SL ▲	1,200	2,000	2,500	3,000	4,000	5,000	—	—	—
SL ▼	1,000	1,500	2,000	2,500	3,500	4,000	—	—	—
SC ▲	2,000	2,500	3,000	3,500	4,500	6,000	—	—	—
SC ▼	1,500	2,000	2,500	3,000	4,000	5,000	—	—	—
LS/L100 ▲	—	—	—	4,500	5,500	7,000	—	—	—
LS/L100 ▼	—	—	—	4,000	5,000	6,000	—	—	—
LW/LW200 ▲	—	—	—	5,000	6,000	8,000	9,500	—	—
LW/LW200 ▼	—	—	—	4,000	5,000	7,000	8,500	—	—
L300 ▲	—	—	—	—	—	—	—	13,500	16,000
L300 ▼	—	—	—	—	—	—	—	12,500	14,500
Ion ▲	—	—	—	—	—	—	6,500	7,500	9,000
Ion ▼	—	—	—	—	—	—	5,500	6,500	8,000
Reliability	1	1	1	1	2	2	2	2	2
Crash Safety (F)	4	5	5	—					
L-series	—	—	—	—	4	5	4	4	4
Ion	—	—	—	—	—	—	5	5	5
Side	3	3	3	—	—	—	—	—	—
L-series	—	—	—	—	2	3	3	3	3
Ion	—	—	—	—	—	—	3	3	3

All ratings on a numbered scale where 5 is good and 1 is bad. See pages 130–132 for a more detailed description.

Side (IIHS)									
L-series	—	—	—	—	1	1	1	1	1
Ion	—	—	—	—	—	—	1	1	1
Offset	3	3	3	—	—	—	—	—	—
L-series	—	—	—	3	3	3	3	3	3
Ion	—	—	—	—	—	—	—	3	3
Head Restraints	1	1	1	1	1	1	—	—	—
L-series	—	—	—	—	1	1	1	1	1
Ion	—	—	—	—	—	—	1	1	2
Rollover Resistance	—	—	—	—	4	4	4	4	4

Honda

CIVIC, DEL SOL, INSIGHT, CIVIC HYBRID ★ ★ ★ ★ ★ / ★

The Honda Civic Si.

RATING: *Civic, del Sol:* Recommended (1992–2006); Above Average (1972–91). If you want to get a reliable, fuel-frugal buy at a cheap price, the 1992–96 models are your best bet for their lighter weight and tighter handling. Any CRX represents a good buy, as well. Earlier Civics have been downgraded because of the increasing number of safety- and performance-related defects reported by owners as these vehicles put on the years. Defects include airbags that fail to deploy, or deploy with such force that they cause severe injuries; ABS brake failures, and constant rotor and pad maintenance; sudden acceleration; original-equipment tire failures; and considerable instability on wet roads. *Insight:* Not Recommended (2001–06); 2006 was its last model year. *Civic Hybrid:* Not Recommended (2003–06). **"Real" city/highway fuel economy:** *Civic:* 7.5/5.7 L/100 km with a manual transmission or 8.0/5.7 L/100 km when equipped with an automatic. Manuals hit these figures consistently, while Civics with automatics burn about 10 percent more gas than the figures show. *High-performance SiR versions:* 9.2/7.0 L/100 km. *Hybrids:* These models get nowhere near their estimated 4.9/4.6 L/100 km fuel consumption; expect to burn as much as 30–40 percent more. **Maintenance/Repair costs:** Average. Independent garages can carry out repairs, but the 16-valve engine's complexity means that more expensive dealer servicing may be unavoidable. Owners should check the engine-timing belt every 3 years/60,000 km and replace it every 100,000 km ($300). **Parts:** Parts are a bit more expensive than most other cars in this class; airbag control modules and body panels may be back-ordered for weeks. **Extended warranty:** A waste of money. **Best alternatives:** GM Firefly or Metro; Hyundai Accent or Elantra; Mazda Protegé; Nissan Sentra; Suzuki Aerio, Esteem, or Swift; and Toyota Echo or Corolla. The CRX's '93 del Sol replacement was a cheapened spin-off that carried over the CRX's faults without its high-performance thrills. Si models are Honda's factory hot rods (the Acura 1.6 EL is an Si clone), which provide lots of high-performance thrills without the bills. Despite four-wheel disc brakes, the Si's mediocre braking and its lack of low-end torque are the car's main performance flaws. **Online help:** *www.cartrackers. com/Forums/live/Honda*, *www.carsurvey.org/model_Honda_Civic.html*, and *www. epinions.com/auto_Make-Honda*.

Strengths and Weaknesses

Civics have distinguished themselves by providing sports-car acceleration and handling with excellent fuel economy and quality control that is far better than what American, European, and most other Asian automakers can deliver. Other advantages: a roomy, practical trunk; a smooth-shifting automatic transmission; a comfortable ride; good front and rear visibility; high-quality construction; bullet-proof reliability; and simple, inexpensive maintenance. Also, these cars can be easily and inexpensively customized for better driving performance, or to gain a racier allure.

Some Civic disadvantages: The Si's suspension may be too firm for some, and its spoiler may block rear visibility. It's hard to modulate the throttle without having the car surge or lurch. The base engine loses its pep when the Overdrive gear on the automatic transmission engages in city driving, and the VTEC variant is noisy. Seats lack sufficient padding, rear access is difficult, rear seatroom is limited to two adults, there's lots of engine and road noise, and an unusually large number of safety-related complaints include airbag malfunctions, sudden acceleration, and complete brake failure.

The 1984–95 Civics suffered from failing camshafts, crankshafts, and head gaskets, as well as from prematurely worn piston rings.

What are minor body faults with recent models turn into major rust problems with older Civics, where simple surface rust rapidly turns into perforations. The underbody is also prone to corrosion, which leads to severe structural damage that compromises safety. The fuel tank, front suspension, and steering components, along with body attachment points, should be examined carefully in any Civic more than a decade old.

The 1996 redesign improved overall reliability and handling and increased interior room, but engine head gasket failures on non-VTEC engines continued to be a problem through the 2000 model year.

The 2001–04 models move from the subcompact to the compact class and increase interior volume while also providing seats that are wider and higher. They are also marginally better performers, from a power and handling standpoint. Although steering feedback is a bit vague and over-assisted, the softly sprung suspension still gives the base car a floating feel, and there's excessive body lean when cornering under speed (EX and Si models have a firmer stance). Drivers will find that parking is more of a chore because the car's increased size makes it difficult to see its rear corners.

Quality control still needs improvement. Heading the list of owner complaints are engine crankshaft failures; transmission malfunctions; weak front springs and shocks; and early strut failure, resulting in degraded handling. Owners also complain of frequent brake repairs (rotor warpage and pad replacement); AC failures; suspension knocks and squeaks; a subpar stereo system; erratic fuel gauge readings; delaminated paint; chronic water leaks; trunk hinges that steal storage room and damage cargo; a constantly lit Check Engine light; a faulty engine computer module and oxygen sensor; early replacement of the crankshaft pulley and timing belt; and fuel- and electrical system failures.

Other common problems include windshield air leaks and noise; warped windshield mouldings; hard-to-access horn buttons; windows that fall off their tracks; side mirrors that vibrate excessively; headlights that can't be focused properly and are prone to water leaks; gas-tank fumes that leak into the interior; and premature rusting, uneven paint application, chalky spots, and paint delamination. Here's what this owner of a 2001 Civic discovered:

> Paint is developing crow's feet in four separate places...body shop said it was due to bird droppings or sap. I believe this to be impossible and believe it to be a defect in the paint. Blemishes and loss of gloss continue to develop in the paint.

Insight and Civic Hybrid

Stay away from used hybrid vehicles regardless of whether they're made by Ford, GM, Honda, or Toyota. Build quality is inconsistent, the electrical and braking systems can be quite hazardous, maintenance is highly dealer-dependent, depreciation is a bit faster than with comparable makes, and fuel economy is illusory. Says this owner of a 2003 Honda Hybrid:

> The Hybrid is supposed to get 48 mpg/city [4.9 L/100 km] and 47 mpg/highway [5.0 L/100 km]. Even the fine print states that the actual mileage should range between 40–56 [5.9–4.2] in the city and 39–55 [6.0–4.3] on the highway.

I have been tracking/documenting my actual mpg. My mpg has never exceeded 35 [6.7 L/100 km]. Since fuel economy is the primary reason for purchasing the Hybrid, potential customers should be extremely skeptical of the claims.

Honda was the first automaker to introduce gas-electric hybrid technology to North American consumers when it launched the Honda Insight in the States in December 1999, followed by the Civic Hybrid in March 2002. Neither vehicle has sold as well as the Toyota Prius.

The Insight, a two-passenger hatchback coupe, uses a small electric motor to assist the 3-cylinder gasoline engine during hard acceleration. The engine recharges the battery pack when coasting or braking and returns to battery power when the car is stopped. The car has very little interior room and poor rear visibility, is slow to accelerate, has a harsh ride and little soundproofing, and is tossed about by moderate crosswinds. Toyota's Prius seats four and uses a more versatile hybrid system, wherein the electric motor is dominant and gasoline and electric power vary, depending upon driving conditions.

The Civic Hybrid looks and feels just like a regular Civic, both inside and out. It carries a 3-year/60,000 km base warranty, a 5-year/100,000 km powertrain warranty, an 8-year/160,000 km battery pack warranty, and emissions-related equipment that's covered by a more extensive warranty. But it comes in second to the Toyota Prius, a much more refined hybrid. Good alternatives are a Honda Civic HX or base Toyota Echo—two cars that sell for about half the price, get great gas mileage, and don't depreciate as much. Some of the Civic Hybrid's advantages are that it does offer some fuel savings, it's smooth-shifting, it gives a comfortable ride, and it provides good front and rear visibility.

On the other hand, the Hybrid's fuel economy may fall short by 25 to 45 percent, says *Consumer Reports*; cold weather performance isn't as fuel-efficient as advertised; and the AC increases gas consumption and shuts off at stoplights, encouraging drivers to sneak up on lights. *Car and Driver* magazine concluded in its September 2004 issue that one would have to drive a Toyota or Honda hybrid 265,500 km (165,000 mi.) to amortize its higher costs. Furthermore, the car's unique dual powerplants can make for risky driving, as this Hybrid owner warns:

> [With a] 2003 Honda Civic Hybrid on a snowy road, coming over a small rise while going around a moderate curve under 40 mph [64 km/h], the battery charging function, activated by driver taking foot off the gas before cresting the hill, produced progressively stronger engine braking effect on the front wheels, equivalent to an unwanted downshift and causing fishtailing and poor response to corrective steering, so that the car slid across the road and into a snow bank and concrete abutment, causing $6,000 (US) in damage. If there had been oncoming traffic, there could have been serious injuries or fatalities.

Repairs and servicing are very complicated to perform; highway rescuers are wary of cutting through the 500-volt electrical system to save occupants; and there's no long-term reliability data. Honda Hybrid performance and overall quality issues include rough shifting; a rotten-egg smell that intrudes into the cabin; premature brake and rear strut wear; a constantly lit Airbag light; poor-quality radio speakers; a rear bumper cover that may fall off, be misaligned, or come loose; and chipped paint.

VEHICLE HISTORY: **1992**—A driver-side airbag, a base 102-hp 1.5L 4-cylinder, plus a frugal CX and VX with 70- and 92-hp 4-cylinder engines, and a sporty Si with ABS. **1994**—A standard passenger-side airbag. **1996**—ABS for EX sedans, upgraded engines, a longer body with better soundproofing, and split folding rear seatbacks. **1999**—The Si is upgraded with new front and rear styling. **2001**—More interior room, additional horsepower, and fresh styling; no more hatchback; Insight hybrid is launched in Canada a year after its American debut. **2002**—Arrival of the 160-hp SiR sporty hatchback, improved fit and finish, a firmer suspension, and a rear stabilizer bar (except on the base model). Front suspension uses MacPherson struts, which increases interior space while watering down the car's sporty performance. Insight given a continuously variable transmission (CVT). **2003**—New gauges, a CD player for the HX, and the arrival of the Civic Hybrid. **2004**—Revised styling and upgraded features, such as larger tires. **2006**—Redesigned with an emphasis on new styling, new safety equipment, and more power. The sedan is larger outside and somewhat smaller inside; the coupe is a bit smaller overall. Side curtain airbags and ABS are standard features.

Safety Summary

All models: 1995–2005—Spoiler and head restraint restricts rear visibility, and large rear-view mirror restricts forward visibility for tall drivers. • Numerous safety defects, including sudden acceleration, engine and transmission malfunctions, and airbags that fail to deploy, deploy inadvertently, or deploy with such force they cause severe injuries:

> My 2002 Honda Civic EX hit another vehicle squarely in the rear end while traveling approximately 15 mph [24 km/h]. Neither of the front airbags deployed! The collision repair centre could find nothing wrong with my airbags. The tow truck operator and the collision repair centre told me that there was some sort of alert out for 2001 and 2002 Honda Civics where the airbags didn't deploy after a front-end collision.

• Ball joints on these vehicles don't have a castellated nut to secure the ball in position; the nut can back off, and the ball pulls out of the steering arm. • Other safety-related complaints: dangerous instability on wet roads; sudden acceleration or stalling; faulty cruise control; ABS brake failures, and constant rotor and pad replacement; defective automatic transmissions; transmission may suddenly jump into Reverse; surging when brakes are applied; vehicle may roll away when parked on an incline; original-equipment tire failures; hood and trunk lids that come crashing down; inoperative door locks; cracked windshields; and headlights and interior lights that suddenly go out. **2000**—Accelerator pedal sticks; cables mounted too tight. • Accelerator cable got hung up in the cruise control, causing the vehicle to suddenly accelerate. • While driving, vehicle suddenly accelerated because of the throttle sticking open, and brakes couldn't stop the car. • Car suddenly accelerated when passing another vehicle. • Gas pedal keeps sticking while driving at a low speed. • Transmission popped out of gear, and brake pedal went right to the floor without any braking effect. • Brakes locked up and vehicle pulled to the left when coming to an emergency stop. • Sudden steering loss while driving. • Excessive vibration because of engine main bearing failure. • Transmission sometimes fails to change gear. • Vehicle suddenly went into Reverse even though shift lever was put into Drive. • While stopped at a light on a hill, vehicle suddenly shifted into Reverse. • Another driver had the same thing happen, except this time the transmission shifted into Neutral. • Transmission was stuck in Reverse. • Faulty power door lock makes it impossible to open door from the inside or outside. • Tail lights don't work when the headlights and dash lights are on. • Rear-view mirror is poorly located and is non-adjustable, creating a large forward blind spot for tall drivers. • Exterior rear-view mirror becomes loose, despite dealer efforts to tighten it. **2001**—Car caught on fire near where the oxygen sensor wires are located. • Child became entangled in rear-seat shoulder belt and had to be cut free. • Car hesitates or stalls when decelerating. • Vehicle surged forward when put into Reverse and engaged Reverse when put into Drive. • Transmission may suddenly pop out of Second gear while underway, or refuse to shift into Third or Fourth gear. • Sudden brake failure (master cylinder replaced). • When brakes are applied first thing in the morning, they don't "grab," resulting in extended stopping distances. • Leaking front strut causes poor handling and front-end noise. • Incorrect fuel gauge and speedometer readings. • Airbag warning light is constantly lit (heating coil or core is suspected). • Loose door latches. • Interior lights dim when AC is engaged. • Water leaks into trunk through tail lights or onto driver-side carpet through door or firewall, or wets front passenger-side carpet (AC condensate suspected). **2002**—Vehicle downshifts on its own. • Sudden failure of the front tie-rod. • Complete loss of steering. • Seat belt doesn't fully retract. • Windshield cracked for no apparent reason. **2003**—Braking can cause the car to accelerate. • Vehicle suddenly accelerated with complete brake loss. • Sudden steering lock-up. • Transmission jumps into Neutral; multiple transmission failures. • Power-window failure. • Faulty Firestone tires. • Loose driver's seat. • Seat belts ratchet up uncomfortably. • The head-high interior support handle may injure the driver in a collision. **2004**—Stuck accelerator pedal. • Sudden, unintended acceleration, loss of brakes; hit a brick wall head-on, and front airbags didn't go off. • Problems with the main rear crankshaft seal. • Excessive steering-wheel vibration/shimmy and vehicle pulling to one side blamed on tires and bad brake rotors. • Drivetrain bucks and jolts when descending a hill. • Loose tie-rod bolts. • Premature leakage, failure of the front struts. • Sudden front wheel bearing failure. • Weak trunk springs allowed lid to drop on owner's fingers. • Dunlop original-equipment tire's (SP20FE P185/70R14) side wall blew; these tires are also frequently blamed for causing excessive vibration/shimmy. • Weak seatbacks collapse when the vehicle is rear-ended at moderate speeds. • Rear seat belt unlatched on its own. • Defective door lock actuators. • Driver-side quarter window shatters from freezing temperatures. • Head restraints restrict driver's rearward visibility.

2005—Fire ignited in the seat belt wiring under the passenger seat. • Sudden front wheel lock-up:

> Our new 2005 Honda Civic had both front wheels lock while my wife was going to work, driving down the freeway in Fort Worth TX. The car was totalled, crashing into a guard rail, blowing the air bags, spinning around, starting a fire at the left front wheel and spreading to my wife's coat as she was getting out.

• Brake and accelerator pedals mounted too close together. *Insight:* **2001**—Random events of power loss cause significant reduction of engine power when it is most needed. • CVT transmission failure. • Steering becomes abnormally unstable when vehicle is driven above 50 km/h over uneven or grooved roadways. • Vehicle is prone to hydroplaning on wet roads. • Tire-tread separation. *Civic Hybrid:* **2003**—Vehicle lost all forward power while cruising on the highway. • Chronic stalling. • Excessive brake vibration; vigorous brake pumping needed to get adequate braking. • Hazardous braking system. • Seat belt locks up. • In cold weather, power windows won't roll back up until vehicle warms up. • Prematurely worn shock absorbers. • Driver seat's design can cause serious back pain. • Electromagnetic field may be a health hazard:

> With the use of a gaussmeter, an instrument used to measure electro magnetic fields, the consumer found that vehicle had a high electromagnetic field. The highest level occurred when the engine draws power from the battery via the integrated motor assist or when the battery was charging.

2004—Airbag suddenly deployed for no reason:

> The airbag deployed while driving at about 5–7 mph [8–11 km/h]. Consumer was attempting to park the vehicle and had not hit anything, no curve or debris in the road or no potholes. Consumer went to turn into the parking space and the air bags deployed and the consumer crashed into a wall. Driver sustained burns to the arm from the force of the air bag and was treated by the emergency crew on site of the accident. The vehicle sustained $10,000.00 worth of damage.

• Trunk caught fire while vehicle was parked. • Sudden, unintended acceleration when foot was taken off of the accelerator pedal, or when braking:

> I was driving up the CA I 5, stopped over and pulled in, in front of a 7/11 and the car slowed down and I pulled up to the cement stop, with foot on brake. All of a sudden the car lurched at a high speed three times, and I was trying to brake it to make it quit and it wouldn't quit or brake. My car bashed in the window of the 7/11 and my foot was not on the gas...it was a horrible experience. However, Honda dealer is saying they cannot find anything wrong with it. I was just on the forum and there are lurching problems. I am sick over this whole thing.

• Front wheels locked up when brakes were tapped lightly. • Excessive vibration caused by prematurely worn brakes. • Vehicle wanders all over the road:

> Civic drifts to the side while driving. All of the uneven, worn out tires were replaced as well as the rims. Even though the tires and rims were replaced, it still did not correct the problem.

Secret Warranties/Internal Bulletins/Service Tips

All models/years: Most Honda TSBs allow for special warranty consideration on a "goodwill" basis, even after the warranty has expired or the car has changed hands. Referring to the "goodwill" euphemism will increase your chances of getting some kind of refund for repairs that are obviously related to a factory defect. • Seat belts that are slow to retract will be replaced for free under Honda's seat belt lifetime warranty, says TSB #03-062, issued September 16, 2003. **All models: 1988–2000**—A rear suspension clunk can be silenced by replacing the rear trailing arm bushing. **1996–98**—A poorly performing AC may need a new condenser fan motor and shroud. **1996–2000**—Poor AC performance. • Harsh shifts. **1996–2001**—Oil pressure switch Product Update Campaign (secret warranty) is another free fix, if the dealer is on your side. **1998–2004**—Deformed windshield moulding. **2000**—Steering pull or drifting. • Whistling or howling noise coming from the top middle of the windshield at highway speeds. • Moonroof seal sticks up or leaks. • Key is difficult to remove from the ignition switch; rear-door lock tab is hard to open. **2001**—Delayed upshift after a cold start. • Stiff manual transmission shifter; pops out of gear. • Rear main seal leak troubleshooting tips. • Separation of the lower control arm ball joints. • Noisy or stiff steering. • Front suspension noise. • Clutch pedal squeaks or clicks when pressed. • Erratic fuel gauge readings, especially when parked on an incline; fuel gauge won't read full. • Sticking speedometer and tachometer needles. • Windshield cracking at the lower corners. • Damaged or cracked foglight lens. • AC condensate drips onto passenger-side carpet. • Seat belt slow to retract. **2001–02**—Engine hesitation when accelerating is often caused by low oil pressure. • A growling noise from the engine area is likely caused by a worn alternator bearing. • Troubleshooting front brake groan or squeal. • Rear suspension squeak (replace the rear knuckle bushing). **2001–04**—If vehicle won't move in Drive, it's likely caused by excessive Second clutch wear (see first bulletin on following page). **2001–05**—Starter grinds while engine cranks. • Inoperative or erratically operating power windows. • Driver's seat rocks back and forth (see second bulletin on following page). • Water leaks into the trunk (see third bulletin on following page). • Hard-to-close trunk lid. • A-pillar rattles. **2002**—Automatic transmission slippage. • Shift lever may be difficult to move. • Troubleshooting a noisy clutch. • Creaking or ticking from the dash or front strut; clean and install shims. • Hard-to-turn seatback lock. • Front windows won't fully roll down. **2003–04**—Sticking door lock cylinder. • Inaccurate fuel gauge (see fourth bulletin on following page).

VEHICLE WON'T MOVE/MIL ON/DTC P0730

BULLETIN NO.: 04-036

DATE: JANUARY 7, 2005

WON'T MOVE IN DRIVE; MIL COMES ON OR D INDICATOR BLINKS WITH A/T DTC P0730

2001–04 Civic

SYMPTOM: The vehicle does not move when you select Drive. The MIL comes on ('01-03 models) or the D indicator blinks ('04 models) with "A" DTC P0730 (shift control system) set.

PROBABLE CAUSE: Excessive wear in the 2nd clutch.

CORRECTIVE ACTION: Replace the A/T. Use the Honda Interface Module (HIM) to update the PGM software ('01–03 models only).

DRIVER'S SEAT ROCKS BACK AND FORTH

BULLETIN NO.: 01-057

DATE: FEBRUARY 22, 2005

2001–05 Civic

SYMPTOM: The driver's seat rocks back and forth during normal driving.

PROBABLE CAUSE: Worn bushings in the height adjustment mechanism.

CORRECTIVE ACTION: Install new seat bushings, nuts, and spacers.

BODY—WATER LEAKING INTO TRUNK

BULLETIN NO.: 03-067

DATE: FEBRUARY 18, 2005

WATER LEAKS INTO THE TRUNK FROM A BODY SEAM

2001–05 Civic

SYMPTOM: Water in the trunk.

PROBABLE CAUSE: Lack of sealer at various seams.

FUEL GAUGE INACCURATE

BULLETIN NO.: 05-002

DATE: MARCH 4, 2005

2003–04 Civic 4-Door EX and LX

SYMPTOM: At any fuel level, the fuel gauge reading drops by 1/4 tank, or 3 to 4 graduation marks. In some cases, the fuel gauge indicates "E" and the low fuel warning light is on. After driving for several minutes, or cycling the ignition switch off/on, the fuel gauge returns to the correct reading. This problem is intermittent, and it affects only Civics with Visteon gauge assemblies.

PROBABLE CAUSE: The software specification for calculating the current fuel level is incorrect.

CORRECTIVE ACTION: Replace the gauge assembly.

IN WARRANTY: The normal warranty applies: Defect Code: 03214.

OUT OF WARRANTY: Any repair performed after warranty expiration may be eligible for goodwill consideration by the District Parts and Service Manager or your Zone Office. You must request consideration, and get a decision, before starting work.

Insight: **2000–01**—Free replacement of the Park brake lever, battery condition monitor, and motor control module. **2001–02**—Water leaks into the trunk. *Civic Hybrid:* **2003**—A CVT transmission update. • Sticking door lock cylinder. • Notchy-feeling clutch. • Deformed windshield molding. **2003–05**—Inoperative or erratically operating power windows. **2004**—Hard-to-close trunk lid. • A-pillar rattles. • Sticking door lock cylinder. • Deformed windshield moulding.

CIVIC, DEL SOL, INSIGHT, CIVIC HYBRID PROFILE

	1997	1998	1999	2000	2001	2002	2003	2004	2005
Cost Price ($)									
Civic	13,495	14,000	14,200	14,200	15,800	15,900	16,000	16,150	16,200
Si	17,895	17,995	18,800	18,800	19,800	19,902	20,700	20,800	21,600
SiR	—	—	—	—	—	25,500	25,500	25,500	—
del Sol	20,995	—	—	—	—	—	—	—	—
Insight	—	—	—	—	26,000	26,000	26,000	26,000	26,000
Hybrid	—	—	—	—	—	—	28,500	28,500	28,500
Used Values ($)									
Civic ▲	4,000	4,500	5,000	6,000	7,000	8,000	9,000	10,500	12,500
Civic ▼	3,500	4,000	4,500	5,500	6,500	7,000	8,000	9,500	11,000
Si ▲	5,500	6,500	6,500	7,500	8,500	10,000	12,000	13,500	16,000
Si ▼	5,000	6,000	6,000	7,000	8,000	8,500	10,500	12,500	14,500
SiR ▲	—	—	—	—	—	11,000	13,500	16,500	—
SiR ▼	—	—	—	—	—	9,500	12,000	14,500	—
del Sol ▲	5,500	—	—	—	—	—	—	—	—
del Sol ▼	4,500	—	—	—	—	—	—	—	—
Insight ▲	—	—	—	—	10,000	12,000	14,000	16,500	19,000
Insight ▼	—	—	—	—	8,500	10,500	12,500	15,000	17,000
Hybrid ▲	—	—	—	—	—	—	15,000	18,000	21,000
Hybrid ▼	—	—	—	—	—	—	13,500	17,000	19,000
Reliability	3	3	4	4	4	4	4	4	4
Insight	—	—	—	—	3	3	3	3	3
Hybrid	—	—	—	—	—	—	3	3	3
Crash Safety (F)	4	4	4	4	5	5	5	5	5
4d	4	4	4	4	5	5	5	5	5
Insight	—	—	—	4	4	4	4	4	4
Side	—	3	2	2	5	3	3	3	4
4d	3	3	3	3	4	4	4	4	4
Insight	—	—	—	—	4	4	4	4	4
Offset	3	3	3	3	5	5	5	5	5
Head Restraints	2	—	2	—	2	3	1	1	1
4d	—	—	—	—	5	3	1	1	1
del Sol	4	—	—	—	—	—	—	—	—
Rollover Resistance	—	—	—	—	4	4	4	4	4
Insight	—	—	—	—	—	—	4	4	4

Hyundai

RATING: Above Average (2001–06); Average (1995–2000). Having inflicted its Pony, Stellar, and Excel misadventures on Canadians, it's about time Hyundai got a product right. Just as Honda and Nissan have improved since bringing out their '70s rustbuckets, Hyundai has learned from its mistakes and brought out more-reliable cars with better warranties—at bargain prices. Think of the Accent as a refined GM Firefly/Metro/Sprint from South Korea, but with more standard features. The absence of ABS is no big loss and should lead to cheaper maintenance costs as the car ages. However, the skinny tires and small engine relegate the car to an urban environment. **"Real" city/highway fuel economy:** 8.9/6.2 L/100 km. Owners report fuel savings may undershoot this estimate by about 10 percent. **Maintenance/Repair costs:** Average. **Parts:** Reasonably priced and easily found. **Extended warranty:** Consider getting an optional powertrain warranty as protection from occasional engine head gasket and tranny failures. **Best alternatives:** GM Firefly or Metro, Honda Civic (an old Honda CRX in good condition would be a master stroke), Hyundai Elantra, Mazda Protegé, Nissan Sentra, Suzuki Esteem, and Toyota Echo or Corolla. **Online help:** *www.carsurvey.org/model_Hyundai_Accent.html.*

Strengths and Weaknesses

Launched as a '95 model, the early Accent was basically an Excel that had been substantially upgraded to provide decent performance and reliability at a phenomenally low price. Of course, with its small 4-cylinder engine, the Accent is no tire-burner, but it will do nicely for urban commuting and grocery shopping. Invest in larger wheels and tires that equip the GT for safer highway handling.

VEHICLE HISTORY: Until the redesigned 2000 models arrived, the Accent hadn't changed much over the years. **1996**—Height-adjustable seat belts and a 105-hp GT hatchback. **1997**—Models saw the debut of a GS hatchback and a GL sedan. **1998**—New engine mounts to cut down vibration, in addition to restyled front and rear ends. **1999**—Power steering and longer warranties. **2000**—A smoother-shifting automatic transmission; a stiffer, better-performing suspension; a stronger and quieter-running engine; and a more comfortable driving position with good visibility. **2001**—Engine got 16 additional horses. **2003**—A slightly larger engine, and restyled front and rear ends. **2005**—Optional ABS brakes. **2006**—Redesigned to be safer, larger, and more powerful (six more horses). Front side airbags, side curtain airbags, ABS, and four-wheel disc brakes are standard features.

Owner complaints are surprisingly rare; however, the following problem areas have been noted: the engine cooling system and cylinder head gaskets (engine overheating), engine sputtering, a Check Engine light that constantly comes on, and chronic automatic transmission failures (an extended transmission warranty is suggested for models no longer under warranty). Owners also frequently complain of excessive front-end vibration; wheel bearing, fuel system, and electrical component failures; premature front brake wear; and excessive noise when braking, particularly an annoying clicking emanating from the rear brake drums.

Safety Summary

All models/years: Airbags fail to deploy, or deploy inadvertently. • Horn controls may be hard to find in an emergency. • Rear head restraints appear to be too low to protect occupants. • Rear seat belt configuration complicates the installation of a child safety seat (pre-2001 models). **All models: 1998–99**—Complete brake failure. • Sudden transmission failure. • Headlights flicker when turning and high beam is inadequate. • Engine control monitor melted. • Fuel gauge failures. **2000**—Fire erupted in the dashboard area. • Accelerator sticks. • Hood flew up and smashed through the windshield. • Left and right axles broke while vehicle was underway. • Transmission sticks between First and Second gear and pops out of Fifth gear. • No shifting because of a failure of the control shaft assembly. • In snowy, icy, or wet road conditions, there's an unpredictable loss of rpm and powertrain response, making for difficult handling and control. • Windshield wipers fail because of the wiper linkage disconnecting from the wiper motor. • Seat belts tighten uncomfortably. **2000–04**—Automatic-transmission-equipped cars lurch into Reverse (TSB #05-36-003-2). **2001**—Gas pooled underneath the rear seat. • Airbags fail to deploy. • Steering shook so badly that driver lost control of vehicle. • Transmission jumps from Drive to Neutral. • Gearshift jumps out of Reverse. • Seat belts unlatch during impact; passenger seat belt tightens uncomfortably. • Windshield and rear window suddenly shattered. • Early ignition coil replacement. **2002**—Throttle body sensor failure causes car to accelerate on its own; intermittent high engine revs. • Chronic stalling. • Automatic transmission failures characterized by slippage, free-wheeling, jerky shifts, and a clunking noise. • Rear brake drums may be out of round. • When stopped, brake pedal sinks slowly to the floor and car rolls away (possibly faulty brake master cylinder). • Manual windows fall down. **2003**—Under-hood fire. **2004**—Sudden stalling and total loss of power while driving. • Airbag failed to deploy. • Airbag deployed when passing over railroad tracks. • Small original-equipment wheels and tires make the car unstable at high speeds or when cornering. • Automatic transmission downshifts abruptly or won't shift at all. **2005**—Fire ignited in the engine compartment. • Fuel sloshes out from the fuel-filler pipe. • Rear window shattered as car was warming up.

Secret Warranties/Internal Bulletins/Service Tips

All models/years: Tips on troubleshooting excessive brake noise. • Apparent slow acceleration on cold starts is dismissed as normal. • A new AC "refresher" will control AC odours. **All models: 1995–98**—Harsh shifting may be fixed by installing an upgraded transaxle control module (TCM). **1995–2001**—TSB #03-40-018 says a defective kickdown servo switch could cause automatic transmission malfunctions.

1996–2004—A defective pulse generator may cause harsh, delayed, and erratic shifting, says TSB #03-40-022. • A TSB published in March 2004 says many automatic transmission breakdowns can be traced to faulty transaxle solenoids. 2000–01—Hyundai has a kit that will free up stiff manual transmission shifting. 2000–06—Automatic transaxle oil leak behind the torque converter. 2002—Harsh or delayed automatic transmission shifting.

ACCENT PROFILE

	1997	1998	1999	2000	2001	2002	2003	2004	2005
Cost Price ($)									
L/GS	10,995	11,295	11,565	11,565	11,995	12,395	12,395	12,895	12,995
GL 4d	12,995	12,995	13,245	13,595	13,595	13,795	13,795	14,195	13,995
Used Values ($)									
L/GS ▲	2,000	2,500	3,000	3,500	4,000	5,000	5,000	6,000	8,000
L/GS ▼	1,700	2,000	2,500	3,000	3,500	4,500	4,500	5,500	6,500
GL 4d ▲	2,500	3,000	3,500	4,000	4,500	5,500	6,000	7,000	9,000
GL 4d ▼	2,000	2,500	3,000	3,500	4,000	5,000	5,500	6,500	7,500
Reliability	3	4	4	4	4	5	5	5	5
Crash Safety (F)	3	3	—	—	—	—	—	5	5
4d	3	3	3	—	—	4	4	4	4
Side	—	—	—	—	—	3	—	4	4
4d	—	—	—	—	3	3	3	5	5
Head Restraints	1	—	1	—	3	3	3	—	—
Rollover Resistance	—	—	—	—	4	4	4	4	4

ELANTRA ★★★★★

RATING: Recommended (2001–06); Above Average (1996–2000); Average (1994–95); Below Average (1991–93). Shhh! This is the car auto columnists laugh at and then buy themselves. They know that Hyundai's quality is the best of the South Korean automakers' and is generally much better than what Detroit offers. Another advantage is that the Accent, Elantra, and Tiburon fly under most buyers' radar, making them more available and much more reasonably priced than better-known brands. There's only a $1,000–$3,500 difference between the high-end and entry-level models. Try to find a 2002–05 model with an unexpired comprehensive 5-year/100,000 km base warranty, or buy any post-1996, pre-2001 version, but give up some of your savings to buy an extended powertrain warranty to protect your wallet from the occasional transmission failure. **"Real" city/highway fuel economy:** 8.9/6.4 L/100 km with a manual transmission, but expect 9.6/6.7 L/100 km with an automatic. **Maintenance/Repair costs:** Average. Dealer servicing has improved considerably, and independent garages find the Elantra's

simple mechanical layout quite easy to diagnose and service. **Parts:** Reasonably priced and easily found. **Extended warranty:** Not needed on post-2001 models. The base warranty is sufficient, though insensitive warranty administrators could use an attitude adjustment. **Best alternatives:** Honda Civic; Hyundai Accent; Mazda Protegé; Nissan Sentra; Suzuki Aerio, Esteem, or Swift; and Toyota Echo, Tercel, Corolla, or Yaris. **Online help:** *www.autosafety.org* and *www.carsurvey.org*.

Strengths and Weaknesses

This conservatively styled, "high-end," front-drive sedan was launched as a 1992 model, carrying a 113-hp 1.6L 4-cylinder engine. It's only marginally larger than the failure-prone Hyundai Excel, but its overall reliability is much better, making it a credible alternative to GM Saturns and the Mazda Protegé, Nissan Sentra, and Toyota Corolla. The redesigned 1996 and later versions actually narrow the handling and performance gap with the segment leader, Honda's Civic. Elantra's 1993 4-cylinder gained 11 more horses and is fairly smooth and efficient when mated with the 5-speed manual transmission.

There is some excessive body lean when cornering, but overall handling is fairly good, mainly because of a relatively long wheelbase and sophisticated suspension. Brakes are adequate, though sometimes difficult to modulate. Conservative styling makes the Elantra look a bit like an underfed Accord, but there's plenty of room for four average-sized occupants.

VEHICLE HISTORY: 1996—Totally redesigned with additional interior room, improved performance and handling, and a quieter-running engine; a wagon and 130-hp 1.8L engine were added, along with dual airbags and upgraded seat belts. **1999**—Mildly revised styling. **2001**—Another revision saw the wagon disappear, increased interior and engine size (now a 140-hp 2.0L 4-cylinder), and added four-wheel disc brakes and ABS. **2002**—Debut of a GT hatchback, which is a bargain when one totes up the cost of its standard features. **2003**—The GT adds a four-door sedan. **2004**—Minor interior and exterior revisions. **2005**—A new base GLS hatchback comes online. **2006**—The sporty GT sedan is gone; front side airbags are standard, but no side curtain airbags.

Owners of 1996–2000 model Elantras report few serious defects; however, as with most Hyundai products, transmission failures are commonplace and have been the object of numerous service bulletins (see the Accent "Secret Warranties/ Internal Bulletins/Service Tips") and recalls. Airbag failures are another frequent complaint. Other problem areas include body deficiencies (fit, finish, and assembly), a leaking sunroof, paint cracking, engine misfire and oil leaks (some oil burning), hard starting, and warped brake rotors. Post-'96 models' passing power with the automatic gearbox is perpetually unimpressive, and the trunk's narrow opening makes for a relatively small storage space. The power problem is attenuated with the revamped 2001 versions.

This having been said, the above-noted problems are in no way as severe or as frequent as what you would find with the Detroit Big Three competition.

The 2001–05 Elantras are noted for chronic stalling; early manual transmission clutch burnout; prematurely worn-out rear brake drums, cylinders, and shoes; and excessive brake noise and chassis vibration (see "Secret Warranties/Internal Bulletins/Service Tips"):

> Strong steering wheel vibration on 2004 Hyundai Elantra at speeds over 60 mph [97 km/h]. Have taken car to dealer 5 times, in which they have rotated wheels, balanced tires, and road-force balanced tires with no improvement. Numerous other Elantras from 2001–2005 suffer from this problem, as a simple Google search will yield many. Hyundai will not acknowledge problem even though there is a TSB for this issue.

Vehicles may also suffer from a passenger-side scraping noise when underway; wind howling in the interior when encountering a crosswind; a humming noise emanating from the corners of the windshield; tire thumping; delayed window defrosting; rainwater seeping in under the door, and paint/clearcoat cracking.

Safety Summary

All models/years: Airbags failed to deploy or deployed for no reason. • Chronic stalling. • Erratic transmission shifting and excessive noise. • Sudden brake loss. • Warped front brake rotors, and master cylinder failure. • Passenger seat belt retracts and locks so that passengers are unable to move. **All models: 1998–99**—Faulty speed sensor. • Cracked transmission case. • Low beam headlights give poor illumination. • Poorly designed jack. **1999**—Defective heater fan and motor assembly. • Trunk lid doesn't close properly. • Loose driver seat. • Defective door handle. **2000**—Vehicle rolled forward even though emergency brake was applied.

• Clutch slave cylinder failure. • Vehicle pulls left continually. • Sudden steering failure; loose steering. • Low beam doesn't light up driver's view; instead, the light reflects outward to the left or right. • Tire jack is too small and weak. **2001**— Sudden, unintended acceleration. • Child had to be cut free from jammed rear centre seat belt. • Seat belt failed to lock up in a collision. • Brakes randomly engage by themselves and overheat/pulsate. • Rear doors freeze shut in cold weather. **2002**—Seatback failure when car was rear-ended. • Brake and gas pedals are set too close together. • While driving in a rainstorm, all interior and exterior lights shut off. **2003**—Engine surging while on the highway. • Vehicle suddenly lost all power. • Complete loss of brakes. • Headlights will read "dim" but will actually be on high. • Distracting windshield glare. • Seat belts fail to lock. **2004**— Under-hood fire:

> Vehicle caught on fire in the engine compartment while driving 40 mph [64 km/h]. The local fire department arrived to extinguish the fire. Dealer and the manufacturer were notified. The consumer stated that she smelled smoke coming through the vents while driving. The engine light came on, and the vehicle lost all power. Vehicle brakes went out. The consumer stopped the vehicle, and her and the passengers got out of the vehicle within seconds of flames.

• Airbag fails to deploy or deploys for no reason. • Almost 100 complaints that the passenger-side front airbag is disabled when a normal-sized adult is seated; recall doesn't correct the problem for all claimants:

> Repeated intermittent illumination of "passenger airbag off" beginning within days of purchase. Failures occur when anyone sits in passenger seat. Adults weighing 190, 170, and 140 have turned airbags off. Poodle weighing 9 lbs turned airbags on!

• Chronic stalling. • Sudden, unintended acceleration. • Back cover on passenger seat pops out. • Faulty crankshaft position sensor causes the engine to stall. • Engine surging. • Stabilizer bar snapped, causing vehicle to fishtail. • Warped brake rotors. • Defective batteries corrode cables and leak acid. • Passenger seat collapsed in a frontal collision at moderate speed. • Roof buckled while car was underway. • Seat belt extenders not available. **2005**—Faulty sensor continues to disable airbag when the seat is occupied. It is designed to disable the system *only* when an under-weight occupant is seated. • Sudden acceleration. • Rear brake wheel cylinder fluid leaks.

Secret Warranties/Internal Bulletins/Service Tips

All models/years: Hyundai has a brake pad kit (#58101-28A00) that the company says will eliminate squeaks and squeals during light brake application. • A harsh downshift when decelerating (bulletin #98-40-001). • Poor shifting may be caused by an inhibitor switch short circuit. • Intermittent slippage in Fourth gear. • Troubleshooting vibration and ride harshness. **All models: 1996–2002**— Harsh or delayed Park–Reverse or Park–Drive engagement. **2001**—Troubleshooting harsh shifting with the automatic transmission (TSB #05-40-011). **2001–02**—Troubleshooting 2–3 shift flaring usually requires a simple updating of the transaxle control module (TCM), says TSB #02-40-001. **2001–05**—Automatic transaxle oil leak behind the torque converter. **2002–03**—Excessive chassis vibration when cruising. **2002–04**—Poor engine performance when driving in high-altitude regions may require a free upgraded fuel pump:

FREE FUEL PUMP REPLACEMENT

BULLETIN NO.: 05-01-009   DATE: SEPTEMBER 2005

2002–04 ELANTRA AND TIBURON FUEL PUMP REPLACEMENT—SERVICE CAMPAIGN T13

Some 2002 through 2004 MY Elantra and 2003 to 2004 Tiburon vehicles may experience rough engine running as a result of reduced fuel pressure when operated in high ambient temperatures at high elevations. A new fuel pump and filter sub-assembly has been made available to correct this condition. This bulletin describes the steps necessary to replace the fuel pump and filter sub-assembly.

2003—Automatic transmission sticks in Second gear. • Harsh shifts into Drive or Reverse. • Rough-running engine may require an upgraded fuel pump. • Corrosion in the front-door wiring connector. **2004**—To eliminate a driveline "bump" when accelerating, reprogram the PCM.

ELANTRA PROFILE

	1997	1998	1999	2000	2001	2002	2003	2004	2005
Cost Price ($)									
GL	13,995	14,295	14,595	14,875	14,875	15,295	15,295	15,630	14,995
GLS/VE	17,245	17,545	17,695	17,475	17,075	16,995	16,995	17,525	17,365
GT	—	—	—	—	—	18,495	18,495	19,015	19,895
Used Values ($)									
GL ▲	2,500	3,000	3,500	4,000	5,000	6,000	7,500	8,500	10,000
GL ▼	2,000	2,500	3,000	3,500	4,500	5,500	6,500	7,500	8,500
GLS/VE ▲	3,500	4,000	5,000	5,500	6,500	7,500	8,500	9,500	11,500
GLS/VE ▼	3,000	3,500	4,500	5,000	6,000	6,500	8,000	9,000	10,000
GT ▲	—	—	—	—	—	8,000	9,000	11,000	13,000
GT ▼	—	—	—	—	—	7,500	8,000	9,500	11,500
Reliability	4	4	4	4	4	5	5	5	5
Crash Safety (F)	3	3	3	—	4	4	4	5	5
Side	—	3	—	—	5	5	5	5	5
Side (IIHS)	—	—	—	—	1	1	1	1	1
Offset	3	3	3	3	1	1	1	5	5
Head Restraints	1	—	3	—	1	1	1	1	1
Rollover Resistance	—	—	—	—	—	—	4	4	4

Kia

After going bankrupt in 1998, Kia was bought by Hyundai (it's also partly owned by Ford through Ford's Mazda affiliation) and now sells a full lineup of vehicles that includes small cars, mid-sized sedans, a minivan, and several sport-utility vehicles. With Hyundai's infusion of cash and better-quality components, 2006 and later Kias have been transformed into remarkably dependable performers.

Not so with earlier models. 2004 and earlier models are known for their poor quality control and below-average crashworthiness scores. Mediocre, erratic automatic transmission performance and durability (a Daewoo bugaboo, too) has also been a well-known Kia trait ever since these vehicles were first imported into Canada over a decade ago. The 2005 versions are more reliable, however, and the 2006 model redesign has improved the cars' performance considerably.

RIO ★ ★ ★

RATING: Average (2005–06); the 2005 will give you better reliability, but the 2006 provides both improved reliability and a fuller array of safety and performance features for almost the same price. Not Recommended (2001–04). Why am I so hard on the early Rios? Simple: They don't offer a modicum of the crashworthiness, safety features, performance, or reliability that other cars deliver for the same price or less. Try a Hyundai Accent or a Toyota Echo instead. **"Real" city/highway fuel economy:** 8.9/6.6 L/100 km with a manual transmission or 9.3/6.7 L/100 km with the automatic tranny. **Maintenance/Repair costs:** Average. **Parts:** Average cost, and parts are easily found, despite the small dealer network. **Extended warranty:** A bumper-to-bumper warranty is a must-buy, which wipes out your low sales-price savings. **Best alternatives:** GM Firefly or Metro; Honda Civic; Hyundai Accent or Elantra; Mazda Protegé; Nissan Sentra; and Toyota Echo, Tercel, or Corolla. **Online help:** *www.autosafety.org* and *www.carsurvey.org*.

Strengths and Weaknesses

A bit smaller than the earlier Kia Sephia and Spectra, the Rio was originally a South Korean spin-off of the Aspire, marketed from 1995 to 1997 under the Ford nameplate. It's one of the cheapest cars on the market and offers both sedan and wagon versions, a limited number of standard safety and performance features, and cheap interior and exterior materials. 2004 and earlier versions put a low base price before safety, reliability, and performance.

Base Rios are equipped with a puny 104-hp 1.6L 4-cylinder engine teamed with a 5-speed manual transmission. Options available include a 4-speed automatic transaxle; ABS; air conditioning; power steering, door locks, and windows; and foglights. Side airbags aren't offered.

Highly manoeuvrable in city traffic and quite fuel efficient, this small car is, nevertheless, poorly suited for highway cruising or driving situations that require quick merging with traffic. Kia's horsepower ratings may be just as suspect as Hyundai's, and reports of chronic stalling sap owner confidence even more. The car's Poor head-restraint rating from IIHS through 2007 and two-star side crashworthiness score from NHTSA on 2003–05 models are also worrisome (2006–07s manage to eke out a three-star rating).

VEHICLE HISTORY: You may be wondering how such a low-quality car originally saw the light of day, so I will digress a bit. Vehicles like the Rio are built and propped up through import tariffs to prevent foreign automakers from capturing the home country's market and jobs. Quality isn't a consideration when you're one of the few players in the game. To keep the factories humming, these cars are exported to developing countries where a low purchase price gives them a huge advantage. When they arrive in Europe and North America, price takes a backseat to quality, reliability, and safety, and auto shoppers look elsewhere for their "bargains." This has been the story with Daewoo, Kia, Fiat, Lada, Dacia, and Yugo.

Kia's products, unlike Daewoo's, do have a track record—and it's not good. In fact, *Consumer Reports* reported on the cars' debut and said in its April 1999 New Car edition, "You'd have to search far and wide to find a car that's worse than this small Korean model." And the proportionally large number of safety-related complaints recorded by NHTSA through 2005 confirms *CR*'s early conclusion.

2003—Subtle styling changes, a slightly larger engine, and extra standard and optional features. Kia claims engineering updates reduce noise and vibration, suspension alterations improve ride comfort, and larger front brakes increase stopping power. None of these pretensions are supported by driver feedback, however. **2006**—A complete redesign gives the car more room, power, and safety features. A four-door hatchback called the Rio5 also joins the lineup. The sole engine is a 110-hp 4-cylinder mated with a standard 5-speed manual transmission; a 4-speed automatic is optional. Front side airbags and side curtain airbags are standard for 2006, though anti-lock four-wheel disc brakes are optional.

Owners report problems with the automatic transmission, seat belts, and electrical and fuel systems; frequent front-end alignments; unreliable tires; and weak, prematurely worn, and noisy brakes. Writes this owner of a 2002 Rio:

> I had the front brakes replaced due to a clip that fell off and got between the brake pad and drum, and the rear brakes replaced due to brake dust and glazing of drums. Now less than two weeks later, I'm starting to have the same grinding noise in the rear brakes again.

Other areas of complaint involve weak and noisy engine performance; a busy, harsh ride; slow and imprecise highway handling; limited passenger room and problematic entry and exit; tire thumping; small audio controls and a missing remote trunk release; low-budget interior materials; small door openings and limited rear headroom and legroom; the trunk's small opening that doesn't take bulky items and doesn't offer a pass-through for large objects; the optional tilt steering wheel that doesn't tilt much; poor body construction; and a small dealer network that may complicate servicing and warranty performance.

Safety Summary

All models/years: Airbag non-deployment. • Chronic stalling. **All models: 2001–03**—Defective fuel line ignited an under-hood fire. • Hood flew up and broke front windshield. • Side airbag failed to deploy. • Vehicle disengages from Overdrive because of a missing transmission control modulator. • Transmission jumps out of gear when brakes are applied. • Brakes stick and pedal goes to the floor without vehicle stopping. • Brakes are noisy. • Excessive shaking and vibration; vehicle swerves all over the road. • Rear seat belt shreds or jams. • Steering binds and grinds when turned; on other occasions it's too loose. • Premature tire wear. • Various mechanical and electrical problems, including clock spring failure. • Check Engine light, Airbag warning light, and Fuel light constantly stay lit. • Bent wheel rims. **2003**—Sudden steering loss. • No-starts, particularly in cold weather, due to faulty engine computer module. • Premature failure of the engine and transmission. • In damp weather, brakes grab abruptly and won't release, or they don't "catch" at all.

> The brake fell off the pad. In most normal cars the brakes are held on with a pop rivet. Not this car. They are held on with thin pieces of aluminum. Everyone knows how easy aluminum bends and twists and that's exactly how mine were. And the brake is held onto the pad with glue!!!

• Steering-column bolt snapped. • Seat belt cuts across the driver's and passenger's throats. • Wheel lug nuts sheared off. • Windshield wiper nuts often come off. **2004**—Mass airflow sensor failures are the likely cause of chronic stalling. • Windshield wiper nut loosened and caused the wiper to fail:

> The retaining nut on the windshield-wiper arm loosens, causing the windshield wipers not to function. The dealership inspected and tightened the retaining nut, but the problem still exists.

2005—Airbag deployed for no reason. • Stalling complaints continue unabated. • Manual transmission clutch replaced at 9,000 km. • Child safety door lock failure; door could not be opened.

Secret Warranties/Internal Bulletins/Service Tips

All models: 2001—Revised transmission shift lever and bushing spacer. • Reinforced fuse-box cover latch. • Troubleshooting automatic transmission concerns. **2001–02**—Special Service Campaign addresses premature transmission failures. **2001–04**—*KIA Technician Times* (Volume 7, Issue 6, 2004) says some vehicles may develop a vacuum leak that will cause the car to run rough. The main cause of this concern is a broken plastic vacuum-line Y-Connector (P/N 0K30C13744A), located below the fuel rail. **2003–04**—TSB #013 addresses different remedies for curing hard starts in cold weather (reprogramming software is one field fix).

RIO PROFILE

	2001	2002	2003	2004	2005
Cost Price ($)					
S	11,995	12,095	12,351	12,650	12,995
RS	12,995	13,095	13,251	13,550	13,995
Used Values ($)					
S ▲		3,000	4,000	5,000	6,500	8,000
S ▼		2,500	3,500	4,000	5,000	7,000
RS ▲		3,500	4,500	5,500	7,000	8,500
RS ▼		3,000	4,000	5,000	5,500	7,500
Reliability	①	②	②	③	④
Crash Safety (F)	—	④	④	④	④
Side	③	③	②	②	②
Head Restraints	①	①	①	①	①
Rollover Resistance	—	④	④	④	④

Note: IIHS gives the 2006–07 Rio a Poor side crashworthiness score, even though NHTSA bumped up its rating to three stars.

Mazda

MAZDA3, PROTEGÉ ★ ★ ★ ★

RATING: *Mazda3:* Above Average (2004–06). The rating has dropped a notch due to the high number of service bulletins sent out to correct the first two years of production glitches. Interestingly, there hasn't been a comparable increase in owner complaints, which continue to be remarkably few in number. Nevertheless, make sure AC cools the car sufficiently. *Protegé:* Recommended (1999–2003); Above Average (1991–98); Average (1985–90). These cars are plentiful at bargain prices; the best buys of all, however, are the totally revamped, better-performing 1999–2003 model Protegés. **"Real" city/highway fuel economy:** There isn't a lot of variation in fuel economy among the different model years, except for the turbocharged engine that wastes gas at a rate of 10.0/7.3 L/100 km. Owners say they burn about 10 percent more fuel than the following estimates indicate. *Protegé:* 8.5/6.7 L/100 km with the 1.6L manual transmission engine or 9.3/6.9 L/100 km with the automatic. The 2.0L engine's estimated fuel consumption is slightly higher at 9.6/7.3 L/100 km with the manual or 9.9/7.4 L/100 km with the automatic. *Mazda3:* 8.5/6.2 L/100 km for the 2.0L manual transmission engine or 9.1/6.4 L/100 km with the automatic gearbox. The 2.3L engine's estimated fuel consumption is slightly higher at 9.2/6.7 L/100 km with the manual or 9.8/7.5 L/100 km with the automatic. **Maintenance/Repair costs**: Higher than average. Repairs are dealer-dependent. **Parts:** Expensive, but easily found. **Extended warranty:** Not necessary. **Best alternatives:** GM Firefly or Metro; Honda Civic; Hyundai Accent or Elantra; Nissan Sentra; Suzuki Aerio, Esteem, or Swift; and Toyota Echo or Corolla. **Online help:** *www.autosafety.org* and *www.carsurvey.org*.

Strengths and Weaknesses

Protegés are peppy performers with a manual transmission hooked to the base engine. As with most small cars, the automatic gearbox produces lethargic acceleration that makes highway passing a bit chancy. Overall durability started improving with the 1991 and later Mazda 323 and Protegé, both of which were also sold as Ford Escorts. Nevertheless, pollution-control components and the electrical system have been troublesome. Watch out for automatic transmission malfunctions, air-conditioner breakdowns, and engine oil leaks, as well.

VEHICLE HISTORY: 1991–95—Reasonably reliable and inexpensive. **1995–98**—Redesigned versions are better buys for cheapskate shoppers looking for more reliability with a dash of additional performance at an affordable price. Powered by a standard, fuel-efficient 1.5L engine mated with a manual 5-speed transmission, these econoboxes are among the roomiest and most responsive small cars around. **1999**—A restyled interior and exterior and a more powerful engine lineup. **2000**—Premium models received front-seat side airbags and an improved ABS system. **2002**—The introduction of the Protegé5 four-door hatchback sport wagon and the MP3, a higher-performing sedan variant. **2003**—A turbocharged 170-hp MazdaSpeed Protegé debuted and sold in small quantities. **2004**—Protegé was replaced by the 2004 Mazda3.

Although 1996–2003 Protegés are far more reliable than most American-made small cars, their automatic transmissions continue to be their weakest link (a problem also seen with Ford's Escort and Hyundai's lineup), with erratic shifting and locking up in Fifth gear. Owners also report fuel-system glitches, electrical problems, front brake vibration, rotor warping, and premature pad wear. Other generic deficiencies are weak rear defrosting, chronic engine stalling (a secret warranty applies up to seven years), AC failures, and body defects, including wind and water leaks into the interior.

Mazda3

An econobox with flair, the front-drive 2004 Mazda3 is a totally new entry-level small car that replaces the Protegé. With considerable engineering help from Ford and Volvo, these cars use a platform that will also serve future iterations of the Ford Focus and Volvo S40. Powered by 150-hp 2.0L or 160-hp 2.3L 4-cylinder engines, coupled with either a 5-speed manual or a 4-speed Sport-mode automatic transmission, the car offers spirited acceleration and smooth, sporty shifting. Handling is enhanced with a highly rigid body structure, front and rear stabilizer bars, a multi-link rear suspension, and four-wheel disc brakes. Interior room is also quite ample with the car's relatively long 263.9 cm (103.9 in.) wheelbase, extra width, and straight sides, which maximize headroom, legroom, and shoulder room.

The Mazda3 is a "thief magnet" with door locks that don't lock. On top of that, their cargo ship tipped over. The automaker has suggested the recovered cars will be sold for parts, and then it recently announced that failure-prone RX-8 engines may need to be replaced.

The Mazda3 is a breeze to break into. Bizarre, but true—all it takes is a blow to the door on either side of any 2004–07 model, and the lock is popped. The Internet is full of reports telling how easily the cars and their contents are stolen. This information first came to light in the fall of 2006 in Western Canada, and now the police and insurers like the Insurance Corporation of British Columbia (ICBC) are scrambling to answer complaints coming in from all over the country.

Mazda has been mum over the issue and hasn't announced any programs to compensate victims, though the automaker is working behind the scenes to improve the lock mechanism, writes Fabrizio Pilato in the January 19, 2007, online issue of Mobile Magazine (*www.mobilemag.com/content/100/354/C11410*):

> This problem is with all Mazda 3 cars, and it may even be to other models, we just don't know the extent of this issue yet. Mazda has known about this problem for over 4 months, according to local Victoria Police. All that is being done at the moment is if you have been subject to a break-in, you can get a reinforced door lock assembly and a protective plate that will stop this from happening again. One victim on A Channel News Victoria claims that Mazda will repair his locking assembly, but not the dent in his door caused by the break in itself.

One Calgary owner actually videotaped the break-in and describes in a March 20, 2007, email sent to the above site how easily the car was opened:

> My car has been broken into 6 times in a little over a month. Even happened 2 days in a row (yesterday morning and this morning). I haven't left anything of value in my car since the first incident. I did have a tire gauge in it the other week and that got stolen! I never have any valuables in view. I have the last 2 incidents videotaped. I could see this car driving slowly down my street with no headlights on. Stops at my car, gets out, lights flash on my car (like they do when unlocking), total time of 20 seconds. It was too dark to see what the guy looked like. The Mazda dealer in Calgary is getting me the part to resolve this issue.

The door dent can cost about $300 to fix, though Mazda owners shouldn't have to pay a cent, because Mazda is legally responsible for claims arising from their wacky no-lock door locks. Insurers can claim their payouts from Mazda, and owners, using the small claims courts if necessary, should get their deductible refunded. Under no circumstances should this claim be used as a pretext to raise the premium when the insurance coverage is renewed. Mazda owners who want the door fixed at no charge and the free installation of Mazda's countermeasure alarm and protective plate should contact the automaker and then get an appointment with the nearest dealer. If Mazda balks at rendering assistance, simply threaten to use the small claims court to get compensation for the stolen items and dent repair, plus an additional mount needed to make the door secure, and a small amount for your inconvenience.

Other websites that will help in your negotiations with Mazda Canada are: *www. havelaptopwilltravel.com/mazda-offers-to-fix-door-lock, townhall-talk.edmunds.com/ direct/view/.f1212da, www.autoblog.com/2007/01/19/mazda3-may-be-vulnerable-to-break-ins, www.mazdausa.com/MusaWeb/contactMazda.action?bhcp=1, www. mazda3forums.com,* and *www.icbc.com.* Doug Henderson is the media relations spokesman for ICBC, and Angelo Carusi is the research and training coordinator. Mr. Carusi can confirm this issue and knows what measures are being taken to help other Canadian Mazda3 owners.

Other Mazda minuses

There aren't a lot of owner complaints. However, some drivers say the car could use a bit more passing power with the standard engine; prematurely worn out brake rotors and pads continue unabated; there are some minor fit and finish deficiencies; a high deck cuts rear visibility; there's limited rear footroom; and some Mazda dealers have been accused of overcharging for scheduled maintenance. Other reported problems for the Mazda3 include excessive fuel consumption, which is about 15 percent more than advertised; the 5-speed manual gearbox sometimes has trouble shifting from First to Second gear; the gas and brake pedal are too close together; drivers easily catch the side of their shoe against the brake when accelerating (consider getting customized racing pedals); the driver's right knee rubs the console; a front-end clunk is felt upon hard acceleration; a popping/creaking/rattling noise emanates from the rear end (hatch struts may be the culprit); the dash and driver's door rattle; a steering clicking/ ticking sound; cracked dashboards; broken window regulators; excess brake dust on rear wheels; the Door Ajar light comes on for no reason; paint is unusually thin, and aluminum rims peel; the CD changer is failure-prone; wimpy AC performance; and the passenger-side wiper may not clean the windshield sufficiently (top 7 cm of arch untouched). Original-equipment and Goodyear tires perform poorly in rain and slush (Kumho Escta, Michelin Pilots, and Hakkapeliittas winter tires are better performers; check with *www.tirerack.com* for the best tire combination).

Safety Summary

All models/years: Airbags failed to deploy. • Transmission failures and malfunctions. • If you stop or park on an incline, vehicle will likely roll away even with brakes applied. **All models: 1995–99**—Cracked fuel line caused fire. • Sudden tire-tread separation (Firestone). • Chronic stalling. • Excessive brake fade. • Metal rods in driver's seat could cause severe back injuries in a rear-end collision. • Driver's seat belt buckle wouldn't unlatch. • Brake pedal pad is too narrow. **2000–02**—Delayed braking. • Vehicle constantly pulls to the right. • Passenger unable to disengage seat belt. • Bucket seat seatbacks contain metal support bars that are extremely uncomfortable. **2001**—Loss of brakes. • Gear shift lever jumped from Drive to Neutral while driving. • Defective steering-column coupling. • Broken rear axle causes severe pulling to one side. • Windows take a long time to defrost. • **2002**—Continual stalling. • Brake line split, leading to rear-ender. **2003**—Nauseating fumes entered the vehicle. • Brake pedal pushed almost to the floor before brakes work; they produce excessive noise. • Passenger seat belt won't disengage. • Passenger seat belt broke; seat belt case and release button broke while trying to release belt. *Mazda3:* **2004**—Premature wearout of brake pads and rotors, and excessive brake-dust accumulation. • The transmission can be hard to shift, especially from Third to Fourth gear. • Transmission replaced during the first year. • Huge accumulation of brake dust on the rear wheels. • Brake rotors are prematurely grooved. • Chronic hard starts, stalling, and poor idling. • AC doesn't cool the car and compromises acceleration. **2005**—When car stalls on the highway, both steering and brakes fail. • Brake failures. • Windshield wiper flew off the car. • AC cooling is still inadequate:

> Inadequate air conditioning cooling compressor cycles on for only 10 seconds regardless of environmental conditions. Dealers/Mazda HQ denies any issue.

• Vehicle stalled and then crashed:

> I was going about 35 mph [56 km/h] and all of a sudden the power went out. I had no brakes, no steering, nothing…once again, and in front of me was an above ground cement manhole we have on the base and I knew I was going to hit it so I just held on tight. The next thing I remember is people screaming "Are you OK" and when I opened my eyes I was upside down. I flew in the air and landed on the car behind me and came within an inch of going into his windshield but that also saved my life, the firefighters said. So now my car is totaled.

• In a collision, some safety features perform poorly, or not at all:

> 1. The driver's seatback broke during impact. 2. The airbag did not deploy when she struck the vehicle in front of her. 3. The emergency switch that shuts down the fuel system did not activate. Our vehicle was totalled from all the damage…

Secret Warranties/Internal Bulletins/Service Tips

All models: 1995–98—Poor engine performance may require a new intake valve. • Erratic shifting may signal that the valve body harness is defective. • If the gear selector lever is hard to operate, it's likely that the lower manual shaft in the transfer case has excessive rust. **1998–2003**—Dealing with musty, mildew-type AC odours. **1999**—No-shift from Second to Third gear. • Manual transmission jerking or hesitation. • Inoperative wiper motor. **1999–2000**—Mazda will replace the mass airflow sensor free of charge up to 7 years/112,000 km (70,000 mi.). Problems with this component include a lack of power, hesitation, or a poor idle. Don't argue, simply tell the dealer you are aware of the replacement campaign, and anyway, it's a part covered by the more comprehensive emissions warranty. **2003**—Cold engine rattling. • Wind noise around doors. *Mazda3:* **2004**—Poor AC performance. • Mazda-upgraded shock absorbers will reduce suspension knocking when passing over bumps. • A splashing sound comes from the dash area. • Trunk lid difficult to open. • Power-window failures require a new window motor. • Fix for squeaking rear brakes. **2004–05**—Hard starts and poor idle are tackled in TSB #01-013/05, and the correction is covered by the warranty. • Possible causes for a noisy, smelly engine coming from any Mazda3 equipped with a manual transmission. • Installing countermeasure washers can stop drivetrain clicking. • Excessive engine vibration fix:

ENGINE VIBRATION ON ACCELERATION/IDLING
BULLETIN NO.: 01-021/05

ENGINE VIBRATION / NO. 3 ENGINE MOUNT RUBBER BROKEN

2004–05 Mazda3

DESCRIPTION: Some vehicles may experience engine vibration. This symptom could be observed under any condition such as accelerating, idling, and/or engine hot or cold. The No. 3 engine mount rubber has been modified to address this concern.

• Rear brake squeal and grinding has been remedied with upgraded brake pads, says Mazda's bulletin #04-003/05. • Modified pads and a mounting support for the front brake calipers have been introduced to correct front brake squeaking. • Front-door rattles correction guidelines. • One-touch window stops halfway down. **2004–06**—Hard starts in cold weather require a software recalibration under warranty. • Rough idle and engine hesitation. • Troubleshooting a snap or clunk noise when operating the windows.

MAZDA3, PROTEGÉ PROFILE

	1997	1998	1999	2000	2001	2002	2003	2004	2005
Cost Price ($)									
Protegé	14,685	14,675	14,970	15,095	15,795	15,795	15,795	—	—
Mazda3	—	—	—	—	—	—	—	16,195	16,295
Used Values ($)									
Protegé ▲	3,000	3,500	4,500	5,000	6,000	7,000	9,000	—	—
Protegé ▼	2,500	3,000	4,000	4,500	5,000	6,000	7,500	—	—
Mazda3 ▲	—	—	—	—	—	—	—	10,500	12,000
Mazda3 ▼	—	—	—	—	—	—	—	9,000	10,500

All ratings on a numbered scale where **5** is good and **1** is bad. See pages 130–132 for a more detailed description.

Reliability	4	4	4	4	5	5	5	4	4
Crash Safety (F)	3	3	—	4	5	5	5	4	4
Side	—	—	—	3	3	3	3	3	3
Side (IIHS)	—	—	—	—	—	—	—	—	1
Offset	3	3	3	3	3	3	3	5	5
Head Restraints (F)	1	—	2	2	3	3	3	2	2
Rear	—	—	—	—	2	2	2	2	2
Rollover Resistance	—	—	—	—	—	—	4	4	4

Nissan

SENTRA ★ ★ ★ ★

RATING: Above Average (1995–2006); Average (1988–94); Not Recommended (1983–87). **"Real" city/highway fuel economy:** *1.8L:* 8.5/6.1 L/100 km with the manual gearbox or 8.3/6.2 L/100 km with the automatic. *2.5L:* 10.2/7.3 L/100 km with the manual or 10.2/7.7 L/100 km with the automatic. Owners report fuel savings vary little from the above estimates. **Maintenance/Repair costs:** Higher than average on early models, but anybody can repair these cars. **Parts:** Reasonably priced, but some owners report waiting weeks for parts. **Extended warranty:** Not required. **Best alternatives:** GM Firefly or Metro, Honda Civic, Hyundai Elantra, Mazda Protegé, Suzuki Esteem or Swift, and Toyota Echo or Corolla. **Online help:** *www.autosafety.org* and *www.carsurvey.org*.

Strengths and Weaknesses

Until the 1991 models arrived, early Sentras were a crapshoot; more recent models give good fuel economy and are cheap, generally reliable, and inexpensive to repair. So what's not to like? Rudimentary ride and handling and subpar build quality, that's what. Quality improved considerably with the 1991 version, yet the vehicle's base price rose only marginally, making these later model years bargain buys for consumers looking for a reliable "beater."

The 1991–94 model year vehicles handle better, although some quality problems remain. These include faulty fuel tanks, leaking manual and automatic transmissions, and noisy engine timing chains and front brakes—problems that have all afflicted these cars over the past decade. Fortunately, with the exception of computer failures and ABS malfunctions, repairs are still relatively simple to perform. The redesigned 1995–97 models introduced fresh styling, a longer wheelbase, a peppier powerplant, standard dual airbags, and side door beams.

VEHICLE HISTORY: 1995—Larger and better performing. **1998**—New front and rear ends, and a new 140-hp SE sedan. **2000**—Underwent a major redesign, offering more powerful engines, a better ride, and enhanced handling. It's well worth the $1,000–$2,000 increase from the '99 version and is basically identical to the costlier 2001 version. **2002**—The 145-hp SE model was replaced at the top of the line by the SE-R and SE-R Spec V; the latter offers a 180-hp engine, a limited slip differential, and a sport-tuned suspension to compete against the Honda Civic SiR and Mazda's high-performance spin-offs. Four-wheel disc brakes also become a standard feature. **2003**—Arrival of the GXE, equipped with a 165-hp 2.5L engine, ABS, and front side airbags. **2004**—Minor exterior styling changes. **2005**—New upholstery fabrics, and the 1.8 S gets standard cruise control.

The 1995–2002 owner complaints concern stalling and hard starting; engine rattles; electrical glitches; premature brake wear and excessive brake noise; automatic transmission whine; AC solenoid failures and AC that blows hot air or freezes up; and accessories that malfunction. Owners have also had to contend with a recurrent steering clunk noise and clutch, clutch-switch, suspension-strut, wheel-bearing, and catalytic converter failures. Crank position sensor malfunction may prevent vehicle from being started. Body assembly is also targeted with some complaints of loose windshield mouldings, poor body fits, paint defects, and air and water leaks into the interior through the trunk and doors.

The 2003–06 models are just as problem-prone. One gets the impression Nissan held back many quality improvements for later inclusion into the 2007 model redesign. Owners of these versions are plagued by cylinder head gasket leaks; cracked #4 cylinder heads on the 1.8L engine; a misfiring #3 cylinder; engine pinging and rattling; and automatic transmission, fuel-system, and electrical problems. Front brake pads and rotors also wear out quickly; there's excessive noise, bouncing, and vibration caused by prematurely worn struts and control arm bushings; the doors vibrate noisily; passenger-side windows leak; the hood allows water to leak onto the drivebelt; rear bumpers may fall off; and there are many incidents of excessive wind noise around the windshield moulding.

 ## Safety Summary

All models/years: Brake and accelerator pedals set too close together. • Airbags fail to deploy or deploy inadvertently. • Steering lock-up. • Chronic stalling. • Sudden acceleration. • Premature tire wear. • Horn blows on its own. **All models: 1998–99**—ABS failures. • Defective brake master cylinder. • Excessive stopping distances. • Sticking throttle. • Ignition key breaks off in the ignition. • Faulty power-door locks. • Vehicle leaks when it rains. • Front seats jam when moved back. **1999**—Loss of braking; extended braking distance. • Fuel-filler flap fell into fuel-filler tube. **2000**—Suspension attachment bolts broke off. **2001**—Brakes easily lock up at all speeds. • Warped brake rotors. **2002**—Fire ignited in the headlight assembly:

> I am a professional fire investigator. This vehicle fire originated with the headlight assembly. The burn patterns clearly indicate this to be the area of origin and the supporting burn patterns indicate the fire originated in the headlight assembly. Even

though this recall does not specifically address a possible fire hazard, I believe the fire is related to the recall problem.

• Fire erupted in the engine compartment. • Sudden acceleration and frequent stalling. **2003–04**—Windshield wipers, turn signals, headlights, horn, and hazard lights may suddenly fail. • Continental tire-tread separation. • The gas and brake pedals may be set too far apart for some. • ABS brake failure. • Brakes lock up at low speed, particularly on wet roads. **2004**—Stalling; repeatedly loses all engine power; and high-speed bucking (surging). • Erratic, rough idling. • Early automatic transmission replacement. • Keyless remote doesn't work, and back door doesn't open from the inside, apparently due to a short in the electrical system. • Continental and Firestone tire tread peeling off. **2005**—Brake failure and then complete rear wheel lockup. • Warped rear brake drums. • Front seatback collapsed from a rear-end collision. • Frequent horn malfunctions. • Inoperative driver's door handle.

Secret Warranties/Internal Bulletins/Service Tips

All models/years: Faulty master cylinder causes brake pedal to slowly drop to the floor. **All models: 1995–99**—Harsh shifts and low power with the automatic transmission may be due to reduced movement of the A/T throttle wire cable inside the cable housing. • A self-activating horn can be fixed by replacing the horn springs and spring insulators. **1997–99**—Harsh shifts and low power with the automatic transmission. • More tips on silencing squeaks and rattles. • Diagnosing causes of brake judder and steering-wheel shimmy. • Slow retraction of the front seat belt. **1999–2001**—Hard starting in cold weather or at high altitudes. • Engine pings with light to moderate acceleration. • Exhaust manifold heat-shield rattle. • Automatic transmission won't upshift. • Tips to improve downshifting (modified downshift spring). • Brake pedal slowly drops to floor (master cylinder check). • Vehicle wanders or pulls to one side. • Water condensation from AC. • Anti-theft system prevents starting. **2000**—Vehicle lacks power; transmission sticks in Third gear. • Slow fuel fill; pump nozzle clicks off continually. • Erratic AC vent flow. • Front suspension squeak and rattling. • Windshield hum or whistle. **2000–04**—TSB #AT04-002, published March 10, 2004, says abnormal shifting of the automatic transmission is likely due to a defective control valve assembly. **2000–05**—Alternator chirping or squealing is caused by a defective alternator drivebelt; "goodwill" adjustment available. **2000–06**—Front-door windows may not work properly. **2001–02**—Low power or poor running. • Water leak in trunk area. • Rear brake caliper knock, clunk, or rattle. **2002–05**—A 2–3 shift chirping noise can be silenced by pouring in two bottles of Nissan's special ATF transmission treatment fluid. Do this first, before spending big bucks on unneeded repairs, inspections, etc. **2003**—Anti-theft system may make for hard starts or no-starts. • Troubleshooting tips for a lit MIL. • AC may operate erratically and have a sticking case door. **2003–05**—A harsh-shifting automatic transmission apparently afflicts a large part of Nissan's lineup:

HARSH 1–2 SHIFT/DTC P0745 STORED

BULLETIN NO.: NTB05-001

DATE: JANUARY 3, 2005

4-SPEED AUTOMATIC TRANSMISSION HARSH 1–2 SHIFT

2003–05 Altima, Sentra; 2003–04 Maxima and 2004 Quest

The transmission fluid is full (correct level) and in good condition (not burnt), and

- There is a harsh shift from 1st to 2nd gear, and/or
- DTC P0745 (line pressure solenoid circuit) is stored,

ACTIONS:

1. Drain and remove the transmission oil pan.
2. Push/pull the ground terminal and wire for the solenoid valve assembly (see Service Procedure step 4).
   - If it doesn't come off, solder the terminal.
   - If it does come off, replace the solenoid assembly.
3. After soldering, recheck the ground terminal and wire
   - If it's tight, repair is complete.
   - If it's loose, replace the solenoid assembly.

2004–06—Nissan's remedy for excessive brake squeaking. **2005**—Cold engine stumbling, stalling fix.

SENTRA PROFILE

	1997	1998	1999	2000	2001	2002	2003	2004	2005
Cost Price ($)									
Sentra	13,698	14,498	15,398	15,398	15,298	15,598	15,598	15,798	15,598
Used Values ($)									
Sentra ▲	2,000	2,500	3,500	4,000	4,500	5,500	7,000	9,000	11,000
Sentra ▼	1,700	2,000	3,000	3,500	4,000	5,000	6,000	8,000	10,000
Reliability	4	4	4	4	4	3	3	3	3
Crash Safety (F)	4	3	—	—	4	4	4	4	4
Side	—	3	—	—	—	—	2	2	2
Side (IIHS)	—	—	—	1	1	1	1	1	1
Offset	—	2	2	2	2	2	2	2	2
Head Restraints	2	2	2	2	2	1	1	1	1
Rollover Resistance	—	—	—	—	—	4	4	4	4

All ratings on a numbered scale where **5** is good and **1** is bad. See pages 130–132 for a more detailed description.

Subaru

RATING: *Forester:* Above Average (2006); Average (1994-2005). *Impreza:* Average (1997–2006), Below Average (1994–96). *WRX:* Below Average (2002–06). The WRX has tricky handling and reliability issues (powertrain, brake, and steering). Except for the Forester, Subaru's model lineup is mostly the bland leading the bland. There's nothing remarkable about Subaru except for its early use of AWD for its entire lineup as a desperate move to stave off bankruptcy in the mid-'90s. Incidentally, the company isn't in great financial shape right now. Quality control has declined markedly over the past few years, and customer service has suffered equally. Smart shoppers will choose a cheaper Asian or South Korean SUV until Subaru lowers its prices and raises performance and quality control levels. The 2006 Forester improvements are a good start. **"Real" city/highway fuel economy:** *Forester:* 10.9/7.9 L/100 km. The turbocharged models are fuel-thirsty, although the automatic transmission actually uses less fuel: 13.0/9.3 L/100 km with a manual transmission or 12.5/9.3 L/100 km with an automatic. Generally, owners report actual gas consumption is often 20 percent higher than the above estimates. *Impreza:* Equipped with a 2.5L engine, this vehicle gets 11.2/7.7 L/100 km with a manual transmission or 10.6/7.6 L/100 km with an automatic. *WRX:* 11.8/8.0 L/100 km. **Maintenance/Repair costs:** Higher than average. Expensive servicing is hard to overcome because independent garages can't service key AWD components. **Parts:** Parts aren't easy to find and can be costly; delayed recall repairs. **Extended warranty:** Not needed. **Best alternatives:** If you don't need the AWD capability, you're wasting your money. Here are some front-drives worth considering: the Honda Civic; Hyundai Elantra; Mazda Protegé; Nissan Sentra; Suzuki Aerio, Esteem, or Swift; and Toyota Echo or Corolla. Some recommended small vehicles with 4×4 capability that are set on a car's frame, not a truck's (to provide more carlike handling), include the GM Vibe, Honda CR-V, and Toyota Matrix or RAV4. **Online help:** *techinfo.subaru.com/html/shoppingHome.jsp, www.autosafety.org, www.carsurvey.org,* and *www.i-club.com.*

Strengths and Weaknesses

These well-equipped small cars have one of the most refined AWD drivetrains you'll find (prior to 1996, they were mostly mediocre front-drive economy cars). With their four-wheel traction, Subarus provide lots of storage space with the wagons, good fuel economy, and good handling without any torque steer. On the other hand, Subaru makes you pay dearly for the AWD capability, overall mechanical reliability is so-so, body workmanship is barely average, and braking can get downright scary. Furthermore, small doors and entryways restrict rear access, the coupe's narrow rear window and large rear pillars hinder rear visibility, heat and air distribution is often inadequate, and front- and rear-seat legroom may be insufficient for tall drivers. Without their AWD capability, these cars would be "back-of-the-pack" used-car picks.

The full-time 4×4 Impreza is essentially a shorter Legacy with additional convenience features. It comes as a four-door sedan, a wagon, and an Outback Sport wagon, all powered by a 135-hp 2.2L or a 165-hp 2.5L 4-cylinder engine. The 2.5L performs much better with the Impreza and Forester than with the Legacy Outback. It is smooth and powerful, with lots of low-end torque for serious off-road use. The automatic transmission shifts smoothly. The manual transmission's "hill holder" clutch prevents the car from rolling backward when starting out. These Subarus hurtle through corners effortlessly, with a flat, solid stance and plenty of grip. Tight cornering at highway speeds is done with minimal body lean and no loss of control, and steering is precise and predictable.

The rally-inspired WRX models have a more powerful 227-hp 2.0L turbocharged engine, lots of standard performance features, a sport suspension, an aluminum hood with a functional scoop, and higher-quality instruments, controls, trim, and seats. The 2003 Impreza and WRX were carried over unchanged.

Another Subaru spin-off, the Forester, is a cross between a tall wagon and a sport-utility. Based on the shorter Impreza, the Forester adds eight horses to the Legacy Outback's 165-hp 2.5L engine and couples it to a 5-speed manual transmission or an optional 4-speed automatic. Its road manners are more subdued, and its engine provides more power and torque for off-roading than do most vehicles its size.

VEHICLE HISTORY: 1993—Impreza's first year on the market. **1995**—Entry-level Imprezas got a coupe and an Outback model, and optional AWD. **1996**—A mix of front-drives and all-wheel drives, along with a new sport model, a new Outback Wagon (for light off-roading), and larger engines. **1997**—Additional power and torque, a restyled front end, and a new Outback Sport Wagon. **1998**—The Impreza got a revised dash and door panels. The Brighton was dropped, and the high-end 2.5 RS was added. **1999**—Stronger engines, more torque, and upgraded transmissions. **2002**—2.2L 4-cylinder was dropped, along with Subaru's pretensions for making affordable entry-level cars. Totally redesigned models include the 2.5 TS Sport Wagon, 2.5 RS sedan, Outback Sport Wagon, the WRX sporty sedan, and the Sport Wagon. There is no longer a two-door version available. *Impreza:* **2004**—New front end with larger headlights and a restyled interior and exterior. **2006**—A small horsepower increase, enhanced front end, additional airbags, and a freshened interior. *Forester:* **1999**—A quieter, torquier engine; a smoother-shifting transmission; and a more solid body. **2000**—Standard cruise control (L) and limited slip differential (S). **2003**—Improved interior materials, an upgraded suspension, and enhanced handling and ride quality. You'll also find larger tires and fenders, and revised head restraints and side-impact airbags. **2004**—A turbocharged 210-hp 2.5L 4-banger and a racier appearance. **2006**—More power and a slightly restyled interior and exterior. The 2006 turbocharged XT adds 20 hp via a redesigned engine intake manifold (this could be troublesome in the future); other models get eight more horses, for a total of 173. A retuned suspension enhances ride smoothness and handling response, and there's improved braking feel on all models. Ground clearance has been slightly increased, and an alarm system is now standard. The 5-speed manual transmission isn't available with L.L. Bean models. *WRX:* **2003**—An AWD car for the high-performance crowd, the WRX is a goofy-looking, squat little wagon/SUV with a large rear end and a 227-hp 2.0L 4-cylinder engine mated to a high-boost turbocharger. **2004**—A 300-hp engine. **2006**—2.5L gets 20 extra horses (up to 230).

Post-'95 Subarus are noted for improved, though only average, quality control, spotty servicing, and serious automatic transmission and brake deficiencies. There's also a history of premature clutch failures and shuddering, particularly after a cold start-up. Owners report poor engine idling; frequent cold-weather stalling; manual transmission malfunctions; rear wheel bearing failures; excessive vibration caused by the alloy wheels; premature exhaust system rust-out and early brake caliper and rotor scoring and wear; minor electrical short circuits; catalytic converter failures; doors that don't latch properly; body panel and trim fit and finish deficiencies, characterized by water leaks and condensation problems from the top of the windshield or sunroof; the windshield cracking and scratching too easily; and paint peeling. In addition to the paint peeling from delamination, owners report that Subaru paint chips much too easily.

Safety Summary

Impreza: **All years:** Sudden acceleration, stalling, transmission failures, steering loss, airbag malfunctions, brake and engine lights continually on, and front seats move fore and aft. **1999**—Engine failure caused by a cracked #2 piston. • When accelerating or decelerating, vehicle will jerk because of excessive play in the front axle. • Front bumper skirt catches on parking blocks; the bumper twists and rips off. • Total loss of braking capability. • The centre rear seat belt's poor design prohibits the installation of many types of child safety seats. **2000**—A mountain of complaints relative to loss of braking and premature wearout of key brake components. **2001**—ABS overreacts when braking over an irregular surface. • Rear wheel bearings fail repeatedly. • Factory-installed anti-theft device disables the starter. **2002**—Chronic brake failures. • Brake rotors are frequently scored after only a few kilometres. • Many reports of blown transmissions. • First gear is hard to engage. **2003**—Unintended sudden acceleration; brake pedal wouldn't respond. • Very poor braking when passing over rough surfaces:

> On my 2003 Subaru Impreza Outback Sport, the anti-lock brakes are dangerous. If you hit a bump while braking, it will trigger the ABS—and result in an almost complete loss of braking ability. I notice a bulletin is listed for the WRX only, but this is a major problem in my car as well.

• Seat belt ratchets tighter; refuses to unlock. • Windshield chips easily. **2004**—Airbags failed to deploy. • Vehicle won't go into gear. • Complete loss of brakes. • Raw fuel smell in the cabin. • Car wanders all over the road because of defective suspension struts. • Windshield is easily cracked. **2005**—Chronic rear strut failure. • Fuel odour inside the cabin. • Windshield is easily cracked, and side window shatters spontaneously. *Forester:* **2000**—Driver burned from airbag deployment. • Sudden loss of transmission fluid. • Driver's seatback may suddenly recline because seat belt gets tangled up in the recliner lever. • Frequent wheel bearing failures. • Fuel-filler cap design is too complicated for gas station attendants to put on properly, which causes the Check Engine light to come on. Driver, therefore, has to pay dealer to reset the Check Engine light. **2001**—Rear wheel bearings broke. • Brake and accelerator pedals are too close together. • In a collision, airbags failed to deploy and seat belt didn't restrain occupant. • In a similar incident, shoulder belt allowed driver's head to hit the windshield. • Headlights don't illuminate the edge of the road and are either too bright on High or too dim on Low. • Alarm system self-activated, trapping a baby inside the car until fire rescue arrived. **2002**—Dangerous delay, then surging, when accelerating forward or in Reverse. • Surging at highway speeds, and stalling at lower rpm. • Transmission failure; gears lock in Park intermittently. • Intermittent backfire when shifting manual transmission. • Open wheel design allows snow and debris to pack in the area and throw wheel out of balance, creating dangerous vibration. • High hood allows water onto the engine. (Note: The preceding comments apply to the Forester but can be relevant to Impreza owners, too.) **2003**—When backing vehicle into a parking space, the hill-holder feature activates, forcing the driver to use excessive throttle in Reverse. • Brake pedal went to floor without braking. • Heater, defroster failure. • Five doors but only one keyhole makes for difficult access when the keyless entry fails. *WRX:* **2001**—Brake rotors are easily grooved, degrading braking ability. **2002**—First gear is hard to engage. • **2002–03**—Windshield cracking. • Chronic ABS brake failures. • Fuel smell in the cabin caused by fuel pooling in the engine manifold recess. **2003**—Increased braking distance when brakes are applied on an uneven surface. **2004**—Defective Bridgestone tires. • Failure-prone, clunking struts will not rebound, causing the rear end to sag and degrading handling. **2005**—Tricky handling is still a problem.

Secret Warranties/Internal Bulletins/Service Tips

All models/years: Bulletins relate to automatic transmission popping out of gear. • At least three bulletins deal with manual transmission malfunctions. • Diagnostic and repair tips are offered on transfer clutch binding and/or bucking on turns. • Troubleshooting tips on a sticking anti-lock brake relay are offered. This problem is characterized by a lit ABS warning light or the ABS motor continuing to run and buzz when the ignition is turned off. • A rotten-egg smell could be caused by a defective catalytic converter. It will be replaced, after a bit of arguing, free of charge up to five years under the emissions warranty. **All models: 1999**—A broken air intake chamber box will cause stalling during start-up and the Check Engine light to remain lit. **1999–2002**—Sliding seat belt latch. **2000**—Growling noises from the engine area. • Automatic transmission light flashing. • Low brake pedal adjustment procedure. **2000–01**—Front oxygen air/fuel sensor cracking. **2001–03**—Premature brake pad wear. **2002–03**—Insufficient AC cooling. **2003**—Defective 4EAT transmission parking pawl rod. • Clutch pedal sticking. *WRX:* **2004–05**—Tips on silencing a noisy rear differential.

FORESTER, IMPREZA, WRX PROFILE

	1997	1998	1999	2000	2001	2002	2003	2004	2005
Cost Price ($)									
Forester	—	26,695	26,695	26,895	28,395	28,395	28,395	27,995	27,995
Base/Brighton	16,991	16,240	17,795	—	—	—	—	—	—
Impreza 4×4	21,395	21,395	21,995	21,995	22,196	21,995	22,995	22,995	22,995
WRX	—	—	—	—	—	34,995	34,995	35,495	35,495
Used Values ($)									
Forester ▲	—	6,000	7,000	8,500	11,500	14,000	16,000	18,000	21,000
Forester ▼	—	5,500	6,500	7,500	10,000	12,500	14,500	16,500	19,000
Base/Brighton ▲	3,500	4,500	5,000	—	—	—	—	—	—
Base/Brighton ▼	3,000	4,000	4,500	—	—	—	—	—	—
Impreza 4×4 ▲	4,500	5,000	6,000	7,000	8,000	10,000	12,000	14,000	16,000
Impreza 4×4 ▼	3,500	4,500	5,500	6,500	7,000	8,500	10,500	12,500	15,000
WRX ▲	—	—	—	—	—	14,000	17,000	21,000	25,000
WRX ▼	—	—	—	—	—	12,500	15,500	19,000	23,500
Reliability	3	3	3	3	3	4	4	4	4
Crash Safety (F)									
Forester	—	—	4	4	4	4	5	5	5
Impreza	4	—	—	—	—	4	4	—	—
Side (Forester)	—	—	—	—	5	5	5	5	5
Impreza	—	—	—	—	—	4	4	—	—
Side (IIHS)	—	—	—	—	—	5	5	5	5
Offset	—	—	—	—	—	5	5	5	5
Forester	—	—	5	5	5	5	5	5	5
Head Restraints	2	—	—	—	2	3	3	—	5
Forester	—	—	2	—	3	3	3	—	—
WRX	—	—	—	—	—	—	—	2	2
Rollover Resistance (Forester)	—	—	—	—	3	3	3	4	4
Impreza	—	—	—	—	—	4	4	—	—

LEGACY, OUTBACK ★ ★ ★

RATING: Average (1997–2006); Below Average (1989–96). A competent full-time 4×4 performer for drivers who want to move up in size, comfort, and features. Available as a four-door sedan or five-door wagon, the Legacy is cleanly and conventionally styled, with a hint of the Acura Legend in its rear end. The AWD is what this car is all about. It handles difficult terrain without the fuel penalty or clumsiness of many truck-based SUVs. The Outback is a marketing coup that stretches the definition of "sport-utility" by simply customizing the all-wheel-drive Legacy to give it more of an outdoorsy flair. Interestingly, what was a $10,000 gap between the high-end and entry-level model narrows to a couple thousand dollars after a few years. **"Real" city/highway fuel economy:** 11.0/7.8

L/100 km with a manual transmission or 10.9/7.9 L/100 km with an automatic. The 3.0L 6-cylinder engine burns 12.4/8.4 L/100 km. Owners say their fuel consumption is about 15 percent more than the estimates given above. **Maintenance/Repair costs:** Higher than average. Repairs are dealer-dependent. **Parts:** Parts aren't easily found and can be costly. **Extended warranty:** You should invest in an extended warranty to cover likely powertrain deficiencies after the base warranty has expired. **Best alternatives:** The Honda CR-V, Hyundai Tucson or Santa Fe, and Toyota RAV4. **Online help:** *www.autosafety.org* and *www.carsurvey.org*.

Strengths and Weaknesses

Costing a bit more than the smaller Impreza, these Subaru models are well-appointed, provide a comfortable ride and acceptable handling with the right options, and have lots of cargo room. On the downside, owners report problematic automatic transmission performance when it's hooked to the base engine; sluggish performance from the 2.5L, undoubtedly because of the car's heft; excessive engine noise; sloppy handling on base models; excessive 4-cylinder engine noise; cramped back seats, with a tight fit for the middle rear-seat passenger; limited rear headroom for tall passengers; trunk hinges that can damage cargo and cut into storage space; seat belts that may be too short for large occupants; and very dealer-dependent servicing.

First launched in 1989 as front-drives, these compacts are a bit slow off the mark. The 5-speed is a bit "notchy," and the automatic gearbox is slow to downshift, has difficulty staying in Overdrive, and is failure-prone. Early Legacy models are noisy, fuel-thirsty cars with bland styling that masks their solid, dependable AWD performance. Actually, the availability of a proven 4×4 powertrain in a compact family sedan or wagon makes these cars appealing for special use. In spite of their reputation for acceptable dependability, however, Subarus are not trouble-free—engine, clutch, turbo, and driveline defects are common on the early models through to the 1998 versions.

VEHICLE HISTORY: 1995–98—These redesigned models have sleeker styling, additional interior room (though legroom is still at a premium), a bit more horsepower with the base engine, and a new 2.5L 4-cylinder engine driving the 1996 AWD GT and LSi. The Outback, a Legacy/Madison Avenue spin-off, was transformed into a sport-utility wagon with a taller roof. Even with the improvements noted above, acceleration is still only passable (if you don't mind the loud engine). The 1997 models marked a return to the company's 4×4 roots, with the repackaging of its Legacy and Impreza 4×4 lineup as Outbacks. A Legacy 2.5L GT all-wheel-drive sporting sedan and wagon variant also joined the group that year. **1999**—Debut of an upgraded 2.2L engine. **2000**—Longer and carrying a new 2.5L engine. **2001**—Two new Outback wagons, featuring a more powerful 3.0L engine, joined the lineup. **2002**—The addition to the lineup of the H6-3.0 VDC Outback sedan, equipped with a standard 3.0L engine. **2003**—New front end styling; GT gets an upgraded engine and a semi-manual Sport Shift; Outback suspension is upgraded to improve cornering and reduce front-end plow. **2005**—Subaru's mid-sized cars are restyled and have larger dimensions, additional features, and more power. In fact, 2.5i models use a 168-hp 4-cylinder with a manual transmission or optional 4-speed automatic. However, a new 250-hp turbocharged version of that engine powers the Legacy 2.5 GT/GT Limited and Outback 2.5 XT models, and it's mated with a manual or an optional 5-speed automatic. The Outback 3.0 R sedan, L.L. Bean Edition wagon, and VDC Limited wagon come only with the 5-speed automatic and a 250-hp 3.0L 6-cylinder engine (up from 212 hp). The automatic transmissions include a manual-shift feature. On the safety front, all these Subarus have anti-lock brakes, front side airbags, and side curtain airbags. An anti-skid system is standard on the Outback 3.0 R VDC wagon but is otherwise unavailable.

The 6-cylinder engine is adequate but doesn't feel as if it has much in reserve. The automatic transmission shifts into too high a gear to adequately exploit the engine's power, and it's reluctant to downshift into the proper gear. On pre-2005 models, the 2.5L engine is a better performer with the manual gearbox, although its shift linkage isn't suitable for rapid gear changes. The 4-cylinder has several drawbacks as well: It's noisy and rough running, and it's tuned more for low-end torque than speedy acceleration.

Base models don't handle well. They bounce around on uneven pavement, the rear end tends to swing out during high-speed cornering, and there's too much body lean in turns at lesser speeds. Higher-end models handle well, though there's some excessive lean when cornering. The GT's firmer suspension exhibits above-average handling.

The Legacy and the Outback have had more than their share of reliability problems over the years. Powertrain defects can sideline the car for days. Engine and transmission problems keep showing up. Servicing can be awkward because of the crowded engine compartment, particularly on turbocharged versions.

Automatic transmission front seals and clutch breakdowns are most common through 2004; the transmission sometimes downshifts abruptly while descending a long grade or travelling on snow-packed highways; and the front brakes require frequent attention. Check Engine and ABS warning lights come on constantly, for no reason. Shock absorbers, constant velocity joints, and catalytic converters also often wear out prematurely. Other problems that appear over most model years include chronic electrical and fuel-system malfunctions; hard starting, surging, and stalling in cold weather; starter and ignition relay failures; and snow packing inside the wheelwells, binding steering. Misadjusted door strikers make for hard closing/opening.

Safety Summary

All models/years: Many reports of sudden acceleration in Drive and in Reverse, severe pulling to one side, ABS brake failures, and premature wearout of brake components. • Small horn buttons may be hard to find in an emergency. **All models: 1999**—Chronic cold engine hesitation, stalling. • Engine failure because of cracked #2 piston. • When accelerating or decelerating, vehicle will begin to jerk because of excessive play in the front axle. • Front bumper skirt catches on parking blocks, resulting in bumper twisting and ripping off. • The centre rear seat belt's poor design prohibits the installation of many types of child safety seats. **2000–01**—Igniter failure allowed unburned gasoline to flow into catalytic converter and resulted in chronic stalling. • Vehicle suddenly veers to the right when accelerating or braking. • Cruise control failed to disengage when brake pedal was depressed. • During a collision, airbags deployed but failed to inflate. • Excessive steering and vehicle vibration when passing over uneven pavement. • Steering lock-up while driving. • Vehicle's rear end bounces about when passing over bumps. • Engine failure because of a cracked #2 piston. • Frequent surging from a stop. • Cracked seat belt buckle. • Seat belts are too short for large occupants. • Rear centre seat belt prevents the secure attachment of child safety seats. **2002**—While idling in Park, vehicle suddenly jumped into Drive. **2003**—Chronic stalling in forward gear and in Reverse, particularly with 6-cylinder-equipped models:

> On multiple occasions, and with multiple drivers, I have had two 2003 Outbacks with frequent stalling when moving from Neutral to First, or to Reverse. This is potentially dangerous when moving out into traffic. Subaru denies receiving prior complaints (despite the material on your site) and in general denies that there is any problem. They also compelled me to sign a "gag" clause as part of a deal whereby they exchanged car #1 for car #2.

2004—Believe it or not, owners still complain of engine hesitation when accelerating from a coastdown or a stop, then sudden surging as the transmission hunts for a lower gear. This has been a generic problem with many Subarus for almost a decade. • Automatic transmission failure. • Seat belt came undone during a collision. • ABS doesn't prevent wheel lock-up.

Secret Warranties/Internal Bulletins/Service Tips

All models/years: Troubleshooting tips on a sticking anti-lock brake relay are offered. This problem is characterized by a lit ABS warning light or the ABS motor continuing to run/buzz when the ignition is turned off. • Diagnostic and repair tips are offered on transfer clutch binding and/or bucking on turns. • A rotten-egg smell is likely caused by a defective catalytic converter. It will be replaced, after a bit of arguing, free of charge under the emissions warranty. **All models: 1997–99**—Excessive driveline vibration is covered in TSB #05-33-98R. Subaru's fix requires modifying the differential. **2000–01**—Loose bolts on the front seat belt retractor. • Inlet heater hose leaks engine coolant. • Probable causes for the automatic transmission Temperature light flashing. • Measures that will eliminate brake squeal. **2000–04**—Door mirror makes wind noise. **2002**—Excessive blower motor noise. • More countermeasures to reduce brake squeal. **2003**—Defective engine water pump. • Improved Sport Shift cold-weather operation. • Defective transmission parking pawl rod. • Roof-rack wind noise. • Premature suspension corrosion:

Certain rear suspension subframe components were produced with poor paint quality, which, after continued exposure to corrosive road salts for a period of several years, could result in rust-out of the component and possible breakage of the subframe. If such breakage occurs while the vehicle is being operated, control of the vehicle could be affected, increasing the risk of a crash.

Remedy: Dealers will clean and rustproof the rear suspension subframe.

2004—Possible causes of transfer clutch binding when cornering. **2005**—Seat belt chime when seat is unoccupied. • AC filter will be replaced free of charge.

LEGACY, OUTBACK PROFILE

	1997	1998	1999	2000	2001	2002	2003	2004	2005
Cost Price ($)									
Legacy 4×4	19,995	19,995	20,495	23,595	24,295	27,395	27,295	27,295	27,995
Outback	30,195	30,895	30,895	34,695	35,195	31,995	37,995	26,995	32,995
Used Values ($)									
Legacy 4×4 ▲	4,000	4,500	6,500	8,500	10,500	13,000	15,000	18,000	21,000
Legacy 4×4 ▼	3,000	4,000	5,500	7,000	9,000	11,500	13,500	17,000	19,000
Outback ▲	5,000	6,500	8,000	9,500	12,000	14,000	15,500	17,000	23,000
Outback ▼	4,000	6,000	7,500	8,500	10,500	13,500	14,000	16,000	21,000
Reliability	3	3	3	3	3	3	3	3	3
Crash Safety (F)									
Legacy 4d	4	4	4	—	4	4	4	4	5
Side	—	3	3	—	4	4	3	4	—
Wagon	—	—	—	—	—	—	4	4	—
Side (IIHS)	—	—	—	—	—	—	—	—	2
Offset	3	3	3	5	5	5	5	5	5
Head Restraints	2	2	2	2	3	3	3	4	3
Rollover Resistance	—	—	—	—	—	4	4	4	—

Suzuki

AERIO, ESTEEM, SWIFT, SWIFT+ ★ ★ ★ ★ ★

RATING: *Aerio:* Recommended (2003–06). *Esteem:* Recommended (1996–2002). *Swift and Swift+:* Recommended (2002–06); Above Average (1995–2001). With the Esteem, getting the most horsepower bang for your buck means shopping for an Esteem sport model or looking at the upgraded 2000 model year or newer versions. Wagons are especially versatile and reasonably priced for the equipment provided. Both the base GL and upscale GLX come loaded with standard features

The Suzuki Aerio.

that cost extra on other models. **"Real" city/highway fuel economy:** *Esteem:* 8.3/6.0 L/100 km with a manual transmission or 9.0/6.3 L/100 km with an automatic. *Aerio:* 9.4/7.0 L/100 km with a manual or 9.3/7.0 L/100 km with an automatic. *Aerio AWD:* 9.9/7.6 L/100 km. **Maintenance/Repair costs:** Average. **Parts:** Average cost, and parts are easily found. **Extended warranty:** A toss-up. Some long-term powertrain protection would be helpful. **Best alternatives:** GM Firefly or Metro; Honda Civic; Hyundai Accent or Elantra; Mazda Protegé; Nissan Sentra; and Toyota Echo, Tercel, or Corolla. **Online help:** *www.autosafety.org* and *www.carsurvey.org.*

 ## Strengths and Weaknesses

The Esteem is a small four-door sedan that is a step up from the Swift. Smaller than the Honda Civic and Chrysler Neon, it has a fairly spacious interior, offering rear accommodation (for two adults) that is comparable to or better than most cars in its class. It stands out, with its European-styled body and large array of such standard features as AC, a fold-down back seat, and remote trunk and fuel-door releases. The roomy cabin has lots of front and rear headroom and legroom for four adults. Cargo space is fairly good with the sedan and exceptional with the wagon's rear seats folded.

The small 95-hp engine delivers respectable acceleration, and overall performance is acceptable, thanks to the Esteem's four-wheel independent suspension, which gives just the right balance between a comfortable ride and no-surprise handling. For a bit more power, look for a '96 or later sport variant that carries a 125-hp powerplant.

Suzuki's Aerio entry-level, front-drive sedan and wagon replaced the Esteem for the 2003 model year. Equipped with optional all-wheel drive, it is one of the lowest-priced AWD vehicles available in Canada. Both models come with a 145-hp 4-cylinder engine that's among the most powerful standard engines in this class. Every Aerio comes with AC, power windows and mirrors, tilt steering wheel, CD player, and split folding rear seats.

Suzuki's Swift is built at CAMI Automotive in Ingersoll, Ontario, and was first launched in 1995 for the American and Canadian markets. It was dropped in the States in 2001, but continues to be sold in Canada as the Swift and the Swift+. The Swift+, essentially a GM/Daewoo Aveo knock-off, was first launched as a 2004 model. It has posted good reliability scores, though crashworthiness info is quite sparse.

VEHICLE HISTORY: 1998—A wagon version joined the lineup. 1999—New front-end styling, 14-inch wheels, and an upgraded sound system. 2000—More power provided by a 122-hp 1.8L engine. 2003—Aerio makes its debut. 2004—The 145-hp 2.0L is replaced by a 155-hp 2.3L engine. Swift+ debuts. 2005—Standard front side airbags and a host of new exterior styling touches. 2006—ABS becomes a standard item.

Here are some of the drawbacks to owning one of these econoboxes: Small tires compromise handling, and power steering doesn't transmit much road feedback. The automatic transmission may shift harshly and vibrate excessively between gear changes. Braking is mediocre for a car this light.

During the relatively short time the Esteem has been around, it has proven to be a high-quality, reliable small car. In this respect, it competes well with its Detroit-built rivals such as the Chevrolet Cavalier, Dodge Neon, and Ford Escort, while being outclassed by the Honda Civic, Mazda Protegé, and Toyota Corolla. Problems reported by Esteem and Aerio owners include premature transmission, clutch, tire, and brake wear; noisy front brakes; occasional electrical short circuits; wind and water intrusion into the passenger compartment; and fragile body panels and trim items. Owners also complain of paint peeling.

Safety Summary

All models: 1998—Airbag failed to deploy. • Seat belt failed to lock up in a collision. • Vehicle is unstable at high speeds. • Door handle failures. **1999**—Engine oil leak sprays oil throughout the engine compartment. • Loss of power when accelerating. • Stuck accelerator pedal. • Chronic stalling. • Transmission and brake failures. **2000**—Sudden acceleration from a stop. • Automatic transmission bangs into gear. • Gearshift lever fell from Drive to Neutral and is hard to move. • Windshield seal vibrates and cracks in cold weather. **2001**—Automatic transmission stuck in lower gear. • Brake failure. • Complete electrical failure fixed temporarily by lifting the hood and jiggling the master control fuse. **2002**—Brake caliper may leak fluid, and early rotor wear. • Faulty wheel bearings. • Ball joints may fall out. • Lower control arm snapped. • Loose heat shield bolts. • Premature tire wear. **2003**—Many complaints of broken, cracked, or bent aluminum wheel rims and wheel bearing failures. • Delayed shifts. • Vehicle refuses to go into Reverse gear. • CV axle joint separation. • Misaligned power-steering bracket. • Trunk pops up while driving. **2004**—Sudden, unintended acceleration. • Original-equipment tires wear out prematurely. **2005**—Passenger-side airbag deployed for no reason. • Front brake failure; faulty brake pads. • Excessive body shake caused by defective stabilizer bushing, bracket, and mount. • Engine was damaged after Aerio was driven through a puddle of water. • Prematurely worn brakes and Yokohama and Michelin tires continue to top the list of owner complaints:

> When my vehicle had 11,295 miles [18,000 km] on it I had to replace the tires as they had excessive wear. The viscous coupling was replaced and the alignment was changed per my work order as recommended by the TS bulletin 11225. Now my car has 30,000 miles [48,000 km] on it and I have to replace my tires again. Obviously there is something wrong with the manufacturing of the vehicle itself as to cause to sets of tires to be worn bare after only 30,000 miles.

Secret Warranties/Internal Bulletins/Service Tips

All models: 1998–99—Remote-entry battery failure because of defective key fob diode. **1999–2002**—Voluntary emissions recall, replacing the vapour control valve. **2000–04**—Battery discharge can be avoided by installing an upgraded alternator, says TSB #TS-03-06304. **2004–05**—Changed alignment specifica-tions. **2004–06**—Suzuki admits that its own faulty suspension may cause abnormal tire wear (TSB #TS 05-11225). **2005**—The stabilizer-bar mount bushing may cause a clunking sound to be heard coming from underneath the vehicle.

AERIO, ESTEEM, SWIFT, SWIFT+ PROFILE

	1997	1998	1999	2000	2001	2002	2003	2004	2005
Cost Price ($)									
Aerio	—	—	—	—	—	—	15,785	15,995	17,995
Aerio SX (AWD)	—	—	—	—	—	—	19,785	20,395	20,995
Esteem GL	13,495	13,895	13,995	15,495	15,695	16,195	—	—	—
Esteem GLX	15,495	16,895	17,195	18,491	18,795	19,795	—	—	—
Swift	10,995	11,495	11,495	11,595	11,595	—	—	—	—
Used Values ($)									
Aerio ▲	—	—	—	—	—	—	7,000	9,000	12,000
Aerio ▼	—	—	—	—	—	—	6,000	7,500	10,500
Aerio SX (AWD) ▲	—	—	—	—	—	—	9,000	11,000	14,000
Aerio SX (AWD) ▼	—	—	—	—	—	—	7,500	9,500	13,000
Esteem GL ▲	2,000	2,500	3,000	4,000	5,000	6,500	—	—	—
Esteem GL ▼	1,500	2,000	2,500	3,000	4,000	5,500	—	—	—
Esteem GLX ▲	3,000	3,500	4,000	4,500	5,500	7,500	—	—	—
Esteem GLX ▼	2,500	3,000	3,500	4,000	4,500	6,500	—	—	—

	1	2	3	4	5	6	7	8	9
Swift ▲	500	700	1,000	2,000	2,500	—	—	—	—
Swift ▼	500	500	800	1,400	1,700	—	—	—	—
Reliability	4	4	4	4	5	5	5	5	5
Crash Safety (F)	—	—	—	—	—	—	—	4	
Side	—	—	—	—	—	—	—	5	
Side (IIHS)	—	—	—	—	—	—	—	—	1
Offset	—	—	—	—	—	5	5	5	5
Head Restraints	—	—	—	—	—	2	2	2	2

Toyota/General Motors

COROLLA, MATRIX/VIBE ★ ★ ★

RATING: *Corolla:* Average (1985–2006). This model is no longer a paragon of high quality, so be wary of serious safety deficiencies that include airbag malfunctions, airbag-induced injuries, sudden acceleration, hesitation and then surging, brake failures, seat belt failures, windshield reflections, dash gauge "wash out," poorly designed headlights that misdirect the light beam, and hard starting:

> I bought a new 2005 Toyota Corolla from…Funks Toyota, Manitoba, Canada. On a number of occasions a lot of cranking is required before the car starts when the engine is warm. A number of owners have the same problem as reported on various forums on the Internet. I have had multiple incidents. The dealer was contacted and I was told that it is just normal to crank for longer periods occasionally.

Since the 1997 model was "de-contented" through the use of lower-quality materials, less soundproofing, and fewer standard features, there has been a noticeable reduction in quality control. The 1995–96 models combine the best array of standard features, quality control, and reasonable (for a Toyota) used prices. 1998–2001 models are good second choices with their horsepower-enhanced engines. But ditch the poor-performing or failure-prone Bridgestone, Firestone, and Goodyear Integrity tires. *Matrix/Vibe:* Average (2003–06). Aimed at the youth market, these versatile spin-offs don't provide enough horsepower to justify their sporty pretensions, and they aren't suitable for any place more rugged than Vancouver's Stanley Park. Higher Vibe prices quickly fall near the Matrix level after a few years, and the Vibe also generates more owner complaints than the Matrix does (possibly due to higher-quality Matrix manufacturing in the Ontario plant and better servicing by Toyota dealers). **"Real" city/highway fuel economy:** *Corolla:* 7.1/5.3 L/100 km with a manual transmission or 8.1/5.8 L/100 km with an automatic. *Matrix:* 7.7/6.0 L/100 km with a manual or 8.3/6.4 L/100 km with an automatic. The 6-speed manual burns 9.5/6.8 L/100 km. *Vibe:* 7.7/6.0 L/100 km with a manual tranny or 8.3/6.4 L/100 km with an automatic. *AWD:* 9.1/6.9 L/100 km. Owners report that their fuel consumption is about 10 percent higher than these estimates. **Maintenance/Repair costs:** *Corolla:* Lower than average, and repairs can be done anywhere. *Matrix/Vibe:* Powertrain and body part supply is a bit problematic, plus owners complain that they cost more than similar parts used on the other models. **Parts:** Corolla parts can be expensive, but they are easily found; Vibe parts aren't easily found and are frequently back-ordered several weeks in Western Canada. **Extended warranty:** Not needed. **Best alternatives:** Matrix and Vibe third-year depreciation is brutal—a bargain for buyers, but a disappointment come trade-in time. Instead of the Matrix/Vibe or Corolla, consider the GM Firefly or Metro; Hyundai Accent or Elantra; Mazda Protegé; Nissan Sentra; and Suzuki Aerio, Esteem, Forsa, or Swift. For the cabin storage space and all-wheel drive, check out the Suzuki Aerio AWD or the Subaru Forester. **Online help:** *www. matrixowners.com, www.autosafety.org,* and *www.carsurvey.org.*

Strengths and Weaknesses

A step up from the Tercel/Echo, the Corolla has long been Toyota's standard-bearer in the compact-sedan class. Over the years, however, the car has grown in size, price, and refinement to the point where it can now be considered a small family sedan. All Corollas ride on a front-drive platform with independent suspension on all wheels.

Post-1987 models are much improved over earlier versions, and many are still on our roads after 15 years. The two-door models provide sporty performance and good fuel economy, especially when equipped with the 16-valve engine. The base engine, however, lacks power and is agonizingly slow when merging or passing on the highway. Owners report problems with premature front suspension strut and brake wear; brake vibration; faulty defrosting that allows the windows to fog up in winter; and rusting of body seams, especially door bottoms, side mirror mounts, trunk and hatchback lids, and wheel openings.

The 1990–94 Corolla's problems are limited to harsh automatic shifting, early front brake pad and strut/shock wearout, AC high-pressure tube leaks, electrical glitches, ignition problems, windshield wiper linkage failures, and some interior squeaks and rattles. They do, however, still require regular valve adjustments to prevent serious engine problems. Less of a problem with these later models, rusting is usually confined to the undercarriage and other areas where the mouldings attach to sheet metal.

The 1995–99 models have chronic seat belt retractor glitches and airbag malfunctions. Additionally, owners report powertrain, brake, and electrical problems; poor rear windshield defrosting; vibrations, squeaks, and rattles afflicting the brakes, steering, and suspension; and body trim imperfections that include water leaking through the doors.

The 2000–02 models continue to have relatively serious quality problems that include engine hesitation and surging; oil leaks; stalling out after a refuel; tire failures; transmissions that pop out of Drive into Neutral, or refuse to shift at all;

a suspension that easily bottoms out; the vehicle wandering all over the road; faulty strut assemblies; warped brake rotors; fenders that are easily dented; a windshield that's easily cracked; and seat belt shoulder straps mounted too high, cutting across the driver's neck.

Year 2003–05 Corolla, Matrix, and Vibe owners report many more mechanical and body problems, with the Vibe leading the way in incidents listed. Problems cited for all three vehicles include hard starts; engine hesitation and surging; engine sludge buildup, requiring expensive repairs; excessive steering wander; transmission/clutch failures and thumping; the vehicle rolling away with the transmission in Park; loss of braking; defective crankshafts; power-steering-pump and fuel-pump failures (a new fuel pump can cost $771 U.S.); electrical short circuits; dash and tail lights that don't come on right away; AC condenser that's vulnerable to road debris damage; loose driver's seat; seat belts that lock up when in use; front dash noise; hubcaps that continually fall off; sunroof and door rattles; paint that chips off the hood; and a rotten-egg smell that comes from the exhaust or through the vents. Owners also say the Corolla is hard to control in inclement weather, and it surges whenever the AC is enabled:

> The 2005 Toyota Corolla has a defective temperature control system in that whenever the vehicle's air conditioning activates or while...the two defrost settings are on, at idle speeds the vehicle surges or accelerates forward to the extent it overrides the braking action at a stopped position.

VEHICLE HISTORY: 1993—Redesigned model is larger and equipped with a driver-side airbag and optional ABS. **1994**—A passenger-side airbag and improved seat belt retractors. **1995**—A torquier 1.8L engine added, with 10 fewer horses (105) than the '94. **1996**—Five fewer horses (100), new front and rear ends, and an upgraded manual transmission. **1997**—An upscale CE version debuts, while the wagon is axed. **1998**—Another redesign produced a slightly more powerful engine (120 horses), an additional 5 cm in vehicle length, and optional front-passenger side-impact airbags. **1999**—Addition of a front stabilizer bar to improve handling. **2000**—Five additional horses and tilt steering on the CE and LE. **2001**—A slight face-lift, and the addition of a new sport-oriented variant called the Corolla S. The VE was dropped, and the formerly mid-level CE replaced it, carrying fewer standard features. The LE was dropped to the CE's former level and was also "de-contented," losing its standard AC and power windows, locks, and mirrors. **2003**—Corolla redesigned to be taller, wider, and longer; adds a new 4-speed automatic transmission; and gets five more horses. The launch of the Matrix/Vibe. **2004**—Matrix XRS lose ten horses (to 170). **2005**—A light restyling and side curtain airbags are optional for all models. Toyota also launched its new high-performance Corolla XRS sedan.

Matrix/Vibe

These small front-drive or all-wheel-drive sporty wagons are crosses between mini SUVs and station wagons, but they're packaged like small minivans. Vibe is built in Fremont, California, at GM's NUMMI factory. The nearly identical Toyota Matrix is manufactured in Toyota's Cambridge, Ontario, plant alongside the Corolla, whose platform it shares, though it provides a larger interior volume.

The front-drive Matrix/Vibe is equipped with a 1.8L 130-hp engine, a 5-speed manual overdrive transmission, and lots of standard features; however, the weak, buzzy base engine can be felt throughout the car. The 4×4 models are about 10 percent heavier and get seven fewer horses (123) than the already power-challenged 130-hp front-drive. Says *Forbes* magazine:

> [B]oth all-wheel-drive cars are saddled with a really wretched 4-speed automatic that almost has to be shifted manually to get the car moving. To put it bluntly, the AWD Vibe and Matrix are so pokey, they feel like they're towing Winnebagos. To boot, the 1.8L engine doesn't hit its paltry torque peak...until a screaming 4200 rpm, at which point the vibration—did somebody say Vibe?—in the cabin is worse than a little off-putting.

The Matrix XRS and Vibe GT are the top-of-the-line performance leaders, with a 170-hp 4-cylinder engine and a high-performance 6-speed manual gearbox, plus ABS, a premium six-speaker stereo, an anti-theft system, 17-inch alloy wheels, and unique exterior cladding.

These vehicles hail from factories that have garnered high quality ratings, and they also come with similar warranties. If you really need additional horsepower, get either the XRS or GT. But keep in mind that there are better-quality high-performance choices out there, such as the Honda Civic Si, Mazda5, or a base Acura RSX. Other front-drives worth considering are the Chrysler PT Cruiser, Hyundai Elantra or Tiburon, Honda Civic, Nissan Sentra, and Toyota Corolla. Of course, the Subaru Impreza or Forester are other good choices for the 4×4 variant.

Safety Summary

All models/years: Chronic airbag malfunctions; they deploy when they shouldn't, or don't deploy when they should. • Sudden, unintended acceleration. • Engine hesitation and surging. **All models: 1998**—Engine compartment fires, gas fumes in the interior, brake and power-steering failures, and excessive steering-column noise. • Excessive drifting and high-speed instability because of the lack of a stabilizer bar. • Premature control arm failure. • Seat belt released in accident. • Rear wheel broke at the axle. • Random honking. **1998–2000**—Brakes lock up. • Vehicle continues to wander and sway at moderate speeds; side winds increase the vehicle's instability. • Gearshift dropped from Drive to Neutral while driving. • Floor mat jams the accelerator. • Engine stalls after refuelling. • Front strut assembly failure. • Inadequate headlight illumination; one side will be aimed too high, the other side too low. **1999**—Engine compartment fire. • Loss of braking ability. • Cruise control self-activates. • Automatic transmission locked up while driving. • Vehicle went out of control after rear control arm failure. • At cruising speed, vehicle tends to wander all over the road. • Windshield shattered when door was closed. • Poor headlight design causes blind spot and poor visibility. • Defective engine camshaft gets inadequate oil lubrication and loses compression. • Rear seat belts aren't compatible with many child safety seats. **2001**—Stuck accelerator pedal. • Headlight illumination problem continues; high beam shoots skyward and is especially hazardous in rain or fog. • Rear driver-side axle sheared in half; vehicle rolled over. • Excessive front brake pad wear; premature failure of the brake proportioning valve and rear brake shoes. • Hole in the oil pan. • Failure of all four Goodyear Integrity tires. • Inside trunk release handle doesn't glow as advertised. **2002**—Fuel leakage:

> On 04/29/02 consumer discovered that vehicle was leaking fuel. Vehicle was repaired by dealer who advised consumer that the fuel lines had come loose. On 07/29/02 while driving, engine compartment caught on fire as a result of fuel leaking.

• In one deployment, airbag ripped and allowed child to be seriously injured. • Unable to shift out of Park. • While using cruise control, gas pedal suddenly went to the floor. • Left rear tire fell off while driving. • Vehicle tends to wander at highway speeds:

> Vehicle wanders and sways back and forth. Vehicle was taken to dealership, and mechanic stated that all four wheels were bent. Vehicle came from factory that way. Goodyear, Integrity, P185/65R14. Right front tire had a bulge on outside.

• Early fuel-pump replacement led to rotten-egg smell. • Strong sulfur smell in the interior. • Weak climate-control system. • Both headlights have stray beams that project upward at a 45-degree angle; very distracting, particularly in mist. • Poor-quality wiper blade. **2003**—Fire ignited because of loose fuel line. • Vehicle suddenly shut down while underway at 100 km/h; in another case, vehicle suddenly accelerated while cruise control was engaged. • Several owners report that a hole in the oil pan caused vehicle to stall. • When the vehicle was parked, the parking brake was released and both airbags deployed; both airbags deployed right after driver turned on the ignition switch; airbags deployed after car passed over a bump in the road; in a rear-end collision, front airbag came out but failed to deploy; side airbag failed to deploy in a side impact; both airbags failed to deploy in a frontal collision:

> [Our] [t]hirteen-year-old daughter sustained [a] severe traumatic brain injury after [a] head-on collision. Her airbag deployed, [but the] top of passenger-side airbag was completely blown apart from one side to the other, allowing her head to strike [the] dash.

> We both had seat belts on. I sustained bruising of [my] hips and right rib. She was in [a] coma and [is] just now beginning to move [her] left side. She still cannot sit up, stand, walk, talk coherently, eat, or do anything for herself.

• Faulty seat belt wiring could cause a fire. • Floormat catches accelerator pedal. • Brake failure when decelerating. • Pedal goes soft when brakes are applied, and brakes lock up when coming to a gradual stop, resulting in extended stopping distances. • Rear welding broke away from the frame, resulting in complete loss of control. • Sudden collapse of the rear axle. • Rear control arm broke while driving at 110 km/h. • Left rear tire fell off. • Defective Uniroyal and Goodyear Integrity tires. • Warped wheels. • Shifter refused to go into gear while driving; transmission sometimes goes from Drive to Neutral while driving; refuses to shift out of Park. • Vehicle wanders all over the road and pulls to the left or right at moderate speeds. In windy conditions, vehicle becomes hard to steer, veering left or right. • Glow-in-the-dark inside trunk release doesn't glow in the dark because it is rarely exposed to light (owner actually crawled inside trunk to test it out!). • Poor-quality wiper blades. • Poorly designed headlights have stray high beams that project upward at a 45-degree angle, and low-beam headlights are too dim. • Sunlight washes out dash readings. **2004**—Hand brake doesn't hold very well. • Vehicle crashed after suddenly accelerating on the freeway. • Engine surges when stopped at a traffic light and AC compressor is engaged. • Noisy, ineffective, and prematurely worn brakes. • Misaligned steering wheel. • Brake and gas pedals are mounted too close together. • Rotten-egg exhaust smell. • Front passenger-side windshield frame obstructs visibility. • Sun visor interferes with the rear-view mirror. • Sunroof came unglued from the metal frame; glass from the sunroof flew off. • Windshield very susceptible to cracks. **2005**—Sudden brake lock-up. • Power-steering failure. • Passenger-seat sensor is too sensitive and rings an alarm when there is the slightest pressure on the seat. • Water pools in the ventilation system:

> [S]evere mildew growth has occurred in ventilation system. This mildew creates an awful sewage smell, and is extremely irritating to my allergies. Dealer sprayed Lysol disinfectant in ventilation intake. The problem came back a week later. To this day, I continually must spray Lysol in the ventilation system. Many types of mildew can be toxic to any human (not just allergy sufferers), and are *known* to cause cancer, which is very concerning to me. Toyota's "official" solution to this problem is to keep spraying Lysol in the ventilation system, and to open the window when the [sewage] smell becomes unbearable. I personally know other 2005 Corolla owners, and their Corollas suffer from the same problem.

• Car will not slow down when foot is taken off the accelerator pedal. • Low engine intake ingests water when going through puddles, causing severe engine damage. • Steering-wheel lock-up. • Excessive play in rear hub bearings. *Matrix:* **2003**—Engine surges when braking with AC engaged. • Excessive steering wander; feels a bit vague, with too much play; some torque steer (twisting) evident, especially on wet roads. • The manual shift lever's upward and forward position is counterintuitive and feels a bit ragged. • Instrument panel lights are dimmed by automatic sensor to the point where they can't be read in twilight hours, and the automatic headlights come on and go off for no apparent reason. **2004**—Hand brake doesn't hold very well. • Windshield very susceptible to cracks. • Clutch failures with the manual transmission. • Car drifts out of control and crashes; steering is non-responsive:

> Matrix drifted to the left while driving, resulting in the consumer losing control and the vehicle flipping over. As the consumer attempted once more to gain control of the steering, the vehicle veered off to the left, hit a ditch, went airborne, and flipped. Toyota determined that there were steering problems.

Dealers have blamed a defective steering yoke and poor-quality original-equipment tires as the causes for this instability and steering loss. • Sudden, unintended acceleration:

> While at a stop sign, the sudden acceleration happened again, and I was unable to immediately stop my car from lurching forward. It moved several inches into oncoming (perpendicular) traffic before I finally threw it into Park and pulled the emergency brake to stop it. No accident occurred, but it came close, and I had my toddler in the back seat, so I consider this [to be] a serious matter. I took it to my dealership (Ourisman Toyota in Chantilly, VA) that Monday, and they kept it for two days. They ran all diagnostic tests possible and found no problem. Nothing was fixed because no test showed a problem, but I am scared to drive my car—the sudden acceleration happens only randomly and cannot be predicted. I drive with only one foot, so this is not a case of two-footed driving and accidentally stepping on the accelerator. In each case, my foot was off the accelerator and on the brake.

• Warped front brake rotors. • Dashboard reflected onto the windshield. • Front bumper/spoiler drags on the ground over any uneven surface. • Ice collects in wheel rims, throwing tires out of balance. **2005**—Hard starting and chronic stalling. • Engine began racing while vehicle was stopped. • Alloy wheel split in half. • Complete brake loss. *Vibe:* **2003**—The Vibe has generated a few more safety-related complaints than the Matrix, and they are in response to different failures, for the most part. • Vehicle surges when foot is taken off the accelerator; several accidents caused by sudden acceleration. • Vehicle will roll while in Park. • Faulty ABS. • Dash gauges can't be read when wearing sunglasses. • Automatic headlight sensor turns the headlights on and off, about 20 times per day, depending on sun and shade variations. • When the lights go on, dash lights become unreadable. • Transmission indicator isn't lit at night. • When driving away after start-up, 15–20 seconds elapse before headlights and tail lights are automatically turned on. • Sunroof suddenly exploded. • Excessive condensation on interior glass. • Wet windows aren't wiped clean when rolled back up. • Refuelling cannot be done without a large amount of fuel being spit out. • Rear outboard seat belts constantly tighten. • Windshield is easily cracked by small stones. **2004**—Again, owners say there is too much steering play, making the Vibe, like its Toyota counterpart, highly unstable on the highway. • Rear-passenger seat belt may be hazardous to children:

The rear-passenger seat belt twisted around the child's abdomen and would not release. Every time the child moved, it clicked tighter. The child had to be cut out of the seat belt.

• Loose driver's seat. • Automatic door locks don't secure the door shut. • Instrument-cluster chrome finish reflects into windshield. • Power side window cracked as it was being raised. • Speedometer needle can't be seen on sunny days. • Headlights are too dim for night driving. • Original-equipment battery is inadequate for winter start-ups. • The original-equipment Continental tires produce excessive vibration and "cupping," and fail prematurely. • Wheel lug nuts may fail:

We took our 2004 Pontiac Vibe all-wheel drive in to Discount Tire to buy four new tires. Discount Tire called us later to inform us that four lugs snapped off while torquing the lugs to 80 ft. lbs. They checked their torque stick and used two other sticks, which continued to snap off the lugs. They sent the car over to Midas to have [it] repaired, and days later when we went to pick it up, I had them check all the lugs again...at 80 ft. lbs. one more lug snapped. So, again, we waited for a new lug to arrive. A total of five lugs snapped off the back end of the car, well before 80 ft. lbs. of torque was applied. I work at a steel plant, and had our lab check a broken lug, and their results were that the lugs were [so] brittle that there was no longation of the bolt before it broke. Discount Tire did an outstanding job in taking care of their customer; I am concerned with how many more lugs out on the roads are too brittle and may snap.

• Many electrical shorts. • Loose firewall shield screws. **2005**—Engine surging when braking. • Poor rear visibility:

On a trip to Cleveland we found out it is not safe. There is not enough visibility in the rear because of a poor design. I had to avoid 4 potential accidents. The driver cannot see others approaching in other lanes at high speeds.

• Hard starts. • Power steering malfunctions. • Severe pulling to one side when accelerating or braking. • Premature tire wear. • Mice can crawl into the dash/air vents.

Secret Warranties/Internal Bulletins/Service Tips

All models/years: Improved disc brake pad kits are described in TSB #BR94-004. • Brake pulsation/vibration, another generic Toyota problem, is fully addressed in TSB #BR94-002, "Cause and Repair of Vibration and Pulsation." • Complaints of steering-column noise may require the replacement of the steering-column assembly, a repair covered under Toyota's base warranty. • AM static noise on all vehicles with power antennas usually means the antenna is poorly grounded. • Toyota has developed special procedures for eliminating AC odours and excessive wind noise. These problems are covered in TSBs #AC00297 and #BO00397, respectively. *Corolla:* **1990–2001**—Toyota has developed a special grease to eliminate clicking when the vehicle goes into Drive or Reverse. **1998**—

Tips on reducing excessive engine V-belt noise. • Delayed upshift to Overdrive with cruise control engaged can be fixed by changing the cruise-control ECU logic. • Water leakage into the rear cab can be plugged by installing an improved C-pillar moulding clip. • If the rear door glass malfunctions when temperatures dive, install an upgraded mounting channel insert bar. • Toyota will replace the airbag computer under a service campaign. **1998–99**—A front suspension squeaking noise can be silenced by replacing the steering-rack end shaft under warranty, but Toyota tells dealers to do the repair only if the customer demands it. **1998–2000**—In an attempt to reduce brake vibration complaints, Toyota will install a new front disc brake pad kit, says TSB #BR002-00, issued March 10, 2000. **1999**—A single-cylinder misfire that causes a rough idle or the activation of the MIL will be fixed under Toyota's base warranty. **1999–2002**—Accessory drivebelt/belt tensioner assembly noise is addressed in TSB #EG015-01, published December 7, 2001. The service bulletin claims the squeak or rattle noise will be corrected free of charge up to 3 years/58,000 km (36,000 mi.) if the owner complains. • Vibration troubleshooting tips. • Sulfur exhaust odour remedies. • Countermeasures for vehicle pulling to one side. **2002–04**—Troubleshooting tips for fixing a poorly performing AC. **2002–07**—Repair tips for correcting a severe pull to one side when underway (TSB #ST005-01). **2003–04**—Deformed roof mouldings. • Sulfur exhaust odour countermeasures. **2003–05**—Ways to silence front- and rear-door wind noise and a rear hub axle bearing humming. • Toyota admits poor heater performance may be a problem and suggests that its upgraded AC will increase the heat (TSB #AC002-05). **2003–06**—Excessive transmission noise:

WHISTLE/HOOT NOISE BETWEEN 35–40 MPH (56–64 KM/H)

BULLETIN NO.: TC012-05   **DATE: SEPTEMBER 1, 2005**

WHISTLE/HOOT NOISE FROM AUTOMATIC TRANSAXLE

2003–06 Corolla

INTRODUCTION: Some 2003–06 model year Corolla vehicles equipped with the 1ZZ-FE engine and an automatic transaxle (ATM) may exhibit a "whistle" or "hoot" noise under light acceleration at 35–40 mph (56–64 km/h) with the ATM at normal operating temperature. ATM cooler lines have been modified to reduce this condition on customer complaint vehicles.

2003–07—Remedy for a windshield ticking noise. **2004–07**—Fixing front-seat squeaking. **2005–06**—Engine vibration/drone when accelerating. • Toyota's correction for hard starts:

EXTENDED CRANK TIME/HARD START

BULLETIN NO.: EG053-06   **DATE: SEPTEMBER 4, 2006**

2005–06 Corolla & Matrix

Some 2005 and 2006 model year Corolla and Matrix vehicles equipped with a 1ZZ-FE engine may exhibit a "no start" or "extended crank" condition. This may be caused by insufficient fuel pressure after the vehicle has been parked for a period of time. The fuel pump assembly manufacturing process has been improved to correct this condition.

• A free grill mesh is available to protect the AC condenser from damage from road debris (TSB #AC002-06). *Matrix:* **2003**—Most of the Corolla bulletins also apply to the Matrix. The following Matrix items may affect the Corolla and Vibe, as well. • Upper suspension tapping noise. • No airflow from centre vents. • Loose or deformed front or rear glass door run. • AC doesn't put out sufficient cool air. • Headlights come on when turned off. • Sulfur odour in the interior. • Discoloured wheelhouse moulding. **2003–04**—Rotten-egg exhaust remedy. • Console door won't stay closed. *Vibe:* **2003**—Poor engine performance after 7000 rpm. • Transmission shifts too early when accelerating at full throttle and the engine is cold. • Harsh shifting. • Water leak from the A-pillar or headliner area. • Upper suspension tapping noise. • Low voltage display or dim lights. **2003–04**—Harsh 1–2 upshifts. • Slipping transmission. • Rotten-egg exhaust remedy. **2004**— Reverse servo cover leak.

COROLLA, MATRIX/VIBE PROFILE

	1997	1998	1999	2000	2001	2002	2003	2004	2005
Cost Price ($)									
Base Corolla	13,968	14,928	15,090	15,625	15,625	15,765	15,290	15,410	15,490
Matrix	—	—	—	—	—	—	16,745	16,745	16,925
XR AWD	—	—	—	—	—	—	24,115	24,210	24,550
XRS AWD	—	—	—	—	—	—	24,540	24,640	25,560
Vibe	—	—	—	—	—	—	20,995	21,150	19,900
GT AWD	—	—	—	—	—	—	27,000	27,140	25,670
Used Values ($)									
Base Corolla ▲	3,500	4,000	4,500	5,000	6,500	7,500	9,000	10,000	11,500
Base Corolla ▼	3,000	3,500	4,000	4,500	6,000	7,000	7,500	9,000	10,500
Matrix ▲	—	—	—	—	—	—	9,500	11,000	12,500
Matrix ▼	—	—	—	—	—	—	8,000	10,000	11,000
XR AWD ▲	—	—	—	—	—	—	13,500	16,000	18,000
XR AWD ▼	—	—	—	—	—	—	12,000	14,500	17,000
XRS AWD ▲	—	—	—	—	—	—	14,000	16,500	19,000
XRS AWD ▼	—	—	—	—	—	—	13,000	15,000	17,500
Vibe ▲	—	—	—	—	—	—	9,000	11,000	13,000
Vibe ▼	—	—	—	—	—	—	7,500	9,500	11,500
GT AWD ▲	—	—	—	—	—	—	11,000	14,000	16,500
GT AWD ▼	—	—	—	—	—	—	9,000	12,500	15,000
Reliability	3	3	3	3	3	3	3	3	3
Crash Safety (F)	4	4	—	4	4	4	5	5	5
Side	3	3	—	4	4	4	4	4	4
Side (IIHS)	—	—	—	—	—	—	1	1	3
Offset	—	3	3	3	3	3	5	5	5
Head Restraints	1	3	3	—	2	2	3	3	1
Matrix	—	—	—	—	—	—	5	5	—
Rollover Resistance	3	3	3	3	3	3	4	4	4

Toyota

ECHO ★ ★ ★ ★ ★

RATING: Recommended (2000–05). An incredibly practical small car, if you can get by the tall, function-over-form styling. Echo represents an excellent alternative to the similarly styled, glitch-ridden Ford Focus and the recently discontinued Chrysler Neon. Now that the Echo has been replaced by the larger and slightly better-performing 2006 Yaris, Echo resale values will decline a bit faster than usual (see Appendix I for the Yaris rating). **"Real" city/highway fuel economy:** 6.7/5.2 L/100 km with a manual transmission or 7.1/5.5 L/100 km with an automatic. Owners report these estimates are correct. **Parts:** Easily found. **Maintenance/Repair costs:** Extraordinarily low. **Extended warranty:** A waste of money. **Best alternatives:** GM Firefly or Metro; Honda Civic; Hyundai Accent; Mazda Protegé; Nissan Sentra; and Suzuki Forsa, Swift, Esteem, or Aerio. **Online help:** *www.autosafety.org* and *www.carsurvey.org*.

Strengths and Weaknesses

Toyota scrapped its stripped-down Tercel in favour of the 2000 Echo, an entry-level, five-passenger model that gives good fuel economy without sacrificing performance. Both two- and four-door models are available, and the car costs substantially less than the Corolla. The Echo also offers about the same amount of passenger space as the Corolla, thanks to a high roof and low floor height.

Cockpit controls and instrumentation are particularly user-friendly, located high on the dash and more toward the centre of the vehicle, rather than directly in front of the driver, where the steering column would hide many gauges and controls. A 108-hp 1.5L DOHC 4-cylinder engine, featuring variable valve-timing cylinder-head technology, powers the Echo. Normally, an engine this small would provide wimpy acceleration, but thanks to the Echo's light weight, acceleration is more than adequate with the manual gearbox, and acceptable with the automatic.

Standard safety features include five three-point seat belts (front seat belts have pretensioners and force limiters), two front airbags (side airbags are not available), four height-adjustable head restraints, rear child-seat tether anchors, and rear door locks.

VEHICLE HISTORY: 2003—A major restyling adds 4 cm to overall length via new front and rear sheet metal and revised bumpers, hood, front fenders, headlights, tail lights, trunk lid, and grille. **2006**—Yaris replaces the Echo.

The Echo has more usable power than the Tercel and provides excellent fuel economy and lots of interior space. There's plenty of passenger room, along with an incredible array of storage areas, including a huge trunk and standard 60/40 split folding rear seats. All models are reasonably well equipped with good-quality materials, well-designed instruments and controls, comfortable seating, easy rear access, and excellent fore and aft visibility. It's quite nimble when cornering, very stable on the highway, and surprisingly quiet for an economy car. The car hasn't changed much since its 2000 model debut and has generated almost no complaints—an amazing feat when compared with the quality decline in Corollas, Camrys, and Siennas since 1997.

So what's not to like? Well, the tall profile and light weight make the Echo vulnerable to side-wind buffeting, base tires provide poor wet traction, excessive torque steer makes for sudden pulling to one side when accelerating, and the narrow body width limits rear bench seating to two adults. There have also been a few complaints about hard transmission shifts, engine ticking, rattling, some interior and brake squeaks, a high-pitched whine when underway, leaking shock absorbers, and broken door latches.

 ## Safety Summary

All models/years: Airbag malfunctions. • Sudden acceleration. **All models: 2000**—Vehicle blown out of control by side winds. • Inoperative horn. • Brake loss said to be caused by a faulty master cylinder. • Warped brake rotors. • Broken steering-wheel tilt mechanism. **2000–01**—Brake pedal is mounted too close to the accelerator pedal. **2001**—Partial brake loss. • Fuel line came undone; fuel line cracked. • Driver's seat belt failed to lock in a collision. **2002**—Several incidents of sudden, unintended acceleration:

> While driving, the Echo will accelerate to 60 mph [100 km/h] without [my] hitting the gas pedal. I have to put the vehicle in Neutral to stop it. I contacted [the] dealer, but he cannot locate the cause.

The sudden acceleration incident occurred three times. The dealer was unable to duplicate the problem in test-driving, but removed the cruise control. The problem was not corrected by removing the cruise control.

• Sudden steering loss led to crash. • Vehicle often jumps out of Drive into Neutral. **2003**—Engine hesitates when shifting gears. • Chronic stalling when decelerating. • Dash lights are not bright enough. **2005**—A gasoline smell permeates the interior.

Secret Warranties/Internal Bulletins/Service Tips

All models/years: Brake vibration caused by rotor rust requires the installation of new pads and rotors as a set. **All models: 2000**—Toyota has a Special Service Campaign (secret warranty) that allows for the free replacement of the brake booster and front brake pads on vehicles equipped with an automatic transmission. Confirmation of this campaign can be found in Toyota Service Bulletin #TC01027, Bulletin Sequence #625, published December 2001 and recorded in the NHTSA database as Item #SB625616. • MIL may indicate a single-cylinder misfire (modify the ECM). • Probable causes for interior squeaks and rattles. • Wheel covers may click or squeak. • Excessive wind noise. • Fuel gauge and speedometer malfunctions. • Brake-clicking countermeasures. • Defective airflow rotary control knob. **2000–02**—Improved carpet design. **2001**—Special Service Campaign to inspect the rear brake tubes, free of charge. • Roof moulding may come loose or become deformed. **2002–07**—Fixes for a vehicle that pulls to one side. **2003**—Hood lock assembly will be replaced free of charge to prevent snow entry and cable rusting (see TSB #BO018-03). **2003–05**—AC evaporator leaks water into the cabin (see bulletin at right). **2003–07**—Windshield ticking noise. **2004–07**—Front seat squeaks.

WATER IN PASSENGER FOOTWELL AREA

BULLETIN NO.: AC005-05   DATE: SEPTEMBER 13, 2005

FRONT PASSENGER FOOT AREA WET

2003–05 Echo and 2004–06 Scion xA & xB

On some ECHO, Scion xA, and Scion xB vehicles, a condition may exist that allows the evaporator drain hose to become detached, causing the passenger foot well to become wet.

ECHO PROFILE

	2000	2001	2002	2003	2004	2005
Cost Price ($)						
Base	13,835	13,980	14,084	13,690	12,995	12,995
Used Values ($)						
Base ▲	4,000	5,000	6,000	7,500	8,500	9,500
Base ▼	3,500	4,500	5,000	6,000	7,500	8,000
Reliability	4	5	5	5	5	5
Crash Safety (F)	—	4	4	4	4	4
Side	—	3	3	3	3	3
Rollover Resistance	—	4	4	4	4	4

Volkswagen

CABRIO, GOLF, JETTA / DIESEL MODELS ★ ★ ★ / ★

RATING: Average (1999–2006); Below Average (1993–98); Not Recommended (1985–92). *Diesel versions:* Not Recommended (all years). In addition to aging badly, these small cars are much more expensive than their competition, despite VW's efforts to bring down actual transaction prices over the past few years. Golfs are entry-level models that are the cheapest of the lot and depreciate fairly rapidly. A Jetta is a Golf with a trunk, the most popular configuration, which fetches fair resale prices; a Cabrio is a Golf without a roof, which depreciates steeply after its first five years of use. Old-technology diesel versions' resale prices are average and will likely ratchet upwards as buyers shy away from the new diesels over the next few years. **"Real" city/highway fuel economy:** *Golf:* 9.8/7.2 L/100 km with a manual transmission or 9.6/7.2 L/100 km with an automatic. *Golf TDI:* 6.2/4.6 L/100 km with a manual or 7.1/4.2 L/100 km with an automatic. *GTI:* 9.8/6.9 L/100 km with a manual transmission; 11.1/7.3 L/100 km with the 6-speed manual. *Jetta 1.8:* 9.9/6.9 L/100 km with a manual or 10.8/7.4 L/100 km with an automatic. *Jetta 2.0:* 9.8/7.0 L/100 km with a manual or 9.6/7.2 L/100 km with an automatic. *Jetta 2.8:* 11.1/7.3 L/100 km with a manual. *Jetta TDI:* 6.2/4.6 L/100 km with a manual or 7.1/4.9 L/100 km with an automatic. *Diesel versions:* Although owners report that their consumption is about 15 percent higher than these estimates, the TDI engine still burns about 40 percent less fuel than an equivalent 4-cylinder gasoline engine and has an impressive 1,000 km (600 mi.) or more range. You'll need that range, however, since only one fuel station out of three or four sells diesel fuel. **Maintenance/Repair costs:** Higher than average. Repairs are very dealer-dependent and expected to be more so as VW changes its diesel technology in 2007. **Parts:** Expensive, but generally available from independent suppliers. Recall campaign parts may be back-ordered for months. Maintenance costs are unreasonably high; for example, TDIClub (*www.tdiclub. com*) says the power-steering fluid, the brake fluid, and the special automatic transmission fluid (they warn to not ever use a Dexron-type fluid in later-model VW automatic transmissions!) should be purchased only from the dealer, even though the VW power-steering fluid is 10 times more expensive than power-steering fluid sold by independents. **Extended warranty:** A smart idea. "Goodwill" warranty repairs are practically non-existent in Canada because of the absence of a VW head office. **Best alternatives:** Any small car that doesn't punish backseat passengers as much as this VW trio does. Try the Honda Civic, Hyundai Elantra or Tiburon, Mazda Protegé, Nissan Sentra, and Toyota Corolla. The only viable diesel alternative is a Jeep Liberty—a different kind of vehicle entirely. **Online help:** *www.autosafety.org*, *www.carsurvey.org*, *www.vwvortex.com*, *www.tdiclub.com*, and *www.myvwlemon.com*.

Strengths and Weaknesses

On the positive side, these small imports are fun to drive and provide good fuel economy. Both engines are easily started in cold weather. But here's the rub: Golfs and Jettas, like the failure-prone Rabbit they replaced, aren't reliable once the warranty expires. What you save in fuel, you lose in the car's high retail price, which is carried over into the used-car market, and the ever-mounting maintenance costs as the vehicle gains years and mileage will easily wear you down.

VW reliability is about average—for the first few years. Then your wallet gets lighter as the brake components and fuel and electrical systems start to self-destruct. Exhaust system components aren't very durable, body hardware and dashboard controls are fragile, the paint often discolours and is easily chipped, and window regulators constantly fail:

> I bought my '96 Jetta GLS in 1999. I have replaced eight window regulators in three years, one power window motor, and I can't get the Check Engine light off for the life of me. I have also had to put the door moulding on the driver's side back door three times.

> I found that the windows falling into the door is always due to a broken window regulator, which are less than half the price if you order them from anyone other than the VW dealer and are not hard to put in yourself.

Volkswagens have terrible quality problems that can't be repaired at the corner garage. Owners report electrical short circuits; heater/defroster resistor and motor failures; leaking transmission and stub-axle seals; and defective valve-pan gaskets, head gaskets, timing belts, steering assemblies, suspension components, alternator pulleys, and brake and electrical systems. Body problems are legion, with air and water leaks, faulty catalytic converters, inoperative locks and latches, poor-quality body construction and paint, and cheap, easily broken accessories and trim items.

Factory defects on 1990–98 Golfs and Jettas are so numerous that they make these models particularly risky buys. Problems include automatic transmission, engine, suspension component, and catalytic converter failures; electrical short circuits; AC malfunctions; and fragile trim items. Body assembly and paint are second-class, leading to rattles and air leaks as the vehicles age.

The redesigned 1994–98 models are a bit safer, though just as unreliable and expensive to fix—if you can find a mechanic brave enough to face parts shortages and diagnostic hell. Problems disclosed in service bulletins for these model years show that serious defects continue to accumulate along with the years. Powertrain failures; never-ending electrical shorts; poor driveability caused by fuel, electrical, and electronic system glitches; water leaks; and trim defects are all addressed. Owners also report the following: electric door locks that take a long time to lock; paint that is easily nicked, chipped, and marked; a variety of trim defects; premature rear tire wear; and poor-quality seat cushions.

VEHICLE HISTORY: 1991—Debut of the 134-hp 2.0L Golf GTI 16V; mandatory 5-speed manual transmission. **1992**—Upgraded diesel engine gets seven more horses (up to 59). **1994**—Dual airbags; the top-line GLX model got a 172-horsepower V6. **1995**—Golf GTI VR6, plus two other Golf models, make their debut; height-adjustable manual front seat belts with emergency tensioners; and side-impact door beams. **1996**—Dashboard-mounted glove box returns; improved seat belt retractors and door locking system. **1997**—The 116-hp 4-cylinder engines got a redesigned cylinder head that cuts engine noise; the Golf GTI VR6 rides lower, thanks to new shocks, springs, and anti-roll bars; the Cabrio Highline received standard AC and a few other amenities; and a cheapened base convertible lost its standard ABS and a few other goodies. **1999**—Updated interior and exterior styling, and a more powerful engine; Cabrios were given new European styling. **2001**—A 150-hp 1.8L turbo four became available for the GLS and was standard in the base GTI; a Jetta wagon was added, along with steering-mounted audio controls (on some models). **2002**—Debut of a more powerful 1.8L 4-cylinder engine, a 5-speed automatic transmission, and an optional 6-speed manual transmission; 2.8L V6 horsepower boosted (200). **2003**—An anti-skid system became standard with the V6 engine; GL got power windows, heated power mirrors, and cruise control; GLS versions come with alloy wheels and a sunroof. **2004**—Jetta got minor styling changes, and an all-wheel-drive Golf arrived. **2005**—Jetta's GLI VR6 sedan and the limited-edition all-wheel-drive V6 Golf R32 were ditched.

Jettas provide slightly more comfort and better road performance than their Golf hatchback counterparts. The 1.6L 4-cylinder found on early Jettas was surprisingly peppy, and the diesel engine is very economical, although quite slow to accelerate. Two nuisance problems are that the cupholder sticks (and coffee drips down the radio stack) and the glove box breaks.

> Since I bought the car, I have spent a few extra dollars on getting it oil-sprayed (Krown) and replacing the tires (Michelin Hydroedge—very good).
>
> There is one other problem that plagues all the VWs I have seen that are more than about two years old. And that is the metal divider in the back windows that rusts prematurely. Almost without exception, every VW on a used car lot has this rusty component on both sides.
>
> C.T.
> OTTAWA

Jettas and Golfs do rust prematurely. They suffer from rapid body deterioration and increasingly frequent mechanical/electrical failures after their fourth year in service. For example, starters often burn out because they are vulnerable to engine heat; as well, sunroofs leak, door locks jam, window cranks break, and windows bind. Owners also report engine head gasket leaks as well as water-pump and heater-core breakdowns. It's axiomatic that all diesels are slow to accelerate, but

VW's Fourth gear often can't handle highway speeds above 90 km/h. Engine noise can be deafening when shifting down from Fourth gear.

The 1999–2005 models are more reliable for the first few years and then they start falling apart about the time the warranty expires, requiring expensive repairs that are often ineffective.

> Even the driver's side leather seat has the seams popping loose, and a part of the frame is pushing through the leather.

Owners still report chronic automatic transmission/clutch, diesel-engine turbocharger, brake, and extensive electrical-system problems; noisy brakes and wheel bearings; subpar body construction and paint; leaky sunroofs and assorted water leaks from other areas (when it rains, both the front and rear floors are soaked); malfunctioning gauges and accessories; fragile, non-responsive locks and latches; bumpers that become brittle and crack as the temperature falls; defective security systems; and disagreeable interior odours. The following Toronto VW owner had this to say:

> I recently purchased a used 1999 VW Jetta (one of the new model types), and after talking to some co-workers, there seems to be a problem with the AC in both Jettas and Golfs. The problem is that condensation builds up on one of the filters, and after a little while bacteria will start to grow, and then when you turn on the fan for the AC the air being pumped out starts to stink. One of my co-workers said it was so bad in her VW Jetta that she thought her husband had left his old hockey equipment in the car!

The Diesel Dilemma

People who buy a diesel-powered vehicle such as VW's TDI usually cite at least one of these three reasons for their decision: lower fuel costs, lower maintenance costs, and the popular notion that diesel engines are more durable. Unfortunately, none of these reasons stands up to close scrutiny.

Higher operating costs

Diesel-fuelled vehicles *do* provide 20–30 percent better fuel economy than gasoline-burners. But that savings is being progressively wiped out by higher diesel fuel prices and maintenance costs. For example, in June 2007, diesel fuel cost about 93 cents per litre in Toronto, while regular gasoline sold for $1.07 per litre. In British Columbia, prices were higher: Diesel fuel averaged 99 cents a litre, and regular fuel sold for about $1.21 a litre.

And diesel fuel costs are going even higher: North American refiners are being forced to produce cleaner, more expensive fuel, and the U.S. refining industry will likely fail to generate enough diesel fuel to accommodate a significant increase in the number of vehicles that burn it.

Michael Tusiani, a senior fellow at Columbia University's Center for Energy, Marine Transportation, and Public Policy, gave these specifics in the August 8, 2005, edition of The Washington Post:

> At this year's auto show in New York, a DaimlerChrysler executive responsible for research and technology cited the success of diesel-engine automobiles in Europe while suggesting that these vehicles could gain a 5 to 10 percent share of the U.S. market. He made those comments at the introduction of a Mercedes-Benz station wagon scheduled to land in America in 2006. He did not mention, however, that because of the popularity of diesel-powered autos, diesel oil prices in Europe are soaring as demand pushes past the amount refiners can make.
>
> In 2004 trucks and other diesel-burning vehicles required about 150,000 barrels per day more than in 2003—a one-year increase of almost 5 percent. If America continues to prosper, this commercial use of diesel will keep growing. Like their European counterparts, U.S. refiners have not seen any reason to invest in greater diesel production. In fact, they have a strong disincentive to build diesel-making equipment: Unless refiners can increase crude oil processing capacity, which seems unlikely, making more diesel will reduce gasoline production. Furthermore, they have gasoline production hardware that has only recently started to make solid profits for them as the price of gasoline rises.

Servicing price-gouging

Diesel owners decry the high cost of regular maintenance and claim that parts and fluids can cost many times what a non-diesel engine would require. Furthermore, dealerships' service personnel are in a monopolist "take it or leave it" position because few independent mechanics will be available to service diesel cars—good diesel mechanics are rare in most dealerships, and diesel engine diagnostic tools and parts inventories are often wanting.

Reliability: The dark side of diesels

Diesel engines are promoted by automakers for their fuel-efficient and dependable performance; however, recent studies and owner complaints indicate diesels burn more fuel than advertised, are more likely to break down than gasoline-powered engines, and produce emissions that exacerbate lung diseases like emphysema and may be responsible for 125,000 cases of pulmonary cancer in the States.

J.D. Power's 2004 Vehicle Dependability Study found that the most fuel-efficient vehicles—diesels and gas-electric hybrids—have more engine problems than similar gasoline-powered vehicles. And this conclusion is backed by automaker service bulletins and owner complaints sent to NHTSA. The discrepancies are an eye-opener:

- Ford and Chevrolet diesel pickups had more engine problems than similar gas-powered models, while Dodge and GMC trucks were better overall.

- Owners of 2001 model year Toyota and Honda hybrids reported twice as many engine problems than did owners of Toyotas and Hondas with gas-powered engines.
- Owners of Volkswagen diesels reported up to twice as many engine problems than did owners of VWs that burn gas.

Diesels have serious quality shortcomings, especially with emissions components such as the mass air sensor, as this reader relates:

> I have a 2001 VW Jetta TDI, and [it has] been losing power.... The dealership...said that it is carbonization (build-up of carbon). They told me that they have to take apart and clean the EGR valve and also replace the mass airflow sensor. I was told it would cost me at least $1,000 to $2,000. They said that it's the "ingredients in the fuel" that are causing the problem. I do know that in Alberta, there are strict guidelines that need to be followed when it comes to emissions and the sort. I feel like I am getting hosed [by] the dealership!!! I heard rumours that other owners in Alberta...[have] had the exact same problem and that they got the work done for free.

> R.Y.
>
> ALBERTA

VW diesel owner clubs have published long lists of failure-prone components found in the TDI over the years. Here is a catalogue of the problems that the TDIClub found:

1. Hard starts or no-starts.
2. Engine stalls and may not restart; Check Engine light comes on, or glow plug light is flashing.
3. Engine lacks power.
4. High fuel consumption.
5. Oil leaks onto ground.
6. Smokes on cold start-up, when accelerating, or at any time.
7. Bucks and jerks at low speeds when cold.
8. Noisy exhaust system.
9. Shuddering, misfiring, and stumbling once underway.
10. Surging, hesitation during acceleration; turbo-boost pressure varies.

Cancer dangers

Diesel exhaust contains more than 40 chemicals that are listed by the U.S. Environmental Protection Agency as toxic air contaminants—including known or suspected human carcinogens, reproductive toxins, and endocrine disrupters. In the United States, two national associations, the State and Territorial Air Pollution Program Administrators and the Association of Local Air Pollution Control Officials, estimate that over a lifetime of exposure to diesel fumes, an estimated 119,570 people in metropolitan areas plus 5,540 people in suburban and rural areas will develop cancer.

There are also hundreds of different chemical compounds that wreak havoc on air quality, playing a role in ozone formation in the air we breathe and in creating particulate matter, regional haze, and acid rain.

Normally, diesel emissions could be cleaned by the exhaust system's catalytic converter. However, diesel fuel that's used in North America is so high in sulfur content that it disables the converter. Sulfur is a poison for diesel pollution control devices, much as lead was a poison to catalytic converters in the '70s. Although cleaner fuel is expected by the end of 2006, there is no guarantee it will be clean enough to work with present-day emissions-control devices.

Both VW and Mercedes-Benz say they will use upgraded diesel engines within the next two years to meet stricter emissions-control laws. A worrisome announcement, when one considers that the next generation of diesels will be using unproven new designs and will also have to contend with new diesel fuel formulations.

 Safety Summary

All models/years: Volkswagen Golfs and Jettas, as well as many Audis, are easily stolen due to a flawed door lock mechanism design, reports *Lemon-Aid* reader and British Columbia resident Susan O.:

> Basically, it is a factory-installed flaw in the design that if you pop the silver cylinder off the only keyed door, you can remove the lock mechanism, which allows anyone to get into the vehicle. Further to that, you are also able to deactivate the alarm, so the VW/Audi consumer would not hear anyone gaining entry. This is a problem not only in Vancouver and Toronto, but in other pockets across the country, according to a Volkswagen head office spokesperson [names withheld].... There is a temporary solution that VW pointed out and quickly also pointed out is not sanctioned by them. The solution is to put a cover plate over the lock, in essence having all the doors resemble each other. The only way of entry then is with the fob. In an emergency, the station wagon hatch may be opened without activating the alarm. This is not the case for the sedans, unfortunately.
>
> These are not such isolated incidences, as they would like us to think. Many go unreported to the police, and the consumer just pays the $300 for a new lock and hopes it doesn't happen again, or goes for the above option at $500 and hopes their fob

battery never dies while out and about.... People I know who have had their VW/Audi cars broken into either in Toronto or here have identified the means of break in as the same, popping off the casing and removing the cylinder. Something is definitely wrong, yet VW doesn't see it the same way. My last letter from them, dated August 10, says they have reviewed the customer service files and do not see cause for repair at their expense. Personally, I think it should be a total recall. It doesn't matter the year or model.

• The NHTSA database shows that the following problems are reported repeatedly: fires; airbags that fail to deploy or cause severe injuries when they go off; inadvertent deployment; Airbag light that stays on for no apparent reason; transmission and wheel bearing failures; transmission pops out of gear; electrical malfunctions leading to chronic stalling; self-activating alarms; lights going out; erratic cruise-control operation; brake, tire, and AC failures; inadequate defrosting; AC mould and mildew smell; poor-quality body components; window regulator failure; and inoperable power windows. Also, doors may open suddenly; locks jam shut, fall out, or freeze; power-window motors and regulators self-destruct; hoods suddenly fly up; cigarette lighters pop out of their holders while lit; the seat heater may burn a hole in the driver's seat; and battery acid can leak onto the power-steering reservoir and cause sudden steering loss. **All models: 1998**—Engine damaged after water was ingested through the air intake system. • Transmission locked into Third gear. • ABS brake failures. • Head restraints suddenly drop down. • Inaccurate fuel gauge. **1999**—Plastic fuel line fails in cold weather. • Chronic stalling in traffic with Engine Warning light lit. • Headlight failure; no low beam. **2000**—Sudden acceleration. • Cracked axle. • Early replacement of the rear brake pads. • Dashboard causes excessive windshield glare. **2000–03**—Airbag cover pops off while driving. • Cracked oil pan. • Engine burns oil. • Chronic stalling in traffic. • Hard starting. • Noisy, prematurely worn brakes. • Sudden headlight failure; poor headlight illumination. • Faulty power-window regulators cause windows to fall down into door panels. **2001**—Timing chain exploded. • Frequent stalling because of defective airflow sensor. • Premature constant velocity joint replacement. **2001–03**—Stalling, no-starts because of faulty ignition coils. **2002**—Fires under the bumper and in the engine compartment. • Sudden, unintended acceleration. • Many reports that the front/side airbags deployed for no reason; driver burned:

> Driving on the turnpike, the driver-side airbag deployed without any sort of impact. There is no visible damage to the vehicle, which was only two months old at the time. Fortunately, the only injury was a burn from the airbag on the side of my arm. My biggest fear is knowing relatives and friends who drive Jettas and who have young children in their car. This incident could have easily been fatal.

• Brake failure. • Vehicle hesitates on acceleration. • Engine Warning light is constantly lit. • Broken window regulator; window falls into the door panel:

On three separate occasions the driver-side front window (twice) and the passenger-side front window (once) has fallen down into the door. On the first occasion, the window shattered inside the door and had to be replaced.

2003—Driver's seat burst into flames. • Vehicle will suddenly veer to the left or right. • Clutch pedal slips; vehicle won't change gears. • Early replacement of the rear axle. **2004**—Golf totally destroyed by a fire of unknown origin. • Jetta fire ignited in the seat-heater control, which was shut off at the time. • Brake failures. • Chronic engine stalling and no-starts, often due to defective ignition coils. • VW says engines need a special oil to prevent engine sludge. • Transmission clutch slipping:

> This is the second time we have had issues with our 2004 VW Jetta wagon. Both times, the car has suddenly, with no warning, had a clutch failure. The first time this happened was [at] 16,000 miles [26,000 km], now a second occurrence [at] just 29,000 miles [47,000 km]. VW tries to pass blame as driver error, but since I drive tractor/trailers for a living and in my 15 years of driving have never had a clutch failure prior to this car, I do not think that my driving is to blame. It is apparent from the numerous experiences I have read about that there is a serious defect in the quality or build of the VW clutch system in newer models.

• There is such a long delay when shifting the automatic transmission in Reverse or Drive, the vehicle is free to roll as if it were in Neutral. • Harsh downshifts. • Transmission locks up between Third and Fourth gears. • Tread separating from the front-passenger tire. • Frequent electrical shorts (windows, lights, gauges, alarm system, etc.). • Dash gauges cannot be read in sunlight. • There is a distracting reflection from the chrome shifter panel. **2005**—Engine surges when shifted into Reverse. • Faulty fuel gauges. • Driver's seat became unattached. *TDI: 2004*—Many reports of engine overheating, chronic stalling, and EGR/turbocharger failures:

> TDI engine will stall at times due to coolant leaking internally into [the] intake manifold through [a] faulty EGR cooler, causing vehicle to lose steering and brake assist. I have looked on VW web forums, and many owners have had a similar incident.

•

> TDI engine and manual transmission: While driving, vehicle lost power intermittently. Pressed accelerator; no change in rpm—just idled. [The] "glow plug" flashed and [the] Engine Warning light...lit after [the] first two occasions, not on [the] third. Restart solves problem for 30 seconds. Dealership was notified, but did not resolve the problem in two attempts. Vehicle is in for third attempt.

The EGR problem is so rampant and expensive to correct that VW owners are pleading for relief, so enterprising independent repair shops are seizing the opportunity to make a profit by offering cheaper fixes for the ensuing turbocharger problems:

Mr. Edmonston,

Thank you for all the great work you do. Are you aware of the potential problems owners of the newer VW TDI may be facing? I took mine (2002/85,000 km) in for service to my VW mechanic (not the dealer), and he informed me that my turbo air intake, and the turbo itself, needed cleaning to the tune of $470.00—oil change included. This was the first time I had heard anything about the turbo clogging up on these engines. He took off the hose connected to the air intake and showed me the accumulation of soot that was choking off the intake. This leads to poor performance and possibly to failure of the turbo if it isn't dealt with in a timely manner. This is caused by a combination of not enough highway driving and poor-quality fuel. VW Canada doesn't seem to recognize this as a service issue. If your car's turbo isn't working properly, they just swap the turbo and exhaust manifold (one piece) to the tune of about $2,000.00. My mechanic subscribes to the BG service and cleaning.... Apparently, this is recommended [at] about every 40,000–50,000 km. This doesn't appear to be an issue with the older turbo diesels prior to the TDI models. I hope it's not going to become another of VW's fiascos like the water-cooled engine in the older Vanagons.

VINCE B.

•

The No. 9250 diesel intake and exhaust cleaning system kit provides an example of profitable maintenance and repair service you can perform. Exhaust soot builds up in the EGR cooler, EGR valve and intake manifold, and even cokes the intake valves. This could cause the turbo to stick, affecting engine performance.

Expensive parts replacement had previously been the only choice. Remove the EGR valve and feeder tube for bench cleaning. Then the kit comes into the picture. If there's a really thick soot buildup in the manifold, thread a special auger from the kit through the EGR valve port to remove the bulk. Next, attach adapters to the cooler and EGR port of the intake manifold. Follow a specific engine-running procedure, using tanks of BG-supplied chemicals to clean the manifold, valves, and cooler, often even a stuck turbo. Diesels have virtually no manifold vacuum, so the intake manifold adapter includes a shop air-powered Venturi vacuum to help draw cleaner through to the valves.

Although the kit's adapters fit only the VW diesel, new adapters will be introduced for the DaimlerChrysler (Mercedes), Ford, and GM diesels now sold in Europe when they reach the U.S. market. Incidentally, TDIClub (see *www.tdiclub.com*) says the EGR soot problem can be eliminated by ensuring that the EGR system is operating at the minimum allowable level. The adjustment procedure doesn't affect performance or emissions legislation. It is found in section 7.h of their FAQ pages. • Stripped manifold bolts are another cause of the turbo's demise. **2005**—The clutch disengages from the flywheel. • TDI's fuel-filler pipe is too small for most truck stop gas stations. • Chronic surging and stalling.

Secret Warranties/Internal Bulletins/Service Tips

All models/years: It's surprising that, despite the many owner complaints, VW has issued few service bulletins. That means these problems don't exist in Volkswagen's opinion, or the automaker doesn't have corrective fixes to apply and will simply carry on as if all systems are "normal." **All models: 1998–99**—Noisy, vibrating blower motor. • Defective instrument cluster. • Radio volume control malfunction. **1998–2006**—Possible reasons why the car won't start or is hard to start. **1999**—Humming noise from front of vehicle when turning may be caused by the differential spider gear. • Sunroof binding or noise will be fixed with replacement slides. **1999–2000**—An engine rapping noise or throttle pedal vibration. **1999–2001**—Malfunctioning instrument cluster. **1999–2006**—Inoperative window regulator. • **2000**—Automatic transmission may go into limp mode without MIL activated. • Vibrating shifter. **2000–01**—Troubleshooting prematurely worn rear brake pads. **2001**—Leaking intake hoses. • Inoperative secondary air pump (blown fuse). • Troubleshooting "defective control module" indication. • Leaking transmission pan gasket. **2000–03**—Faulty ignition coils (chronic stalling, no restart) covered reluctantly by a warranty extension after VW first denied the problem existed. **2002**—Inoperative fresh air blower. • Broken armrest lid. • Defective VI radio controls. **2003–06**—Causes for excessive vibration when braking (a warranty item, admits VW). **2004–06**—Shift delay upon acceleration. **2005**—Humming noise when turning at low speeds. • Rattling noise from the AC front centre air outlets. • Fuel-tank lid won't close. • Musty odours from vents. **2005–06**—Inoperative rear window defogger. **2006**—Faulty door lock cylinders.

CABRIO, GOLF, JETTA PROFILE

	1997	1998	1999	2000	2001	2002	2003	2004	2005
Cost Price ($)									
Cabrio	25,230	25,300	25,300	25,300	28,530	28,530	—	—	—
Golf	14,690	16,765	15,610	18,950	19,040	19,230	17,950	18,300	18,530
Jetta	18,050	18,620	18,620	21,170	21,280	21,490	24,260	24,520	24,750
Jetta TDI	18,550	19,220	19,945	23,100	23,220	23,450	25,860	26,080	26,310
Jetta TDI wagon	—	—	—	—	—	—	25,860	27, 550	27,780
Used Values ($)									
Cabrio ▲	5,500	7,000	8,500	10,500	12,500	15,000	—	—	—
Cabrio ▼	4,500	6,000	7,500	9,000	11,000	13,000	—	—	—
Golf ▲	2,500	3,000	3,500	4,000	5,000	7,000	9,000	11,000	13,000
Golf ▼	2,000	2,500	3,000	3,500	4,500	6,000	7,500	9,000	11,500
Jetta ▲	3,500	4,500	5,000	6,500	8,000	10,500	12,500	15,000	18,000
Jetta ▼	3,000	4,000	4,500	5,500	6,500	8,500	11,500	13,000	16,500
Jetta TDI ▲	4,500	5,500	6,500	7,500	9,000	12,000	14,500	17,000	19,000
Jetta TDI ▼	4,000	5,000	6,000	6,500	7,500	10,500	13,000	15,500	17,500
Jetta TDI wagon ▲	—	—	—	—	—	—	14,500	17,000	20,000
Jetta TDI wagon ▼	—	—	—	—	—	—	13,000	15,500	18,500

Reliability	2	2	3	3	3	3	3	3	3
Crash Safety (F)									
Golf	3	3	3	5	5	5	5	5	5
Jetta	3	—	—	5	5	5	5	5	5
Side									
Golf	—	—	—	—	—	—	4	4	4
Jetta	—	3	3	4	4	—	4	4	5
Side (IIHS)	—	—	—	—	—	—	—	—	5
Offset	2	2	5	5	5	5	5	5	5
Jetta	2	2	5	5	5	5	5	5	5
Head Restraints (F)									
Golf 2d	—	—	2	—	5	5	5	5	—
Golf 4d	1	—	3	—	3	3	3	3	—
Jetta	—	—	—	—	3	3	3	3	3
Rollover Resistance	—	—	—	—	4	4	4	4	—

MEDIUM CARS

Medium-sized cars, often referred to as family cars, are trade-offs between size and fuel economy, offering more room and convenience features but a bit less fuel economy than small cars. They're popular because they combine the advantages of smaller cars with those of larger vehicles. As a result of their versatility, as well as both upsizing and downsizing throughout the years, these vehicles overlap both the small and large car niches. The trunk is usually large enough to meet average baggage requirements, and the interior is spacious enough to meet the needs of the average family (seating four people in comfort and five in a pinch). These cars are best for combined city and highway driving, with the top three choices traditionally dominated by Japanese automakers: the Honda Accord, the Mazda 626/Mazda6, and the Toyota Camry. South Korean automakers, however, are catching up fast, with Hyundai's Elantra, Tiburon, and Sonata leading the pack.

The Hyundai Sonata.

But there are lots of bad cars in this group too. Take the Ford Taurus and Sable, for example. Bestsellers for many years and easily found used at incredibly low prices, these two models don't cost much because they are no longer built and are generally unreliable. Engine, transmission, brake, electrical, and body problems are legion, and repair costs for the automatic transmission alone can easily run about $3,500. GM's lineup isn't much better. On the other hand, Chrysler's Sebring, Breeze, Cirrus, and Stratus have improved in quality during the past several years and generally offer fair reliability and competitive used prices. Actually, Chrysler is the best of the Detroit Big Three from a quality and price standpoint. Its models have significantly improved in quality control, although they are nowhere near as dependable as vehicles made by Asian automakers.

What the Heck Is a Crossover?

Advertising hype for a tall wagon, the term describes most family-sized vehicles that incorporate unibody construction, a relatively high seating position, four-wheel drive (usually), a good amount of cargo space, and seating for at least four. Crossover models embrace a wide range of sizes and configurations, from the compact Dodge Caliber to the seven-passenger Buick Enclave. Some models are styled like traditional SUVs, others may look like downsized SUVs or upsized wagons (Pontiac Vibe and Toyota Matrix), and an emerging fourth type resembles a mini-minivan (Mazda5).

The Pontiac Vibe GT.

MEDIUM CAR RATINGS

Recommended

Acura 1.6, 1.7L EL (1997–2005)

Acura CSX (2006)*

Acura Integra (1994–2001)

Honda Accord (2000–02)

Mazda 626 (1999–2002)

Above Average

Acura CL-Series (1998–2003)

Acura Integra (1986–93)

DaimlerChrysler Avenger,
      Sebring (2002–06)

Honda Accord (1990–99; 2003–06)

Hyundai Sonata (1999–2006)

Mazda6 (2003–06)

Mazda 626, MX-6 (1996–98)

Mitsubishi Gallant (2005–06)*

Nissan Altima (1998–2001)

Toyota Camry (1985–96)

Average

Acura CL-Series (1997)

Acura RSX (2002–06)*

DaimlerChrysler Avenger,
Sebring (2000–01)

General Motors Achieva, Alero, Grand Am,
      Skylark (2000–05)

General Motors Allure (2005–06)*

General Motors Bonneville, Cutlass,
      Cutlass Supreme, Delta 88, Grand Prix,
      Impala, Intrigue, LeSabre, Lumina,
      Malibu, Monte Carlo, Regal (1984–87;
      (2000–06)

General Motors Century (1998–2005)

Honda Accord (1985–89)

Hyundai Sonata (1995–98)
Mazda 626, MX-6 (1994–95)
Mitsubishi Gallant (2005–06)*
Nissan Altima (1993–97; 2002–06)

Toyota Camry, Solara (1997–2006)
Volkswagen New Beetle (2000–06)
Volkswagen Passat (2006)

Below Average

DaimlerChrysler Avenger, Sebring
   (1995–99)
DaimlerChrysler Breeze, Cirrus,
   Stratus (1999–2000)
Ford Freestyle (2005–06)*
General Motors Achieva, Alero, Grand Am,
   Skylark (1995–99)

General Motors Century (1997)
General Motors G6 (2005–06)*
General Motors Lucerne (2006)*
General Motors/Suzuki Epica/Verona
   (2004–06)
Volkswagen New Beetle (1998–99)
Volkswagen Passat (1998–2005)

Not Recommended

DaimlerChrysler Breeze, Cirrus,
   Stratus (1995–98)
Ford Sable, Taurus (1986–2006)
General Motors Achieva, Alero, Grand Am,
   Skylark (1985–94)
General Motors Bonneville, Cutlass,
   Cutlass Supreme, Delta 88, Grand Prix,
   Impala, Intrigue, LeSabre, Lumina,
   Malibu, Monte Carlo, Regal (1988–99)

General Motors Century (1982–96)
Hyundai Sonata (1986–93)
Mazda 626, MX-6 (1985–93)
Volkswagen Passat (1989–97)

*See Appendix I.

Acura

1.6, 1.7 EL	★ ★ ★ ★ ★

RATING: Recommended (1997–2005). Basically a gussied up Honda Civic, Acura's EL series (EL signifying "entry-level") was originally a rebadged version of Honda's Domani subcompact, sold exclusively in Japan. The redesigned 2001 EL and later models offer the most for your money. They are closely based on the Honda Civic EX sedan and offer more features and a slightly more powerful, torquier engine. Acura's latest iteration, the 2006 CSX (see Appendix I) is a twin of the 2006 Civic. As the Civic grew in size from a subcompact to a compact during the past decade, so did the EL. The 1.7L engine designation was dropped from the 2005 model name, and headlight and tail light styling became more distinctive. **"Real" city/ highway fuel economy:** *1.6L:* 7.8/6.1 L/100 km with a manual transmission or 7.9/6.0 L/100 km with an automatic. *1.7L:* 8.1/6.3 L/100 km with a manual transmission or 7.9/6.0 L/100 km with an automatic. **Maintenance/Repair costs:**

The Acura EL.

Average. Repairs aren't dealer-dependent. **Parts:** Average costs, thanks to the use of generic Honda Si parts sold through independent suppliers. **Extended warranty:** Not needed. **Best alternatives:** Chevrolet Cavalier; Honda Civic EX or Si; Hyundai Elantra wagon, Sonata, or Tiburon; Mazda3, 626, or Protegé; Mitsubishi Lancer; Pontiac Sunfire; and Toyota Camry or Corolla. **Online help:** For the latest owner reports, service bulletins, and money-saving tips, visit *www. acuraworld.com/forums* and *www.autosafety.org.*

Strengths and Weaknesses

The first Japanese automobile built exclusively in and for the Canadian market, the EL is essentially an all-dressed Civic sedan, built in Alliston, Ontario, and sold under the Acura moniker. It was created in response to Canadian Acura dealers' pleas for a more affordable Acura.

VEHICLE HISTORY: **1997**—Since its '97 model launch, the EL has been immensely popular—and, thus, hard to find on the used-car market. **2001**—The 1.7L 2001 model is an all-new incarnation (like the 2001 Civic) that is roomier, more fuel-efficient, and better equipped. Buyers get standard side airbags, four-wheel disc brakes, and front seat belt pretensioners, which tighten the belts during a collision. The standard 5-speed manual transmission is revised for smoother shifts and quieter operation, and the 4-speed automatic transmission boosts fuel economy by almost 3 percent. Even though horsepower remains the same, torque increases by almost 8 percent. **2003**—A retuned suspension and steering system for better handling and enhanced ride comfort reduce engine vibration through improved engine mounts and upgraded brakes. Additionally, the 2003 models are given adjustable head restraints and upgraded instrument clusters, centre console armrests, and front seats.

First generation ELs come with a peppy 127-hp VTEC 1.6L 4-banger that's both reliable and economical to run. Add the Civic's chassis and upgraded suspension components, and you have competent performance that's as good as or better than that of the Civic Si. But the 1.6 EL does have a few weak points, such as a narrow interior, with seats and seatbacks that are not to everyone's liking; emergency braking that's only average; head restraints rated Poor by IIHS; an overly soft suspension; and excessive engine noise intruding into the passenger compartment despite upgraded soundproofing.

The 1.6 and 1.7 EL have done quite well over the years they've been on the market, even though there haven't been many changes since the second-generation 2001 model was launched. The cabin is quieter than the Civic's, the steering is quick and responsive, handling is quite nimble with 15-inch tires versus the Civic's 14-inchers, and the suspension is firmer. Braking and acceleration have also improved; however, the engine's maximum torque is reached at only about 5000 rpm, which means lots of downshifting with a full load of passengers and cargo. Interestingly, Honda recommends premium gasoline, yet the equivalent Civic gets by with regular fuel. One major safety complaint targets premature strut failures that degrade handling (see "Honda Civic" section). Otherwise, the few owner complaints recorded have typically concerned premature suspension wear (mostly springs and bushings), merely adequate engine power, wind noise, easily dented body panels, malfunctioning accessories (AC, audio system, electrical components, etc.), and fragile trim items. Some minor turn-offs with the 2001 model include the car losing power when the AC is activated, the lack of stereo controls on the steering wheel, and the driver-seat armrest interfering with the gearshift lever.

Secret Warranties/Internal Bulletins/Service Tips

All models/years: Most Honda/Acura TSBs allow for special warranty consideration on a "goodwill" basis even after the warranty has expired or the car has changed hands. Referring to this euphemism will increase your chances of getting some kind of refund for repairs that are obviously related to a factory defect. Keep in mind that many Honda bulletins often apply to Acuras, as well. So check out the Civic's and Accord's TSBs and safety complaints before assuming that a particular Acura problem doesn't exist or that it's your responsibility. • Acura says that it will replace any seat belt's tongue stopper button for the life of the vehicle. • Interestingly, the automatic transmission failures afflicting 2000–03 Acuras and Hondas don't seem to be much of a problem with this entry-level Acura. Still, should you have a tranny breakdown within 7 years/160,000 km, don't hesitate to cite Honda's latest transmission extended warranty, applicable to the Civic and Accord, to back up your claim. • Seat belts that are slow to retract will also be replaced for free, says TSB #91-050. **All models: 2003–04**—A soft brake pedal feel or any noise from the brake assembly when braking may indicate there's a problem with the brake-booster master cylinder.

1.6, 1.7 EL PROFILE

	1997	1998	1999	2000	2001	2002	2003	2004	2005
Cost Price ($)									
1.6/1.7 EL	17,800	18,800	19,800	20,005	21,500	21,700	22,000	22,200	23,000
Used Values ($)									
1.6/1.7 EL ▲	3,500	4,500	5,500	7,000	9,000	10,500	13,000	15,000	17,000
1.6/1.7 EL ▼	3,000	4,000	5,000	5,500	7,500	9,000	11,000	13,000	15,000
Reliability	5	5	5	5	5	5	5	5	5

Note: These vehicles have not been crash-tested.

CL-SERIES ★ ★ ★ ★

RATING: Above Average (1998–2003); Average (1997). Be wary of the overpriced, hard-to-find, failure-prone automatic transmission on all model years; it's one reason that the CL doesn't get a five-star rating like its little brother. **"Real" city/ highway fuel economy:** 2.2L: 9.5/7.0 L/100 km with a manual transmission or 10.4/7.5 L/100 km with an automatic. 2.3L: 9.7/6.9 L/100 km manual or 10.6/7.3 L/100 km automatic. 3.0L: 12.7/7.0 L/100 km with an automatic transmission. 3.2L: 12.0/7.4 L/100 km manual or 12.3/7.7 L/100 km automatic. Owners report fuel savings on the two 6-cylinder engines may undershoot the above estimates by about 10 percent. **Maintenance/Repair costs:** Higher than average, but repairs can be done practically anywhere. **Parts:** Costs are much higher than average if purchased from an Acura dealer:

> I have a 2003 Acura CLS that required replacement of a headlight at 66,000 miles [106,000 km]. This headlight cost $928.85.

Extended warranty: Not needed since Honda/Acura already covers transmission failures via "goodwill" warranty extensions. **Best alternatives:** BMW 318, Honda Accord, Lexus SC 300, Nissan Maxima, and Toyota Camry. **Online help:** For the latest owner reports, service bulletins, and money-saving tips, look at *www. acuraworld.com/forums* and *www.autosafety.org*.

Strengths and Weaknesses

The only difference between the 2.2L CL and the 3.0L CL is the 3.0L CL's larger engine, different wheels, and larger exhaust tip. The 2.2L CL's engine was upgraded to 2.3L on the 1998 models.

These are stylish front-drive, five-passenger luxury coupes that are American-designed and built. They have a flowing, slanted back end and no apparent trunk lock (a standard remote keyless entry system opens the trunk from the outside, and a lever opens it from the inside). And while other Japanese automakers are taking content out of their vehicles, Acura has made the CL one of the most feature-laden cars in its class. Sure, we all know that the coupe's mechanicals and platform aren't that different from the Accord's, but when you add up all of its standard bells and whistles, you get a fully loaded medium-sized car that costs thousands of dollars less than such competing luxury coupes as the BMW 318 and the Lexus SC 300.

VEHICLE HISTORY: CLs have changed little since they were launched as 1997 models. **1998**—Debut of the 2.3L engine. **2003**—CL soldiers on with the two-door coupe and Type S coupe, both equipped with stronger base 3.2L V6s.

Recent model CLs get plenty of power from the smooth-running and quiet 3.2L V6. Handling is better than average, thanks to an upgraded suspension, variable assisted steering, and 16-inch wheels. The ride is comfortable and well controlled. Braking is first-class (100–0 km/h in 35 m). Front and rear bucket seats are supportive and easily adjusted. There's plenty of room up front, controls and most gauges are user-friendly (the navigation system and tachometer placement are the only exceptions), and the climate controls are efficient and within easy reach. Owners appreciate the large trunk with its low liftover and a locking ski pass-through that enhances the CL's cargo space.

On the down side, this is not a car designed with rear seat passengers in mind. Adults will likely find their heads pressed against the top of the back-light glass, and legroom and footroom are at a premium. Rear access is a crouch-and-crawl affair. In the trunk, lid hinges intrude into the trunk area and risk damaging cargo when the trunk is closed.

Here are some of the problems reported with the 1997–99 models: faulty transmission control unit; transmission downshift problems; chronic brake rotor pulsation and other brake problems leading to resurfacing of brake rotors and early replacement of brake pads, rotors, calipers, and springs; repeated front-end realignments; door and wind noise leading to replacement of door; and a sunroof that won't stop at the closed position, requiring replacement of sunroof switch and controller.

Owners have reported that the 2002–03 models equipped with both manual and automatic gearboxes can be troublesome. Manuals don't shift smoothly into Second and Reverse gears, and the automatic transmissions are known to fail completely, as the following owner relates:

> Car started free revving and erratically upshifting and downshifting with hard jerks. All malfunction indicators lit up. Almost lost control on the freeway. Was told transmission is shot on a car that is a bit over a year old.

Even if the automatic transmission remains intact, its erratic performance creates a serious safety hazard, says another 2002 3.2L CL owner:

> The transmission downshifted by itself to a lower gear, causing the vehicle to decelerate in a dangerous manner. Sooner or later someone is going to get killed if this problem is not corrected.

Sudden, unintended acceleration and hesitation complaints are also thought to be transmission-related (see "Secret Warranties/Internal Bulletins/Service Tips").

Owners of these newer models also report that premature brake pad and caliper wear and warped brake rotors continue to be a serious problem.

Safety Summary

All models: 1998—When driving on a flat surface at 45 km/h, or 1500 rpm, vehicle will jerk and pull for about 30 seconds. • Transmission seals fail. • Chronic electrical shorts. • Premature shock failure. • Sudden power-steering loss. • Excessive steering play because of faulty steering-column coupling. • Vehicle will sometimes accelerate when slowing for a stop. **1999**—Airbags don't deploy. • Transmission failure; inoperative gearshift because of water on the horn. • Steering locks up intermittently. • Short drivers may be seriously injured by the front airbag's deployment. **2002**—Transmission slips out of gear and suddenly downshifts; engine surges. • Sudden, unintended acceleration accompanied by loss of braking ability. • Window slides down into door. **2003**—Engine timing-belt failure. • Stalling. • Tire-tread separation. • Transmission corrective repairs are inadequate and simply reduce the vehicle's overall performance and handling:

> I have a 2003 Acura CL Type S. Acura has replaced the automatic transmission twice, and the 3rd transmission currently in the car is having problems. Although the manufacturer extended the warranty to 7 years and 100,000 miles [160,000 km], they sent service bulletins requesting service-induced slippage between gears and reduction of horsepower to reduce strain on the transmission. This car is advertised as a high-performance automobile, and, unknown to the customer, to take care of a manufacturing defect, they are adjusting the overall performance of the car. My car has been in for repair in excess of 15 times.

Secret Warranties/Internal Bulletins/Service Tips

All models/years: Most Honda/Acura TSBs allow for special warranty consideration on a "goodwill" basis, even after the warranty has expired or the car has changed hands. Referring to this display of "good will" increases your chances of getting some kind of refund for repairs that are obviously related to a factory defect. • Acura says it will replace any seat belt's tongue stopper button for the life of the vehicle. • Seat belts that are slow to retract will also be replaced for free, says TSB #91-050. **All models: 1997–98**—Power-seat noise. • Power windows don't work. • Window rattling. **1998–99**—Steering wheel remote audio switches may not work properly. **2001–03**—In September 2002, Honda extended its warranties to 7 years/256,000 km (160,000 mi.) on automatic transmissions on about 1.2 million cars and minivans because the components may fail or wear out early. The new retroactive warranty includes 2000 and 2001 model year Accords, Preludes, and Odysseys; 2000–02 Acura 3.2L TLs; 2001–02 Acura 3.2L CLs; and some 2003 models of both Acuras, spokesman Kurt Antonius said. He admitted that about 25,000 vehicles have experienced transmission problems, which include slow or erratic shifting. What's most disappointing about Honda's warranty extension is that it doesn't go back to cars from the 1997 model year, in which transmission breakdowns are also quite common. **2002**—Airbag light may remain lit. • Moonroof squeaks. • Seatback panel may loosen. • Missing speed sensor plug. • Troubleshooting engine oil leaks. *2.2L:* **1999**—Coolant leak from the engine block. *3.0L:* **1997–99**—A Product Update Campaign calls for the re-routing of the PCV hose to prevent the intake manifold EGR port from clogging. This is especially applicable to vehicles using fuel sold in the United States. **1997–2003**—Troubleshooting V6 engine oil leaks, and rules for applying the "goodwill" warranty. **1998–99**—Troubleshooting the inadvertent activation of the MIL (malfunction indicator light). **2001–03**—A secret warranty extension covers the automatic transmission up to 7 years/160,000 km (100,000 mi.), says TSB #02-027, issued September 15, 2003. Although limited to the torque converter, this extension creates a benchmark for all major tranny components. • The cost of a broken stabilizer-link replacement may also be covered under an Acura "goodwill" warranty extension:

BROKEN REAR STABILIZER LINK

BULLETIN NO.: 05-015   DATE: JUNE 24, 2005

1999–2003 3.2 TL, 2001–03 3.2 CL, and 2004–05 TSX

PROBLEM: A rear stabilizer link is broken.
CORRECTIVE ACTION: Replace both stabilizer links with improved parts.
PARTS INFORMATION: Rear Stabilizer Link Kit (includes both links and new self-locking nuts): P/N 06523-S84-A00
IN WARRANTY:
The normal warranty applies.
OUT OF WARRANTY:
Any repair performed after warranty expiration may be eligible for goodwill consideration by the District Parts and Service Manager or your Zone Office. You must request consideration, and get a decision, before starting work.

• In TSB #01-017, Acura says its new revised brake pads will reduce vibration when braking. This admission means Acura should share costs for this replacement. • Brake Alert lights intermittently. **2003**—Free replacement of the power control module (PCM), fuel pressure regulator (TSB #03-017), and front engine camshaft (TSB #02-033).

CL-SERIES PROFILE

	1998	1999	2000	2001	2002	2003
Cost Price ($)						
2.2L/2.3L CL	27,800	30,000	30,900	35,000	36,000	37,800
3.0L CL	30,650	34,000	35,000	—	—	—
Type S CL	—	—	—	40,000	40,000	41,800
Used Values ($)						
2.2L/2.3L CL ▲	5,500	7,500	9,000	12,000	15,500	18,000
2.2L/2.3L CL ▼	4,500	6,000	8,000	11,000	13,500	16,000
3.0L CL ▲	6,500	8,500	10,500	—	—	—
3.0L CL ▼	5,500	7,500	9,000	—	—	—
Type S CL ▲	—	—	—	13,500	16,500	19,000
Type S CL ▼	—	—	—	12,000	15,000	17,000
Reliability	4	4	4	4	4	4
Head Restraints	1	—	1	1	1	1

Note: These vehicles have not been crash-tested.

INTEGRA ★ ★ ★ ★ ★

RATING: Recommended (1994–2001); Above Average (1986–93). The Integra's rating is unusually high because of the few owner complaints recorded, the car's all-around competent performance, and the ease with which it can be customized through inexpensive ground effects and other options. Interestingly, there's little price difference between used entry-level and high-end models, despite the $4,000 premium when the cars were new. **"Real" city/highway fuel economy:** *1.8L:* 9.3/7.0 L/100 km with a manual transmission or 10.0/7.1 L/100 km with an automatic. Owners report fuel savings may undershoot the above estimates by at least 15 percent. **Maintenance/Repair costs:** Lower than average. Repairs can be done practically anywhere. **Parts:** Costs are a bit higher than average, but most parts can be bought from cheaper independent Honda suppliers. **Extended warranty:** Not necessary; save your money for performance tires (see *www.tirerack.com*). **Best alternatives:** Honda Accord; Mazda 626; Hyundai Elantra wagon, Sonata, or Tiburon; and Toyota Camry or Solara. **Online help:** *www.acuraworld.com/forums* and *www.autosafety.org*.

Strengths and Weaknesses

A Honda spin-off, early Integras (1986–89) came with lots of standard equipment and are a pleasure to drive, especially when equipped with a manual transmission. The 4-speed automatic saps the base engine's power considerably, but there is usually sufficient reserve power to accomplish most tasks. Surprisingly, these early models corner better and are more agile than later 1990–93 models. The hard ride can be softened a bit by changing the shocks and adding wide tires. The front seats are very comfortable, but they're set a bit low, and the side wheelwells leave little room for your feet. Rear seatroom is very limited, especially on the three-door version.

VEHICLE HISTORY: 1986–89—Redesigned in 1989, engines become smoother running and pick up 12 more horses (130). **1990**—Four-door sedan replaces the four-door hatchback, adding a bit more interior room; the GS debuts. **1992**—140-hp engine. **1994**—142-hp engine adds variable valve timing for extra power and smoothness. **1997**—The G-SR gains a 170-hp engine; a high-performance 195-hp Type R debuts. **1998**—A slight front-end restyling. **1999**—RS version dropped. **2000**—Return of the Type R, and the addition of an upgraded 4-speed automatic transmission to the general lineup. **2001**—Emergency trunk release. **2002**—Replaced by the RSX.

For model years 1990–93, the high-revving 1.7L powerplant growls when pushed and lacks guts (read "torque") in the lower gears. The 1.8L engine runs more smoothly but delivers the same maximum horsepower as the 1.7L it replaced, until the '94 model year, when it gains 10 extra horses. Surprisingly, overall performance has been toned down and is compromised by the 4-speed automatic gearbox. Interior design is more user-friendly, with the front seating roomier than in previous years, but the reduced rear seating is still best for small children.

Mechanical reliability is impressive, but that's also the case with most Hondas, which sell for far less, and many mechanical components are so complex that self-service can pretty well be ruled out. The Integra's front brakes may require more attention than those of other Hondas. What Integras give you in mechanical reliability and performance, however, they take away in poor quality control on body components and accessories. Water leaks, excessive wind noise, low-quality trim items, and plastic panels that deform easily are all commonplace. Owners also report severe steering shimmy, excessive brake noise, premature front brake-pad wearout, and radio malfunctions.

The 1994–2001 models offer a smoother ride than previous versions. However, the powerful VTEC engine requires lots of shifting, and interior room is still problematic. Overall, there are too few improvements to justify the high prices that post-1999 models command; therefore, target cars in the 1997–99 model year range for optimum savings and performance.

Owners report that some steering wheel shimmy, fit and finish deficiencies, and malfunctioning accessories continue to be problematic on later models. Only a smattering of automatic transmission defects have been mentioned, though any glitches within 7 years/160,000 km should be fixed free of charge (see preceding "CL-Series" section). Premature front brake wear is also an ongoing concern, often fixed for free if the client is the least bit threatening. Squeaks and rattles frequently crop up in the door panels and hatches, and the sedan's frameless windows often have sealing problems.

Safety Summary

All models/years: No airbag deployment, or inadvertent deployment; sudden acceleration; automatic transmission defects; poor headlight illumination; and chronic brake failures are common in every model year. • Prematurely warped rotors are the cause of excessive vibration and pulling. **All models: 1998**— Sudden steering lock-up. • Driver's seat belt won't loosen. • Horn failure. • Sunroof malfunctions. • Window motor inoperative. **1999**—Front windshield distorts vision. • Check Engine light comes on constantly. **2000**—Small horn buttons are difficult to activate in an emergency. • Automatic transmission failure. • Rear brake-pad failure. • Steering wheel obstructs view of speedometer. **2001**— Complete transmission failure. • Early engine computer and idling valve replacements. • Michelin tires don't have sufficient traction on wet roads.

Secret Warranties/Internal Bulletins/Service Tips

All models/years: Most Honda/Acura TSBs allow for special warranty consideration on a "goodwill" basis, even after the warranty has expired or the car has changed hands. • Vehicle cranks but won't start. • Severe and persistent steering wheel shimmy is likely due to an imbalanced wheel/tire/hub/rotor assembly. • Check Engine light constantly lit. • Headlight fogging. • Debris in blower motor (install protective screen). • Window guide channel comes loose. • Front brake squeal countermeasures. • Reducing rattles from the rear shelf area. •

Noisy power steering. • Seat belts that are slow to retract will be replaced for free, says TSB #91-050. **All models: 1990–2001**—Remedy for a rear suspension clunk or squeak. **1992–99**—A defective seat belt tongue stopper will be replaced free of charge with no ownership, time, or mileage limitations. **1997–2001**—Brake light comes on intermittently.

INTEGRA PROFILE

	1997	1998	1999	2000	2001	2002	2003
Cost Price ($)							
RS	18,595	18,795	19,500	21,000	—	—	—
LS/SE	23,095	23,245	23,800	23,800	21,800	22,000	22,500
Used Values ($)							
RS ▲	2,500	3,000	4,000	5,500	—	—	—
RS ▼	2,000	2,500	3,500	4,500	—	—	—
LS/SE ▲	3,500	4,500	5,000	6,500	7,000	8,000	10,000
LS/SE ▼	3,000	3,500	4,500	5,500	6,500	7,500	8,500
Reliability	4	4	4	4	5	5	5
Crash Safety (F)	—	4	—	—	—	—	—
Head Restraints (F)	2	—	3	—	3	—	3
Rear	—	—	—	—	2	—	—
Rollover Resistance	4	—	—	—	—	—	—

DaimlerChrysler

AVENGER, SEBRING ★ ★ ★ ★

RATING: Above Average (2002–06); Average (2000–01); Below Average (1995–99). The Avenger and its more luxuriously appointed Sebring twin have had fewer factory-related defects than other new Chrysler designs, though this is faint praise, indeed. Drive a hard bargain, because the money you save will be eaten up in transmission, engine head gasket, engine sludging (1998–2002 models), and AC evaporator repair bills unless you get the 7-year powertrain warranty, threaten small claims court action, or use your service manager successfully to get "goodwill" assistance. The Sebring convertible is an attractively styled bargain ragtop. **"Real" city/highway fuel economy:** *Sebring convertible:* 11.9/7.9 L/100 km with a manual transmission or 11.2/7.8 L/100 km with an automatic. *2.4L sedan:* 11.1/7.7 L/100 km. *2.7L sedan:* 10.6/7.3 L/100 km. Fuel savings may be lower by about 15 percent. **Maintenance/Repair costs:** Average. Avenger repairs must be done at a Chrysler dealer. **Parts:** Average cost and availability.

All ratings on a numbered scale where 5 is good and 1 is bad. See pages 130–132 for a more detailed description.

Extended warranty: Yes, if Chrysler's base warranty has expired. **Best alternatives:** Ford Mustang or Probe, GM Camaro or Firebird, Hyundai Tiburon, Mazda Miata, Nissan 240SX, and Toyota Celica. **Online help:** *www.autosafety. org/autodefects.html, www.datatown.com/chrysler, www.wam.umd.edu/~gluckman/ Chrysler/index.html* (The Chrysler Products' Problem Web Page), *www.daimlerchrysler vehicleproblems.com* (The Truth Behind Chrysler), *www.sebringclub.net/board, www. asog.net* (Avenger/Sebring Owners Group), and *www.intrepidhorrorstories.blogspot. com* (Dodge Intrepid Owner? Read This!).

Strengths and Weaknesses

These coupes, sedans, and convertibles are good buys mainly because they've had fewer new-model teething problems than other Chrysler-built vehicles. Sebring is a reasonably priced luxury model equipped with standard amenities, including AC, bucket seats, and a tilt steering wheel.

These front-drives use powertrains and platforms from Mitsubishi's Eclipse and Galant and also share most safety features and mechanical components, including standard dual airbags and a 150-hp 2.4L 4-banger along with a 2.7L V6, a 200-hp 3.0L V6, and a 3.5L V6.

VEHICLE HISTORY: 1995–99—Minor restyling touches and the dropping of the 4-cylinder engine in mid-1999. **2000**—Sebring convertible's suspension is retuned to give a more comfortable ride, and the same year's base Avenger is given additional standard equipment—notably, the ES's 2.5L V6 and an automatic transmission. **2001**—The redesigned Sebring adds a sedan, a more powerful V6, and a premium sound system. The Avenger is dropped. **2002**—Sebrings are joined by a 200-hp 2.7L V6 R/T sedan equipped with a manual 5-speed gearbox. **2003**—Addition of four-wheel disc brakes. **2004**—Restyled front ends for the convertibles and sedans. **2005**—Coupes are dropped.

Acceleration is fairly good, though noisy, with the base 4-cylinder engine and a manual transmission; however, the 3.0L and 3.5L V6 are the engines of choice to overcome the power-hungry automatic transmission and to avoid a persistent 4-cylinder engine head gasket defect affecting all model years through 1999. Handling is better than average, and the ride is generally comfortable, except for a bit of choppiness because of the firm suspension.

The 2.7L V6 would normally be a good alternative to the small 4-cylinder; however, it is subject to early engine primary timing-chain tensioner and tensioner O-ring failures and oil sludging on 1998–2002 models—a problem covered by a secret "goodwill" warranty. Owners also report automatic transmission failures, grinding when shifting, shuddering from a stop, and defaulting to Second gear; engine oil leaks; loss of steering and a clanking or rattling heard when turning over rough pavement; premature suspension replacement, brake wear, and brake failures; ignition, electrical system, and PCM glitches; sunroof malfunctions; and sloppy body construction (water leaks and lots of wind noise) as the areas most needing attention. Would you believe that the driver's seat motor burns out because it doesn't have a fuse? Replacement cost: $2,000!

As with 2005–06 Corvettes, the convertible tops can fly off on early models, plus they leak water and air and operate erratically. A faulty window regulator allows the window to run off its track. Poor design and sloppy construction allow water into the vehicle when the window is partly opened; rear windshield sealant lets water leak into the vehicle; wheel rims are easily bent and leak air from normal driving; there's excessive brake dust; a black goo oozes from body panels and the undercarriage; side door mouldings melt; and the chrome wheels and airbag coating peels.

Safety Summary

All models: 1996–99—Mitsubishi-built Avengers have had few safety-related incidents reported to NHTSA. Sebring safety failures over the same period were frequent and serious. *Sebring:* **1996–99**—Engine head gasket failures. **1998–2002**—The same old complaints, such as electrical short circuits and brake and airbag woes. • Reports concerning sudden acceleration, loss of steering control caused by the floormat blocking the steering column, bent wheel rims causing tire blowouts, seat belt lock-up, and alternator/battery failures increase. • Many complaints that the side door panel cladding falls off while cruising. • 2.7L engine oil sludging has generated over 1,000 complaints and is covered by a secret warranty (see "Secret Warranties/Internal Bulletins/Service Tips"). • Timing chain failures occur with the same engine. **1999**—Vehicle catches fire after hitting bumper of other car at 8 km/h (5 mph). • Another fire caused by a leaking fuel hose. • Front airbags fails to deploy upon impact. • Many incidents where the throttle sticks while engaging Reverse. • Premature replacement of the lower lateral sway bar. • Automatic transmission rebuild after 61,000 km (38,000 mi.). • Split transmission line. • Delayed, noisy transmission shifting. • Slips into Reverse and rolls downhill, despite being in Park with ignition off. • Constant velocity joint flies off in heavy traffic on interstate. • Brakes don't grab sufficiently; complete loss of braking caused by loss of vacuum. • Defective rear defroster clip. • Windshield wipers suddenly stop working. • Convertible boot flies off while vehicle is underway. • Brake failure and extended stopping distance caused by defective wheel speed sensor, modulator, or master cylinder and brake pad disintegrating, causing rotor scoring. • Automatic transmission slips out of gear while vehicle is cruising at 120 km/h; suddenly goes to 50 km/h. • Transmission fluid leakage through a crack in the transmission case. • Driver's seat belt often unlatches and seatback side latch may fail. **2001**—Brake failure accompanied by sudden, unintended acceleration. • Brake caliper bolt falls off. • Brake and accelerator pedals are too close to each other. • Window shatters when convertible top is lowered. **2002**—When putting vehicle into Reverse, it sometimes surges forward. • Engine stalls out after fill-ups. • Sudden brake failure. • Suspension feels loose at high speeds when passing over bumps or potholes. • Steering wheel catches and pulls right when turning. • Back windows suddenly explode. • Brake and gas pedals are too close together. • Coupes have the driver's seat set at an angle that's disorienting. **2003**—Sudden loss of steering. • Driver's airbag deploys for no reason. • Tapping brakes locks them up. • ABS brake failure. • Rodents can get into the heater blower area. • Headlights dim and shut off intermittently. **2004**—Electrical wiring in the rear defroster ignites a fire. • Airbags fail to deploy. • Tall front occupants may suffer considerable trauma despite airbag deployment. • Sudden, unintended acceleration when stopped or accelerating. • Sticking accelerator pedal. • Firewall fuel line leakage. • Engine overheating and stalling. • Transmission slippage—not engaging the gear selected and shifting to a higher and then a lower gear, making the car surge. • Transmission sticks in Park. • Steering failure. • Excessive steering shake at idle. • Seat heater overheats. • Windshield wiper switch breaks away from steering column. • Wiper sprayer hoses break after hood is opened a few times. • Dash lights flicker and headlights may suddenly go off. • Key sticks in the ignition. • Seat belt buckle breaks when latched. • Horn may not work properly. • Warped driver-side airbag cover. • Chrome door handles can cut a finger. • Bumper falls off car. **2005**—Airbags deploy and start a fire. • Delayed shifts. • Steering failure caused by broken steering knuckle. • Left front wheel breaks away from vehicle. • Filler pipe collapses while vehicle is refuelling. • Inaccurate fuel gauge readings. • Seat belt light comes on for no reason. • Seatback springs forward with excessive force. • Passenger-side window spontaneously explodes. • Horn sounds on its own.

Secret Warranties/Internal Bulletins/Service Tips

All models: 1995–98—Delayed transaxle engagement can be corrected by installing an upgraded trailing-arm bushing. **1995–2001**—Front coil spring creak, pop, or squeak can be silenced by putting in coil spring insulators. • Intermittent loss of speed control can be prevented by installing new speed sensors. • Wind noise coming from the front windshield area is caused by wind lifting the windshield moulding at the glass. • Tips on reducing excessive front brake pulsation or shudder. • Paint delamination, peeling, or fading. **1997–99**—New software will prevent the transmission from shifting erratically or falling into a Second gear "limp" mode. *Sebring:* **1996–99**—Upgraded engine head gasket. **1996–2000**—Steering wheel clunk or rattle. • Wet carpet (convertible). **1998–2002**—The 2.7L V6 engine sludging "goodwill" warranty isn't yet confirmed by any service bulletin. Nonetheless, Chrysler spokesman Sam Locricchio told *AutoWeek* on September 3, 2004, that the automaker is working hard to "find a reasonable and appropriate resolution" for individual complaints. This problem may not go away. Chrysler hasn't shown any production changes that guarantee engines will not sludge up in the estimated 10 percent of 2005 Chrysler 300 and Dodge Magnums that are sold with the same V6 (mounted front-to-back rather than sideways). **2001**—Rough 2.7L engine idle. • Automatic transmission bump, sag, and surge. • Rear suspension squawk. **2001–02**—Moderate to severe highway engine surge. • Exhaust rattle, vibration. • Low or no cabin heat. • Loose, warped front door trim panel. **2001–03**—Erratic AC operation. **2001–04**—Poor AC operation. • Suspension or body pop or clunk noise. • Window fogging. **2001–06**—Musty AC smell. • Wind noise from the dash area. **2002**—Hard-to-remove fuel cap. **2002–04**—Delayed gear engagement:

DELAYED GEAR ENGAGEMENT

NUMBER: 21-004-05   DATE: JANUARY 22, 2005

TRANSMISSION DELAYED ENGAGEMENT

2004 Pacifica; 2002–04 Sebring Convertible/Sebring Sedan/Stratus Sedan; 2003 Liberty; 2002–04 300M/
Concorde/Intrepid; 2002–03; Neon 2002–03 PT Cruiser; 2002–03 Town & Country/Caravan/Voyager; 2003
Wrangler

This bulletin involves replacing the front pump assembly in the automatic transmission and checking the
Transmission Control Module (TCM) for the latest software revision level.

2003—Horn blows on its own. • Rear brake clunk. **2003–04**—Harsh down-shifts. **2003–05**—Automatic transmission whine at 100 km/h. **2004**—Driveability improvements to fix engine stumbling and rough running, idle fluctuations, and surging when at idle or coming to a stop. • Harsh 4–3 downshifts. • Low-speed transmission bumps. • New spark plug for 2.4L engine. • Pop/clunk sound from front of vehicle; engine snapping noise. • Steering-column click. • Revised suspension lateral-control links. • Door clunk noise. • Power seat won't adjust; front seat movement. • Intermittent loss of accessories. • Customer Satisfaction No. C30, relative to the PCM connector seal. • Window fogging. **2004–05**—Inoperative AC. **2004–06**—AC leaks water onto passenger floor.

AVENGER, SEBRING PROFILE

	1997	1998	1999	2000	2001	2002	2003	2004	2005
Cost Price ($)									
Avenger	18,780	19,280	20,360	—	—	—	—	—	—
Avenger V6	23,820	24,320	23,545	—	—	—	—	—	—
Sebring	21,420	21,500	23,380	27,685	23,240	23,320	23,610	24,115	24,560
Sebring V6	24,135	24,360	28,675	26,525	30,095	27,380	27,795	28,415	28,855
Convertible	27,030	27,530	32,100	32,585	33,595	33,580	34,305	35,195	35,795
Used Values ($)									
Avenger ▲	2,500	3,000	3,500	—	—	—	—	—	—
Avenger ▼	2,000	2,500	3,000	—	—	—	—	—	—
Avenger V6 ▲	3,500	4,000	5,000	—	—	—	—	—	—
Avenger V6 ▼	3,000	3,500	4,500	—	—	—	—	—	—
Sebring ▲	3,500	4,000	4,500	5,000	6,000	7,000	8,000	9,500	12,500
Sebring ▼	3,000	3,500	4,000	4,500	5,000	6,000	7,000	8,500	11,000
Sebring V6 ▲	3,500	4,500	5,500	6,500	7,500	8,500	9,500	11,500	14,000
Sebring V6 ▼	3,000	4,000	4,500	5,500	6,500	7,500	8,500	10,500	13,000
Convertible ▲	5,500	6,500	6,500	8,500	9,500	13,000	14,500	18,000	20,000
Convertible ▼	5,000	6,000	6,000	7,000	8,500	11,000	12,000	16,500	18,500

Reliability	2	3	3	3	3	3	4	4	4
Crash Safety (F) (Avenger)	5	—	—	—	—	—	—	—	—
Sebring 2d	5	—	—	—	4	4	4	4	4
Sebring 4d	—	—	—	—	5	5	5	5	5
Sebring cvt.	4	—	—	—	3	3	3	3	3
Side (Sebring)	—	—	—	—	3	3	3	3	3
Sebring 4d	—	—	—	—	3	3	3	3	3
Sebring cvt.	—	—	—	—	3	3	3	3	3
Side (IIHS)	—	—	—	—	1	1	1	1	1
Offset	—	—	—	—	3	3	3	3	3
Head Restraints									
Avenger	2	—	2	—	—	—	—	—	—
Sebring 2d	1	—	3	—	2	3	2	2	2
Sebring (R)	—	—	2	—	1	2	—	—	2
Rollover Resistance	—	—	—	—	5	5	5	5	5
Sebring 2d	—	—	—	—	—	—	4	4	4
Sebring cvt.	—	—	—	—	—	—	5	5	5

BREEZE, CIRRUS, STRATUS ★ ★

RATING: Below Average (1999–2000); Not Recommended (1995–98). When these cars were new, they were not very reliable and were only so-so highway performers. Now that they have been off the market for about seven years, they are even worse choices. That said, these cars have fewer mechanical and safety problems, believe it or not, than the Ford competition. Nevertheless, be prepared to experience a number of nasty safety-related failures such as airbags that don't deploy, sudden acceleration, a jerky automatic transmission that suddenly drops out of gear, and loss of braking. Be especially wary of any model carrying the anemic and failure-prone 4-cylinder engine, and watch out for engine sludging with the 2.7L V6. **"Real" city/highway fuel economy:** The 2.4L automatic transmission engine gets 11.3/7.1 L/100 km, and the 2.5L 6-cylinder automatic gets 12.3/7.9 L/100 km. **Maintenance/Repair costs:** Higher than average, but repairs aren't dealer-dependent. **Parts:** Higher-than-average costs (independent suppliers sell for much less), but they aren't hard to find. Recall parts, however, tend to dribble in; a month's wait isn't unusual (as has been the case with the transaxle oil cooler hose campaign for 2001 models). Don't even think about buying any of these cars without a 3- to 5-year supplementary warranty. **Extended warranty:** A good idea. **Best alternatives:** Acura Integra, Hyundai Elantra Wagon or Sonata, Mazda 626, Nissan Altima or Stanza, and Toyota Camry. **Online help:** For the latest owner reports, safety reports, complaint strategies, and money-saving tips, look at *www.autosafety.org/autodefects.html, www.wam.umd.edu/~gluckman/Chrysler* (The Chrysler Products' Problem Web Page), and *www.daimlerchryslervehicleproblems.com* (The Truth Behind Chrysler).

Strengths and Weaknesses

Roomy, stylish, well appointed, and comfortable, the Chrysler Cirrus and Dodge Stratus were 1996 mid-sized sedan replacements for the LeBaron. The Breeze, launched as a 1996 model and dropped after its 2000 model run, is essentially a "de-contented" version of the more expensive Cirrus. For 2001, the Stratus and the Cirrus coupe, sedan, and convertible fell under the Sebring moniker. Other improvements for the renamed models were a smoother ride and the addition of a 2.7L engine.

Most components have been used for some time on other Chrysler models, particularly the Neon subcompact and the Avenger and Sebring sports coupes. Power is supplied by one of four engines: a 2.0L 4-cylinder engine (shared with the Neon), a 2.4L 4-banger, or the recommended 2.5L and 2.7L V6. Carrying Chrysler's "cab forward" design a step further up the evolutionary ladder, these cars have short rear decks, low noses, and massive sloping grilles. A wheelbase that's 5 cm longer than the Ford Taurus makes these cars comfortable for five occupants, with wide door openings and plenty of trunk space.

Judged by their styling and roominess alone, these cars would appear to be great buys. They are, in fact, high-risk choices from both a performance and a quality-control standpoint. Problems reported by owners include the following: chronic automatic transmission failures; early and frequent engine head gasket failures through the 1998 models (no doubt part of the Neon engine legacy), plus erratic engine operation; ABS malfunctions and sudden brake and steering loss; paint delamination and peeling; electrical short circuits; weak headlights; underperforming AC; water leaks into the trunk area and interior; easy-to-break trim items; lots of squeaks and rattles; and head restraints that are set too far back. In 1999, the manual seat-height adjuster was dropped, making it difficult for short drivers to distance themselves safely from the airbag deployment. This also complicates both forward and rearward visibility, which is already seriously compromised by the cars' styling.

VEHICLE HISTORY: 1996—Horsepower boosted to 163 on the 2.5L engine. **1997**—Sebring convertible launched on Cirrus sedan platform. **2000**—Stratus and Breeze nameplates dropped. **2001**—4-cylinder engine and manual transmission are no longer available; Cirrus nameplate dropped.

Safety Summary

All models: Sudden acceleration; stuck throttle. • Airbags fail to deploy. • Frequent complaints of ABS failures. **1998**—Airbag explodes rather than inflates. • Floormat jams the steering-column assembly, causing the steering to lock up. • Automatic transmission (floor console design) throw from Drive to Reverse to Park is too long, resulting in driver thinking vehicle is in Park when it's really in Reverse. • Floor shift indicator on the dash doesn't give a true reading of which gear is engaged. • Gearshift lever can be moved into Drive without putting foot on brakes to engage the transmission/brake interlock system. • High trunk lid makes it impossible to see directly behind the vehicle. **1999**—Airbag deployed inadvertently, knocking driver out and causing an accident. • Stalling upon acceleration and when foot is taken off of the gas pedal. • Steering locks up when making left-hand turns. • Automatic transmission has a short lifespan; sensors are the first to go. • Transmission lever can be shifted into Drive without first depressing brake pedal. • Cracked axle. • Many incidents reported of sudden brake failure without any prior warning. • Chronic brake rotor warpage around 8,000 km (5,000 mi.), resulting in severe brake vibrations, noise, and extended stopping distance. • Engine fumes invade the cabin, causing driver drowsiness. • Frequent electrical shorts cause gauges, wipers, and windows to function erratically. • Engine, ABS, and Airbag warning lights often come on for no reason. • Seat belts fail to tighten. **1999–2000**—Several trunk fires reported from an overly intense trunk-mounted light bulb. • Dash reflects onto front windshield. • While driving, brake vacuum hose separates, causing complete brake failure. **2000**—Electrical system fire. • Timing belt slips, causing valves to seize in the engine. • Brake lock-up; no airbag deployment in resulting collision. • Low-speed gear whine. • Automatic transmission has a hard 3–2 shift. • Transmission drops out of gear at 75 km/h. • Warped brake drums and rotors make for very noisy braking and cause vehicle to pull dangerously to one side:

> Vehicle's driver-side front caliper seized and refused to release fully, causing vehicle to pull strongly to the left and causing overheating of the rotor and substantial loss of braking.

• Wheel lug nuts loosen on their own. • Excessive rear-window fogging. • Windshield wiper doesn't clear snow adequately from driver-side windshield. • Driver's door jams because of faulty door panel. • Seat belts too tight. • Chronic dead battery. • Space-saver spare tire is only good for a few kilometres and at slow speeds.

Secret Warranties/Internal Bulletins/Service Tips

All models/years: Anecdotal reports confirm Chrysler has a 7-year/160,000 km secret warranty covering paint delamination, peeling, and fading. • Chrysler will replace AC evaporators up to 7 years/115,000 km. **All models: 1995–99**—Intermittent loss of speed control. **1995–2000**—A steering-column clunk or rattle can be silenced by changing the steering-column retainer-coupling bolt. • A poorly operating engine may only need a new EGR valve emissions component (covered by the emissions warranty). **1997–98**—Excessive cold crank time, start die-out, or weak run-up may be corrected by replacing the powertrain control module (PCM), according to TSB #18-18-98. **1999**—A metallic noise heard from the rear doors can be silenced by modifying the window regulator channel. **1999–2000**—No-starts and stalling may be caused by a malfunctioning entry-key immobilizer system.

BREEZE, CIRRUS, STRATUS PROFILE

	1997	1998	1999	2000	2001	2002
Cost Price ($)						
Breeze	—	18,200	18,865	19,505	21,090	—
Cirrus	22,115	23,235	24,125	24,765	22,180	22,365
LXi	24,555	25,695	26,465	26,465	24,840	25,050
Stratus	17,895	18,200	18,865	19,505	21,090	—
V6	19,750	20,100	24,060	24,475	25,025	—
Used Values ($)						
Breeze ▲	—	1,000	2,000	2,500	3,000	—
Breeze ▼	—	700	1,500	2,000	2,500	—
Cirrus ▲	700	1,200	2,000	2,500	3,000	4,000
Cirrus ▼	500	1,000	1,500	2,000	2,500	3,000
LXi ▲	1,000	1,500	2,500	3,000	3,500	4,500
LXi ▼	700	1,200	2,000	2,500	3,000	4,000
Stratus ▲	1,000	1,500	2,000	3,000	3,500	—
Stratus ▼	500	1,200	1,500	2,500	3,000	—
V6 ▲	900	1,500	2,500	3,500	4,000	—
V6 ▼	600	1,200	2,000	3,000	3,500	—
Reliability	2	2	2	2	2	3
Crash Safety (F)	3	3	3	3	3	5
Side	—	—	3	3	3	3
Offset	1	1	1	1	1	1
Head Restraints						
Stratus (F)	1	—	1	—	2	—
Stratus (R)	—	—	—	—	1	—

Note: Crash ratings are applicable to all models.

Ford

SABLE, TAURUS ★

RATING: Not Recommended (1986–2006). Wow! A used Taurus for less than $2,000? What a bargain—NOT! These quintessential lemons make the Ford "You Light Up My Life" Pinto and Vauxhall Firenza look good. They are easy to find and dirt cheap because their owners can't wait to get rid of them before they pay another $3,000 in powertrain repairs (if they're lucky). And the extra engine and transmission warranty protection you must buy will wipe out any savings realized from a low selling price. The high-performance Taurus SHO (Super High Output) is worse. It's a double-whammy wallet buster with major engine deficiencies that can cost up to $15,000 to remedy; plus it shares most of the other generic safety- and performance-related defects that have long plagued the Taurus and Sable. The last model year for the Sable and the Mercury brand in Canada was 1999; Taurus managed to hold on through the 2006 model year. The restyled and slightly upgraded 2008 Ford Five Hundred and Ford Freestyle will be renamed the Taurus and Taurus X, respectively. **"Real" city/highway fuel economy:** The 3.0L engine with an automatic transmission gets 12.4/8.2 L/100 km. These Fords are real gas hogs; owners report fuel savings may undershoot the above estimate by at least 20 percent. **Maintenance/Repair costs:** Much higher than average, but repairs aren't dealer-dependent. Shopping at engine, transmission, brake, and muffler shops offering lifetime warranties can prevent some repeat repair costs. **Parts:** Average costs (independent suppliers sell for much less) and very easy to find, except for the discontinued SHO engine and Taurus parts such as the fuel pumps and electrical components needed to correct chronic stalling and electrical shorts. **Extended warranty:** Nothing less than a bumper-to-bumper extended warranty will do. Even with additional protection, you're taking a huge risk with your wallet. **Best alternatives:** Honda Accord, Hyundai Elantra wagon or Sonata, Mazda 626, Nissan Sentra or Stanza, and Toyota Camry. Good alternatives to the SHO and its failure-prone engine would be the Ford Mustang GT or Probe GT and the Probe's twin, the Mazda MX-6. **Online help:** *www.fordlemon.com* (Disclaimer: FordLemon is an effective consumer rights organization, but you may find some of the content on their website offensive), *www.tgrigsby.com/views/ bymodel.htm* (The Anti-Ford Page), *www.carsurvey.org/modelyear_Ford_Taurus_ 1999.html*, *www.consumeraffairs.com/automotive/ford_taurus_gaskets.htm*, *www. lemonlawclaims.com/Ford%20Taurus%20cowl%20leak.htm*, *www.crash-worthiness. com/ford/ford_recalls.html*, *www.autosafety.org/autodefects.html*, and *www.v8sho.com*.

Strengths and Weaknesses

Although they lack pick-up with the standard 4-cylinder engine, these mid-sized sedans and wagons are competent family cars, offering lots of interior room, nice handling, a good crash rating, and many convenience features. From a performance standpoint, the best powertrain combination for all driving conditions is the 3.0L V6 hooked to a 4-speed on the family sedan. The Yamaha powerplant harnessed to a manual gearbox on the high-performance SHO is a recipe for disaster. Total engine rebuilds are the norm, not the exception.

Yet the first generation Taurus LX was *Motor Trend* magazine's Car of the Year for 1986 and placed on *Car and Driver*'s annual Ten Best list from 1986 to 1991. Two examples of why most automobile journalists can't be trusted.

These cars are extremely risky buys, and they are getting worse as they age. To see just how badly time is taking its toll, take a look at the NHTSA website link listed in Appendix III. Chronic engine head gasket/intake manifold and automatic trans- mission failures; a plethora of hazardous airbag, fuel-system, brake, suspension, and steering defects; and chronic paint/rust problems are the main reasons their rating is so low. Owners are also reporting that engine and transmission repairs don't last: Some owners are routinely putting in new engines or transmissions every few years.

Up until 2001, Ford's "goodwill" programs usually compensated owners for most of the above-noted failures (except for self-destructing SHO engines) once the warranty had expired. Unfortunately, these refund programs have dried up as Ford puts stonewalling before integrity. Owners are routinely faced with $3,000 engine or automatic transmission repair bills in addition to thousands of dollars in repairs for defective fuel systems, brakes, and suspension and steering assemblies. Ford rejects many owner complaints on the grounds that repairs were done by independent agencies, or the vehicle was bought used, or it is no longer under the original warranty—three reasons that are often rejected by small claims court judges.

SHO

The Taurus SHO high-performance sedan, debuting in 1989 and sold through the 1999 model year, carried a Yamaha 24-valve 3.0L V6 with 220 hp; a stiff, performance-oriented suspension; and a 5-speed manual transmission. As of 1993, a 4-speed automatic transmission became available. In mid-1996, a redesigned SHO debuted with a standard Yamaha 32-valve V8 and 15 additional horses (235). Ford dropped the manual transmission at that time, a move that turned off most die-hard performance enthusiasts. The SHO is an impressive high-performance car that, unfortunately, has its own unique Yamaha-sourced engine problems, in addition to carrying Ford's failure-prone automatic transmission and sharing a host of other deficiencies with the Taurus and Sable.

Automatic transmission failures

Since 1991, Ford's automatic transmissions have been just as failure-prone as Chrysler's; they function erratically and are slow to shift—an annoying drawback if you need to rock the car out of a snowbank, and fairly dangerous if you need to pull out onto a busy roadway. A cracked aluminum forward-clutch piston principally causes these problems, although dozens of other causes, including flaws in major hardware and software components, have been linked to the above failures. Breakdowns usually occur after three years of use, around the 80,000–120,000 km mark, and can cost $3,000–$3,500 to repair at the dealer, or half that much at an independent garage (which I recommend) if no after-warranty assistance is proffered.

Engine failures

Ford's other major powertrain problem is the 3.8L engine's chronic head gasket failures, first seen in a major way on 1994–95 models, and on 1995–96 and later Windstars. Faulty engine intake manifold defects afflict other engines on more recent models. Both kinds of engine failures have similar symptoms: engine overheating, poor engine performance, and a reduction in night-driving visibility caused by a thin film deposited on the inside of the windshield. Repairs range from $700 to $1,000, depending upon what other damage has occurred from overheating. Left untreated, the failure can cook your engine, requiring repairs costing from $3,000 to $4,000. And, even if treated in time, this defect can cause failures in emissions components (oxygen sensors and various computer modules) and other hardware malfunctions that can lead to expensive repairs.

Other problems

The 4-cylinder engine is a dog that no amount of servicing can change. It's slow, noisy, prone to stalling and surging, and actually consumes more gas than the V6. The 3.0L 6-cylinder is noted for engine head bolt failures and piston scuffing and is characterized by hard starting, stalling, excessive engine noise, and poor fuel economy. Transmission cooler lines leak and often lead to the unnecessary repair or replacement of the transmission.

Other things to look out for are blown heater hoses, malfunctioning fuel-gauge sending units, and brakes that need constant attention—they're noisy, pulsate excessively, tend to wear out prematurely, require a great deal of pedal effort, and are hard to modulate. Master cylinders need replacing at around 100,000 km.

The 1988–95 models continue to have defective ignition modules, oxygen sensors, and fuel pumps, which cause rough running, chronic stalling, hard starting, and electrical system short circuits. Other problem areas include the following: disintegrating tie-rods, ball joints, coil springs, and motor mounts; an automatic transmission that is slow to downshift, hunts for Overdrive, and gives jerky performance; air conditioners that are failure-prone and can cost up to $1,000 to fix; malfunctioning heaters that are slow to warm up and don't direct enough heat to the floor (particularly on the passenger side); a defective heater core that costs big bucks to replace (buy from an independent supplier); and noisy, prematurely worn rack-and-pinion steering assemblies. Front suspension components also wear out quickly. Electrical components interfere with radio reception. The automatic antenna often sticks, electric windows short circuit, power door locks fail, and the electronic dash gives inaccurate readings. Owners report that electrical short circuits—which illuminate the Check Engine light and cause flickering lights and engine surging—are frequently misdiagnosed. Body/trim items are fragile on all cars (did somebody mention door handles?). Paint adherence is particularly poor on weld joints, plastic components, and the underside—even with mudguards. Owners also report that water leaks into the trunk through the tail light assembly, and there's an annoying sound of fuel sloshing when accelerating or stopping.

VEHICLE HISTORY: 1986—Taurus and Sable debut with a wimpy 2.5L 4-cylinder, an adequately powered but failure-prone 3.0L V6, and an optional and even more unreliable 3.8L V6 (offered through 1996). **1989**—SHO high-performance model, with a self-destructing Yamaha engine, is introduced. **1990**—Driver-side airbag. **1992**—This second-generation redesigned model adopts a more rigid chassis and drops the 4-banger. **1993**—SHO gets an automatic transmission, and engines and transmissions start breaking down on all models. **1994**—Dual front airbags;

powertrain continues to self-destruct. **1995**—A watershed year for engine head gasket failures and cooked engines. **1996**—A third-generation redesign highlighted by an ugly ovoid restyling where windows look like portholes, headroom is reduced, and entry/exit becomes more problematic. The 3.8L V6 is dropped, leaving two mediocre V6 engines to choose from. Other changes include upgraded engines, new electronic controls for the LX, better handling and ride quality, more effective soundproofing, and some transmission refinement. **1997**—SHO gets a V8 and an automatic transmission. **2000**—Redesigned and restyled to provide a more comfortable ride, a more powerful and quieter powertrain, upgraded airbags, adjustable pedals, seat belt pretensioners, and improved child safety-seat anchors. Ford drops the oval design and reduces sales prices in a futile effort to win back sales lost to the Japanese automakers. **2001–03**—Minor upgrades. **2004**—A slight restyling of the front and rear. **2005**—LX and SES versions are dropped. **2006**—Ford ditches the wagon and 201-hp V6 engine.

Owners of third-generation 1996–99 models still report serious safety-related deficiencies and other performance-related problems, such as engine and transmission seal leaks; the automatic transmission shifting erratically or not at all; front-end failures, including the outer tie-rods, ball joints, and stabilizer bar links; power windows that fail one after the other and cost $300–$500 each to repair; and "possessed" windshield wipers.

Who needs a radio? Each Taurus and Sable provides a symphony of rattles, buzzes, whines, and moans to keep you company on long drives. The most annoying? The incessant snapping and creaking of the plastic in the centre console and dash caused by the plastic sections binding against each other when the body flexes, especially if the sun has been shining on it. The reliability of 2000 model year vehicles continues to go downhill. Fuel-system failures result in surging, stalling, and a gasoline smell that invades the interior; electrical shorts cause the vehicle to suddenly shut down and not start again; the ABS and airbag malfunction; Check Engine lights stay lit; powertrain and body components have a short lifespan; and owners have found that the restyled head restraints block rear and side visibility.

Fourth-generation 2000–06 models use an adequate, though dated, base 155-hp 3.0L Vulcan V6. Other nice standard features include heated outside mirrors, a 60/40 split-fold rear seatback for additional cargo space, a driver's footrest, and reserve power to operate the power windows and moonroof after the engine is shut off. The suspension is softened and four-wheel disc brakes are eliminated.

These cars are generally quiet running, provide good handling and road holding, and offer a comfortable ride along with better-than-average crash protection. Of course, they are also heavily discounted (we know why). Some of the minuses include insufficient storage space, limited rear headroom and access, and a history of serious transmission and engine failures. Engine intake manifold defects top the list, accompanied by sudden engine shutdown. Furthermore, Flex-Fuel models may be difficult to start:

Car won't start properly on E-85 even though car is advertised as E-85 Flex-Fuel capable. Ford Motor has said they are working on repair for the problem.

The automatic transmission often shifts out of First gear too soon, shifts slowly, constantly bangs through the gears, and frequently chooses the wrong gear. Also expect chronic warped brake rotors; AC failures; electrical system shorts (lots of blown fuses); steering, front suspension, fuel (faulty fuel pumps), and brake system deficiencies; and extremely poor fit and finish, highlighted by numerous water leaks into the interior.

Getting compensation

Canadian owners still have to threaten small claims court action to get Ford Canada to accept repairs done by independent garages or to compensate for repeat failures or failures that occur in the 100,000–160,000 km ("no man's land") range, where warranty decisions are particularly inconsistent.

Anyone who has just been blown off on the phone by a Ford Customer Assistance rep should keep in mind what one Ford whistle-blower whispered in my ear:

> The only thing that gets our attention is if a small claims lawsuit is threatened or has been filed. These are kicked upstairs to Legal Affairs and are settled right away by staffers who have far more latitude and much less attitude.

 Safety Summary

All models/years: Tie-rod may collapse suddenly. Although the 1992 models were recalled to fix this defect, many other model years are affected and haven't been recalled. The son of a West Coast Taurus owner relates this incident:

> The right inner tie-rod, a piece of the suspension critical to the steering and thus safety of my 1992 Taurus, broke while my father was attempting to make a right turn from a stop sign. The car lost all steering control and the front wheels were seized. Fortunately, the car was barely moving, and no collision occurred…. I hope you can inform all Taurus and Sable owners of the inherent dangers lurking in their steering system.

• Front coil springs may fracture because of excessive corrosion. Ford has replaced many coils for free under a secret warranty. Interestingly, Ford's Windstars have the same problem and benefit from the same 10-year extended warranty. Use that as your Taurus coil benchmark, as this Whitby, Ontario, engineer should do:

> I have a 1995 Mercury Sable that has developed two broken coil springs, on front right and rear left wheel. The fracture surfaces on the front spring show no fatigue bands and are compatible with intergranular stress corrosion or hydriding, both indicating a manufacturing defect. Microscopic examination would be required to confirm the cause of failure.

This car has seen only light-duty service, is low mileage, and has always been garaged. I feel this is a significant safety issue. The failures have given no warning signs, and only the front one was detected during routine maintenance. The front spring has broken in two places, leaving a broken spring end only a quarter inch [0.6 cm] from the tire. I cannot easily see what is stopping it [from] going right into the tire, and suspect it would have worked its way in over the course of a few more miles. I am also concerned that a local independent mechanic says he has seen several spring failures on the Taurus/Sable, but that the local dealer's service rep has not. I note from the *Lemon-Aid* website that Transport Canada is investigating spring failures on this vehicle type.

• Strong fuel odour seeps into the interior. • Power steering suddenly fails. • These vehicles eat brake rotors, calipers, and pads every 8,000 km (5,000 mi.). • Warped rotors. • Transmission slips out of Park. • Frequent complaints of sudden acceleration or high idle when taking the foot off the gas pedal at a standstill, shifting into Reverse, slowly accelerating, or applying the brakes. • Chronic stalling and brake failures. • Airbag fails to deploy or is accidentally deployed. • Dash reflects onto windshield. **All models: 1999**—Engine fires. • Many reports of no-starts or sudden stalling caused by fuel pump failure. • Defective power-steering pump causes sudden steering lock-up. • ABS brakes lock up when applied, and vehicle suddenly accelerates. • Many reports of brake pedal being pushed to the floor with no braking effect. One '99 Taurus owner recounts the following tragic experience in his NHTSA complaint:

Sudden brake loss, cruise control wouldn't disengage, brakes to floor, emergency brake pulled to no effect, death of four.

Every element of this owner's story is repeated throughout the NHTSA database in reports from other Taurus and Sable owners. • Cruise control fails to disengage when vehicle is going downhill. • Frequent automatic transmission failures that include slipping, hesitation, lurching into gear, failure to engage First gear, and a defective fluid pump destroying the catalytic converter. • Transmission in Park position allows vehicle to roll downhill. • Transmission may leak fluid onto the exhaust manifold. • Front-passenger seat belt won't retract or lock into position. • Seat belt breaks. • Seat belts fail to retract in a collision. • Rear defroster/defogger works poorly. • Rear windshield explodes when defroster/defogger activated. • Rear windshield explodes while vehicle is underway. • Headlights dim when brakes are applied. • Trunk light bulb burns part of luggage. • Electrical system shorts lead to the erratic operation of power door locks (they unlock while vehicle is underway) and windows. • AC discharges a foul odour that causes eyes to water and burn. • Fuel tank leaks. • Vehicle will stall out when fuel gauge shows the tank is one-quarter full. In fact, the gauge is so inaccurate that it will vary its reading by a half a tank depending upon whether you are going uphill or downhill. **2000**—As of April 2007, 1,140 safety failures have been reported to NHTSA for the first year of the Taurus' latest redesign (a few hundred complaints would be normal). Most of the problems are similar to those reported for previous years. Gas fumes in the interior (driver found it exceeded CO_2 monitor limits and caused drowsiness and headaches); constantly lit warning lights; complete electrical failures; and sudden acceleration, surging, and stalling accompanied by brake failures continue to be the most frequent complaints:

> I released the brake after stopping at a stop sign, and turned the wheel to the right, the vehicle suddenly accelerated to what seemed about 100 km/h in about 10 seconds. The vehicle went toward the right and struck a curb, and the brakes did not appear to work. Once the vehicle came to a rest, the engine then shut off, the windshield broke, and the driver's side door wouldn't open. I suffered minor injuries.

• Whatever you do, don't ignore the Check Engine light. In another recorded incident, the car didn't run away, stall, or lose its brakes—it simply exploded:

> At start-up the intake manifold exploded, resulting in total destruction. Shrapnel was embedded in the insulation cover on the hood and found throughout the engine compartment. The windshield washer module on the right side was blown off and found approximately five feet [1.5 m] from the car. This vehicle has been in for service for hard starting and fuel system Check Engine light for the past year.

2001—Complaints continue unabated and echo those from previous years. • When coming to a stop, vehicle continues to accelerate because foot presses brake and gas pedal at the same time. • Car accelerates while backing up. • Airbag warning light comes on for no reason. • Rear-view mirror too low on windshield; blocks view to the right. • Driver-side seat belt tightens by itself while driving. • Left rear wheel came off in transit; lost control of car. **2002**—Engine compartment fire. • Sudden acceleration; vehicle surges and then shuts off when fuel tank is filled. • Frequent stalling, hard starts, and poor idle caused by chronic fuel pump failures or a contaminated fuel pressure sensor. • Strong fuel smell comes from the air vents. • Fuel gauge stuck on Full. • Fuel tank is easily punctured • Interior rear-view mirror location obstructs visibility. • Seat belts may not reel out or retract. • Seat belt continually tightened around child and had to be cut. • Adjustable brake and accelerator pedals are set too close together and are often too loose. • Rear brake lines rub together. • High beam lights are too dim. • Cigarette lighter pops out and falls under passenger seat. **2003**—Airbag warning light stays lit. • Rear left wheel and rim flies off because of defective lug nuts. • Engine has to be replaced because block heater is incorrectly mounted on the engine. • Engine belt tensioner shatters. • Excessive steering vibration. • Right rear wheel almost fell off because of faulty stabilizer bolt. • Firestone tire blowout. **2004**—Replacing the original radio will render the airbag inoperative since the controls run through the original equipment radio supplied by Ford. • Several reports of coil-spring breakage causing loss of steering control (a problem for over a decade—see "Secret Warranties/Internal Bulletins/Service Tips"). • Driver's seat catches on fire. • Chronic stalling. • Automatic transmission shifts erratically and slips. • Seat belt choked passenger in a collision. • Brake failure and engine surging occur simultaneously along with a lit ABS and Traction Control warning light. • Only driver's side door has a key-operated lock. • Sunroof opens and closes on its own. • Continental tire sidewall blows out; other reports that the belts slip and the sidewalls bulge outward. **2005**—Engine compartment fire. • Engine rpms decrease whenever the brakes are applied. • Transmission shifts erratically:

> The transmission started slipping around 38,500 miles [62,000 km]. It has been repaired 3 times. Hopefully it is fixed at this point. I was almost hit twice because the transmission slipped from 50 mph to 25 mph [80 to 40 km/h] in a matter of seconds. The vehicles behind me had to slam on brakes and jump lanes to keep from hitting me.

• Vehicle wanders all over the road. • Side windows implode while driving. • Inaccurate fuel gauge. • Static electricity shocks driver exiting vehicle. • Ventilation system allows polluted air to enter the cabin. • Driver's seat belt fails to latch. • Child safety seat tips to the side when car corners at 15–20 km/h.

Secret Warranties/Internal Bulletins/Service Tips

All models/years: Many reports of sudden coil-spring breakage puncturing tires and throwing vehicles out of control; there are no confirming TSBs, however. Writes the owner of a 1999 Taurus SE:

> Driver side coil spring failed, cutting the tire in half. Not too bad at 60 km/h but would have been a disaster at 100 km/h. Seems there were "not enough failures" to require recall earlier, but ANOTHER investigation has been opened by [the] government. Dealer said it was a "common" failure!!! I would not drive a Taurus/Windstar until I put something other than Ford springs on them. There are also reports of similar failures in Contours, Escorts, Focus, and F-150s. Problems with Ford coil springs and corrosion date from at least 1993. So, 11 years later, they clearly have done NOTHING to fix the problem. The corrosion where my spring broke was NOT visible externally, but was clearly rusted internally at the point where it broke.

• Repeated heater core leaks. • A rotten-egg odour coming from the exhaust probably means that you have a faulty catalytic converter; replacement may be covered under the emissions warranty. • A buzz or rattle from the exhaust system may be caused by a loose heat shield catalyst. • A sloshing noise from the fuel tank when accelerating or stopping requires the installation of an upgraded tank. • Paint delamination, fading, and peeling. **All models: 1994–98**—No Fourth gear may signal the need to install an upgraded forward clutch-control-valve retaining clip. **1994–99**—Service tips to silence wind noise around doors. **1995–99**—Tips for sealing windshield water leaks and reducing noise, vibration, and harshness while driving. **1995–2000**—A harsh 3-2 downshift/shudder when accelerating or turning may have a simple cause: air entering the fluid filter pick-up area because of a slightly low ATF fluid level. **1996–98**—Troubleshooting tips for a torque converter clutch that won't engage. • Hard starts or long cranks may be caused by a miscalibrated power control module (PCM), a faulty air control motor (IAC), or a malfunctioning fuel pump. • Install a power-steering service kit to silence steering moan. • A rattle heard when accelerating may be corrected by replacing the exhaust pipe flex coupling. • Water leaking onto the passenger floor area is likely caused by insufficient sealing of the cabin air filter to the cowl inlet. **1996– 99**—Frequent no-starts, long cranks, or a dead battery may be caused by excessive current drain or water entry in the ABS module connector. **1996– 2001**—Inoperative power windows may need a new motor and lubrication of the glass run weather stripping. **1996–2003**—Repair tips for when the torque converter clutch doesn't engage. **1997–2007**—Remedy for chronic heater core leaks. **1999**—Owner Notification Program regarding transmission rear lube-tube and bracket replacement. • Engine buzz or rattle. • Slight vibration upon acceleration. • Lack of engine braking. • Excessive spark knock with the 3.0L engine. • Engine oil pan leaks. • No Reverse engagement is likely caused by the Reverse clutch lip seals shearing or tearing during cold-weather Reverse engagement. • No 3–4 shifts, or 3–4 shift shuddering. • Inoperative speed control and blower motor. • Self-activating front wipers need an upgraded multifunction switch (covered under warranty or "goodwill"). • Hard-to-turn ignition key. • Wagons display a false Door Ajar light warning. • Intermittent loss of instrument panel illumination. • Separation between the layers of the instrument panel. • Premature deterioration of the front seat trim. • Power window binding. • Inaccurate fuel tank gauge; fuel tank causes gas pump to shut off prematurely. **2000**—Engine-pan oil leaks. • Automatic transmission may operate erratically. • A hissing sound may be heard coming from the intake manifold. • A growling or scraping sound may be heard during acceleration. **2000–01**—3.0L engines may exhibit a rough start or poor idle or excessive spark knock, or they may backfire on start-up. • 3–4 shift shudder. • The exhaust pipe contacts the rear control arm, resulting in rear end buzzing, groaning, and rattling. • Fuel smell permeates the interior. **2000– 03**—Power window "grunting." • No-starts or hard starts. **2000–07**—An inaccurate fuel gauge will be repaired under the emissions warranty (see page 66). **2001**—Side airbag light may remain lit. • Rough idle. • Check Engine light remains lit. • Automatic transmission fluid leakage from the main control cover area. • Rough shifting and engine surging. • Sticking/binding ignition-key lock cylinder. **2001–04**—Malfunctioning blower motor. **2001–05**—Tips on eliminating an engine ticking noise. **2002–03**—A faulty cooling fan may cause engine noise, excessive vibration, and a rough idle. **2002–05**—Troubleshooting transmission malfunctions. • Engine-cooling-fan-induced body boom. • Rough engine idle sensation; unusual engine noise at idle. • Incorrectly installed gear-driven camshaft position-sensor synchronizer assemblies may cause engine surge, loss of power, or MIL to light. • Rattling, clunking front suspension. **2003**—Transmission may not go into Reverse. **2003–06**—Inoperative AC compressor; **2004**—3.0L engine oil leaks; cold hard start, no-start, and surging. • Hesitation when accelerating. • Wipers won't shut off. • Inoperative rear window defroster. • Accelerator pedal vibration. • Speedometer malfunctions. • Wheel cover and front suspension noise. **2005–07**— Troubleshooting a misfiring engine.

	1997	1998	1999	2000	2001	2002	2003	2004	2005
Cost Price ($)									
Sable GS	23,595	24,395	24,595	—	—	—	—	—	—
LS Wagon	26,596	25,096	25,795	—	—	—	—	—	—
Taurus GL	23,195	—	—	—	—	—	—	—	—
Taurus LX	26,195	23,295	23,495	24,495	24,250	24,550	24,750	24,995	—
GL/SE Wagon	23,196	23,995	24,695	26,495	26,555	27,285	27,630	28,355	26,345
SHO	32,695	37,795	37,995	—	—	—	—	—	—
Used Values ($)									
Sable GS ▲	2,000	2,500	3,500	—	—	—	—	—	—
Sable GS ▼	1,700	2,000	2,500	—	—	—	—	—	—
LS Wagon ▲	2,500	3,500	4,000	—	—	—	—	—	—
LS Wagon ▼	2,000	2,500	3,000	—	—	—	—	—	—
Taurus GL ▲	1,700	—	—	—	—	—	—	—	—
Taurus GL ▼	1,400	—	—	—	—	—	—	—	—
Taurus LX ▲	2,500	3,000	3,500	5,000	7,000	8,500	10,500	13,500	—
Taurus LX ▼	2,000	2,500	3,000	4,500	5,500	7,500	9,000	11,500	—
GL/SE Wagon ▲	3,000	3,500	4,000	4,500	5,000	6,500	8,500	11,000	13,000
GL/SE Wagon ▼	2,500	3,000	3,500	4,000	4,500	5,500	7,500	9,500	11,500
SHO ▲	4,000	4,500	5,000	—	—	—	—	—	—
SHO ▼	3,500	4,000	4,500	—	—	—	—	—	—
Reliability	1	1	1	1	2	2	2	2	2
Crash Safety (F)	4	5	—	5	5	5	4	4	4
Side	3	3	—	3	3	3	3	3	3
Offset	5	5	5	5	5	5	5	5	5
Head Restraints (F)	1	—	1	3	5	2	3	2	2
Rear	—	—	—	3	3	3	—	—	—
Rollover Resistance	—	—	—	—	4	4	4	4	4

General Motors

ACHIEVA, ALERO, GRAND AM, SKYLARK ★ ★ ★

RATING: Average (2000–05), with the right powertrain set-up and an extended powertrain warranty; Below Average (1995–99); Not Recommended (1985–94). Only the Grand Am and its Alero twin survived the 1999 model year. Despite its post-2004 phase-out, the Olds Alero's resale value has remained remarkably high. Keep in mind that the 4-cylinder engines are noisy and rough running. "**Real**" city/highway fuel economy: *Grand Am and Alero:* With a 2.2L engine, these vehicles get 9.4/6.0 L/100 km with a manual transmission or 9.8/6.6 L/100 km with an automatic; with a 3.4L 6-cylinder and an automatic tranny, the figures are 11.7/6.7 L/100 km. *Skylark:* 10.7/6.7 L/100 km with a 2.2L engine and an automatic; 12.3/7.8 L/100 km with a 3.1L 6-cylinder and an automatic. Owners report Grand Am and Alero fuel savings may undershoot the above estimates by at least 20 percent. **Maintenance/Repair costs:** Higher than average. Repairs aren't dealer-dependent. **Parts:** Higher-than-average costs, but parts can be bought from independent suppliers for much less than from the dealership. **Extended warranty:** A toss-up. Extended powertrain coverage should be sufficient protection. **Best alternatives:** Acura Integra; Honda Accord; Hyundai Elantra wagon, Sonata, or Tiburon; Mazda 626; Nissan Altima; and Toyota Camry. **Online help:** For the latest owner reports, service bulletins, and money-saving tips, look at *www.autosafety.org/autodefects.html*, or type "GM paint delamination," "piston slapping," or "manifold defects" into a search engine such as Google.

Strengths and Weaknesses

These cars originally came with a failure-prone 150-hp Quad SOHC engine, a 5-speed transaxle, and ABS. The basic front-drive platform continues to be a refined version of the Sunfire (Sunbird) and Cavalier J-body. They are too cramped to be family sedans (rear entry/exit can be difficult), too sedate for sporty coupe status, and too ordinary for inclusion in the luxury car ranks.

In their basic form, these cars are unreliable, unspectacular, and provide barely adequate performance. An upgraded 3.1L V6 powerplant gives you only five more horses than the base 4-banger and frequently requires intake manifold gasket repairs covered by a 6-year/100,000 km secret warranty. There's been a lot of hype about the Quad 4 16-valve engine, available with all models, but little of this translates into benefits for the average driver. A multi-valve motor produces more power than a standard engine, but always at higher rpm and with a fuel penalty and excess engine noise.

These cars ride and handle fairly well, but mostly share chassis components with the failure-prone J-bodies. This explains why their engine, transmission, brake, and electronic problems are similar. Fortunately, manual transmissions are much more reliable and are also the better choice for fuel economy. Water leaks and body squeaks and rattles are so abundant that GM has published a six-page troubleshooting TSB that pinpoints the noises and lists fixes.

VEHICLE HISTORY: All models: 1991–95—Potentially unsafe door-mounted front seat belts. **1992**—A major redesign offers new styling and a 3.3L V6. **1994**—A revised 3.1L V6 replaces the 3.3L V6 and a driver-side airbag was added. **1996**—Restyled and given standard AC, dual airbags, and three-point seat belts; a new twin-cam engine replaced the 2.3L Quad 4. **1998**—De-powered airbags. *Alero:* **2004**—Last model year. *Grand Am:* **1999**—Given better engines, a new platform, more standard equipment, and a restyled, more comfortable interior. **2002**—A quieter, more efficient 140-hp 2.2L base engine with 10 fewer horses than the engine it replaced; a revised console storage area. **2004**—An MP3 speaker upgrade. **2005**—Dropped from production.

The 2.5L 4-cylinder engine doesn't provide much power and has a poor reliability record. Avoid the Quad 4 and 3.0L V6 engines with SFI (sequential fuel injection) because of their frequent breakdowns and difficult servicing. Poor engine cooling and fuel system malfunctions are common; diagnosis and repair are more complicated than average, however. The engine computer on V6 models has a high failure rate, and the oil pressure switch often malfunctions. The electrical system is plagued by gremlins that cause gauges and controls to go haywire, and this results in the car shutting down on the highway. Seals and pumps in the power-steering rack deteriorate rapidly. Front brake discs, rotors, and pads need replacing every 8,000 km (5,000 mi.). Locks and headlights self-activate.

Among body deficiencies, owners note that windshield mouldings fall off, water leaks into the trunk and through the doors, door panels often need replacing, the sun visor fails to stay in place, seat cushions aren't durable, and paint defects are quite common.

Alero and Grand Am (1999–2005)

These redesigned cars aren't very impressive. The best engine choice for power, smoothness, and value retention is the 207-hp 3.4L V6; it gives you much-needed power and is quite fuel efficient. The new 2.2L engine is quieter, but its lack of power is noticeable, particularly when coupled with an automatic transmission. Stay away from the Computer Command Ride option; true, it allows you to choose your own suspension settings, but the settings aren't quite what they pretend to be.

Taking their styling cues from GM's Grand Prix, the Grand Am and its Alero twin offer a roomy, comfortable interior in two- and four-door body styles. They share the same platform and mechanical components, and the base Grand Am SE uses a 140-hp 2.2L powerplant, while other trim levels use the 150-hp 2.4L Quad DOHC engine. A 170-hp 3.4L V6 engine is standard on the SE2. The upscale Alero, Oldsmobile's entry-level model, debuted in 1999 as the replacement for the slow-selling Achieva—often referred to as the "under-Achieva." The Alero shares the Grand Am's chassis and powertrains, although only the 2.2L and 3.4L V6 are offered. The V6 may be teamed with either a 5-speed manual or a 4-speed automatic transmission.

Grand Ams from 1999 to 2005 are well appointed with many more standard features than previous versions, like traction control. They have a competent V6, good steering and handling, and average quality control. Some of their disadvantages include a mediocre ride over rough terrain, excessive 4-cylinder noise, and a noisy interior. Also, expect difficult rear-seat access (coupe), awkward radio controls, rear visibility that's obstructed by the spoiler, problematic trunk access, annoying body creaks and rattles, and doubtful long-term powertrain reliability.

Equally well equipped, Aleros give impressive V6 acceleration (even though it's the same engine found in the Grand Am, it performs better in the Alero). You'll find logical, user-friendly gauges and controls, a fairly spacious interior for cargo and passengers, standard traction control, and a quiet-running V6 powertrain. Here's the Alero's downside: excessive 4-cylinder engine noise and torque steer, steering that's not as crisp as the Grand Am's, difficult rear-seat access (coupe), and questionable long-term durability. The Alero was dropped during the 2004 model year after GM's phase-out of its Oldsmobile division.

Overall quality control is poor. Owners warn of powertrain malfunctions, including sudden transmission failure and poor shifting, engine overheating, and premature brake pad and rotor wear.

Owners also mention electrical problems; suspension squeaks; and substandard body assembly that produces squeaks and rattles, water leaks, and poor paint adhesion. There are reports that the sunroof may leak water into the electrical panel, causing short circuits. The spoiler may obstruct rear visibility.

Safety Summary

All models/years: Airbag fails to deploy. • Inadvertent airbag deployment. • Sudden acceleration and stalling. • Frequent brake failures and extended stopping distance; brake-caliper seizure damages pads and rotors. • Power-steering failures and fluid leakage. • Transmission jumps out of gear. • Shoulder belt rides across driver's neck. • Erratic fuel gauge operation. • Headlights suddenly shut off or don't provide enough illumination. • Head restraints block rear vision. • Dash is reflected onto the windshield. • Water leaks everywhere. **All models: 1998–99**—Vehicle catches fire while parked. • Cruise control is either inoperative or fails to disengage. • Chronic hesitation and stall-out, accompanied by dash lights and other electrical components going haywire. • Enhanced traction system engages when not needed. • Complete electrical system shutdown while vehicle is underway. • Rainwater leaks through the dash panel into the fuse box. • Wheel lug nuts shear off, causing wheel to fall away. • Severe brake, steering, and body vibrations; vehicle intermittently jerks violently to one side. • Steering-pump failure. • Fuel pressure regulator leaks fumes into the interior. • Sunroof explodes when side window is opened while vehicle is underway. • Windows run off their channels and shatter. • Windshield washer fluid freezes because of poor tubing design. • Locks and headlights self-activate. • Faulty fuel-level sensor gives a false Empty reading. • Seat belts tend to twist when retracting. **2000**—Although there aren't an unusually large number of complaints recorded, the same problems keep appearing. They include frequent brake light burnout; poor braking or the complete loss of braking; overheated, warped brake rotors and excessive vibration when braking; chronic stalling; the trunk lid opening on its own while the vehicle is underway; and water leaks through the doors and sunroof. The sunroof leaks result in the electrical system shorting out and the vehicle shutting down. **2001**—Stalling, brake rotor warpage, and sunroof leaks appear once again. Other problems include fires igniting at the right rear of vehicle; fuel tanks being easily punctured; and rear axles bending or breaking, leading to a loss of control. **2002**—Frequency of safety complaints has increased substantially. • Transmission suddenly fails while cruising at speeds over 100 km/h. • Chronic stalling. • Vehicle continues accelerating after passing another car on the highway. • Car constantly surges and hesitates. • Vehicle tends to wander all over the road; pulls to one side when accelerating. • Steering shudders upon braking or acceleration; faulty power steering pump; steering feels too loose. • ABS light comes on, followed by brake failure; brake pedal set too low; parking brake failure. • Fuel-pump failure. • Shoulder belts twist in their housing; in the GT two-door, they ride abnormally high on the shoulder/neck area. • Power doors lock on their own. • Headlights blink on and off. • Middle rear lap seat belt is too short to secure a child safety seat. • Loose driver's seat. • Windshield wipers shut off intermittently. • Rear windshield shatters when defogger is activated; side door glass shatters behind mirror for no reason. • Inside door edge is razor sharp. • Slight front impact causes the battery tray to break off or results in the battery sliding off the tray. *Alero:* Engine compartment fire. • Right front wheel separates because the lug nuts and bolts shear off. • Tapped brakes to turn cruise control off, and vehicle accelerated. • Rear main oil seal leak blows oil onto exhaust pipe. • Fuel tank leakage. • Water leakage onto the back of the instrument panel causes the instruments and gauges to malfunction; other electrical shorts cause instrument panel gauges and controls to fail. • Windshield water leaks cause electrical shorts. • Hard to find horn "sweet spot" in an emergency.

Secret Warranties/Internal Bulletins/Service Tips

All models/years: A rotten-egg odour coming from the exhaust may be the result of a malfunctioning catalytic converter—possibly covered by the emissions warranty. Stand your ground if GM or the dealer claims you must pay. • Tips on removing AC odours; GM has a special kit to keep AC odours at bay. • Paint delamination, peeling, or fading. • Reverse servo cover leaks. **All models: 1990–2000**—Countermeasures for water collecting in the tail lights. **1995–98**—A steering squeak or squawk may be reduced by installing a rack-and-pinion service kit. **1996–98**—Install a seat belt webbing stop button if the seat belt latch slides to the anchor sleeve. • Passenger compartment water leaks can be plugged by applying silicone sealer to the top vent grille assembly. **1997–98**—Hard starting or a weak or dead battery may signal the need to repair the B+ stud and/or starter wiring. **1999–2000**—No Third or Fourth gear may signal a defective direct clutch piston. • Upgraded pads and rotors will fix brake pulsation/vibration. • A wet front or rear carpet may mean the front door water deflectors need to be replaced. • Simply changing the radiator cap may cure your hot-running engine. *Skylark:* **1995–98**—Intermittent Neutral/loss of Drive at highway speeds can be fixed by replacing the control valve body assembly. *Grand Am, Alero:* **1998–2003**—Automatic transmission flaring. **1999**—Hesitation or lack of power when accelerating on vehicles equipped with the 3.4L engine may simply require reprogramming the PCM. • Paint chipping from the Grand Am SE's rocker panel and lower quarter panel can be prevented by installing upgraded driver- and passenger-side rocker mouldings. **1999–2001**—A front-end clunk or rattle can be silenced by replacing the brake pedal assembly under warranty. • Water leak troubleshooting. • Wind rush from the front windshield. **1999–2002**—Excessive pedal or steering wheel pulsation when braking can be eliminated by using GM's Front Pad Kit #18044437, says TSB #00-05-23-002A. **1999–2004**—Faulty rear lights cost up to $300 to repair, but GM will cover the cost through a secret warranty, a recall, and its implied warranty obligations. • Poor automatic transmission performance and slipping. • Faulty front door window glass and power window motor. • Front wheel tire noise may be silenced by replacing Goodyear Eagle tires. **1999–2005**—Side windows won't roll up. **2000**—If the vehicle stalls, hesitates, or won't start, you may need to replace the modular fuel sender strainer. **2000–01**—If the Check Engine light comes on, it may mean the fuel-sender-to-tank O-ring is defective. • Install a fuel tank sender kit if the fuel gauge gives inaccurate readings. **2000–03**—Firm transmission shifts and shudders or transmission slips or fails to shift. • Loss of power steering. • Noisy front suspension. • Inaccurate fuel gauge readings. • Front door window glass comes out of run channel; wind noise from rear of vehicle. **2001–04**—Silencing a creaky door. **2001–05**—Harsh upshifts. **2002**—No-starts; harsh transmission shifts. • Transmission fluid leakage. • Premature failure of the transaxle converter pump. • A Customer Service Campaign will pay for the inspection and correction of a transaxle converter bearing failure, detailed in TSB #01031. • Remedy for suspension noise or malfunctions. • Shift indicator doesn't show correct gear selection. • Engine alerts stay lit. • Brake pedal, underbody, or suspension clunk or rattle noise. • Door creaking. • Windshield glass distortion. **2002–04**—Poor transmission performance can be caused by a defective driven sprocket support assembly. • Popping noise emanating from the suspension. **2002–05**—Water leaking on the floor requires a clean drain hose to correct. **2003**—Poor shifting and inaccurate gauges. **2004**—No-starts, stalling. • Transmission growl or howl when accelerating from a stop. • Trunk water leaks.

ACHIEVA, ALERO, GRAND AM, SKYLARK PROFILE

	1997	1998	1999	2000	2001	2002	2003	2004	2005
Cost Price ($)									
Achieva S	20,735	21,200	—	—	—	—	—	—	—
Alero	—	—	20,995	20,445	21,335	21,745	22,285	22,335	—
Grand Am/Coupe GT	19,035	19,610	21,795	20,625	20,915	21,405	21,640	21,885	27,000
Skylark	21,220	22,965	—	—	—	—	—	—	—
Used Values ($)									
Achieva S ▲	2,500	3,000	—	—	—	—	—	—	—
Achieva S ▼	2,000	2,500	—	—	—	—	—	—	—
Alero ▲	—	—	4,000	4,500	6,000	8,000	9,500	10,500	—
Alero ▼	—	—	3,500	4,000	4,500	7,500	8,500	9,000	—

	3,500	4,000	4,500	5,000	6,000	7,500	9,000	10,000	14,500
Grand Am ▲	3,500	4,000	4,500	5,000	6,000	7,500	9,000	10,000	14,500
Grand Am ▼	3,000	3,500	4,000	4,500	5,000	6,000	8,000	8,500	13,000
Skylark ▲	2,500	3,000	—	—	—	—	—	—	—
Skylark ▼	2,000	2,500	—	—	—	—	—	—	—
Reliability	2	3	3	3	3	3	3	3	3
Crash Safety (F)									
Grand Am 2d	4	—	—	—	4	4	4	4	4
Grand Am 4d	5	—	4	4	4	4	4	4	4
Skylark 2d	4	—	—	—	—	—	—	—	—
Skylark 4d	5	—	—	—	—	—	—	—	—
Side									
Achieva 4d	1	1	—	—	—	—	—	—	—
Grand Am 2d	—	—	2	1	3	1	3	1	1
Grand Am 4d	1	1	1	3	3	3	3	3	3
Skylark 4d	1	—	—	—	—	—	—	—	—
Offset	—	—	1	1	1	1	1	1	1
Head Restraints									
Grand Am 2d	—	1	—	2	1	1	1	1	1
Grand Am 4d	—	1	—	2	1	1	1	1	1
Alero	—	—	—	—	—	—	2	—	—
Rollover Resistance									
Grand Am 2d	—	—	—	—	—	—	4	4	4
Grand Am 4d	—	—	—	—	—	4	4	4	4

BONNEVILLE, CUTLASS, CUTLASS SUPREME, DELTA 88, GRAND PRIX, IMPALA, INTRIGUE, LESABRE, LUMINA, MALIBU, MONTE CARLO, REGAL ★★★

RATING: Average (2000–06); Not Recommended for front-drives (1988–99); Average for rear-drives (1984–87). Although these GM models are generally classed as medium-sized cars, some of them move in and out of the large-car class as well. Overall, the Intrigue, Malibu, Monte Carlo, and Grand Prix provide the best quality at the highest depreciation rate (for used-car bargain hunters). Nevertheless, use some of the savings for extra powertrain protection, or get close to the service manager. **"Real" city/highway fuel economy:** *Malibu 2.2L:* 9.9/6.6 L/100 km with an automatic transmission. *Malibu 3.5L:* 10.4/6.8 L/100 km with a 6-cylinder engine and an automatic transmission. *LeSabre and Bonneville 3.8L:* 11.9/7.3 L/100 km with a 6-cylinder and an automatic tranny. *Monte Carlo 3.4L:* 11.8/7.1 L/100 km with the 6-cylinder automatic. Owners report fuel savings may undershoot the above estimates by about 20 percent. **Maintenance/Repair costs:** Higher than average, but repairs aren't dealer-dependent. **Parts:** Higher-than-average costs (independent suppliers sell for much less), but not hard to find. Nevertheless, don't even think about buying one of the front-drives without a supplementary 3- to 5-year powertrain warranty. **Extended warranty:** Yes, mainly for the engine and automatic transmission. **Best alternatives:** Acura Integra;

Honda Accord; Hyundai Elantra Wagon, Sonata, or Tiburon; Mazda 626; and Toyota Camry. **Online help:** The Center for Auto Safety has a huge database of service bulletins and owner complaints at *www.autosafety.org/autodefects.html*, or once again, you can use a search engine like Google to look for information on GM paint delamination, engine piston slapping, or manifold defects.

Strengths and Weaknesses

The following problems are common to all models: no-start or no-crank conditions caused by a defective ignition and start switch assembly; hot engine idles poorly; engine oil pan leaks; harsh shifting, harsh 1–2 upshifts; poor engine performance and transmission slipping (clean out debris in valve body and case oil passages); some transmissions may produce a grinding or growling noise when engaged on an incline with the engine running and the parking brake not applied; delayed shifts, slips, flares, or extended shifts in cold weather; erratic shifting; excessive vibration on smooth roads; generator whine, hum, moan, or vibration; premature alternator failure; steering vibration, shudder, or moan during parking manoeuvres.

Body assembly on all models is notoriously poor and is no doubt one of the main reasons why GM has lost so much market share over the past decade. Premature paint peeling and rusting, water and dust leaks into the trunk, squeaks and rattles, and wind and road noise are all too common. Accessories are also plagued by problems, with defective radios, power antennas, door locks, cruise control, and alarm systems leading the pack. Premature automatic transmission failures and excessive noise when shifting have been endemic up to the 1998 model year. Since then, the company's powertrain problems have been less frequent. Engine intake manifold gaskets, though, have a high failure rate and are covered by a 6-year/100,000 km secret warranty (see the confidential GM service bulletins on pages 77–79).

Rear-drives

The rear-drives are competent and comfortable cars, but they definitely point to a time when handling wasn't a priority and fuel economy was unimportant. Nevertheless, interior comfort is impressive, overall reliability is pretty good, repairs are easy to perform, defects aren't hard to troubleshoot, and servicing can quite easily be done by cheaper independent garages. Electrical malfunctions increase proportionally with extra equipment. The AC module and condenser and wheel bearings (incredibly expensive) also have short lifespans. Windshield posts, the rear edges of trunk lids, and roof areas above doors rust through easily.

Front-drives

Front-drive technology is not GM's proudest achievement, so it's not surprising to see the company embrace rear-drives in its post-2004 models. Its front-drives, phased into the lineup in the '80s, are a different breed of car: less reliable and more expensive to repair than rear-drives, with a considerable number of mechanical (e.g., brake, steering, and suspension components) deficiencies directly related to their front-drive configuration. Nevertheless, acceleration is adequate, fuel economy is good, and handling is better than with their rear-drive cousins—except in emergencies, when their brakes frequently lock up or fail, notwithstanding ABS technology. The Detroit Big Three's front-drive designs and manufacturing weaknesses make for unimpressive high-speed performance, a poor reliability record, and expensive maintenance costs. That's why most fleets and police agencies use rear-drives when they can get them. They've seen the rear-drives' safety and operating cost advantages.

GM's medium-sized front-drives aren't particularly driver-friendly. Many models have a dash that's replete with confusing push buttons and gauges that are washed out in sunlight or reflect annoyingly upon the windshield. At other times, there are retro touches, like the Intrigue's dash-mounted ignition, that simply seem out of place. The keyless entry system often fails, the radio's memory is frequently forgetful, and the fuel light comes on when the tank is just below the one-half fuel-level mark. The electronic climate control frequently malfunctions, and owners report that warm air doesn't reach the driver-side heating vents. Servicing, especially for the electronic engine controls, is complicated and expensive, forcing many owners to drive around with their Service Engine, Airbag, and ABS warning lights constantly lit.

Other major problem areas found over the past decade include engine head gasket leaks; plastic intake manifold cracking; automatic transmission failures and clunking; leaking and malfunctioning AC systems (due mainly to defective AC modules); faulty electronic modules; rack-and-pinion steering failures; weak shocks; excessive front brake pad wear; warping rotors; seizure of the rear brake calipers; rear brake/wheel lock-ups; myriad electrical failures, requiring replacement of the computer module; leaking oil pans; and early replacement of the suspension struts.

The base 2.3L and 2.5L engines found on pre-'95 models provide insufficient power. The more powerful 3.1L V6 is peppier, but it's seriously hampered by the 4-speed automatic transaxle. The high-performance 3.4L V6, available since 1991, gives out plenty of power, but only at high engine speeds. Overall, the 3.8L V6 is a more suitable compromise. One major powertrain problem found over the past decade involves the 3.1, 3.4, and 3.8L V6 engines: specifically, engine head gasket leaks and plastic intake manifold cracking. These engine defects affect almost all GM and Saturn models, as well as Ford's 1994–2002 lineup (see the "Crown Victoria, Grand Marquis" and "Town Car" sections).

Other deficiencies: The instruments and steering column shake when the car is travelling over uneven road surfaces, and lots of road and wind noise comes through the side windows, thanks to the inadequately soundproofed chassis. Seating isn't very comfortable because of the lack of support caused by low-density foam and knees-in-your-face low seats combined with the ramrod-straight rear backrest. The ride is acceptable with a light load, but when fully loaded, the car's back end sags and the ride deteriorates. Owners report that 3.8L engines won't continue running after a cold start, the exhaust system booms, 3T40 automatic transmissions may have faulty Reverse gears, and the instrument panel may pop or creak.

On one hand, 2002–05 models do have a nice array of standard features, a good choice of powertrains that includes a supercharged 3.8L engine, a comfortable ride, and an easily accessed, roomy interior. On the other hand, they continue to have noisy engines at high speeds, rear seating that's uncomfortable for three, bland styling, and obstructed rear visibility because of a high-tail rear end. Most important, these cars are hobbled by a chintzy powertrain warranty that's clearly insufficient, knowing GM's past engine and transmission deficiencies. Imagine having to pay $3,000–$5,000 for a new engine or transmission just as your used-car "bargain" passes its fifth year.

Intrigue

Strikingly similar to the Alero, the Oldsmobile Intrigue was GM's replacement for the Cutlass Supreme and represents the most refined iteration of the W-body shared by the Century, Grand Prix, Lumina, and Regal. It's more luxurious than the Lumina and performs as well as the Accord, Camry, or Maxima. Its rigid chassis has fewer shakes and rattles than are found on GM's other models, and its 3.8L engine provides lots of low-end grunt but lacks the top-end power that makes the Japanese competition so much fun to toss around. The '99 versions got a torquier 3.5L V6 coupled with standard traction control. This engine's a bit more refined, but it's still not smooth, and the automatic transmission still struggles to get past its first two gears. Year 2001 models dropped standard traction control and added automatic headlights.

1995–2005 Impala, Lumina, and Monte Carlo

These models are popular two- and four-door versions of Chevy's "large" mid-sized cars, featuring standard dual airbags, ABS, and 160-hp V6 power. The Monte Carlo was formerly sold as the Lumina Z34. Powertrain enhancements have increased horsepower and fuel efficiency. Each car has been given a slightly different appearance and a distinct personality. A 3.1L V6 is the standard engine, a standard 3.4L 210-hp V6 powers the coupe and is optional with the LS Lumina, and a 3.8L V6 equips the more upscale versions. The 2004 SS comes with a supercharged 3.8L engine.

VEHICLE HISTORY: All models: 1996—The 3.4L gets a slight horsepower boost, and all-disc braking is adopted on the Monte Carlo Z34 and upscale versions of the LS. 1997—A better-performing transmission mated to the 3.4L engine gives smoother shifts. 1998–99—Few changes, except for the addition of the 3.8L V6 to the Monte Carlo Z34 and Lumina LTZ. *Bonneville:* 1992—A slight restyling, and plastic front fenders. 1994—Dual airbags and more SSE features. 1995—A 205-hp 3.8L engine. 1996—A more powerful supercharged engine, and restyled front and rear ends. 2000—Restyled similarly to the Buick LeSabre, with a larger wheelbase and longer platform but less headroom. Also new this year are standard front seat side-impact airbags, four-wheel disc ABS brakes, a tire-inflation monitor, and an anti-skid system (SSEi). **2001**—SLE is given standard traction control. **2003**—Revised bucket seats. **2004**—Arrival of a 275-hp V8, and the dropping of the 240-hp V6. *Impala:* **2001**—Standard OnStar with the LS, and emergency inside trunk release on all. **2002**—Standard dual-zone climate controls, and a CD player. **2003**—OnStar and driver-side airbags become optional. **2004**—A new SS model equipped with a 240-hp supercharged V6. **2005**—Minor trim changes and different front headrests. *Lumina:* **2000**—Lumina's standard 3.1L engine gets a bit more torque and a small horsepower boost, in addition to the model getting more standard equipment. This is the Lumina's last year before the Impala replaces it. But the Monte Carlo soldiers on, having been reworked and brought out on the Impala platform for 2000. It is carried over unchanged. *Malibu:* **1998**—Aluminum wheels. **1999**—Automatic, brighter headlights and tail lights, and added soundproofing. **2000**—A restyled front end, and no more 4-cylinder engine. **2001**—Standard power door locks and defogger, an improved sound system, and remote keyless entry. **2002**—A CD player and floormats. **2003**—ABS becomes optional. **2004**—Completely redesigned. The sedan uses Saab's 9-3 platform and a base 145-hp four-cylinder engine (a 200-hp V6 comes with the LS and LT) hooked to a 4-speed automatic transmission. A Maxx hatchback uses the same powertrain but adds a sliding rear seat with a reclining seatback, a cargo cover that transforms into a tailgate table, a glass skylight, four-wheel disc brakes, and head-protecting side curtain airbags. *Monte Carlo:* **2001**—Standard driver-side airbag, traction control, OnStar, and emergency inside trunk release. **2002**—Standard dual-zone climate controls and a rear-seat centre shoulder belt. **2003**—Remote keyless entry for the LS. **2004**—A supercharged 3.8L SS.

Except for the automatic transmission upgrade, owners report that newer versions still have many of the same shortcomings seen on earlier front-drive models, though the 2005 Monte Carlo has far fewer problems than the Malibu or the Impala. Body construction is still below par, with loose door panel mouldings, poorly fitted door fabric, misaligned panels, and water accumulation in the backup lights. Other common problems are fuel pump whistling, frequent stalling, vague steering, premature paint peeling on the hood and trunk, heavy accumulation of hard-to-remove brake dust inside the honeycomb-design wheels, scraped fenders from contact with the front tires when the wheel is turned, and hard starts due to delayed cranking:

> The vehicle hesitated to start therefore you have to hold the key several seconds to start. The car has a rough idle. Only had the car three month[s] and have return[ed] it about 10 times for the same issues. I was told that it's normal for it to run that way.

Despite its own recent redesign, the 3.1L engine isn't entirely problem free. Engine controls, faulty intake manifold gaskets (a chronic problem affecting the entire model lineup; see "Secret Warranties/Internal Bulletins/Service Tips"), and electronic fuel-injection systems have created many problems for GM owners. The 4-speed automatic transmission still has some bugs. The front brakes wear quickly, as do the MacPherson struts, shock absorbers, and tie-rod ends. Steering assemblies tend to fail prematurely. The electrical system is temperamental. The sunroof motor is failure prone. Owners report water leaks from the front windshield. Front-end squeaks may require the replacement of the exhaust manifold pipe springs with dampers.

1997–2005 Cutlass and Malibu

These two front-drive, medium-sized sedans are slotted in between the Cavalier and Lumina in both size and price. They are boringly styled cars that use a rigid body structure to cut down on noise and improve handling. Standard mechanicals include a 2.4L twin-cam 4-cylinder engine or an optional 3.1L V6. These cars offer plenty of passenger and luggage space. Although headroom is tight, the Malibu can carry three rear passengers, and gives much more legroom than either the Cavalier or Lumina. The 1998 model year was Cutlass' last, while its Malibu twin continues on.

Here are other points to consider: The base 4-cylinder is loud, handling isn't on par with the Japanese competition, there's lots of body lean in turns, outside mirrors are too small, there's no traction control, and the ignition switch is mounted on the dash (a throwback to your dad's Oldsmobile).

In the 2004 model year, there are two vehicles thought of as Malibus. The "old" Malibu (N-body) was called Malibu through the 2003 model year. In 2004, it was renamed the Classic. The "new" Malibu (Z-body) was called Malibu in 2004. The redesigned 2004 Malibu's engine feels underpowered for highway cruising, with constant shifting with the 4-cylinder hooked to the 4-speed automatic transmission (which is the only set-up available). Good handling, but the ride is a bit firm. Its tires don't inspire confidence. Interior seating is okay up front, but knees-to-chin in the rear. The Maxx version excels at providing rear-seat comfort.

In addition to the generic front-drive problems listed previously, owners also report the following: early failures of the exhaust and intake manifold gaskets (see "Secret Warranties/Internal Bulletins/Service Tips"); fuel-injector deposits that cause chronic stalling, poor idling, or hard starts; excessive vibration at any speed; a transmission that doesn't lock when the key is in the accessory position; very loose steering; sensors failing throughout the vehicle; premature suspension strut failures (vehicle bottoms out with four or more passengers aboard); excessive AC noise; and an intermittently failing high-beam light switch.

Safety Summary

All models/years: Airbag fails to deploy. • Sudden engine failure or overheating (faulty intake manifold). • Vehicle suddenly accelerates or stalls in traffic. • Brake failures. • Frequent loss of braking, and premature rotor warpage and pad wearout. • Vehicle rolls downhill when parked on an incline. • Dash reflection in the windshield obstructs view. • Automatic trunk lid flies up and falls down on one's head. • Improper headlight illumination. • Horn is difficult to activate because of the hand pressure required. **2000–01**—Sudden electrical shutdown. • Exhaust/gas fumes in the interior. • Automatic transmission failure. • Front control arm breakage. • Blurred windshield. • Tires mounted on aluminum wheels tend to leak air. • Vehicle wanders or "floats" on the highway. • Heater gives out insufficient heat. • Headlight switch overheats. *Bonneville:* **2000–01**—Battery located in the back of the rear seat goes bad, causing sulfuric acid fumes to escape into the passenger compartment, making passengers ill. • Weak spring design allowed trunk lid to fall on person's head, causing injury. **2003**—Defogger was activated and fire ignited. • Fire erupted in the rear deck speaker. • Shifter can be moved without key in the ignition or brakes applied. *Impala:* **2003**—Frequent complaints of dash area and engine compartment fires. • Front harness wires overheat; excessive current load from fuel pump may burn the ignition block wire terminal; inhalation injuries caused by the melting of the wiring harness plastic. • Electrically heated seat burns the driver's back. • The connection that goes to the brake pedal piston collapses, causing total brake failure. • Chronic stalling; engine sputters, hesitates; Service Engine and battery lights come on (dealer unable to correct problem). • When traction control is activated, wheel slip computer is also activated, and security system kills the engine and prevents it from being restarted. • Driver's side wheel falls off. • Vehicle jerks when passing over rough pavement. • Car rolls back at a stop. • Excessive steering-wheel vibration. • Left and right control arm, lower control arm, ball joint, and steering failures. • AC refrigerant leaks into car interior. • Driver-seat adjuster failed, and seat suddenly moved backward, causing loss of vehicle control. • The rubber seal on the windows, which sometimes acts as a squeegee when lowering and raising the window, has been replaced with a new design that allows road salt to enter and short-circuit the window mechanism. • Front driver-side windshield wiper doesn't clean the windshield completely; poor design allows dirty windshield washer fluid to be deflected off the windshield and cuts the view from the side windows. • A hazy film collects on the inside of all the windows (usually a sign of intake manifold gasket failure). **2004**—Crankshaft position sensor failures cause vehicle to stall and not restart. • Vehicle can be shifted out of Park without applying the brakes. • Vehicle hydroplanes easily, wanders all over the road, and jerks to one side when braking. • Steering wheel suddenly jerks to one side and resists driver's pull in the other direction. • Unreliable steering assembly replaced twice. • Defective front-end suspension. • Lights dim when power windows are raised or lowered. • Poorly designed daytime running lights blind oncoming drivers. • Fuel-tank failures. • Moisture in headlights reduces illumination (dealer says defect affects all Impalas). • Static electricity shocks occupants as they leave the vehicle. **2005**—Inadvertent airbag deployment:

> A 2005 Chevy Impala police car was traveling on a gravel road in rural Ogle County, Illinois when both front air bags deployed, the car never made contact with anything, there are at least 30 pictures of the car and the roadway. Since the 30th I personally have called General Motors about my concerns involving the rest of my 2005 squad cars, I've called every day since the 30th, with no response...

• Engine surging. • Fuel pressure regulator may leak fuel. • Intermediate steering shaft is a sealed unit, yet requires frequent lubrication. • Steering pump failure. • Parking brakes won't hold on an incline and the transmission fails to hold the vehicle in Park or in Reverse. • Car can be shifted into any gear without depressing the brake pedal. • ABS failure. • Frequent traction control system failures. • Headlights suddenly go out. • Windshield wipers fail to go down into the parked position. • Automatic window could easily kill a child:

> The way that the window switch is designed it can easily shut on a child's body or body part. There was something about this six months ago on TV. This was a rental vehicle for a trip for vacation.... When the consumer's son leaned his head out the window, his elbow hit the switch, and the window began to go up. The consumer suggested that a different type of switch be installed, the type that one would have to pull in order to close the window.

• Inadequate headlight illumination. • AC blower seizes, causing an electrical fire. *LeSabre:* **2000–01**—Under-hood fire ignited as driver was parking car. • When the fuel tank is full, fuel leaks from the top. • False airbag deployment injured driver. • Airbag deployment when key inserted into the ignition. • Car stalls because fuel lines leak. • Cruise-control cable disconnects from cruise-control module, jamming the accelerator cable to full throttle. • Accelerator cable pops out of its bracket, causing vehicle to go to full throttle. • Brake pedal goes all the way to the floor because of missing brake shaft retainer clip. • When applying brakes, pedal becomes very hard, resulting in extended stopping distance. • Sudden steering loss. • Excessive highway wander. • Shoulder belt crosses at driver's neck. • Hard-to-read speedometer. • Difficulty seeing dashboard controls because of dash-top design. • ABS and Service Engine lights come on for no reason. • Intermittent windshield wiper failure. • Horn is hard to operate, unless driver balls her hand into a fist and pounds on it. • Headlight design creates a shadow, impeding visibility. **2003**—Engine surging while driving on the highway. • Brake pedal goes almost to the floor without stopping the vehicle. **2004**—Wipers fail intermittently. • Dash panel lights dim constantly. • Uncomfortable seats are too slippery. • Headlight failure. • Poorly performing General Tires. *Monte Carlo:* **1995–2001**—Under-hood fires. • Airbag deployment caused driver's shirt to catch on fire. • Side airbag flap material falls off, leaving a large hole. • Side airbag falls out of its mounting. • Extremely poor wet traction. • Although GM TSB asks dealers to re-weld the subframe engine cradle, owners say that the fix isn't effective. • Early fuel pump and water pump failures. • Dash gauges go haywire from chronic electrical shorts. • Check Engine, ABS, and Airbag lights stay lit despite dealers' best troubleshooting attempts. • Shoulder belt crosses at neck and seat belts don't retract properly. • Horn is hard to access. **2002**—Fire ignites from overheated seat heater. • Sudden steering loss; excessive steering effort required. • Vehicle rolls back on an incline. • Excessive brake pulsation. • Constant headlight flickering. **2003**—Fire ignited in the trunk area. • Engine cradle mounting welds come apart from the steering gear. • Hard shifting. • Automatic transmission slips in First gear because of faulty pressure valve. • Sudden loss of braking. • Because brake pedal sits a bit higher than it would on other makes, foot can easily slip under the pedal. • Bent stabilizer bar. • Driver and passenger seat belts tighten up progressively to the point where they are extremely uncomfortable. • Horn takes excessive force to activate; malfunctions in the winter. • Tail light failures. • Sunroof cracks. • Moulding separates from the rest of the body. **2004**—Engine fails and then catches fire. • Mushy brakes; pedal goes to the floor when brakes are applied:

> Car would not stop. No warning lights came on. Noise from front right brakes when going forward or in reverse. Pedal to floor happened in good dry weather on both occasions. ABS was not active at time of incident. Took car to dealer, and it was repaired at no cost to me since the car is under warranty...dealer gave me a loaner for the day. Dealer stated..."brake caliper was seized to pads."

• Warped dash, and radio face gets extremely hot. • Excessive vibration when cruise control is engaged.

Secret Warranties/Internal Bulletins/Service Tips

All models/years: Keep in mind that some of the following service bulletins may apply to more than one model and to subsequent model years. • Reverse servo cover seal leak (transmission). **All models: 1993–2003**—AC-induced odours can be eliminated by using a coil coating kit. • A rotten-egg odour coming from the exhaust is probably caused by a malfunctioning catalytic converter (covered by the emissions warranty). • Paint delamination, peeling, or fading. **1993–2004**— TSB #01-08-42-001A covers the causes and remedies for moisture in the headlights. **1995–2001**—Troubleshooting engine oil pan leaks. **1995–2004**— Five GM service bulletins confirm a pattern of engine intake manifold gasket defects, which are covered by a 6-year/100,000 km secret warranty (see pages 77–79). In the most recent bulletin, #04-06-01-017, GM says that its revised intake manifold gasket is more "robust" and adds 2004 models to the list of afflicted models. This is another admission of liability under the implied warranty statutes. Internet references are *www.talkaboutautos.com/group/alt.autos.chevrolet.malibu/ messages/5867.html* and *www.alldatapro.com*. But don't break out the champagne over GM's apparent recognition of its engine defects yet. This 2003 LeSabre owner says GM's intake manifold fix is no fix at all:

> I recently received a letter from GM stating that there may be a problem with coolant leaks around gaskets at the upper intake manifold or at the lower intake manifold, which might "cause high engine temperatures." The letter says it is a "voluntary customer satisfaction program." The suggested fix is to take the vehicle in to the local dealer and have them change some of the fasteners and then "add cooling system sealant" to the radiator. It seems to me that putting cooling system sealant in a brand new car (and thus reducing the life of the radiator) is an unacceptable fix for a possible gasket problem.

1998—A wet right rear floor signals the need to reseal the stationary glass area. • Engine runs rough. • Power-steering shudder and vibration. • Front suspension scrunch/pop. • Reducing AC odours. • Inaccurate speedometer. **1998–99**—Power-steering shudder/vibration may be fixed by replacing the pressure pipe/hose assembly. **2001–02**—Poor engine performance and erratic shifting. • Intermittent no-starts. **2001–04**—Erratic shifting, slipping transmission. • Troubleshooting a noisy blower motor. **2001–05**—Harsh 1–2 upshifts. **2001–07**—Correcting a shift shudder during light acceleration. **2003–05**—Remedy for side window binding. **2004–05**—Troubleshooting an inoperative horn. **2004–06**—Assorted steering noises. **2005**—AC compressor noise. *Cutlass, Malibu:* **1997–99**—Front disc brake pulsation will be corrected by installing upgraded pads and rotors, says TSB #00-05-23-002. **1997–2003**—Inoperative tail lights due to water intrusion. • Automatic transmission flaring. **1999–2002**—Troubleshooting tips for plugging water leaks into the trunk and interior. **2000–01**—Faulty fuel gauge. **2002**—Dash rattling correction. **2003**—Firm shifts, no downshifts, or shudder. **2004**—Noisy steering column, and lack of steering assist. • Wind noise caused by the transmission shift cable. • Ignition key hard to remove in cold weather. • Instrument-panel rattle or buzz. **2004–05**—Correcting increased steering effort on start-up. • Steering pop or snap noise when turning. • Hood won't latch in the primary position. • A special lube must be applied to prevent door latches from freezing. **2004–06**—Poor instrument panel backlighting. • Inoperative tail/turn lights. • Front end clunk/rattle. **2005–07**—Rear brake creak or squeak. *Grand Prix:* **2004–06**—Correcting AC compressor growl/whine. **2006–07**—Correcting a shift shudder during light acceleration.

BONNEVILLE, CUTLASS, CUTLASS SUPREME, DELTA 88, GRAND PRIX, IMPALA, INTRIGUE, LESABRE, LUMINA, MALIBU, MONTE CARLO, REGAL PROFILE

	1997	1998	1999	2000	2001	2002	2003	2004	2005
Cost Price ($)									
Bonneville	31,175	33,255	29,000	30,740	32,065	32,365	33,430	34,345	35,310
Cutlass Supreme	26,355	—	—	—	—	—	—	—	—
Delta 88 LSS	32,185	32,950	32,515	—	—	—	—	—	—
Grand Prix	26,305	26,035	27,489	28,050	28,110	28,050	28,277	28,125	27,865
Impala	—	—	—	24,595	24,490	24,875	26,020	26,810	26,405
Intrigue	—	27,998	27,994	28,365	28,450	28,365	—	—	—
LeSabre	32,370	33,100	28,845	30,465	32,120	32,960	33,720	33,935	34,550
Lumina	22,340	22,980	23,074	—	—	—	—	—	—
Malibu	19,995	20,595	20,895	22,050	22,495	22,760	22,980	22,370	22,375
Malibu Maxx	—	—	—	—	—	—	—	26,320	26,495
Monte Carlo	24,275	24,895	24,715	26,090	26,165	26,525	27,620	28,200	27,840
Regal	27,795	28,410	27,695	29,120	28,895	29,080	29,980	29,975	—

Used Values ($)									
Bonneville ▲	3,500	4,500	5,500	6,000	7,500	9,000	11,000	14,000	18,000
Bonneville ▼	3,000	4,000	5,000	5,500	6,500	8,000	9,500	12,500	16,500
Cutlass Supreme ▲	3,000	—	—	—	—	—	—	—	—
Cutlass Supreme ▼	2,500	—	—	—	—	—	—	—	—
Delta 88 LSS ▲	3,500	4,000	5,000	—	—	—	—	—	—
Delta 88 LSS ▼	3,000	3,500	4,000	—	—	—	—	—	—
Grand Prix ▲	2,500	3,500	4,500	5,500	7,500	9,500	11,500	14,000	16,000
Grand Prix ▼	2,000	3,000	4,000	5,000	6,000	7,500	10,000	12,500	15,000
Impala ▲	—	—	—	5,000	6,500	8,000	10,000	12,000	15,000
Impala ▼	—	—	—	4,000	5,500	7,000	8,500	10,500	13,500
Intrigue ▲	—	2,500	3,500	4,500	6,000	8,500	—	—	—
Intrigue ▼	—	2,000	3,000	4,000	5,000	6,500	—	—	—
LeSabre ▲	3,500	4,000	4,500	6,000	8,000	11,000	14,000	17,000	20,000
LeSabre ▼	3,000	3,500	4,000	5,000	6,000	8,500	11,500	15,000	18,000
Lumina ▲	1,500	2,500	3,500	—	—	—	—	—	—
Lumina ▼	1,200	2,000	3,000	—	—	—	—	—	—
Malibu ▲	2,000	3,000	3,500	4,500	5,500	7,000	8,500	10,500	13,500
Malibu ▼	1,500	2,500	3,000	3,500	4,500	6,000	7,500	9,000	11,500
Malibu Maxx ▲	—	—	—	—	—	—	—	12,000	15,000
Malibu Maxx ▼	—	—	—	—	—	—	—	10,500	13,000
Monte Carlo ▲	2,000	3,000	4,000	5,000	6,500	8,000	10,000	13,000	15,000
Monte Carlo ▼	1,500	2,500	3,500	4,500	5,500	7,000	8,500	11,500	13,500
Regal ▲	3,000	4,000	5,000	6,000	7,000	9,500	12,500	15,000	—
Regal ▼	2,500	3,500	4,500	5,500	6,500	7,500	10,500	13,000	—
Reliability	2	2	3	3	3	3	3	3	3
Crash Safety (F)									
Bonneville 4d	5	5	—	—	4	4	4	4	4
Cutlass 4d	—	—	4	4	—	—	—	—	—
Grand Prix 4d	4	—	—	—	4	4	4	3	3
Impala	—	—	—	5	5	5	5	5	5
Intrigue	—	4	4	4	—	—	—	—	—
LeSabre 4d	4	4	4	—	—	4	4	4	4
Lumina 4d	5	4	4	4	4	—	—	—	—
Malibu	4	4	4	4	4	4	4	4	5
Monte Carlo	4	—	—	5	5	—	5	5	—
Regal 2d	—	—	—	—	—	—	—	—	—
Regal 4d	—	—	4	4	4	4	4	4	—
Side									
Bonneville 4d	—	—	—	—	4	4	4	4	4
Grand Prix	—	—	—	—	—	2	2	3	3
Impala	—	—	—	4	4	4	4	4	4
Intrigue	—	—	—	—	3	3	—	—	—
LeSabre 4d	—	3	3	4	4	4	4	5	4
Lumina	4	4	4	4	4	—	—	—	—
Malibu	1	1	1	2	2	3	3	4	4

All ratings on a numbered scale where 5 is good and 1 is bad. See pages 130–132 for a more detailed description.

Monte Carlo	4	—	—	—	3	3	—	3	3
Regal 4d	—	3	3	3	3	3	3	3	—

Side (IIHS)

Malibu 4d	—	—	—	—	—	—	—	5	5

Offset

Bonneville 4d	—	—	—	5	5	5	5	5	5
Cutlass 4d	3	3	3	—	—	—	—	—	—
Grand Prix 4d	3	3	3	3	3	3	3	5	5
Impala	—	—	—	5	5	5	5	5	5
Intrigue	—	3	3	3	3	3	—	—	—
LeSabre	—	3	3	5	5	5	5	5	5
Regal	3	3	3	3	3	3	3	3	—

Head Restraints

Bonneville	1	—	1	—	—	—	1	1	1
Cutlass	1	—	1	—	—	—	—	—	—
Cutlass Sup.	1	—	—	—	—	—	—	—	—
Grand Prix	2	—	3	—	2	2	2	1	1
Intrigue	—	—	1	—	1	1	—	—	—
Impala	—	—	—	1	1	1	1	1	1
LeSabre 4d	1	—	1	—	—	—	1	1	1
Lumina	1	—	1	—	—	—	—	—	—
Malibu	2	—	2	—	2	2	2	3	3
Malibu Classic	—	—	—	—	—	—	1	1	1
Monte Carlo	1	—	1	—	2	2	2	2	—
Regal 4d	—	—	1	—	1	1	1	1	—

Rollover Resistance

Bonneville	—	—	—	—	—	—	5	5	5
Grand Prix	—	—	—	—	—	—	4	4	4
Impala	—	—	—	—	4	4	4	4	4
LeSabre	—	—	—	—	—	—	—	—	5
Malibu	—	—	—	—	—	4	4	4	4
Monte Carlo	—	—	—	—	—	—	—	4	4

CENTURY ★ ★ ★

RATING: Average (1998–2005); Below Average (1997); Not Recommended (1982–96). With the older models, the same failure-prone components were used year after year. The 1996 Century isn't in the same league as the revised 1997 version, which adopted the W-platform used by the Chevrolet Lumina, Pontiac Grand Prix, and 1998 Oldsmobile Intrigue. The '97 is more refined, but also more glitch-ridden during the first year of its redesign. GM replaced the Century with the 2005 Buick Allure and the upscale 2006 Lucerne (see Appendix III). **"Real" city/highway fuel economy:** *3.1L:* 11.7/7.2 L/100 km with an automatic transmission. Owners report fuel savings may undershoot the above estimate by about 15 percent.

Maintenance/Repair costs: Higher than average, but repairs aren't dealer dependent. **Parts:** Higher-than-average costs (independent suppliers sell for much less), but not hard to find. Nevertheless, don't even think about buying one of these front-drives without a 3- to 5-year comprehensive warranty. **Extended warranty:** Yes, for the powertrain. **Best alternatives:** Acura Integra; GM Cavalier or Sunfire (Sunbird); Honda Accord; Hyundai Elantra Wagon, Sonata, or Tiburon; Mazda 626 or Protegé; Nissan Sentra or Stanza; and Toyota Camry. **Online help:** Owner reports and service bulletins can be found at *www.autosafety. org/autodefects.html*, or you can use a search engine such as Google to find information on GM paint delamination, engine piston slapping, or manifold defects.

Strengths and Weaknesses

The Century was always outclassed by the competition because of its low-quality components, ho-hum highway performance, and bland styling. Nevertheless, it was always popular with fleet buyers and car rental agencies because owners wanted a comfortable and affordable family sedan or wagon. Although handling and other aspects of road performance varied considerably, depending on the suspension and powertrain chosen, overall reliability remained a constant—abysmally poor.

The 1988–96 models are particularly unreliable. The 2.5L 4-cylinder engine suffers from engine-block cracking and a host of other serious defects. The 2.8L V6 engine hasn't been durable either; it suffers from premature camshaft wear and leaky gaskets and seals, especially the intake manifold gasket, a problem carried over to GM's entire 2004 model lineup (see Part Two, pages 77–79). The 3-speed automatic transmission is weak, and the 4-speed automatic frequently malfunctions. Temperamental and expensive-to-replace fuel systems, including the in-tank fuel pump, afflict all models and years, causing chronic stalling, hard starting, and poor fuel economy (use the emissions warranty as leverage to get compensation). Fuel-system diagnosis and repair for the 3.0L V6 can be difficult, and the electronic controls are often defective. Air conditioners frequently malfunction, and the cooling system is prone to leaks.

Prematurely worn power-steering assemblies are particularly commonplace. Brakes are weak and need frequent attention because of premature wear and dangerously rapid corrosion; front brake rotors warp easily; excessive pulsation is common; and rear brake drums often lock up, particularly when damp. Shock absorbers and springs wear out quickly. Rear wheel alignment should be checked often. Electric door locks frequently malfunction. Water leaks onto carpeting. Premature and extensive surface rust—caused by poor paint application, delamination, and defective materials—is common for all years. Far more disturbing are the scattered reports of severe undercarriage/suspension rusting, possibly making the vehicles unsafe to drive—and costing lots of money to correct.

VEHICLE HISTORY: 1982–96—Early 125–150-hp V6 engines are replaced by a 3.3L V6 in 1989. A failure-prone 4.3L diesel engine is carried over from 1982–85 (beware!). A 3.1L V6 comes on the scene in 1994 along with a driver-side airbag and ABS. **1997**—Given a complete make-over that includes the following: a spunkier 160-hp 3.1L V6 engine; gobs of room and trunk space (rivalling that of the Taurus, Concorde, Accord, or Camry); sleeker styling; a much quieter interior; and an upgraded standard ABS system that produces less pedal pulsation. Engine noise is also reduced, although insufficient firewall insulation means a considerable amount of noise still gets into the interior. Other new features include upgraded door seals, steering wheel–mounted radio controls, and additional heating ducts for rear passengers. **1998**—Reduced-force airbags. **1999**—Adoption of a revised ABS system, better traction control, and an enhanced suspension to reduce body roll. **2000**—Given a small horsepower boost to 175. **2003**—A minor face-lift and a freshened interior. **2004**—Standard four-wheel disc brakes. **2005**—An abbreviated model year; replaced by the Allure (LaCrosse in the States).

On the downside, the 1996–2004 Century's engine intake manifold gaskets have a short lifespan (see preceding "Bonneville, Grand Prix, et al." section), the speed-dependent power steering is too light and vague, and its suspension and handling are more tuned to comfort than to performance. The front air-deflector shield has also been the object of many complaints. Its low placement causes the shield to hit the roadway whenever passing over a small dip or bump. Furthermore, the bumper pulls off when passing over parking blocks.

Overall reliability has improved a bit since the 1997 model changeover glitches were corrected. However, powertrain breakdowns are still commonplace, and fit and finish remain subpar, particularly when compared with the Japanese competition. The 2000–05 models aren't much improved. They continue to have premature engine head gasket failures, piston slap noise, early transmission breakdowns, electrical system and computer module malfunctions, and front and rear brakes that rust easily and wear out early, with discs that warp far too often. Shock absorbers and MacPherson struts wear out or leak prematurely. The power rack-and-pinion steering system degenerates quickly after three years and is characterized by chronic leaking. Poor body fit, particularly around the doors, leads to excessive wind noise and water leaks into the interior. Door locks also freeze up easily.

Safety Summary

All models/years: Vehicle suddenly accelerates on its own. • Horn buttons difficult to access and depress because of their small size. • Dash reflection in windshield causes poor visibility. • Headlights provide poor visibility. • Head restraints won't stay in the raised position. **All models: 1998**—Idle surge after releasing brake because of faulty oxygen sensor. • Leaking lower intake manifold. • Engine oil pan leakage. • Chronic stalling. • Transmission shifts erratically. • Transmission hard to put into Reverse; faulty gearshift lever. • Sudden loss of electrical power. • Climate control switch failures. • Headlight switch failure. • Windshield wiper-arm failures. • Horn blows on its own when car is not running. **1999**—Engine fire on start-up. • Chronic engine hesitation when accelerating or changing gears. • Cruise control fails to disengage. • Premature transmission failure: won't go into Reverse; shift lever hangs up; Drive gear won't hold vehicle when stopped on an incline. • In one incident, seat belt trapped child around waist; child had to be cut free. • Front right window suddenly explodes. • Tire jack won't hold vehicle's weight. **2000**—Engine replaced twice. • Transmission has a tendency to shift often, whether it's necessary or not. • If vehicle is driven with the windows down, there is a loud shaking noise and the vehicle vibrates violently. • Steering wheel heats up when both the radio and headlights are on. • Driver's seat leans to the side. • Large head restraints block vision. • Low beams don't illuminate the highway adequately; the light spreads only to the side end of the front fender, resulting in poor visibility. • Air scoop/spoiler hits or scrapes the ground. • If vehicle is parked on uneven ground, the doors stick because of body flexing. • Driver-side window suddenly explodes, as from decompression, while underway. • Wipers can't be aligned. **2001**—Brakes fail. • Transmission won't hold vehicle parked on an incline. • Cannot drive car with rear windows down because the air pressure hurts eardrums. **2002**—Sun visors are hard to use. • Gas pedal may be mounted too low for some drivers. • Reverse and tag lights fail because of frayed wiring at trunk hinge. **2003**—Sudden brake failure. • Car rolls backward when stopped in gear on an incline. • Passenger-side windshield wiper channels water directly in the line of vision on the upstroke, temporarily blocking driver's vision. • Vent behind shifter handle becomes very hot when heater is on. • Gearshift lever continually sticks. • Air dam deflector on the front of the vehicle is mounted too low and hits the road on dips. **2004**—Electrical shorts cause the headlights to shut off or dim while driving. **2005**—Head restraints are mounted too high. • Driver's seat sinks in the middle.

Secret Warranties/Internal Bulletins/Service Tips

All models/years: An upgraded low-level fuel sensor will fix a fluctuating fuel gauge that bedevils GM's entire car lineup; it's an expensive repair that's covered by a GM "goodwill" warranty, if you insist on it. • Reverse servo cover seal leak (transmission). **All models: 1993–2005**—A rotten-egg odour coming from the exhaust is probably the result of a malfunctioning catalytic converter; replacement cost may be covered by the emissions warranty up to eight years. • Eliminate AC odours by installing an evaporator cooling-coil coating kit. • Paint delamination, peeling, or fading. **1994–98**—A cold-engine tick or rattle heard shortly after start-up may be fixed by replacing the piston/pin assembly. **1997–99**—A low-speed steering shudder or vibration may be corrected by replacing the steering pressure and return lines with revised "tuned" hoses. • Front disc pads have been upgraded to reduce brake squeal. • A shaking sensation at cruising speed may be fixed by replacing the transmission mount. • TSB #00-03-06-001 gives a comprehensive listing of common front-end noises and what's needed to silence them. • Install a new steering wheel inflatable restraint module to make it easier to sound the horn. **1997–2001**—Binding automatic transmission shift lever (see TSB 01-07-30-017). **1998**—A wet right rear floor signals the need to reseal the stationary glass area. **1998–2000**—Simply changing the radiator cap may cure your hot-running engine and prevent coolant loss. **2000–01**—GM's TSB says the best way to eliminate an engine ticking noise is to replace the engine's pistons (covered by a secret warranty, of course). **2000–02**—Exhaust system ping, snap. • Poor transmission performance. • No-start remedy. **2001–04**—Erratically shifting, slipping transmission. **2001–05**—Harsh 1–2 upshifts. **2003**—Firm shifts, no downshifts, shudder. **2003–04**—GM's service bulletin recommends the fuel tank be changed under warranty when the rear end produces a clunking or banging noise:

CLUNK/BANG FROM VEHICLE REAR

BULLETIN NO.: 04-06-04-066A   DATE: AUGUST 3, 2005

CLUNK/BANG FROM REAR OF VEHICLE (REPLACE FUEL TANK AND REFLASH PCM)
2003–04 Century, Grand Prix, Impala, Monte Carlo, and Regal.

CONDITION: Some customers may comment on a clunk/bang type noise coming from the rear of the vehicle. This noise will be most noticeable when the vehicle comes to a stop or during parking lot maneuvers. Customers may also comment that the noise occurs when the fuel tank is between 1/2 and full.
CAUSE: The noise may be caused by fuel sloshing around in the fuel tank.
CORRECTION: Replace the fuel tank with P/N 15141578. Refer to the Fuel Tank Replacement procedure in the Engine Controls sub-section of the service manual. This new tank has internal baffles to prevent the fuel from sloshing around.

CENTURY PROFILE

	1997	1998	1999	2000	2001	2002	2003	2004	2005
Cost Price ($)									
Century	24,545	25,215	25,199	25,570	25,200	25,325	25,820	26,300	26,445
Used Values ($)									
Century ▲	2,500	3,000	3,500	5,000	6,500	8,500	10,000	12,000	14,500
Century ▼	2,000	2,500	3,000	4,000	5,500	7,000	8,500	10,500	13,000
Reliability	2	2	2	2	3	3	4	4	4
Crash Safety (F)									
Century 4d	—	—	4	4	4	4	4	4	4
Side (Century 4d)	—	3	3	3	3	3	3	3	3
Offset	3	3	3	3	3	3	3	3	3
Head Restraints (F)	1	—	1	—	1	1	1	1	1
Rollover Resistance	—	—	—	—	—	—	4	4	4

General Motors/Suzuki

RATING: Below Average (2004–06). This is a middle-of-the-road performer that's seriously outclassed by the Japanese competition. **"Real" city/highway fuel economy:** 2.5L: 11.9/7.9 L/100 km with a 6-cylinder engine and an automatic transmission. No owner reports of excessive fuel consumption, but the owner sampling is still quite small. **Maintenance/Repair costs:** Estimated to be average. Repairs aren't dealer dependent. **Parts:** Average costs, and generic parts can easily be found for much less from independent suppliers. **Extended warranty:** Not needed. **Best alternatives:** Hyundai Sonata and Kia Magentis. **Online help:** Owner reviews can be found at *www.carforums.com/forums*, *www.cartrackers.com/Forums*, and *www.carsurvey.org/model_Chevrolet_Epica.html*.

Strengths and Weaknesses

This South Korean mid-sized sedan competes with the Hyundai Sonata and the Kia Magentis, and originally cost $24,710 (plus a $930 freight fee) for a 2004 model, or about $11,000 more than the cheapest Aveo. Used, these cars have depreciated quite a bit: A 2004 Epica LS Sedan is now worth between $10,000 and $12,000, whereas the slightly more upscale 2004 LT will bring in between $11,000 and $13,000.

For your money, you get an inline 6-cylinder DOHC engine with a 4-speed automatic transmission that produces 36 more horsepower than the Optra does. Other standard goodies include air conditioning; AM/FM/CD player; power seats, locks, windows, and mirrors; remote entry; projector-beam headlights; foglights; 15-inch tires; and four-wheel disc brakes.

Epica's 6-cylinder engine is both smooth and quiet. When under load, though, it still takes an inordinate amount of time to pass other cars or merge into traffic. Gear changes aren't always smooth, especially in city traffic and when downshifting. Also, the automatic transmission's "hold" button doesn't have much effect. The ride is comfortable, thanks to the standard four-wheel independent suspension (front double wishbones/rear multi-link). Speed-sensitive power steering is a bit numb and provides little feedback. Nevertheless, the car handles predictably and corners well. Four-wheel disc brakes are standard, and ABS is optional on LS models, standard on LT trim.

Under GM's stewardship, the exterior is beautifully styled and the interior has been upgraded. Fit and finish have improved, but the poor choice of interior materials creates a trashy, mismatched look. Front and rear headroom and legroom are barely adequate for four or five adults, and room is unacceptably cramped in cars that carry the space-stealing sunroof. A pass-through from the cabin to the trunk is a good idea that's badly executed due to the narrow opening. Climate control gauges and controls are confusing, the heater output doesn't stay constant, and the rear defogger is inadequate. Epica owners complain of automatic transmission, electrical system, brake, and fit and finish deficiencies.

Safety Summary

All models/years: Optional ABS on the Epica LS and Verona GL, but standard on the Epica LT and on the Verona GLX. • The standard seat-mounted side airbags on the Verona are optional on the Epica. • Rear seat belts on either car may not be long enough to carry large passengers. • NHTSA tests give the 2005 and 2006 Veronas three- and four-star ratings for driver and passenger protection in frontal collisions, four- and three-star ratings for front and rear occupant protection in side impacts, and four stars for rollover resistance. In IIHS tests, the Verona is rated Acceptable in the stringent frontal offset impact test and Poor in side impact collisions, ranking 10th of the 13 cars in its class. • Dash-mounted white face gauges are easy to read, and the headlights provide exemplary lighting. **All models: 2004**—Airbags fail to deploy properly. • Seat belts lock in the retractor. • Sudden acceleration when automatic transmission is shifted from Reverse to Drive. • Chronic engine stalling not fixed by recall correction, and many vehicles excluded from the program. • Hard starting. • Early replacement of the intake manifold and oxygen sensor. • Engine throws a piston rod. • Difficulty downshifting. • Inoperative heater. • Crooked fuel cap causes Check Engine light to illuminate.

Secret Warranties/Internal Bulletins/Service Tips

All models: 2004—Upshift/downshift delay. **2004–05**—Tips for troubleshooting numerous electrical problems. • Erratic fuel gauge readings (replace the sender). • Front suspension crunching or squeaking.

Honda

| ACCORD | ★ ★ ★ ★ |

RATING: Above Average (2003–06, 1990–99); Recommended (2000–02); Average (1985–89). Most knee-jerk "anything Japanese is good" car guides give the Honda Accord and Toyota Camry equally positive ratings. Not *Lemon-Aid*. For the past decade, Toyota has been asleep at the switch and allowed the Camry's quality to decline. That's why the Accord has higher scores with both the 16-valve 4-cylinder and the V6 engine. In a nutshell, the Accord is one of the most versatile compacts you can find. Think of it as a better-performing Toyota Camry with better-quality components and fewer powertrain defects, especially Toyota's dreaded delay/surge problem acceleration. Nevertheless, the 2003 through 2006 models don't get top scores because of redesign glitches that are still being addressed by the company.

These deficiencies include powertrain defects, sudden acceleration and stalling, brake failures, and airbag malfunctions. **"Real" city/highway fuel economy:** 2.4L: 9.1/6.4 L/100 km with a manual transmission or 10.0/6.4 L/100 km with an automatic. 3.0L: 9.1/6.4 L/100 km with a 6-cylinder engine and a manual transmission; 11.5/6.3 L/100 km with a 6-speed manual or 11.4/7.3 L/100 km with an automatic. Owners report actual fuel economy doesn't vary much from the above estimated figures. **Maintenance/Repair costs:** Lower than average. Repairs aren't dealer-dependent. Recall repairs may be delayed. **Parts:** Higher-than-average costs, but parts can easily be found for much less from independent suppliers. **Extended warranty:** Not needed. **Best alternatives:** Acura Integra; Hyundai Elantra wagon, Sonata, or Tiburon; Mazda 626; and Toyota Camry. **Online help:** Owner complaints and service bulletins can be found at *www. autosafety.org/autodefects.html*, and helpful owner forums can be found at *www.vtec. net* (The Temple of VTEC), *www.kbb.com* (Kelley Blue Book), *www.edmunds.com*, *www.carforums.com/forums*, and *www.cartrackers.com/Forums*.

Strengths and Weaknesses

Fast and nimble even without a V6, this is the mid-sized sedan of choice for drivers who want maximum fuel economy and comfort along with lots of space for grocery hauling and occasional highway cruising. With the optional V6, the Accord is one of the most versatile mid-sized cars you can find. It offers something for everyone, and its top-drawer quality and high resale value mean there's no way you can lose money buying one.

Accord Hybrid

After successfully launching its 2003 Civic Hybrid, Honda introduced the 2005 Accord Hybrid. Equipped with a 255-hp V6 engine, the Hybrid is assisted as needed by an electric motor and a 5-speed automatic transmission. An innovative Variable Cylinder Management System automatically deactivates three cylinders when cruising or on deceleration. Like the Civic Hybrid, the Accord Hybrid can't be driven on electricity alone.

The primary complaint of Hybrid owners is that the vehicle gets nowhere near the advertised gas mileage; owners say it's about 30 percent worse than promised. Other Hybrid-specific complaints involve electrical short circuits and premature brake wear. Overall, though, there are proportionately fewer complaints from Accord Hybrid owners than from Toyota Prius owners, and the complaints are less serious in nature. Because Hybrid sales are stagnant, Honda has confirmed that 2007 will be the car's last model year.

Whether hybrid or gasoline-powered, the Accord doesn't really excel in any particular area; it's just very, very good at everything. It's smooth, quiet, mannerly, and competent, with outstanding fit and finish inside and out. Other strong points are comfort, ergonomics, reliability, driveability, and impressive assembly quality. Unlike Toyota's lineup, there's no acceleration delay and surge. Nevertheless, Accords do have some problems: insufficient torque with the base engine on early models makes for constant highway downshifting; the automatic transmission tends to shift harshly and slowly (covered by a "goodwill" warranty); rear passenger room is tight; and there have been a number of safety-related complaints reported to NHTSA (see below).

During the '80s, Accords were beset with severe premature rusting, frequent engine camshaft and crankshaft failures, and serious front brake problems. Engines leaked or burned oil and blew their cylinder head gaskets easily, and carbureted models suffered from driveability problems through 1986. If left untreated, rust perforations will develop unusually quickly. Especially vulnerable spots are front fender seams, door bottoms, and areas surrounding side-view mirrors, door handles, rocker panels, wheel openings, windshield posts, front cowls, and trunk and hatchback lids.

VEHICLE HISTORY: 1990–93—More room and additional power through a new and quieter 2.2L 4-cylinder engine. Rear seating space remains inadequate, the added weight saps the car's performance, and the automatic transmission shifts harshly at times. Owners report numerous air and water leaks, and prematurely worn automatic transmissions, constant velocity joints, and power-steering assemblies. **1994**—Redesign adds dual airbags, increases interior room, and boosts 4-cylinder horsepower from 125–130 to 145. **1995**—Addition of a 175-hp 2.7L V6. The automatic transmission still works poorly with the 4-cylinder, producing acceleration times that are far from impressive, and owners still complain of excessive road noise and tire whine. Nevertheless, no significant reliability problems have been reported with this redesign. **1996**—Slightly restyled, the trunk opening is enlarged, and a rear-seat pass-through feature increases cargo space. **1998**—Substantially reworked, with more powerful engines (150–200 hp), including a new 200-hp 3.0L V6; a more refined suspension and automatic transaxle; upgraded ABS; additional interior space; and more glass. Wagon version dropped. **1999**—ABS on the LX. **2000**—Side airbags with all V6-equipped models. **2001**—A restyled exterior, dual side airbags, V6 traction control, and improved soundproofing. **2003**—This larger, totally restyled model offers a V6 and 6-speed manual tranny combo, and increased 4-cylinder and V6 horsepower (160 and 240, respectively) and fuel economy. **2004**—V6 models add traction control. Head-protecting side curtain airbags are standard on EX V6 models, and for now also available on EX 4-cylinders. **2005**—Introduction of the Hybrid sedan, standard side curtain-type airbags along with front torso airbags, and better interior sound-proofing. EX-L, EX V6, and Hybrid models come with leather upholstery, dual-zone automatic climate control, and heated front seats.

Confidential technical service bulletins show that the 1994–97 models are susceptible to AC malfunctions, engine oil leaks, the Check Engine light coming on for no reason, transmission glitches, power-steering pump leaks, windows falling off their channels, and numerous air and water leaks. Usually, these problems are simple to repair and Honda customer relations staff are helpful; however, Honda staffers and dealers are reluctant to admit their mistakes and may be getting a bit too arrogant in their dealings with the public. Witness the company's failure to publicly disclose its 1994–97 engine oil leak problems, which now affect the 2004 Accord and Odyssey.

Bulletins and owner complaints relating to the reworked 1998–2000 models show a surprisingly large number of factory-related powertrain and body defects, undoubtedly a result of the Accord's redesign. Some of those deficiencies, which affect both safety and performance, are chronic lurching, hesitation, and stalling while on the highway, accompanied by the Check Engine light coming on, hard starting, frequent transmission failures, poor tracking that allows the vehicle to wander, defective rear computerized motor mounts, electrical shorts, coolant and brake master cylinder leakage, ABS and AC failures, and poor radio reception.

Body and accessory problems for these same model years include a plethora of squeaks, creaks, groans, and rattles; wind noise; water leaks; fuel gauge defects; paint chipping, bubbling, and peeling on hood, trunk, and roof (Honda blames it on bird droppings); leaky sunroofs; windshields with vertical lines of distortion; driver-side mirrors that shake excessively; faulty fuel-sending units that make for inaccurate fuel readings (when full, indicates three-fourths full); and speedometers that are off by 10 percent.

Owners of 2001 and 2002 models report that sudden, unintended acceleration remains a serious problem and can occur at any time, as the owner of this 2001 Accord relates:

> While taking the car through a car wash, vehicle accelerated and ran into two other cars and through a fence.

Other performance-related problems include automatic transmission breakdowns, expensive and frequent servicing of the brake rotors and pads, and electrical glitches.

The 2003 redesign has contributed to a continued decline in quality through the 2005 model year, resulting in the Accord losing its Recommended rating for those model years. Up to 268 safety-related complaints have been registered by NHTSA, when merely one-quarter of this number is considered normal. Sadder still, Honda promised us better-performing, more durable transmissions in its redesigned 2003 models. The company lied, and then later reluctantly extended the warranty up to eight years. Furthermore, some 2003–05 model year Accord owners say their cars have similar problems but haven't been included in the new warranty program; others complain that the corrective repairs haven't fixed the tranny problems and that they were forced to pay a deductible, which should be Honda's responsibility. So far, the 2006 models appear to be improving, but we'll need more owner feedback before restoring a Recommended rating to the Accord.

And here are other problems related to this last redesign: a rotten-egg exhaust smell in the cabin; coolant in the engine oil pan; frequent hard starts; erratic transmission shifts; engine oil leaks onto the manual transmission clutch, causing shifting slippage (the problem is caused by a low vent valve on the 6-speed tranny); brake shuddering, grinding, and squealing; warped brake rotors; a popping noise heard when accelerating; a steering-column ticking; AC condenser that's easily punctured by road debris; defective CD changer; stereo speaker hum or popping and frequent speaker blowouts; passenger-side seat heater coming on by itself and overheating; windshield creaks in cold, dry weather; the moonroof not closing all the way; non-stop rattles, squeaks, and vibrations in door panels, tops of windows, rear shelf, and in the B-pillars around the top seat belt anchor; wrinkled, bubbling door window moulding; doors closing on occupants as they leave the vehicle; rear headliner becoming unglued and sagging, causing water to leak into cabin and trunk (carpeting and rear seat saturated after moderate rainstorms); defective paint; and roof buckling:

> 2005 Honda Accord EXL experienced a buckling roof. The consumer's wife was driving and had run over a pot hole when she heard a loud noise. The consumer found the roof severely buckled. The consumer had taken the vehicle to the dealer when they found other 4 door Honda Accords with the same problem. Currently the consumer vehicle has big buckles in the roof.

The increase in engine, transmission, and brake failures is worrisome. Nevertheless, CAA surveys have shown that customer satisfaction is at an impressive 88 percent, compared to 85 percent for both the Toyota Camry and Mazda 626. Also, to its credit, Honda puts a "goodwill" clause in almost all of its service bulletins, allowing service managers to submit any claim to the company long after the original warranty period has elapsed.

Safety Summary

All models/years: Sudden acceleration, stalling. • Airbags fail to deploy, or deploy for no reason. • Check Engine light is always on. • Excessive windshield glare. • AC failure. • Premature front/rear brake wear. • Gas and brake pedals are too close together and often get pressed at the same time. • Faulty power windows. • Seat belt continually ratchets tighter. **All models: 1999–2000**—Airbag deployment causes extensive neck and head injuries. • Sudden brake loss. • Emergency brakes failed to hold on hill, allowing car to roll into lake. • Brake master cylinder leakage. • Driver's seatback suddenly falls back. • Steering knuckle breaks while driving. • Bolt that holds the lower control arm assembly breaks away from the frame, causing wheel to come out of fender. • Many complaints of chronic lurching, hesitation, and stalling while on the highway, accompanied by Check Engine light coming on (dealers say they can't duplicate the problem). • Engine sputters at half throttle. • Hard starting. • Frequent transmission failures. • Vehicle doesn't track well; wanders all over the road. • Exhaust pipe runs under oil pan plug, causing dripped oil to burn off exhaust. • Seat belts fail to retract, or continually tighten up, choking occupant. • Right front passenger window explodes while driving. • Windshield has vertical lines of distortion. • Driver-side mirror shakes excessively. **2001**—Excessive front-end vibration and wandering over the highway. • Automatic transmission leaks and jerks into gear. • Rear stabilizer bar links break. • Vehicle rolls back when stopped on an incline. • Complete brake loss. • Check Engine and Airbag warning lights remain lit. • Incorrect fuel gauge readings. • The front windshield has a UV-protective coating that gives the windshield a wavy appearance. **2002**—Car suddenly shuts down in traffic because of a defective immobilizer system. • Automatic transmission failures. • Seat belt won't retract, or continually tightens; in one incident, child had to be cut free. • Child safety seat can't be installed because buckle latch is located too far into the seat. • Partial brake failure; brakes fail to catch at first, then suddenly grab. • Vehicle pulls sharply when braking. • Trunk lid may suddenly fall. **2003**—Sudden, unintended acceleration while car is in motion or when put into Reverse. • Axle suddenly snaps. • Severe pulling to the right. • Power steering groan believed to be caused by the steering pump. • Console overheats and smells burnt. • Keys overheat in the ignition. • Complete brake failure. • ABS and traction-control lights stay lit and corrective parts aren't easily found. • Frequent Michelin tire blowouts. • Rear vision is obstructed by head restraints, high rear deck, and roof pillar. **2004**—Several reports of fires igniting in the insulation material:

> While driving vehicle caught fire. Dealership found that the sound deadening material came too close to the heat of the engine.

Also, one report of fire igniting behind the right front tire while vehicle was underway. • Brake light bulb drops down into the trunk area and burns through luggage. • Axle collapses while vehicle is underway. • Vehicle accelerates when brakes are applied. • Engine surges when shifting gears. • Complete brake failure; brake alert is constantly lit. • In one incident, brakes applied, car jerked to the side, total loss of braking (other complainants say the brakes lock up), and Accord hit guardrail. • Steering suddenly locks up. • Seat belt failed to retract in a rear-end collision; several complaints allege the front seat belts failed to restrain occupants in frontal collisions. • Frequent no-starts. • Passenger-side mirror slipped off; another one "exploded." • Steering pulls to one side while driving. • Side window shatters after morning moisture is wiped off. • Side-airbag sensor won't warn you if passengers are improperly seated:

> The consumer stated the side airbag off light does not signal an improper leaning of a passenger against the window. The Honda technical department recommended replacing the sensor in the seat, however, that did not rectify the problem. The technical dept. then told the consumer the side airbag off light was purposely deleted in order to spare the driver any alarm....

• If you put your purse on the front passenger-side seat, the airbag is disabled. The same thing occurred when a driver's 90-pound daughter sat in the same seat. • Driver's seat moves forward on its own. • Carbon monoxide fumes invade the passenger compartment. • Defogger causes condensation on inside windshield, which then freezes. • Firestone and Michelin tire sidewall bubbling. **2004–2005**—

Brakes may be overly sensitive and grab too quickly; vehicle jerks to a stop. • Key sticks in the ignition. • Distorted windshield:

> A new windshield was installed, and that one was also distorted. In total, five replacement windshields were ordered but they all had the same defect.

2005—Sudden acceleration after a cold start. • Intermittent stalling. • Cell phone interference can affect airbag sensors. • Right front wheel comes apart. • Cracks in the steering wheel just above the airbag. • Intermittent power steering failure. • Honda's jack is a knuckle-buster that won't hold the car. • Shifter slips by Drive mode into D3, or sticks in second gear. • Michelin MXV4 tire sidewall blowout. • Poorly lit heating and cooling control panels. *Hybrid:* **2005**—Instead of a spare tire, owners are given a can of sealant that won't work if the puncture is located outside the tread.

Secret Warranties/Internal Bulletins/Service Tips

All models/years: Steering-wheel shimmy is a frequent problem and is taken care of in TSB #94-025. • A slow-to-retract seat belt will be replaced for free under Honda's lifetime warranty, says TSB #03-062. • Deformed windshield moulding. **All models: 1998–2001**—Tips on silencing a moonroof squeak. **1998–2004**—V6 engine oil leaks (an extension of a problem first noticed on 1994–97 models). **1998–2006**—Vehicles with broken rear stabilizer links are eligible for a free replacement under a Honda "goodwill" program. **1999**—Glove box door rattle, wheel click, and clutch-pedal and rear wheel-bearing noise. • Loose AC, heater, temperature, and fan control knobs. • Inaccurate fuel gauge. **1999–2000**—Engine hard starts. • Coolant leaks from the water passage near the EGR valve. • PCM needs to be recalibrated under warranty to prevent MIL from coming on for no reason. • TSB #00-038 says a transmission shudder or judder will be fixed for free under a "goodwill" program. **1999–2003**—Automatic transmission malfunctions and failures will be fixed or replaced under a more recent and comprehensive "goodwill" extended warranty program (see Part Two, "The Wacky World of Secret Warranties"). **1999–2006**—Repair tips applicable to vehicles that pull/drift to one side. **2001**—Windshield hum or whine. • Cracked, damaged foglight lens. • The horn plate bolts on the driver's airbag may not have been properly torqued and could cause a rattle in the steering wheel. **2002–06**—Honda has offered American owners a warranty extension of 5 percent off the indicated mileage because its vehicles' odometers were found to over-register mileage. Canadian owners haven't yet been notified. **2003**—"Goodwill" campaigns to replace automatic transmissions and multiplex integrated control units (MICUs) that regulate door locks, trunk alarm, etc. • Corrective action for coolant leakage into the engine oil pan; oil leaks at the cylinder head cover. • A faulty air-intake air-breather pipe hose may cause the engine warning light to remain lit. Its replacement is covered by a special Honda Product Update Campaign. • An automatic transmission that won't go into Reverse is eligible for a free correction under another Honda "goodwill" campaign (TSB #03-042). • Automatic transmission leaks on the cooler lines. • Hard starts. • Troubleshooting calipers, rotors, and pads, following complaints of excessive brake vibration (wait a minute, weren't these the same chronic problems present before Honda's much-vaunted 2003 brake upgrade?):

> My 2003 Accord has been in the Honda dealer with problems with the front brakes (warped rotors). After having the front rotors resurfaced and pads replaced twice, it was found that the front calipers were hanging up. My car just turned 17,000 miles [27,200 km] and it has had problems with the front brakes since it had 8,000 miles [12,800 km], at that time I was told by the dealer that I was "riding" my brakes and they would only take care of this problem for me at no cost just this "one time."

• Troubleshooting ABS brake-light illumination. • Inaccurate gauges and odometer. • Vehicle pulls to the right. • Excessive steering vibration. • Noisy power steering countermeasures. • Investigating owner reports of cracked windshields. • Doors don't unlock in cold weather. • Poor AC cooling. • Rear shelf rattling. • Dash or pillar creaking or clicking. • Roof moulding channel leaks water; roof water leak fix. • Wrinkled door window moulding. • Remedies for front brake noise or judder when braking. **2003–04**—If the brake pedal is stiff, a new booster vacuum hose may be required. • Loose steering or clunky performance:

LOOSENESS FELT/CLUNKING NOISE WHEN TURNING

BULLETIN NO.: 05-013   DATE: MARCH 25, 2005

2003–04 ACCORD V6—CLUNKING OR LOOSENESS IN THE TIE ROD INNER JOINT

While turning, clunking is heard from the steering or looseness is felt in the steering wheel.

PROBABLE CAUSE: Water entered the tie-rod inner ball joint, causing rust that wore the plastic liner inside of the socket.

CORRECTIVE ACTION: Inspect the tie-rod ball joints, and replace the boots and tie-rod ball joints as required.

• Troubleshooting dim headlights. • Remedies for a sulfur smell in the interior. **2003–05**—Low fuel warning is activated even though fuel tank is a quarter full. **2003–06**—Guidelines for fixing dashboard/A-pillar creaks and clicks. **2004**—Excessive engine vibration in idle. • Noisy steering. • No-starts and faulty power windows. • Door rattles. • Wheel-bearing humming or growling. • Heater blower overheats or blows a fuse.

ACCORD PROFILE

	1997	1998	1999	2000	2001	2002	2003	2004	2005
Cost Price ($)									
LX sedan	20,995	23,800	23,800	23,000	22,800	23,000	25,000	25,100	25,500
EXi/EX V6	23,495	26,800	26,801	31,300	30,800	31,100	32,500	32,900	33,600
Hybrid	—	—	—	—	—	—	—	—	36,990

Used Values ($)

LX sedan ▲	5,000	6,000	7,000	8,500	10,500	12,000	14,000	16,500	18,500
LX sedan ▼	4,000	5,000	6,000	7,000	9,000	10,500	12,500	15,000	17,000
EXi/EX V6 ▲	6,000	7,500	8,500	10,000	12,500	15,500	18,000	21,000	23,000
EXi/EX V6 ▼	5,000	6,500	7,500	9,000	10,500	14,000	16,000	19,500	21,500
Hybrid ▲	—	—	—	—	—	—	—	—	27,500
Hybrid ▼	—	—	—	—	—	—	—	—	26,990
Reliability	4	4	4	5	5	5	4	4	4
Crash Safety (F)	4	4	4	—	5	5	5	5	5
4d	4	4	4	4	5	5	5	5	5
Side (2d)	—	—	3	3	4	4	5	4	4
4d	2	4	4	4	4	4	5	5	4
Side (IIHS)	—	—	—	—	—	—	1	5	5
Offset	3	3	3	3	3	3	5	5	5
Head Restraints (2d)	2	—	3	—	—	—	3	3	1
4d	—	—	2	—	3	3	1	1	1
Rear	—	—	—	2	2	2	1	1	1
Rollover Resistance	—	—	—	5	5	5	4	4	4

Note: The Accord Hybrid rate of depreciation is similar to that of the Civic Hybrid and Toyota's Prius.

Hyundai

SONATA ★ ★ ★ ★

RATING: Above Average (1999–2006); Average (1995–98); Not Recommended (1986–93). The 1994 model year was skipped. Recent iterations of the Sonata haven't registered one-tenth the number of safety complaints of the highly rated Honda Accord or Toyota Camry. On the other hand, Sonata's crashworthiness ratings aren't impressive. For maximum savings, I suggest you buy a 1999–2004 version, keep it at least five years to amortize the depreciation, and put some of the savings on the purchase price into a comprehensive supplementary warranty to protect yourself when the warranty ends. **"Real" city/highway fuel economy:** *2.4L:* 10.9/7.2 L/100 km with an automatic transmission. *2.7L:* 12.3/7.9 L/100 km with a 6-cylinder engine and an automatic tranny. *3.5L:* 13.9/8.4 L/100 km with a 6-cylinder and an automatic. Owners report fuel savings may undershoot the above estimates by at least 10 percent, or up to 20 percent with the larger 3.5L engine. **Maintenance/Repair costs:** Higher than average. Repairs aren't dealer-dependent. **Parts:** Higher-than-average costs, and parts are often back-ordered. **Extended warranty:** An extended powertrain warranty would be a smart buy. **Best alternatives:** Acura Integra, GM Cavalier or Sunfire, Honda Accord, Hyundai Elantra wagon or Tiburon, Mazda 626, and Toyota Camry.

Online help: For the latest owner reports, service bulletins, and money-saving tips, look at *www.automotiveforums.com/vbulletin/f741*, *www.autosafety.org/autodefects.html*, *www.kbb.com* (*Kelley Blue Book*), *www.edmunds.com*, *www.carforums.com/forums*, and *www.cartrackers.com/Forums*.

Strengths and Weaknesses

This mid-sized front-drive sedan has gone from bad to good in an incredibly short period of time. Could it be just a coincidence that major improvements were made several years ago, once Hyundai hired Toyota's top quality-control engineer, who brought with him a bushel basket of internal quality reports? It's a moot question now. The papers were returned to Toyota's lawyers late last year following threats of legal action. Hyundai assured Toyota the documents went unread (wink wink, nudge nudge).

Corporate intrigue aside, the Sonata is a decent performer in most areas, with some notable exceptions. Acceleration is impressive with the manual gearbox and passable with the automatic. Handling and performance are also fairly good, although emergency handling isn't confidence-inspiring, particularly because of the imprecise steering and excessive lean when cornering. As with other early Hyundai models, the automatic transmission continues to shift erratically up through the 2005 model, the engine is noisy, and reliability is a problem for the 1989–93 models, while the 1995–98 models are only marginally improved.

VEHICLE HISTORY: 1995—Redesigned for additional interior room, plus more horsepower and an upgraded automatic transmission. Nevertheless, acceleration with the automatic is still below average with the 4-banger, and the automatic gearbox downshifts slowly (the manual transmission is still more reliable and fuel efficient). **1996**—More standard features, such as air conditioning, power steering, a split folding rear seatback, liquid-filled engine mounts, and additional sound-proofing. **1999**—Arrived with a redesigned body and suspension, side airbags, two new engines, and a huge price increase that's not reflected in its low resale value. **2000**—Side airbags and larger wheels. **2001**—A new grille and additional standard features of minor importance. **2002**—GL given four-wheel disc brakes. **2003**—Standard front side airbags.

Throughout the Sonata's history, Hyundai's technical service bulletins have been replete with references to automatic transmissions that exhibit what Hyundai describes as "shift shock" as well as delayed shifting. In addition to the tranny problems, owners of pre-1995 models report poor engine performance (hard starting, poor idling, stalling); a hot-running engine (when you're stopped at a traffic light, it shakes like a boiling kettle); a #3 spark plug that often needs replacing or cleaning; rough engine rattles; high oil consumption (one litre every two to three months); excessive front brake pulsation and premature wear; steering defects (when the steering wheel is turned to either extreme, it makes a sound like metal cracking); cruise control malfunctions and electrical short circuits; a battery life of only 18 months; malfunctioning lights; radio failures; falling interior roof liners; faulty hood locks; a rotten-egg smell coming from the catalytic converter; broken mufflers; faulty resonators; defective exhaust pipes; poor door and window sealing (water leaking into the interior when the car is washed); and premature paint peeling and rusting.

The 1995–2006 Sonatas have elicited very few quality-control and safety complaints and represent the better buys in this group, following the '95 and '99 models' redesign. However, automatic transmissions, brakes, airbags, steering, and fuel- and electrical-system components still top the list of parts most vulnerable to premature failure or malfunctioning. Airbag and Check Engine lights are constantly lit, and fit and finish continue to be only average.

Safety Summary

All models/years: Airbags don't deploy when they should, or deploy when they shouldn't. • Frequent automatic transmission failures. **All models: 1999—** Complete brake failure. • Airbag warning light comes on for no reason. • Sudden alternator failure causes entire vehicle to shut down. • **2000**—Driver-side airbag deploys when driver slams the door. • Airbag warning light stays lit. • Sudden brake loss; brakes don't hold in a panic situation. • Warped front brake rotors produce excessive steering shimmy. • Stalls when in low gear or when decelerating (recall campaign didn't remedy the problem). • Power-steering leaks and early replacement. • Window often comes off its track. • In one incident, power window caught child's head and neck. • Headlights dim when AC engages. **2001**—Hood flies up and shatters windshield. • Engine sleeves can come loose, causing pistons to smash spark plugs. • Engine bucks and hesitates before rpm suddenly increase and car takes off. • Frequent stalling upon deceleration. • Faulty crankshaft position sensor is blamed for the poor engine performance. • Automatic transmission may suddenly shift into Neutral, or the shift lever sometimes pops out of gear. **2002**—Problems getting recall work done. • Axle (U-bolt) fails while car is underway. • Seat belt latch releases when jostled by passenger's elbow. **2003**—Driver-side seat belt buckle suddenly releases. • Large rear-view mirror obstructs the view. • Tire valve stem failure (cut) on both front tires:

> I purchased BFGoodrich Touring T/A Pro series (size P205/65R 15) for my 2003 Sonata at Sam's Club. In a month and a half, I had 4 flat tires and 10 valves replaced because the hubcaps spin and slice the valves. I lost 7.5 hours of work and received a back injury while trying to change one of the tires. I've spoken to Hyundai and BFGoodrich—both of which suggested getting the H rated tires instead of the S rated. I did that, but it didn't work. I also paid $75 for a diagnostician [who told] me that I had the wrong bead on the tires but [who] couldn't suggest a solution. My owner's manual simply states, "always replace your tires with those of the recommended size," [and] lists the tire size specifications as P205/65R 15. There is no recommended replacement brand named and no mention about having the correct size beading. I took my car to another dealer and learned that the BFGoodrich tires have a bead protectant [that] causes the hubcaps to rest directly against my tires, thus causing them to spin. There should be a gap between the hubcap and tire. I switched to a

Goodyear tire and have not had problems since. The problem with slicing valve stems only occurs on the 15-inch tires with hubcaps (as opposed to the 16-inch tires on aluminum wheels).

2004—Gas fumes enter the cabin. • Sudden, unintended acceleration. • Stalling because of faulty throttle sensor. • Early clutch failure. • Automatic transmission slippage and seizure. • Complete brake loss. • Rear wheel bearing seizure. • Seat belt came loose during a collision. • Side mirrors are no longer clear. • Frequent complaints of Michelin tire premature wear and blowouts. **2005**—Failure of the passenger-side front suspension. • No brakes. • Loose front passenger seat. • Vibration caused by loose engine mount bolts. • Excessive heat generated under the driver-side dash. • Windshield is easily scratched.

Secret Warranties/Internal Bulletins/Service Tips

All models/years: Troubleshooting tips for delayed engagement of the automatic transmission. • Harsh shifting when coming to a stop or upon initial acceleration is likely caused by an improperly adjusted accelerator pedal switch transmission control unit (TCU). • A faulty air exhaust plug could cause harsh shifting into Second and Fourth gears on vehicles with automatic transmissions. • Brake pedal pulsation can be corrected by installing upgraded front discs and pads. • Troubleshooting tips for reducing brake noise. **All models: 1999–2000**—No-starts, hard starting, or erratic idling may all be caused by a canister purge valve that's stuck open. • Correcting hard manual shifting into First or Second gear and shudder on acceleration (CV joints). **1999–2001**—Correcting erratic shifts. • Key sticks in ignition cylinder. • Silencing gear whine. **1999–2002**—Harsh, delayed shifts. **1999–2006**—Troubleshooting tips relative to differential seal oil leaks. **2000**—Rear suspension produces a metallic rubbing noise. **2000–01**—Correcting droning or rumbling brake noise at freeway speeds. **2001–02**—Hyundai will fix a noisy rear suspension by replacing the rear stabilizer bar bushing. **2002**—Troubleshooting poor shifting and torque converter clutch malfunctions. • 2–3 shift flare. • Erratic operation of the automatic climate control. **2003**—Harsh shifts into Drive or Reverse. • Sticks in Second gear. **2003–04**—Low-speed driveline "bump." **2004**—Engine hesitation requires a reprogrammed PCM. **2005**—Oil leak from the bell housing/torque converter area. **2006**—Front drive axle snapping noise.

SONATA PROFILE

	1997	1998	1999	2000	2001	2002	2003	2004	2005
Cost Price ($)									
Base	16,995	17,495	19,495	19,995	20,495	21,195	21,595	22,395	22,395
Used Values ($)									
Base ▲	2,500	3,000	3,500	4,500	5,000	7,500	10,000	12,000	14,000
Base ▼	2,000	2,500	3,000	4,000	4,500	6,500	8,500	10,500	12,500

Reliability	3	3	3	4	4	4	4	4	4
Crash Safety (F)	3	3	—	—	—	4	4	4	4
Side	1	1	—	4	4	4	4	4	4
Side (IIHS)	—	—	1	1	1	1	1	1	1
Offset	1	1	3	3	3	3	3	3	3
Head Restraints (F)	1	—	3	—	1	1	1	1	1
Rear	—	—	1	—	—	—	—	—	—
Rollover Resistance	—	—	—	—	—	5	5	5	5

Mazda

626, MX-6, MAZDA6 ★ ★ ★ ★

RATING: *Mazda6:* Above Average (2003–06). *626:* Recommended (1999–2002). *626, MX-6:* Above Average (1996–98); Average (1994–95); Not Recommended (1985–93). Tall drivers should be wary of the low headrests, which can be hazardous in a collision, and short drivers will want to ensure they can see adequately without getting dangerously close to the airbag housing. **"Real" city/highway fuel economy:** *Mazda6 2.3L:* 9.6/6.7 L/100 km with a manual transmission or 10.4/7.5 L/100 km with an automatic. *Mazda6 3.0L:* 12.1/8.1 L/100 km with a manual or 12.3/8.1 L/100 km with an automatic. *Mazda 626 2.0L:* 9.4/6.8 L/100 km with a manual or 11.3/7.9 L/100 km with an automatic. *Mazda 626 2.5L:* The 6-cylinder gets 11.8/8.5 L/100 km with a manual or 12.2/8.5 L/100 km with an automatic. There isn't a lot of difference in fuel consumption rates between these models. Although the newer versions like the Mazda6 are a bit more fuel frugal, their higher price tag means any savings are illusory. Owners also say fuel savings vary by at least 15 percent. **Maintenance/Repair costs:** Higher than average. Repairs aren't dealer dependent, however, so save bagfuls of loonies by frequenting independent repair shops. **Parts:** Easily found, but sometimes costly. Although Mazda has promised to cut prices, you should still compare prices with independent suppliers. **Extended warranty:** An extended powertrain warranty is recommended as protection against automatic transmission breakdowns and other factory-related defects. **Best alternatives:** Acura Integra; GM Cavalier or Sunfire; Honda Accord; Hyundai Elantra wagon, Sonata, or Tiburon; and Toyota Camry. **Online help:** Owner reports, customizing tips, performance upgrades, and service bulletins can be found at *www.automotiveforums.com*, *www. autosafety.org/autodefects.html*, *www.kbb.com* (*Kelley Blue Book*), *www.edmunds.com*, *www.car-forums.com/forums*, and *www.cartrackers.com/Forums*.

Strengths and Weaknesses

Although far from being high-performance vehicles, these cars ride and handle fairly well and still manage to accommodate four people in comfort (except for the MX-6 coupe). The 1988–92 versions incorporate a third-generation redesign that adds a bit more horsepower to the 4-banger. Apart from that improvement, these cars have changed little over the years and are still easy riding, fairly responsive, and not hard on gas. On the downside, the automatic transmission downshifts roughly, the power steering is imprecise, and the car leans a lot in turns.

Four-wheel steering was part of the sedan's equipment in 1988, and it was added exclusively to the MX-6 a year later. Wise buyers should pass over this option and look instead for anti-lock brakes and airbags on 1992 LG and GT versions. The manual transmission is a better choice because the automatic robs the engine of much-needed horsepower, as is the case with most cars this size. A passenger-side airbag was added to all '94 models.

The MX-6 is a coupe version of the 626. It has a more sophisticated suspension, more horsepower, and better steering response than its sedan alter ego. The 1993 model gained a base 2.5L 165-hp V6 powerplant. Overall reliability and durability are on par with the 626.

The 1995–97 models offer improved performance, handling, and overall reliability plus reasonable fuel economy. Owners still complain, though, of subpar body construction, electrical system and cruise control glitches, dim headlights, brakes and AC compressors that wear out prematurely, and automatic transmissions that shift poorly and are prone to premature failure. The Check Engine light comes on and goes off repeatedly because of oil spilling into the airflow sensor or leaking of the intake manifold gasket. Expect jerky downshifts when the 4-cylinder is at full throttle. Shocks and struts (MacPherson) aren't very durable and are expensive to replace (especially when the model is equipped with the electronic adjustment feature).

Body problems include windshield mouldings that flake and fall off; door and hatch locks that often freeze up; a loose dash on the right side; an interior door panel that pulls away; fading interior colours; headliner rattles; and metal surrounding the rear wheelwells that is prone to rust perforation, as are hood, trunk, and door seams. The paint seems particularly prone to chipping. The underbody and suspension components on cars older than five years should be examined carefully for corrosion damage. The exhaust system rarely lasts more than two years, and wheel bearings fail repeatedly within the same period.

VEHICLE HISTORY: 1998—Attractive Mazda Millenia-type styling, a longer wheelbase and larger cabin, a reinforced body to keep creaks and rattles to a minimum, and more powerful engines. **1999**—A larger selection of standard accessories. **2000**—Restyled and substantially improved with a small horsepower boost (5), and enhanced handling, steering, and interior appointments. **2001**—Improved sound system, an emergency trunk release, and user-friendly child safety seat anchors. **2003**—Arrival of the Mazda6. **2004**—A four-door hatchback and wagon are added and some models come with larger wheels. **2005**—Standard antilock braking and traction control; a 6-speed automatic transmission replaces the 5-speed unit for "s" models.

Owners of 1998–2002 models report malfunctioning automatic transmissions, engine head gasket failures, fuel system glitches that cause sudden acceleration and stalling, faulty airbags, and electrical shorts that result in the Check Engine light staying lit and engine stalling or shutdown.

Other complaints point out that shifting isn't all that smooth, nor is the automatic gearbox very reliable; the car is hard-riding over uneven pavement; there's too much body lean in turns; excessive torque steer (pulling) to the right often occurs when accelerating; road noise intrudes into the cabin; the rear spoiler blocks rear visibility; and the trunk opening isn't conducive to loading large objects. As if that wasn't enough, Mazda has a history of automatic transmission and fit and finish deficiencies and scheduled maintenance overcharges (check out the CBC TV *Marketplace* archives).

Mazda6

The 2003 through 2005 Mazda6 is offered with one of two powerplants: an impressive 160-hp inline 4-cylinder that equals the Accord's entry-level engine, or a 220-hp V6 that trumps the Camry's 192 horses but comes up a bit short when compared with the 240 horses unleashed by the Accord and Altima. Either engine can be hooked to a 5-speed manual or automatic transmission that also offers a semi-manual "Sport Shift" feature.

Don't get the idea that this is a warmed-over 626. It's set on an entirely new platform and carries safety and convenience features never seen by its predecessor, such as two-stage airbags and a chassis engineered to deflect crash forces away from occupants. Wider than the Accord, the Mazda6's interior allows for a comfortable ride and carries an unusually large trunk.

During its first year on the market, there was a wide range of owner complaints that have become fewer with more recent models. Owners mention various water leaks, omnipresent interior and exterior clunks (suspension), and a number of driveability concerns that include poor engine and transmission performance (clutch failures, predominantly):

> In early June my Mazda6 MTX began to experience a problem with the transmission. Whenever I would accelerate, the rpms would increase by 1k [1000] then decrease by about the same amount before the transmission would catch and the power would be distributed to the wheels. Now a little over a month later, my clutch is almost completely worn out. I'm taking my car in to get this checked out, but the car shouldn't be experiencing any problems with the clutch/transmission when it's still under 26,000 miles [42,000 km].

Also, the 5-speed transmission is difficult to shift in its lower gears, hesitates when accelerating or decelerating, and gets stuck in gear. Many owners report chronic stalling and hard starts, defective engine knock sensors, noisy brakes and steering, electrical shorts everywhere, a rotten-egg smell that pervades the interior, window motor failures, wipers that don't sweep fast enough to remove rain, rust-like stains in the door sashes and trunk lids, excessive condensation on the inside bottom of the front windshield, paint bubbling, dash rattles, the separation of the radiator's bottom seam, and waits of a month or more for replacement parts.

Safety Summary

All models/years: The 626's different iterations have registered far fewer complaints than their Asian, European, or American counterparts. • One Canadian neurologist told *Lemon-Aid* that early 626 head restraints are set too low and cannot extend to a safe level • Inadvertent airbag deployments or airbags that fail to deploy in a collision. • Sudden, unintended acceleration. • Frequent automatic transmission malfunctions and failures. **All models: 1999**—Left lower strut bolts loosen, bend, and break, causing the driver-side wheel to fall. • Premature tire wear. • When AC engages, engine hesitates and causes car to jerk. • Automatic transmission shift shock. • Transmission fails upon deceleration; it downshifts harshly, O/D (Overdrive) light flashes, and then engine compartment starts to fill with transmission fluid. • Headlights dim intermittently. • Excessive vibration at low speeds. • Seat belts won't properly secure a child safety seat. **2000**—Cylinder head failures at the #2 cylinder. • 4-cylinder engine stumbles badly in cold weather. • Automatic transmission jerks during 2–1 shifts, lurches into gear because of sudden high revs, and sometimes won't go into gear. • Cracked passenger-side rear axle. • Check Engine light stays on. **2001**—Automatic transmission jerks into gear. • Seat belts fail to retract. **2002**—Driver's side seat belt unlatched during an accident. • Jerky automatic transmission shifts. • Loose front wheel bearing. • AC constantly blows cold air. • Excessive right-side vibration when vehicle is underway. • Bridgestone tire tread separation. *Mazda6:* **2003**—Hard starts. • Steering failures. • Sickening exhaust fumes smell like rotten eggs. • Centre defroster vent doesn't close completely, allowing condensation to form and impair visibility. • Child injured hand in door handle. **2004**—Injury from airbag:

Driving in stop and go traffic. Speed of about 15 mph [24 km/h] when a car 3 cars ahead of me quick[ly] stopped. I hit the car in front of me, and both airbags deployed. Fumes and powder or dust of some sort came out of airbag, landed on my hand and gave me a 2nd degree burn.

• Fuel line detached from engine on two occasions:

I have a 2004 Mazda6 S. I have had two incidents where the fuel line has detached from inside the engine and the car has stalled and gasoline has poured out from underneath the car. The first time, the dealership told me that there was a recall and I should receive [notification] in the mail. I later found out there was no recall. They then fixed the car supposedly, and three months later it happened again.

• Dangerous automatic transmission design cuts engine power when passing another vehicle:

> Vehicle design problem that could easily result in fatality. 2004 Mazda6 S. This is the transmission that can either be run as full automatic or as a semi-manual shift. When in a passing situation with the throttle fully open, the engine jumps into action and the transmission down shifts as it should. However, if the gas pedal is kept pressed down as in a passing situation, the transmission will not up shift at any point. The result is that the engine rpms will increase to the point of hitting the red line. At that point another feature shuts down the engine until the rpms are significantly below the red line. The result is loss of power at the most critical time in the passing maneuver.

• Total brake failure. • Brakes suddenly disengage and then re-engage with a severe jolt. • Early severe brake rotor warpage. • Airbag light comes on due to cracked front sensors that short out from water ingress. • Rear windshield shatters because the defroster shorts out. • AC fogs up the windshield. • Passenger-assist handle above the rear seat breaks off. • Driver electronic door lock often will not allow occupant to open car door from the inside (help!). **2005**—Car is slow to accelerate from low speeds. • Harsh shifts, automatic transmission slippage, getting stuck in gear (has to be put into manual mode), and dropping into the next lower gear for no reason. • Manual transmission seizure.

Secret Warranties/Internal Bulletins/Service Tips

2002—Rough idle, hesitation, and stumble. • Grinding, rubbing noise at front of vehicle. • Tips to silence wind noise around doors. *Mazda6:* **2003**—Seat fails to heat. • Doors hard to close in cold weather. • Sticking traction-control system switch. • Trunk lid staining. • Wind noise around doors. **2003–04**—Inoperative turn signals. **2003–05**—Procedures to cure an engine camshaft ticking noise. • 1–2 gear shift shock with automatic transmission. • Engine speed fluctuation when shifting. • Manual transmission clutch noise, vibration upon warm-up. • Front brake squeaks and moans. • Erratic seat heater operation. • Driver-side kick panel falls off. • Lower windshield fogging. **2003–06**—Rough idle and hesitation. • Excessive body vibration. • AC won't go into recirculation mode. **2004**—Engine surging at 80 km/h. • Hesitation or rough idle at high altitudes. • Remedies for brake judder and moan. • Special Service Program #60 to replace the fan control module. • Special Service Program for evaporative emission-system leak monitoring failures. • Special Service Program for O_2 sensor failure. • Front suspension popping, clunking. **2005**—Surging at 60–90 km/h with the 2.3L 4-cylinder engine.

626, MX-6, MAZDA6 PROFILE

	1997	1998	1999	2000	2001	2002	2003	2004	2005
Cost Price ($)									
626	19,995	19,995	20,140	20,140	23,175	23,470	—	—	—
MX-6	23,325	—	—	—	—	—	—	—	—
Mazda6	—	—	—	—	—	—	24,295	24,395	23,795
Used Values ($)									
626 ▲	4,000	4,500	5,500	7,000	8,000	10,000	—	—	—
626 ▼	3,500	4,000	5,000	6,000	7,500	8,500	—	—	—
MX-6 ▲	3,500	—	—	—	—	—	—	—	—
MX-6 ▼	3,000	—	—	—	—	—	—	—	—
Mazda6 ▲	—	—	—	—	—	—	13,000	15,500	18,000
Mazda6 ▼	—	—	—	—	—	—	11,500	14,500	16,500
Reliability	3	3	4	4	4	4	4	4	4
Crash Safety (F)	—	4	4	4	4	4	5	5	5
Side (626 4d)	3	3	3	3	3	3	3	3	3
Side (IIHS)	—	—	—	—	—	—	1	1	1
Offset	—	3	3	5	5	5	5	5	5
Head Restraints	1	—	1	—	1	1	1	1	1
Rollover Resistance	—	—	—	—	—	—	5	5	5

Note: The 2003–05 Mazda6 earns a higher "Marginal" score for head-restraint protection if the vehicle doesn't have optional lumbar adjustment.

Nissan

ALTIMA ★ ★ ★

RATING: Average (2002–06, 1993–97); Above Average (1998–2001). Here's the Altima dilemma: Until 1997, these cars were bland-looking but fairly reliable, though so-so, performers. Thereafter, performance was improved incrementally as prices remained quite reasonable. Then the totally new, stylish, high-performance 2002 Altima changed everything. Sure, it's a great highway performer, but few can pay the $24,000–$30,000 entry fee. Moreover, safety- and performance-related defects are extraordinarily frequent and difficult to diagnose. And finally, word has gotten around that these redesigned models are troublesome and resale value has plummeted. Writes this owner of a 2003:

> Is it possible that Nissan's commitment to quality, customer service, and related policies to customer satisfaction are only window dressing, and is it possible that they have adopted Ford's policies to quality and customer satisfaction?

Nevertheless, at my "wit's end" with the Altima, and after less than two years of problem-plagued ownership, last night I visited a local Hyundai dealer, only to learn that the black book value of my 2003 Altima is only $15,000.

Watch out for early model bargains: The 140-hp 4-cylinder engine barely provides the necessary versatility needed to match the competition. Although the SE gives the sportiest performance, the less expensive GXE is the better deal from a price/quality standpoint. You will need an extended powertrain warranty, though, to protect you from automatic transmission failures on 1998–2001 models and a more extensive warranty to protect you from post-2001 Altima defects. **"Real" city/highway fuel economy:** *2.5L:* 10.3/7.3 L/100 km with a manual transmission or 10.3/7.4 L/100 km with an automatic. *3.5L:* 11.3/8.3 L/100 km with a manual or 12.3/8.3 L/100 km with an automatic; 11.5/7.3 L/100 km when equipped with a 6-speed manual tranny. *1.8L:* 8.8/6.2 L/100 km with a manual or 9.0/6.5 L/100 km with an automatic. *2.0L:* 9.9/7.0 L/100 km manual or 9.8/7.2 L/100 km automatic. *2.4L:* 10.9/7.6 L/100 km with the automatic. Although the upgraded 2002 versions are peppier, owners say fuel savings are much less than estimates show—sometimes they are off by as much as 20 percent. **Maintenance/Repair costs:** Higher than average. Repairs are dealer-dependent. **Parts:** Owners complain of parts shortages on the 2002 and later versions. Parts on earlier models are relatively inexpensive. **Extended warranty:** A comprehensive extended warranty is a must-have for all model years. **Best alternatives:** Acura Integra; later model GM Cavalier or Sunfire; Honda Accord; Hyundai Elantra wagon, Sonata, or Tiburon; Mazda 626 or Mazda6; and Toyota Camry. **Online help:** For the latest owner reports, service bulletins, and money-saving tips, look at *www.autosafety.org/autodefects.html*, *www.alldata.com*, *www.kbb.com* (*Kelley Blue Book*), *www.edmunds.com*, *www.carforums.com/forums*, and *www.cartrackers.com/Forums*.

Strengths and Weaknesses

The 1993–97 Altima's wheelbase is a few centimetres longer than the Stanza's, and the car is touted by Nissan as mid-size, even though its interior dimensions put it in the compact league. The small cabin seats only four, and rear-seat access is difficult to master because of the slanted roof pillars, inward-curving door frames, and narrow clearance.

Expect only average acceleration and fuel economy with the pre-2002 4-cylinder engine. It has insufficient top-end torque and gets buzzier the more it's pushed. In order to get the automatic to downshift for passing, for example, you have to practically stomp on the accelerator. Manoeuvrability is good around town but twitchy on the highway. There are no reliability problems reported with the 16-valve powerplant; however, the 5-speed manual transmission is sloppy and the automatic transmission's performance has been problematic through the '97 model year. Later years through 2001 are a better choice from reliability and fuel-economy standpoints. The uncluttered under-hood layout makes servicing easy. Body assembly is only so-so, with more than the average number of squeaks and rattles.

The 2002–05 redesigned models are shaped like Passats with Maxima hearts, and provide scintillating V6 acceleration, flawless automatic transmission operation, good braking, well laid-out instruments and controls, and better-than-average interior room and craftsmanship.

Highway handling isn't impressive. The 4-cylinder engine isn't as refined as the competition and is noisy when pushed, and the V6 acceleration overpowers this car and causes excessive rear-end instability and steering pull to one side. Brakes tend to lock up on wet roads; interior appointments lack panache; there's limited rear headroom; expect snug rear seating for three adults and obstructed rear visibility; the dashboard reflects onto the windshield; dash gauges wash out in sunlight; and parts are often back-ordered. Quality problems multiply as these cars age. Says this owner of a 2003 Altima:

> I have reported: abysmal floating, wander, and continual correction at highway and in-town speeds; an overabundance of torque steer; and exorbitant amounts of buffeting leading to excessive driver correction and fatigue, uncertainty, and fear.

> I have reported intermittent clanks in the front end when getting into the vehicle and coming to a stop, all of which cannot seem to be duplicated by Nissan techs or service managers. This is further exacerbated by well known and documented facts that the rear struts are faulty and are commonly replaced, faulty front struts also require replacement, and there is a fix for faulty front suspension components. I have previously reported the handling characteristics to that of a full-size minivan towing a boat or trailer driving behind a transport truck. Certainly not the same characteristics communicated by Nissan. I have also reported the ride to be extremely harsh. Traversing bumpy roads with or without occupants in the rear seat, the ride is unstable. Road noise and small cracks and bumps are also amplified and quite apparent.

The car's 175-hp 2.5L 4-cylinder engine is almost as powerful as the competition's V6 powerplants, and the optional 245-hp 3.5L V6 has few equals among cars in this price and size class. And when you consider that the Altima is much lighter than most of its competitors, it's obvious why this car produces sizzling (and sometimes uncontrollable) acceleration.

Owners report engine surging, stalling, and hard starting, possibly because of a defective engine crank sensor or throttle switch; an annoying and hazardous dash reflection onto the windshield; electrical glitches; and excessive brake wear, noise, and pulsations. Snow builds up in the small wheelwells, making steering difficult and causing excessive shimmy; the clutch pressure plate throw-out bearing and flywheel may fail when downshifting into Fourth gear; rear shocks are noisy and failure-prone; the ABS warning light stays lit; and there's lots of ignition noise in the radio speakers.

VEHICLE HISTORY: 1993—Altima debuts with a 140-hp 2.4L 4-cylinder engine, a driver-side airbag, and poorly designed, uncomfortable motorized shoulder belts. **1994**—Dual airbags and no more motorized belts. **1995**—Freshened styling.

1998—Slightly restyled with a barely larger interior, de-powered airbags, and degraded handling. 2000—Slightly restyled again to look longer and wider; engine gets five more horses (155 hp); and suspension/chassis enhancements improve handling somewhat and make for a quieter ride. 2002—Completely revised with two high-performance engines (a 180-hp 2.5L 4-cylinder or an optional 240-hp 3.5L V6), a larger interior, and a more supple ride combined with sportier handling. Quality declines. 2003—Inconsequential trim changes. 2005—The sporty new SE-R model arrives with a 260-hp V6. Other V6 models now use a 5-speed automatic, and the interior trim is also upgraded throughout the lineup.

Problem areas with early models are prematurely worn, noisy front brakes, fuel system malfunctions, transmission and electrical system failures, and body glitches. The 1998–2001 models have generated fewer complaints, but owners still report sudden acceleration and stalling; front brakes locking up or failing completely; failure of the airbags to deploy; transmission breakdowns; and poor body fit and finish, notably causing water leaks (mainly in the trunk) and body squeaks and rattles.

Safety Summary

All models: 2000—Exhaust fumes enter vehicle. • Dashboard bursts into flames while vehicle is underway. • Vehicle continues to accelerate when slowing down to a stop or when put into Reverse. • Chronic stalling. • Automatic transmission won't stay in gear. • The rear wheelwell's inner fender has sharp, jagged edges. • Windshield cracks frequently. **2001**—Sudden, unintended acceleration. • Engine will suddenly shut down. • Engine motor mount failure. • Automatic transmission makes a grinding or clunking noise when shifting. • Defective sway-bar bushing. • In one incident, wheel fell off, causing vehicle to slam into a wall. **2001–03**—Airbags fail to deploy. **2002–03**—Safety defects become more common as these cars age. • Dealerships said to be aware of redesigned Altima's tendency to catch fire. On one occasion, fire erupted after collision; fire ignited because of a faulty fuel injection system on another occasion, and also ignited while vehicle was cruising on the highway. • Vehicle was idling and then suddenly went into Reverse and accelerated as groceries were being unloaded from the trunk (dash indicator showed car in Park). • Driver run over by his own car when it slipped into Reverse. • Sudden acceleration when brakes are applied. • Transmission slips and engine hesitates when accelerating. • Chronic stalling. • Windshield distortion. • Exhaust-pipe hanger pin catches debris that may ignite. • Crankshaft position sensor failure. • Tail lights constantly fail. • Battery suddenly blows up. • Seat belt fails to retract. • Instrument panel gauges wash out in sunlight. **2004**—Sudden stalling and hard starts. • Vehicle starts, but won't move forward. • Brake rotors completely wear out during first year. • Rear windshield shatters as door is closed. • Rear seat belt will not slacken when pulled gently. • Right front tire falls off vehicle. • Car is a "hostage-taker":

> The problem that I face now is that I cannot get out of my car!!!!!! I arrived home one day and found that the driver's side door would not open from the inside. I am

7 months pregnant and was very scared when I found this problem. What if there is ever a car fire or an accident and I cannot get out? You can open the door from the outside but not the inside. Hyannis Nissan claims it's a door latch problem and it had to be replaced. So since my warranty just ran out I have to pay $192.00 to get this repaired. Are you kidding me?

2005—Sudden, unintended acceleration while parking. • Seat belts fail to lock when Altima is rear-ended. • Rear control bar breaks (see TSB #NTB05-114b in "Secret Warranties/Internal Bulletins/Service Tips," below):

Rear passenger control bar (2 rods) broke at the weld while driving and caused my car to spin out of control, causing damage to the tire, and the rear housing. I had my car towed to a Nissan dealership. This was the poorest customer service ever. I was told it would not be covered under either warranty that I carry. I was told to turn it over to my insurance company. I feel that Nissan is not taking responsibility for something that was a manufacturer's problem. This same part has a recall in other states, just not Florida?

• Transmission hesitates and then slams into gear. • Excessive steering vibration resolved:

I have a 2005 Nissan Altima 3.5 SL. Last summer I was having problems with the car's handling at highway speeds. I had the car aligned, replaced all 4 tires, one by one and was still having [problems] with the car—which was shaking at speeds over 60 mph [97 km/h]. I took it to the dealer again and they determined that the shaking was like a turbulence effect. The spoiler under the car was not allowing the wind to flow through properly, which was causing the shaking effect at highway speeds.

Secret Warranties/Internal Bulletins/Service Tips

All models/years: Diagnostic and correction tips for brake vibration and steering wheel shimmy. • TSB #NTB99-028 outlines the procedures necessary to fix slow-to-retract seat belts. • TSB #NTB00-037a covers possible causes of the vehicle's pulling to the side. **All models: 1998–2000**—Troubleshooting a rattling in the engine compartment. • Tips for eliminating brake vibration and shudder. **1999–2000**—A sunroof that jams when opening rearward requires a readjustment of the sunroof links. • Guidelines as to what constitutes suspension strut leakage qualifying for warranty coverage are found in TSB #NTB99-001. • Remedies for a noisy automatic transmission. **2002–03**—Hard starting (see first bulletin on following page). • Chronic loss of power (see second bulletin on following page). • Excessive engine, fuel-sloshing, and suspension noise. • Front door trim fabric separation. • Low power, poor running, and MIL stays lit. • Inoperative AC; warm air flows from vents. • Poor heater performance. • AC temperature isn't adjustable. • AC drain hose may leak into interior. • Howling noise when clutch is released. • Rear suspension and radio speaker noise. • Sunroof wind noise and water leaks. • Water leakage on front floor area. • Wind noise from doors. • Sunroof won't close at highway speeds. • Faulty Airbag warning light. • Wheel cover squeak, click. •

ENGINE WON'T CRANK IN PARK/WILL CRANK IN NEUTRAL

BULLETIN NO.: EL02-028; NTB02-083   DATE: JULY 30, 2002

2002–03 Altima (L31) with automatic transmission

SYMPTOMS: If an applied vehicle shows all of the following symptoms:

- Engine does not crank when the gear shift selector lever is in Park (P) position,
- Engine does crank when the gear shift selector lever is in Neutral (N),
- Incident usually happens if the engine is at normal driving temperature rather than cold,

The Service Procedure has two steps: Part A—Check the Park/Neutral Switch Adjustment, adjust if necessary; Part B—Adjust the Automatic Transmission Control Cable, at the Slotted Transmission Control Arm. Remove any play or "slack" in the cable.

Automatic transmission slips in Reverse and won't brake when in Drive 1 range, also makes a clicking noise. • Headliner rattle. • Poor heater performance. **2002–04**—The control valve assembly may be the culprit responsible for erratic shifting. • Grease streaks on front-door glass. **2002–05**—Secret 13-year extended warranty on the rear subframe:

HESITATION ON ACCELERATION

BULLETIN NO.: EC03-003; NTB03-022   DATE: MARCH 15, 2003

2002–03 Maxima (A33) only with manual transmission; 2002–03 Altima (L31) only with V6 (VQ35) engine and manual transmission

SYMPTOMS: An Applied Vehicle has a momentary hesitation when accelerating between 2000 and 3000 rpm.

ACTIONS: Replace the Mass Airflow Sensor; Perform ECM reprogramming.

CAMPAIGN—REAR SUSPENSION MEMBER, BUSHING REPLACEMENT

BULLETIN NO.: NTB05-114B   DATE: MARCH 24, 2006

VOLUNTARY SERVICE CAMPAIGN REAR SUSPENSION REPLACEMENT/BUSHING REPLACEMENT AND SEALING

On some model year 2002–05 Nissan Altima and 2004–05 Nissan Maxima vehicles, there is a possibility that corrosion of the rear sub-frame may occur. Corrosion is most likely in cold climates where heavy salting of roads is common practice in freezing conditions. A mixture of road salt and water can promote corrosion in the rear sub-frame bushings of some vehicles. In severe cases, cracking of the rear sub-frame may occur, which may result in a knocking noise coming from the rear of the vehicle. The performance or handling characteristics of the vehicle are not affected and it is safe to drive the vehicle. On most vehicles, Nissan will replace the rear sub-frame assembly. On some 2005 Model Year vehicles, where sub-frame replacement is not necessary, Nissan will replace and seal the front bushings and seal the rear bushings.

WARRANTY EXTENSION: To ensure the highest levels of customer satisfaction, Nissan is also extending the warranty for cracking of the rear sub-frame due to corrosion to a total of 13 years with unlimited mileage on all model year 2002–05 Nissan Altima and 2004–05 Nissan Maxima vehicles. Vehicles included in the Service Campaign (as described above) are also covered by the Warranty Extension.

• If the automatic shifter is hard to move or the sliding plate is deformed, replace both. • Replacing the seal and insulation can eliminate front-door wind noise. **2002–06**—Oil cooler oil leaks do *not* require the replacement of the complete engine oil cooler assembly, says TSB #NTB06-029. **2003–05**—Nissan's bulletin admits that a harsh-shifting condition is factory-related:

A/T—HARSH 1–2 SHIFT

BULLETIN NO.: AT04-014 AND NTB05-001   DATE: JANUARY 3, 2005

4-SPEED AUTOMATIC TRANSMISSION HARSH 1–2 SHIFT
2003–05 ALTIMA; 2003–04 MAXIMA; 2003–05 SENTRA; 2004 QUEST.

IF YOU CONFIRM: The transmission fluid is full (correct level) and in good condition (not burnt), and
- There is a harsh shift from 1st to 2nd gear, and/or
- DTC P0745 (line pressure solenoid circuit) is stored,

ACTIONS:
1. Drain and remove the transmission oil pan.
2. Push/pull the ground terminal and wire for the solenoid valve assembly (see Service Procedure step 4).
   - If it doesn't come off, solder the terminal.
   - If it does come off, replace the solenoid assembly.
3. After soldering, recheck the ground terminal and wire (see Service Procedure step 8).
   - If it's tight, repair is complete.
   - If it's loose, replace the solenoid assembly

2004—Hard starts or no-starts may signal the need for a new fuel pump assembly. • Engine won't crank in low temperatures. • Alternator noise after engine shut off. • Window noise when engine activated. **2004–05**—Measures that will silence a rattling, buzzing exhaust system.

ALTIMA PROFILE

	1997	1998	1999	2000	2001	2002	2003	2004	2005
Cost Price ($)									
XE/S	20,798	19,398	19,898	19,998	19,998	23,498	23,798	23,798	23,798
GXE/SE	21,398	21,998	22,698	22,698	22,698	27,698	24,675	24,298	29,098
Used Values ($)									
XE/S ▲		2,000	3,000	4,500	5,500	7,000	8,500	12,500	15,000	17,500
XE/S ▼		1,500	2,000	3,000	4,500	5,500	7,000	11,000	14,000	16,000
GXE/SE ▲		3,500	4,000	5,500	6,500	8,000	9,500	14,500	17,500	21,000
GXE/SE ▼		3,000	3,500	4,500	5,500	6,500	8,500	13,000	16,000	19,500

Reliability	4	4	4	4	4	2	2	2	2
Crash Safety (F)	4	3	3	—	4	4	4	4	5
Side	—	3	3	3	3	3	3	3	3
Side (IIHS)	—	—	—	—	—	1	1	1	1
Offset	—	—	—	2	2	5	5	5	5
Head Restraints (F)	2	—	2	1	1	3	3	3	3
Rear	—	—	—	—	—	2	2	2	—
Rollover Resistance	—	—	—	—	—	4	4	4	4

Toyota

CAMRY, SOLARA ★ ★ ★

RATING: Average (1997–2006); Above Average (1985–96). Interestingly, the older models offer more quality than the latest versions. The Solara, a two-door Camry clone, is outrageously overpriced when bought new; however, the 1999–2003 models are good buys because they are more reasonably priced. Of all the model years, I'd go for the 2001 Solara (its third year out) for a few thousand more and a better build quality. The LE V6 sedan, particularly the 2001 version, is one of the best Camrys from a quality/price standpoint. Just a word of caution: 1997–2005 model Camrys and Solaras have elicited an unusually high number of safety complaints that are carried over from one model year to the next. The complaints include hesitation followed by sudden acceleration; engine compartment fires; V6 engine failures from sludge buildup; automatic transmission breakdowns; transmission interlock failures, which allow a parked vehicle to roll away; severe wandering at highway speeds; loss of braking; and poor headlight illumination. There is nothing you can do to prevent these failures, and you may have to force Toyota to pay for their correction through CAMVAP arbitration or small claims court. **"Real" city/highway fuel economy:** *Camry and Solara 2.4L:* 10.1/6.7 L/100 km with an automatic transmission. *3.3L:* 11.7/7.4 L/100 km with a 6-cylinder engine. *Camry 2.2L:* 10.0/6.8 L/100 km with a manual tranny or 9.0/6.5 L/100 km with an automatic. *2.4L:* 10.4/7.3 L/100 km with an automatic. *3.0L:* 11.9/7.3 L/100 km with an automatic. These estimates may be off by as much as 20 percent. **Maintenance/Repair costs:** Higher than average, but repairs aren't dealer-dependent. **Parts:** Parts can be more expensive than for most other cars in this class, making it worth your while to shop at independent suppliers. Parts availability is excellent. **Extended warranty:** Not needed for 1996 and earlier models, but essential for 1997 and later vehicles. **Best alternatives:** The Acura Integra; Honda Accord; Hyundai Elantra wagon, Sonata, or Tiburon; and Mazda6 or 626. **Online help:** Owner feedback, service bulletins, and complaint strategies can be accessed at *www.autosafety.org/autodefects.html*, *www.automotiveforums.com*, *www.kbb.com* (*Kelley Blue Book*), *www.edmunds.com*, *www.carforums.com/forums*, *www.cartrackers.com/Forums*, and through a search engine like Google, using "engine sludge" as the key phrase.

Strengths and Weaknesses

The Camry is basically a Japanese Oldsmobile (the old rear-drive kind); it drives and coddles you. Safety complaints aside, it's an excellent small family hauler because of its spacious, comfortable interior; good fuel economy; and impressive reliability and durability. Just make sure you change the oil more frequently than Toyota (or Lexus, for that matter) suggests for its V6 engine.

The 1985–93 models have few problems, although they're far from perfect. Main areas of concern are failure-prone cylinder head gaskets; suspension and electrical system failures; defective starter drives and ring gear; leaking low-pressure and high-pressure power-steering lines; outer CV boots that split, causing grease to leak; premature brake wear; and some paint peeling and rusting. Premature brake wear, excessive noise and vibrations, and stinky exhaust emissions are persistent problems with all Toyota vehicles, including the current models.

The 1995–96 Camrys are fairly reliable and reasonably priced, but they too have their shortcomings and are getting pretty old. Owners report premature brake failures, excessive brake vibration and wear, faulty window regulators, smelly ACs, and myriad rattles, clunks, and groans that seem to come from everywhere. There is also the first evidence of what will become a decade-old safety defect: surging and shuddering when decelerating, and an automatic transmission that slips out of gear when parked. Still, the number of chronic breakdowns is nowhere near that seen with 1997–2005 Camrys.

"De-contenting" hit Toyota's 1997 and later lineup hard, resulting in many changes that cheapened the Camry and precipitated a huge increase in owner complaints over problems that had never appeared on Toyota vehicles before. Many of these defects continue to reappear to this day. One of the worst problems, first showing up in 1997 and continuing through the year 2000 models, is engine sludge buildup, leading to engine failures that may cost as much as $7,000 to correct (see the "Sienna" section). Toyota has also admitted to engine head gasket leaks for the first time.

Quality problems continue to plague the 1997–2005 models, giving the impression that Toyota is riding on a reputation it no longer deserves. Specifically, owners report failure-prone engine head gaskets and automatic transmissions (to Toyota's credit, both problems are covered by an extended "goodwill" warranty, but this is little solace for the hazardous predicaments, inconveniences, and out-of-pocket expenses they cause); frequent hesitation or stalling out when accelerating or braking; front power windows that often run off their channels; excessive steering-wheel vibrations; constantly irritating brake pulsations, plus brake components (calipers, rotors, pads, master cylinder, and the ABS valve) that wear out early; self-destructing AC; warning lights that constantly come on; charcoal canisters that need early replacement (covered by the emissions warranty, if you insist on it); a suspension that bottoms out when carrying four adults; leaky, noisy struts; water leaking into the car on the driver's side after a hard rain; and moonroofs that are prone to water leaks and annoyingly loud wind noise. Side pillar rattling is also a chronic annoyance.

VEHICLE HISTORY: 1992—No more AWD. Only a hatchback and wagon are offered with a 130-hp 2.2L 4-banger or a 185-hp 3.0L V6, plus a driver-side airbag. **1997**—Totally redesigned to be taller, longer, wider, more powerful, and cheaper (in both senses of the word). Gone are the coupe and station wagon variants. The wheelbase has been extended by 5 cm, giving backseat passengers more room. Other changes—it's powered by a base 133-hp 2.2L 16-valve 4-cylinder engine (taken from the Celica) and an optional 3.0L 24-valve V6 that unleashes 194 horses. Either engine can be mated to a 5-speed manual or an electronically controlled 4-speed automatic. ABS and traction control is standard on all V6-equipped Camrys, rear seats have shoulder belts for the middle passenger, and low beam lights are brighter. **1998**—Optional side airbags and an improved anti-theft system. **1999**—Debut of the Solara; adjustable front headrests; new upholstery. **2000**—Slightly restyled with larger tires and a small horsepower boost (4-cylinder engines). The following year's models remain unchanged. **2002**—Car gets larger and now carries a 157-hp 2.4L 4-cylinder engine. **2003**—Power-adjustable foot pedals are offered. **2004**—SE version gets a 225-hp 3.3L V6 hooked to a revised 5-speed automatic, improved fuel injection, and additional soundproofing. The 3.0L V6 available in the LE and XLE also gets the new 5-speed automatic and gains 18 hp, giving it 210 hp. Standard foglights and an in-dash six-disc CD changer are new to the XLE and XLE V6. **2005**—Standard ABS, and an upgraded automatic transmission for models equipped with a 4-cylinder engine. Less effective rear drum brakes are kept on the entry-level models, while other Camrys have four-wheel discs. Other minor changes include standard steering-wheel audio controls and a rear centre headrest. SEs have a new grille and a firmer suspension. Leather upholstery is a standard feature with the V6 XLE.

Solara

Introduced in the summer of 1998 as a '99 model, the Solara is essentially a longer, lower, bare-bones, two-door coupe or convertible Camry with a sportier power-train and suspension and a more stylish exterior. But don't let this put you off. Most new Toyota model offerings, such as the Sienna, Avalon, and RAV4, are Camry derivatives. Year 2000 models returned unchanged, except for the addition of a convertible version and three additional horses; 2001 models were carried over without any significant improvements.

Relatively rare on the used-car market, a base model Solara will cost you $3,000–$4,000 more than an entry-level Camry sedan. And if you get one with the Sienna and Lexus ES 300's V6 powerplant, you're looking at a few thousand dollars more. You have a choice of either four or six cylinders. Unfortunately, vehicles equipped with a V6 also came with a gimmicky rear spoiler and a headroom-robbing moon-roof. The stiff body structure and suspension, as well as tight steering, make for easy, sports-car-like handling with lots of road feel and few surprises.

Safety Summary

All models/years: Airbag fails to deploy or is accidentally deployed. • Sudden acceleration when braking, shifting, or parking. • Stalling, then surging when accelerating or braking. • Car rolls away when parked on an incline. • Owners report that Firestone original-equipment tires fail prematurely. • Vehicle wanders all over the road or drifts into oncoming traffic. **All models: 1999**—There are 521 safety-related incidents logged into NHTSA's database. Incredible as it may seem, the Camry continues to have serious safety-related defects that aren't much different from what's been recorded for previous model years. They include, in order of frequency: sudden unintended acceleration; airbags not deploying during a collision; inadvertent airbag deployment, injuring occupants; complete brake failure, or extended stopping distances caused by poor braking; chronic engine hesitation when accelerating, or stalling; Check Engine, Airbag, and ABS warning lights coming on constantly; optically distorted windshield; and the transmission not holding when stopped on a hill. **2000**—There are 364 safety-related incidents logged into NHTSA's database. **2001**—There are 193 safety-related incidents logged into NHTSA's database. • Under-hood fire (left side) while vehicle is parked overnight. • Fire ignites from underneath vehicle while driving. • Excessive grinding noise and long stopping distances associated with ABS braking. • Brake pedal pushed to floor, but no braking effect. • ABS brakes suddenly lock up when coming to a gradual stop. • Defective rear brake drum. • Vehicle tends to drift to the right at highway speeds. • Excessive steering wheel vibrations at speeds over 100 km/h. • Entire vehicle shakes excessively when cruising. • Vehicle's weight is poorly distributed, causing the front end to lift up when the vehicle's speed exceeds 90 km/h. • Suspension bottoms out too easily, damaging the undercarriage. • Too-compliant shock absorbers make for a rough ride over uneven terrain. • Rear suspension noise at low speeds. • Automatic transmission slippage. • In once incident, with engine running and transmission in Park position, car rolled down a hill. Two small girls inside of car jumped out, but one was then run over. • Car rolls backward after it is put into Park and ignition key is removed. • Vehicle parked overnight has its rear window suddenly blow out. • Windshield distortion is a strain on the eyes. • Floor-mounted gearshift indicator is hard to read. • Seat belts are too tight on either side and tighten up uncomfortably with the slightest movement. • Shoulder belt twists and won't lie straight. • Leaking suspension struts and strut-rod failure. • Trunk lid may suddenly collapse. • Faulty driver's window track. • Driver-side door latch sticks. • Sulfuric acid odour enters the interior. • Fuel tank makes a sloshing noise when three-quarters full. • Clunking noise heard from rear of vehicle when gas tank is half full. • Tire jack collapses during change of tire. **2002**—An astounding 620 owner complaints up to May 2007 puts the Camry in Ford Focus territory for safety-related failures. • Starter caught on fire in the parking lot; under-hood fire (left side) while vehicle was parked overnight; fire ignited from underneath vehicle while driving. • Airbags fail to deploy:

My brother was involved in a fatal crash in a new 2002 Toyota Camry XLE. The accident occurred in North Carolina and is being investigated by the highway patrol. The car left the highway and rolled over, eventually impacting a tree. The car was equipped with front, side, and side curtain airbags. No airbag deployed in this accident. I believe the lack of airbag deployment was contributory to my brother's death.

• Faulty cruise control causes vehicle to suddenly accelerate. • Sudden acceleration without braking effect. • Brake pedal goes to floor with no braking effect. • ABS brakes suddenly lock up when coming to a gradual stop. • Defective rear brake drum. • Many owners complain of poor brake pedal design:

> Arm that holds up brake pedal is interfering with the driver's foot. Driver stated if consumer had a large size foot, it could easily get wedged and stuck on brake pedal. Foot gets caught between the floormat and the brake arm, needs to be redesigned.

• Front right axle broke six months after car was purchased. • High rear end cuts rear visibility. • Turn signal volume is too low. **2003**—376 safety-related complaints were registered by NHTSA that are mostly identical to the 2002 model's incidents already detailed.

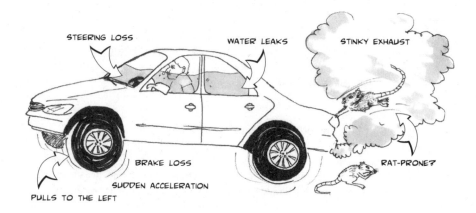

2004—263 safety-related complaints were logged into NHTSA's database, almost double what one would expect for a so-called top quality car. • Fire ignites in the side wheelwell. • Airbags fail to deploy:

> On April 26, 2005, my daughter driving a 2004 Toyota Camry LE (V6) rear-ended another vehicle (an Acura) at a speed of 50+ mph [80+ km/h], and none of the airbags in the Camry were deployed. Drivers of both cars were taken to hospital for further evaluation. Later, I contacted Toyota Corp., which had one of its inspectors inspect the wrecked vehicle and determined "the airbags operated as designed." I have requested on at least two occasions a copy of the inspection report and other related documents and memos from Toyota Corp., and they have refused to provide me with the requested documents. In a May 16, 2005, letter sent to me by Toyota, they have stated that "the SRS airbags are not designed to inflate if the vehicle is subjected to a rear impact, if it rolls over, or if it is involved in a low-speed frontal collision." In

reality, our Camry was not rear-ended, did not roll over, and had a high-speed frontal collision of 50+ mph [80+ km/h].

• Sudden, unintended acceleration when using the cruise control, braking, shifting from Park to Reverse, or pulling into a parking space:

Difficulty shifting from Park to Reverse, then upon shifting into Drive the car accelerated uncontrollably, would not stop, collided with a mobile home, airbags did not deploy, resulting in the death of one passenger and injury of driver.

•

While parking the car, the steering locked turning the car to the right. The car accelerated and surged despite depressing the brake (same as ODI PEO4021), the car broke a metal flag pole, damaged a retaining wall, and fell seven feet [2 m] into a major street. The airbags did not deploy.

•

Caller's mother-in-law just got her car washed and when she pulled out of the car wash, the vehicle accelerated without warning. She pumped the brakes and tried to stop the car, and it would not stop. The car went into an 8-lane highway and was hit by an 18-wheeler and a pickup truck. Driver sustained injuries and so did the driver of the pickup truck.

• Steering U-joint bearing fell out. • Steering knuckle defective:

Steering knuckle defective on 2004 Toyota Camry...a major safety issue. Problem has been going on for two weeks. Now after taking it to an official Toyota dealer repair shop, problem still not fixed. Now at least two weeks to a month wait on part. Was told we were number 536 on waiting list, and was told it was not a safety issue in short term, but do not believe that. Steering is loose, and a catch occurs in steering. Passenger can even feel when this occurs. Dealer has reported three exact same problems with other Camrys in the same week.

• Brake and gas pedal are mounted too close together. • Sudden brake failure. • Brake pedal goes all the way to the floor, and braking distance is increased. • Many complaints that the car drifts to the left into oncoming traffic:

If you don't keep constant pressure on the steering wheel the car will go left at an alarming rate. The amount of drift is so bad that if you remove your hand from the wheel, the steering wheel will turn left by itself. The amount of auto wheel turn is between 3 to 12 inches [7.5–30 cm].

• When in Drive on a hill, the vehicle rolls backward. • When shifted into Reverse, vehicle goes forward. • Transmission shudders when shifted from First to Second gear. • When accelerating, engine and transmission will hesitate for up to four seconds, then will surge forward. This problem extends over several model years and also includes the Lexus ES 300/330:

> Severe hesitation on acceleration. The car reminds me of a 1970s Volkswagen I had that would stall when the gas pedal was depressed. It can be scary accelerating across an intersection with cars coming or pulling out into traffic because of the unpredictability.

• Poorly designed, misadjusted headlights cause a blinding glare. • Backup lights are too dim. • Repeat failures of the cruise-control, odometer, and speedometer control modules. • Airbags are disabled even when a heavy adult sits in the seat. • Inside cabin hood release latch not attached to release mechanism. • The bumpers are easily dented. • Several cases where a Firestone/Bridgestone tire sidewall unravelled. • Premature wearout of Firestone tires. • Original-equipment Goodyear Integrity "all-season" tires perform poorly in snow, and Bridgestones don't have much traction on wet roads:

> I have a new 2004 Camry 4 cyl. LE sedan with 5,500 miles [8,800 km] on the original Bridgestone tires. These tires have very poor traction on rainy roads, and with even light snow you can slide easily at 3 mph [5 km/h] as we did. These tires are dangerous and should not be allowed on the market. Shame on Toyota for putting such sub-standard equipment on their cars. Advertisement says these tires are all-season tires. Bridgestone suggested I pay for upgraded tires. I say why should I pay again for proper all-season tires that were supposed to come on the car?

• Unstable tire jack. • Odometer over-registers by 3 percent (affects warranty, etc.). • Electronic gas mileage calculator is off by 2 km per litre (4.7 miles per gallon). Dealer says they are all off and no repair is being contemplated. • Are 2004 Camrys "rat-prone?" Read the following owner's complaint and decide for yourself:

> O_2 sensors failed due to rodents or rabbits chewing the plastic wiring housing the internal electrical wires. O_2 sensors had to be replaced at a cost of about $600. The outside coatings, or sheaths, for the wiring is made of a soy-based plastic and possibly contains a "fish oil" in the sheath, which attracts rodents and rabbits, and they chew on the plastic wire coverings, thereby destroying the O_2 sensor's wiring mechanism. This problem is prevalent in the Denver and mountain state areas and should be corrected as the problem could lead to engine fires or engine failures. The wiring housing should be changed to a "retardant" type of wiring to prevent other incidents of this problem, and not just for Toyota but for all manufacturers.

2005—157 safety-related complaints have been logged into NHTSA's database, about a third more than usual for a top-quality car. • Vehicle hesitates and then surges. • Sometimes, the Camry will suddenly lurch forward when easing into a parking space:

Our Camry surged forward from its parking space where my mother had pulled in into the opposite parking space and into a parked Ford Explorer SUV, knocking off the Explorer's front license plate completely onto the ground. My sister said she looked down to see if my mother's foot was on the accelerator and it was not, it was on the brake pedal. She heard my mother say "I can't stop!" as she stood on the brake pedal. The car surged forward into the parked Explorer on its own acceleration. We had a Toyota in the early 1980's and had this exact problem resulting in another crash.

•

I was slowly turning right to park in front of a store with my foot on the brakes preparing to stop when my 2005 Camry accelerated, jumped the curb and crashed into a storefront window.

• V6 has chronic hesitation problem at lower speeds. • Engine surges when slowing for a traffic light, or when applying moderate brake pressure. • Airbag panels on some units may have a hole in them. • Car constantly veers left. • Transmission shifts with a jolt when car slows down and then accelerates. • Brake pedal will sink to the floor intermittently. • Windshield has hash marks that obstruct vision when sun shines through. • Continental tire suddenly separates from the rim. • Other Continentals are replaced due to dry rot.

Secret Warranties/Internal Bulletins/Service Tips

All models/years: To reduce front brake squeaks on ABS-equipped vehicles, ask the dealer to install new, upgraded rotors (#43517-32020). • Owner feedback over the last decade as well as dealer service managers who wish to remain anonymous tell me that Toyota has a secret warranty that will pay for replacing front disc brake components that wear out before 2 years/40,000 km. If you're denied this coverage, threaten small claims court action. • Toyota has a special kit to reduce AC odours. **All models: 2002**—Special Service Campaign to replace the driver-side front airbag. • Automatic transmission shift quality improvements. • Catalytic converter heat-shield rattle. • Free replacement of the JBL sound system amplifier addresses popping noise. • Gas cap sticks. • Campaigns to repair the washer reservoir tank; remove coil-spring spacers. • Tips on eliminating sulfur exhaust odours. **2002–04**—Intake manifold rattle. **2002–05**—No more tips on removing odours. Toyota finally "comes clean" and authorizes the free replacement of the catalytic converter on almost its entire lineup. The Camry bulletin is shown at left. **2002–06**—Plugging a front door water leak. • Sunroof binds or squeaks. **2003**—Poor shift quality can be corrected by updating the ECM calibration (TSB #TC008-03). • Engine running lean. •

STINKY SULFUR DIOXIDE ODORS

BULLETIN NO.: EG011-04   DATE: MAY 13, 2004

EXCESSIVE SULFUR DIOXIDE ODORS

2002–05 Camry

Some customers may complain of excessive sulfur dioxide odor on 2002–05 model year Camry vehicles equipped with 1MZ-FE engines under the following conditions:

- Stop and go driving.
- Heavy acceleration.

In order to reduce the sulfur dioxide odor, a new catalytic converter has been developed.

Vibration during 1–2 upshift. • Accessory drivebelt squeal; belt tensioner rattle. • MIL warning light constantly comes on. • ECU-updated calibration. **2003–06**— Tips for silencing intermediate steering shaft noise. • Remedy for a windshield ticking noise. **2004–05**—Could this be the long-awaited fix for the Camry's hesitation in traffic when accelerating?

ENGINE CONTROLS—A/T DOWNSHIFT LAG/GEAR HUNTING

BULLETIN NO.: TC005-05   DATE: JUNE 21, 2005

ECM CALIBRATION: SHIFT FEELING ENHANCEMENT

2004–05 Camry

To improve the transmission shift feeling during specific operating modes, the Engine Control Module (SAE term: Powertrain Control Module/PCM) calibration has been revised. These improvements include:

- Reduced downshift lag when accelerating at speeds from 10 to 20 mph [16–32 km/h].
- Less gear hunting when driving on/off accelerator pedal at 20 to 30 mph [32–48 km/h] (for example: during heavy rush-hour traffic).
- Improved response rate during heavy acceleration from a stop.

• Correction for vehicle drifting or pulling into oncoming traffic:

VEHICLE PULLS/DRIFTS TO THE LEFT

BULLETIN NO.: ST002-04   DATE: FEBRUARY 4, 2004

VEHICLE PULL/DRIFT IMPROVEMENT PROCEDURE (NEW SPRINGS AND IMPROVED STRUTS)

2004 Avalon and 2004–05 Camry and Solara

TSB REVISION NOTICE:

- February 16, 2005: The 2004–05 Solara table in the Parts Information section has been updated.
- December 2, 2004: Title has been changed ("Pull" changed to "Pull/Drift"); VINs have been updated in Production Change Information section; 2005 model year added for Camry & Solara; Parts Information added; and Repair Procedure has been expanded and clarified, including rotation angle of Front Coil Spring Seat Upper.

2004–06—Rear suspension thumping. • Front seat squeaking. *Solara:* **All years:** Water leaking into the trunk area. • Poor durability of rear-view mirrors. **2002– 03**—Harsh automatic transmission shifts (see bulletin on following page). • Excessive brake vibration. • Sliding-roof repair tips (TSB #BO002-03). • Power front seat feels loose (TSB #BO004-03).• Poor AC/heating. **2002–05**—Fuel door hard to open. • Remedy for rotten-egg smelling exhaust. **2004–06**—Convertible top hard to close.

LIGHT THROTTLE SECOND–THIRD GEAR SHIFT SHOCK/SHUDDER

2002–03 Camry

OVERVIEW: Some 2002 and 2003 model year V6 Camry vehicles produced at TMMK may exhibit a triple shock (shudder) during the 2–3 upshift under "light throttle" acceleration. Follow the repair procedure in this bulletin to adjust the condition on applicable vehicles.

CAMRY, SOLARA PROFILE

	1997	1998	1999	2000	2001	2002	2003	2004	2005
Cost Price ($)									
Base Sedan CE	21,178	21,348	21,680	22,180	24,565	—	—	—	—
LE	25,458	25,268	26,508	27,070	27,695	23,755	24,800	24,800	24,990
LE V6	—	—	—	—	—	27,585	27,070	27,070	27,475
Base Solara	—	—	26,245	26,665	27,580	28,175	28,175	28,800	26,850
V6	—	—	29,815	30,270	33,075	33,990	34,290	27,777	30,950
Used Values ($)									
Base Sedan CE ▲	4,000	5,000	6,500	8,000	9,000	—	—	—	—
Base Sedan CE ▼	3,000	4,500	6,000	7,000	8,000	—	—	—	—
LE ▲	5,500	6,500	7,500	9,000	10,500	11,500	14,000	16,000	18,000
LE ▼	5,000	6,000	7,000	7,500	9,500	10,500	12,500	14,500	17,000
LE V6 ▲	—	—	—	—	—	13,500	15,500	17,500	20,500
LE V6 ▼	—	—	—	—	—	12,000	14,000	16,000	19,000
Base Solara ▲	—	—	7,500	9,000	10,500	11,500	15,000	17,500	20,000
Base Solara ▼	—	—	6,500	8,000	10,000	10,500	14,000	16,500	18,500
V6 ▲	—	—	9,000	10,500	12,000	14,500	17,000	19,000	22,500
V6 ▼	—	—	8,000	10,000	10,500	13,000	15,500	17,500	21,000
Reliability	3	3	3	4	3	3	3	3	3
Crash Safety (F)	4	4	4	4	4	5	5	4	5
Solara	—	—	3	3	3	—	3	5	—
Side	3	3	3	4	3	2	3	4	4
Solara	—	—	3	3	3	3	3	5	5
Side (IIHS)	—	—	—	—	—	1	1	1	1
Offset	5	5	5	5	5	5	5	5	5
Head Restraints	—	3	3	—	4	2	2	5	5
Solara	—	—	3	—	3	3	3	3	—
Rollover Resistance	—	—	—	—	5	4	4	4	4

Note: Without head- and torso-protecting side airbags, 2002–06 Camrys receive a side crashworthiness rating of "Poor" from IIHS.

Volkswagen

RATING: Average (2000–06); Below Average (1998–99). The New Beetle's cute styling is no longer a sufficient enticement to draw buyers. Beetle sales are suffering because hard-nosed shoppers want reliability and fuel economy, and they are finding that VW's products are not making the grade. Safety-related complaints registered by NHTSA include electrical fires, chronic stalling, and transmission failures. **"Real" city/highway fuel economy:** *1.8L:* 9.6/7.2 L/100 km with a manual transmission or 10.3/7.3 L/100 km with an automatic. *2.0L:* 9.8/7.0 L/100 km with a manual or 9.6/7.2 L/100 km with an automatic. *1.9L diesel:* 6.2/4.6 L/100 km with a manual or 6.5/5.2 L/100 km with an automatic. Owners report gasoline fuel savings may undershoot the above estimates by at least 10 percent, or 15 percent for diesel fuel. **Maintenance/Repair costs:** Average, but only a VW dealer can repair these cars. **Parts:** Usually easily found, since they're taken mostly from the Golf parts bin, but body parts are harder to find. **Extended warranty:** A good idea. **Best alternatives:** Acura Integra; GM Cavalier or Sunfire; Honda Accord; Hyundai Elantra wagon, Sonata, or Tiburon; Mazda 626; Nissan Sentra; and Toyota Camry. **Online help:** For the latest reports from Beetle owners on their love/hate relationships, plus service bulletins and money-saving tips, look at *www.myvwlemon.com*, *www.vwvortex.com*, *www.autosafety.org/autodefects.html*, *www.alldata.com*, *www.kbb.com* (*Kelley Blue Book*), *www.edmunds.com*, *www.carforums.com/forums*, and *www.cartrackers.com/Forums*.

Strengths and Weaknesses

Why so much emotion for an ugly German import that never had a functioning heater, was declared "Small on Safety" by Ralph Nader and his Center for Auto Safety, and carried a puny 48-hp engine? The simple answer is that it was cheap—it was the first car many of us could afford as we went through school, got our first jobs, and dreamed of…getting a better car. Time has taken the edge off the memories of the hardships the Beetle made us endure—such as having to scrape the inside windshield with our nails as our breath froze—and left us with the cozy feeling that the car wasn't that bad after all.

But it was.

Now VW has resurrected the Beetle and produced a competent front-engine, front-drive compact car set on the chassis and running gear of the Golf hatchback. It's much safer than its predecessor, but, oddly enough, it's still afflicted with many of the same deficiencies that we learned to hate with the original. Again, without the turbocharger, the 115-hp base engine is underwhelming when you get it up to cruising speed (the 90-hp turbodiesel isn't much better), plus there's still not much room for rear passengers, engine noise is disconcerting, front visibility is hindered by the car's quirky design, and storage capacity is at a premium.

On the other hand, the powerful optional 1.8L turbocharged engine makes this Beetle an impressive performer; the heater works fine; steering, handling, and braking are quite good; and the interior is not as spartan or as tacky as it once was.

VEHICLE HISTORY: 2000—Addition of a 150-hp turbocharged 4-cylinder engine, firmer suspension, and improved theft protection. **2001**—Larger exterior mirrors and a trunk safety release. **2002**—Introduction of the 180-hp Turbo S and a new Electronic Stabilization Program. **2003**—Convertible and turbodiesel arrive. **2004**—Upgraded head-protecting airbags and front head restraints, improved spoiler, and new wheels. The GLX model is axed. **2005**—Audio systems include a jack for connecting digital music players.

In a nutshell, here are the New Beetle's strong points: standard side airbags; easy handling; sure-footed and comfortable, though firm, ride; impressive braking; comfy and supportive front seats with plenty of headroom and legroom; and a cargo area that can be expanded by folding down the rear seats.

On the minus side, owners have reported serious safety defects (see NHTSA data, below), powertrain performance is unimpressive, and body construction is second-rate. Here are specific owner gripes: The base engine runs out of steam around 100 km/h and may overheat; diesel engines lack pep and produce lots of noise and vibration; faulty O_2 sensor causes the Check Engine light to come on; frequent ECM failures; axle oil pan and oil pump failures; delayed shifts from Park to Drive, or failure to shift into Fourth gear; car is easily buffeted by crosswinds; optional high-mounted side mirrors, large head restraints, and large front roof pillars obstruct front and rear visibility; limited rear legroom and headroom; difficult rear entry/exit; excessive engine and brake noise; early brake component replacement; malfunctioning dash gauges; awkward-to-access radio buttons and door-panel-mounted power switches; faulty window regulators; skimpy interior storage and trunk space; interior vent louvre loosens and breaks; hatchback rattles and sometimes fails to open; AC disengages when decelerating; front lights retain water and short out; and the low-slung chassis causes extensive undercarriage damage when going over a curb.

Safety Summary

All models: 2000–01—Many complaints of prolonged hesitation when accelerating. • Steering suddenly locks up. • Prematurely worn rear brake pads (TSB #00-01, November 27, 2000). • Low-mounted fuel tank is easily punctured. • Mass airflow sensor and secondary air injection pump motor failures. • Back glass suddenly shatters. • Windows fall into door channel because of defective regulators. • Hard to keep rear window free of rain, snow, or dew. • Windshield distortions impede vision. • Airbags fail to deploy. • Airbag warning light stays lit constantly. • Rear seat-belted passengers hit their heads on the unpadded side pillars. **2002**—ABS failure. • Window goes up and down on its own. • Brake fluid leakage. • Harsh downshifts; vehicle loses power (mass airflow sensor is the suspected cause):

> Car downshifts extremely hard when coming to a stop, causing driver and passengers to be lunged forward in their seats. Dealer states that this is a characteristic of the car. Problem is intermittent and increases when vehicle is warmed up. On one occasion downshift occurred so hard that I thought I was just rear-ended by another car. I bought the car for my wife and now she is afraid to drive it.

2003—Sudden acceleration, stalling. • Side airbag deploys for no reason. • Driver-side airbag fails to deploy. • Punctured fuel tank leaks fuel. • Steering-wheel lock-up; excessive shake; constant pulling to the right (torque steer). • Back glass suddenly explodes. • Rear windshield is hard to see through. • Dash warning lights come on constantly for no apparent reason. • Head restraints still sit too high to be comfortable and obstruct rear visibility. • Open sunroof sucks exhaust into the cabin. • Left front strut slips down through the spindle, causing the spindle to hit the wheelwell. **2004**—Airbags fail to deploy. • Complete transmission failure; replaced transmission also shifts poorly. • Delayed shifting and long hesitation when accelerating. • Sudden stalling and loss of electrical power while underway. • Complete loss of steering. • Electrical shorts cause the odometer and other accessories to malfunction. • Wiper suddenly quits working. • Airbag warning light comes on constantly. • Annoying beep when seat belt isn't buckled. • Driver-side window lowers on its own. • On convertible models, the windows catch on the top when the doors are opened. **2005**—Airbags fail to deploy in a collision. • Owners report the worst of both worlds when describing engine performance. For example, there are reports of the car suddenly accelerating when coming to a stop, or, conversely, losing power when accelerating. • Airbag warning light comes on constantly. • Driver's window exploded.

Secret Warranties/Internal Bulletins/Service Tips

All models/years: Sudden, unintended acceleration. • Airbags fail to deploy when they should. • Door windows separate from regulators. • Lousy radio reception. **All models: 2000–01**—Turn signal blinks too fast. • Prematurely worn rear brake pads. **2000–06**—Removing a musty smell emanating from the air vents. **2001**—Inoperative secondary oil pump. **2002**—Transmission appears to leak fluid. • Inoperative fresh-air blower motor. **2003–04**—Erratic performance of manual transmission's Reverse gear. **2003–05**—Corroded rotors may be the cause of excessive brake vibration. • Convertible top may not operate correctly. **2004**—Hard starting, no-starts, rough running when wet; may emit light gray smoke. • Front-seat passenger airbag disabled when full-sized passenger is seated. • Inoperative rear window heating element. • Monsoon radio amplifier doesn't automatically switch off.

	1998	1999	2000	2001	2002	2003	2004	2005
Cost Price ($)								
Base	19,940	21,500	21,950	21,950	21,950	23,210	23,690	23,910
Used Values ($)								
Base ▲	4,500	5,500	7,000	8,500	10,500	12,500	14,500	17,000
Base ▼	4,000	5,000	6,000	7,000	9,000	11,000	13,000	15,500
Reliability	2	2	3	3	3	3	3	3
Crash Safety (F)	—	4	4	4	4	4	4	4
Side	—	5	5	5	5	5	5	5
Side (IIHS)	—	—	—	—	—	—	1	1
Offset	5	5	5	5	5	5	5	5
Head Restraints (F)	5	5	—	5	5	5	3	3
Rear	3	3	—	—	3	3	3	—
Rollover Resistance	—	—	—	—	—	4	4	4

Note: Used diesel models will cost from $500 to $1,000 more than the gasoline-powered versions. A base 1999–2004 convertible will cost a whopping $5,000 to $7,000 more than a hardtop. Head restraints with adjustable lumbar support on the 2004–05 New Beetle are rated "Good."

PASSAT ★ ★ ★

RATING: Average (2006); Below Average (1998–2005); Not Recommended (1989–97). Don't listen to the car journalists who love European cars like the Passat. They don't pay for service visits. Read owner opinions and you'll see that the Passat is a big disappointment. Word has gotten out that these cars are over-hyped for their performance prowess, that they aren't very dependable, and that they cost a lot to maintain. Consequently, Passats have lost their lustre to Japanese luxury cars, and they now depreciate quickly. But beware; their low price won't cover the extraordinarily high repair bills you'll get from Otto and Hans. **"Real" city/highway fuel economy:** *1.8L:* 9.8/6.9 L/100 km with a manual transmission or 11.7/7.3 L/100 km with an automatic. *2.8L:* 12.7/8.3 L/100 km with a 6-cylinder engine and an automatic tranny. *4.0L:* For an 8-cylinder engine, 14.0/8.9 L/100 km with a 6-speed manual or 13.4/8.8 L/100 km with a 6-speed automatic. Owners say the 8-cylinder engines burn at least 20 percent more fuel than the above figures show. **Maintenance/Repair costs:** Higher than average costs; dealer-dependent. **Parts:** Parts and service are more expensive than average; long waits for parts are commonplace. **Extended warranty:** Yes, principally for the powertrain. **Best alternatives:** Acura Integra, Audi A4 or A6, and Honda Accord. **Online help:** For owner feedback detailing the dark side of VW ownership, go to *www.myvwlemon.com, www.vwvortex.com, www.autosafety.org/autodefects.html, www.alldata.com, www.kbb.com (Kelley Blue Book), www.edmunds.com, www.carforums.*

com/forums, and *www.cartrackers.com/Forums*, or consult a search engine such as Google, using "VW coil pack stalling" or "engine sludge" in your search.

Strengths and Weaknesses

These front-drive compact sedans and wagons use a standard 2.0L engine and other mechanical parts borrowed from the Golf, Jetta, and Corrado. However, a 2.8L V6 becomes the standard powerplant beginning with the '99 wagon. Its long wheelbase and squat appearance give the Passat a massive, solid feeling, while its styling makes it look sleek and clean. As with most European imports, it comes fairly well-appointed.

As far as overall performance goes, the Passat is no slouch. The multi-valve 4-cylinder engine is adequate, and its handling is superior to that of most of the competition. The 2.8L V6 provides lots of power when revved and is the engine that works best with an automatic transmission.

VEHICLE HISTORY: 1990—Debuts with a 134-hp 2.0L 4-cylinder engine. **1993**—A 172-hp 2.8L V6 powers the GLX. **1994**—The 4-cylinder engines are axed. **1995**—Redesigned model adopts dual airbags, a restyled interior, rear headrests, a softened suspension, and a much-improved crashworthiness rating; the 4-cylinder engine returns, and a TDI wagon and sedan debut. **1998**—Based upon the Audi A4 and A6, this model offers more usable interior space, better handling, and better engine performance with its 150-hp turbocharged 1.8L engine and 190-hp 2.8L V6. **2000**—An AWD model, heated front seats, a brake wear indicator, and an improved anti-theft ignition. **2001**—Mid-year changes include a new nose, upgraded tail lights and dash gauges, chassis improvements, and the debut of a 170-hp engine alongside a new W8 270-hp AWD luxury car. **2002**—Given a 134-hp 2.0L turbocharged diesel coupled to either a front-drive or an all-wheel-drive powertrain. Also new is a 5-speed automatic transmission with manual capability. **2003**—W8 is given a 6-speed manual transmission. **2004**—A diesel powerplant joins the lineup, and AWD is offered on more models. **2005**—No more W8 series, GL models only come with a turbodiesel, and the GLX gets 17-inch wheels.

Passats are infamous for automatic transmission failures, engine ignition coil/fuel system stalling and no-starts, and engines gummed up by oil sludge—all costly-to-repair items covered by secret warranties. Even when they're operating as they should, the Passat's manual and automatic gearboxes leave a lot to be desired; for example, the 5-speed manual transmission gear ranges are too far apart (there's an enormous gap between Third and Fourth gear), and the 4-speed automatic shifts poorly with the 4-banger. Also, owners report that the transmission won't shift from lower gears, as well as problems with clutch slave cylinder leaks, front brakes (master cylinder replacements, brake booster failures, rotor warpage, premature wear, and excessive noise), MacPherson struts, and fuel and electrical systems as the car ages. Additionally, defective tie-rod and constant velocity joint seals allow debris to enter into the vehicle's system, effectively causing premature wearout of internal components; engines often leak oil; early replacement of the power-steering assembly is often needed; and fuel and computer module problems lead to hard starts and chronic stalling.

On the body side, there's a helicopter-type wind noise when cruising with the windows or sunroof open; the sunroof rattles; the front spoiler and rear trim fall off; water leaks persistently from the pollen filter; interior trim and controls are fragile; heated seats are a pain in the...well, you know; the driver's seat memory feature fails; door speakers need frequent replacing; rear door mouldings warp easily; the fuel gauge malfunctions, indicating fuel in the tank when it's empty; windshields may be optically distorted; and the rear-view passenger-side mirrors are too small and cause several blind spots.

Owners report that VW dealer servicing is the pits. Cars have to be brought in constantly to fix the same problem, recall campaign repairs are often slow because parts aren't available, and warranty coverage is spotty because VW headquarters doesn't empower or pay dealers sufficiently to take the initiative. Competent servicing and parts are particularly hard to find away from large cities, and many of the above-mentioned deficiencies can cost you an arm and a leg to repair.

Safety Summary

All models/years: Sudden, unintended acceleration. • An incredible number of automatic transmission malfunctions, breakdowns, and early replacements. • Airbags fail to deploy, or deploy for no reason. One VW employee told U.S. federal investigators he was fired shortly after complaining about the airbag hazard:

> The driver-side head airbag (air curtain) of a 2003 Volkswagen Passat W8 sedan deployed spontaneously while I was driving the car...a few minutes later, when the car was stopped, the steering wheel airbag deployed spontaneously...I suffered a permanent wrist injury and am suffering from post-traumatic stress syndrome...the incident, which happened during a test drive, was reported to the management of the VW dealership for which I was working and to the VW of America by the management.

• Airbag light comes on for no reason. **All models: 2000–03**—Many reports of fire erupting in the engine compartment. • Excess raw fuel flows out of the exhaust system. • Hard starts and chronic stalling. • Check Engine light comes on intermittently and then engine shuts down. • While cruising, vehicle speeds up; when brakes applied, it slows down until foot is taken off the brake, then surges again. Owners describe it this way:

> Dangerous situation. When accelerating from a complete stop, vehicle does one of three things: 1) gasps for gas and goes nowhere (dangerous when making left-hand turns), or 2) tries to move ahead like a carbureted car with vapour lock, or 3) performs normally.

• Braking doesn't disengage cruise control. • Hesitation and long delays when accelerating. • Automatic transmission suddenly drops out of gear. • Many complaints of windshield distortion (there's an accordion effect where letters and objects expand and contract as they pass by). • Passenger window suddenly explodes just after being rolled up. • Windshield wipers cut out. • Plastic engine nose shield falls off. • Rear tire failure damages the fuel-filler neck, causing a fuel leak. **2002**—Premature CV joint failure. • Oil pan is easily punctured because of low ground clearance. • Some electrical and fuel system glitches cause chronic stalling (ignition coils still seem to be a primary cause); loss of engine power. • Gas pedal remains stuck to the floor. • Brakes don't grab as well when vehicle is cold; premature brake wear; noisy braking. **2003**—Vehicle runs out of fuel despite the fuel gauge showing one-quarter tank of gas. • Super-heated seats. **2004**—Vehicle lurches forward when braking or accelerating:

> When slowing to a stop transmission/drivetrain occasionally will demonstrate a jarring and potentially dangerous "clunk" as if the transmission is dropping out of the car. The car also lurches forward slightly. We have read that some dealers tell their customers the problem is due to a faulty transmission control module. Our dealer said they could do nothing, denying ever hearing about the problem. We contacted VW-USA and they said they had no knowledge of such a problem. This is clearly untrue!!! There are complaints of this problem all over the Internet. VW is setting itself up for tremendous liability issues should injuries occur because of this problem.

• Engine seizes because of oil sludging. • Transmission control module and clutch failure, hard shifting, and gears slam into place with a clunking sound. • Automatic transmission tends to hesitate and then jumps forward. • Loss of power steering; grinding noise. • Prematurely worn rear brake pads. • Electrical short circuits shut off lights. • Seat heater burns through seat:

> The heated drivers seat in my 2004 VW Passat caught on fire and burned through my wife's jeans. This occurred after driving only 1/4 mile [0.4 km]. She felt something on her leg, and when she looked down there was smoke coming out of the seat. She stopped and got the fire out, but it had burned her (left a red mark on her leg), her jeans, and put a hole in the seat. The local VW dealer was contacted and made aware of the problem, and they are replacing the defective parts on the driver seat. However, when questioned about the passenger seat being defective, it was explained that they have only had a problem with the driver seat. I would think that they used the same materials in both seats and that the reason there has not been a problem with the passenger seat is due to the possibility that it is not used as much.

• Insufficient space between the footrest and clutch pedal; foot gets trapped. • Windshield wiper collects snow and ice in wiper groove. • Water leaking into interior causes serious electrical shorts, primarily affecting the drivetrain:

> Water coming into front passenger seat resulting in damages to the TCM (transmission control module), wet carpeting, and rust under the passenger seat. The transmission module failure resulted in vehicle not able to shift into higher gear, and delay[ed] acceleration. The TCM and carpeting was replaced.

• Tire tread separation; defective valve stems. • Continental tire sidewall bubbling. • Low-mounted oil pan is easily damaged when passing over uneven terrain. **2005**—Chronic stalling may cause engine failure. • Seat belts fail to retract:

> The front and rear seat belts on the left side of my Passat are defective. The driver's belt has been "lazy" in retracting from time to time but it's "normal" now. However, my left rear seat belt has been laying detracted on my seat for about 3 months now simply because nobody ever sits back there and I'm always driving this car for work. By reading message board[s] such as *www.tdiclub.com* this is a very common complaint for the 2004 and 2005 VW Passat.

Secret Warranties/Internal Bulletins/Service Tips

All models/years: Failure-prone, malfunctioning automatic transmissions. **All models: 1995–99**—An erratically shifting automatic transmission may be caused by an improper throttle angle setting. **1996–2006**—Condensation inside exterior lights. **1998–99**—Tips on fixing a door speaker rattle or vibration. • VW says a delayed upshift after a cold start is normal and a wait of 40 seconds isn't too long. (Typical of company logic: "Our cars are perfect; our customers aren't.") **1998–2000**—Defective fresh-air control lever light affects operation of heating/AC system. **1998–2001**—Malfunctioning radio volume control and instrument cluster. **1999**—Engine cranks, but won't start. • Malfunctioning windshield wipers. • Engine misfire. **2000–01**—Airbag warning light remains lit. **2000–06**—Ridding musty odours emanating from the air vents. **2001**—Noisy sunroof. • Broken armrest lid latch. **2003**—Updates for the ECM and TCM modules. **2003–06**—Excessive vibration when braking may be caused by corroded brake rotors. *Diesels:* **2004–05**—Engine hesitation on acceleration.

PASSAT PROFILE

	1997	1998	1999	2000	2001	2002	2003	2004	2005
Cost Price ($)									
Sedan	28,620	28,450	29,100	29,100	29,500	29,550	29,550	29,550	30,190
Used Values ($)									
Sedan ▲	3,500	5,000	6,000	8,000	10,000	13,000	15,500	18,000	21,500
Sedan ▼	3,000	4,000	5,500	7,000	8,500	11,500	14,000	16,500	19,500
Reliability	2	2	2	2	3	3	3	3	3
Crash Safety (F)	4	—	—	5	5	5	5	5	5
Side	—	—	—	4	4	4	4	4	4
Offset	1	5	5	5	5	5	5	5	5
Head Restraints (F)	1	2	2	—	1	1	1	1	1
Rear	—	1	1	—	—	—	—	—	—
Rollover Resistance	—	—	—	—	—	—	4	4	4

Note: The wagon version sells for about $500 more than the Passat sedan.

All ratings on a numbered scale where 5 is good and 1 is bad. See pages 130–132 for a more detailed description.

LARGE CARS

Back to the future. Chrysler has rediscovered rear-drives, after badmouthing them for two decades as they pushed front-drive junk. The final irony is that the rear-drive 300 and Magnum models have their own subset of crappy, failure-prone components (drivetrain, steering, electrical system, suspension, and brakes), leaving drivers with no choice whatsoever.

Honest, officer, I wasn't going that fast… Hey, does that patrol car have a Hemi?

Quintessential highway cruisers for law enforcement agencies, travelling sales-people, large families, or retirees, full-sized American cars are icons of a time long passed. No longer able to compete due to high fuel costs and the availability of more versatile crossover minivans and small sport-utilities, most of these "land yachts" have been axed or are being phased out, as is the case with Ford's Crown Victoria and Grand Marquis.

Chrysler has stayed in the game with its spacious and attractively styled Concorde, Intrepid, and 300M sedans. Unfortunately, these family sedans are several notches below Ford's and GM's when it comes to dependability and highway performance. Chrysler hopes to climb back up the performance and quality ladder with its 2005 rear-drive Magnum wagon and 300 Series equipped with Hemi engines. Early reports, though, aren't all that positive, with 2005's 300 Series racking up a total of 249 safety-related complaints. The 2006s have generated far fewer complaints (60), but more owner feedback is needed to assess their long-term viability.

Owners once had to pay a premium for these behemoths, which usually came fully loaded with performance and convenience features, but they were happy to do so because these vehicles offer considerable comfort and stability at high speeds. They also depreciate relatively quickly (making Fords great used-car bargains), they can seat six adults comfortably, and they're ideal for motoring vacations. Repairs are a snap and can be done almost anywhere, and there's a large reservoir of reasonably priced replacement parts sold through independent agencies.

The downside? Terrible fuel economy, mediocre highway performance, and handling that's neither precise nor exciting. The interior is comfortable but not as versatile as in a minivan or SUV, seniors find entry and exit physically challenging, and you don't get as commanding a view of the road as in taller vehicles.

LARGE CAR RATINGS

Average

DaimlerChrysler Charger (2006)*
DaimlerChrysler SRT8 (2006)*

Ford Cougar, Thunderbird (1985–97)
Ford Crown Victoria, Grand Marquis
    (1996–2006)

Below Average

DaimlerChrysler 300, 300C, 300M,
    Concorde, Intrepid, Magnum
    (2005–06)

Ford Cougar, Thunderbird (2003–05)
Ford Five Hundred (2005–06)*

Not Recommended

DaimlerChrysler Concorde, Intrepid,
    LHS, Vision (1993–2004)

Ford Cougar, Thunderbird (1999–2002)

*See Appendix I.

Station Wagons (Full-Sized)

If passenger and cargo space and carlike handling are what you want, a large station wagon may not be the answer. A used minivan, van, light truck, downsized SUV, or compact wagon can meet your needs and be just as cheap, and it will probably still be around a decade from now. Once-popular rear-drive, full-sized wagons—such as the GM Caprice and Roadmaster (both axed in 1996)—lost out to sport-utilities and minivans a decade ago, and have now been reincarnated as crossover front-drives.

Some disadvantages of large station wagons include difficulty in keeping the interior heated in winter, atrocious gas consumption, sloppy handling, and poor rear visibility. Also, rear hatches and rear brake supporting plates tend to be rust-prone, and the bodies become rattletraps.

DaimlerChrysler

RATING: Below Average (2005–06); Not Recommended (1993–2004). What a disappointing lineup of front- and rear-drives. One would have thought the Mercedes connection would have seen the sharing of top-quality front- and rear-drive components by Daimler. No such luck. Chrysler has gone from subpar front-drive vehicles to rear-drive 300 and Magnum models that are just as unreliable. Sure, they are smartly styled, but that's about all the 2005–06 models offer. Although all of the above-named cars are bargain priced, factory glitches can steal away most of your savings—and endanger your life too. Be especially wary of the discontinued Intrepid, LHS, New Yorker, and Vision. Parts are rare, and mechanics cringe when these hard-to-service cars arrive in their service bays. **"Real" city/highway fuel economy:** *Concorde 2.7L:* 12.6/8.0 L/100 km. *3.5L:* 12.5/7.9 L/100 km. *Intrepid 2.7L:* 11.0/7.4 L/100 km. *3.5L:* 12.5/7.9 L/100 km. Owners report fuel savings may undershoot the above estimates by at least 20 percent. **Maintenance/Repair costs:** Higher than average, but most repairs aren't dealer-dependent. **Parts:** Higher-than-average costs (independent suppliers sell for much less), but not hard to find for models still in production. **Extended warranty:** If you can't get a powertrain warranty, don't give these cars a second glance. In fact, what you really need is bumper-to-bumper protection— a $2,000–$3,000 extra expense. **Best alternatives:** GM Bonneville, Caprice, LeSabre, or Roadmaster, and Ford's early Cougar, T-Bird, Crown Victoria, or Mercury Grand Marquis. **Online help:** *www.datatown.com/chrysler, www.wam. umd.edu/~gluckman/Chrysler/index.html* (The Chrysler Products' Problem Web Page), *www.daimlerchryslervehicleproblems.com* (The Truth Behind Chrysler), *www.intrepidhorrorstories.blogspot.com* (Dodge Intrepid Owner? Read This!), and *www.autosafety.org/autodefects.html.*

Strengths and Weaknesses

DaimlerChrysler's lineup of full-sized cars share the same chassis and offer most of the same standard and optional features. They provide loads of passenger space and many standard features, such as four-wheel disc brakes and an independent rear suspension. Since their 1998 redesign, base models are equipped with a failure-prone 2.7L V6 aluminum engine that delivers 200 hp. Higher-line variants get a more powerful 3.2L V6 225-hp power plant or a 242-hp 3.5L V6. Earlier models also carried a 3.3L 153-hp 6-banger, but 70 percent of buyers chose the 3.5L for its extra horses. Both engines provide plenty of low-end torque and acceleration, but this advantage is lost somewhat when traversing hilly terrain—the smaller V6 powerplant strains to keep up.

The early cars have a better handling and steering response than the Ford Sable and Taurus or GM mid-sized front-drives, but the difference is marginal when you tote up the $3,000–$10,000 cost of powertrain, brake, and AC repairs.

Furthermore, these cars can be as unsafe as they are unreliable. Read the following owners' experiences, which are both scary and typical:

> Travelling on the freeway at 100 km/h, my 1999 Chrysler 300M's rear windshield was sucked out and flew to the side of the road. I had no prior problems with the windshield. Entire rear windshield and casing flew off.

·

> My 2000 Concorde accelerated on its own. I had to hit a tree to stop the car. The airbags did not deploy upon impact. Tires continued spinning after impact, until I turned off the ignition.

Owner reports confirm that there are chronic problems with leaking 3.3L engine head gaskets, engine sludge gumming up the works of the 2.7L engine, and noisy lifters that wear out prematurely around 60,000 km. Water pumps often self-destruct and take the engine timing chain along with them (a $1,200 repair). Complaints of engine surging and unintended acceleration are also frequent refrains regarding all model years. However, the one recurring safety problem affecting almost all model years concerns the steering system. As you can read at *www.daimlerchryslervehicleproblems.com* (The Truth Behind Chrysler):

> Chrysler has been under investigation by NHTSA for more than 55,000 warranty claims for steering problems with these vehicles and 1,450 reports of steering control problems, some including complete loss of steering control....

> Many consumers have also paid over $1,200 (U.S.) for replacement steering assemblies.... Common symptoms of steering problems with these vehicles are typically loose steering, excessive play in the steering, vibration, wandering, steering out of alignment, clunks, rattle, rubbing, or binding.

The 4-speed LE42 automatic transmission is a spin-off of Chrysler's failure-prone A604 version, and owner reports show it to be just as unreliable. Owners tell of chronic glitches in the computerized transmission's shift timing and other computer malfunctions, which result in early replacement and driveability problems (stalling, hard starts, and surging).

Body problems abound, with lots of interior noise; uneven fit and finish with misaligned doors and jagged trunk edges; poor-quality trim items that break or fall off easily; exposed screw heads; faulty door hinges that make the doors rattle-prone and hard to open; distorted, poorly mounted windshields; windows that come off their tracks or are misaligned and poorly sealed; power window motor failures; and steering-wheel noise when the car is turning.

AC failures are commonplace and costly to repair. The problem has become so prevalent that Chrysler has a little-known warranty extension that will pay for the replacement of the evaporator up to seven years. Chrysler has tried to limit compensation to certain models only, but the company is stuck with its 7-year benchmark, first announced over a decade ago, which owners can now cite for any AC failure.

VEHICLE HISTORY: 1994—Debut of a sporty LHS and redesigned New Yorker equipped with variable-assist power steering; Concorde gets the touring suspension and a small horsepower boost (8). **1997**—New Yorker dropped along with the 3.3L V6 on the base LX model. **1998**—Concorde and Intrepid are completely redesigned and given two new V6s (a 200-hp 2.7L and a 225-hp 3.2L), ABS, traction control (on the LXi), and dual front airbags. **1999**—Improved steering and ride. **2000**—Suspension upgrades, a freshened instrument panel, and standard variable-assist steering on the LXi. **2001**—Steering-mounted audio controls, a rear-seat centre shoulder belt, and an internal trunk release. **2002**—The 300M Special performance model comes with a new grille, upgraded ABS, and more user-friendly child safety seat anchors. Concorde gets the LHS's styling and most of the other LHS amenities, including a 250-hp 3.5L V6, leather trim, high-tech gauges, ABS, traction control, and 17-inch alloy wheels. The LXi acquires the 3.2L V6 with a 234-hp variant of the 3.5L V6. **2003**—Intrepid gets a 244-hp 3.5L V6, Concorde horsepower goes to 250, and the 300M's power is boosted to 255 hp. **2004**—All models adopt rear-drive in late-2004, forcing Chrysler to admit that rear-drive models are still very much in demand. **2005**—Debut of the rear-drive 300, 300C, and Magnum.

300M and LHS

These two models represent the near-luxury and sport clones of the Chrysler Concorde. Although they use the same front-drive platform as the Concorde, their bodies are shorter and they're styled differently. In fact, the 300M is the shortest of Chrysler's mid-sized sedans. Both cars are powered by a 253-hp 3.5L V6 mated to Chrysler's AutoStick semi-automatic transmission. Mechanical and body deficiencies generally mirror those of the Concorde and Intrepid.

300, 300C, and Magnum

These rear-drive, full-sized, and feature-laden (standard traction control, electronic stability control, and ABS) sedans and wagons were first launched as 2005 models. Their first year on the market was accompanied by numerous factory-related problems, as well as limited parts supply and problematic servicing due to the cars' new design and relatively small sales volume. With fuel costs rising, the residual value for these cars is plummeting as more buyers flock to more fuel-efficient, light-weight front-drives.

The Chrysler Magnum.

The top-of-the-line Chrysler 300 shares its platform with the sportier Dodge Magnum wagon and comes in three packages: the base model with a 190-hp V6; a Touring version with a 250-hp V6; and the high-performance 300C with a 340-hp V8 Hemi engine. The V8 is rather exceptional and scary. It features Chrysler's Multi-Displacement System, which theoretically uses eight cylinders under load and then switches to 4-cylinder mode when cruising. This is unsettling, because the last time this was offered by (Cadillac in the '80s), owners found their cars running on four cylinders along freeways and then switching to eight cylinders in traffic. AWD is available on Touring and 300C models. V6-equipped models have a 4-speed automatic transmission. AWD and V8 versions use a 5-speed automatic with a manual shiftgate.

Crash test scores are quite good: Frontal crash protection was given five stars, and side-impact protection and rollover resistance scored four stars. 2005 model-year safety-related complaints archived by NHTSA, however, are far more numerous than one can accept, even for a brand new model (249 complaints logged for the 300 Series and another 178 related to the Magnum, as of May 2007). Owner complaints include burns from the seat heater; premature tire wear; chronic stalling and hard starting (especially in vehicles with the Hemi engine); automatic transmission failures; a transmission that hesitates, then slams into gear; steering that freezes or breaks in low temperatures; stabilizer bar separation; persistent electrical shorts; lights that suddenly shut off; a horn that doesn't work; a pulling to the right while driving (the camber bolt service bulletin fix doesn't help); and a rear hatch that seizes shut so that the owner has to crawl through the back of the vehicle to open it.

 Safety Summary

All models/years: No airbag deployment in a collision. • 2.7L engine suddenly self-destructs because of excess oil sludge and overheating. Owners describe the failure this way:

> The primary symptom is that the car heater, for no reason, does not blow hot air. If this has been happening it is likely that your car engine has been overheating and causing sludge to build up in the top half of the engine. Ultimately your engine will fail with very little warning. Some symptoms are: car starts to burn oil, very light traces of white smoke from exhaust, and the engine may seem to run a little rough at idle.

Examine your oil fill cap to see if there is any buildup of a black, grease-like gunk. If you see this, ask a mechanic to check for sludge buildup. If sludge is present, your engine may fail with little or no warning. Cost for repairs averages $6,500 (U.S.). Two excellent websites that cover this problem from both a Canadian and an American perspective are *www.intrepidhorrorstories.blogspot.com/2003_11_01_archive.html* (Dodge Intrepid Owner? Read This!) and *www.autosafety.org/article.php?did=961&scid=122*. Interestingly, Mercedes-Benz recently settled a class-action lawsuit for $32 million (U.S.) over engine sludge breakdowns affecting its 1998–2001 lineup of luxury cars. See *www.legalnewswatch.com/news_182.html*. •

Engine rod bearing failure. • Engine surging and sudden, unintended acceleration. • Many reports of sudden transmission failures, often because of cracked transmission casings. • Transmission fluid leakage caused by defective transmission casing bolt. • Gas fumes enter the interior. • Windshields are often distorted and may fall out while vehicle is underway. • A high rear windowsill obstructs rear visibility. • Headlights may be too dim for safe motoring, may cut out completely, or may come on by themselves. Defrosting may also be inadequate, allowing ice and moisture to collect at the base of the windshield. Chrysler has a fix for these two problems that requires the installation of a new headlight lens and small foam pads into the defroster outlet ducts. • Both ABS and non-ABS brakes perform poorly, resulting in excessively long stopping distances or the complete loss of braking ability. • Brake rotors rust prematurely and warp easily, and pads have to be changed every 15,000 km. • The overhead digital panel is distracting and forces you to take your eyes from the road. • The emergency brake pedal catches pant cuffs and shoelaces as you enter and exit the vehicle. **All models: 1999**—The bolt that holds the fan and engine pulley comes loose, resulting in complete loss of steering ability. • Brakes continually lock up, grind when applied, and result in extended stopping distance. • Vehicle will suddenly shudder or lurch violently while underway at cruising speed. • Fuel smell invades the interior. • Shifter pin to interlock cable breaks off, causing the ignition key to be removable while vehicle is in gear. • Frequent failure of the power window motors. **2000–01**—Transmission won't shift to Reverse, and engine stalls. • Side seat belts don't retract. • Front and rear windshields distort view; there may be an annoying reflection on the inside of the windshield, particularly evident on vehicles with beige interiors. **2002**—Yikes! Transmission malfunctions continue unabated. • Steering drifts; sometimes takes undue effort or squeaks and clunks. • Seat belt button is too sensitive; belt is easily unlatched inadvertently. *300M:* **1999**—Airbags suddenly deploy for no reason when changing lanes. • Transmission jumps from Park to Reverse with engine running. • One driver's son took shifter out of Park without key in ignition, and vehicle rolled down hill. • Vehicle constantly shakes and shimmies, wobbles and bobbles on the highway. **2001**—Sudden stalling in traffic. • Unstable driver's seat. • Fuel tank easily overflows. **2002**—Brake failure, then engine surges. • No-starts. • Sunroof explodes. • Right front wheel disconnects from vehicle. **2003**—Sudden brake and automatic transmission failure. • Surging when stopped. • Rear visibility compromised by narrow rear windows. **2004**—Airbag fails to deploy. • Chronic stalling when driving on the highway, believed to be caused by a faulty camshaft position sensor. • Engine sludge causes engine to seize:

> The 2.7L engine seized without any warning while driving 30–35 mph [48–56 km/h]. The consumer was able to pull over to the side of the road. The vehicle was towed to the dealer. The mechanic informed the consumer [that,] while checking the oil, they noticed sludge and metal flakes....

• Steering-wheel vibration and clicking. • Automatic rear-view mirror operates erratically. • Trunk collects water, interferes with spare-tire access. • Premature wearout of Continental and Goodyear tires. **2005**—Sudden acceleration with the Hemi engine:

> I have a new 2005 Dodge Magnum. The car has the 5.7L Hemi motor. My wife cranked the car and put it in reverse. She then depressed the accelerator and the engine did not respond with any rpm change until the accelerator pedal was depressed in excess of 50%. When the engine did respond, it was violent, causing the car to spin tires and accelerate backward at a high rate of speed, hitting another car in our driveway. This has happened about 6 times and actually happened while the insurance appraiser was in the car... I have posted this problem on a Dodge talk forum and am finding additional people with very similar problems.

• Chronic stalling. • Transmission failure; the car suddenly downshifts to First gear while the vehicle is underway. • Bolts fall from the drive shaft. • Many complaints that the car always pulls to the right. • Seat belts do not restrain a child safety seat sufficiently. • Passenger-side airbag is disabled when a normal-sized passenger sits in the seat. • Rear windows won't go down.

Secret Warranties/Internal Bulletins/Service Tips

All models/years: A rotten-egg odour coming from the exhaust is probably caused by a malfunctioning catalytic converter; this is covered by Chrysler's original warranty and by the emissions warranty. Don't take no for an answer. The same advice goes for all the squeaks and rattles and the water and air leaks that afflict these vehicles. Don't let Chrysler or the dealer pawn these problems off as maintenance issues. They're all due to factory-related defects and should be covered for at least five to seven years. • Paint delamination, peeling, or fading. **All models: 1993–2000**—If the vehicle leads or pulls at highway speeds, TSB #02-16-99 suggests a whole series of countermeasures, including replacing the engine mounts if necessary. • Loose or noisy steering may be corrected by servicing the inner tie-rod bushings or by simply replacing the tie-rod. • Harsh, erratic, or delayed transmission shifts can be corrected by replacing the throttle position sensor (TPS) with a revised part. **1993–2001**—More tips on fixing loose or noisy steering. **1993–2006**—Troubleshooting complaints of a musty odour coming from the AC (TSB #24-006-06). **1995–99**—More troubleshooting tips are offered on diagnosing and fixing trunk water leaks. **1998–99**—Delayed shifts and other transmission malfunctions affecting a broad range of models are addressed in TSB #21-03-98. • Troubleshooting tips for lack of hot or cold air; the PCM may need to be reprogrammed. • Countermeasures for correcting excessive road noise and a variety of squeaks, rattles, and squawks. • Troubleshooting tips for correcting water leaks on top and/or under floor carpets. **1998–2000**—Poor AC performance can be fixed by first carrying out Customer Satisfaction Recall #857 and then reprogramming the PCM. • Repair procedures are outlined for reattaching the rear door trim panel. • Guidelines for silencing wind noise emanating from the sunroof and the area in front of the B-pillars. • Front suspension strut squeaking can be stopped by installing a revised front strut striker cap. **1998–2001**—Loose driver's seat. • Window sticks in the up position. **1998–2004**—Remedy for a 3.5L engine that stumbles or misfires, according to TSB #09-002-03. • Rear headliner sags or rattles. • Erratic AC operation:

AC—ERRATIC OPERATION

BULLETIN NO.: 24-009-01   **DATE: AUGUST 3, 2001**

1998–**2002** (LH) LHS/300M/Concorde/Intrepid

NOTE: PERFORM CUSTOMER SATISFACTION RECALL NO. 857, REPROGRAM PCM, FOR 2000 MODEL YEAR VEHICLES BUILT PRIOR TO AUGUST 30, 1999 (MDH 0830XX).

SYMPTOM/CONDITION: Erratic operation of the AC and heater systems including: lack of cold air, lack of hot air, unrequested mode change (Automatic Temperature Control [ATC] only), no control of mode or temperature control or dithering/tapping blend door noise. These symptoms may be accompanied by the following Diagnostic Fault Codes (DTCs): Blend Door Feedback, Blend Door Stall, A/C Control Mode Door Input Shorted To Battery, In-Car Temp Sensor Failure, ATC Messages Not Received, or Mode Door Stall.

• Remedy for an engine ticking noise (TSB #09-002-04). **1999–2002**—Snapping sound when opening or closing door. **2000–01**—Erratic engine idle. • Front strut noise. • Front suspension or steering gear rattle. • Vehicle leads or pulls. **2000–04**—Fuel tank slow to fill; this has been a chronic problem affecting five model years:

FUEL SYSTEM—FUEL TANK SLOW TO FILL

BULLETIN NO.: 14-001-03   **DATE: JANUARY 24, 2003**

2000–04 (LH) LHS/300M/Concorde/Intrepid

OVERVIEW: This bulletin involves correcting any or all of the following items as necessary:
- Kinked/plugged fuel tank vent lines
- Replacing the fuel tank control valve
- Replacing the Leak Detection Pump (LDP) filter
- Unplugging or replacing the fuel tank fill tube assembly

• Rear strut squeaks. **2001**—Troubleshooting automatic transmission surge and sag and shift bump complaints (TSB #18-007-01). **2002**—Transaxle limp-in; engine misfire; engine no-start. • Discoloured window moulding. **2002–04**—Vehicles equipped with a 3.5L engine that has a rough idle when cold may need the PCM re-calibrated or replaced, a free service under the emissions warranty (see TSB #18-042-03). **2003**—Engine stumbling or misfire. • Defective PCM. • Delayed or temporary loss of transmission engagement after initial start-up. • Transmission goes into "limp" mode. • Harsh 4–3 downshift. • Headliner sag or rattle. • Front brake noise or pulsation. • Poor AC performance. • Rear strut squeaks. • Wind noise from sunroof or B-pillar when driving. **2003–04**—Harsh downshifts. • Poor transmission shifting:

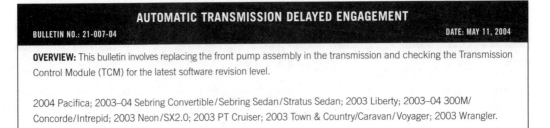

AUTOMATIC TRANSMISSION DELAYED ENGAGEMENT

BULLETIN NO.: 21-007-04   DATE: MAY 11, 2004

OVERVIEW: This bulletin involves replacing the front pump assembly in the transmission and checking the Transmission Control Module (TCM) for the latest software revision level.

2004 Pacifica; 2003–04 Sebring Convertible/Sebring Sedan/Stratus Sedan; 2003 Liberty; 2003–04 300M/Concorde/Intrepid; 2003 Neon/SX2.0; 2003 PT Cruiser; 2003 Town & Country/Caravan/Voyager; 2003 Wrangler.

2005–06—Hard starts with the V6. • Automatic transmission 1–2 upshift shudder or rough shift. • Transfer case shudder on slow-speed turns. • Transmission shudder or buzz due to water contamination; torque converter may require replacement. • Inoperative power-steering tilt. • Sunroof glass not flush with roof; will not close. • Sunroof rattles. • Upper windshield buzz, hum. • Headliner sags. • Gap between rear fascia and body side tail light. • Loose body cladding. • Poor radio reception with the defroster on.

300, 300C, 300M, CONCORDE, INTREPID, LHS, MAGNUM, VISION PROFILE

	1997	1998	1999	2000	2001	2002	2003	2004	2005
Cost Price ($)									
300	—	—	—	—	—	—	—	—	29,995
300C	—	—	—	—	—	—	—	—	43,095
300M	—	—	39,150	39,675	40,900	39,900	40,335	40,910	—
Concorde	26,815	26,915	27,635	28,115	28,485	29,690	30,240	30,775	—
Intrepid	24,055	24,395	25,060	25,520	25,910	25,765	25,095	25,615	—
LHS	40,500	40,500	41,150	41,370	41,655	—	—	—	—
Magnum	—	—	—	—	—	—	—	—	27,995
Vision	24,775	—	—	—	—	—	—	—	—
Used Values ($)									
300 ▲	—	—	—	—	—	—	—	—	19,000
300 ▼	—	—	—	—	—	—	—	—	17,500
300C ▲	—	—	—	—	—	—	—	—	28,000
300C ▼	—	—	—	—	—	—	—	—	26,000
300M ▲	—	—	5,000	6,000	8,000	11,000	13,000	16,000	—
300M ▼	—	—	4,500	5,500	6,500	8,500	10,500	14,500	—
Concorde ▲	3,000	3,500	4,000	4,500	6,500	8,500	10,500	12,500	—
Concorde ▼	2,500	3,000	3,500	4,000	5,000	7,500	9,000	11,000	—

Intrepid ▲	2,500	3,000	3,500	4,000	5,500	7,000	9,000	10,500	—
Intrepid ▼	2,000	2,500	3,000	3,500	4,500	6,000	7,500	9,000	—
LHS ▲	3,000	4,000	5,000	6,000	8,000	—	—	—	—
LHS ▼	2,500	3,500	4,500	5,500	6,500	—	—	—	—
Magnum ▲	—	—	—	—	—	—	—	—	17,500
Magnum ▼	—	—	—	—	—	—	—	—	15,500
Vision ▲	3,000	3,500	—	—	—	—	—	—	—
Vision ▼	2,500	3,000	—	—	—	—	—	—	—
Reliability	1	1	1	1	2	2	2	2	2
Crash Safety (F)	4	—	4	4	4	4	4	4	5
300M	—	—	—	—	3	3	3	4	—
Side	4	—	4	4	4	4	4	4	4
Side (IIHS)	—	—	—	—	—	—	—	—	1
Offset	—	—	—	3	3	3	3	3	5
LHS/300M	—	—	1	1	3	3	3	3	—
Head Restraints									
300/Magnum	—	—	—	—	—	—	—	—	1
300M (F)	—	—	2	—	2	1	1	1	—
300M (R)	—	—	1	—	—	—	—	—	—
Intrepid (F)	1	—	—	2	4	4	4	4	—
Intrepid (R)	—	—	—	—	—	3	3	3	—
LHS	1	—	2	—	3	—	—	—	—
Vision	1	—	—	—	—	—	—	—	—
Rollover Resistance									
300/Magnum	—	—	—	—	—	4	4	4	4
300M	—	—	—	—	—	4	4	4	—
Concorde	—	—	—	—	—	—	5	5	—
Intrepid	—	—	—	—	—	—	5	5	—

Note: All these vehicles are practically identical and should have similar crashworthiness scores, even though not every model was tested in each year.

Ford

COUGAR, THUNDERBIRD ★ ★

RATING: Below Average (2003–05); Not Recommended (1999–2002); Average (1985–97). Flashy, but from a reliability and performance perspective, not one of Ford's better ideas. For readers wondering how these cars could go from Average to Not Recommended, remember that we are reviewing distinctly different vehicles. The early rear-drives improved over the years; however, the 1999–2002 front-drive iteration carries all of the deficiencies of Ford's front-drives coupled with the Contour's and Mystique's own subset of problems. As a first-year vehicle, the Cougar's quality control declined even more (see "Safety Summary" and "Secret Warranties/Internal Bulletins/Service Tips"). As for the resurrected 2003–05's low rating, it has little to show for its high price tag from a performance perspective. **"Real" city/highway fuel economy:** *3.8L: 12.7/8.4 L/100 km. 4.6L: 13.6/8.6 L/100 km with an 8-cylinder engine. 2004 Thunderbird 3.9L: 14.0/9.4 L/100 km.* Owners report fuel savings may undershoot the above estimates by at least 15 percent, or by 20 percent for the 2004 model. **Maintenance/Repair costs:** About average, and most repairs aren't dealer-dependent. **Parts:** Moderately priced (independent suppliers sell for much less) and not hard to find for rear-drives. Front-drive parts, however, are more expensive and not as easily found. And with both the Contour and the Cougar taken off the market, they will likely become rarer. **Extended warranty:** Yes, for the front drives. **Best alternatives:** GM Caprice, LeSabre, or Roadmaster, and Ford's early Cougar, T-Bird, Crown Victoria, or Mercury Grand Marquis. **Online help:** *www.thunderbirdnest.com, www.autosafety.org/autodefects.html, www.blueovalnews.com,* and *www.cougarsunroof.com/faqs.php.*

Strengths and Weaknesses

These are no-surprise, average-performing, two-door rear-drive luxury cars that have changed little over the years. Handling and ride are far from perfect, with considerable body lean and rear-end instability when taking curves at moderate speeds or on wet roadways.

Overall reliability of these models has been average, as long as you stay away from the turbocharged 4-cylinder engine and watch out for 3.8L V6 engine head gasket failures and automatic transmission glitches.

True, these cars offer lots of power, but excessive noise and expensive repairs are the price you pay when they're pushed too hard. Front suspension components wear out quickly, as do power-steering rack seals. Owners of recent models have complained of ignition module defects, electrical system bugs, premature front brake repairs, steering pump hoses that burst repeatedly, erratic transmission performance, early AC failures, defective engine intake manifolds, numerous squeaks and rattles, faulty heater fans, and failure-prone power window regulators.

VEHICLE HISTORY: *Thunderbird:* **1989**—Trimmed down and equipped with a fully independent suspension and a 3.8L V6. A 210-hp Super Coupe (SC) model debuts. **1991**—A 200-hp 5.0L V8 arrives. **1994**—A 4.6L V8 debuts along with dual front airbags and restyled front and rear ends. **1996**—Super Coupe is dropped and more restyling tweaks are added. **1997**—Four-wheel disc brakes and dash/interior touch-ups. **2002**—A new Thunderbird debuts. **2003**—28 more horses for the 3.9L V8 (280), the 5-speed automatic is offered with optional manual-shift capability, and the instrument cluster is upgraded. **2004**—Revised interior trim, restyled wheels, and a new garage-door opener. *Cougar:* **1999**—First year on the market. **2000**—Interior trunk release handle. No more driver-door map pockets. **2001**—Interior and exterior styling revisions.

1999–2002 Cougar

Essentially a Contour spin-off, this Cougar's main attributes are its attractive styling and pleasant handling. However, owners have to accept mediocre acceleration with the base models; problematic transmission performance; a narrow, claustrophobic interior for a four-seater; limited rear seat room; obstructed rear visibility; an ugly and superfluous trunk-lid spoiler; and excessive interior noise.

The front-drive Cougar, restyled as a hatchback, is equipped with a 16-valve, 125-hp 2.0L inline-four or a 24-valve, 170-hp 2.5L V6, later replaced with an upgraded 200-hp powerplant, and optional ABS and side airbags. It shares the Contour's chassis (with 2.5 cm added), base 4-banger, and V6, but its suspension and steering are much tighter. Emergency handling is acceptable, but it's not in the same league as Japanese sedans. The firm suspension and quick, responsive steering make the Cougar both nimble and stable when cornering under speed, especially with the optional Sport Group's rear disc brakes and larger wheels (you'll have to put up with a harder, noisier ride, though). The car is also quite peppy around town, with a good amount of low-end torque. Braking is also good, with little fading after successive stops.

Acceleration is only so-so with the base 4-cylinder or V6 engine, and they both run roughly; the 4-banger is not as refined or fun to push as is the Japanese competition. The 170-hp V6 lacks passing or merging power; 0–100 km/h takes about 10 seconds. The automatic transmission tends to hunt for the proper gear when going over hilly terrain, and there's no way to lock out Overdrive in Fourth gear. The 5-speed hooked to the V6 also shifts roughly. The base suspension doesn't absorb bumps very well, and the optional Sports Group tires produce a busy, jostling ride on any surface that's less than perfect. Steering is also a bit heavy in city traffic.

Owner-reported problems include chronic engine stalling; automatic transmission failures accompanied by slipping or hunting during the 1–2 shift; humming and clanking noises; a manual transmission that's hard to shift from one gear to another; electrical glitches; an engine that increases rpm when shifting; chronic stalling, rough running, and hard starts; premature front and rear brake wear with a low grinding noise or squeak when the brakes are applied; a misaligned trunk lid; sunroof, door, and side-window jamming; door latch failures; doors that lock and unlock themselves; faulty driver-side door weather stripping that produces excessive wind noise; and water leakage into the interior (be wary of car washes).

2002–05 Thunderbird

After a brief hiatus, the Thunderbird name returned affixed to a $56,775 retro-styled two-seater rear-drive convertible that looks nothing like its 1955–57 namesake or the $25,095 '97 model it replaced (now worth about $5,000). This T-Bird shares variations of the engine and chassis used by the Lincoln LS and Jaguar S-Type as well as their 5-speed automatic transmission. Power is supplied by a retuned 280-hp 3.9L V8.

The car is way overpriced. Sure, first owners got lots of bells and whistles for their $50,000, but other cars offer just as much for far less money. Second, this is one dull-looking luxury roadster with few features that distinguish it from half a dozen cheaper imports in the same genre. Other minuses: a tiny, shallow trunk; a cheap-looking, boring instrument panel; limited headroom; an unwieldy folding top cover; and excessive air turbulence when driven with the top down. Ford wants you to believe that the new Thunderbird iteration is true to the heritage of its classic forebears and represents good value for your money. Unfortunately, this Thunderbird proves just the opposite. Head restraints are rated Poor by IIHS, the official launch and delivery was delayed several times because of factory-related problems, the base manufacturer's suggested retail price was double what the original Thunderbird cost just a few years ago, and the car was discontinued in 2005.

Safety Summary

All models/years: Airbags fail to deploy. • Inadvertent airbag deployment. • Transmissions are noisy, won't shift properly, and often won't shift at all. • Frequent reports of sudden brake failures, front brake rotor warpage, and noisy brakes. • Brake pedal sinks below the accelerator pedal level, causing driver to depress the accelerator. • Power window regulator failures. • Electric door locks are failure-prone. • Speedometer and fuel gauge work erratically. • Horn is hard to activate. **All models: 1999**—Driver's airbag deploys after collision, and seat belt fails to lock up. • Sticking throttle causes sudden, unintended acceleration. • Cruise control won't disengage. • Chronic hesitation or stalling; electrical shorts or a faulty fuel pump, fuel regulator, intake gaskets, or idle air control (IAC) solenoid are the prime suspects. • Power steering fails and dash lights go out when car is driven through a rain puddle. This may be caused by the serpentine belt getting wet. • Steering failures because of a broken suspension strut or the tie-rod bolt shearing off. • Plastic fuel tank is prone to early disintegration, contributing to stalling. • Gas tank seal swells and breaks, spilling fuel. • Fuel tank wiring harness melts. • Wheel may crack, causing a tire blowout. • Lug nut wrench doesn't work. • Trunk won't open or close, and remote release is useless. **2000–01**—Broken stabilizer-bar bracket allows wheel to drop under car. • Intermittent brake failure. • Automatic transmission hesitates as it hunts for the correct gear and then shifts with a jerk. • Faulty seal causes fuel tank leakage. • Fuel smell in the interior comes in through the vents; fuel also leaks onto the ground. • Engine hangs in higher rpm when foot is taken off the gas pedal and clutch is depressed. • Lights flicker; loss of all electrical power. • Headlight failures. • Key won't work in the ignition. • Hard to find a child safety seat that fits in the rear. • The silly, non-functional rear spoiler is distracting and cuts rearward vision. **2001**—Engine compartment fire ignites while in traffic. • Brake lights often fail. *Cougar:* **1999–**

2000—Faulty sunroofs. **2002**—Gas fumes seep into the cabin. • Chronic stalling. • Transmission fails. • Frequent failure of the sway bar bushing. • When brakes are applied, vehicle hesitates, then car surges forward. • Fuel pump failures; incorrect fuel gauge reading. *Thunderbird:* **2002**—Water leaks onto the airbag housing. • Frequent stalling, especially when making a left turn. • Driver's seat belt fails to release. • Sun visor can't be tilted toward the driver or passenger. • Convertible top flies up while car is underway. **2003**—Erratic shifting. • Transmission failure. • ABS failure; vehicle hops all over the road. • Front brake caliper comes off and locks wheel up. • Vehicle accelerates when brakes are applied. **2004**—Several reports of sudden acceleration accompanied by loss of brakes. • Passenger-side rear airbag deploys for no reason, burning passenger. • Brake and accelerator pedals are mounted too close together. **2005**—Airbag deploys for no reason:

> We are seeking authorization for repairs to this vehicle. It is very fortunate no one was seriously injured due to the faulty operation of this device. Further, the dealer tells us that the deployment of the side air bag now disables all of the air bags leaving the driver and any passengers in a very vulnerable situation.

Secret Warranties/Internal Bulletins/Service Tips

All models/years: Ford's "goodwill" warranty extensions cover engine and transmission breakdowns up to about seven years. There's nothing like a small claims court action to focus Ford's attention. The same advice applies if you notice a rotten-egg odour coming from the exhaust. **All models: 1993–2000**—Brake vibration diagnosis and correction. **1993–2002**—Paint delamination, peeling, or fading. **1999**—Three bulletins target automatic transmission failures, suggesting that either the Overdrive/Reverse ring gear be replaced or an upgraded transaxle assembly be installed. **1999–2000**—Engine knock. • An exhaust sulfur odour evident just after highway cruising may signal the need to replace the catalytic converter. • Automatic transmission fluid leaks. • Water leaks and wind noise troubleshooting tips. **1999–2001**—No forward gear:

NO FORWARD GEAR ENGAGEMENT

BULLETIN NO.: 00-18-2   **DATE: SEPTEMBER 4, 2000**

1994–97 Probe; 1994–2000 Contour; 2001 Escape; 1994–2000 Mystique; 1999–2001 Cougar

ISSUE: Some vehicles may exhibit no forward gear ranges due to the misalignment of the forward/coast clutch cylinder snap ring with respect to the legs of the forward clutch piston.

ACTION: During assembly of the forward/coast clutch cylinder, the gap in the select fit retaining ring should be located midway (i.e., 45 degrees) between adjacent legs of the forward clutch piston.

• Rear brakes moan or groan:

1999–2001 Cougar

ISSUE: Some vehicles equipped with rear disc brakes may exhibit a "moaning/groaning" noise on initial brake application (cold soak). This may be caused by the rear brake pads vibrating in the caliper. Braking performance is not affected by this condition.

ACTION: Install revised rear disc brake service kit.

• Brake warning light stays lit. **1999–2002**—Harsh, delayed upshifts. • Repeated failure of the heater core. • There's a 10-year secret warranty on fuel pumps:

Ford

Frank M. Ligon
Director
Service Engineering Operations
Ford Customer Service Division

Ford Motor Company
P. O. Box 1904
Dearborn, Michigan 48121

May 2004

TO: All U.S. Ford and Lincoln Mercury Dealers

SUBJECT: Extended Coverage Program 04N02: Supplement #1
Certain 1999 through 2002 Model Year Cougar Vehicles
Fuel Delivery Module – New Design

Ref: Extended Coverage Program 04N02: Dated April 2004
Certain 1999 through 2002 Model Year Cougar Vehicles
Fuel Delivery Module

PURPOSE OF THIS SUPPLEMENT
- Notify dealers of the availability of the new design fuel delivery module.
- Revised technical instructions for the new design fuel delivery module.
- Revised labor times and part information.
- Special required cutting tool – (same cutting tool supplied and used for 03N01).

PROGRAM TERMS
This program extends the coverage of the fuel delivery module (FDM) to 10 years from the original warranty start date of the vehicle, with no limit on the number of miles that the vehicle has been driven. This program provides one-time replacement coverage, and is automatically transferred to subsequent owners.

VEHICLES COVERED BY THIS PROGRAM
Certain 1999 through 2002 model year Cougar vehicles built at the Flat Rock Assembly Plant from May 25, 1999 through November 30, 2001. Affected vehicles are identified in OASIS.

REASON FOR PROVIDING ADDITIONAL COVERAGE
Some of the affected vehicles may experience engine hesitation, loss of power, surging, and other similar symptoms as a result of contamination of the fuel pump. Because the contamination of the fuel pump is progressive, it may ultimately become sufficiently blocked to cause the engine to stall completely. Although the symptoms noted above can occur under a variety of driving conditions, they are most likely to occur when there is less than one-quarter tank of fuel and/or when the driver is attempting to accelerate while making a turning maneuver (such as entering a highway through a cloverleaf) or while driving uphill.

All ratings on a numbered scale where **5** is good and **1** is bad. See pages 130–132 for a more detailed description.

2000—Airbag warning light remains lit. • Low Engine Coolant light on for no apparent reason. • Automatic transmission fluid leakage. • Water leak or wind noise at the upper corner of the B-pillar. 2002–05—Engine misfire may be caused by water in the coil on plug (COP) or the coil wells. • Hard starting or low battery. • Water leaks from convertible top. • Cracked brake lever boot. • Heater core leakage. 2003—No-starts; discharged battery. • Harsh shifting. 2003–05— Steering noise, vibration. 2004—Rough-running, misfiring engine. • Harsh shifts. • Driveline vibration. • Rear brake squealing. 2004–05—Harsh, delayed shifts continue to plague these cars. 2005—Engine knock, ticking.

COUGAR, THUNDERBIRD PROFILE

	1997	1998	1999	2000	2001	2002	2003	2004	2005
Cost Price ($)									
Cougar	23,495	24,995	19,995	20,595	23,655	26,995	—	—	—
T-Bird	23,595	25,095	—	—	—	51,550	56,615	56,775	56,775
Used Values ($)									
Cougar ▲	3,000	3,500	4,000	4,500	6,500	9,000	—	—	—
Cougar ▼	2,500	3,000	3,500	4,000	4,500	7,000	—	—	—
T-Bird ▲	3,500	4,000	—	—	—	23,000	25,000	28,000	34,000
T-Bird ▼	3,000	3,500	—	—	—	20,500	23,000	25,000	32,000
Reliability	3	3	2	2	2	2	2	3	3
Crash Safety (F)	5	5	—	—	—	4	—	4	4
Side	—	3	—	—	3	5	—	5	5
Cougar	3	—	—	—	3	3	—	—	—
Rollover Resistance	—	—	—	—	—	—	—	5	5

CROWN VICTORIA, GRAND MARQUIS ★ ★ ★

RATING: Average (1996–2006). Downgraded from Recommended to Average during the past decade because powertrain failures and other safety-related deficiencies are on the rise. Yet, dollar for dollar, these are good choices, particularly now that high gas prices are stampeding owners into selling their large cars at rock-bottom prices. **"Real" city/highway fuel economy:** 13.9/8.7 L/100 km. Owners report fuel savings may undershoot this estimate by about 20 percent. **Maintenance/ Repair costs:** Average, but some electronic repairs can be carried out only by Ford dealers. **Parts:** Higher-than-average costs (independent suppliers sell for much less), but they're not hard to find. **Extended warranty:** Yes, invest in an extended powertrain warranty. **Best alternatives:** Buick LeSabre, early Ford Thunderbird or Cougar, GM Caprice or Roadmaster, and Toyota Avalon. **Online help:** www.autosafety.org/autodefects.html, www.tgrigsby.com/views/ford.htm (The

Anti-Ford Page), *www.flamingfords.info*, *www.crownvictoriasafetyalert.com*, and *www.blueovalnews.com*.

Strengths and Weaknesses

These rear-drive cars are especially well suited to seniors, who will appreciate the roomy interiors and oodles of convenience features (although entry and exit may require some acrobatics). The high crash protection scores and ease of servicing are also major advantages. Handling, though, is mediocre and can be downright scary on wet roads, where the car can quickly lose traction and fishtail out of control. Passing over small bumps is also a white-knuckle affair—the car bounces around, barely controllable.

Both the 4.6L and 5.0L V8s provide adequate, though sometimes sluggish, power, with most of their torque found in the lower gear ranges. The Lincoln Town Car shares the same components and afflictions as the Crown Vic and Grand Marquis.

As is the case with most full-sized sedans, high insurance premiums and fuel costs have walloped the resale value of both models, making these cars incredibly good used buys. The only caveat is to make sure the undercarriage, powertrain, electronics, and brakes are in good shape before you ink a deal.

VEHICLE HISTORY: 1995—Restyled and given standard heated outside mirrors and a new interior treatment. **1997**—Improved steering and rear air suspension (a horror to diagnose and repair). **1998**—More power steering and suspension improvements. **1999**—ABS and a new stereo system. **2000**—An emergency trunk release, user-friendly child safety seat anchorages, and an improved handling package for quicker acceleration. Last model year for the Crown Victoria in Canada, as the Grand Marquis continues alone. *Grand Marquis:* **2001**—A small horsepower boost, minor interior improvements, adjustable pedals, seat belt pretensioners, and improved airbag systems. **2002**—Traction control to offset the car's notoriously poor wet-weather traction. **2003**—A revised frame and upgraded suspension, plus the debut of a high-performance Marauder equipped with a 302-hp V8, sport suspension, and exclusive trim. **2005**—A sporty LSE version joins the lineup.

On the downside, a number of factory-related problems appear year after year. These include failure-prone fuel pump, sender, fuel filter, and fuel hose assemblies; ignition module and fuel cut-off switch malfunctions that cause hard starting and frequent stalling; brakes (rotors, calipers, and pads), shock absorbers, and springs that wear out more quickly than they should; and chronic front suspension noise when passing over small bumps. Inadequate inner fender protection allows road salt to completely cover engine wiring, brake master cylinder, and suspension components; therefore, frequent inspection and cleaning is required. Hubcaps frequently fall off. Finally, there is such a high number of safety-related complaints concerning brake and fuel lines, suspension, and steering components that an undercarriage inspection is a prerequisite to buying models three years or older. Other annoying body defects include poor fit and finish, trunk leaks, subpar interior materials, and flimsy plastic trim.

Safety Summary

All models/years: Since 1991 to the present, Ford has known that the fuel tanks on these cars are easily punctured in a rear-end accident. Unfortunately, the company has not seen fit to recall the vehicles, even after losing a $43-million lawsuit for the death of the owner of a Lincoln Town Car that burst into flames after being rear-ended. • Fuel line and electrical fires. • Sudden, unintended acceleration. • Cracked intake manifolds cause loss of coolant. • Airbags fail to deploy or deploy for no reason. • ABS brake failures. • Premature brake rotor warpage and pad wearout cause excessive brake noise (grinding), vibration, and extended stopping distances:

> Fleet of 15 police cars, Crown Victoria had the front brake, rotors, and pads replaced every 20,000 miles [32,000 km].

• Brake and accelerator pedals mounted too close together. **All models: 1992–2001**—Rear-end impact may puncture fuel tank; two TSB repairs already carried out. **1998**—NHTSA investigators are looking into reports that the inertia fuel cut-off switch operates when it shouldn't, stalling the vehicle. • Sudden loss of power; stalling. • Traction control engages for no reason, causing loss of power and control. • Steering too sensitive when changing lanes, making it easy to lose control. • Dome light switch is poorly designed; it can be activated only by the driver because of its location. • Loss of lighting caused by sudden electrical system failure. • Rubber hose leading from the fuel tank is easily hit when going over a bump or pothole. **1999**—Sudden stalling while underway (fuel inertia cut-off switch self-activates when vehicle hits a pothole or goes over a small bump). • Steering shaft failure when turning. • Cracked rear trailing-arm assembly frames. • Transmission jumps from Park into gear. • Sticking front calipers cause vehicle to veer to the right or left. • Premature wear of the lower control arm. • Loose rear outer door handles. • Driver's seat misalignment places steering wheel and gas/brake pedals too far to the right. **2000**—Over-sensitive steering causes vehicle to wander. • Power window failures in cold weather. • Headlights short out intermittently. **2001**—When the car is driven in rainy weather, water gets into the engine compartment, causing the water pump to throw the fan belt and leading to loss of control of the vehicle. • Frequent complaints of little traction on wet roads. • ABS failure leading to brake lock-up or loss of braking ability. • Spongy brakes sink to floor with little braking effect. • Vehicle moves forward when shifted into Reverse. • Vehicle rolls back when stopped on an incline. • Windshield wipers fail intermittently and easily freeze up in sleet. **2002**—There continue to be many Crown Victoria complaints concerning the powertrain, fuel tank fire fears, cracked wheel rims, and poor rainy weather performance. • There are also many Grand Marquis complaints concerning sudden acceleration, cruise control not disengaging, and tire sidewall separation (Michelin and others). **2003**—Vehicle struck from behind exploded into flames. • Tire-tread separation. • Missing upper control arm bolt. • Brake booster fails. • Fan belt comes off in rainy weather, causing overheating and loss of power steering, water pump, and other accessories. • Horn "sweet spot" too small; horn takes too much effort to sound. • Sunlight causes a reflection of the defrost vents onto the windshield and poor dash panel illumination. **2004**—Transmission slips; shifts into Reverse on its own. • Excessive steering vibration may be caused by original-equipment wheels and faulty tires. • Turn signal fails intermittently. **2005**—Sudden, unintended acceleration:

> This car has a dangerous defect. Randomly, when in a stationary position, by holding the brakes, the engine and transmission sometimes suddenly accelerate powerfully, making it difficult to hold the car.

• Stuck accelerator. • Fuel tank punctured by road debris. • Brake pedal travel is excessive before brakes are applied. • Horn does not blow.

Secret Warranties/Internal Bulletins/Service Tips

All models: 1985–2002—Repeated heater core failure. **1992–2001**—Measures to protect the fuel tank from puncturing and fuel from igniting during a rear-end collision. Ford has offered free protective shields to police fleets and limousine owners. Motorists can go to dealers to ask for them to be installed at their own expense. This covers every model year for the three regular car types going back as far as 1992. **1993–2001**—An exhaust buzz or rattle may mean you have a loose catalyst or muffler heat shield. • Paint delamination, peeling, or fading. **1994–99**—Tips on preventing wind noise around the doors. **1995–99**—Tips on reducing noise, vibration, and harshness as well as plugging windshield water leaks. **1996–2001**—Faulty intake manifold repairs will be refunded up to $1,000, and a free, retroactive 7-year/unlimited mileage warranty will apply. **1997–98**—Lack of AC temperature control may require a new air door actuator. **1997–99**—Delayed upshifts may require a new 2–3 accumulator along with a revised piston. • A rough idle or exhaust system resonance may be fixed by installing an exhaust system mass damper. **1997–2006**—Hard starts. **1998–99**—A pull or drift when braking in rainy weather can be corrected by installing upgraded front brake linings that are less sensitive to water, says TSB #98-13-4. • A poorly performing AC that also makes a thumping noise may need a new suction accumulator and suction hose assembly. **1998–2000**—Ford Special Service Campaign 00B60 (January 31, 2002) allows for the free installation of control-arm reinforcing brackets or new control arms, regardless of mileage. Ask for a partial refund. **1998–2001**—A Ford Special Service Campaign will replace the engine mounts free of charge on vehicles in fleet service. **1998–2002**—In a separate campaign, the automaker has extended the intake manifold warranty to seven years without any mileage limitation. This campaign is in response to complaints of coolant leakage leading to engine overheating. • Inoperative shift interlock. **1998–2005**—Troubleshooting engine misfires (TSB #04-16-1). **1999–2001**—Correcting a 2–1 shift clunk noise. **1999–2002**—Engine head gasket leakage:

1999–2002 Crown Victoria, Mustang; 1999–2001 E Series, Expedition, F-150, Super Duty F Series; 2000–01 Excursion; 1999–2002 Town Car; 1998–99 Navigator; 1999–2002 Grand Marquis

ISSUE: Some vehicles equipped with the Romeo-built 4.6L 2V engine or 5.4L 2V Windsor and 5.4L Supercharged engine may exhibit an oil leak or oil weepage from the cylinder head gasket at the right hand rear or the left hand front of the engine. Oil weepage is not considered detrimental to engine performance or durability. An oil leak may be caused by metal chip debris lodged between the head gasket and the block, chip debris between the cylinder head and the head gasket, or by damage to the cylinder head sealing surface that occurred during the manufacturing process.

ACTION: Once an oil leak is verified with a black light test at the head gasket joint, replacement of the head gasket can be performed. If the head was damaged by chip contamination, the head should be replaced. A revised "Service-Only" gasket is now released for both of these cases.

2000–01—Troubleshooting a ticking noise in First gear. **2000–03**—Excessive engine grinding noise. **2000–04**—Lack of cooling, or low airflow from the vents. **2000–06**—A special kit will fix seat belts that are slow to retract. **2001**—Correcting a 3–4 shift flare. **2001–02**—Front-end accessory drivebelt slips off water pump pulley when splashed with water (TSB #02-5-4). **2001–04**—Tips on silencing engine ticking (includes replacing the cylinder head). **2003**—Ford says rear axles "may be noisy or exhibit rear axle shaft and/or axle bearing premature wear. This is caused by excessive load, temperature, and inadequate lubrication." Ford will replace the axle bearings under dealer operation code 030505A. • Water in the headlights and erratic headlight operation. • Inaccurate fuel gauge. • Power-steering assist calibration. • Excessive power-steering pump noise. • Front wheel area click or rattle. • Anti-theft system may cause the transmission to stick in Park or the steering wheel to lock. • Defective front coil springs may cause the vehicle to have a harsh ride or the suspension to sit low in the front. Ford will install free revised front coil springs: #3W1Z-5310-EA and #3W1Z-5310-HA. • Cracked wheel rims. Call 1-800-325-5621 to replace the affected wheel(s) up to five years or 240,000 km (150,000 mi.) from the vehicle's warranty start date. **2003–04**—Countermeasures for suspension squeaking or rubbing. • Excessive engine vibration at idle. • An engine knock after a cold start can be silenced by installing a free exhaust shield kit, says TSB #04-2-1. • Ignition-lock cylinder binding. • AC rattling. **2003–06**—Noisy suspension air compressor. **2004**—Vehicle won't shift into Overdrive. **2004–05**—Delayed shifting into Reverse (see bulletin on following page). • Catalytic converter buzzing or rattling. **2005–06**—Sagging driver's seat cushion. • Steering too light at highway speeds. • Premature corrosion of the aluminum body panels.

DELAYED REVERSE ENGAGEMENT

BULLETIN NO.: 05-2-3   DATE: FEBRUARY 7, 2005

2004–05 Crown Victoria, Town Car, and Grand Marquis.

Some 2004–05 Crown Victoria/Grand Marquis/Town Car vehicles may exhibit a delayed reverse engagement, greater than 2 seconds, after shifting the gear selector lever into reverse.

ACTION: It may be necessary to replace the detent spring and adjust the shifter linkage.

CROWN VICTORIA, GRAND MARQUIS PROFILE

	1997	1998	1999	2000	2001	2002	2003	2004	2005
Cost Price ($)									
Crown S/LTD	29,895	30,995	31,895	32,095	—	—	—	—	—
Grand Marquis GS	32,195	32,895	33,695	31,195	34,125	35,120	35,800	36,720	36,735
Used Values ($)									
Crown S/LTD ▲	4,000	5,000	6,000	7,000	—	—	—	—	—
Crown S/LTD ▼	3,500	4,500	5,500	6,500	—	—	—	—	—
Grand Marquis GS ▲	4,500	5,000	6,000	6,500	8,500	11,000	13,500	16,000	19,000
Grand Marquis GS ▼	4,000	4,500	5,500	6,000	7,000	9,500	12,500	14,500	17,000
Reliability	3	3	3	3	3	3	4	4	4
Crash Safety (F)	5	5	5	5	5	5	5	5	5
Side	—	4	4	4	5	4	4	4	5
Side (IIHS)	—	—	—	—	—	—	1	1	1
Offset	—	—	—	—	—	—	5	5	5
Head Restraints	1	—	1	—	1	1	2	2	2
Rollover Resistance	—	—	—	—	5	5	5	5	5

LUXURY CARS

Money Doesn't Matter

The Beatles got it right. Money doesn't buy you love (nor safety, if your 2001–06 Toyota or Lexus hesitates, delays upshifting, and then surges when pulling away from a stop)—and it certainly doesn't buy you quality and reliable performance in many other luxury cars, either. Ask any Audi, Cadillac, Jaguar, Lincoln Continental, Mercedes, Saab, or VW owner. They now know that more dependable and better-performing cars can be bought for half the price from Asian automakers. Heck, surveys show even the Germans prefer Asian brands over their own BMW and Mercedes "luxo-toys."

Same cars, different names

Used luxury cars can be great buys if you ignore most of the hype and remember that many high-end models don't give you much more than the lower priced entry-level versions. For example, the Lexus ES 300 is a Toyota Camry with a higher sticker price; the Audi A4 isn't much different from the Volkswagen Passat; Lincoln's front-drive Continental uses mostly junky Ford Taurus and Sable power-trains; and the Acura 3.2 TL, Infiniti I35 (formerly called the I30), and Jaguar X-Type are fully loaded, high-tuned versions of the Honda Accord, the Nissan Maxima, and the European Ford Mondeo, respectively.

Both high- and low-end models project a flashy cachet; come loaded with high-tech safety, performance, and comfort features; and can be bought, after three years or so, for half of what they sold for as new. Furthermore, if you can get servicing and parts from independent garages, you'll save even more. On the downside, there are overpriced luxury lemons out there (such as the Lincoln Continental and the Cadillac Allanté and Catera) that aren't built anymore and are unreliable, with hard-to-service engines and transmissions and servicing costs that rival Neiman Marcus.

Mercedes-Benz owners, for example, can't say they weren't warned. Over a decade ago, a $5-million study conducted over five years by the Massachusetts Institute of Technology said that the German automaker had begun making lousy cars by committing the same assembly-line mistakes as American automakers: allowing workers to build poor-quality vehicles and then fixing the mistakes at the end. As one reviewer of *The Machine that Changed the World*, by James P. Womack, Daniel T. Jones, and Daniel Roos (HarperCollins, November 1991), wrote:

This study of the world automotive industry by a group of MIT academics reaches the radical conclusion that the much vaunted Mercedes technicians are actually a throwback to the pre-industrial age, while Toyota is far ahead in costs and quality by building the automobiles correctly the first time.

Readers of *Lemon-Aid SUVs, Vans, and Trucks* know from the internal service bulletins I quote extensively that Mercedes' C-Class compacts and M-Class sport-utilities have been plagued by serious factory defects, running the gamut from powertrain failures to fit and finish deficiencies. However, a confidential January 2002 quality survey leaked to the press confirms that Mercedes' quality problems now affect its entire vehicle lineup.

The survey, commissioned by European automakers from TÜV Rheinland, a German auto-inspection and research association, ranked Mercedes 12th in quality control, just behind GM's much maligned Opel. You have to be European to appreciate what a slap in the face this represents to Mercedes-Benz. A few weeks earlier, J.D. Power and Associates had released an American-based study of 156,000 car owners that showed that 5-year-old Mercedes vehicles had a higher-than-average number of problems (engine oil sludge being foremost on 1998–2001 models). Power subsequently lowered the company's rating for quality control to "fair" from "good."

Several years later, German drivers reached the same conclusion as J.D. Power and Associates. The 38,454 members of ADAC, Germany's largest automotive club, who responded to a December 2003 survey rated Volkswagen as number 31, Mercedes as number 32, and Land Rover as number 33 among the 33 brands polled regarding overall customer satisfaction.

European automakers were understandably shocked by their low ADAC rankings, yet they still haven't taken the quality-control steps needed to produce vehicles that can compete with Asian automakers. Industry insiders believe Mercedes' quality problems are symptomatic of a malaise affecting many luxury-car manufacturers: rushing too many new models into production and building cheaper, smaller, bare-bones knock-offs of popular models.

Traditionally, the luxury-car niche has been dominated by American and German automakers. During the past decade, however, buyers have gravitated toward Japanese models. This shift in buyer preference has forced Chrysler out of the market, has made Ford drop its problem-plagued Lincoln Continental, and has GM returning to rear-drive Cadillacs. BMW, Audi, and Porsche are the only European automakers with respectable sales.

Depreciation is your friend

Okay, so you're well advised to choose a Japanese model, but doesn't that mean you'll have to dig deep in your wallet, wiping out most of your expected savings from buying used? Not necessarily. Smart buyers can pick up a fully equipped 2001 Toyota V6 Camry or Avalon for between $10,500 and $12,000, or two-thirds less than what these models originally cost. Similar savings are realized by the purchase of a Honda Accord, Nissan Maxima, or Mazda 626, all of which offer similar equipment, reliability, and performance to Acura, Infiniti, and Lexus models, but for much, much less.

My favourite luxo-toys

I am not a big fan of luxury cars. If I were, however, I would limit my choice to several vehicles that look good, are reliable, and can be relatively easy to maintain. For me, that would be the BMW 325 and the Lexus SC 400.

Older BMWs are almost all good buys, but the 325 series stands out because it comes as a two-door, a four-door, a wagon, and a convertible, and has gradually evolved over the years. A 2001 in good condition can be found for less than $14,000, and models from the mid-1990s cost less than half that. The quality of the cars, the durability of their powertrains, and their overall performance cannot be faulted.

The 2005 BMW 325xi.   The 1995 Lexus SC 400.

The Lexus SC 400 is another luxury car I would have my eye on. A 1993 model sells for just under $15,000, while an equivalent model today would cost over $100,000, including tax. This Lexus gives you gobs of smooth V8 power, first-class build quality, and classic styling.

It's sad but true: There aren't any American luxury cars that can match an equivalent Japanese model for overall reliability, durability, and value. And this isn't because Japanese products are that well made; far from it, as anyone who's purchased an engine-sludged Lexus will attest. No, it's simply because GM, Ford, and Chrysler vehicles are so poorly made that they make everyone else's look better. This fact has been reflected in the head-spinningly high depreciation rates and plummeting market share seen with most large-*cum*-luxury cars put out by the Big Three. GM's rear-drive Cadillac DeVille and Lincoln's Town Car come closest to meeting the imports in overall reliability and durability, yet they still come nowhere near the quality level of many entry-level imports. Examples of lousy American luxury cars abound: The front-drive Chrysler New Yorker and LHS are unremarkable and are plagued by serious powertrain reliability problems, and most GM Cadillacs have been characterized by innovative, albeit unreliable, technology like variable-cylinder engines (the 4-6-8 engine); cobbled-together diesel powerplants; and poorly engineered, high-maintenance, low-quality front-drive components.

What does this foretell for the future of used luxury cars? Prices for American entries will plummet as high fuel and insurance costs take their toll. And Cerberus, Chrysler's new owners, will certainly flood the market with heavily-rebated new cars, trucks, and minivans. A flood of cheap off-lease cars will further cut into prices and give buyers a wider choice among imports and the Detroit Big Three. Finally, we'll likely see the renaissance of rear-drives, with Cadillac and Ford leading the parade, while the equity investors who now own Chrysler decide whether rear-drives are worth the investment.

LUXURY CAR RATINGS

Recommended

BMW 5 Series (1992–2003)
BMW M Series (1997–2006)
BMW Z4 (2003–06)

Infiniti I30 (2000–03)
Lexus ES 300/330, GS 300, IS 300, LS 400/430,
   SC 400/430 (1996–2001)

Above Average

Acura RL (1996–2004)
Acura TL (1996–99)
BMW 3 Series (2001–06)
BMW Z3 (1996–2002)
Ford/Lincoln Mark VII, Mark VIII
   (1995–98)
General Motors Aurora (2001–03)
Infiniti I30 (1997–99)

Infiniti I35 (2002–04)
Infiniti J30 (1994–97)
Infiniti M35, M45 (2006)
Infiniti Q45 (1991–96; 2001–05)
Lexus ES 300/330, GS 300, IS 300, LS 400/430,
   SC 400/430 (1990–95; 2002–06)
Toyota Avalon (1995–2004)

Average

Acura RL (2005–06)
Acura TL (2000–06)
BMW 3 Series (1994–2000)
BMW 5 Series (1985–91; 2004–06)
Ford/Lincoln Continental
   (2000–02)
Ford/Lincoln LS (2005–06)
Ford/Lincoln Mark VII, Mark VIII
   (1994)
Ford/Lincoln Town Car (1995–2006)
General Motors Park Avenue
   (1998–2005)
General Motors Aurora (1995–99)

General Motors Concours,
   DeVille (2002–05)
General Motors Riviera (1995–99)
General Motors STS (2005–06)*
Infiniti I30 (1996)
Infiniti J30 (1993)
Infiniti M35, M45 (2003–05)
Infiniti Q45 (1997–2000)
Kia Magentis (2005–06)
Mercedes-Benz 300 series, 400 series,
   500 series, E-Class (1985–91)
Nissan Maxima (1989–2001)
Toyota Avalon (2005–06)

Below Average

Audi A4, A6 (100), A8, S4, S6,
  TT Coupe (1996–2006)
BMW 3 Series (1984–93)
Ford/Lincoln Continental
  (1988–99)
Ford/Lincoln LS (2000–04)
Ford/Lincoln Mark VII, Mark VIII
  (1986–93)
Ford/Lincoln Town Car (1988–94)
General Motors Park Avenue
  (1991–97)
General Motors CTS (2003–06)

General Motors Eldorado,
  Seville (1992–2004)
General Motors Concours,
  DeVille (1985–2001)
Infiniti G35 (2003–06)
Kia Magentis (2001–04)
Mercedes-Benz 300 series, 400 series,
  500 series, E-Class (1992–2006)
Nissan Maxima (1986–88; 2002–06)
Volvo 850, C70, XC70, XC90, S40, S60,
  S70, V40, V70 (1993–2006)
Volvo 900 series, S80, S90, V90 (1989–2006)

Not Recommended

Audi A4, A6 (100), A8, S4, S6,
  TT Coupe (1984–95)
General Motors Park Avenue
  (1985–90)
General Motors Catera (1997–2001)
General Motors Eldorado,
  Seville (1986–91)

General Motors Riviera (1986–93)
Infiniti G20 (1994–2002)
Jaguar S-Type (2000–06)*
Mercedes-Benz C-Class (1994–2006)

*See Appendix I.

Acura

RL ★ ★ ★

RATING: Average (2005–06), and the RL's price-gouging is almost a felony; Above Average (1996–2004). Basically a fully loaded, longer, wider, and heavier TL equipped with a larger engine that produces less horsepower than its smaller brother. Watch out for the failure-prone, notchy 6-speed manual transmission. There is no justification for pricing the redesigned 2005 version almost $15,000 higher than the 2004. Interestingly, a 2001 can be had for around $10,000. **"Real" city/highway fuel economy:** There's not much difference in gas consumption between the old and new V6 engines. *2004 and earlier V6 models:* 13.0/9.1 L/100 km; *2005 and 2006 V6 models:* 12.9/8.4 L/100 km. These estimates are fairly accurate, according to owners' actual experiences. **Maintenance/Repair costs:** Average; most repairs are dealer dependent. **Parts:** Most mechanical and electronic components are easily found and moderately priced. Some owners report that recall repairs are often delayed because corrected parts aren't available (transmission/transfer case, for example). Body parts may be hard to come by and can be expensive. **Extended warranty:** No, save your $2,000. **Best alternatives:** Consider the departed Acura Legend, BMW's 5 Series, Infiniti's I30 or I35, and the Lexus GS 300/400. You may want to take a look at the TL sedan: It's not as expensive, and it's a better performer, though passenger room is more limited. **Online help:** *www.cbel.com/acura_cars* and *www.acurasucks.com*.

 ## Strengths and Weaknesses

Good (though not impressive) acceleration that's smooth and quiet in all gear ranges, exceptional steering and handling, comfortable ride, loaded with goodies, and top-quality body and mechanical components. The steering can be numb, however, and manual and automatic transmissions are sometimes problematic.

The 3.5 RL is Honda's—oh, I mean, Acura's—flagship sedan. It's loaded with the innovative high-tech safety and convenience features one would expect to find in a luxury car. These include heated front seats, front and rear climate controls, a rear-seat trunk pass-through, xenon headlights (get used to oncoming drivers flashing you with their headlights), "smart" side airbags, ABS, traction control, and an anti-skid system. The 3.5L 210–225-hp V6 mated with a 4-speed automatic transmission provides good acceleration that's a bit slower and more fuel-thirsty than the TL, partly because of the RL's extra pounds. The 2005's 300-hp V6 coupled to a 5-speed automatic (a manual shifter wasn't offered) resolves this problem. The car handles nicely, with a less firm ride than the TL, although steering response doesn't feel as crisp. Interior accommodations, which fit four occupants, are excellent up front and in the rear because of the RL's use of a larger platform than the TL's. Headroom is a bit tight, though, and the 2005's smaller dimensions may irk some buyers who don't mind sacrificing performance for extra room.

VEHICLE HISTORY: 1996—RL replaces the Legend. **1998**—A sportier suspension, alloy wheels, and a three-point rear centre seat belt. **1999**—Side airbags, high-intensity discharge headlights, larger brakes, and a retuned suspension. **2000**—A Vehicle Stability Assist system and upgraded side airbags. **2001**—An in-trunk emergency opener. **2002**—A small horsepower boost (15), OnStar assistance, wider tires, larger brakes, and more sound deadening. **2003**—Improved child safety seat anchors, wheels, and tail lights. **2004**—Minor equipment upgrades. **2005**—A major redesign reduced the car's size, but made it more feature-laden. The '05 model is 10 cm shorter in wheelbase and overall length than its predecessor, but offers standard all-wheel drive, a 300-hp V6 hooked to a 5-speed automatic, more safety and convenience features, and refreshed styling. Safety features include standard front side airbags and side curtain airbags, anti-lock four-wheel disc brakes, anti-skid control, steering-linked xenon headlights, navigation system, and keyless access and ignition.

Owner-reported problems include frequent stalling, a failure-prone, misshifting manual transmission, noisy transmission engagement and steering, malfunctioning accessories, electrical shorts, premature brake wear, and front-wheel liner cracking.

Safety Summary

All models/years: It's interesting to note that the RL has had remarkably few complaints registered by NHTSA. **All models: 1998**—Premature wearout of the front and rear brake pads at around 24,000 km (15,000 mi.). **1999**—ABS failed to respond, resulting in rear-end collision. **2000**—Vehicle suddenly stalls when decelerating or cruising on the highway; transmission replaced, but problem returned. • Premature transmission replacements. **2001**—Transmission shifts poorly when accelerating or decelerating; vehicle stalls at slower speeds. • 6-speed manual transmission misshifts when going from Third to Fourth gear; it engages Second gear instead, causing extensive engine damage. • In cold weather, Second gear is hard to engage and produces a grinding noise. • Sometimes transmission pops out of Second gear. **2002**—Extensive engine damage caused by downshifting into Second gear, grinding:

> Very bad "grind" going into Second gear when the transmission is cold. It takes about 25 minutes of driving until it starts to shift smoothly. The colder the weather is outside, the worse the problem. You can feel the gears grinding in the transmission. I have a petition with over 60 signatures from other RSX owners. This problem can be very dangerous if you are trying to get into Second gear and the transmission is grinding so bad it locks you out.

• Chronic stalling when decelerating. **2003**—Vehicle suddenly stalls while exiting a freeway. • Dashboard display is unreadable in daylight. • Seat belt does not restrain driver. **2004**—Xenon headlights are blinding. **2005**—Inadequate headlight illumination:

> The vertical self-adjusting headlights pose serious safety concerns on unlit roadways, often illumination only 40 feet [12.2 metres] in front of the car. On hilly terrain, the headlights will adjust down as the vehicle starts uphill, illuminating approximately 40 feet [12.2 metres] in front of the vehicle. This also occurs when the vehicle travels over bumps and [with] any minor changes in vehicle attitude. It is very easy to overdrive the headlights, often at speeds less than 20 mph [32 km/h]. You simply cannot see road hazards or pedestrians.

• Suspension bottoms out with a full load and damages the undercarriage:

> I believe the vehicle has a fundamental design flaw. The clearance below the front of the car is insufficient and furthermore [it's] possible the suspension is not strong enough for the weight of the engine. What happened is that I used the car under normal operating conditions and it got damaged. I had three normal size adult passengers and a normal size 9 year old child in the car. No luggage. I pulled into a parking lot at normal speed and there was a loud noise from the front of the vehicle. I have noticed before that the front of the vehicle hits curbs when you park and scrapes when you go up sidewalk ramps, so I was aware that it does not have ample clearance and or/suspension, but in this case with those passengers on board it was worse, the right corner of the bumper got badly damaged.

All models/years: Like Honda's, most of Acura's TSBs allow for special warranty consideration on a "goodwill" basis, even after the warranty has expired or the car has changed hands. Referring to this euphemism will increase your chances of getting some kind of refund for repairs that are obviously factory defects. • Seat belts that fail to function properly during normal use will be replaced for free under the company's lifetime seat belt warranty. • Diagnostic procedures and correction for off-centre steering wheels. **All models: 1996–2002**—A guide to diagnosing and fixing intermittent electrical shorts. **1997–2001**—Master cylinder clutch fluid leakage. **1999**—A navigation system that locks up or resets can be corrected by rewriting the unit's software; a remanufactured unit may also be considered. **1999–2000**—A squeaking, creaking driver's seat is addressed in TSB #00-010. **1999–2006**—Diagnosis and correction of drift/pull problem. **2000**—Troubleshooting noisy automatic transmissions. • Moonroof rattles. • Driver-seat noise. • Steering-wheel clunk. **2000–01**—Stability Assist may activate too soon. • Engine starts and dies when ignition is released. **2000–02**—Low-speed stalling. **2002–06**—Mileage warranty extended by 5 percent. **2003**—Airbag light comes on for no reason. • Troubleshooting automatic transmission malfunctions. **2004**—Sticking fuel-filler cap. **2005**—Hot weather may cause stalling, hard starts caused by vapour lock. **2005–06**—Front brake rattle, squeal. • Defective automatic door locks.

RL PROFILE

	1997	1998	1999	2000	2001	2002	2003	2004	2005
Cost Price ($)									
Base	54,600	55,000	52,000	52,000	53,000	54,000	55,000	55,800	69,500
Used Values ($)									
Base ▲	5,000	7,000	9,000	11,000	13,000	17,000	21,000	27,500	47,000
Base ▼	4,500	5,500	7,500	9,500	11,500	15,000	19,000	26,000	44,000
Reliability	4	5	5	5	5	5	5	5	5
Crash Safety (F)	—	—	4	4	4	4	4	4	5
Side	—	—	—	—	—	—	—	4	5
Offset	3	3	3	3	3	3	3	3	5
Head Restraints	2	—	2	—	1	1	1	1	2
Rollover Resistance	—	—	—	—	—	—	4	4	5

RATING: Average (2000–06); Above Average (1996–99). Every year that these Acuras are redesigned, quality takes a hit and the purchase price becomes even more out of reach. **"Real" city/highway fuel economy:** 11.7/7.7 L/100 km. Owners report fuel savings may undershoot this above estimate by about 10 percent. **Maintenance/Repair costs:** Average cost, but many repairs are dealer dependent. **Parts:** Higher-than-average costs (some independent suppliers sell for much less under the Honda name), but not hard to find. **Extended warranty:** Not needed. **Best alternatives:** Consider the Acura Integra, BMW's redesigned 3 Series, Infiniti's redesigned I30 or I35, Mazda Millenia, and Lexus ES 300. You may want to take a look at Acura's CL coupe: It's not as expensive, and it's as close as you can get to the Accord with lots of standard bells and whistles thrown in. **Online help:** *www.vtec.net* (The Temple of VTEC), *www.acuraworld.com/forums, www.cbel.com/acura_cars*, and *www.autosafety.org/autodefects.html*.

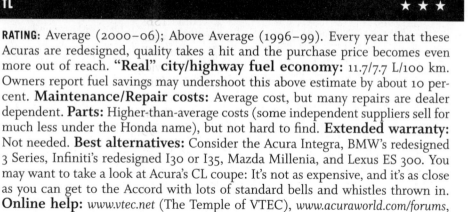

Strengths and Weaknesses

The TL has impressive acceleration, handles well, rides comfortably, and is well put together, with quality mechanical and body components. However, the suspension may be too firm for some, and the vehicle creates excessive road noise and has uncomfortable rear seating and problematic navigation-system controls.

Filling the void left by the discontinued Vigor, the TL combines luxury and performance in a nicely styled front-drive, five-passenger sedan that uses the same chassis as the Accord and CL coupe. Base models will likely carry an adequate, though unimpressive, 2.5L inline 5-cylinder engine. Performance enthusiasts will opt for versions equipped with the more refined 3.2L 225/270-hp V6 mated to a 6-speed manual transmission and a firmer suspension introduced with the 2004 model. It provides impressive acceleration (0–100 km/h in just over 8 seconds) in a smooth and quiet manner, without any fuel penalty. Handling is exceptional with the firm suspension but can be a bit tricky when pushed. Bumps are a bit jarring, and the ride is somewhat busier than other cars in this class, but this is a small price to pay for the car's high-speed performance.

VEHICLE HISTORY: 1998—TLs come with a bit more standard equipment than in previous years. **1999**—The 2.5L engine is dropped, and practically everything else is upgraded. **2000**—Enhanced performance features that include a better-performing 5-speed transmission, a free-flowing intake manifold, side airbags, and depowered front airbags. **2002**—A new performance version based on the CL Type S, a minor face-lift, new wheels and headlights, and more comfortable seat belts. **2004**—New styling, 10 more horses, and more standard safety features. Although the length is shorter by 16 cm, interior room remains unchanged despite the addition of head-protecting curtain side airbags. Other changes include a 6-speed manual tranny, a sportier suspension, high-performance tires, Brembo front brakes, and a limited slip differential.

Interior accommodations are better than average up front, but rear occupants may discover that legroom is a bit tight and the seat cushions lack sufficient thigh support. The cockpit layout is very user-friendly, due in part to the easy-to-read gauges and accessible controls (far-away climate controls are the only exception). Standard safety features include ABS, traction control, childproof door locks, three-point seat belts, and a transmission/brake interlock.

Common complaints involve chronic automatic and manual transmission failures (covered by a "goodwill" warranty), the 6-speed manual transmission shifting roughly into Third gear and sometimes popping out of gear, engine surging and stalling, malfunctioning airbags and accessories, electrical shorts, premature brake and tire wear, and poor body fits. Owners point out that the window regulator may need replacing, the ignition switch buzzes, the trunk lock jams, and the rear bumper is often loose.

Safety Summary

All models/years: Horn is difficult to locate in emergency situations. • Airbags fail to deploy in a collision. • Sudden, unintended acceleration. • Frequent tire failures. **All models: 1998–2001**—Clutch master cylinder fluid leakage. **1999**—Airbags deployed in a collision and severely burned driver's hands. • Seat belt failed to retract in a collision, allowing driver to hit windshield. • Transmission fails to downshift or upshift. • Front rotors warp within 160,000 km (100,000 miles). • Door locks operate erratically. • Wiper blades leak graphite, smearing windshield. • Instrument panel is washed out in sunlight, making odometer practically invisible. **2000**—Brake pedal feels spongy, and it's easy for drivers to confuse the brake and gas pedals. **2001**—Automatic transmission failures that leave the engine revving high (like when passing), but the car doesn't accelerate (it actually slows down). **2002**—Driver's seat belt unreeled during accident. • Automatic transmission failures at high speed. • Transmission grinds when shifting from First to Second gear. **2004**—Side airbags fail to deploy. • Erratic automatic transmission shifting. • Stability control activated right front brake, causing the vehicle to swerve suddenly. • Excessive steering-wheel shake and chassis vibration often blamed on tires, but it can be caused by a defective transmission torque converter. • Cracked alloy wheel rim caused tire failure. • Headlight low beam creates a dark/blind spot. • Multiple malfunctions with the hands-free phone system. • Windshield is easily broken. • Many complaints of hydroplaning and excessive vibration from the Bridgestone Turanza EL42 tires:

> This tire exhibits unsafe characteristics in wet weather, with noticeable drift and hydroplaning in any amount of standing water, even as little as 1/16 inch [1.6 mm]. In heavy rains, even with no standing water present, the tire seems incapable of dispersing water as quickly as it falls, again leading to vehicle instability. From a ride quality point of view, the tire is also unsatisfactory in that it flat spots every morning, especially in cool weather but even in warmer weather as well.

• Windshield wiper washer, power-seat position memory, power mirrors, and auto-dimming mirror often malfunction due to the system's fuse constantly blowing. **2005**—Car pulls to either side when it is underway. • Severe rear brake corrosion and grooving extends stopping distance:

> This could lead to an accident due to the diminished braking capacity. Almost identical pattern on left and right rear rotors. Found during 21K dealer service but was there to lesser extent at about 12–15K.... Rotors and pads were replaced to correct the problem.

• Premature failure of Bridgestone and Michelin tires:

> Tire failure complaint against Acura and Michelin Tire Corporation. The right front tire dislodged completely off of the rim. The portion of the tire which comes in contact with the road surface completely separated from the remainder of the tire. The dislodge[d] portion of the tire passed completely over in front of the consumer's vehicle and proceeded to roll in the pathway of three adjacent lanes of traffic. The consumer's vehicle was damage[d] due to [losing] some control of the vehicle when the incident occurred. The tire was inspected by a tire dealer and it was determined that there was [no] puncture to the tire or any prior damage to the tire, it was clearly a defect with the tire.

• Early replacement of the side window motor and regulator.

Secret Warranties/Internal Bulletins/Service Tips

All models/years: Like Honda's, most of Acura's TSBs allow for special warranty consideration on a "goodwill" basis, even after the warranty has expired or the car has changed hands. Referring to this euphemism will increase your chances of getting some kind of refund for repairs that are obviously factory defects. • Seat belts that fail to function properly during normal use will be replaced for free under the company's lifetime seat belt warranty. • Diagnostic procedures and correction for off-centre steering wheels. **All models: 1999–2000**—A squeaking, creaking driver's seat is addressed in TSB #00-014. • A wrinkled rear door sash trim will be covered under a "goodwill" policy, even if correction is done by an independent body shop. • Tips on replacing a leaking torque converter. • Troubleshooting moonroof creaks. **1999–2002**—Front, middle, or rear engine oil leaks likely caused by a too-porous cast aluminum engine block (TSB #01-041). • Loose front seat back panel. **1999–2006**—Diagnosing and fixing a drift/pull to one side. **2000**—Excessive cranking when restarting. • Faulty front and rear water passage gaskets at the cylinder head can cause a coolant leak next to the EGR valve. • Radiator/condenser fan runs continuously, discharging battery. • Vehicle clunks when going over bumps. **2000–01**—MIL (malfunction indicator light) and Airbag warning light may stay lit for no apparent reason. • V6 engine oil leaks. • Speed sensor plug may be missing. • Panic alarm activates inadvertently. • Brake pedal pulsation. • Windshield wiper smearing and streaking. **2000–03**—Honda extends its warranties to 7 years/160,000 km (100,000 miles) on automatic transmissions (see "CL" section, pages 247–251). **2001**—A booming sound may be heard when the moonroof is opened while the car is underway. • Moonroof squeaks. • Climate control changes intermittently. **2002–06**—Acura has extended the mileage warranty by 5 percent. **2004**—A Fifth-gear vibration or drone may require the installation of a dynamic damper (P/N 50207-SEP-305). • A lit ABS warning light may indicate that there's moisture in the sensor. **2004–05**—TSB #05-033 says you should install a #10A fuse if the windshield wiper washer, power seat position memory, power mirrors, and auto-dimming mirror don't work. • A faulty outside temperature gauge probably needs a new gauge control module. • A clicking or popping brake pedal may have a misaligned brake-pedal position switch plunger. Turn it around so the connector lock faces the 5 o'clock position. • Prematurely worn Bridgestone tires will be replaced for free under a "goodwill" policy. **2004–06**—Tips on silencing front brake squeal. • Inoperative, noisy side window regulators.

TL PROFILE

	1997	1998	1999	2000	2001	2002	2003	2004	2005
Cost Price ($)									
Base	36,600	37,000	35,000	35,000	36,000	37,000	37,800	40,800	41,000
Used Values ($)									
Base ▲	6,000	7,000	8,000	10,500	12,000	15,500	18,500	25,000	29,000
Base ▼	5,500	6,500	7,000	9,500	10,500	14,000	16,000	23,000	27,000
Reliability	4	4	4	3	4	4	3	3	4
Crash Safety (F)	4	4	—	—	4	4	4	5	5
Side	—	—	—	—	4	4	4	4	4
Side (IIHS)	—	—	—	—	—	—	—	5	5
Offset	—	—	5	5	5	5	5	5	5
Head Restraints	1	—	1	—	1	1	1	2	2
Rollover Resistance	—	—	—	—	—	5	4	4	4

Audi

A4, A6 (100), A8, S4, S6, TT COUPE ★ ★

RATING: Below Average (1996–2006); Not Recommended (1984–95). The rating has dropped because of poor wet weather braking performance, serious transmission and engine failures, and chronic electrical shorts. **"Real" city/ highway fuel economy:** *A4 1.8L:* 11.2/7.2 L/100 km with a manual transmission. *Quattro 3.0L:* 13.5/8.7 L/100 km with a manual tranny (this version burns a lot more fuel than the A4!). *S4:* 15.8/10.2 L/100 km with a manual. *A6 3.0L:* 11.5/

8.1 L/100 km. *TT Coupe 1.8L:* 11.3/7.5 L/100 km with a Selectronic transmission. *TT Coupe 3.2L:* 10.9/8.1 L/100 km. Owners report fuel savings are fairly accurate for those models equipped with a manual transmission. Estimates for vehicles equipped with an automatic transmission may be off by about 10 percent. **Maintenance/Repair costs:** Higher than average, and almost all repairs have to be done by an Audi dealer. Expect long delays for recall repairs. **Parts:** Way higher-than-average costs, and independent suppliers have a hard time finding parts. Don't even think about buying one of these front-drives without a 3- to 5-year supplementary warranty backed by Audi. **Extended warranty:** A good idea, considering how badly past engine, coil pack, and sludge problems were handled by Audi in Canada. VW and its different divisions work from the States. **Best alternatives:** Acura Integra, TL, or RL; BMW 3 Series; Infiniti I30/I35; and Lexus ES300. TT Coupe shoppers may also want to look at the BMW Z3, Honda S2000, and Mazda Miata. **Online help:** *www.audiworld.com, www.vwvortex.com, MyAudiTTsucks.com,* and *www.thetruthaboutcars.com.*

Strengths and Weaknesses

Audi's best-selling line, these cars are attractively styled and comfortable to drive, handle well, and provide a fairly comfortable interior. But you'd better know how to separate the wheat from the chaff, since some model years can be wallet-busters due to their rapid depreciation, poor quality, and high servicing costs.

The early '90 models, including the old 90 and 100, have a worse-than-average reliability record and are plagued by mechanical and electrical components that don't stand up to the rigors of driving in cold climates. Look for the better-built and more recent A4 and A6 models. Although most dealers don't want to service these relics, many independent garages (staffed by former VW mechanics) will go the extra mile to keep them on the road.

The 1996 and later models are the pick of the Audi litter (dating from when all-wheel drive became an optional feature on all entry-level models). The A6, the reincarnation of the 100 Series, is packed with standard features and is a comfortable, spacious front-drive or all-wheel-drive luxury sedan that comes with dual airbags and ABS. It uses the same V6 powerplant as the A4, its smaller sibling, but has 47 additional horses. Unfortunately, the engine is no match for the car's size (0–100 km/h in 13 seconds), and steering and handling are decidedly trucklike. The A8, the first luxury car with an all-aluminum body, competes with the BMW 7 Series and the Mercedes S-Class. Equipped with a WHO 174-hp 2.8L V6 or a 300-hp V8, the A8 is a decent buy. Its drawbacks—it comes with a high price, its steering is a bit imprecise for an Audi, and its aluminum body can only be repaired by an Audi dealer.

Launched in 1994 and powered by a turbocharged 227-hp 2.2L 5-cylinder engine, the S6 is a high-performance spin-off of the A6. Its reliability is better than average, and its sporty performance leaves the A6 in the dust.

VEHICLE HISTORY: *A4:* **1997**—The A4 V6 sedan is renamed the 2.8 and joins a new entry-level A4 1.8T. An improved 190-hp DOHC V6 also debuts that year. **1998**—The addition of the A4 2.8L V6 wagon, equipped with a 5-speed Triptronic transmission. **1999**—Addition of an A4 1.8L wagon, and the base 1.8L model receives additional insulation. **2000**—A high-performance S4 joins the A4 lineup, and A4 2.8Ls are given a power-assisted front passenger's seat. The S4 is a limited-production, high-performance spin-off that carries a 227-hp turbocharged rendition of the old 5-cylinder powerplant. **2001**—The base 1.8L engine gets 20 extra horses; an all-new 2001 S4 sedan and Avant, featuring a 250-hp 2.7L twin-turbocharged V6, also join the lineup. **2002**—A4 totally revamped, getting a roomier interior, a 10-hp boost to the base engine, and a 3.0L all-aluminum, 5-valve-per-cylinder, 220-hp V6 engine hooked to a new 6-speed manual transmission. Other features: a more rigid body, an upgraded independent rear suspension, and brake assist. **2003**—Addition of a convertible. **2004**—More high-performance models and greater all-wheel drive availability. Plus, Quattro models dropped the old 5-speed for a 6-speed manual transmission. *A6:* **1999**—Carried over with minor changes. **2000**—Addition of two performance sedans and side curtain airbags (standard on the 4.2). **2001**—2.7T and the 4.2 A6 models get Audi's electronic stabilization program, which prevents fishtailing and enhances traction control. **2002**—Debut of all-wheel drive, a 2.7L engine, and adjustable air suspension. **2003**—The new RS6 debuts equipped with a 450-hp 4.2L V8; the sporty S6 Avant adds a more powerful V8, sport suspension, and special trim; and the 2.7T gets 17-inch wheels. On the downside, front-passenger seat memory is no more, and steering-wheel shift buttons are gone. **2004**—A V8 for the all-road Quattro and a new sports model, the 2.7T S-line sedan. **2005**—Refreshed styling and additional room and power. Wheelbase is increased by 8 cm and models are equipped with either a 255-hp V6 or a 335-hp V8, coupled to 6-speed automatic transmission with manual-shift capability and all-wheel drive. Audi's MMI operating system, like BMW's iDrive, uses a centre console knob to control many of the car's accessories. All A6s now have front side airbags, side curtain airbags, and optional rear side airbags. Antilock four-wheel disc brakes and an anti-skid system are both standard. *TT:* **2001**—A two-passenger softtop Roadster debuts; addition of Electronic Stability Program (ESP), a rear spoiler, and a 225-hp turbocharged 4-cylinder engine. **2002**—A new radio with in-dash CD. **2003**—All-wheel drive now only found on uplevel models; a revised grille. **2004**—A 250-hp 3.2L V6 Quattro model hooked to a new Direct Shift Gearbox—a clutchless manual that can shift like an automatic.

These alphabetically named cars are conservatively styled, often slow off the mark (in spite of the V6 addition when hooked to an automatic), and plagued by electrical glitches. The 4-speed automatic shifts erratically (delayed and abrupt engagement), and the 2.8L V6 engine needs full throttle for adequate performance. Handling is acceptable, on a par with the BMW 3 Series, but the ride is a bit firm and the car still exhibits considerable body roll, brake dive, and acceleration squat when pushed, although acceleration times beat out those of the Mercedes.

Overall quality control improved markedly with the 1996–99 model years and then started going downhill. Through the 2005 models, there have been an inordinate number of safety- and performance-related defects reported by owners. The automatic transmission and electrical system are the cars' weakest links and have plagued Audi's entire lineup for the past decade. Normally this wouldn't be catastrophic; however, as the cars become more electronically complex, with more functions handled by computer modules, you're looking at some annoying glitches to say the least (failure to go into gear, false obstacle warnings, etc.). Here are some other "annoyances": the transmission suddenly downshifting or jerking into Forward gear, brake failures in rainy weather, premature brake wear and grinding when in Reverse, fuel-system malfunctions leading to surging and stalling, early lower control arm replacement, steering grinds, defective mirror memory settings, distorted windshields, and body glitches. Furthermore, servicing is still spotty because of the small number of dealers in Canada and the fact that these cars are extremely dealer dependent. Owners report long servicing delays.

TT Coupe

The best of the Audi lineup, the TT Coupe is a sporty front-drive hatchback with 2+2 seating set on the same platform used by the A4, Golf, Jetta, and New Beetle. A two-seat convertible version, the Roadster, was launched in the spring of 2000. The base 180-hp 1.8L engine (lifted from the A4) is coupled with a manual 5-speed, while the optional engine uses a 6-speed manual transaxle. Shorter and more firmly sprung than the A4, the TT's engines are turbocharged.

More beautifully styled and with better handling than the Prowler, the TT comes with lots of high-tech standard features that include four-wheel disc brakes, airbags everywhere, traction control (front-drive models), a power top (Quattro), a heated-glass rear window, and a power-retractable glass windbreak between the roll bars (convertible). An alarm system employs a pulse radar system to catch prying hands invading the cockpit area.

Problem areas reported by owners include premature transmission failures and grinding of the Second gear synchronizers, early tie-rod wearout, excessive brake noise, electrical shorts causing dash gauges and instruments to fail, premature wheel bearing failures, poorly performing window regulators, steering-wheel clunks, and loose bolts that cause the subframe to move while driving over bumps and while braking.

Safety Summary

All models/years: Extremely poor wet braking on later models, caused by water contaminating the brake rotor and disc; braking delay is almost two seconds. • Chronic stalling. • Many cases of distorted windshields. **All models: 1998—** Stuck gas pedal. • Premature transmission failure; car pops out of gear. • Front and rear brake rotor and pad fail. • Premature upper and lower control arm failures (50 complaints found on *www.audiworld.com*). • Sunroof opens by itself. **1999—**

Sudden, unintended acceleration when backing up. • Vehicle will roll away even though parking brake is engaged. • Brakes suddenly lock up. • Engine loses power when shifting. • Door locks don't work. • Airbag failures. • Headlights burn out prematurely and don't provide sufficient illumination. • Booming noise heard if the sunroof or any window is open when car is underway. **2001**—Brakes fail to stop vehicle. • Headlights blind oncoming drivers. • Hood latch breaks, allowing hood to smash into windshield. **2002**—Frequent coil pack failures forced Audi to pay for their replacement, but the problem continues on other models (see *www. audiworld.com/search/index.html*):

> I have been in contact with close to 100 other 2002 Audi owners through the AudiWorld website and the coil pack problem is a serious issue. The ignition coil packs have been failing on at least 10 percent of the 2002 vehicles and Audi says they are all isolated cases. When they fail the car barely runs and can create a lot of personal safety issues.

> •

> I have learned that Audi had a product recall for this exact problem, however my 2003 A4 components are not covered by those under recall. I was told I have the "newer" versions of the ignition coils already in my car. While they might be newer, they sure haven't solved the underlying problem! Two blown ignition coils in less than 2 months and I can't get the…[manufacturer] to replace the other 2 coils that I'm certain will go out at some point soon too.

• Sudden acceleration. • No airbag deployment. **2003**—Stuck accelerator pedal. • No-starts believed to be caused by instrument cluster or steering lock/ignition cylinder failures. • Ignition coil packs continue to blow (see above complaint). • Stalling believed to be caused by a defective fuel pump. • CVT hesitates before engaging. • Parking brake fails to hold. • Outside mirrors don't automatically readjust. • Ice glazes the brake rotors. • Frequent failure of the windshield wiper motor and washer. • Faulty Pirelli tires. • Doors fill with water when it rains. **2004**— Sudden, unintended acceleration. • Stuck accelerator causes sudden acceleration. • Tire jack stand collapsed. • Pirelli tire-tread separation. • Convertible top failures. **2005**—Airbag fails to deploy. • Airbag sensor light stays lit. • Car constantly drifts to the right side of the roadway. • Car is a rodent magnet:

> At 2,200 miles [3,500 kilometres], a headlight warning light came on, and I took my car to the dealership. I was told that a mouse had climbed into my engine, built a nest out of the hood insulation, and chewed through wires. Audi refused to cover any damages. This incident cost me $1,400.

• Vehicle hesitates for two to three seconds when accelerating from a complete stop:

> I have almost been T-boned while trying to make a left hand turn, 3 times. The car is dangerous!! I took it in to the dealer on July the 1st. They told me then that that is the way the car is designed to operate.

A6 Sedan: **1998–99**—During refuelling, gasoline spits back violently from the filler pipe. **2003**—Car fails to start (not coil-related, they say). • Sudden acceleration. • Airbags fail to deploy. • Numerous complaints of delayed braking; no brakes in rainy weather; parking brake failure; and premature replacement of the front brake rotors. • Sudden headlight failure. • Blue-white headlights blind oncoming drivers. **2004**—More Pirelli tire failures. **2005**—Acceleration is still plagued by engine hesitation. • Right outside mirror tilts down in Reverse gear for parking, but does not go back to normal until up to speed in second gear. Result: no mirror while entering traffic. *TT Coupe:* **2000**—Engine compartment howling or moaning heard when accelerating. • Periodic grinding of the Second gear synchronizers is a common failure, said to affect many Audi and VW models. • Parking brake failure. • Engine explodes following a computer malfunction. • Electrical short causes vehicle to lose power. • Fuel gauge shows full, even though fuel is low. **2001**—Defective fuel gauge gives false reading (A6 models recalled for the same defect). • All windshields have some kind of visual distortion (anything viewed, especially straight lines, is distorted). Audi has a secret warranty to replace the windshields for free, regardless of mileage. • Sudden clutch failure (Audi pays half the replacement cost). • Central computer failure causes door locks to jam, trapping occupants. • Sudden windshield wiper failure. **2002**—Serious drivetrain failures:

> When traveling at 60 mph [96 km/h] my front left axle fell out of the drive system, and my car was thrown into a spin. I barely missed several other vehicles as well as a highway divider. I was told at the service center the axle never was pinned in place properly. The second and more recent incident involves the transmission. While driving in moderate traffic, as I shifted through the gears, nothing happened, and then finally when it felt like the car shifted into gear, the entire transmission froze up, and I almost was hit from the back.

• Owners report a multitude of electrical shorts affect the radio, horn, lights, dash gauges, and controls. • Ignition coil failures. • Xenon headlights don't adequately light the roadway. **2003**—Engine threw a rod at 80,000 km. **2004**—Original equipment tires found to have extensive sidewall cracks.

Secret Warranties/Internal Bulletins/Service Tips

All models/years: Defective catalytic converters that cause a rotten-egg smell may be replaced free of charge under the emissions warranty. • Inoperative radio; dash light is too dim. • Underbody wind noise. **All models: 2001–03**—Faulty ignition coils cause sudden stalling/no-starts; replacement coils will be installed free of charge without prior ownership or mileage restrictions; consequential damages (towing, alternate transport, ruined vacation, etc.) will also be refunded if you stand your ground. **2002–04**—Broken, missing audio knobs will be replaced free of charge (TSB #04-05, April 2004). *A4, A6, S6:* **1996–2004**—Moisture accumulation in headlights is Audi's responsibility (TSB #03-03, November 2003). *A4, A6:* **1998–2000**—Diagnostic and repair procedures for disc brake squeals, an engine that will crank but not start, and engine misfires. **1999**—AC doesn't provide enough cooling. • Tips to silence rear window creaking or popping. **2002–03**—Automatic transmission jerks going into Reverse. **2002–05**—Bucking when accelerating with vehicles equipped with the Multitronic automatic transmission. **2005**—Cold engine stumble; warm engine stall. **2005–06**—Oil leak from oil filter housing. *A4:* **2002**—Poor AM band reception. **2002–04**—Oil leak at camshaft adjuster. **2002–06**—Faulty glove compartment door. • Noisy power steering. **2003–04**—Free service campaign to replace the engine wire harness. **2004**—3.0L engine misfiring troubleshooting tips. **2004–06**—Remedies for power-steering system noises. **2005–06**—Remote won't lock/unlock doors. *A6:* **1997–2001**—Erratic engine-idle fluctuation. **1998–2002**—Inoperative fresh-air control lever. **1998–2004**—Noisy power steering. **2000**—Automatic transmission goes into limp mode and won't shift. **2001**—Inoperative self-levelling system. • Stained D-pillar trim. **2003**—Inoperative keyless entry transmitter and faulty fresh-air control lever light. **2004**—Troubleshooting tips to correct inadequate AC cooling. **2005**—AC whining, howling. • Fuel gauge reads empty with a full tank. **2005–06**—Rough-running cold engine. • Inoperative sunroof. • Crackling noise from speakers. *TT:* **2004**—Front stabilizer bar upgrade to reduce noise. **2004–05**—Xenon headlight failure. **2004–06**—Momentary delay when accelerating. • Vehicle won't go into gear.

A4, A6 (100), A8, S4, S6, TT COUPE PROFILE

	1997	1998	1999	2000	2001	2002	2003	2004	2005
Cost Price ($)									
A4	31,600	32,700	32,700	32,990	33,785	37,225	37,310	34,435	34,985
A6 (100)	49,270	48,800	48,880	49,170	49,835	54,235	51,740	51,950	59,500
A8	89,840	90,540	90,540	86,250	86,500	86,500	86,500	97,750	93,900
S4	—	—	—	56,000	57,200	57,200	—	67,950	68,250
S6	63,550	—	—	—	—	88,500	88,500	—	—
TT	—	—	—	49,500	50,400	50,400	48,650	49,975	64,950
Used Values ($)									
A4 ▲	5,000	7,500	9,000	11,000	12,500	16,000	17,500	23,000	26,000
A4 ▼	4,000	6,500	8,000	9,500	11,500	14,000	16,000	21,000	24,000
A6 (100) ▲	8,500	9,500	11,000	12,500	17,500	22,000	29,000	35,000	43,000
A6 (100) ▼	7,500	9,000	10,000	11,500	15,500	20,000	27,000	33,000	41,000
A8 ▲	11,000	12,500	14,000	16,000	20,500	29,000	39,000	55,000	63,000
A8 ▼	10,000	11,500	13,000	14,000	18,500	27,000	36,000	52,000	60,000
S4 ▲	—	—	—	14,000	20,000	25,000	—	43,000	50,000
S4 ▼	—	—	—	12,500	18,000	23,000	—	40,000	48,000
S6 ▲	9,000	—	—	—	—	31,000	43,000	—	—
S6 ▼	8,000	—	—	—	—	28,000	41,000	—	—
TT ▲	—	—	—	13,000	16,000	21,000	26,000	31,000	38,500
TT ▼	—	—	—	11,000	14,000	19,500	24,000	29,000	36,000

Reliability	2	2	2	2	3	3	3	3	3
Crash Safety (F)									
A4	4	—	—	—	—	4	4	4	4
A6 (100)	5	—	—	—	—	—	—	—	5
A8	—	5	5	5	5	5	5	—	—
Side (TT)	—	—	—	—	—	5	5	5	5
A4	—	—	—	—	—	5	5	5	5
Side (IIHS)	—	—	—	—	—	—	—	—	5
Offset (A6)	—	3	3	3	3	3	3	3	5
A4	—	—	—	—	—	5	5	5	5
Head Restraints									
A4 (F)	1	—	3	—	5	5	5	1	2
A4 (R)	—	—	—	—	3	—	—	—	—
A6	1	—	3	—	5	5	5	5	3
A8	1	—	3	—	3	2	2	5	5
TT Coupe	—	—	—	—	—	3	3	3	—
TT Roadster	—	—	—	—	—	5	5	5	—
Rollover Resistance									
A4	—	—	—	—	—	4	4	4	4
TT	—	—	—	—	—	—	5	5	5

BMW

3 SERIES, 5 SERIES, M SERIES, Z SERIES ★ ★ ★ ★ / ★ ★ ★ / ★ ★ ★ ★ ★

RATING: *3 Series:* Above Average (2001–06); Average (1994–2000); Below Average (1984–93). *5 Series:* Average (2004–06, 1985–91); Recommended (1992–2003). *M Series:* Recommended (1997–2006). *Z3:* Above Average (1996–2002). *Z4:* Recommended (2003–06). Sorry, but *Lemon-Aid* can't jump on the "BMW is best" bandwagon for every model year. Although these are the best models Europe has to offer, that's faint praise, indeed. First of all, there's no reason why Bimmers should be so over-priced. For example, why does the 2004 series cost $10,000 more than the previous year's models and what genius priced the Z8 at almost $200,000? Adding to the negative vibes, owner feedback and internal service bulletins show these cars come with a performance and quality reputation that far exceeds what they actually deliver. Some of the websites listed below show the dark side of the BMW driving experience. **"Real" city/highway fuel economy:** *2.2L:* 11.3/7.2 L/100 km with a manual transmission or 11.6/7.4 L/100 km with an automatic. *2.5L:* 11.7/7.4 L/100 km with a manual tranny or 12.3/8.0 L/100 km with an automatic. *3.0L:* 11.7/7.2 L/100 km with a manual or 12.2/8.0 L/100 km with an automatic. *5 Series 2.5L:* 11.7/7.4 L/100 km manual or 12.5/7.6 L/100 km automatic. *3.0L:* 11.7/7.2 L/100 km manual; 12.9/7.8 L/100 km automatic. *4.4L:* 14.4/8.6 L/100 km manual; 13.0/8.2 L/100 km automatic. BMW owners report fuel savings estimates are relatively accurate for vehicles equipped with manual transmissions. Other models burn about 10 percent more fuel than estimated. **Maintenance/Repair costs:** Higher than average, but many repairs can be done by independents who specialize in BMWs. Unfortunately, these experts are usually concentrated around large urban areas. **Parts:** Higher-than-average costs, and parts are often back-ordered. **Extended warranty:** Not needed. **Best alternatives:** There are a number of credible alternatives to the Z Series, such as the AWD 3 Series and the Mazda6. Also look at the Acura Integra, TL, or RL; Infiniti I30 or I35; Mazda Millenia; and Toyota Avalon. *Wagons:* Get a Mercedes E-Class. Sure, BMW makes better sedans, but the E-class gives a more comfortable ride; offers a huge trunk, a flat floor, and a low loading sill; and doesn't infuriate you with a confusing high-tech iDrive gizmo. **Online help:** *www.straight-six. com, www.mwerks.com, www.bmwnation.com, www.roadfly.com, yoy.com/yoy/auto/ m3_failure_index.html* (BMW M3 Engine Failures Page), *www.bmwboard.com,* and *www.bmwlemon.com.*

 ## Strengths and Weaknesses

3 Series

The 3 Series vehicles exhibit great 6-cylinder performance with the manual gearbox, and ride and handling are commendable. The 318's small engine is seriously compromised, however, by an automatic transmission. The 325e is more pleasant to drive and delivers lots of low-end torque. Through 1998, rear passenger and cargo room is limited. After a redesign of the '99 models, passenger and cargo space was increased.

The 1991 and later models provide peppy 4-cylinder acceleration only with high revs and a manual transmission. Keep in mind that city driving requires lots of manual gear shifting characterized by an abrupt clutch. If you must have an automatic, look for a used model with the 6-cylinder engine. The larger 1.9L 4-cylinder that went into the mid-'96 models doesn't boost performance all that much.

Although the 1997 models come with traction control, it is not very effective in giving these vehicles acceptable wet pavement traction. A problem since the early '90s, the rear end tends to slip sideways when the roadway is wet (much like Ford's rear-drive Mustang). Smart shoppers who opt for the improved 2000 models will keep in mind that rear interior room is still a joke—unless you happen to be sitting there. Various upgrades make the 2001 and later models the better choices.

VEHICLE HISTORY: 1998—Given a 2.5L inline 6-cylinder and side airbags. **1999**—Revamped with a better-performing base engine and 2.8L 6-banger and a more refined transmission and chassis. **2000**—A redesigned lineup of coupes, convertibles, and wagons; the hatchback is gone. **2001**—Receives an engine upgrade, larger brakes and wheels, and optional 4×4 capability. High-performance M3 Coupe returns with a 330-hp engine. **2002**—M3 gets a new 6-speed sequential manual transmission; entire lineup gets recalibrated steering, reshaped headrests, and an in-dash CD player. **2003**—Coupes and convertibles are restyled, along with a transmission upgrade and a new sedan performance package. **2004**—Expanded availability of the sequential manual transmission.

Handling with all model years is still tricky on wet roads, despite the ASC+T traction control; rear-seat access is problematic; rear passenger space continues to be disappointing; and styling is the essence of bland. The brakes, electrical system, and some body trim and accessories are the most failure-prone components. Engine overheating is a serious and common failure.

5 Series

Essentially a larger, more powerful 3 Series, the 5 Series has made its reputation by delivering more performance in a larger, more versatile interior. The 6-cylinder and V8 engines are somewhat fuel-thirsty and occasionally a bit noisy, but they are quite remarkable, durable performers. There is no problem with rear-seat or cargo room with the 5 Series Bimmer. Handling and ride are superb, although these weighty upscale models do strain when going over hilly terrain if they have the automatic gearbox.

5 Series owners report numerous electrical and fuel glitches, faulty turn signal indicators, starter failures, self-activating emergency flashers, rotten-egg odours from the exhaust, and excessive steering-wheel or brake vibrations.

Overall reliability was very poor with early Bimmers but, except for numerous electrical shortcomings, has improved during the past few years. Nevertheless, whenever a problem arises, repair costs are particularly high because of the small number of dealers, the relative scarcity of parts, and the acquiescence of affluent owners. Electrical and fuel system, automatic transmission, and front brake failures are the primary weak spots of the 1984–93 models. Chronic engine surging at idle is also commonplace. Door seams, rocker panels, rear-wheel openings, and fender seams are particularly prone to rust. Check the muffler bracket for premature wear and the weather seals and door adjustments for leaks.

The '94 and later models still have reliability problems affecting the automatic and manual transmissions, brakes, and fuel and electrical systems. Owners report that premature brake wear causes excessive vibration and noise when the brakes are applied. The 4.0L engines are known to sometimes click, rattle, and knock due to faulty crankshaft main bearing shells or poor oil viscosity. The 3.0L 6-cylinder engines were also noted for producing an irregular clicking noise. There are some reports of water leaks through the doors.

Year 2000–03 models are plagued by cooling fan malfunctions, leading to engine overheating and fires; airbag malfunctions; a manual transmission that's hard to shift into Second gear, pops out of gear, and grinds when shifting; automatic transmission screeches when shifting; steering degradation when braking at slow speeds; and front-door water leaks.

The 5 Series 2004 models seem to have hit a quality plateau, and the addition of parts of the 7 Series' iDrive feature is downright scary. It uses a console "joystick" knob to control entertainment, navigation, communication, and climate functions, which annoys and distracts drivers who aren't so techno-savvy.

VEHICLE HISTORY: 1997—The redesigned model is longer and comes with an enlarged V6 or V8 engine, dual front and side airbags, anti-lock brakes, and traction control. **1998**—Head protection system introduced. **1999**—Station wagons get both 6-cylinder and V8 power, xenon headlights, memory for power seats and mirrors, a Park Distance Control that warns of obstacles when backing up, and a self-levelling rear suspension. Standard on V8 models and newly optional for 528i versions is BMW's Dynamic Stability Control. **2000**—Return of the high-performance M5 Sedan; 528i versions get a standard anti-skid system; rear side airbags for the M5. **2001**—525i Sedan and Wagon debut. **2002**—540i's V8 gets an extra 8 hp. **2003**—A sunroof for all 6-cylinders and a new Sport Package with the manual transmission 540i Sedan. **2004**—Redesigned with new styling, new features, and a more powerful V8. The 545i 6-speed was given a sport suspension teamed with run-flat tires, plus Active Steering and Active Roll Stabilization to counteract body lean. All models have BMW's controversial iDrive console joystick to control entertainment, navigation, communication, and climate functions. Critics say that the iDrive takes a University of Waterloo degree in engineering to operate, plus it's a safety hazard. The 545i and 545i 6-speed models use a 4.4L V8 with 325 hp, up from 290 in last year's 540i. The wagon is gone. **2005**—Minimal changes; coupes (except M3) get a standard sunroof, and coupes and convertibles join the M3 in getting a standard tire-pressure monitor.

M Series

Launched in 1996 as a four-door model, the M3 is a high-performance coupe originally equipped with a potent 240-hp 3.0L engine (later bumped up to 3.2L), a manual shifter, a firm suspension, and 17-inch tires.

VEHICLE HISTORY: 1997–2000—Re-designed the M Series. **2000**—The M5 is mostly a renamed 540i Sports Sedan. **2001**—Arrival of a new 315-hp inline-six, Dynamic Stability Control, and a tighter suspension (watch those kidneys), while the M3 returns in convertible and coupe formats, equipped with a high-performance 333-hp engine. **2002**—All models are given a modified aluminum suspension, wider 18-inch tires and wheels, a new limited-slip differential, and a refreshed interior.

Overall M3 reliability is quite impressive; however, these cars have one fatal flaw: Their engines self-destruct. In fact, 128 failed engines have been registered with the *yoy.com/yoy/auto/m3_failure_index.html* (BMW M3 Engine Failures Page) website, which dubs the powerplant "The Engine of Damocles."

Watch out for main bearing or connecting rod problems with M3 engines built from 2001 through 2002. The problem is real, has been confirmed by BMW, and is extensively documented online at *members.roadfly.com*. BMW extended the warranty to 6 years/161,000 km (100,000 mi.).

Other reported problems include a loud clunking from the rear end when shifting or decelerating, said to be caused by a faulty driveshaft attachment at the differential, and delamination and poor paint application. 1996–99 models are known for being more difficult to tune for performance due to slightly smaller intake manifold runners and more complicated electronics.

Z Series

BMW's first sports car, the two-seater Z3 debuted in early 1996 and was based on the 3 Series platform. Its 138-hp 1.9L 4-banger is outclassed by the competition (such as the Porsche non-S Boxster, the Mercedes-Benz 3.2L V6 SLK, and the Honda S2000), and you have to get the revs up past 3000 rpm to get adequate

passing torque. The 2001 model, with its 2.5L 184-hp 6-cylinder engine, is an all-around better performer and offers more features at a fairly depreciated price.

Dynamic Stability Control, large 17-inch wheels, and Dunlop SP Sport performance tires don't enhance handling as much as BMW pretends they do: Get used to lots of steering corrections.

The Z4 is a more feature-laden convertible, equipped with an inline 6-cylinder engine and a standard manual softtop. It still carries a base 184-hp 2.5L engine coupled with a 5-speed manual transmission; the higher-end Z4 3.0i has a 225-hp 3.0L mated to a 6-speed manual gearbox. Run-flat tires, ABS, and an anti-skid system are standard features.

In 2000, BMW launched its $195,000 super-luxury Z8: a limited-production, fully equipped model with a power softtop, a removable hardtop, a body made largely of aluminum, and a 4.9L V8 hooked to a mandatory 6-speed manual transmission. The car lasted four model years and is now worth about $80,000.

VEHICLE HISTORY: 1996—BMW's Z3 1.9L roadster arrives on the scene. **1997**—An optional 2.8L engine is added, along with standard traction control. **1998**—Standard rollover bars and upgraded sport seats. **1999**—Standard side airbags

(318Ti excepted) and a new 2.8L coupe. A 2.5L inline-six replaces the 1.9L 4-cylinder engine. **2000**—A slight restyling and standard Dynamic Stability Control. **2001**—Debut of the Z8. Roadsters and coupes adopt a 3.0L powerplant (instead of the 2.8L), and bigger brakes and wheels are added. Also, the 2.5L engine is tweaked to unleash 14 additional horses. **2003**—Launch of the Z4. The Z8's last model year.

Owners report frequent stalling when decelerating, faulty right-side seat switches, and a squeaking, popping noise from the driver's door or in the shoulder area of the convertible top.

Safety Summary

All models/years: Sudden acceleration. • Airbag malfunctions include bag deploying inadvertently or failing to go off in an accident, and a constantly lit warning light. • Transmission pops out of gear. **All models: 2002**—Many incidents where cooling fan failure causes engine to overheat or a fire to ignite (see *www.roadfly.com/bmw*). • Premature replacement of the front control arms. *318:* **1998**—In one incident, a finger was cut off when caught in the power window. • Glass comes out of door channel. • Headlights provide poor illumination of the roadway. • Severe suspension hop when passing over small bumps. • Car's rear end slides out during turns. • Incorrect fuel gauge readings. **1999**—Front plastic grille piece falls off car and damages the windshield while vehicle is underway. • Automatic transmission failures. • Seat belt doesn't retract as it should. • Horn sounds when vehicle is put in Reverse. • Headlights come on and off intermittently. • Several incidents of fire igniting when high beams are activated. • Heated seats get too hot. **2000**—Poor wet braking. • Faulty steering damper and control arms. • Seat belt warning light stays on. • Seat belt doesn't retract properly. • Drivebelts may suddenly fail. **2001**—Fire ignites because of defective fan assembly. • Defective cooling fan causes engine to overheat; seen as a widespread problem on the bulletin board at *www.roadfly.com/bmw*. • Premature replacement of the control arms. • Defective gas pedal assembly causes jerky acceleration; BMW will replace it on a case-by-case basis. *320:* **2002**—Distorted windshield. *323:* **2002**—Premature failure of the magnesium alloy control arms and steering damper. • Poor steering when braking at slow speeds. • In rainy weather, brakes stiffen as they are applied, leading to extended stopping distances. • Faulty sunroof. *325i:* **All years:** Transmission failure within five days of purchase. • Electrical system fire. • Steering column is kinked to the left. • In one case, right-door airbag deployed even though vehicle was hit on the left. • Sunroof glass suddenly explodes (several incidents reported):

Urgent—my 2002 325i's first sunroof glass exploded on me on 1/25/02. The replacement glass has two surface hairline cracks and two hairline cracks beneath the surface of the glass. This cannot be an isolated incident. Please examine your sunroof carefully for defects. No one at BMW is taking this seriously enough.

• Doors lock without prior warning. *328:* **2002**—Sudden acceleration; when accelerating, engine cuts out, then surges forward (suspected failure of the throttle assembly). • Severe engine vibrations after a cold start as Check Engine light comes on. • If driver wears a size 12 shoe or larger and their foot is flush against the accelerator pedal, the top of the shoe rubs up against the panel above the pedal, preventing full pedal access. • Rear-quarter blind spot with the convertibles. *330i:* **2002**—Side airbag deploys when vehicle hits a pothole. • Vehicle overheats in low gear; tires lose air. • Vehicle slips out of Second gear when accelerating. **2003**—Chronic stalling, rough idle. • Transmission slipping. **2004**—Constant stalling. *M3:* **1998**—Brake failure. • Chronic horn failures. • Rear-view mirror blocks a substantial portion of the field of vision. **1999**—ABS failure. **2001**—Rear-end clunking, leading to failure of the driveshaft attachment at the differential (confirmed by other complaints on *www.roadfly.com/bmw*). *Z3:* **1998**—Defective rear stabilizer bar. • Automatic transmission jumps out of gear. • Intermittent headlight and instrument cluster failures. • Rear-view mirror creates a huge blind spot. **1999**—Seat belts don't spool out or retract as they should. **2000**—Computer keeps engine at high revs when throttle is released. • Passenger-side seat belt jams. **2000–01**—Faulty speedometer. **2001**—Engine stalls when decelerating. • Interior and exterior lights dim when AC engages. • Passenger's seat belt doesn't fit snugly. • Driver's seat rocks to and fro. • Exterior and interior lights dim and engine loses power when AC is engaged.

Secret Warranties/Internal Bulletins/Service Tips

All models/years: Rear sway-bar links may come off the sway bar. • Front brake squeal. • Steering wheel buzz. • Door brake doesn't hold. • Driver's seat is loose. **All models: 1996–99**—Frequent crankshaft position sensor failures result in chronic Check Engine light illumination. Changing the sensor and installing an adapter harness under warranty or under a BMW "goodwill" policy can correct this problem. **2001–04**—Engine cylinder head oil leaks. *3 Series:* **1998**—A no-start condition may signal that the oil level sensor is faulty. • A clunk heard during downshifts, when releasing the accelerator pedal, or when shifting into Reverse is likely caused by excessive axial clearance at the transmission output. • Inoperative sunroof. **1998–2000**—Hard shifts or no-shifts can be corrected by exchanging the valve body. **1999**—Tips for improving AM radio reception. • An inoperative cruise control may need a new brake light switch (strange but true). **1999–2000**—Guidelines for plugging manual transmission oil drain plug leaks. **2000**—Idle speed and headlight brightness fluctuate when seat heater is activated. • Low airflow through vents. • Erratic automatic transmission shifting. **2002**—Incorrect fuel gauge readings. • Rattling, tapping engine noise. • Troubleshooting navigation system malfunctions. • No 1–2 upshifts. **2003**—Harsh 3–2 and 2–1 downshifts (reprogram EGS module). **2004**—Delayed Park to Drive shift. • Low oil level false alert. • Numerous malfunctions of telematics components. *5 Series:* **All years:** Centre dash humming or buzzing when accelerating. • Water inside of headlight. • Erratic performance of the navigation system. **1996**—Oil level sensor may give an incorrect reading. **1997**—Airbag warning light stays lit for no reason. **1998**—A no-start condition may signal that the oil level sensor is faulty. **2004**—

Defective ignition coils. • The 3.0L engine loses power at 4000 rpm. • Harsh automatic transmission downshifts. • Engine drivebelt tensioner noise can be eliminated by installing a hydraulic-style tensioner and a new ribbed V-belt. • An under-hood steering clicking, ratcheting noise can be silenced by replacing the Active Front Steering (AFS) control module and steering gear. • AC stops working after a long drive. • The AC compressor may have been contaminated by moisture if cooling is delayed. • Dunlop SP Sport run-flat tires with less than 30,000 km will be replaced free of charge if they wear out prematurely or cause excessive vibration and noise. • Trunk lid won't latch. • Erroneous flat-tire warning. *525i:* **2000**—No 1–2 upshifts. *540:* **1999**—Air-mass meter warranty extended to 7 years/120,000 km (75,000 miles). **2002**—Rattling, tapping engine noise. • Passenger-side airbags may not line up with the dash. • Steering groaning and grinding. • Troubleshooting navigation system malfunctions. *M Series:* **2001–03**— After a plague of self-destructing engines, BMW put out SIB #11-04-02 in June 2003 that extended the warranty to 6 years/161,000 km (100,000 miles) on all 6-cylinder engines, initiated a Service Action to replace key components free of charge, and recalibrated software for easier cold starts. Owner repair bills were also paid retroactively, including demands for consequential damages. **2004**—Door locks lock and unlock on their own. • Convertible-top creaking. • Inoperative xenon headlights.

3 SERIES, M SERIES, Z SERIES PROFILE

	1997	1998	1999	2000	2001	2002	2003	2004	2005
Cost Price ($)									
318ti	26,900	27,800	27,800	—	—	—	—	—	—
318i 4d	32,300	33,300	—	—	—	—	—	—	—
Convertible	43,900	44,900	45,900	—	—	—	—	—	—
320i 4d	—	—	—	—	33,900	34,500	34,900	34,950	34,950
323 Coupe	—	39,900	—	—	—	—	—	—	—
325i, 328i	46,900	47,900	50,902	44,900	37,950	41,200	39,300	39,450	39,900
Convertible	57,900	58,900	58,900	—	52,500	52,800	53,400	53,950	54,400
330CI Convertible	57,900	58,900	58,900	—	62,800	62,900	63,500	63,950	64,400
M/M3 2d	61,900	62,900	62,900	62,900	69,800	73,500	73,800	73,950	73,950
M Performance	—	—	—	—	—	—	—	—	54,300
M5 4d	—	—	—	102,650	104,250	105,500	105,500	—	—
Z3 1.9L/2.3L	40,500	41,500	43,900	45,901	46,900	47,200	—	—	—
Z3 2.8L	49,900	51,900	52,900	54,900	55,900	56,200	—	—	—
Z4 2.5L	—	—	—	—	—	—	51,500	51,800	51,900
Z4 3.0L	—	—	—	—	—	—	59,500	59,900	59,900
Z8	—	—	—	190,000	190,000	195,000	195,000	—	—

Used Values ($)

318ti ▲	6,500	7,500	9,000	—	—	—	—	—	—
318ti ▼	5,500	6,500	7,500	—	—	—	—	—	—
318i 4d ▲	8,000	9,500	—	—	—	—	—	—	—
318i 4d ▼	6,500	8,500	—	—	—	—	—	—	—
Convertible ▲	10,000	12,000	14,000	—	—	—	—	—	—
Convertible ▼	9,000	11,000	13,000	—	—	—	—	—	—
320i 4d ▲	—	—	—	—	12,000	15,500	18,500	22,000	26,000
320i 4d ▼	—	—	—	—	10,000	13,500	16,000	20,000	24,000
323 Coupe ▲	—	9,000	—	—	—	—	—	—	—
323 Coupe ▼	—	8,500	—	—	—	—	—	—	—
325i, 328i ▲	7,500	8,500	11,000	13,000	14,500	18,000	21,000	25,500	28,500
325i, 328i ▼	7,000	8,000	9,500	11,500	13,500	16,000	18,500	23,500	30,500
Convertible ▲	13,000	16,000	19,500	—	22,500	27,000	31,500	36,500	43,000
Convertible ▼	12,000	14,000	18,000	—	20,500	24,500	29,000	34,500	40,500
330CI Convertible ▲	15,000	18,500	23,000	—	25,500	32,000	38,000	43,500	50,000
330CI Convertible ▼	14,000	16,500	21,000	—	23,500	30,000	35,500	41,500	48,500
M/M3 2d ▲	9,500	11,000	14,500	18,000	22,500	28,500	37,000	47,000	54,000
M/M3 2d ▼	8,500	10,000	13,500	16,500	21,000	26,500	36,000	45,000	52,000
M Performance ▲	—	—	—	—	—	—	—	—	41,000
M Performance ▼	—	—	—	—	—	—	—	—	38,000
M5 4d ▲	—	—	—	27,000	35,000	43,000	52,000	—	—
M5 4d ▼	—	—	—	25,000	33,000	41,000	49,000	—	—
Z3 1.9L/2.3L ▲	10,000	12,500	16,500	18,000	21,500	25,000	—	—	—
Z3 1.9L/2.3L ▼	8,500	11,000	14,500	16,000	19,000	23,000	—	—	—
Z3 2.8L ▲	—	13,500	18,000	19,000	22,500	26,000	—	—	—
Z3 2.8L ▼	—	11,500	16,000	18,000	20,000	24,000	—	—	—
Z4 2.5L ▲	—	—	—	—	—	—	30,000	35,000	39,000
Z4 2.5L ▼	—	—	—	—	—	—	28,000	33,000	37,000
Z4 3.0L ▲	—	—	—	—	—	—	35,000	41,000	47,000
Z4 3.0L ▼	—	—	—	—	—	—	33,000	39,000	45,000
Z8 ▲	—	—	—	60,000	73,000	90,000	110,000	—	—
Z8 ▼	—	—	—	55,000	68,000	85,000	105,000	—	—
Reliability	3	3	3	4	4	4	4	4	4
Crash Safety (F)	—	—	—	—	—	4	4	4	4
328i	4	—	—	—	—	—	—	—	—
Side	—	—	—	—	—	—	3	3	3
Offset	—	—	—	5	5	5	5	5	5
Head Restraints	1	—	1	3	3	1	1	1	1
M3	—	—	—	—	2	2	2	2	—
Convertible	—	—	1	—	—	—	—	—	—
Z3	1	—	3	—	3	3	—	—	—
Z4	—	—	—	—	—	—	5	5	—
Rollover Resistance	—	—	—	—	—	4	4	4	4

Note: The huge price difference between entry-level models and their top-of-the-line variations narrows to almost nothing after seven years. Additionally, when friends point out how little Bimmers depreciate, point to the above price chart, singling out the Z8's freefall—from $190,000 for a new 2000 to a shocking $60,000 as of May 2007.

	1997	1998	1999	2000	2001	2002	2003	2004	2005
Cost Price ($)									
525i, 528i, 530i	54,900	56,200	57,200	55,500	54,700	55,200	55,500	66,500	66,500
Used Values ($)									
525i, 528i, 530i ▲	8,000	10,000	12,000	14,500	19,000	24,000	29,000	41,000	49,000
525i, 528i, 530i ▼	7,000	8,500	10,500	12,500	18, 500	22,000	27,000	38,000	46,000
Reliability	5	5	5	5	5	4	4	4	4
Crash Safety (F)									
Offset	5	5	5	5	5	5	5	5	5
Head Restraints (F)	3	—	3	—	5	5	5	1	1
Rear	2	—	—	—	—	—	—	—	—

Note: NHTSA hasn't crash-tested the 5 Series; however, European crash tests have rated the 1994–2007 models "Good" to "Excellent," and the U.S.-based IIHS has rated it "Good" since 1997.

Ford/Lincoln

CONTINENTAL, LS, MARK VII, MARK VIII, TOWN CAR ★ ★ ★

RATING: *Continental:* Average (2000–02); Below Average (1988–99). *LS:* Average (2005–06); Below Average (2000–04). *Mark VII, Mark VIII:* Above Average (1995–98); Average (1994); Below Average (1986–93). *Town Car:* Average (1995–2006); Below Average (1988–94). In a nutshell: Rear-drives are generally more reliable buys than front-drive versions. But there are other important factors to consider. For example, the discontinued 1988–2002 front-drive Continentals are theoretically average buys and dirt-cheap. However, servicing problems will likely increase as parts dry up and knowledgeable mechanics die off, leaving you with a garaged car that's more of a sculpture than a conveyance. The rear-drive Town Car and LS are the best choices for quality and performance, and the Mark series isn't a bad choice either, particularly when you consider its incredibly low cost. A really smart move would be to buy a fully equipped Grand Marquis or Crown Victoria and escape the luxury price penalty altogether. **"Real" city/highway fuel economy:** *Town Car:* 13.9/8.7 L/100 km. *LS 3.9L:* 14.0/9.4 L/100 km. Owners report fuel savings may undershoot these estimates by at least 20 percent. **Maintenance/Repair costs:** Higher than average, if done by a Ford or Lincoln dealer. **Parts:** Higher-than-average costs, but not hard to find (except electronic components and body panels). **Extended warranty:** Yes, for the front-drive Continental; no, for any of the rear drives. **Best alternatives:** Acura Integra or RL; Cadillac DeVille; and Infiniti I30 or I35. **Online help:** *www.autosafety.org/autodefects.html* and *www.blueovalnews.com.*

Strengths and Weaknesses

These large luxury cruisers are proof that quality isn't always proportional to the money you spend. Several designer series offer all the luxury options anyone could wish for, but the two ingredients most owners would expect to find—high quality and consistent reliability—are sadly lacking, especially with the front-drive versions. All models have poor-quality automatic transmissions, electrical systems, brakes, body hardware, and fit and finish. NHTSA-recorded safety complaints also target more front-drive than rear-drive Lincolns, with engine, transmission, airbag, and brake failures cropping up repeatedly over the years.

Continental (front-drive)

When the Continental converted to front-drive in 1988, what was a mediocre luxury car became a luxury lemon with serious safety-related deficiencies. The frequency and cost of repairs increased considerably, and parts became more complex, complicating easy diagnosis and repair. The automatic transmission tends to self-destruct, particularly on 1988–2000 models; engine head gaskets blow (see Part Two); electrical components are unreliable, with intermittent loss of all electrical power; stopping performance is compromised by premature brake wear and wheel lock-up; and body hardware is an embarrassment. The redesigned 1995 Continental featured a new V8 powerplant, more aerodynamic styling, and fibreglass panels. That redesign engendered an upsurge in complaints relative to engine, transmission, electrical system, and brake deficiencies until the year 2000. Thereafter, owner complaints trailed off considerably until the Continental was ditched after the 2002 model year run.

VEHICLE HISTORY: 1996—Anti-theft alarm. **1997**—Traction control added, and failure-prone air springs dropped. **1998**—A shorter nose and 2.5 cm less rear legroom. **1999**—Front side airbags and a 15-hp boost (to 275). **2000**—Rear child seat anchors and an emergency trunk release.

These cars don't offer the kind of trouble-free driving one would normally expect in a luxury vehicle selling for over $40,000. The failure-prone and expensive-to-repair automatic levelling air-spring suspension system makes for a stiff ride (especially on early models) while still allowing the Continental to "porpoise" because of its heavy front end. The Continental's anemic V6 powertrain is poorly suited to a car of this heft. The engine hesitates in cold weather, and the automatic transmission shifts roughly.

Mechanical defects include frequent engine flywheel and transmission forward clutch piston replacements; failure-prone ABS, electrical, suspension, and steering systems; and glitch-ridden electronic modules causing hard starts and sudden stalling. The mass of electrical gadgets increases the likelihood of problems as the cars age. For example, automatic headlight doors fail frequently, and the electronic antenna and power windows often won't go up or down. The computerized dashboard is particularly glitch-ridden.

Other reliability complaints concern transmission fluid leakage, rough upshifting caused by a defective valve body, and inadequate air conditioning and heating.

Town Car

The rear-drive Town Car is the best of a bad lot, sharing most of its parts with the Crown Victoria and Grand Marquis and easily found with little mileage and at bargain prices. Cheaper high-mileage units are frequently sold by airport limousine companies and taxi services that run the airport shuttle service. Transport authorities force the companies to update their fleet every few years, creating a flow of perfectly suitable luxury cars sold at next-to-nothing prices. The car's rear-drive configuration is relatively inexpensive to repair, and parts aren't hard to find. Nevertheless, the Town Car is still afflicted with many generic problems that appear year after year. Some of the more common problems are engine head gaskets that warp because a plastic part in the intake manifold has failed; transmission, AC, and electrical system failures; disintegrating tie-rod ends; and body hardware fit and finish deficiencies.

VEHICLE HISTORY: 1996—Engine upgraded, and revised climate controls. **1997**—Steering refinements, but loss of dual exhausts cuts horsepower by 20 (drops to 190 hp). **1998**—Redesigned for a faster, lower, and stiffer ride. **1999**—Side airbags. **2000**—Improved child seat anchorages and a trunk emergency escape release. **2001**—25 horses added to engine; adjustable pedals; and seat belt pretensioners. **2003**—Restyled; a revised frame, suspension, and steering system; and 17-inch tires. Also new are four-wheel, fully assisted ABS disc brakes, front side airbags, an upgraded navigation system, and a 14-hp boost. **2004**—Standard rear obstacle detection system; base Executive model dropped.

Incidentally, Ford Canada announced on December 19, 2005, that it would pay all engine intake manifold gasket repair claims going back seven years (enter "Ford intake manifold extended warranty" into a search engine such as Google). Nevertheless, this warranty extension leaves some customers in the lurch.

LS

The LS rear-drive sedan comes with a high-performance 200-hp variant of the Taurus 3.0L V6 mated with an optional manual or standard automatic gearbox. Also available is a 250-hp 3.9L V8, based on that of the Jaguar XK8 coupe, coupled with a semi-automatic transmission. Both engines are identical, but the Lincoln produces 30 fewer horses than the Jag equivalent. There is very little difference between the 2000 and 2001 models, except that the 2001 carries standard traction control. The 2002 models came back unchanged.

The LS offers a lot for a reasonable base price. The V6 version is priced in the range of the BMW 3 Series, Lexus ES 300, and Mercedes C-Class while delivering standard equipment and interior space that rivals the 5 Series, GS, and E-Class.

Lincoln's return to rear-drive opened up a Pandora's box of powertrain, AC, electrical system, and body glitches. Owners report jerky transmission shifting, excessive drivetrain and body noise and vibrations, inconsistent braking response, and erratic AC performance. The 2005–06 models have generated few complaints. The LS was dropped in mid 2006.

VEHICLE HISTORY: 2001—Standard traction control. **2002**—The V6 got 10 more horses. Debut of an LSE version with a rear spoiler, special wheels, and new lower-body trim. **2003**—More powerful engines; restyled; quieter running. The manual transmission is dropped. **2004**—Suspension tweaked to reduce vibration, harshness, and noise.

Safety Summary

All models/years: Sudden, unintended acceleration; gas pedal sticks. • Sudden forward acceleration when shifter placed into Reverse is a common theme that has affected the entire model lineup, including the 2005 Town Car. It is believed to be a software or pedal position problem and not confined to front- or rear-drives only. • Loss of braking. • Inadvertent deployment of airbags, or airbags don't deploy when they should. • Gas and brake pedal are mounted too close together. • Sudden loss of electrical power. • Severe pull and vibration when braking. • Brake failures caused by premature wear of rear drums and rotor warpage. • Steering control degrades or locks up when car passes through puddles. • Annoying reflections onto the front windshield. • Horn is hard to activate. • Mirrors vibrate excessively and don't adjust easily. *Continental:* **1999**—Brake line ruptured. • Headlights fail to adequately light side of the road. • Visual image speedometer can't be seen by colour-blind drivers. **2000**—Warning lights come on constantly, and car's central computer module often malfunctions. • Brakes don't work well; require extended stopping distance. • Side-view mirror can't be adjusted properly because of a design defect. **2001**—Car suddenly accelerated while in Reverse; brake/transmission interlock not connected. • Driver's foot can be snared by two console cables when going from the gas pedal to the brakes. • Instrument panel washes out in bright sunlight. **2002**—Car speeds up while going downhill with cruise control engaged. • In one incident, while in Park with the brakes applied, vehicle rolled back into another car. • Sticking, binding shoulder belt. • AC freon may escape from the unit and cause windshield to fog up. • Plastic front air dam is easily broken:

> Damage to the engine could occur if it is not replaced, because it directs the air through the engine compartment. We have personally inspected other Lincoln vehicles and numerous have...either completely missing or damage[d] air dams. It appears this is a quick $80.00 profit for the company that could be easily fixed using softer material.

LS: **2000–01**—Lurching, hesitating automatic transmission shifting. • Brakes fail during the first five minutes after a cold start. • Brake pedal becomes hard and resists application or turns mushy and goes to the floor. • Warning lights come on for no reason. • Defective steering causes violent swerving from side to side. • Automatic door locks engage by themselves, locking out driver. **2002**—Sudden shutdown while on the highway. **2003**—Transmission suddenly seizes. • Loss of steering due to computer malfunction. • Head restraints obstruct visibility. **2004**—Airbag deploys for no reason. • Stalling continues to be a chronic problem. • Hard starts. • Brake failure. • Harsh upshifts and gear hunting. • When accelerating, vehicle hesitates and then surges. **2005**—Fuel leak from a cracked fuel tank. • Side airbag deploys for no reason. • Sudden loss of power. • Broken wheel lug nuts. • Defective sidewall (Continental tires). *Town Car:* **1998**—Traction control engages at the wrong time, making driver lose control of the vehicle. • Fuel may spit out of filler pipe when refuelling. • Easy to get foot stuck on accelerator pedal because of placement of partition. • Fuse panel location interferes with applying the brake pedal. • Rear-view mirror creates a large blind spot. • Passenger-side door won't open close to a curb because of the car's low stance. **1999**—Loss of all electrical power while cruising on the highway. • Chronic stalling. • Head restraints won't lock into position. **2000**—Vehicle suddenly accelerates when cruise control is engaged and brakes are applied. The following NHTSA report is rather typical of other similar complaints:

> Driver was going 75 mph [120 km/h] with cruise control set. When approaching a curve, driver applied the brakes to slow down, and as brake pedal was pressed, vehicle [sped] up. Driver was coached from limousine service on a two-way radio how to control vehicle. Driver turned off cruise control switch and vehicle returned to normal.

• Inadvertent airbag deployment. • Frequent brake failures (brake pedal will fade and not hold). • Horn is hard to activate. • Vehicle pulls hard to one side when braking. • Faulty trunk light bulb ignited clothing in trunk. • Power windows fail intermittently. **2001**—Sudden acceleration when brakes are applied. • Inadvertent airbag deployment:

> Passenger side airbag deployed at 70 mph [110 km/h] with no impact to vehicle. Lost control of vehicle temporarily and crossed traffic to other side of road. Regained control after crossing back to original lane shoulder and braking hard. Very frightening experience considering the noise, surprise, and dust from the airbag deploying. Only good thing was that no traffic was coming in other lane.

NHTSA is looking into side-impact airbags deploying for no reason. There are 76 complaints and nine injuries reported. • Frequent brake failures. • Wheel lug studs break off at the hub. • Ignition locks up when key is inserted. • Broken driver's seat. • Headlights can't be aimed properly. • Brake and accelerator pedal set too close together. Dash reflects onto windshield. **2002**—Repeated brake master cylinder failures. • Brake pedal not responsive until pressure is reapplied. • Head restraints set too low. • While driving, sunroof blew off. **2003**—Sudden, unintended acceleration. • Complete brake failure. • Brake light causes an annoying reflection onto the rear windshield. • Hood latch snapped while driving. **2004**—Only 33 safety-related complaints recorded by NHTSA—half of what one would normally expect. • When key was turned in the ignition, fire ignited immediately. • No airbag deployment. • Sudden, unintended acceleration; many reports that the vehicle accelerates when brakes are tapped (also many complaints that accelerator and braking pedals are mounted to close together). • Cruise control doesn't hold the car's speed when descending a hill. • Poor braking. • Sunshine reflects on dashboard metal strip creating an annoying glare. • Tires leak air due to faulty chrome wheels. **2005**—Only 23 safety-related problems logged so far. • Engine surges as brakes are applied:

> When pressing hard on brakes 2005 Town Car engine went to full throttle. The incident happened 3 times.

• Vehicle suddenly accelerated when put into Reverse. Dealer saw no computer error code present, so ignored the problem. • Vehicle hesitates a few seconds before going into passing gear. • Due to the front seat belt's location, the buckle cuts off circulation causing right leg numbness. • It can take up to 15 minutes to put in a few gallons of gas due to a faulty fuel tank valve. • Trunk slams shut due to a dislodged torque rod in the closure assembly.

Secret Warranties/Internal Bulletins/Service Tips

All models: 1985–2002—Repeated heater core leaks. **1993–99**—Paint delamination, peeling, or fading. *Continental:* **1994–99**—Tips on plugging door, window, and moonroof wind noise. **1995–98**—No Fourth gear may mean you have a defective forward clutch-control valve retaining clip. • Condensation buildup on the inside of windows may be stopped by installing an upgraded pressure cycling switch. • An intermittent shifting into Neutral or loss of Forward or Reverse gear is likely caused by a defective forward clutch piston (a problem that has haunted Ford and Lincoln for over a decade). **1998–2002**—Hard-to-turn ignition switch. • Troubleshooting tips for engine misfiring. **1999**—No Reverse engagement with the automatic transmission may be caused by torn reverse clutch lip seals. **1999–2002**—Engine hesitation, surging, and bucking can be fixed under warranty by reprogramming the PCM. *LS:* **2000–01**—Hard starts or no-starts. • Frequent bulletin references to automatic transmission defects producing delayed engagement (PCM module seen as likely culprit), driveline vibration and buzz/clunk/drone, and fluid leakage. • Trunk may suddenly open. • Inaccurate ambient temperature display. • Inoperative AC dual zone heater. • ABS, Airbag, and Service Engine lights come on for no apparent reason. • Noisy front power windows. • Steering wheel "nibble," hum, or boom noise. • 3.9L oil leak from the bell housing area. • Poor braking on V6-equipped models. • V6 engine noise on acceleration, and highway drone noise. • Instrument panel squeaks and rattles. **2000–02**—Inoperative power windows. • Oil pan drain plug leaks. • Correction for a noisy suspension. **2000–05**—Troubleshooting engine misfires. • Inoperative defroster. **2000–06**—AC heater core leakage or electrolysis. • Aluminum body panel corrosion "goodwill" warranty. **2001–02**—A faulty cooling fan is the likely cause of engine overheating. **2003–04**—Harsh upshifts require the reprogramming of the PCM. • An engine stumble or backfire may also be corrected in the same way. • Moisture in the Reverse tail light. • Steering gear noise, vibration. **2004**—Harsh upshifts. • The water pump hose is prone to bursting on 3.0L-equipped models. Ford's extended the warranty. *Mark VII, Mark VIII:* **1985–99**—An exhaust buzz or rattle may be caused by a loose heat-shield catalyst. **1993–94**—Automatic transmissions with delayed or no forward engagement, or a higher engine rpm than expected when coming to a stop, are covered in TSB #94-26-9. *Town Car:* **1995–2006**—Ford will install for free a fuel-tank fire shield on all limos. **1997–2006**—AC heater core leakage or electrolysis. **1998–2005**—Troubleshooting tips for engine misfiring. **2000–06**—Aluminum body panel corrosion "goodwill" warranty:

ALUMINUM BODY PANELS—CORROSION

BULLETIN NO.: 06-25-15   **DATE: DECEMBER 11, 2006**

FORD: 2000–07 CROWN VICTORIA, TAURUS; 2005–06 FORD GT; 2005–07 MUSTANG; 2000–03 RANGER; 2000–07 EXPEDITION; 2002–07 EXPLORER; 2004–07 F-150; 2007 EXPLORER SPORT TRAC; LINCOLN: 2000–06 LINCOLN LS; 2000–07 TOWN CAR, NAVIGATOR; MERCURY: 2000–07 GRAND MARQUIS AND SABLE.

ISSUE: Some vehicles may exhibit a bubbling or blistering under the paint on aluminum body parts. This is due to iron contamination of the aluminum panel.

ACTION: This TSB provides service tips and procedures, outlining methods to properly prepare and protect aluminum body parts from cross contamination.

BACKGROUND: Ford's Scientific Research Laboratory has performed a number of tests on vehicle body parts returned for corrosion related concerns. Testing has revealed that the aluminum corrosion was caused by iron particles working their way into the aluminum body part, prior to it being painted.

Ford cannot deny its own responsibility. It was negligent in painting over the contaminated panels in the first place.

2001–04—Engine ticking countermeasures. **2002–05**—Rear axle shudder or chatter. **2003**—Premature wear of the axle shaft or axle bearing. • Erratic AC blower motor operation. • Blower motor whistling. • Inaccurate fuel gauge. • Power steering assist calibration; excessive power steering pump noise. • Front wheel area click or rattle. • Anti-theft system may cause the transmission to stick in Park or the steering wheel to lock. • Rear parking-brake clicking. **2003–04**—Cold-start engine knocking. • Suspension squeaking and rubbing. • Erratic operation of the AC blower. **2003–05**—Inoperative parking-assist. **2004**—Exhaust manifold to converter leak. **2004–05**—Delayed Reverse engagement. **2005–06**—Hesitation, lack of power during the 1–2 shift.

CONTINENTAL PROFILE

	1995	1996	1997	1998	1999	2000	2001	2002
Cost Price ($)								
Continental Ex.	50,995	51,896	49,995	51,995	52,795	52,895	51,920	52,900
Used Values ($)								
Continental Ex. ▲	2,500	3,000	4,500	5,000	6,000	7,500	10,000	11,500
Continental Ex. ▼	2,000	2,500	3,000	4,500	5,500	6,000	8,000	10,000
Reliability	1	1	2	2	2	3	3	3
Offset	3	3	3	3	3	3	3	3
Head Restraints	1	—	1	—	1	—	2	2

LS PROFILE

	2000	2001	2002	2003	2004	2005
Cost Price ($)						
LS	40,595	40,870	42,300	42,500	43,750	43,865
Used Values ($)						
LS ▲	8,000	11,000	14,000	16,500	18,000	21,000
LS ▼	6,500	9,000	11,500	14,500	16,000	18,500
Reliability	3	3	3	3	4	4
Crash Safety (F)	5	5	5	—	5	5
Side	—	4	4	4	4	4
Offset	5	5	5	5	5	5
Head Restraints	1	2	2	3	3	3
Rollover Resistance	—	5	5	5	5	5

MARK VII, MARK VIII PROFILE

	1991	1992	1993	1994	1995	1996	1997	1998
Cost Price ($)								
Mark VII, VIII	38,895	41,010	43,968	47,995	50,996	51,895	53,695	56,595
Used Values ($)								
Mark VII, VIII ▲	2,000	2,500	3,000	3,500	4,000	5,000	6,000	7,000
Mark VII, VIII ▼	1,500	2,000	2,500	3,000	3,500	4,500	5,500	6,500
Reliability	2	2	2	2	2	3	3	3
Head Restraints	—	—	—	—	1	—	1	—

Note: The Mark series hasn't been crash-tested by NHTSA.

	1997	1998	1999	2000	2001	2002	2003	2004	2005
Cost Price ($)									
Town Car	45,895	50,195	52,195	51,495	53,970	53,445	55,205	57,645	58,865
Used Values ($)									
Town Car ▲	5,000	6,000	8,500	10,500	12,000	15,000	18,500	23,000	26,000
Town Car ▼	4,000	5,500	7,500	9,000	11,000	13,000	16,000	21,000	24,000
Reliability	3	3	3	4	4	4	5	5	5
Crash Safety (F)	4	—	—	4	5	5	5	5	5
Side	—	—	4	4	4	4	5	5	5
Offset	—	—	—	—	—	—	3	5	5
Head Restraints	1	—	1	—	1	1	2	2	2
Rollover Resistance	—	—	—	—	—	—	5	5	5

General Motors

PARK AVENUE ★ ★ ★

RATING: Average (1998–2005); Below Average (1991–97); Not Recommended (1985–90). **"Real" city/highway fuel economy:** 11.9/7.3 L/100 km. Owners report fuel savings may undershoot this estimate by at least 20 percent. **Maintenance/Repair costs:** Higher than average, but repairs aren't dealer dependent. **Parts:** Higher-than-average costs (independent suppliers sell for much less), but not hard to find. Nevertheless, don't even think about buying one of these front-drives without a 3- to 5-year extended warranty backed by the automaker. **Extended warranty:** A must-have. **Best alternatives:** Acura Integra or RL, Cadillac DeVille, Infiniti I30 or I35, Nissan Maxima, and Toyota Avalon. **Online help:** *www.autosafety.org/autodefects.html.*

Strengths and Weaknesses

Full-sized luxury sedan aficionados love the flush glass, wrap-around windshield and bumpers, and clean body lines that make for an aerodynamic, pleasing appearance. But these front-drive cars are more than a pretty package: They provide lots of room (but not for six), luxury, style, and—dare I say—performance. On one hand, plenty of power is available with the 205-hp 3.8L V6 engine and the 240-hp supercharged version of the same powerplant. On the other hand, owners decry the car's ponderous handling, caused partly by a mediocre suspension and over-assisted steering with the base model; obstructed rear visibility; hard braking accompanied by a severe nosedive; interior gauges and controls that aren't easily deciphered or accessed; and surprisingly high fuel consumption.

Although the 1991–96 Park Avenue models improved over the years, they compiled one of the worst repair histories among large cars. Main problem areas are the engine, automatic transmission, fuel system, steering, brakes, electrical system (including defective PROM and MEMCAL modules), starter, and alternator, plus the badly assembled, poor-quality body hardware. The 3.0L V6 engine is inadequate for cars this heavy, and the 3.8L has been a big quality disappointment.

Under-hood servicing is complicated. Other problems: Automatic transmission and engine computer malfunctions are common, the fuel-injection system is temperamental, window mechanisms are poorly designed, the power-steering assembly is failure-prone, there are frequent electrical failures, front brake pads and rotors require frequent replacement, and shock absorbers leak or go soft very quickly. Extensive surface corrosion has been a problem because of poor, and often incomplete, paint application at the factory.

VEHICLE HISTORY: 1996—All models get variable-assist steering and the Ultra gains 20 more horses. **1997**—Park Avenue and Ultra are redesigned to include a reworked powertrain, a stiffer body, improved interior amenities, upgraded four-wheel disc brakes, and an upgraded ventilation system. **1998**—De-powered airbags. **1999**—A tire-monitor gauge for the Ultra. **2000**—StabiliTrak stability control is added. **2002**—Steering-wheel controls for the climate and sound systems. **2003**—Ultra gets side VentriPorts, a new grill, and chrome exhaust tips.

Plenty of power is available with the 205-hp 3.8L V6 engine and the Aurora's 240-hp supercharged powerplant, if you don't mind burning the extra fuel. This configuration enables the car to do 0–100 km/h in under 9 seconds (impressive, considering the heft of these vehicles) and improves low- and mid-range throttle response. Both the Park Avenue and Ultra use a stretched version of the more rigid Riviera and Aurora platform. The revised 1998–2004 models continue to have serious engine intake manifold and transmission problems in addition to airbag, AC, fuel, and electrical system failures. Poor fit and finish is characterized by leaks, squeaks, rattles, moans, and whines.

Safety Summary

All models: 1998—Chronic stalling and loss of electrical power, particularly when braking. • Vehicle also suddenly accelerates when braking. • With cruise control engaged, vehicle picks up speed when going downhill. • Faulty fuel-sending unit; fuel gauge failure. • Cracked engine head gasket. • Transmission failures. • Brakes or steering fail in rainy weather. • ABS failure may be caused by defective computer module. • Steering failure caused by broken serpentine belt. • Premature failure of brake rotors, pads, and calipers. • Goodyear tire-tread separation. • Faulty air level ride fills up rear shocks so that rear end sticks up high in the air. • Seat belts jam in the retractor; fail to extend or retract. • Door locks don't work properly. • Windshield dash glare. **1999**—Frequent stalling; Check Engine light comes on. • Loss of steering because of premature steering-pump failure. • Brake rotor overheating and warpage creates excessive vibration and pulling to one side when brakes are applied. • Transmission jerks when going from Reverse to Drive. • Airbag warning light comes on for no reason. • Shoulder belt twists in retractor. • Keys won't lock or unlock the doors. • Battery often goes dead. **2000**—Airbags deploy when they shouldn't and fail to deploy when they should. • Steering may suddenly lock up. • Excessive steering-wheel vibration numbs hands. • Horn is hard to activate, especially in cold weather. • Front seat lapbelts may be too short; GM will give owners a free extension if they sign a waiver of liability. • Windshield wipers suddenly quit working. **2001**—Sudden, unintended acceleration. • Delayed and extended shifts, slippage in cold weather; early transmission replacement. • Intermittent windshield wiper shut-off. • Trunk lid fell on driver's head. • Excessive dash reflection onto windshield. • Hard to find horn button in an emergency. • Windshield wiper malfunctions. • Driver's seat belt locks up. **2002**—Intermittent horn failure in cold weather. **2003**—Multiple brake failures. • Chemical used to combat AC mould may cause an allergic reaction. • Rear window defroster doesn't defrost entire windshield. **2004**—Headlight high and low beams are a fixed unit, not allowing mechanic to aim them independently and this resulting in inadequate illumination.

Secret Warranties/Internal Bulletins/Service Tips

All models/years: Automatic transaxles on front-drive models equipped with V6 engines are particularly failure-prone. • Reverse servo cover leak. **All models: 1993–2002**—AC odours can be reduced by applying a cooling-coil coating or by installing a special kit. • A rotten-egg odour coming from the exhaust is probably caused by a malfunctioning catalytic converter and may be covered under GM's emissions warranty. • Paint delamination, peeling, or fading. **1993–2005**—No Reverse, Second, or Fourth gear. **1995–2001**—Engine oil pan leaks. **1996–2004**—GM admits it has a "goodwill" warranty covering engine intake manifold failures (see Part Two, pages 77–79). **1997–2001**—Troubleshooting steering vibration, shudder, or moan. **1997–2005**—Oil leaks from transmission vent. **1998**—A fuel gauge that gives inaccurate readings probably needs a new fuel level sensor. **1998–99**—Re-calibrating the PCM can cure low power, stalling, or stumbling when accelerating. **1998–2000**—A hard-to-shift gearshift lever may need a new cable assembly. **1999–2000**—An engine that runs hot, overheats, or loses coolant may simply need a new radiator cap. • Slips, launch shudders, and harsh upshifts or garage shifts have a variety of causes and corrections, says TSB #00-07-30-002. • Diagnostic procedures for an engine that runs hot, overheats, or loses coolant are outlined in TSB #00-06-02-001. **1999–2001**—Tips on correcting excessive engine vibration and silencing generator whine, hum, and moan. **2001**—Delayed and extended shifts, slippage in cold weather. **2001–02**—Poor engine performance and erratic shifting (TSB #02-07-30-013). **2001–04**—Transmission slippage, and harsh 1–2 shifts. **2002–03**—Door lock falls into door panel. **2003**—Erratic automatic transmission shifting. • Transmission grind/growl when vehicle is parked on an incline. • Defective front outer tie-rod ends.

	1997	1998	1999	2000	2001	2002	2003	2004	2005
Cost Price ($)									
Park Avenue	40,865	41,850	41,060	42,075	43,000	43,700	45,790	47,550	47,610
Used Values ($)									
Park Avenue ▲	3,000	4,000	5,500	7,000	9,500	13,500	16,500	20,000	24,000
Park Avenue ▼	2,500	3,500	4,500	6,000	7,000	11,000	14,000	18,000	22,000
Reliability	2	3	3	3	3	4	4	4	4
Crash Safety (F)	—	—	—	—	4	4	4	4	4
Side	—	—	—	—	4	4	4	4	4
Offset	5	5	5	5	5	5	5	5	5
Head Restraints	1	—	1	—	1	1	1	1	1
Rollover Resistance	—	—	—	—	—	—	4	4	4

AURORA, RIVIERA ★ ★ ★ ★

RATING: *Aurora:* Above Average (2001–03); Average (1995–99). There was no year 2000 model. Now that GM has phased out its Oldsmobile division, Aurora resale values are falling rapidly, making the second series' revamped 2001 and 2002 models excellent used buys. *Riviera:* Average (1995–99); Not Recommended (1986–93). GM skipped the 1994 model year and introduced an all-new 1995 version. **"Real" city/highway fuel economy:** The Aurora gets 13.5/8.3 L/100 km, but, interestingly, a 1999 Buick Riviera gets slightly better fuel economy, at 13.2/7.7 L/100 km. Owners report fuel savings may undershoot these two estimates by about 20 percent. **Maintenance/Repair costs:** Higher than average, but repairs aren't dealer dependent. **Parts:** Higher-than-average costs (independent suppliers sell for much less), but not hard to find. GM's phase-out doesn't affect availability or costs, since these vehicles use the same generic parts found on many other GM products. **Extended warranty:** Yes; powertrain repairs alone can cost double what you will pay for an extra warranty. **Best alternatives:** Acura Integra, TL, or RL; Cadillac DeVille, Fleetwood, or Brougham; Ford Crown Victoria or Mercury Grand Marquis; Mercedes E-Class; Nissan Maxima; and Toyota Avalon. **Online help:** *www.autosafety.org/autodefects.html.*

Strengths and Weaknesses

Although the redesigned 1988–93 cars got performance, handling, and ride upgrades, they kept the same low level of quality control, with multiple design and manufacturing defects, including serious fuel injection, engine-computer, and electrical system problems that haven't been solved to this day. One particularly poor design was the complex Graphic Control Center, which used an oversensitive video screen and small push buttons. It's both distracting and expensive to repair. The automatic transmission is notoriously failure-prone, and brakes wear out prematurely and perform poorly. Surface rust and poor paint quality are the most common body complaints for all model years. Shock absorbers wear out quickly, and the diesel engine seldom runs properly.

VEHICLE HISTORY: 1995—Riviera was totally redesigned with standard dual airbags, ABS, a 3.8L V6, and a supercharged variant. **1997**—Additional standard features and a smoother-shifting automatic transmission. **1998**—A supercharged engine arrives. **1999**—Traction control.

Overall, 1995–99 models offer many more luxury features but continue the checkered repair history. As with many of its front-drives during the latter half of the '90s, GM improved quality somewhat, but there are still many generic deficiencies affecting the automatic transmission (torque converter constantly engages and disengages); engine, fuel, and electrical systems; computer modules; AC compressor; brakes (rotor warpage and premature pad replacement); steering; suspension; and fit and finish. Trunk wheelwell leaks are common. Because of their problematic brakes, these cars usually have a pronounced low-speed shudder/vibration and severe pull that intensifies when passing over uneven terrain or when braking.

Aurora

This front-drive Olds luxury sedan was aimed at the Acura, Infiniti, and Lexus crowd. It uses the same basic design as the Riviera but doesn't share the same major mechanical features or popular styling. Because it was a relatively late entry into the Oldsmobile line, GM took more care in the selection of mechanical, electronic, and body components. This has made the Aurora more reliable and glitch-free than GM's other vehicles, which continue to be hobbled with poor-quality components and subpar fit and finish. Too bad that this progress was all for naught, as Aurora folded along with the entire Oldsmobile line.

VEHICLE HISTORY: 1997—Larger front brakes. **1999**—Additional engine mounts to damper vibration. **2001**—A new platform, and now equipped with a 3.5 V6 or 4.0L V8 engine. **2001**—Mid-year addition of an automatic load-levelling suspension. **2002**—GM phase-out of the V6 in favour of a V8. **2003**—Last model year sees all models powered by a V8.

The Aurora's main advantages are its sporty handling and unusual aero styling. In contrast to the Riviera, the Aurora seats only five and offers a 4.0L V8 derived from the Cadillac 4.6L V8 Northstar engine. Acceleration is underwhelming (this is a heavy car) but adequate for highway touring. Road and wind noise are omnipresent, and the trunk's small opening compromises its ability to handle odd-sized objects.

Model-year 1995–2000 Auroras have similar quality failings to those of the Riviera, but they're not as extensive and they generally become less common with the 2001–03 models. Nevertheless, owners of these recent models complain of engine coolant leaks, chronic electrical and fuel supply glitches, harsh shifting, drivetrain vibrations, brake failures, water leaks through the front corner moulding, and overall high maintenance costs.

Safety Summary

Aurora: **1995–2001**—Chronic stalling. • Horn is hard to access and operates erratically. • Headlights short out or come on inadvertently. **1999**—Water is sucked up into engine when car passes over puddles. • Power steering loses power at low speeds. • Loss of all electrical power, including interior and exterior lights. • Exhaust fumes enter interior. **2001**—Total brake failure. • Electrical shorts cause complete electrical shutdown or erratically operating interior and exterior lights and gauges. • Head restraints block rear vision. • Windshield wipers fail intermittently. **2001–03**—Loss of engine coolant. • Will not go into First gear when cupholder is extended. • Reflection of the defrost grate is very distracting to short drivers. **2002**—Severe front-end vibration at 100 km/h; not tire-related. • Headlights flicker. **2003**—Vehicle suddenly accelerated when started up and put in Reverse. • Sudden loss of steering. • When turning, feels like tire is rubbing underbody. • High headrest obstructs rear visibility. • Interior and exterior lights go out periodically. • Rear tail lights dim intermittently. • ABS and traction control warning lights come on for no reason. *Riviera:* **1998**—Engine mount failure. • Brakes don't stop vehicle; frequent rotor replacement. • Horn won't blow at times.

Secret Warranties/Internal Bulletins/Service Tips

All models: 1993–99—AC odours can be reduced by applying a cooling-coil coating. • A rotten-egg odour coming from the exhaust is likely the result of a malfunctioning catalytic converter. • Paint delamination, peeling, or fading. **1995–99**—Floor pan corrosion perforation in the battery compartment can be corrected by installing a GM repair kit. *Aurora:* **1995–99**—A cold engine knock or ticking may be caused by excessive carbon deposits in the engine. • A steering shudder at idle or during parking may be fixed by installing an anti-shudder power-steering outlet hose assembly. **1996–99**—GM has an enhanced crankshaft rear seal to use for complaints related to leaking or poor sealing. **1997–2005**—Fluid leak from transmission vent. **1999–2000**—Overheating or coolant loss may be corrected by simply replacing the radiator cap and polishing the radiator filler neck. **1999–2003**—Harsh shifts, chuggle (slipping), and no downshifts when decelerating. **2000–01**—If there's a sudden loss of power when accelerating, the transmission fluid pressure switch may be defective. **2000–02**—Seatback squeaks. • Poor shifting. **2001**—Cooler-fitting coolant leaks. • Delayed Reverse engagement. **2001–02**—Shake, vibration at cruising speed. **2001–03**—Premature hood blistering and corrosion. • Inoperative seat heater. **2003**—Intermittent no-start, no-crank condition. • Engine overheating in cold weather. • Sudden engine shutdown. • Harsh shifting remedy. • Automatic transmission grind/growl when vehicle is parked on an incline. • Poor transmission and engine performance may be caused by debris in the transaxle valve body and case oil passages, says TSB #02-07-30-013. • Incorrect First gear ratio; delayed

Reverse engagement; harsh shifting upon start-up; transmission whining noise and cooling line leaks; leakage from the quick-connect fitting at the case cover; no Fourth gear, or slipping in Fourth gear; oil leakage from the oil level sensor; and intermediate shaft clunk. • Water contamination of the ABS sensor. • Excessive vibration on smooth roads. • Broken sunroof deflectors. • Faulty windshield wipers. • Horn blows on its own, or refuses to blow.

AURORA PROFILE

	1995	1996	1997	1998	1999	2001	2002	2003
Cost Price ($)								
Aurora	43,020	43,695	46,045	47,250	46,190	39,590	40,030	46,590
Used Values ($)								
Aurora ▲	2,500	3,000	3,500	4,000	5,000	8,000	11,500	15,500
Aurora ▼	2,000	2,500	3,000	3,500	4,500	5,500	9,000	13,000
Reliability	3	3	3	3	3	3	3	4
Crash Safety (F)	3	3	3	3	3	4	4	4
Side	—	—	—	—	—	3	3	3
Offset	—	—	—	—	—	5	5	5
Head Restraints	1	—	1	—	1	5	5	5

RIVIERA PROFILE

	1993	1995	1996	1997	1998	1999
Cost Price ($)						
Riviera	30,790	39,525	40,700	42,415	44,950	44,125
Used Values ($)						
Riviera ▲		2,000	3,000	3,500	4,000	5,000	6,500
Riviera ▼		1,500	2,500	3,000	3,500	4,500	5,500
Reliability	2	3	3	3	3	3
Head Restraints	—	1	—	1	—	1

CATERA, CTS, ELDORADO, SEVILLE ★ ★

RATING: *Catera:* Not Recommended (1997–2001). *CTS:* Below Average (2003–06). *Eldorado and Seville:* Below Average (1992–2004); Not Recommended (1986–91). **"Real" city/highway fuel economy:** *Catera:* 13.8/9.2 L/100 km. *CTS 3.2L V6:* 12.6/8.2 L/100 km with a manual transmission. *CTS 3.6L V6:* 13.4/7.8 L/100 km with an automatic transmission. *2001 Eldorado and Seville 4.6L:* 14.0/7.9 L/100 km. *2004 Seville 4.6L:* 13.3/8.2 L/100 km. Owners report fuel savings may undershoot

All ratings on a numbered scale where 5 is good and 1 is bad. See pages 130–132 for a more detailed description.

the above estimates by at least 20 percent. **Maintenance/Repair costs:** Higher than average. Catera repairs are more expensive because they are dealer dependent. Long delays for recall repairs on all models. **Parts:** Higher-than-average costs (independent suppliers sell for much less), but most parts aren't hard to find. **Extended warranty:** Don't buy any of these cars without a 3- to 5-year supplementary warranty. **Best alternatives:** Acura Integra or RL; Cadillac DeVille, Brougham, or Fleetwood; Ford Crown Victoria; and Mercury Grand Marquis. **Online help:** *www.autosafety.org/autodefects.html* and *www.supremecourt. nm.org/pastopinion/VIEW/98ca-020.html* (New Mexico Supreme Court and Court of Appeals).

Strengths and Weaknesses

Front-drive Cadillacs are unreliable, cobbled-together embarrassments. The biggest tip-off that GM was conning us with these front-drives was in 1987 when GM sold gussied-up V6-equipped Cavaliers as Cadillac Cimarrons. They flopped, and Infiniti and Lexus carved out a huge chunk of the American luxury car market that they have never given up. Even though later Cadillacs used many of the same mechanical components as the Riviera and Toronado, they continued to be no match for the Asian competition because of their poor quality and complexity.

In recent years, Cadillac has realized its mistake, and now most models are marginally more reliable rear-drives (CTS, Escalade, SRX, and STS); only the 2005 DTS retains front-drive.

Catera

Assembled in Germany and based on the Opel Omega, the rear-drive, mid-sized Catera comes with a 200-hp V6 engine, 4-speed automatic transmission, 16-inch alloy wheels, four-wheel disc brakes, a limited slip differential, traction control, and standard dual front airbags. This conservatively styled car (the uninspired styling has Lumina written all over it) was designed to compete with the BMW 328i, Lexus ES 300, and Mercedes-Benz C280. It was also a flop.

VEHICLE HISTORY: 1998—De-powered airbags. **1999**—More complex electronics and emissions systems to meet federal standards. **2000**—Slight styling changes, side airbags, improved throttle control, and a retuned suspension.

Cateras have a quiet, spacious, and comfortable interior; responsive handling; fine-tuned suspension; and almost non-existent lean or body roll when cornering. On the downside, the steering system lacks balance and allows the vehicle to wander, the controls aren't easy to figure out, some gauges are hard to read, and the driver's rear view is hindered by the large rear head restraints and narrow back windshield. Furthermore, owners report chronic stalling and hard starts, possibly because of a malfunctioning idle control valve; the transmission hunts for the right gear; and dash warning lights are constantly lit. Body fit and finish is subpar: Panels are often misaligned, squeaks and rattles are omnipresent, and wind and water leaks are commonplace. And here are two other performance problems reported by many owners: When you pass over a large expansion joint, the floor pan vibrates annoyingly, and if you drive over a bump when turning, the steering wheel kicks back in your hands.

Another point you may wish to consider: GM dealers are notoriously bad when it comes to understanding and repairing European-transplanted cars (just ask any Saab owner). As well, low-volume cars generally don't have an adequate supply of replacement parts in the pipeline until they've been on the market for a while. Add in the Catera's European connection and the fact it has just been dropped by GM, and you'd best be ready to endure lots of mechanic head-scratching, long service waits, and high parts costs for those repairs not covered under warranty.

It's a safe bet that these cars will be less reliable and more troublesome than the competition. GM first learned that lesson with the British-built, failure-prone Vauxhall Firenza it unleashed on an unsuspecting Canadian public in the '70s. A few years later, it settled out of court on several class actions that I piloted, and paid a $20,000 fine to the federal government for misleading advertising. (On a nationally advertised road trip across Canada, GM said the cars excelled. Truth is, they were a disaster. They required a team of engineers just to get started.)

CTS

Cadillac's entry-level CTS replaced the Catera in 2003. It's a fairly reliable luxury rear-drive car that performs like a European sports sedan, despite being one of the largest, heaviest vehicles in its class. This extra weight makes the CTS a fuel guzzler, with an estimated city/highway fuel economy rating of only 13.4/7.8 L/100 km. Crashworthiness is a more positive story. The 2003–06 models scored four stars for front- and side-impact occupant protection and rollover resistance and five stars for rear-seat occupant protection in side collisions. Suggested alternatives are the Acura TL, Infiniti G35, Lincoln Town Car, and Toyota Avalon.

The CTS's problematic powertrain has been constantly evolving during its few years on the market. First-year models only offered a 220-hp 3.2L V6 coupled to a standard 5-speed manual gearbox or an optional 5-speed automatic transmission. Smart buyers, though, will opt for the smoother and more powerful 255-hp 3.6L V6 engine and automatic transmission that power the 2004 models. That same year, the 2004 CTS-V was launched, carrying a Corvette-derived, 400-hp 5.7L V8 that isn't as reliable as the V6. The 2005 CTS models replaced the 3.2L engine with a 2.8L V6 that delivers 10 fewer horses and a 6-speed manual gearbox instead of the previous year's 5-speed.

The above-noted powertrain changes haven't improved differential reliability, which has been a chronic problem for years:

> At 27,000 miles [43,000 kilometres] I was driving the CTS-V [and] changed gears from 2nd to 3rd [at] approx. 30 mph [48 km/h]. [I] heard a clunk and [the] rear end started to whine...I parked the car, called road side service, they towed the car to

the dealer. Customer service rep called a few days later [and] he said the rear end has failed again and needs complete replacement. [T]he hanger bearing is bent, the main bolt is broken in two pieces and [he] is recommending a complete new rear end. [H]e also said GM refused to pay for service to his surprise. Here we go again. My local dealer has the car, it has not been repaired as of yet, so yes the old parts are available. The Cadillac CTS-V rear differential is weak and may break causing this car to skid or suddenly stop, causing an accident, injury, or death. Cadillac knows of the problem and has provided some customers with warranty repair, offered 100,000 mile [160,000 kilometre] extended warranties for others and yet denied repair for customers with similar problems. This rear differential is under rated for this car's horse power and was designed for use in the standard CTS version of this car[;] the rear tires have also been a problem showing early signs of wear. I had to replace my first set [of] front and rear [tires] at 8,500 miles [13,500 kilometres][.] [T]hese tires are worst rated tire by consumers at *www.tirerack.com* and *www.cadillacfaq.com.*

Other problems include constant rear-end whine (a warning that total failure is just around the corner); stability control and ABS failure; early replacement of the fuel/water pump, radiator, and power windows; electrical system shorts causing lights, gauges, instruments, and power seats to malfunction; and poor fit and finish, highlighted by paint blistering, premature corrosion, and door handle, dash, and radio button plastic peeling.

Eldorado and Seville

Sitting on the same platform as the front-drive Eldorado, the Seville has European-style allure with a more rounded body than the Eldorado. Apart from that, since its redesign in 1992, its engine, handling, and braking upgrades have followed the Eldorado's improvements in lockstep fashion.

Although the base 4.9L V8 provides brisk acceleration, the 32-valve Northstar V8, first found on the 1993 Touring Coupe, gives you almost 100 more horses with great handling and a comfortable ride. Overall, the Touring Coupe or Sport Coupe will give you the best powertrain, handling, and braking features. Of course, you'll have to contend with poor fuel economy, rear visibility that's obstructed by the huge side pillars (a Seville problem, as well), confusing and inconvenient climate controls, and a particularly complex engine that's failure-prone and a nightmare to troubleshoot.

VEHICLE HISTORY: 1998–2001—The only real change was the Eldorado's Northstar engine tweaking for year 2000 models. *Seville:* **2002**—An upgraded suspension. **2004**—300-hp engine is dropped; Seville replaced by the STS.

These cars have generic deficiencies that fall into common categories: poorly calibrated and failure-prone engines, transmissions, and fuel and ignition systems; a multiplicity of electrical short circuits; and sloppy body assembly using poor-quality components. Specifically, engines and fuel systems often produce intermittent stalling, rough idling, hesitation, and no-starts; the Overdrive automatic is prone to premature failure; oil pumps fail frequently; front brakes and shock absorbers wear out quickly; paint is often poorly applied, fades, or peels away prematurely; fragile body hardware breaks easily (front-bumper cracks are commonplace); and there are large gaps between sheet-metal panels and doors that are poorly hung and not entirely square. Other body problems include the cracking of front outside door handles, door rattles (Eldorado), poor bumper fit, loose sun visor mounting, rear tail light condensation, fading and discolouring appliqué mouldings (Seville), interior window fogging, creaking body mounts, water leaking into the trunk from the licence plate holder (Eldorado), noisy roof panels and seatback lumbar motors, and a creaking noise at the front-door upper hinge area.

Safety Summary

Catera: **1997–2001**—Chronic stalling. • Frequent wheel alignments. • Defective brake rotors cause excessive vibration and pull. • Premature tire wear. • Vehicle wanders and pulls to one side. • Door locks don't work, and key sticks in the ignition. • Windshield wipers are inadequate in heavy rain. **1998**—Engine head gasket failures. **1999**—Accelerator can be floored, and vehicle will only creep forward. • Head restraints block vision. • Loss of steering. • Door latch sticks in the closed position. **2000**—Hesitant shifting. • Defective ignition switch. **2001**—Airbags fail to deploy. • Gas pedal sticks. • Fuel line is exposed to road debris. • Windshield orange-peel pattern. • Tires may wear out quickly because the wheels pitch in slightly. *CTS:* **2003**—Airbags fail to deploy. • Unintended acceleration. • Many complaints of rear differential/casing failures and excessive hum or whine; insiders say the differential is overwhelmed by the powerful engine, causing excessive wheel hop. • Electrical shorts. • PCV valve may burst, spewing oil and causing engine to catch fire. • Suddenly runs out of fuel. **2004**—In one incident, key was put into the ignition and the airbag deployed, breaking driver's nose. • Airbags fail to deploy. • Surging when brakes are applied. • CTS-V manual transmission often fails to shift properly. • Rear differential fractures and separates into half shafts:

Rear differential of my 2004 Cadillac CTS-V is too weak. It clunks, and produces excessive wheel-hop, thus not allowing the power to transfer. The whole rear end of the car from the bushings to the rear cradle to the half shafts are too weak for the car. Over 1000s of CTS-Vs of the under approx. 4,000 produced from 2004–2005 have had major issues. Service centers claim everything is normal. My car is continually in the shop. GM refuses to pay for these items and I have a 6-yr 100,000 mile [160,000 km] warranty. Service centers are not equipped to deal with this car, and GM failed to engineer it properly. In addition all of my interior parts rattle when I step on it, and some continue to rattle during daily driving. The paint quality of the exterior is the worst I have [seen]…yet. There are weird blotches all over the place and are obviously due to poor paint application at the factory. I have owned the car for 3 months and so far have had to replace the radiator, the whole nav unit, the rear differential. And already, the nav unit is beginning to show the same indications of why it got replaced in the first place, and the rear differential is starting to make noises again. Also, the dual mass flywheel produces lots of noise.

There needs to be an in-depth investigation regarding the number of CTS and CTS-V rear differentials that have been replaced. I have now been through 2 personally, and an online poll of 65 CTS-V owners showed this: 26% have had 1 replacement, 5% have had 2 or more replaced, and 8% have had 3 or more replaced. The link for this poll is: *cadillacforums.com/forums/showthread.php?p=305662&posted=1 #post305662.*

• Rear child safety seat latches don't latch properly. • Inaccurate "miles remaining" fuel gauge allows driver to run out of gas. • Bose CD player locks up. • Tread separates from Goodyear Eagle sidewalls. • Stability tracking system engages when it shouldn't, suddenly pulling the car into oncoming traffic. **2005**—Headlights are too bright and sometimes flicker. • Faulty run-flat tires. Dash reflects onto the front windshield, obstructing visibility. *Eldorado, Seville:* **1986–2001**—A plethora of electrical short circuits and front axle, ABS brake, and steering failures. • Sudden, unintended acceleration. • Airbag malfunctions (deploying for no reason and injuring occupants). • Brake rotors and pads always need changing. • Excessive vibration at all speeds. • Poor headlight illumination. *Eldorado:* **2002**—No airbag deployment. • Front tires wear out prematurely. *Seville:* **1999**—Front control arm snaps. • Tie-rod end comes apart. • Loss of power steering when driving in the rain. • Front and rear lights collect water. **2000**—Seat belt retractors don't work properly. • Excessive drifting at any speed. • Brake caliper locks up. **2001**—While driving, passenger-side wheel collapsed because of a missing suspension bolt. • Steering column rubbing noise is heard when making a right turn. **2002**—Chronic stalling in traffic. • Many reports of excessive vibration (suspension, driveshaft, wheels, and tires replaced). • Noisy, erratic transmission shifting. **2003**—Display panel can be hard to see. • Excessive oil burning. **2004**—Loose driver's seat.

Secret Warranties/Internal Bulletins/Service Tips

All models/years: Reverse servo cover leak. **All models:** **1993–99**—A cold engine knock or ticking may be caused by excessive carbon deposits in the engine. • AC odours can be reduced by applying a cooling-coil coating. • Paint delamination, peeling, or fading. **1996–2003**—Excessive oil consumption may be caused by dirty piston rings, says GM TSB #02-06-01-009B. **1998–2003**—Water and musty smell in rear compartment. • Inoperative seat heater. **1999–2000**—An engine that runs hot, overheats, or loses coolant may simply need a new radiator cap. • Steering-column clunk. **1999–2004**—Repair tips for a slipping automatic transmission. **2000–01**—If there's a sudden loss of power when accelerating, the transmission fluid pressure switch may be defective. **2000–02**—Power steering noise. • No power when accelerating; 1–2 shift concerns. **2001**—Intermittent inoperative instrument panel (requires replacement of the I/P cluster assembly). • Delayed Reverse engagement. **2001–03**—Loss of engine coolant. • Steering clunk remedy is to replace the intermediate shaft. **2001–05**—Harsh upshifts. **2002–05**—Navigation system screen goes blank. **2003**—Erratic transmission performance. **2004**—Troubleshooting tips for hard starts. *Catera:* **1997–2001**—

Coolant loss; engine overheating. • Rear compartment noise. • Steering-column squeak. • Key can't be removed from the ignition lock cylinder. *CTS:* **2003**— Transmission shudder upon hard acceleration (replace the transmission output shaft flange). • Suspension rattling. • Windshield stress cracking. • An underbody thump noise can be silenced by replacing the engine mounts. **2003–04**— Automatic transmission has no Reverse gear or slips in gear. • Automatic transmission Reverse servo cover leak. • Oil leaks from cam valve cover seal (3.2L V6). **2003–05**—Harsh upshifts. • Intermittent dead battery (replace overhead console assembly). **2003–06**—Aluminum hood blistering. • Noisy suspension when turning (ionstall front lower control arm rear bushing spacer). **2004**— Transmission won't stay in Sport mode. **2004–05**—In TSB #05-04-114-001A, Cadillac admits its CTS models have rear-wheel hop and offers to replace the rear subframe bushings to correct the problem. • Remedy for frozen door locks. • Harsh upshifts. *Eldorado, Seville:* **1996–2003**—Excessive oil consumption can be corrected with new piston rings if a new ring-cleaning process doesn't work (TSB #02-06-01-009C). • Hard to see display panel.

CATERA, CTS, ELDORADO, SEVILLE PROFILE

	1997	1998	1999	2000	2001	2002	2003	2004	2005
Cost Price ($)									
Catera	42,690	43,250	42,310	42,635	42,485	—	—	—	—
CTS	—	—	—	—	—	—	39,900	39,200	37,800
CTS-V	—	—	—	—	—	—	—	70,000	70,700
Eldorado	52,015	53,000	52,660	53,455	56,600	57,450	—	—	—
Seville	57,000	59,900	59,195	60,195	58,710	59,450	62,045	63,400	—
Used Values ($)									
Catera ▲	4,500	5,500	6,500	7,500	8,500	—	—	—	—
Catera ▼	4,000	5,000	6,000	6,500	7,500	—	—	—	—
CTS ▲	—	—	—	—	—	—	19,000	20,500	24,000
CTS ▲	—	—	—	—	—	—	17,000	18,000	22,000
CTS-V ▲	—	—	—	—	—	—	—	32,000	40,000
CTS-V ▼	—	—	—	—	—	—	—	30,000	38,000
Eldorado ▲	4,500	5,500	7,500	9,500	12,000	15,500	—	—	—
Eldorado ▼	4,000	5,000	6,000	7,500	10,500	13,000	—	—	—
Seville ▲	6,000	7,000	9,000	11,500	14,000	17,000	20,500	26,000	—
Seville ▼	5,500	6,500	7,000	9, 000	12,000	15,000	18,000	23,500	—
Reliability	1	1	1	2	2	2	2	2	3
Crash Safety (F)	—	—	—	—	—	—	4	4	4
Side	—	—	—	—	—	—	4	4	4
Offset									
Catera	5	5	5	5	5	—	—	—	—
CTS	—	—	—	—	—	—	5	5	5
Seville	1	—	—	5	5	5	5	5	

Head Restraints									
Catera	3	—	2	—	3	—	—	—	—
CTS	—	—	—	—	—	—	1	1	1
Eldorado	1	—	1	—	1	1	—	1	—
Seville	1	—	1	1	1	1	1	1	—
Rollover Resistance									
CTS	—	—	—	—	—	—	4	4	4

Note: Reliability figures apply to the Eldorado and Seville only; Catera and CTS reliability information is given within the text.

CONCOURS, DEVILLE ★ ★ ★

RATING: Average (2002–05); Below Average (1985–2001). Interestingly, new Concours were sold at a premium over the DeVille, but the difference narrows considerably as the vehicles age. There are two major safety problems affecting 1995–99 models: inadvertent side and front airbag deployment and chronic stalling in traffic. **"Real" city/highway fuel economy:** 13.3/8.2 L/100 km. Owners report fuel savings may undershoot this estimate by at least 20 percent. **Maintenance/Repair costs:** Higher than average, and most repairs must be done by a dealer. Expect long delays for recall repairs. **Parts:** Higher-than-average costs, but parts aren't hard to find. All of these front-drives require a 3- to 5-year supplementary warranty. **Extended warranty:** A good idea for the front-drives, because Cadillac parts are so darned expensive and there aren't a lot of independent suppliers. **Best alternatives:** Acura Integra or RL, Infiniti I30 or I35, and Toyota Avalon. **Online help:** *www.autosafety.org/autodefects.html.*

Strengths and Weaknesses

Although they have better handling and are almost as comfortable as older, traditional Caddies, these front-drive luxury coupes and sedans are barely worth considering because of their dismal reliability and overly complex servicing. Redesigned 1995–99 versions have posted fewer complaints; however, they are still far below the industry norm for quality and reliability. As with the Eldorado and Seville, you get the best array of handling, braking, and performance features with more recent versions, but reliability remains a problem and Cadillac fuel economy is an oxymoron. Also, the dash controls and gauges are confusing and not easily accessible, and the high trunk lid and large side pillars obstruct the rear view.

VEHICLE HISTORY: 1996—DeVilles were given the Northstar V8 and an upgraded automatic transmission and suspension. The Concours received 25 additional horses along with improved steering and suspension. **1997**—Substantially reworked and given new styling, side airbags, and an upgraded interior. **1998**—De-powered airbags. **2000**—A number of high-tech improvements, including refinements to the V8 engine, Night Vision, Rear Parking Assist, and StabiliTrak traction control. **2002**—An enhanced suspension. **2005**—Redesigned and sold as the 2006 DTS.

The 4.3L V6, 4.1L V8, and 4.5L V8 engines and 4-speed automatic transmission suffer from a variety of terminal maladies, including oil leaks, premature wear, poor fuel economy, and excessive noise. The electrical system and related components are temperamental. Steering is noisy, the suspension goes soft quickly, and the front brakes often wear out after only 18 months/20,000 km. Problems with the digital fuel injection and engine control systems are very difficult to diagnose and repair. Premature paint peeling and rusting, excessive wind noise in the interior, and fragile trim items characterize poor body assembly.

Safety Summary

DeVille: **1998**—Inadvertent side airbag deployment. • Wheel flew off car after wheel studs failed. • In one incident, vehicle suddenly accelerated, killing one person and injuring others. • Accelerator sticking. • Cruise control self-activates. • Chronic stalling while underway. • Can't read speedometer in daylight. • Many complaints of front and rear brake rotor warpage and premature pad and caliper failure. • Sudden loss of power steering. • Vehicle tends to wander all over the road. • Leaking engine oil coolant. • Windshield washer fluid doesn't pump high enough. • Gas-tank sensor failure causes inaccurate fuel readings. • Interior lights frequently malfunction. **1999**—Airbags explode when vehicle is started, idles, accelerates, or is parked. Several occupants have been injured. • Incidents where front and side airbags failed to deploy in a collision. • Engine overheating, loose head bolts, and excessive oil consumption. • Stalling when coasting or coming to a stop. • Vehicle rolls backward when in gear. • Fuel tank leaks fuel. • Premature warpage of the front and rear brake rotors. • Failure-prone ignition and electronic control module. • Tire flies off while vehicle is underway. • Factory-equipped jack inadequate to support vehicle. • Instrument panel lighting hard to read in daylight. • Power door locks operate erratically. • Windshield wipers won't come on unless turned on High. • Driver's seat belt constantly tightens up. **2000**—Sudden, unintended acceleration and chronic stalling. • Steering locks up. • Automatic transmission jolts when shifting. • Airbags deploy inadvertently. • A shroud may impede access to brake pedal. • Frequent crankshaft sensor failure. • Digital instrument panel can't be read in daylight. • Sun visor blocks out overhanging traffic lights. • Horn is hard to access. **2001**—Transmission doesn't shift all the way into Drive; it pops out of gear and allows vehicle to roll down an incline. • Brake pedal goes to the floor without braking. • Steering wheel emits a grinding sound. • Side mirror creates a huge blind spot. **2002**—Sudden acceleration in Reverse. • Driver-side wheel fell off. • Chronic stalling after refuelling. • Seat belts are too short for some occupants. • Shoulder belt fits short drivers poorly. • Distorted windshield. • Airbag warning light stays lit. **2003**—Intermittent stalling. • Total brake failure. • Instrument panel shuts down. • Sun visor obstructs vision. • Tire jack collapses. **2004**—Vehicle caught fire while parked. • Transmission fluid leakage is a fire hazard. • Sudden, unintended acceleration:

Car accelerated, crossed 12' [3.7 m] sidewalk, crashed thru glass window front and skidded 12' [3.7 m] to final stop inside pharmacy... Car was repaired at cost of $11,518.46 paid by insurance. Cadillac division of General Motors was notified, without any response. Cadillac dealer in Brunswick, Georgia, and Dew Cadillac in Pinellas Park, Florida vowed that "sudden acceleration" was impossible because the computer did not indicate "any" problems. However, Dew Cadillac did replace the throttle assembly without charge or explanation.

• Hesitation when accelerating. • Airbag fails to deploy. • Chronic stalling caused by electrical failure. • Sudden brake failure. • Early tie-rod replacement. • Hood latch isn't secured tightly. **2005**—Reduced stopping ability due to premature brake disc warpage. • Headlights shut off when turning signals are enabled. • DeVille tail lights blur the vision of drivers of following cars. • Door won't stay open when the car is parked on an incline. • Lengthy delay when transmission is shifted into Reverse. • Sidewall bubbling with original equipment Vogue tires.

Secret Warranties/Internal Bulletins/Service Tips

All models/years: Defective catalytic converters that cause a rotten-egg smell in the interior may be replaced free of charge under the emissions warranty. • Reverse servo cover seal leak. • Paint delamination, peeling, or fading. **All models: 1996–2003**—Excessive oil consumption can be corrected with new piston rings if a new ring-cleaning process doesn't work (TSB #02-06-01-009C). **2000–02**—Loss of power when accelerating. • 1–2 shift concerns. • Noisy steering. • Steering column rubbing noise. • Scratched door glass. • Parking brake won't release; warning light stays lit. **2001**—Intermittent inoperative instrument panel (requires replacement of the I/P cluster assembly). • Cooler-fitting coolant leaks. • Delayed Reverse engagement. **2001–03**—Loss of engine coolant. **2001–05**—Harsh upshifts. **2003**—Erratic transmission shifting. *All models with 5.7L engines:* **1999–2000**—An engine that runs hot, overheats, or loses coolant may simply need a new radiator cap. *DeVille:* **2000–04**—Remedies for excessive vibration, shaking while cruising. • Troubleshooting rear suspension noise. **2000–05**—Silencing a front end clunk. • Hood blistering, premature corrosion. **2003**—Intermittent no-starts; no electrical power (align engine wiring junction block, says TSB #06-03-009). **2003–04**—Right rear-door air leak. **2005**—Difficult to move shifter out of Park. • Moan, squawk during low-speed turns.

CONCOURS, DEVILLE PROFILE

	1997	1998	1999	2000	2001	2002	2003	2004	2005
Cost Price ($)									
Concours	56,985	58,600	57,490	—	—	—	—	—	—
DeVille	49,400	50,495	49,710	51,995	51,895	52,555	54,925	56,235	57,500
Used Values ($)									
Concours ▲	5,000	5,500	7,000	—	—	—	—	—	—
Concours ▼	4,500	5,000	6,000	—	—	—	—	—	—
DeVille ▲	4,500	5,000	6,000	8,500	11,000	14,500	18,000	21,500	26,500
DeVille ▼	4,000	4,500	5,500	6,500	9,000	12,000	16,000	19,500	24,000

Reliability	2	2	2	2	2	2	3	3	3
Crash Safety (F)	4	4	4	3	3	1	1	4	4
Side	4	4	4	4	4	4	4	4	4
Rollover Resistance	—	—	—	—	—	5	5	5	5

Infiniti

G20/G35, I30/I35, J30, M35, M45, Q45   ★ ★ / ★ ★ ★ ★

RATING: *G20:* Not Recommended (1994–2002). *G35:* Below Average (2003–06); *I30:* Recommended (2000–03); Above Average (1997–99); Average (1996). *I35:* Above Average (2002–04). *J30:* Above Average (1994–97); Average (1993). *M34, M45:* Above Average (2006); Average (2003–05); *Q45:* Above Average (2001–05, 1991–96); Average (1997–2000). The 1997–99 Q45s were made more cheaply, came with fewer standard features, and were equipped with a smaller, less powerful engine than previous models. The 2002 I35 exhibits a disturbingly high number of performance- and safety-related defects; other Infinitis, however, demonstrate impressive reliability and quality control. **"Real" city/highway fuel economy:** *G20:* 10.0/6.9 L/100 km. *I30 3.0L:* 12.1/8.1 L/100 km. *I35:* 12.1/8.3 L/100 km. *J30:* 12.8/9.3 L/100 km. *Q45 4.1L:* 13.4/9.2 L/100 km. *Q45 4.5L:* 13.6/ 8.8 L/100 km. Owners report fuel savings may undershoot the above estimates by about 10 percent. **Maintenance/Repair costs:** Higher than average, and repairs must be done by either an Infiniti or a Nissan dealer. **Parts:** Higher-than-average costs, but not hard to find (except body panels and the lighting assembly on the I30t):

> In late October I noticed that one of my headlights would periodically cut out and I was left with just the daytime running light in that particular headlight. It wasn't doing this consistently and I assumed it was probably just a problem with the bulb or perhaps a loose connection/wire.

> When I took it in to the dealer for my next service in mid-Feb I asked them to check it out. They found the problem...but told me that it couldn't be repaired and that the part wasn't sold separately. Instead the entire light assembly needed to be replaced with the light assembly costing $1,500.00 and with taxes and labour the cost would exceed $1,800.00.

Extended warranty: Not necessary. **Best alternatives:** The fully equipped Honda Accord, Mazda Millenia or 929, Nissan Maxima, and Toyota Camry or Avalon are better buys from a price/quality standpoint, but they don't have the same luxury cachet. Also consider the Acura Integra, Legend, or RL, and the Mercedes E-Class. **Online help:** *www.carsurvey.org.*

Strengths and Weaknesses

With its emphasis on sporty handling (diluted somewhat with the '97 and later model years), the Infiniti series takes the opposite tack from the Lexus, which focuses on comfort and luxury. Still, the Infiniti comes fully equipped and offers owners the prestige of driving a comfortable and nicely styled luxury car that's more reliable than what's offered by Lexus, though not quite as refined.

G20

The least expensive Infiniti, the 1994–96 G20 is a front-drive luxury sports sedan that uses a base 2.0L 140-hp 16-valve, twin-cam, 4-cylinder powerplant to accelerate smoothly, albeit noisily, through all gear ranges. Dual airbags came on line midway through the 1993 model year, and ABS is standard. The towing capacity is 450 kg (1,000 lb.). Cruise control is a bit erratic, particularly when traversing hilly terrain. Unlike the engine, the automatic transmission is silent, and power is reduced automatically when shifting. Steering is precise and responsive on the highway. However, the rear end tends to swing out sharply following abrupt steering changes. Early Infiniti G20s rode a bit too firmly, which led to the suspension being softened on the 1994 model. Thereafter, drivers say that the suspension bounced and jiggled occupants whenever the car went over uneven pavement or the load was increased.

VEHICLE HISTORY: 1999—Returning after a 3-year hiatus, the '99 G20 wasn't worth the wait. It's basically a package of unfulfilled expectations with its wimpy 2.0L 140-hp engine, firmer ride, and ordinary styling. On the positive side, the car does handle and ride better. **2000**—A bit more horsepower and an upgraded transmission. **2001**—Standard leather seats and a power sunroof.

1999 and later G20s aren't as refined as their entry-level Lexus counterparts in interior space, drivetrain, or convenience features. The 140-hp engine's lack of low-speed torque means that it has to work hard above 4000 rpm—while protesting noisily—to produce brisk engine response in the higher gear ranges. The automatic transmission shifts roughly, particularly when passing; the power steering needs more assist during parking manoeuvres; and the dealer-installed foglights cost an exorbitant $500 to replace. Tall drivers will find the legroom insufficient, and rear passengers will feel cramped. Trunk space is limited by the angle of the rear window.

Owner complaints target automatic transmission failures, engine coolant leaks, prematurely worn brake rotors and brake pads, excessive noise when braking, malfunctioning power seats, and clunky springs and shock absorbers.

G35

Infiniti's rear-drive, sporty luxury car was introduced in the spring of 2002. The sedan is equipped with a 260-hp engine, versus 280 hp for the coupe. Coupes are feature-laden, stretched versions of Nissan's problem-prone 2003 350Z sports car, with less power and a small fold-down back seat added. Sedans are quite long and provide a sportier performance than Infiniti's front-drive I35. Initially, both G35s offered a 5-speed automatic transmission with manual shift gate, but a 6-speed manual was phased in within a year. Both body styles offer four-wheel ABS disc brakes, front side airbags, and side curtain airbags (only for the front seats in the coupe). Manual transmission coupes come with more performance-oriented upgraded brakes. Alternative choices would be the Acura TL, Audi A4, BMW 3 Series, and Cadillac CTS.

Owner complaints primarily concern automatic transmission failures and erratic shifting, noisy manual 6-speed transmission, radio noise and dashboard clicking, excessive brake dust and squealing, very poor fuel economy, an unstable driver's seat, and early replacement of brake pads and rotors:

> The dealer informed me that most owners must replace brakes and rotors in less than 15000 miles [24,000 kilometres]. I submit two issues with the brakes of G35: 1. Safety—The rotors are substandard and can go under safe limit very easy since most customers [do] not expect extreme early wear. The same point can be made for the pads. It is possible the brake system interacts in unexpected way[s] with VDC [Vehicle Dynamic Control] and [ABS] so the pads become engaged in certain situations. 2. Warranty Coverage—I was charged $510 for front brake pads and new rotors. The Infiniti G35 maintenance and warranty book explicitly list the pads as replaceable items, but does not mention the rotors. The dealer could not point out where in the Infiniti warranty book the rotors are excluded from warranty coverage. Since Infiniti wrote the warranty book, if something is not explicitly excluded from the warranty, it should be covered.

VEHICLE HISTORY: 2004—Debut of an all-wheel-drive sedan with Snow Mode that provides a 50/50 front/rear torque split. All models come with a 5-speed automatic transmission or a 6-speed manual. The AWD model comes only with automatic. For 2004, the base sedan got larger 17-inch wheels; manual-shift coupes received upgraded brakes and 18-inch wheels, while the sedan variant got a limited-slip differential. **2005**—Automatic-transmission-equipped sedans share the coupe's 280-horsepower V6, while manual-equipped models have 18 more horses (298). The all-wheel-drive G35x comes only with an automatic transmission. Models using a manual tranny use a standard limited-slip differential and sport suspension.

J30

Introduced as an early 1993 model and dropped in 1997, the rear-drive, four-door J30 and its high-performance variant, the I30, are sized and priced midway between the G20 and the top-of-the-line Q45. The J30 uses a modified version of the Nissan 300ZX's 3.0L 210-hp V6 engine. Although the vehicle is replete with important safety features and it accelerates and handles well, its engine is noisy, passenger and cargo room have been sacrificed to styling, and fuel economy is underwhelming.

The J30 comes with a standard airbag (or dual airbags, depending on the model year), ABS, and traction control. It has changed very little over the years, meaning that there's no reason to choose a more recent model over a cheaper older version.

Quality problems include airbag malfunctions (inadvertent deployment and failure to deploy), cracked exhaust manifolds, leaking fuel injection systems, and excessive vibration when accelerating.

I30/I35

Introduced as an early '96 model, the I30 is a sport sedan spin-off of the Nissan Maxima with additional sound-deadening material and a plushier interior. The car's interior is also roomier, but its ride is unimpressive and handling is compromised by excessive body lean when cornering. Engine and road noises are omnipresent. The redesigned year 2000 model adds rear seatroom and reduces body lean considerably. I35s have a quieter and better-performing engine, a much improved ride, and more responsive handling.

VEHICLE HISTORY: 1996–99—Models change little, except for front side airbags and new headlights and tail lights added to the '98s. **2000**—Represents the best value from a price/performance perspective. Entirely revamped with more conservative styling, 37 more horses, and a larger cabin. Head restraints are also upgraded, suspension is improved, larger wheels are added, and high-intensity headlights are adopted. **2002**—Renamed the I35 and given a larger V6 engine, new styling, and more standard features.

Incredibly, the recently minted I35 has elicited more performance-related complaints than its I30 predecessor, which was no paragon of quality control. This same phenomenon has been noted with Nissan's new Altima models, which continue to have serious factory-related glitches six years after the model's launch.

I30 owners report chronic suspension failures, drivetrain vibration and clunking, faulty steering, and defective transverse links, springs, and struts. I35s are known for hesitation and surging when accelerating, electrical shorts, excessive front-end play, vibration, drivetrain noise, loose steering, rattling noises, incorrect fuel gauge readings, and inoperative seat memory buttons.

Q45

Faster and glitzier than other cars in its category, this luxury sedan provides performance, while its chief rival, the Lexus LS 400, provides luxury and quiet. Up to the '96 model, the Q45 used a 32-valve 278-hp 4.5L V8 tire-burner not frequently found on a Japanese luxury compact. It accelerates faster than the Lexus, going 0–100 km/h in 7.1 seconds without a hint of noise or abrupt shifting. Unlike the base engine of the G20, though, the Q45's engine supplies plenty of upper-range torque as well. The suspension was softened in 1994, but the car still rides much more firmly than its Lexus counterpart. The four-wheel steering is precise, but the standard limited slip differential is no help in preventing the car's rear end from sliding out on slippery roads, mainly because of the original-equipment "sport" tires, which were designed for 190 km/h autobahn cruising. There's not much footroom for passengers, and cargo room is disappointing. Fuel economy is non-existent. ABS is standard, but a passenger-side airbag wasn't available before 1994.

VEHICLE HISTORY: 1997—A downsized 4.1L V8 was set on a smaller platform, effectively changing the character of the car from a sporty performer to a highway cruiser. **1998**—Front seat belt pretensioners. **2002**—A new 4.5L V8 producing 340 hp (up from 266). The transmission is a 5-speed automatic with a manual shift mode. High-end electronics are standard, including traction control (TCS), Vehicle Dynamic Control (VDC), Electronic Brake Force Distribution (EBD), tire pressure monitors, high-intensity xenon headlights, and Voice Control for the climate control and eight-speaker Bose 300-watt audio system, including a six-disc CD changer. **2003**—A rear-axle upgrade for faster and smoother acceleration. **2004**—A rear-view camera. **2005**—A minor facelift and a recalibrated transmission for smoother shifts.

The Q45 has been exceptionally reliable throughout its model run, despite some reports of premature AC failures, power steering problems, excessive wind noise around the A-pillars, sunroof wind leaks, tire thumping, cellular telephone glitches, faulty CD players, and a popping sound from the radio. Owners say that the paint scratches and flakes off so easily that it has to be constantly touched up.

M35, M45

The 2003 M45 replaced the I30/I35 as Infiniti's mid-size, rear-drive luxury car. Powered by a 340-hp V8 engine and coupled to a 5-speed automatic transmission, the first three model years sold poorly primarily due to the car's bland design and cramped interior. The redesigned 2006 version is dramatically restyled and offers more interior room and high-tech features, like a peppier V8 with 15 fewer horses, four-wheel steering, a performance-tuned suspension/transmission, and upgraded brakes. M35 sedans use a 275-hp V6 that's available with rear-drive or all-wheel drive.

Owners complain of excessive oil consumption, poor tire performance with the Michelin Pilots, and a host of other problems:

> ...(perforated leather seats had mesh coming out, CD changer jammed, AC compressor busted, belts on the motor had to be replaced, glove box had to be readjusted, hood had to be readjusted to stop the squeaking when closing the doors, front window guides and stabilizer-inner door had to be replaced to stop all the squealing when letting the windows up/down) and schedule another visit to see if the engine/exhaust problem could be repaired. The dealership had my car for 3 weeks...and cleaned out the combustion chamber at their cost and the day I got it back, it was still smoking out the pipes. The dealership says they know nothing else to do but to replace the motor if it's consuming oil. I found these other complaints which already state that

Infiniti knows about this oil consumption problem and appears to be giving me the run around. If the motor is replaced with another Nissan V8, the same problem is likely to reoccur. Their product is defective.

Safety Summary

G20: **1999**—Carbon monoxide poisoning. • When car is put into Reverse, driver's seat reclines without warning. **2001**—Foul odour emitted by AC. • Brake failure. • Brake rotors glaze over and need turning. • Airbags fail to deploy. *G35:* **2003**— Despite it's close affinity to the defect-ridden 250Z, 115 owner complaints is a bit fewer than what one would normally expect. In fact, the low-volume 350Z has registered almost twice as many safety-related deficiencies. • Vehicle accelerates when coming to a stop with the AC engaged and a foot on the brake pedal. • Early automatic transmission replacement. • Poor upshifting from First gear. • Loss of front braking capability. • Premature wearout of brake pads and rotors. • Rear window shatters suddenly. • Seat belt cuts across the neck of small-statured drivers. • Driver's seat rocks back and forth. • Poorly illuminated clock. • Headlights shut off when they are dimmed. • Rear defroster takes forever to work. **2004**—Sudden acceleration due to pedal sticking, or when the speed control is engaged. • Transmission failures and premature brake replacement still dominate owner complaints. • Parking brake won't secure vehicle on an incline:

> I stopped my 2004 Infiniti G35 sedan at the end of my driveway, set the parking brake, and got out of the car to retrieve an item left on the ground next to my mailbox. When I walked away from the car, it began rolling. The car rolled off the side of my driveway and into the woods, where it hit a tree, causing considerable damage. Infiniti denies any responsibility for the damage, claiming that the brake is functioning within factory specifications.

• In one incident, ABS system locked up, flipping the car, and killing the driver and two passengers. • Michelin Pilot tires perform poorly in winter conditions. • Heated air is constantly drawn in from the engine compartment. *I30/I35:* **1998**— Airbag malfunctions. • Side window blows out. • Brake failure. **1999**—When using the turn signal, it's easy to turn off the headlights. • Airbag warning light stays on continuously. • Water seeps inside the vehicle from beneath. **2000**— Sudden, unintended acceleration. • Transmission jerks when shifting. • Premature wear of brake rotors. • Sunlight washes out gauges. • Headlight aimed too low. **2001**—Rear suspension fails. • Sudden, unintended acceleration. • Cruise control won't disengage when brakes are applied. **2002**—Airbags fail to deploy. • Steering wheel pulls sharply to one side when accelerating. • Poor braking. • Stalling. *M45:* **2003**—Hesitation when accelerating:

> The vehicle has an unsafe operating characteristic. When calling for immediate acceleration, you get nothing for several seconds. It has a significant lag in throttle response, up to 4 seconds, which when lane changing or merging causes a significant safety problem. We have been nearly rear-ended on several occasions.

Q45: **1996**—Airbag indicator flashes because of ECM failure. • Premature failure of the shock absorber and power window. **1997**—Owner alleges that vehicle design causes the vehicle to hydroplane. • Airbag warning light comes on for no reason. • When car is put into Reverse, driver's seat reclines without warning. • Severe front-end vibration continues after tires are replaced. **1998**—Airbag fails to deploy. • Accelerator pedal sticks while vehicle is stopped. **2000**—Excessive vibration starts at 100 km/h. **2001**—Sudden acceleration when vehicle is shifted into Reverse gear. **2002**—Excessive vibration caused by bent original-equipment wheels. **2004**—Laser-controlled cruise control abruptly cuts power when passing another vehicle and doesn't work in rain or when driving into the sun at sunset.

Secret Warranties/Internal Bulletins/Service Tips

All models/years: Troubleshooting tips to correct brake pedal judder and hard starts. • Vehicles with sunroofs may have wind noise coming from the sunroof area because of a small pinhole in the body sealer at the rear C-pillar. • Windshield cracking. • Erratic operation of the power antenna requires that the antenna rod be replaced. • Slow retraction of the front seat belt can be fixed by wiping off any residue found on the seat belt D-ring. *G20:* **1999**—Excessive blower noise can be reduced by installing a new cover. • Coolant leakage may be caused by a defective intake manifold expansion plug. • Replace the window-glass run rubber if the window makes a popping sound when opened. **1999–2000**—Countermeasures for front-end clunks when turning or braking. **1999–2001**—Power seat won't move, or makes a grinding noise. • Shock absorbers that clunk will be replaced under warranty. **2000**—Engine lacks power; stuck in Third gear. • Correcting a brake judder. • Cloudy, scratched instrument cluster lens. • Parcel shelf rattle or buzz. • Low idle, or engine dies when put into gear. • Preventing a rotten-egg smell emitted by the exhaust. **2001–02**—Rear brake caliper clunk, rattle, or knock. • Defroster not flush, rattles. *G35:* **2003–05**—Rear axle clicking. **2003–06**—No starts in cold weather. **2005**—Dash squeak and rattle repair. **2005–06**—Gap between glove compartment and dash. *I30/I35:* **1996–98**—If either one of the front power seats won't move, check for a broken power-seat drive cable. **1996–2000**—Excessive blower noise can be reduced by installing a new cover. **2000–01**—No-starts may be caused by a faulty engine wire harness. • Transmission slippage. • Brake judder (vibration) is covered by a 4-year/97,000 km (60,000 mi.) warranty, says TSB #ITB00-063b. • Troubleshooting tips to correct self-locking doors. **2000–04**—Poor transmission performance. **2001**—Remedy for a low/no idle after a cold start. **2001–02**—Rear brake caliper clunk, rattle, or knock. **2002**—Faulty sunroof. **2002–03**—Upgraded brake pads to reduce brake judder or other anomalies. *M45:* **2003**—Poor clock illumination. **2003–04**—A ticking or thumping noise coming from the engine area may signal the need to replace the fuel damper assembly. • Diagnosing and correcting an engine knocking or tapping noise. *Q45:* **1997–99**—A lumbar support mechanism that's inoperative should be replaced with an upgraded support mechanism. • If either one of the front power seats won't move, check for a broken power-seat drive cable. • Excessive blower noise can be reduced by installing a new cover. • TSB #ITB98-062 gives an exhaustive listing for a variety of squeak and rattle repairs.

1997–2000—TSB #ITB00-010 gives a detailed list of brake judder countermeasures. 1998–99—An automatic transmission that produces a "double thump" noise when coming to a stop likely needs a new transmission control module (TCM). 2002—Engine hesitation. • Steering pull to the right; excessive vibration. • Difficult to move shift lever. • Front suspension noise. • Rear power-seat grinding noise. • Door sash rusting. • Inoperative rear sunshade. • Trunk lid hard to close. • Hard to read oil gauge. • Smoke from tailpipe. • Airbag warning light stays lit. • Loose driver's seat cushion. • Poor AC performance. • Inoperative headlight low beam. 2002–03—Incorrect shifting. • Navigation system stuck in "please wait" mode. • Upgraded brake pads to reduce brake judder or other anomalies. 2002–04—Remedy for engine knocking after a cold start.

G20/G35, I30/I35, J30, Q45 PROFILE

	1997	1998	1999	2000	2001	2002	2003	2004	2005
Cost Price ($)									
G20	—	—	29,950	29,950	29,900	29,900	—	—	—
G35 Sedan	—	—	—	—	—	—	38,900	39,600	39,900
G35 Coupe	—	—	—	—	—	—	45,000	45,200	46,100
I30/I35	40,600	41,000	41,350	41,950	39,900	39,500	39,700	41,200	—
J30	52,600	—	—	—	—	—	—	—	—
M35	—	—	—	—	—	—	—	—	54,800
M45	—	—	—	—	—	—	62,000	62,000	64,400
Q45	65,000	66,500	71,000	71,000	70,000	73,000	74,900	75,500	88,000
Used Values ($)									
G20 ▲	—	—	5,000	6,500	8,000	10,000	—	—	—
G20 ▼	—	—	4,500	5500	7,000	8,000	—	—	—
G35 Sedan ▲	—	—	—	—	—	—	18,500	24,000	28,000
G35 Sedan ▼	—	—	—	—	—	—	16,500	22,000	26,000
G35 Coupe ▲	—	—	—	—	—	—	21,000	27,000	32,000
G35 Coupe ▼	—	—	—	—	—	—	19,000	25,000	29,000
I30/I35 ▲	5,000	6,000	7,000	8,500	11,000	13,500	17,000	22,000	—
I30/I35 ▼	4,500	5,500	6,500	7,000	9,500	11,000	14,500	20,000	—
J30 ▲	6,500	—	—	—	—	—	—	—	—
J30 ▼	6,000	—	—	—	—	—	—	—	—
M35 ▲	—	—	—	—	—	—	—	—	38,000
M35 ▼	—	—	—	—	—	—	—	—	36,000
M45 ▲	—	—	—	—	—	—	25,000	34,000	44,000
M45 ▼	—	—	—	—	—	—	23,000	32,000	42,000
Q45 ▲	7,000	8,000	9,000	10,000	12,000	21,000	28,000	39,000	52,000
Q45 ▼	6,500	7,500	8,500	9,500	10,500	19,000	26,000	37,000	49,000
Reliability	2	2	2	3	3	3	3	3	3
Crash Safety (F) (I30/I35)	—	4	—	4	4	4	4	4	—
J30	4	—	—	—	—	—	—	—	—
Side (I30/I35)	—	4	—	4	4	4	4	4	—

Offset									
G35	—	—	—	—	—	—	5	5	5
I30/I35	3	3	3	3	3	3	3	3	—
J30	—	—	—	4	4	—	—	—	—
Q45	2	2	2	2	2	—	5	5	5
Head Restraints									
G20	—	—	2	—	1	1	—	—	—
G35	—	—	—	—	—	·	—	—	1
I30/I35	2	—	2	—	—	—	—	—	—
J30	1	—	—	—	—	—	—	—	—
Q45	1	—	1	—	—	—	—	—	2
Rollover Resistance (I35)	—	—	—	—	—	—	4	4	4

Kia

MAGENTIS ★ ★ ★

RATING: Average (2005–06); Below Average (2001–04). Consider buying a competitor with more refinement and a proven history of reliability and good quality control. **"Real" city/highway fuel economy:** 2.4L: 10.9/7.2 L/100 km. V6: 11.7/7.9 L/100 km. Owners say they get about 10 percent less fuel economy than these estimates indicate. **Maintenance/Repair costs:** Average. **Parts:** Average costs, but parts aren't widely available yet. **Extended warranty:** A good idea only if the car will be kept more than five years. **Best alternatives:** A loaded Honda Accord, Nissan Maxima, and Toyota Camry. **Online help:** *www.mycarstats. com/auto_complaints/KIA_complaints.asp.*

Strengths and Weaknesses

Sold in the States as the Optima, this front-drive, five-passenger sedan is basically a Hyundai Sonata without traction control. The Magentis comes with a twin-cam 138-hp 2.4L 4-cylinder or optional 170-hp 2.7L V6 hooked to a 4-speed automatic transmission (V6s have the Sonata's separate gate for manual shifting and four-wheel ABS). Other standard features include front seat belt pretensioners, a tilt steering column, independent double wishbone front suspension and independent multi-link rear suspension, a 60/40 split folding rear seat, and tinted glass.

The Magentis is nicely appointed, provides good V6 performance, handles well, and rides comfortably. There's also plenty of front headroom and better-than-average fuel economy with regular fuel. The car is a bit better built than Kia's other models, but fit and finish is still inferior to other Asian makes.

Unfortunately, this car has some major weaknesses that include a wimpy 4-cylinder engine, a poorly performing 4-speed automatic transmission, mediocre braking, limited rear headroom, considerable body lean when turning, faulty door locks that trap occupants, excessive wind and tire noise, a small trunk opening, and a weak dealer network. Owner complaints deal primarily with poor servicing, sudden acceleration (maybe wimpy is good), harsh shifts, stalling, brake failures, premature brake pad and rotor wear, electrical shorts, AC overheating, faulty door locks, and subpar fit and finish.

VEHICLE HISTORY: 2002—A larger V6 engine with a gain of 8 horses and 15-inch wheels; SE sedans adopt standard automatic headlights. **2003**—Refreshed interior and exterior styling that includes new audio and climate controls, a new grille and hood, larger body mouldings, and restyled taillights. Both engines return with slightly reduced horsepower ratings after Kia and its owner, Hyundai, pleaded guilty to fudging horsepower figures on earlier models. **2004**—Larger wheels and a newly designed grille.

Safety Summary

All models/years: Airbags fail to deploy. **All models: 2001**—Chronic hesitation, stalling, and surging. • Transmission failures. • Excessive AC condensation in the interior. • Inaccurate fuel gauge. • Faulty door locks. **2002**—Delayed acceleration. • Sudden stalling while cruising on the highway. • Complete brake failure. • Windows won't go down. • Faulty door locks. **2003**—Accelerator sticks. • Sudden loss of power. • Brake failures. • Vehicle starts on its own. • Rainy weather causes the car to run roughly. • Large rear-view mirror blocks visibility. • Inoperative headlight high beams. • Doors lock and unlock on their own. • Sticking door locks trap occupants. **2004**—Fire ignites in the dashboard area. • Suspension pulls vehicle into oncoming traffic. • Engine surges when manual transmission is shifted from Second to Third gear. • Vehicle suddenly loses power. • Power-steering leaks. • Delayed acceleration. • Leaking fuel regulator. • Mud compromises EGR valve performance. • Inoperative cruise control. **2005**—Defective steering assembly causes the vehicle to suddenly veer right. • Faulty high beam headlights.

Secret Warranties/Internal Bulletins/Service Tips

2003–04—A hesitation when accelerating can be corrected by recalibrating the engine control module (ECM).

MAGENTIS PROFILE

	2001	2002	2003	2004	2005
Cost Price ($)					
LX Base	20,995	21,295	22,250	22,250	22,450
LX V6	23,995	24,295	25,750	25,750	25,850
SE/EX V6	27,995	29,095	28,750	28,750	28,850

Used Values ($)

LX Base ▲	5,000	7,000	9,000	10,500	13,000
LX Base ▼	4,000	5,500	7,500	9,500	11,500
LX V6 ▲	6,000	7,500	9,000	11,500	14,000
LX V6 ▼	5,000	6,500	7,500	10,000	12,500
SE/EX V6 ▲	7,000	8,500	10,500	13,000	15,500
SE/EX V6 ▼	6,000	7,000	9,000	11,500	14,000

Reliability	2	3	3	3	4
Crash Safety (F)	—	—	4	4	4
Side	—	—	—	4	4
Side (IIHS)	1	1	1	1	1
Offset	3	3	3	3	3
Head Restraints	1	1	1	1	1
Rollover Resistance	—	—	5	5	5

Lexus

ES 300/330, GS 300, IS 300, LS 400/430, SC 400/430 ★★★★

RATING: Above Average (2002–06, 1990–95); Recommended (1996–2001). A bit more refined than the Infinitis, Lexus' lineup offers first-class performance and better-than-average reliability, with the exception of a powertrain that is prone to dangerous stalling and surging. The latest model years have been downgraded because of serious design deficiencies relating to sudden acceleration; chronic engine/transmission stumble, shudder, and surge; and dash gauges that are unreadable during daylight hours. **"Real" city/highway fuel economy:** *ES 300:* 12.3/8.2 L/100 km. *ES 330:* 11.6/7.5 L/100 km. *GS 300:* 13.1/8.6 L/100 km. *GS 400:* 13.4/9.4 L/100 km. *GS 430:* 13.1/8.6 L/100 km. *GS 300 and GS 430 4.3L:* 13.3/9.3 L/100 km. *IS 300:* 13.2/8.8 L/100 km with a manual transmission or 13.1/8.9 L/100 km with an automatic. *LS 430:* 13.2/8.6 L/100 km. *LX 470:* 17.9/12.9 L/100 km. Fuel savings may be lower by about 10–15 percent. The ES 330 burns less fuel than its ES 300 predecessor, even though the ES 300 is equipped with a smaller 3.0L engine. **Maintenance/Repair costs:** Higher than average, and repairs must be done by either a Lexus or a Toyota dealer. **Parts:** Higher-than-average costs, but parts aren't hard to find (except body panels). **Extended warranty:** Not necessary. **Best alternatives:** A fully equipped Acura Legend, Honda Accord, early Nissan Maxima, and Toyota Camry will provide airbags, comparable highway performance, and reliability at far less initial cost, but you don't get the Lexus cachet. Nevertheless, if you do pay top dollar for a used Lexus, its slow rate of depreciation virtually guarantees that you'll get much of your money back. **Online help:** *us.lexusownersclub.com, us.lexusownersclub.com/forums/index. php?act=ST&f=7&t=3584&* (02–06 Transmission Hesitation Problems, the Official Stupid Tranny Thread), *www.carsurvey.org/manufacturer_Lexus.html,* and *yotarepair.*

com/Automotive_News.html. For Lexus engine sludge and other repair hints, type the phrase "Toyota engine sludge" into a search engine such as Google.

Strengths and Weaknesses

These are benchmark cars known for their impressive reliability and performance. Sports cars, they're not. But if you're looking for your father's Oldsmobile from a Japanese automaker, these luxury cars fit the bill. Like Acuras and Infinitis, Lexus models all suffer from some automatic transmission failures; engine sludge buildup (*www.autooninfo.info/VCC200310ToyotaEngineReliability.htm*); early rear main engine seal and front strut replacements (front struts are often replaced under a secret warranty); and front brake, electrical, body, trim, and accessory deficiencies, most of which are confirmed by confidential technical service bulletins.

ES 300/330

Resembling an LS 400 dressed in sporty attire, the entry-level ES 300 was launched in 1992 to fill the gap between the discontinued ES 250 and the LS 400. In fact, the ES 300 has many of the attributes of the LS 400 sedan but sells for much less money. A five-passenger sedan based on the Camry but 90 kg (200 lb.) heavier and with a different suspension and tires, it comes equipped with a standard 3.0L 24-valve engine that produces 181–210 horses coupled to either a 5-speed manual or a 4-speed electronically controlled automatic transmission. Like some Infiniti models, however, the ES 300 hesitates and surges when accelerating. Headroom is also surprisingly limited for a car this expensive.

VEHICLE HISTORY: *ES 300/330:* **1994**—Dual airbags and a new 3.0L 6-cylinder that boosts horsepower (3) to 188. **1995**—A new front air intake, standard foglights, and new brake/signal lights. **1997**—A restyled interior and exterior, increased interior dimensions, improved centre rear seat belt, and horsepower increased to 200. **1998**—De-powered airbags along with side airbags and an upgraded anti-theft system. **1999**—Horsepower increased to 210, upgraded automatic transmission, and traction control. **2000**—Restyled front ends and tail lights, and improved child safety seat anchors. **2001**—An emergency trunk release. **2002**—A longer, taller body; new 5-speed automatic transmission; improved brakes, steering, and suspension; and more standard luxury features. No more standard traction control. **2004**—ES 330 debuts with 15 extra horses and larger head-protecting side airbags. **2005**—Minor styling changes, a memory system for both power front seats, and power door mirrors.

On April 3, 2003, Toyota issued a press release admitting to engine sludge problems with its 1997–2002 Toyota and Lexus vehicles equipped with 3.0L IMZ V6 engines and all 1997–2001 Toyota vehicles powered by 5SFE 2.2L 4-cylinder engines. The automaker pledged to cover claims with an extended warranty. For a vehicle this well made, government-reported safety-related defects are surprisingly omnipresent. These reports include airbag-induced injuries; sudden acceleration;

an unreliable powertrain that surges, stumbles, stalls, and shifts erratically; ABS and Goodyear tire failures; excessive vibration when underway; interior window fogging; unreadable dash gauges; and poor AC performance.

GS 300

The rear-drive GS 300 is a step up from the front-drive ES 300 and just a rung below Lexus' top-of-the-line LS 400. It carries the same V6 engine as the ES 300, except that it has 20 more horses. This produces sparkling performance at higher speeds, though the car is disappointingly sluggish from a start. Fuel economy is sacrificed for performance, however, and the base suspension and tires pass noisily over small bumps and ruts. Visibility is also less than impressive, with large rear pillars and a narrow rear window restricting the view. There's not much usable trunk space, and the liftover is unreasonably high.

VEHICLE HISTORY: 1996—A light rear-end restyling and a 5-speed automatic transmission. **1998**—Restyled once again and given an upgraded V8. **2000**—A new brake assist system and more user-friendly child safety seat anchors. **2001**—Substantially upgraded with a 300-hp 4.3L V8, upgraded transmission controls, standard side curtain airbags, smart airbags, an emergency trunk release, and a host of other convenience features. **2002**—A revised navigation system.

Owner complaints have centred on brake failures, electrical shutdowns, prematurely worn wheel bearings, excessive front-end vibrations, fragile wheel rims, and electrical and fuel system malfunctions resulting in unintended sudden acceleration and hesitation.

IS 300

Targeting BMW's 3 Series, Lexus's latest rear-drive sports-compact sedan comes with similar power and features to the BMW 325I—for a few thousand dollars less. Moreover, there is practically no difference in fuel economy between the manual and automatic transmission modes. The only engine is a 215-hp 3.0L inline-six (borrowed from the GS 300) mated to a 5-speed automatic transmission and incorporating Lexus's E-shift feature for manual shifting. Other important features are four-wheel ABS-equipped disc brakes, 17-inch wheels, performance tires, front seat belt pretensioners, and traction control. Just a bit narrower than the BMW 3 Series, the IS 300 is a competent performer both for routine tasks and in emergency situations. Fortunately, it hasn't been afflicted by the ES 300's and Camry's chronic powertrain defects that cause a dangerous shift delay and surging when accelerating. Look for models equipped with a limited slip differential, but don't pay more for models featuring a sunroof, heated seats, or leather upholstery.

VEHICLE HISTORY: 2002—A SportCross wagon is added, and it comes only with an automatic transmission. Manual-shift sedans have a firmer suspension; ABS is upgraded; side curtain/front side airbags and traction control are standard.

In a nutshell, these cars stand out with a nice array of standard features; quality-looking gauges; good acceleration, handling, and braking; a comfortable ride; a low beltline for a great view; and first-class workmanship. On the other hand, the automatic transmission's manual E-shifter is awkward to use and isn't as sporty as a BMW's; owners report excessive road noise and tire thump; the instrument panel reflects in the windshield; the interior doesn't feel as plush as the competition's; seat cushions don't provide adequate thigh support; rear seating is a bit cramped; trunk hinges eat up trunk space and may damage luggage; no crashworthiness data is available; and premium fuel is required. Other cars worth considering are the Acura TL and BMW's 3 Series.

LS 400/430

The Lexus flagship, the LS 400 rear-drive arrived in 1990 with a 250-hp 4.0L V8. It outclasses all other luxury sedans in reliability, styling, and function. Its powerful engine provides smooth, impressive acceleration and a superior highway passing ability at all speeds. Its transmission is smooth and efficient. The suspension gives an easy ride without body roll or front-end plow during emergency stops, delivering a major comfort advantage over other luxury compacts. Other amenities include anti-lock brakes, a driver-side airbag, and automatic temperature control.

VEHICLE HISTORY: 1995—Increased interior and exterior dimensions, a more powerful engine, and a better-performing drivetrain for quicker acceleration. **1997**—Side airbags. **1998**—An improved V8, a new 5-speed automatic transmission, Vehicle Stability Control (VSC), and a host of interior upgrades. **2001**—Totally redesigned with a sleeker body, a 4.3L V8, an upgraded suspension, and a more spacious, reworked interior. Additional safety and comfort features have also been added. **2003**—A firmer suspension and 17-inch wheels. **2004**—A 6-speed manumatic transmission, driver knee-protecting airbags, steering-linked headlights, a power rear sunshade, and a tire-pressure monitor are added. Suspension, steering, and ABS systems are also upgraded.

The brakes don't inspire confidence, owing to their mushy feel and average performance. Furthermore, there's limited rear footroom under the front seats, and the rear middle passenger has to sit on the transmission hump. This car is a gas-guzzler that thirsts for premium fuel.

Owner complaints deal mainly with sudden, unintended acceleration; stalling caused by a faulty throttle sensor; traction control that causes the vehicle to swerve (usually to the left) unexpectedly; failure of the VSC to activate; main computer failures; spongy brakes; electrical glitches; and door locks that stick shut, trapping occupants.

SC 300, SC 400/430

These two coupes are practically identical, except for their engines and luxury features. The cheaper SC 300 gives you the same high-performance 6-cylinder engine used by the GS 300 and Toyota Supra, while the SC 400 uses the 4.0L V8 engine found in the LS 400. You're likely to find fewer luxury features with the SC 300 because they were sold as options. Nevertheless, look for an SC with traction control for additional safety during poor driving conditions. On the downside, V8 fuel consumption is horrendous, rear seating is cramped, and trunk space is unimpressive. Also, invest in a good anti-theft device, or your Lexus relationship will be over almost before it begins.

VEHICLE HISTORY: 1996—Given the LS 400's V8. **1998**—SC gets the 4.0L V8 engine, while the SC 300 continues to use the previous year's inline-six but ditches its 5-speed manual transmission. Other upgrades are variable valve timing, a more refined 5-speed automatic transmission, a new anti-theft system, and de-powered airbags. **1999**—American-sold models get larger brakes. **2005**—Upgraded shock absorbers and navigation system.

Safety Summary

All models: 1997–2002—Engine warranty extended to eight years to cover engine oil sludge claims (*www.autosafety.org*). *ES 300/330:* **All years:** Sudden, unintended acceleration. **1999**—Rear seat belts don't hold a child safety seat firmly. **2000**—Sudden, unintended acceleration when in Reverse. • Engine stalls or won't accelerate in traffic. • Vehicle suddenly downshifts from Fourth to First in heavy traffic; jerky shifting. • Rolls backward when transmission is in Drive. • Swerves left on a straight road. • Rear-view mirror doesn't move, resulting in poor visibility. **2001**—In one incident, engine fire ignited from what investigator said was fuel leaking from a rubber hose that had disconnected from the fuel filter. • Car suddenly accelerates as driver slows coming to a stop sign or when pulling into a parking space. • Traction control engages much too easily when merging into traffic. • One vehicle started up and began moving down the street in Reverse, despite the fact that there was no key in the ignition cylinder and the vehicle was left in Park. • Vehicle hesitates when applying accelerator after decelerating. **2002**—Airbags fail to deploy. • Impossible to read speedometer and other gauges in sunlight; they have red needles against a black background. • Won't go into gear properly. • Fuel cap won't screw off. • Warped brake rotors. • Defective Goodyear Eagle tires (sidewall bubbling). **2002–03**—Chronic engine/transmission surging and stalling not fixed by computer module recalibration, switching to premium fuel, etc.:

> The transmission of the 2003 Lexus ES 300 is subject to major hesitation, particularly in crowded intersections and with lack of acceleration. Very noticeable when traveling about 27 mph [43 km/h] and then needing to move, there is major delay in the signal telling the engine and transmission to work together and move the car. Around 40 mph [64 km/h] it wants to upshift to the Fifth gear, and just below that hunts to go back to Fourth.
>
> The manufacturer says, as [they] did for the 2002 models, that a software fix is being prepared. They stated the problem from the 2002 was fixed. Evidently that is

not the case. They now tell me that a fix is coming year-end. How many accidents will occur by then? Dealer says that the car will learn from the driver, but that is not working, and hesitation from 0–5 mph [0–8 km/h], from 27–45 [43–72 km/h], etc. is very pronounced. If you "floorboard" it from slow speeds, its hesitation is great, and car almost dies.

2004—Sudden acceleration; brake failure. • Stuck accelerator. • Delayed shift and surging when accelerating still occurs frequently, despite Toyota's special campaign "fix" that involves changing the electronic module:

This car is extremely dangerous. It's either a defective transmission or bad drive-by-wire design. The car hesitates extremely badly on acceleration. For example, when you are entering a limited access highway, if you slow down and then step on the gas, there is a long lag before the car begins to pick up speed. This lag is often a second or more. I have nearly been hit numerous times while the car makes up its mind whether it wants to move or not. The dealer has refused to fix the problem.

• Transmission goes into Reverse when shifted into Drive. • Vehicle lunges forward when transmission is shifted into Reverse. • Steering pulls vehicle into oncoming traffic. • Passenger-side airbag is disabled when adult of any weight sits in the front passenger seat. • Serious blind spots caused by left and right side rear-view mirrors. **2005**—Hesitation and then surging continues to be a major complaint category. • Sudden loss of braking capability. *GS 300:* **1998**—Vehicle surges or suddenly accelerates. • After yaw sensor replacement, as per recall, yaw sensor failure causes an accident. • Rear brake caliper plate for brake pads falls off after brake pins dislodge. • Poor low-beam illumination. • Trunk lid falls down unexpectedly. **1999**—Sudden, unintended acceleration and unexpected delayed acceleration. • Airbags fail to deploy. • Wheels break under normal driving conditions. • Complete brake failure. • Excessive vibration at highway speeds. **2002**—Fire ignites from fuel filter leak. • Sticking accelerator. • Vehicle starts without key. • Traction control engages too easily. • Inadequate headlight illumination. • Digital dash indicator washes out in sunlight. **2003**—Again, reports of sudden, unintended acceleration and hesitation when accelerating.

Secret Warranties/Internal Bulletins/Service Tips

All models: 1999—Excessive engine noise when idling at normal operating temperature. • If the vehicle shudders during a 2–3 shift, consider changing the transaxle valve body. **1999–2001**—Information on correcting automatic transmission fluid leaks. **2000–01**—Procedures for obtaining a free seat belt extender. **2002**—Harsh 2–3 shift. • Tilt steering hard to move from down position. • Troubleshooting steering pull and interior squeaks and rattles. **2002–03**—TSB #TC004-03, issued August 4, 2003, gives recalibration instructions for correcting erratic shifting. This free repair is in effect for 96 months/128,000 km (80,000 mi.) and is limited to the correction of the problem based upon a customer's specific complaint. • Unreadable dash gauges will be corrected free of charge under TSB #EL001-03, issued January 23, 2003. • A shim kit will reduce front brake vibration, says TSB #BR002-02, issued December 24, 2002. • A gas cap sticking fix is detailed in TSB #EG003-02, issued February 8, 2002. • Body creak or snap from top of front windshield. **2002–04**—Inoperative AC; AC warning light comes on. **2002–05**—Countermeasures for poor shift quality. **2002–06**—Troubleshooting tips for vehicles that pull to one side when underway. • Inoperative rear power window. **2003–05**—Steering clunk, pop. **2003–06**—Windshield ticking noise. **2004**—Troubleshooting tips for a malfunctioning front-seat occupant seat belt sensor. • Vehicle pulls into oncoming traffic. **2004–06**—Front-seat squeak. **2005**—Rear seat belt buckle difficult to use. *GS 300:* **2000–02**—Front stabilizer bar noise. **2001–02**—Front coil-spring clicking. **2002**—Steering pull troubleshooting. *LS 400, LS 430:* **1999–2000**—Countermeasures to reduce steering noise and improve smoothness. **2000**—Moonroof water leaks. **2001**—Moonroof rattle, and rear corner air leak. • Instrument panel rattling. • Rear seat and luggage compartment creaking. • False illumination of the MIL. **2002**—No sound from amplifier. **2002–06**—Steering-pull troubleshooting. **2004**—Ignition switch difficult to turn. • No picture displayed by backup camera. • Rear window water leaks.

ES 300/330, GS 300, IS 300, LS 400/430, SC 400/430 PROFILE

	1997	1998	1999	2000	2001	2002	2003	2004	2005
Cost Price ($)									
ES 300/330	42,960	43,820	44,235	43,995	44,000	43,400	43,800	43,800	43,900
GS 300	71,400	58,900	59,220	59,420	60,700	60,700	61,700	61,700	61,700
GS 430	—	—	—	—	71,300	68,800	69,500	69,500	69,500
IS 300	—	—	—	—	40,830	37,820	37,775	37,775	37,900
LS 400/430	78,700	78,300	78,690	78,950	80,000	81,900	82,800	83,200	84,900
SC 400/430	83,000	84,000	—	—	—	84,000	85,500	86,800	89,770
Used Values ($)									
ES 300/330 ▲	6,500	8,000	9,000	11,000	14,000	18,000	21,000	26,000	30,000
ES 300/330 ▼	5,500	7,000	8,000	9,500	12,500	16,000	18,500	24,000	28,000
GS 300 ▲	9,500	11,000	12,000	14,000	18,500	24,500	30,000	38,000	44,000
GS 300 ▼	8,500	10,000	11,000	12,500	17,000	23,000	28,000	36,000	42,000
GS 430 ▲	—	—	—	—	21,000	27,500	34,000	43,000	50,000
GS 430 ▼	—	—	—	—	19,000	25,000	32,000	41,000	48,000
IS 300 ▲	—	—	—	—	13,000	16,500	19,000	23,000	27,000
IS 300 ▼	—	—	—	—	11,000	14,500	17,000	21,000	25,000
LS 400/430 ▲	10,500	13,000	15,000	18,000	25,000	31,000	38,000	48,000	58,000
LS 400/430 ▼	9,500	11,500	13,500	16,000	23,000	29,000	36,000	46,000	56,000
SC 400/430 ▲	13,500	16,000	—	—	—	37,000	45,000	55,000	64,000
SC 400/430 ▼	12,500	15,000	—	—	—	35,000	43,000	53,000	62,000
Reliability	4	4	4	4	4	4	4	4	4
Crash Safety (F)									
ES 300/330	—	4	4	—	—	—	5	5	—
GS 300	3	—	—	—	—	—	—	—	—

Side (ES 300/330)	—	5	5	—	5	—	5	5	5
IS 300	—	—	—	—	—	—	—	—	5
Side (IIHS)									
ES 330	—	—	—	—	—	—	—	5	5
Offset									
ES 300/330	—	—	—	—	—	5	5	5	5
GS 300	—	—	5	5	5	5	5	5	5
LS 400/430	5	5	5	5	5	5	5	5	5
Head Restraints									
ES 300/330	3	—	3	—	3	3	3	1	1
GS 300	—	—	—	—	—	—	2	2	2
IS 300	—	—	—	—	2	2	2	2	2
LS 430	—	—	—	—	2	2	2	2	2
Rollover Resistance									
ES 300/330	—	—	—	—	—	—	4	4	4
IS 300	—	—	—	—	—	—	—	—	5

Mercedes-Benz

C-CLASS ★

bad buy

RATING: Not Recommended (1994–2006). These cars no longer outclass the Detroit Big Three in safety, reliability, or comfort. **"Real" city/highway fuel economy:** *C230:* 10.5/7.2 L/100 km with a manual transmission or 10.2/7.1 L/100 km with an automatic. *C240:* 12.9/8.4 L/100 km with a manual tranny or 12.4/8.9 L/100 km with an automatic. *C32 AMG:* 14.6/10.3 L/100 km. *C320:* 12.7/8.3 L/100 km manual; 11.8/8.2 L/100 km automatic. *CL500:* 14.7/9.1 L/100 km. *CL600:* 18.4/11.6 L/100 km. *CL55 AMG:* 16.6/10.3 L/100 km. Owners report fuel savings are lower than the above estimates by about 15 percent. **Maintenance/Repair costs:** Higher than average, and most repairs must be done by a Mercedes dealer if you don't live in an area where independent shops have sprung up. Look out for electronic glitches and engine oil sludge (see page 69). **Parts:** Higher-than-average costs. Parts are highly dealer-dependent and relatively expensive. **Extended warranty:** An extra warranty is a smart idea. **Best alternatives:** Acura Integra or RL, BMW 3 Series, Infiniti I30, and Toyota Avalon. **Online help:** *www.benzworld. org/forums, www.mercedesproblems.com* (Customer Problems with Mercedes-Benz Production Quality Control), *www.mercedes-benz-usa.com* (Mercedes-Benz Lemon Problem Vehicles), and *www.carsurvey.org/manufacturer_Mercedes-Benz.html.*

Strengths and Weaknesses

Replacing the power-challenged and bland 190 series, the 1994 C-Class gained interior room and two new engines: a base 147-hp 2.2L and a 194-hp 2.8L

6-cylinder—a real powerhouse in this small car when coupled to the manual 5-speed transmission. The 4-speed automatic is a big disappointment—it requires a lot of throttle effort to downshift and prefers to start out in Second gear. Although this series got small, incremental power increases and additional features over the years, you don't see a major redesign until 2001. Unfortunately, the new engines and other features added at that time only add to the car's poor reliability, engine and road noise is still bothersome, and interior space is still inadequate. Since then, these cars have coasted on the Mercedes name and been touted mainly as fuel-sippers with a high-end cachet. That's poor recompense for what little the car actually offers.

VEHICLE HISTORY: 1997—C-Class replaces the standard 2.2L engine with the more robust 2.3L (C230). Revised headlights. **1998**—A new 2.8L engine (C280), BabySmart car seats, Brake Assist, and side airbags. **1999**—Models get the SLK's 2.3L supercharged engine, replacing the C230's normally aspirated powerplant; a better-performing drivetrain; and standard leather upholstery. **2000**—A Touch Shift auto-manual transmission; stability control; and Tele-Aid, a communications system for calling for assistance. **2001**—Completely revamped, gaining two new engines, additional safety features, and more aerodynamic styling. **2002**—Additional rear room and storage space, more high-performance features, a wagon, and an AWD sedan and wagon. **2003**—All-wheel drive and another wagon (C240) are added and the C230 hatchback coupe gets a new supercharged 4-cylinder engine, losing 3 horses in the process. **2004**—Sports coupes adopt a standard three-spoke steering wheel, enlarged chrome exhaust tip, and other pseudo-sporty paraphernalia. **2005**—Restyled and joined by a high-performance 362-hp V8-equipped C55 AMG sedan. The C320 gets a 3.5L V6.

Keep in mind that owner surveys give the entry-level C-Class cars a just-better-than-average rating, while the 300 and higher series have always scored way above average in owner satisfaction. C-Class owners report frequent problems with sudden, unintended acceleration; drivetrain noise and vibration; and slipping or soft shifts. Engines (oil sludge), brakes, the AC electrical system, and computer-controlled electronic components (telematics) are glitch-prone, hell to diagnose, and expensive to repair.

Safety Summary

All models/years: Sudden, unintended acceleration and brake failure. **All models: 1998**—Airbag warning light came on, and then airbag suddenly exploded. • Faulty gas gauge sensor. • Rear suspension bouncing makes it difficult to maintain directional control. • Car is very vulnerable to side-wind buffeting. • Window failures. **1999**—Brakes fail on incline. **2000**—When the vehicle is cold, the automatic transmission slips, sticks in gear, and shifts abruptly. **2002**—Many reports of sudden loss of power, stalling. • Airbags fail to deploy. • Wide rear quarter panel blind spot (C240). • Multiple electrical short circuits. • Differential failure. • Vehicle wanders over highway. • Driver's seat and side rear-view mirror fail to return to preset position. **2003**—Sudden engine surging. • Fuel gauge failure and loss of power. • Faulty fuel tank causes engine warning light to stay lit. • No throttle response, and strong fuel smell pervades the interior. • Vehicle jerks when accelerating. • Weak wheels are easily bent. **2004**—Airbags fail to deploy. • Fire ignites in the electrical wires housed in the dashboard. • Transmission fails to shift into Reverse. • Loose driver's seat. • Windshield wipers fail intermittently. • Front windshield is easily cracked by road debris. • Auto-dimming rear-view mirror sometimes turns pitch black. • AC corrosion produces a noxious odour in the cabin.

Secret Warranties/Internal Bulletins/Service Tips

All models/years: Excessive engine valve-train noise may be caused by a stretched timing chain. After 48,000 km, the camshaft and timing chain drive should be checked carefully, especially if excessive noise is heard. • Water in the oxygen sensor connector in the front-passenger wheelwell. • Ignition key difficult to remove. • Clicking from the front-door lock trim. **All models: 1997–2003**—Tips on correcting window operating noises. **1997–2004**—Engine oil sludge refund guidelines. **1998–2001**—Free engine repair or replacement for oil sludge. **1999**—Hesitation after a cold start and rough 1–2 and 2–3 shifts during warm-up. **1999–2000**—If the brake pedal is hard to apply, replace the brake-booster and crankcase vent hoses. **2001**—Troubleshooting hard starts and poor engine performance. **2002**—Lack of power, engine hesitation. • Inoperative cruise control. • Power-window motor locks up when closing. • Inoperative central locking system. • Tail/brake lights stay on. **2002–04**—Engine rattling. • Inoperative cruise control. • Harsh transmission shifts. • Transmission fluid leaks at the electrical connection. • Scraping noise comes from the transmission tunnel area. • Inoperative trunk/cargo light. • Free corrosion repairs along the door bottoms. • Headlight flickering. • Silencing sliding-roof noises. **2003–04**—Troubleshooting tips for fixing a rough-running engine. • Windshield blistering near rain/light sensor. • Inoperative xenon headlights. • Dome lamp won't come on. **2004**—Engine oil leaks through the cylinder head bolt threads. • Free radiator and radiator hose replacement (230 model). • Steering leaks. • Suspension rumbling. • Exhaust rattling, hissing, and humming. **2004–05**—Campaign to check and replace, if necessary, the automatic transmission pilot bushing. **2005**—The following items may also apply to previous model years. If you have identical problems, ask your dealer service manager to check the files. • Engine won't start. • Engine oil leaks from the oil level sensor. • Rough idle. • Harsh shifts with the automatic transmission. • Transmission fluid leaks at the electrical connector. • Inoperative central locking system and AC heater blower motor. • Steering assembly leaks fluid. • Steering squeal or squeak when turning. • Steering flow noise. • Front seat noise. • Faulty power seats. • Whistling when the brake pedal is released. • Noise from the door checks. • Chattering/noisy windshield wipers. • Sliding roof water leaks, rattling. • Moisture in the turn signal lamps and mirrors. • Tail lights won't turn off; trunk lamp won't turn on. • Inoperative xenon headlights. • Door frames will get free rustproofing under a special Service Campaign (read: "secret warranty"). • Another Service Campaign calls for the free modification of the lower door seal.

	1997	1998	1999	2000	2001	2002	2003	2004	2005
Cost Price ($)									
230	36,950	37,550	37,950	38,450	—	33,950	34,450	35,290	36,450
240	—	—	—	—	37,450	37,950	38,450	41,290	42,250
280	50,995	49,950	49,950	49,950	—	—	—	—	—
320	—	—	—	—	49,950	50,600	49,750	40,700	40,600
Used Values ($)									
230 ▲	5,500	6,500	7,500	10,000	—	14,000	17,000	20,000	24,000
230 ▼	5,000	6,000	7,000	8,000	—	12,000	15,000	18,000	22,000
240 ▲	—	—	—	—	12,000	16,000	19,500	23,000	28,000
240 ▼	—	—	—	—	10,000	14,500	18,000	21,000	26,000
280 ▲	8,000	9,000	10,000	12,000	—	—	—	—	—
280 ▼	7,000	8,000	9,000	10,500	—	—	—	—	—
320 ▲	—	—	—	—	14,500	18,000	23,000	23,000	26,000
320 ▼	—	—	—	—	12,500	16,000	22,000	21,000	24,000
Reliability	2	2	2	3	3	3	3	3	3
Crash Safety (F)									
C230	4	4	—	—	—	—	4	4	4
Side									
C230/C-Class	—	3	3	3	—	—	5	5	5
Side (IIHS)	—	—	—	—	—	—	—	—	3
Offset	—	—	—	—	5	5	5	5	5
Head Restraints (F)	2	—	3	—	5	5	5	2	2
Rear	—	2	2	—	—	—	—	—	—
Rollover Resistance	—	—	—	—	—	—	4	4	4

300 SERIES, 400 SERIES, 500 SERIES, E-CLASS ★ ★

RATING: Below Average (1992–2006); Average (1985–91). Mercedes' quality has deteriorated over the past decade because of the increased complexity of mechanical, emissions, and electronic components. Beware of engine oil sludge. **"Real" city/highway fuel economy:** *E320:* 13.2/8.1 L/100 km. *E500:* 14.4/9.1 L/100 km. *E55 AMG:* 16.6/10.3 L/100 km. Owners report fuel savings are less than the above estimates by about 20 percent. **Maintenance/Repair costs:** Higher than average, but many repairs can now be done by independent garages. **Parts:** Higher-than-average costs and limited availability. **Extended warranty:** A good idea. **Best alternatives:** The natural inclination is to seriously consider one of the BMW variants. Don't. Equivalent 2001 and later 5 Series, 6 Series, 7 Series, and X5 models come with standard iDrive—a complicated cockpit electronic controller that will drive you batty. Says *Electronic Design* Magazine (*www. elecdesign.com/Articles/Index.cfm?AD=1&AD=1&ArticleID=8246*):

BMW's 2001 introduction of iDrive, its pioneering driver information/entertainment system, was arguably the biggest corporate disaster since Coca-Cola Co. decided to tinker with the formula for its eponymous beverage.

Granted, by the time the 5-Series adopted iDrive a few years later, the system was redesigned so the driver could use it without looking at the small LCD panel. The 2007 X5 incorporates iDrive's third redesign in seven years. All this effort does make for a more user-friendly operation, but the learning curve is still rather steep. Instead, consider Acura Integra or RL, Ford Crown Victoria or Mercury Grand Marquis, Infiniti I30, Mazda Millenia, and Toyota Avalon. **Online help:** *www. benzworld.org*, *www.mercedes-benz-usa.com* (Mercedes-Benz Lemon Problem Vehicles), *www.mercedesproblems.com* (Customer Problems with Mercedes-Benz Production Quality Control), *www.troublebenz.com*, *www.carsurvey.org/ manufacturer_Mercedes-Benz.html*, and *www.oil-tech.com/32million.htm* (AMSOIL).

Strengths and Weaknesses

These cars were once ideal mid-sized family sedans until Mercedes started churning out feeble downsized models and installing failure-prone electronic components. Nevertheless, the E-Class sedans are the best of a bad lot and are relatively reliable, depreciate slowly, and provide all the interior space that the early 190 Series and present-day C-Class leave out. Their major shortcoming is a weak dealer network that limits parts distribution and drives up parts and servicing costs.

VEHICLE HISTORY: *E-Class:* **1997**—A new 5-speed automatic transmission, and the E420 gets a V8 engine. **1998**—The addition of a station wagon and all-wheel drive. The 300D adds a turbocharger for extra power; the E320 comes with a new 3.2L V6. Other additions are a BabySmart child protection system, Brake Assist, and an electronic Smart Key feature. **1999**—A new side-impact head protection feature. **2000**—Diesel dropped; a new all-wheel-drive E430 with standard side airbags is added. All models get new wheels, Touch Shift (an auto-manual device), and Electronic Stability. **2001**—One-touch opening sunroofs. **2003**—An E320 Special Edition Sedan arrives. **2004**—Increased availability of all-wheel drive, a revamped wagon body style, and a new 7-speed automatic transmission. **2005**—A turbocharged diesel, the E320CDI, debuts as an early 2005 model.

Quality control has traditionally been better than average with the 300 and higher series; however, it has followed a downward trend during the last decade. Owners point out recurring problems with the fuel and electrical systems, causing lights, instruments, and gauges to shut off and the trunk lid to open when the engine is shut down. Other common problems include premature rusting and paint delamination; stalling and engine surging; engine oil leaks; engine problems caused by a stretched timing chain; oil sludging in 1998–2001 models (see "Secret Warranties/ Internal Bulletins/Service Tips"); computer module failures (in both the engine and transmission); an erratically performing, leaky, and noisy transmission; excessive power steering play; and front window wind noise.

300 series: **1998**—Sudden, unintended acceleration while on the highway. • Airbag fails to deploy in a collision. • In one incident, steering went out while parking and car caught on fire. • Total loss of braking; pedal went to floor. • Premature failure of the automatic transmission, tie-rod, belt tensioner, fuel pump, fuel level sensor, oxygen sensor, window controls, power-assisted sunroof, electric seats, turn signal switch, and brake lights. • Power seat suddenly moved back and reclined while vehicle was underway. **1999**—Sudden acceleration when turning or decelerating to exit the freeway. • Engine fuel line leakage. • Sunroof electrical fire. • Fuel-pump failures. • Inaccurate fuel gauge says tank is full, but almost 23 litres more can be pumped. • Sudden stalling while underway, especially when going over a bump in the road. • Excessive vibration when decelerating. • Transmission leaks oil, disengages, and then suddenly locks up. • ABS suddenly activates, throwing vehicle to side of the road. • Self-activating door locks. • Severe window hazing in rainy weather. **2000**—Panic stops may produce a brake pedal stiffness and loss of braking ability. • Premature brake booster failure. • Poor acceleration said to be caused by fuel injection control module. • Fuel gauge still gives false low readings. • Horn blows on its own, and warning lights are constantly lit. **2001**—Side airbags deploy inadvertently. The following owner of a 2001 300E recounts his surprise at the time:

> While driving down the highway, my passenger side curtain and rear side door airbags deployed for no reason at all…. It scared the hell out of me and nearly caused me to crash the car.

• Water enters the automatic transmission control module, preventing the transmission from changing gears. • Vehicle hesitates when accelerating with gas pedal halfway depressed, then it lurches forward. **2002**—Steering locks up while turning. • Total electrical failure in traffic, leading to vehicle shutdown. • Stalling when accelerating. • Windows don't stay up. **2003**—Faulty gateway module and software cause failure in the braking system and tire pressure feedback. • Electrical failures can leave the vehicle with no rear brakes and limited use of the front brakes. • Erratic transmission shifts. **2004**—Airbags fail to deploy. • Vehicle lurches forward without accelerator depressed. • Sudden loss of power while underway or merging:

> On two occasions on the freeway at highway speeds, the engine shut down without warning. The engine shut off at once and [would] not crank when [tried to start] engine…again. Had to have vehicle towed. Dealer explained he was unfamiliar with this problem. Thought this may be the computer in the car. Made repairs and replaced parts. About 2 weeks afterwards this happened again.

• Total brake failure. • Intermittent failure of the radar-controlled cruise control. • Mirrors tilt down when backing up, but don't tilt up until car goes forward at 14 km/h. **2005**—Side airbag fails to deploy. • Airbag warning light and ABS alert stay lit. • Seat belt chime goes off when the seat is unoccupied. • When decelerating, vehicle lurches forward. • Distracting reflections on the driver side mirror, and of the dash onto the front windshield. • Frequent electrical failures. • Diesel engine is unacceptably slow to accelerate. • Excessive black soot and a tar-like residue generated by the diesel engine. • Faulty AC/defrost blower motor. • Prematurely worn original equipment tires. • Erroneous navigation/GPS directions will get you into serious trouble:

> The problem, as I see it, is that a fair percentage of drivers will blindly follow the verbal instructions with serious consequences. Incidentally, talking with the salesman about this problem, he told me that they already had a woman drive into a lake.

Secret Warranties/Internal Bulletins/Service Tips

All models/years: Engine surges at full load. • Vacuum-pump oil supply modified through the introduction of a second bore in oil spray nozzle. This helps reduce complaints that engine won't shut off. • Airbag Service Campaign. **All models: 1986–98**—Fuel-pump relay failures. **1998**—Engine-rattle countermeasures. **1998–2004**—Free engine repairs or replacement if afflicted by engine oil sludge, following the *O'Keefe* class action settlement in April 2003. Order No: S-B-18.00/16a, published December 2003, gives all the details on the problem and Mercedes' payout rules. **2000**—A Special Service Campaign will replace, free of charge, side airbags that may deploy if the vehicle is left in the sun. **2002–05**—Free replacement of the alternator voltage regulator. **2003**—Piston-slap engine noise. **2004**—No-starts. • Harsh transmission shifts. • Steering leaks. • Sliding roof-rack cover cracks. • Wheelhouse water drain modification. • Rear axle rumbling. • ABS buzzing. • Front door lock rattling. • Exhaust system rattling, hissing, and humming. • Inoperative trunk cargo light. **2005**—Oil leaks from the oil level sensor. • Rough automatic transmission engagement, droning, buzzing noises. • Transmission leaks fluid at the electrical connector. • Campaign to check and repair possible automatic transmission pilot bushing leakage, at no charge to the vehicle owner; another campaign concerns the free cleaning of the front axle carrier sleeve and bolt replacement, a third campaign will reprogram the battery control module, and a fourth campaign will inspect or replace the alternator/regulator. • Foul interior odours. • Steering fluid leaks and steering squeal when turning. • Front seat noise. • Inoperative power seat adjustment. • Cracking noise from the B-pillar area. • Sliding roof water leaks, rattling. • Moisture in the turn signal lights and mirrors. • Erratic windshield wiper operation.

300 SERIES, 400 SERIES, 500 SERIES, E-CLASS

	1997	1998	1999	2000	2001	2002	2003	2004	2005
Cost Price ($)									
300ED	59,950	59,950	59,950	—	—	—	—	—	—
320E 4d	65,900	66,450	66,750	67,150	67,900	68,350	69,950	72,050	73,000
420E, 430	73,300	73,950	74,250	74,750	75,750	76,150	—	—	—
500E/S	132,950	117,900	122,900	112,851	114,650	116,950	81,500	83,500	84,600
55 AMG	—	—	—	98,900	100,550	101,600	113,000	101,150	115,650

Used Values ($)

300ED ▲	9,000	10,000	13,000	—	—	—	—	—	—
300ED ▼	8,000	9,000	11,000	—	—	—	—	—	—
320E 4d ▲	10,500	12,000	14,000	16,000	21,000	26,000	34,000	42,000	50,000
320E 4d ▼	9,500	11,000	13,000	14,500	19,500	24,000	32,000	40,000	48,000
420E, 430 ▲	12,000	14,000	15,000	17,500	22,000	29,000	—	—	—
420E, 430 ▼	11,000	12,500	14,000	15,500	20,500	27,000	—	—	—
500E/S ▲	15,000	18,000	22,000	25,000	29,000	39,000	55,000	46,000	64,000
500E/S ▼	14,000	16,000	19,000	23,000	26,000	36,000	50,000	43,000	59,000
55 AMG ▲	—	—	—	19,000	27,000	36,000	48,000	61,000	74,000
55 AMG ▼	—	—	—	17,000	25,000	33,000	46,000	59,000	72,000
Reliability	3	3	3	3	3	3	3	3	3
Crash Protection	—	—	—	—	—	—	4	4	4
Side	—	—	—	—	—	—	5	5	5
Offset	3	3	3	5	5	5	5	5	5
Head Restraints (4d)	5	—	3	—	5	5	5	3	3
Wagon	—	—	—	—	3	3	—	—	—
Rollover Resistance	—	—	—	—	—	—	5	5	5

Nissan

MAXIMA ★ ★

RATING: Below Average (2002–06, 1986–88); the 2002 and 2004 model redesigns have led to an overall decline in quality. Average (1989–2001); redesigned 1995–2001 versions offer a peppier engine, more rounded styling, and a slightly longer wheelbase. **"Real" city/highway fuel economy:** *3.0L:* 10.8/7.9 L/100 km with a manual transmission or 12.1/8.1 L/100 km with an automatic. *3.5L:* 11.5/7.3 L/100 km manual; 11.6/7.9 L/100 km automatic. Owners report fuel savings are less than these estimates by about 10 percent. **Maintenance/Repair costs:** Higher than average, but repairs can be done practically anywhere for vehicles up to the 2001 models. Thereafter, you are totally dependent upon field fixes, a mountain of service bulletins, and "goodwill" warranties to tackle complicated factory-related goofs. **Parts:** Higher-than-average costs, but parts are easy to find. Xenon headlights are frequently stolen from the car because they are easily accessed and can cost $800 each to replace. **Extended warranty:** A must-have for 2002 and 2004 models. **Best alternatives:** Acura Integra or RL, Infiniti I30, Mazda Millenia, and Toyota Avalon. **Online help:** *www.mycarstats.com/auto_complaints/NISSAN_complaints.asp* and *www.consumeraffairs.com/automotive/nissan.html.*

Strengths and Weaknesses

These front-drive sedans are very well equipped and nicely finished, but they're cramped for their size. Although the trunk is spacious, only five passengers can travel in a pinch (in the literal sense). The 6-cylinder 190-hp engine, borrowed from the 300ZX in 1992, offers sparkling performance; the fuel injectors, however, are problematic. The '93 models got standard driver-side airbags, and the Maxima remained unchanged until the 1995 model's redesign. There was a second redesign for the year 2000 version.

Electrical and front suspension problems afflict early Maximas. Brakes and engine timing belts need frequent attention in all model years as well. Newer models have a weak automatic transmission and ignition system. There have also been reports of cooked transmissions caused by a poorly designed transmission cooler. Mechanics say that installing an externally mounted transmission cooler with a filter and replacing the transmission filter cooler at every oil change can prevent this breakdown.

Owners report that the V6-equipped Maxima is sometimes hard to start in cold weather because of the engine's tendency to flood easily. The cruise control unit is another problematic component. When it's engaged at moderate speeds, it hesitates or drifts to a lower speed, acting as if the fuel line was clogged. It operates correctly only at much higher speeds than needed. Owners say that a new fuel filter will not correct the problem. Additionally, though warped manifolds were once routinely replaced under a "goodwill" warranty, Nissan now makes the customer pay. The warpage causes a manifold bolt to break off, thereby causing a huge exhaust leak. Premature wearout of the muffler is a frequent problem; unlike the warped manifold problem, it's often covered by Nissan's "goodwill" warranty, wherein the company and dealer will contribute 50 percent of the replacement cost.

Most fuel-injector malfunctions are caused by carbon clogging up the injectors; there are additives that you can try that might reduce this buildup. There have also been internal problems with the coil windings on the fuel injectors. Your best bet is to replace the entire set.

Nissan has had problems with weak window regulators for some time. If the window is frozen, don't open it. The rubber weather stripping around the window is also a problem: It cuts easily and causes the window to go off track, which in turn causes stress on the weak regulators. Driver-side window breakage is common and can cost up to $300 to repair. Costly aluminum wheels corrode quickly and are easily damaged by road hazards. There have been a few reports of surface rust and paint problems. Maximas usually suffer from rust perforation on the sunroof, door bottoms, rear wheelwells, front hood edges, and bumper supports. The underbody should also be checked carefully for corrosion damage.

VEHICLE HISTORY: 1995—A longer wheelbase (adding to interior room), a new 3.0L engine, and more rounded styling. The cars compete well with fully equipped Camrys, entry-level Infinitis, and Lexus models. Nevertheless, tall passengers will find the interior a bit cramped, and the automatic transmission is often slow to downshift and isn't always smooth. **1997**—Models get a new front-end restyling. **2000**—Redesigned to offer more power, interior space (particularly for rear-seat passengers), and safety/convenience features. **2001**—Carried over relatively unchanged, except for an Anniversary Edition equipped with a 227-hp 3.0L V6 taken from the Infiniti I30. **2002**—Completely revamped, featuring a 260-hp 3.5L V6 coupled to a 6-speed manual or 4-speed automatic transmission; revised interior trim; larger front brakes; new front-end styling; a power driver's seat; xenon headlights; and 16-inch wheels. **2003**—GLE gets standard front side airbags. **2004**—Another redesign adds to the size and weight, along with 5 more horses. Once again, quality takes a big hit. **2005**—6-speed manual transmission has improved shift action.

The 2005 Nissan Maxima.

Each Maxima redesign has been followed by an increase in owner complaints, a normal occurrence with most revamped vehicles, but unusually severe with Nissan. Usually, after a couple of years, quality rebounds and complaints diminish.

Recent redesigns have hobbled the powertrain. Owners have difficulty controlling the engine speed with the gas pedal; there's engine popping and knocking when accelerating, surging or stalling when braking or decelerating, and transmission malfunctions galore. Premature front brake pad wear and rotor warpage; a choppy, jarring suspension; excessive front-end shaking and shimmy; faulty ignition coils; and inadequate headlight illumination continue to be major problems.

The 2004–05 revamped Maximas continue to have major quality problems, as confirmed on the *maxima.org* website and by Craig, a *Lemon-Aid* correspondent and Maxima owner:

> Phil: attached is my "master listing" of the 6th generation Maxima problems. Many owners are mad as hell the quality has dropped so much from previous versions of the cars. As well, many owners are sick and tired of inept dealers, who cannot fix the problems.
>
> A few problems, such as brake and wheel shimmy, orange peel paint and broken struts, and the "skyview" roof window known for spontaneous shattering, seem to have no Nissan solution....

- Brake shimmy or judder when braking from highway speed
- Wheel shimmy between 45 and 65 mph [72–105 km/h] when driving
- Glove box misalignment
- Left turn signal won't return to centre position
- Orange peel paint
- Grill peeling
- Shift plate scratches too easily
- Display screen scratches too easily, is foggy or has condensation inside
- Rear parcel shelf vibrating and/or noise
- Broken strut(s)
- Harsh automatic shifting (especially when cold) with 5 speed auto
- Gear grind from 1st and 2nd
- Slow seat heaters
- Instrument cluster plastic protectors peel
- Weak radio reception
- Windows slow to roll down
- Side mirrors won't reposition
- Seat shifting
- Rear speaker "beeping"
- Screeching sound—loose heat shield at 2000 rpm
- Transmission failure
- Air bag warning label on visor bubbling up
- Sunroof deflector hitting glass
- Door trim pieces easily get rub marks
- HID lights—high beam won't return to low beam
- HID lights—burn out prematurely
- Fog lights—burn out prematurely
- Car won't start (loose fuel pump connector at fuse panel)
- Right floorboard soaked floor
- Liquid running sound in A/C system, especially after cold start
- Stiff doors after sitting for awhile
- Skyview roof exploding
- Armrest won't stay down and cup holder comes out of track
- Leaking sunroof
- Plastics flexing and squeaking inside cabin
- Stereo buttons on steering wheel don't work

This is clearly a situation where one cure definitely does not fit all. It seems the dealers lean toward all the usual suspects before they resort to the steering-rack friction adjustment that has cured the shimmy for some of the most persistent cases. Hard starting can be traced in some cases to a loose fuel-pump connector at the fuse panel.

Safety Summary

All models/years: Airbag failed to deploy. • Sudden loss of power, resulting in inoperative brakes and steering. • Chronic stalling. • Erratic transmission performance. • ABS failures. **All models: 1998**—Vehicle intermittently accelerates while braking. • Frequent windshield wiper failures. **1999**—Throttle "shock" and transmission hesitation. • Frequent ignition coil failures. • Vehicle pulls constantly to the left. • Cruise-control resume feature doesn't work. • Power door locks cycle from lock to unlock. **2000**—Early replacement of the catalytic converter (alerted by Check Engine light) and the #6 ignition coil. Stand your ground; both are covered by extended warranties. • Poor headlight illumination. • A chlorine-type smell permeates the interior. **2001**—Engine compartment fire. • Steering lock-ups and loss of brakes. **2002**—Vehicle suddenly swings to the right. • Steering wheel overheats. • Sudden acceleration in Reverse with gearshift lever indicating Drive. • ABS and traction control malfunction every time car is washed. • Front wheels lock up or get no power; ABS light remains lit. • Car has pronounced hesitation upon acceleration:

> When driving vehicle out of a parking lot, at about 15 mph [24 km/h], I pressed gas pedal and car did not respond (there seems to be no traction on wheels for about 10 seconds), then "slip" light starts flashing for about 3 seconds. After this, vehicle starts getting traction again and light stops flashing.

• Vehicle accelerates when foot taken off accelerator. • Defective mass air sensor or crank sensor causes sudden loss of power and transmission bucking and jerking. • Vehicle rolls backward when parked on an incline. • Right front wheel buckles when brakes are applied. • In one incident, vehicle surged when brakes were applied while parking, and car hit a brick wall. • Faulty air control valve causes sudden acceleration. • Suspension transverse link failed, causing loss of control; owners report that cars not in the recall have the same defect. • Lower control arm failure as in recall notice, but car isn't among those recalled. • Chronic brake failures. • Xenon headlights are easily stolen and expensive to replace:

> Headlights easily stolen on Nissan Maxima 2002, 2003. I have a 2002 Maxima SE and the other day, my headlights were stolen while the car was parked outside my mother-in-law's house. I found out this has been an ongoing problem with this vehicle and Nissan isn't telling anyone about this problem when purchasing this vehicle...the way the lights are connected they are easily stolen and will be an ongoing problem as long as you own this vehicle. Nissan will retrofit new lights at the owner's expense, about $300.00.

• Moisture collects in the headlights. • Windshield wipers don't work in cold weather; fluid line freezes up. • Sunroof opens on its own, allowing rain and debris to enter. • Front passenger-side window won't stay closed. • Back window suddenly shatters. • Rear quarter window air leaks. • Trunk water leaks. • Original tires leak air. • Hood and front bumper paint chipping. **2003**—O_2 sensor failure. • Hard to read instrument panel lights. • Passenger-side airbag deploys on its own. • Paint chips easily. • Xenon headlight thefts. **2004**—Excessive steering-wheel shimmy. • In one incident, vehicle was underway at 100 km/h when suddenly the steering wheel locked up and the brakes failed. • In another instance, the front wheels locked up while the vehicle was in motion, causing extensive undercarriage damage. • Vehicle suddenly swerves out of control. • Vehicle suddenly accelerates in Reverse when put into Drive. • Sudden acceleration upon start-up (a faulty air control valve is suspected). • Unable to control engine speed with the accelerator pedal. • Vehicle stalls without warning in cold weather (suspect the computer module). • Fuel leaks from seal when over-filled. • Excessive front-end vibrations. • Strong bleach-like odour permeates the interior. • Many complaints that the headlights are poorly designed, placing the high beams too high for adequate visibility; drivers complain they can't see between the high and low beams. • Trunk lid and latch are hazardous when raised. • Several incidents where the SkyView roof shattered:

> While driving a 2004 Maxima, out of nowhere the glass roof exploded outward. Glass covered me and the backseat of the car. Nothing hit the car. I went under no over-passes, there were no other vehicles around me at the time. I nearly lost control of the car and suffered minor scratches to forehead and arm from the shattered glass. I strongly feel that this was some sort of defect and want this documented as to prevent further injury to other drivers of this make [of] vehicle.

• Sunroof opens and closes on its own. • Steering wheel overheats in direct sunlight. • The driver-side windshield washer may not work in cold weather. • Tire-tread separation. **2005**—Stalling and hard starts. • Engine surges when downshifting. • There is a one-second delay from when the accelerator pedal is released to when the car begins to slow down. • Engine threw a rod and had to be replaced. • Erratic transmission shifts. • Change tray is poorly designed: If change falls through the gap, it will cause major electrical damage to the car and possibly ignite a fire. • Strong vibration and shimmy, probably related to faulty suspension strut assemblies that often wear out within a year:

> Started with shaking steering wheel from 55 mph [90 km/h] and above. Took it back several times to Nissan. Replaced brakes, rotors, struts, rims and tyres. Also body repairs like swaying rear fender and vibrating heat shield in engine. Still have shaking problems, cannot rotate tyres and speed balanced over 7 times and no solution. Took for service and Nissan did recalls to rear suspension ABS and child seat anchors. They rotated the tyres and now the car pulls to the left and the right on rough roads (total nightmare).

• Sudden total brake loss. • Accelerator and brake pedals are mounted too close together. • Rack and pinion steering assembly wears out early. • Many incidents where the original-equipment Goodyear/Eagle and Wahl tire sidewalls crack. • Broken axle. • Headlights don't work properly and are a thief magnet:

> The projector lamps utilize a shutter to change from high to low beam. After the lamp has operated for a period of time (30 min–1 hour) the shutter does not move fully, leaving the lamps in a partial or full high beam mode, even when low beam is called for by the control switch. This is a hazard to oncoming drivers, and I get flashed by oncoming traffic frequently.

Secret Warranties/Internal Bulletins/Service Tips

All models/years: Defective catalytic converters that cause a rotten-egg smell may be replaced free of charge under Nissan's emissions warranty; the same principle applies to EVAP canister charcoal leakage. • TSB #P195-006 looks at the many causes and remedies for excessive brake noise. • Troubleshooting MIL alerts. **All models: 1995–98**—An inoperative power seat may require a new drive cable. **1995–99**—Blower-motor noise can be cured by installing a new blower-motor cover. • A front brake groan when stopping is addressed in TSB #99-032. • A rear brake groan or hum can be fixed by readjusting the parking brake cable. • If the rear brakes squeak or squeal when cold, replace the rear brake pads with upgraded ones. • Guidelines for correcting steering pull or drift. • Tips on eliminating a foul odour emanating from the sunroof sunshade. **1996–99**—Diagnostic tips for fixing a front seat belt that's slow to retract. **1998–99**—An On-Off transmission throttle shock can be attenuated by installing an upgraded ECM. **1999**—Guidelines for correcting rocker panel creaking or popping. **2000**—Low idle or stalling in gear. • Excessive brake vibration countermeasures. • Right front strut noise. • Rear bumper scratched by trunk lid. • Tips on silencing interior squeaks and rattles and front brake groan. **2000–01**—Automatic transmission gear slippage. **2000–02**—Doors may intermittently lock by themselves. **2000–03**—Driver's seat won't go forward or backward. • Abnormal shifting (the control valve assembly is the likely culprit, says TSB #NTB04-035). • Oil leaks from the oil cooler seal. **2001–02**—Rear brake caliper clunk, rattle, or knock. • Rear suspension bottoms out (also an Infiniti problem). • Hood vibration. **2002**—Erratic sunroof operation. • Radio ignition static. • Driver's power seat won't move forward or backward. • Clutch howling. **2002–03**—Hesitation upon acceleration. • Lack of engine power. • Sunroof operates on its own. **2003**—Navigation screen stuck on "please wait." • Troubleshooting brake noise and judder. **2003–04**—Harsh 1–2 shifts. **2004**—Cold upshift shock; abnormal shifting. • Fuel system misfires. • Hard start after a cold soak. • Engine won't crank in cold weather. • Front brake noise. • AC gurgling noise. • Exhaust ticking noise. • Water leaks from roof. • Headlight fogging. • Loose headliner. • Howling, humming tires. **2004–05**—Exhaust rattle/buzz when accelerating. • Voluntary service campaign involving the free replacement of the rear suspension and bushing sealing (see bulletin on page 317). **2004–06**—Front power seat malfunction. **2005**—AC clicking.

MAXIMA PROFILE

	1997	1998	1999	2000	2001	2002	2003	2004	2005
Cost Price ($)									
Base	27,998	27,998	28,598	28,598	29,000	32,900	32,900	34,500	34,600
Used Values ($)									
Base ▲	4,000	5,000	5,500	7,000	9,000	11,500	14,500	19,000	22,500
Base ▼	3,500	4,500	5,000	6,000	8,000	9,000	13,000	17,500	21,000

Reliability	4	4	4	4	3	2	2	2	2
Crash Safety (F)	4	4	4	—	4	4	4	5	5
Side	4	4	4	—	4	4	4	4	4
Side (IIHS)	—	—	—	—	—	—	—	2	2
Offset	3	3	3	3	3	3	3	5	5
Head Restraints (F)	2	2	3	3	5	5	5	1	1
Rear	—	—	2	—	—	—	—	—	—
Rollover Resistance	—	—	—	—	—	4	4	4	4

Toyota

AVALON ✷ ★ ★ ★

RATING: Average (2005–06); Above Average (1995–2004). Sorry, Toyota, but your Avalon had already slipped from our Recommended category and now continues to be downgraded in this year's guide. The Avalon suffers from the same "less for more" philosophy we have seen since 1997 with most of Toyota's lineup (with a few exceptions such as the Echo and Celica). Surprisingly, post '97 Avalons fare better than most other Toyotas, but during the past three years, following the car's last major redesign, quality has declined markedly. Avalons have exhibited an unusually large number of safety-related defects in addition to charges that its engines are often sidelined by engine oil sludge. It's a good idea to make sure that headlight illumination is adequate for your driving needs, "green glow" dash reflections onto the windshield aren't too distracting, and windshield visibility is adequate for rainy weather. **"Real" city/highway fuel economy:** 11.0/7.4 L/100 km. Owners report fuel savings match this estimate. **Maintenance/repair costs:** Average. **Parts:** Higher-than-average costs and limited availability. **Extended warranty:** Not needed. **Best alternatives:** A fully loaded Camry, but if you want a more driver-involved experience in a Toyota, consider a Lexus ES 300 or GS 300. Other good choices are the Acura Integra or RL, BMW 3 Series, Infiniti I30, Mazda Millenia, and the early Nissan Maxima. **Online help:** *www.carsurvey.org/model_toyota_avalon.html*, *yotarepair.com/automotive_news.html*, and *www.consumeraffairs.com/automotive/toyota_avalon.html*, or conduct a search for "Toyota engine sludge" using a search engine like Google.

Strengths and Weaknesses

This near-luxury four-door offers more value, interior space, and performance than do other cars in its class that cost thousands of dollars more. A front-engine, front-drive, mid-sized sedan based on a stretched Camry platform, the six-passenger (up to the 2004 model) Avalon is bigger than the recommended rear-drive Cressida it replaced and similar in size to the Ford Taurus. Sure, there's a fair amount of Camry in the Avalon, but it's quicker on its feet, better attuned to abrupt manoeuvres, and 5 cm longer. In fact, there's more rear-seat legroom than you'll find in either the Taurus or the Chevrolet Lumina. It's close to the Dodge Intrepid in this respect.

VEHICLE HISTORY: 1997—More power, torque, and standard features. **1998**—Seat belt pretensioners, side airbags, new headlights and tail lights, and a new trunk lid and grille. **2000**—Restyled and considerably improved. It's more powerful, roomier, and full of more high-tech safety and convenience features. **2003**—More styling upgrades and revised gauges. **2005**—The third-generation Avalon has been restyled, and is larger and more powerful. It seats five instead of six due to new front bucket seats, and offers 2.5 cm more legroom and a floor-mounted shifter. A stretched platform adds 10 cm to the wheelbase, about 15 cm to overall length, and a bit more width and height, but interior room is little changed. Toyota's 280-hp 3.5L V6 coupled to a 5-speed automatic, instead of the previous year's 4-speed, replaces the 210-hp 3.0L V6 transmission. All models come with four-wheel ABS disc brakes, front side airbags, side curtain airbags, and a driver's knee airbag. Traction/anti-skid control is available for most models, except the Touring. Other features added to the 2005 models: reclining backrests for a split folding rear seat, a steering wheel with telescopic as well as tilt adjustment, heated/cooled front seats, keyless starting, and xenon headlights (Touring and Limited).

Quality control up through 2004 is better than average, though steering, suspension, and fuel system components are failure-prone, and many owners have complained of engine sludge forcing them to spend thousands of dollars for engine repairs (now covered by a "goodwill" extended warranty).

Owners of 2005 and 2006 Avalons report their cars have serious safety, performance, and reliability problems. And word is getting around. Says LemonLawClaims.com (*www.lemonlawclaims.com/toyota_avalon_problems_lemon. htm*):

> Toyota Motor Corp., long known for its problem-free cars and trucks, is experiencing quality control problems in a number of its products. Among the troubled models are Avalon, Prius and the FJ Cruiser, but it is the Avalon that has attracted the most industry attention. Toyota introduced the redesigned Avalon in 2005, and ever since it has been beset with problems. For the Avalon, the Japanese automaker has provided service bulletins, which alerts dealers to problems, on bad U-joint welds, faulty catalytic converters and a leak in the oil supply line for variable valve timing. There also have been recalls to correct problems with air bags and the steering column on some Avalons. Transmission hesitation problems, which have plagued the automaker in the past, also have resurfaced with the five-speed automatic transmission installed in the Avalon. While the earlier transmission problems were experienced by consumers in a variety of situations, this round of trouble surfaces particularly when the driver presses the acceleration pedal for greater speed. All the difficulties have resulted in the Avalon being downgrading in its quality rating to "average" by *Consumer Reports*.

Other performance gripes posted by *Lemon-Aid* readers include numerous electrical system glitches, premature front brake repairs and suspension strut failures, power steering that's a bit too light, hydroplaning, excessive body lean, under-steering when cornering, and a problematic Vehicle Stability Control (VSC) and Traction Control system (TRAC):

Toyota's luxury "cherry" is taking on a decidedly lemony flavour.

> Phil: The problem with the 2005 Avalon is that there is no way of disengaging the Vehicle Stability Control (VSC) and the traction control (TRAC) feature to allow you to spin the tires if you become stuck in snow or mud, something we have an abundance of for over 1/2 the year. So, what happens is when you get in snow, the tires refuse to spin and the vehicle just sits there and won't move. Three weeks ago (the last time I drove it) I became stuck in 3" of snow in a service station parking lot at Archerwill, Saskatchewan, and it took three people pushing in order to get me moving. Both the less costly Toyota Camry and 4Runner models have buttons to disengage the Vehicle Stability Control (VSC) and the traction control (TRAC) feature for this purpose or other emergency.

Body construction and assembly are no longer first class, with poor fit and finish, rattles, and water/air leaks the most common complaints. Trunk leaks have been reported on late '90s models, and paint flaking has afflicted some 2001–03 versions. Except for some engine sludge complaints, premature brake wear, and body and accessory glitches (wind noise, AC, and audio system malfunctions), the 2002 and 2003 models have had few problems.

Safety Summary

All models/years: Airbags failed to deploy in an accident. • Sudden, unintended acceleration. • Bridgestone/Firestone, Dunlop, and Michelin tire failures. **All models: 1998**—Vehicle caught fire at fuel-filler neck when getting gas. • Gas-tank fuel hose leaks fuel. • Airbag deployment caused severe chest and chin injuries. • Front seat reclined suddenly when vehicle was hit from the rear. • Engine surges and drops rpm rapidly and unexpectedly when engaging cruise control or when taking foot off the gas pedal. • Power-steering pump failure and fluid reservoir leakage. • Early replacement of brake pads, calipers, and rotors. • Front suspension bangs and clanks when going over a bump of any size, and rear suspension bottoms out. • Constant vibration in steering wheel and accelerator while driving caused by fuel pressure regulator. • Loose driver's seat. • Kick panel falls off repeatedly. **1999**—Airbag warning light comes on for no reason. • Cruise control operates erratically. • Brake pedal goes to floor with little effect. • Car shifts poorly (hesitates and jerks) when you let off the gas and then accelerate or do a rolling stop. **2000**—Automatic transmission slippage. • Brake pedal goes to the floor with no braking effect. • Driver's seat rocks back and forth. • Steering wheel off-centre. • Airbag warning light stays lit. • Dash lights and gauges reflect onto windshield. • Inadequate headlight illumination. • Horn failure. **2001**—Excessive highway wandering. • Engine surging at idle. • Flex hose comes off the charcoal canister, causing warning light to come on when refuelling. • Front and rear suspension bottoms out when carrying four adults. • Insufficient steering feedback. • Jerky acceleration. • Sudden failure of the instrument and information panel lighting and headlights. • Driver's side-view mirror has a small viewing area. • At night, the instrument panel lights and gauges reflect a green glow onto the windshield. **2002**—Cruise control doesn't slow car when going downhill. • Vehicle veers to the left at high speeds; vehicle wanders left and right. • Driver-side seat belt doesn't retract. • Dash lights reflect onto the windshield. • Vehicle emits a strong sulfur odour, which Toyota bulletins claim is normal. **2003**—Extended braking distance caused by improperly installed brake lines. • Front brakes appear to apply themselves. • Steering wheel blocks view of speedometer; hard to read gearshift position gauge at night. • Panel glass overheats while driving. • Incorrect readings from the fuel range finder. **2004**—Rear wheel seizes while vehicle is underway. • Stalling when AC is activated. • Key won't turn in the ignition. • Difficult to judge distance when backing up. **2005**—Throttle stuck to the floor. • Hesitation and surging when accelerating. • Engine surges and then shuts off and can't be restarted. • Cruise control speed drop is hazardous:

> When my car slows down suddenly because of the car in front, there is no warning for the car behind me. Toyota was notified of this problem and told me not to use the sonar in heavy travelled roads. That is no solution. There should be a fix to make the brake lights go on when the car is slowed down by the sonar.

• Brakes suddenly fail due to a faulty master cylinder. • Loose motor mounts cause noise and instability when accelerating from a stop. • Wheel bearing axle grease leaks onto front disc pad, causing poor braking. • Rear windshield distortion causes road to appear wavy and cars to appear to be swerving. • Electrical shorts:

> Three different electrical shorts in a 2005 Toyota Avalon Limited with less [than] 5000 miles [8,000 kilometres]. The shorts were in the brake light switch, the engine control unit, and the fuse box. The first and third short prevented the car from starting. The second short caused the engine to stall while traveling at 55 mph [90 km/h] on a major highway. It is a miracle that there was not an accident. The switch, engine control unit, and fuse box have all been replaced. The car has been towed 4 times during the first year of ownership.

Secret Warranties/Internal Bulletins/Service Tips

All models/years: Poor-fitting, loose trim panels. **All models: 1990–2000**—Brake-pad clicking may be corrected by use of a special Toyota-recommended grease; however, some owners say it's not very effective. **1995–2000**—A power-steering squeak can be silenced by installing a new rack end shaft. **1997–99**—Front suspension noise can be eliminated by changing the suspension support. **1997–**

2002—Extended warranty will pay for engine sludge damage up to eight years, without any mileage limitation. **2000**—Roof leaks water. • Sliding roof and door mirror noise. **2000–01**—Measures to reduce instrument panel luminosity. • Wheel bearing ticking noise. • Door popping and creaking. **2000–04**—Fuel door hard to open. **2003**—Blank navigation screen. **2004**—Correction for vehicle tendency to pull to the left. • Front suspension knocking. **2004–06**—Front seat squeak. **2005–06**—Engine oil leaks. • Water leaks onto the front floor area. • Pull/drift to one side while driving. • Diagnosis and correction of steering column noise. • Creaking and ticking noise heard from base of rear windshield. • Rear suspension thump, clunk. • Inoperative horn. • Loose fog lamps. • Luggage lid won't close properly.

AVALON PROFILE

	1997	1998	1999	2000	2001	2002	2003	2004	2005
Cost Price ($)									
XL	33,718	34,688	35,605	36,595	36,370	38,365	—	—	—
XLS	36,188	37,868	42,515	43,800	44,710	45,135	45,560	45,830	39,900
Used Values ($)									
XL ▲	4,000	5,000	6,500	8,000	10,000	13,000	—	—	—
XL ▼	3,500	4,500	5,500	6,500	8,500	11,000	—	—	—
XLS ▲	5,000	6,000	7,500	9,000	11,000	14,000	19,000	22,000	28,000
XLS ▼	4,500	5,500	6,500	7,500	9,500	12,500	17,500	20,000	26,000
Reliability	5	5	5	5	5	5	5	5	3
Crash Safety (F)	4	4	—	3	3	4	4	4	5
Side	5	5	—	4	4	4	4	4	5
Side (IIHS)	—	—	—	—	—	—	—	—	5
Offset	2	3	3	5	5	5	5	5	5
Head Restraints (F)	1	3	3	3	1	1	1	1	1
Rear	—	1	1	—	—	—	—	—	—
Rollover Resistance	—	—	—	—	—	4	4	4	4

Volvo

850, C70, XC70, XC90, S40, S60, S70, V40, V70 ★★

RATING: Below Average (1993–2006). Surprisingly, for a car company that emphasizes its commitment to safe cars and quality components, Volvo's entire lineup during the past decade has deteriorated from both quality and safety perspectives. There are two reasons for this decline: the use of more complex, failure-prone electronics, and Ford's poor stewardship of the company. As a result, good dealers and technicians have left Volvo in droves, parts suppliers cannot meet Ford quality targets and also make a profit, and customers are chafing at the cold response they get from Ford's owner "assistance" call centres. Safety-related defects reported by owners include engine and seat fires, loss of steering, sudden acceleration, transmission failures, electrical shorts, light failures, and tire blowouts. As if this weren't bad enough, Ford's cost-cutting and sadistic customer relations have left many new and used buyers leery of getting a Volvo. **"Real" city/highway fuel economy:** *850:* 12.2/7.6 L/100 km with a manual transmission or 11.7/7.5 L/100 km with an automatic. *Turbo:* 12.8/8.4 L/100 km with a manual tranny or 12.3/8.4 L/100 km with an automatic. *C70:* 11.7/8.0 L/100 km manual; 11.4/7.6 L/100 km automatic. *XC70 2.5L:* 12.6/8.8 L/100 km. *XC90 2.5L:* 13.3/9.1 L/100 km. *XC90 T6 2.9L:* 15.6/10.6 L/100 km. *S40/V40:* 10.8/7.3 L/100 km manual; 10.7/7.0 L/100 km automatic. *S60:* 10.8/7.3 L/100 km manual; 10.7/7.0 L/100 km automatic. *S60 2.4T AWD:* 11.7/7.9 L/100 km. *S60 R:* 13.1/8.6 L/100 km manual; 13.2/8.6 L/100 km automatic. *S60 T5:* 11.5/8.0 L/100 km. *S70:* 11.2/7.6 L/100 km manual; 10.6/7.7 L/100 km automatic. *V70 2.4L:* 10.8/7.3 L/100 km manual; 10.9/7.1 L/100 km automatic. *V70 2.5LT AWD:* 11.7/7.9 L/100 km. *V70 2.5LT R AWD:* 13.1/8.6 L/100 km manual; 13.2/8.6 L/100 km automatic. Fuel savings may be lower than these figures by about 10–15 percent. **Maintenance/Repair costs:** Higher than average, and repairs must be done by a Volvo dealer. **Parts:** Higher-than-average costs, and limited availability. **Extended warranty:** A good idea, considering that even some of the most mundane repairs can be costly to perform. **Best alternatives:** Don't waste your money on a 1997 850; the 1996 models are virtually identical. The 1998 model 850s were renamed the C70, S70, and V70; they also have a disappointingly high number of safety- and performance-related deficiencies reported to the U.S. federal government. Other choices are the Acura Integra or RL, BMW 3 or 5 Series, Infiniti I30, Mazda Millenia, the early Nissan Maxima, and Toyota Avalon. **Online help:** *www.volvospy.com, www.consumeraffairs. com/automotive/volvo.htm, www.consumeraffairs.com/automotive/volvo_fires.html,* and *www.carsurvey.org/manufacturer_Volvo.html.*

Strengths and Weaknesses

Bland, but practical to the extreme, with plenty of power, good handling, and lots of capacity. For 1997, the 850 GLT got a bit more lower-end torque, while the turbo version was upgraded with electrically adjusted front passenger seats and an in-dash CD player. The base 850 Sedan uses a 24-valve 168-hp 2.4L 5-cylinder engine hooked to a front-drive powertrain. (An all-wheel-drive version is available only in Canada and Europe.) Wagons use the same base powerplant hooked to a 5-speed manual or optional 4-speed electronic automatic. GLTs have a torquier turbo variant of the same powerplant that boosts horsepower to 190.

The sports sedan T5 is a rounder, sportier-looking Volvo that delivers honest, predictable performance but comes up a bit short on the "sport" side. Volvo's base turbo boosts horsepower to 222, but its new T-5R variant uses an upgraded turbocharger that boosts power to 240 horses—for up to 7 seconds. Passenger space, seating comfort, and trunk and cargo space are unmatched by the competition. Braking on dry and wet pavement is also exemplary. The ride of both the sedan and the wagon deteriorates progressively as the road gets rougher and passengers are added. Turbo versions are particularly stiff, and passengers are constantly bumped and thumped.

The 850 hasn't escaped the traditional AC, electrical system, and brake problems that afflict its predecessors. Additionally, owners have complained that the early models have uncomfortable seat belts, insufficient rear travel for the front seats, and many body hardware deficiencies.

70 Series and 90 Series

Making its debut in the 1998 model year, the 70 Series is basically the discontinued 850 using a *nom de plume*. The letters S, V, and C preceding the numerical designation stand for sedans, wagons, and coupes. The 90 Series is a re-designated rear-drive 960, and, as with the 70 Series, sedans are indicated by an S and wagons by a V. Both the 70 and 90 Series are carried over relatively unchanged, except for their names.

With the front-drive 70 Series, all-wheel drive is offered with the wagons, and the base 2.4L 5-cylinder engine comes with three horsepower ratings: 168, 190, and 236 hp. Only two transmissions are available: a manual 5-speed (relatively rare) and an automatic 4-speed. Handling is superb, with the suspension dampened somewhat for a more comfortable ride than what many European imports offer. AWD performs flawlessly, road and body noise are muted, and the cars are well appointed with a full array of standard safety features, with the exception of traction control, which is optional.

VEHICLE HISTORY: *70 Series:* **1999**—An AWD GLT sedan debuts; the R wagon's engine gets 11 more horses (247 hp); automatic transmission shifts and braking performance are improved. A standard engine immobilizer is added, as are "smart" airbags that match the device's explosive force to the car's speed and unlock the car doors after a collision. **2000**—No more base AWD V70 wagon, nor T5. Side airbags are upgraded to protect occupants' heads, and the front seatbacks and headrests are redesigned to minimize whiplash. **2001**—Station wagons get more interior room now that they use the full-size S80 sedan platform. The S70 sedans, base and GLT wagons, and the high-performance R-type are no more, but the C70 coupe and convertible remain. Traction control is standard only on the T5, all models have anti-lock all-disc brakes, front head/chest side-impact airbags, curtain window airbags, and Volvo's WHIPS system that moves the front seat rearward in a rear-end collision to minimize whiplash injury. **2002**—An all-wheel-drive 2.4T AWD comes on board, Volvo's anti-skid system is standard on the T5, and traction control is standard on all front-drives. **2003**—The V70 2.5T AWD and XC70 get a power boost of 11 extra horses, and the T5's power is cranked up to 247 horses. **2004**—Debut of the high-performance 300-hp V70R, equipped with AWD and a 6-speed manual or 5-speed automatic transmission. **2005**—Refreshed styling, optional run-flat tires, wood interior trim, and a firmer suspension for the T5. The AWD V70 2.5T has been discontinued.

On the downside, rear seating is cramped for three adults, and the instrument panel appears overly busy, with a confusing array of gauges, instruments, and controls on the centre console. Plus, the three rear head restraints induce claustrophobia while severely restricting rear visibility.

The 90 Series has plenty of room for three rear-seat passengers, and its 181-hp V6 performs very smoothly and fairly quietly, providing plenty of power for passing and merging. The car's tight turning circle makes parking a snap, and the suspension has been tuned for comfort rather than performance. Still, handling is quite good. Once again, the large rear head restraints obstruct rear visibility.

VEHICLE HISTORY: *940, 960, S90, V90:* **1996**—4-cylinder 940 models are dropped, leaving just the 6-cylinder 960s. Side airbags are a standard feature. Also, the seatbelts are more user-friendly for securing child safety seats. **1998**—Sedans are renamed the S90 and wagons are called V90. The 181-hp inline-six powers both. Volvo also revises the centre consoles and softens the suspension.

As far as quality control and dealer servicing are concerned, Volvo technical service bulletins and owner complaints indicate that factory defects on all models have been on the rise for the past five years. For example, the car's electrical system may go berserk or shut down entirely in rainy weather or when the car is passing over puddles; headlights, turn signal lights, and other bulbs burn out monthly; power window switches and locks fail constantly; wheels are easily bent; the turn signal lever doesn't return; airbags deploy for no reason; and springs are noisy.

The above defects clearly show that quality control is less stringent at the factory level since Ford acquired the company, and that Volvo is counting on Ford and Volvo dealers to repair their engineering mistakes. On the other hand, Volvo has improved service and warranty relations by accelerating service-training programs. But the effort may be too little, too late: Volvo sales have fallen, and many dealers are trying to bail out before Ford's mismanagement ruins them.

C70

The C70's strong points: good acceleration with lots of torque, exceptional steering and handling, first-class body construction and finish, and predicted better-than-average reliability. Its weak points: difficult rear seat entry/exit, some engine turbo lag, excessive engine noise, a jarring suspension, and an uncertain future.

Seating four comfortably, this luxury coupe and convertible is based on the 850 (pardon, S70) platform and marketed as a high-performance Volvo. It comes with two turbocharged engines: a base 2.4L 190-hp inline 5-cylinder and a 2.3L 236-hp variant. Either engine can be hooked to a 5-speed manual or 4-speed automatic transmission. Of the two engines, the 190-hp appears to offer the best response and smoothest performance. Acceleration is impressive, despite the fact that the car feels underpowered until the turbo kicks in at around 1500 rpm—a feature that drivers will find more frustrating with a manual shifter than with an automatic. Steering and handling are first class, fit and finish are above reproach, and mechanical and body components are top quality.

The only things not to like are turbo lag, tire thumping caused by the high-performance tires, excessive engine and wind noise, and power-sliding rear seats that require lots of skill and patience to operate.

S40 and V40

Volvo's latest small sedan and wagon come with a 1.9L 150-hp turbocharged 4-cylinder engine coupled with an automatic transmission. Two side airbags, anti-lock brakes, air conditioning, cruise control, and power windows are also standard. The 2001 model got a minor facelift, an upgraded engine and 5-speed automatic transmission, side curtain airbags, and some handling improvements. The 2002s were carried over unchanged.

These models have also generated an unacceptably high number of complaints concerning chronic brake repairs, automatic transmission failures, fuel system malfunctions leading to poor driveability, and myriad electrical shorts and body defects.

S60

This sporty, mid-range sedan uses the same large car platform as the V70 and S80 but provides more interior room. A 197-hp 5-cylinder engine teamed with an all-wheel-drive powertrain has been added to the lineup, giving buyers AWD benefits without having to choose the taller, more SUV-like Cross Country. Drivers will have the choice of three inline 5-cylinder engines: a 168-hp naturally aspirated version, a 197-hp low-pressure turbo, and a 247-hp high-pressure turbo.

Some of the S60's pluses are fair acceleration; exceptional handling and braking; a good array of user-friendly instruments and controls; comfortable front seating; and very good head-restraint, offset, front, and side crashworthiness scores. Some of the car's deficiencies include lots of turbo throttle hesitation and torque steer pulling when accelerating; an imprecise manual shifter; a jarring ride with some tire thump (worse with the T5) when passing over uneven pavement; rear visibility that's obstructed by a high parcel shelf, obtrusive head restraints, and a descending roofline; cramped rear seating, made worse by rear legroom that disappears when the front seats are pushed back only halfway; a narrow trunk with a small opening; and turbo engines that require premium fuel.

Other cars worth considering are the Acura TL and Infiniti I35. Leftover S60s have been deeply discounted, particularly in view of Volvo's declining sales.

XC70, XC90

Essentially a renamed V70 station wagon, the XC70 is an SUV wannabe that offers five-passenger seating, high ground clearance, sleek styling, and AWD versatility.

Its mechanical components are practically identical to those of Volvo's other sedans. The base engine is a 168-hp (non-turbo) 2.4L 5-cylinder. The turbo version has been replaced by a 208-hp 2.5L turbocharged 5-cylinder hooked to a 5-speed automatic gearbox. It is followed by the 247-hp 2.5L turbocharged T5 and a 300-hp variant found on the V70 R.

XC90 models are based on Volvo's S80 car platform and aren't intended for off-road use. They offer seven-passenger seating along with a base turbocharged 208-hp 2.5L 5-cylinder and an optional 268-hp 2.9L V6 on the T6 version. All transmissions have a manual shiftgate. However, the AWD system lacks low-range gearing. Anti-lock four-wheel disc brakes, anti-skid/traction control, and Roll Stability Control are standard. Also included are front torso side airbags and head-protecting side curtain airbags that cover all seating rows.

Problem areas are limited to frequent brake maintenance (rotors and pads), chronic stalling, and electrical system and body faults (inoperative moonroof, door locks, and gauges), notably excessive windshield/dash glare and side windows that won't close until the control button is pressed three times. Poor fuel economy is also a recurring complaint.

Safety Summary

All models: 1998—Passenger-side airbag suddenly deployed while vehicle was parked. • Front and side airbags failed to deploy in a collision. • Right front-wheel assembly disengaged from car while vehicle is underway, causing loss of control. • Vehicle suddenly accelerated; brakes locked up. • Stalling while underway caused by defective air mass sensor. • A piece of the vacuum brake system came loose, causing engine rpm to surge and spontaneous locking of the brakes. • Transmission randomly fails to engage in Reverse gear or kicks strongly when going into Reverse. • Frequent battery failures caused by battery not holding its charge. • Headlights and other lights burn out frequently. • Two incidents where the front turn-signal socket smouldered and charred. • Driver's seat belt doesn't retract when disconnected. • Continental tire-tread separation. • Frequent tire blowouts. • Wheels are easily bent, causing excessive vibration. • Defective door lock pin makes it difficult to open or close door. • Weak trunk lid struts allow lid to fall. • Dashboard causes excessive glare on windshield. • Tall front seats and head restraints obstruct visibility. **1999**—Sudden acceleration when applying brakes. • Vehicle shuts down when making a left turn. • Airbags fail to deploy. • While underway, driver seat suddenly moved backward. • Fuel fumes leak into interior. • Brake pedal locks up. • Chronic light failures. • Automatic door locked, and trunk lock failed to open. • Automatic gas-tank door jams shut. • Tailpipe extends beyond bumper, burning occupant. • Inside door handles pinch fingers. *XC70:* **2003**—Loose fuel lines. **2004**—While cruising on the highway, engine suddenly starts racing, steering wheel and brakes locked, and all gauges went dead. • Excessive steering-wheel shake. • Steering wheel incapable of facilitating a U-turn. • Rear view mirror auto-dim feature doesn't work. *XC90:* **2003**—Prematurely worn out Pirelli tires. • Unable to turn key in the ignition. • Rusty lug nuts. **2004**—Vehicle's all-wheel-drive feature causes the car to handle erratically and go out of control. • Airbags failed to deploy when car was hit from the side. • When shifting into Park, shifter inadvertently goes into Reverse. • Tire blowout caused fuel line to leak. • Engine seizure due to a buildup of engine sludge. • Transmission interlock becomes disengaged when remote door-lock key fob is activated; one incident caused the car to roll down a hill. • Transmission replacement during car's second year on the road. • Gearshift indicator either goes blank or shows the wrong gear. • Doors suddenly unlock themselves and open while vehicle is underway. • Battery quickly loses its charge. *C70:* **2001**—Power-window noise. *S40, V40:* **2001**— Under-hood electrical fire. • Cracked fuel regulator pump spilled fuel onto hot engine and fumes spread into the interior. • Sudden, unintended acceleration when vehicle put into Drive. • Chronic stalling attributed to faulty idle control valve and air mass meter. • Complete loss of braking. • Brake pedal hard to depress, reducing brake effectiveness. • Brakes don't stop vehicle within a reasonable distance. • Brake pedal is too close to the gas pedal. • Brake pedal snapped, went to the floor while going downhill. • When applying the brakes in cold weather, pedal won't depress, causing extended stopping distances (dealer confirms vacuum-pump motor is defective). • Premature replacement of the front and rear rotors and pads:

> I have a 2001 S40 with 30,000 miles [48,000 km] on it. I have had nothing but problems with the brakes and headlamps. I have replaced the front brakes and rotors three times. I have replaced the rear rotors once and the pads twice. The headlamps constantly blow out. I wrote Volvo and they tell me the brakes go because of the material they use. Apparently it is soft. Too bad they did not tell me I would incur these expenses before I leased it.

• Vehicle pulls to the left when accelerating or coming to a stop. • Repeated automatic transmission failures. • Airbag warning light stays lit. • Faulty forward/backward seat adjustment. • Noisy engine and sunroof. **2002**—Sudden, unintended acceleration. • Airbags fail to deploy. • Annoying reflection of the dash onto the windshield (see *www.volvospy.com*). • ABS failure. • Rear brake pads wear out prematurely and ruin the rotors. • Horn is hard to activate. **2003**— Transmission slips from Second to Third and shifts harshly:

> This transmission slipping usually lasts for 2 to 3 seconds and this loss of power can easily put me into a major accident.

• Faulty engine fuel line. • Michelin tire blowout, allegedly because of a factory defect. *V40:* **All years:** More complaints that the brake pedal won't depress, causing total brake loss or extended stopping distances and premature wearout of the front brake pads (around 20,000 km). • A new wiring harness is available to extend the life of low-beam headlight bulbs. • Under a special program, Volvo will replace the front-door window to prevent excessive noise. This replacement is contingent upon a customer complaint. • Correction for front-seat whining or creaking. **2002**—Poor braking with ABS. • Dash reflects onto windshield. **2004**— Sudden, unintended acceleration. • Airbag warning light is lit for no reason. •

Total loss of braking capability. • Brake and accelerator are mounted too close to each other. • Sun glare washes out dashboard instrument readings. • Gas gauge gives inaccurate readings. • Power windows and doors malfunction. • Windshield wipers cycle on and off. • Tail lights, parking lights, and side marker lights won't come on, and sometimes all of the dash gauges go out. • Radio and climate controls turn off by themselves. • Trunk lid sticks. **2005**—Parking brake won't hold the car on an incline. • Original equipment scissor jack won't hold up the car. *S70, V70:* **2000**—Airbags fail to deploy. • Vehicle suddenly pulls to one side while cruising. • Unexpected total loss of power. • Engine sputters and then shuts off. • Prematurely worn front stabilizer-link rod. • Considerable brake fade at start-up. • Driver's window sticks in the down position. • AC allows exhaust fumes into the vehicle. • Chronic light failures. *V70:* **2001**—Excessive reflection of beige dash onto windshield. • Engine stalls in traffic; dealer says problem is caused by a "weak" fuel pump. • Engine mounts break. • Manual transmission clutch sticks in cold weather. • Vehicle can roll away when parked on an incline. • Brake pedal is too close to gas pedal. • Front door indent doesn't hold door open. • Sunroof blew in while going through a car wash. • Rear tailgate door won't lock. • Coffee spilled from cupholder shorted airbag computer. • Frequent bulb failures. **2002**—Shoulder belt crosses at neck. • Sunroof broke and fell into roof liner. **2003**—Emergency brake bracket comes apart. • Tires continually and prematurely wear out. **2004**—Car easily damaged when going over a bump at low speed:

> Car was damaged going over a speed bump (on public road) at about 5 mph [8 km/h]. There is a recall in Europe to fix this problem (by removing a bracket that...can be forced upwards, damaging the exhaust and driveshaft).

• Pirelli P6 tire sidewall bubbles and cracks. • Fuel gushes out when refuelling. • Vehicle pulls to the right. • Loose steering caused by a prematurely worn out tie-rod. • Harsh shifting when accelerating. • Concussion suffered in an accident when head hit the interior handholds, which are often bumped into. • Poor headlight illumination:

> I am very concerned about the very poor quality of illumination provided by the headlights, particularly the low beam, of my 2004 Volvo V70R. If I drive on a highway with oncoming traffic such that I cannot use my high beams, I will be overdriving my low beams at any speed over 30 mph [48 km/h]. I have already been back to the dealer in Bellingham, WA, to have adjustments, but to no help. Worst headlights I have ever had on a car. And these are HID special lights.

2005—Car frequently stalls out. • Unexpected and intermittent brake failure (*forums.swedespeed.com/zerothread?id=32551*). • Passenger-side airbag is disabled if the occupant moves.

Secret Warranties/Internal Bulletins/Service Tips

All models/years: Check the valve-cover nuts at every servicing interval to prevent oil leakage. • Free front seat belt extenders available. • Rear suspension popping or "boing" noise. **All models: 1999–2004**—Knocking noise when turning. **1999–2005**—Manual transmission may not shift easily into First or Reverse gear. **2001–04**—Remedy for a high-pitched exhaust system squeal. **2002–04**—Engine knock, rattle, and low power. **2003–04**—Xenon headlights may be inoperative due to a faulty ballast. **2003–06**—Eliminating musty odours from the air vents. **2004**—Reasons why engine may run roughly. • Electrically powered seats rock back and forth. • Rear suspension noise. • Front axle pinging when shifting during parking manoeuvres. **2004–05**—Wheel bolt corrosion. **2005**—Engine may have a rough idle, misfire, run roughly, or lack power. • AC stops working intermittently. **2005–06**—Seat backrest play/noise. • Remedy for a faulty alternator. • Vent air temperatures cycle from hot to cold. *850, S70, V70:* **1997–99**—Rear axle whining countermeasures. **1997–2000**—Automatic transmission final-drive whining correction tips. **1998–2000**—Power-window noise can be silenced by following the procedures outlined in TSB #8330033. • Poor FM reception (static) can be improved by modifying the ground strap. **1998–2004**—Manual transmission doesn't easily shift into Reverse or First gear. *C70:* **1997–99**—There are at least half a dozen bulletins addressing water leaks affecting the C70. **2001**—Rough cold starts, long cranking times, tachometer jumps, and engine warning light activates. **2003–05**—Wheel bolt corrosion. *S40, V40:* **2000-01**—Engine oil filler neck may be faulty. • Ticking noise may be heard from the canister purge valve. • The MIL stays on while driving. **2001**—Exhaust manifold retaining nuts may be loose or missing. **2002**—Uneven idle. *S70, V70, C70:* **1997–2000**—Reducing power-seat lateral movement. **1998–2000**—Special Service Campaign to upgrade service life of headlights; free bulb replacement. • Another campaign provides for the free replacement of the headlight wiper stop lug. **1999–2001**—Defective throttles in about 356,000 C70, V70, S60, S70, and S80 Volvos have been failing at unusually high rates, causing the vehicles to stall and fail air emissions tests, and sticking owners with costly repairs. Volvo has "quietly" agreed with U.S. EPA and California authorities to extend the warranty up to 10 years/320,000 km (200,000 mi.). As part of the agreement, Volvo will also reimburse owners who have already had the defective throttles replaced. The cost to replace the throttle can reach up to $1,000. An estimated 21 to 94 percent of throttle modules will fail within that time, depending on vehicle model, according to reports by Volvo to the California Air Resources Board and the U.S. Environmental Protection Agency.

The faulty throttles are also the subject of a class action lawsuit charging that Volvo violated California law by issuing a "secret warranty" to assist some, but not all, owners of vehicles with defective throttles. Volvo's service bulletins claim the problem is caused by improper maintenance. Although this defect falls squarely under the 8-year emissions warranty in Canada and the U.S., Volvo's public statement on the matter says it will allow only one warranty claim per car under the company's 4-year warranty. What weasels! (See the bulletin on the following page.)

1999–2003—Suspension resonance, vibration. **1999–2004**—Brake, exhaust system resonance, vibration. • Front seat loose, noisy. *C70:* **1998–2002**—Uneven

ELECTRONIC THROTTLE MODULE (ETM), CLEANING

S70/V70 1999–2000/C70 1999

S80 1999/V70/S60 2001

Carbon deposits can form in the throttle module bore on cars frequently driven short distances. This residue can cause idle speed to become uneven and noticeable to the driver especially with the increased load produced by the air conditioning compressor cycling on and off. This Service Bulletin describes how to clean the throttle module bore.

WARRANTY STATEMENT: Claims may be submitted under New Car Warranty ONLY one time per vehicle when there is a documented customer complaint, using claim type 01.

idle. *S60, V70*: **2001**—Uneven idle. **2001–04**—Brake, exhaust system resonance, vibration. • Front-seat noise, rocking. **2002–04**—Engine knock and rattle with reduced power.

850, C70, XC70, XC90, S40, S60, S70, V40, V70 PROFILE

	1997	1998	1999	2000	2001	2002	2003	2004	2005
Cost Price ($)									
850	31,995	—	—	—	—	—	—	—	—
Turbo	43,995	—	—	—	—	—	—	—	—
TLA/AWD	48,495	—	—	—	—	—	—	—	—
C70	—	54,675	49,995	50,595	52,995	49,995	59,595	63,995	—
S40	—	—	—	—	31,400	31,495	31,495	31,495	29,995
S60	—	—	—	—	35,995	36,495	36,495	36,495	36,995
S70	33,995	34,995	35,195	—	—	—	—	—	—
S90	46,700	47,400	—	—	—	—	—	—	—
V40/50	—	—	—	—	32,400	32,495	32,495	32,495	31,495
V70	—	33,295	36,295	36,495	37,495	37,995	37,995	37,995	38,495
XC70 AWD	—	—	—	—	—	—	49,495	49,495	46,495
XC90 AWD	—	—	—	—	—	—	54,995	49,995	49,995
Used Values ($)									
850 ▲	5,500	—	—	—	—	—	—	—	—
850 ▼	4,500	—	—	—	—	—	—	—	—
Turbo ▲	6,500	—	—	—	—	—	—	—	—
Turbo ▼	5,500	—	—	—	—	—	—	—	—
TLA/AWD ▲	7,500	—	—	—	—	—	—	—	—
TLA/AWD ▼	6,500	—	—	—	—	—	—	—	—
C70 ▲	—	6,500	8,500	10,000	12,000	18,000	30,000	36,000	—
C70 ▼	—	6,000	7,500	8,500	10,500	16,000	28,000	34,000	—
S40 ▲	—	—	—	—	10,500	12,500	14,500	17,500	19,000
S40 ▼	—	—	—	—	9,000	11,000	13,000	16,000	18,000
S60 ▲	—	—	—	—	11,500	14,500	17,500	20,500	25,500
S60 ▼	—	—	—	—	10,000	12,000	15,000	19,000	23,000

All ratings on a numbered scale where ⬛5 is good and ⬛1 is bad. See pages 130–132 for a more detailed description.

S70 ▲	5,000	6,000	8,000	—	—	—	—	—	—
S70 ▼	4,500	5,500	7,000	—	—	—	—	—	—
S90 ▲	6,000	7,000	—	—	—	—	—	—	—
S90 ▼	5,500	6,500	—	—	—	—	—	—	—
V40/50 ▲	—	—	—	—	11,000	13,000	15,500	18,500	20,500
V40/50 ▼	—	—	—	—	9,500	11,500	14,000	17,000	19,000
V70 ▲	—	6,500	8,000	9,500	12,000	14,500	18,000	21,500	26,500
V70 ▼	—	6,000	7,000	8,500	10,500	13,000	16,000	19,500	24,500
XC70 AWD ▲	—	—	—	—	—	—	22,000	28,000	33,000
XC70 AWD ▼	—	—	—	—	—	—	20,000	26,000	31,000
XC90 AWD ▲	—	—	—	—	—	—	24,000	29,000	34,000
XC90 AWD ▼	—	—	—	—	—	—	22,000	27,000	32,000
Reliability	3	3	3	2	2	2	2	2	2
Crash Safety (F)									
850	5	—	—	—	—	—	—	5	5
S40	—	—	—	—	—	—	—	4	4
S60	—	—	—	—	4	4	4	4	4
S70	—	5	5	5	—	—	—	—	—
V70	—	—	—	—	—	—	—	—	5
XC70 AWD	—	—	—	—	—	—	—	—	5
XC90 AWD	—	—	—	—	—	—	4	4	5
Side									
S40	—	—	—	—	—	—	—	5	5
S60	—	—	—	—	5	5	5	5	5
S70	—	4	4	4	—	—	—	—	—
V70	—	—	—	—	—	—	—	—	5
XC70 AWD	—	—	—	—	—	—	—	—	5
XC90 AWD	—	—	—	—	—	—	5	5	5
Offset (850/S70)	5	5	5	5	—	—	—	—	—
S40	—	—	—	—	—	5	5	5	5
S60	—	—	—	—	5	5	5	5	5
XC90 AWD	—	—	—	—	—	—	5	5	5
Head Restraints									
850	5	—	—	—	—	—	—	—	—
C70	—	—	5	—	5	—	5	5	—
S40/V40	—	—	—	—	5	5	5	5	5
S70	—	—	5	—	—	—	—	—	—
V70	—	—	5	—	5	5	5	5	—
XC90 AWD	—	—	—	—	—	—	5	5	5
Rollover Resistance									
XC90 AWD	—	—	—	—	—	—	—	4	4

RATING: Below Average (1989–2006). The 1998 model 900s were renamed the S90 and V90, and have apparently inherited similar brake and electrical deficiencies. The model was renamed the S80 for the 1999 model year. It's interesting to note that the 960 Series becomes cheaper to acquire than the 940 as the years progress. Although these cars are acceptable buys when bought new and covered by the manufacturer's warranty, their reliability and safety quickly go downhill after the third year of ownership. **"Real" city/highway fuel economy:** *960:* 13.3/8.3 L/100 km. *S90/V90:* 13.2/8.7 L/100 km with a manual transmission or 10.9/7.1 L/100 km with an automatic. *S80 2.9L:* 11.9/7.8 L/100 km. *S80 2.5L AWD:* 11.7/7.9 L/100 km. *T6:* 12.6/8.3 L/100 km. Fuel savings may be lower by about 20 percent. **Maintenance/Repair costs:** Higher than average, and repairs must be done by a (Ford) Volvo dealer. Yikes! **Parts:** Higher-than-average costs and limited availability. **Extended warranty:** A wise purchase simply to avoid expensive surcharges as Ford and Volvo mechanics and claims agents tap dance around who pays for warranty repair costs. **Best alternatives:** Acura Integra, TL, or RL; BMW 3 Series; Infiniti I30; Mazda Millenia; the early Nissan Maxima; and Toyota Avalon. **Online help:** *www.volvospy.com, www.consumeraffairs.com/automotive/volvo.htm,* and *www.carsurvey.org/manufacturer_Volvo.html.*

Strengths and Weaknesses

On one hand, these cars are practical to the extreme, with plenty of power, good handling, lots of carrying capacity, many standard safety features, and impressive crashworthiness ratings and accident-injury claim data. On the other hand, weak points include a jarring ride in vehicles equipped with 16- and 17-inch wheels; limited rear visibility; excessive engine, wind, and road noise; fuel-thirstiness (turbo models); declining quality control and increased frequency of safety-related deficiencies; and limited availability, causing soaring resale prices for recent reworked models with little room for negotiating.

Having debuted as essentially repackaged 760s, the flagship 900 Series rear-drive sedans and wagons have a much better reliability record than do the 240 and 700 Series, and have been on par with the 850, S70, and V70 over the last few model years. Both the 940 and 960 offer exceptional roominess and comfort and are capable of carrying six people with ease. The wagon provides lots of cargo space and manages to do it in great style. The 1996 960s were given front-seat side-impact airbags and upgraded door locking. Here are some owner gripes: The base 114-hp 2.3L engine is overpowered by the car's weight, there's excessive fuel consumption with the turbo option, and vehicles encounter excessive road and wind noise at highway speeds.

Most of the 900 and 90 Series' deficiencies are identical to those seen in the S70s, with some exceptions, such as miscalibrated engine computer modules that cause random misfiring; rotten-egg and other exhaust odours that permeate the interior, even after the catalytic converter is replaced; ignition switch, rear spring, and climate-control unit failures; excessive on-road shudder/vibration, drifting, and hard steering; frequent fuel leaks; the extended tailpipe that can burn children; the battery boiling over, causing acid to spray into the engine compartment; and seat belts that catch in the door after failing to retract properly. Drivers also report that the front bumper is too low; it hits the wheel stop in parking lots, causing extensive bumper and wheelwell damage. Also, brakes continue to require frequent and expensive maintenance because of the poor durability of front and rear pads and the premature warpage of the brake rotors (15,000–30,000 km).

VEHICLE HISTORY: 1999—The S80 is a redesign of the S90 and offers several interesting new features, such as a powerful 268-hp transverse inline 6-cylinder engine and a sophisticated automatic transmission called the Geartronic—a 4-speed automatic with a feature for manually changing gears if one so desires. Additionally, the car is chock full of safety features, has the largest interior of any Volvo, gives impressive performance and handling, and is attractively styled. **2001**—Dual-stage airbags and 16-inch wheels. **2002**—Engine tweaks give more power at a lower rpm, and the base engine drops a few horses. Also an in-trunk emergency release and new alloy wheels. **2004**—Refreshed styling, new gauges, and the addition of all-wheel drive. **2005**—Wood interior trim, optional run-flat tires, and larger wheels on the high-performance models.

Unfortunately, the S80's defects closely resemble the problems reported in prior years' models (see "Safety Summary" below) and seriously undermine Volvo's much-touted safety claims.

Safety Summary

All models: 1998—Engine fire. • Airbags didn't deploy in a collision. • Fuel system leak (T-junctions and clamps replaced). • Other fuel leaks reported, where owners claim problem may relate to the fuel expansion tank or its hoses. • Vehicle suddenly accelerates. • Tire-tread separation. • Premature failure of the headlight, tail light, turn signal, driveshaft, front and rear brake pad and rotor, tailgate struts, window switches, and door locks. • Turn signal bulbs are scorched, and plastic melted. • Total loss of braking ability. • Inappropriate placement of the tailgate handle causes one to pull the tailgate close to one's face, causing nose injury. • Brakes didn't work on an incline after vehicle stalled out. *S80: 1999–2001*—Many complaints of defective throttle control modules causing sudden loss of power and poor idling. **2001**—Engine threw a rod. • Engine surges at idle. • Transmission sticks in Park. • When shifting into Drive, vehicle goes into Reverse. • Power-steering leaks. • Cabin temperature sensor failure. • Key won't turn the ignition. • Battery won't hold its charge. **2001–02**—Lights continually burn out. **2003**—Sudden, unintended acceleration. • Front wheel fell off when the ball joint separated. **2004**—Excessive steering shake caused car to go out of control. **2005**—Cracked oil pump.

Secret Warranties/Internal Bulletins/Service Tips

All models/years: Check bulletin information on Volvo models found in the preceding ratings; Volvo service bulletins often overlap. • Inspect the valve-cover nuts at every servicing interval to prevent oil leakage. • New steering components will reduce power-steering knocking. • AC evaporator odours can be controlled by installing a new fan control module. • Tips on silencing noise from the manual front seats. **All models: 1992–98**—Oil pump leaks are usually because of loose pump retaining screws. **1997–99**—Rear axle whining countermeasures. • Automatic transmission final-drive whining correction tips. • Upgraded rear brake pads to reduce grinding. • Upgraded weather stripping to reduce upper windshield moulding noise. • Installation of protective covers for door locks. • Improvements for door handle operation in cold weather. *S80:* **1999**—Uneven throttle. **1999– 2000**—Automatic transmission shudder during upshifts. **1999–2001**—New rear brake pads have been developed to reduce vibration. • Power seat movement on acceleration and deceleration. • Loose A-pillar trim. • Subframe bushing knocking noise. • Defective electronic throttle module in about 356,000 1999–2001 C70, V70, S60, S70, and S80 Volvos covered by a secret 10-year warranty (see page 454). **1999–2003**—Suspension resonance, vibration. **1999–2004**—Brake, exhaust system resonance, vibration. **2000**—Free engine oil grate inspection. **2001**—Body squeak or crunch noise brought on by wet or cold weather. **2002– 04**—Engine knock and rattle with low power. **2003–06**—Eliminating musty odours coming from the air vents. **2004–05**—Park assist relay free replacement campaign. **2005–06**—Vent temperature cycles from hot to cold.

900 SERIES, S90, V90, S80 PROFILE

	1997	1998	1999	2000	2001	2002	2003	2004	2005
Cost Price ($)									
960	47,400	—	—	—	—	—	—	—	—
S90	—	47,400	—	—	—	—	—	—	—
V90	—	49,075	—	—	—	—	—	—	—
S80	—	—	49,995	55,995	54,395	54,395	54,895	54,895	54,995
Used Values ($)									
960 ▲	4,500	—	—	—	—	—	—	—	—
960 ▼	4,000	—	—	—	—	—	—	—	—
S90 ▲	—	5,000	—	—	—	—	—	—	—
S90 ▼	—	4,500	—	—	—	—	—	—	—
V90 ▲	—	5,500	—	—	—	—	—	—	—
V90 ▼	—	5,000	—	—	—	—	—	—	—
S80 ▲	—	—	6,500	8,500	11,000	16,000	22,000	28,000	35,000
S80 ▼	—	—	5,500	7,000	9,500	13,500	20,000	26,000	33,000
Reliability	2	2	2	2	2	2	2	2	2
Crash Safety (F)									
960	4	—	—	—	—	—	—	—	—
S80	—	—	—	—	5	5	5	5	5

All ratings on a numbered scale where **5** is good and **1** is bad. See pages 130–132 for a more detailed description.

Side (S80)	—	—	—	—	5	5	5	5	5
Offset (S80)	—	—	—	5	5	5	5	5	5
Head Restraints									
960/S90	5	—	—	—	—	—	—	—	—
S80	—	—	5	5	5	5	5	5	5
Rollover Resistance	—	—	—	—	—	—	5	5	5

SPORTS CARS

Throw Common Sense to the Wind

Yes, we all know that these small, low cars with high-powered, fuel-thirsty engines and seating for only two are a dangerous choice for young drivers, and scream out "mid-life crisis" when driven by pony-tailed, open-shirted middle-aged men. They're also usually way overpriced and astronomically expensive to insure, they lose their value quickly, and they beg to be driven too fast.

But they're so much fun to drive, especially for those of us who missed our chance to own one in our youth because we were too poor, practical, or preoccupied with our Corollas and Cavaliers to give in to our primal instincts.

If driving performance is important to you now, consider getting an agile, fun-to-drive small car, such as a mid-1990s version of the Acura Integra, Honda Civic, Mazda Miata, or Nissan Sentra SE-R. If you want to be a little more "in your face," however, it's hard to lose money with a Detroit Big Three muscle car sportster built through 1974 (see Appendix I).

There are three kinds of sports cars to consider: traditional two-seater roadsters, styled much like the MGB of the early '70s or Mazda's Miata; sporty coupes and hatchbacks, such as the Japanese Acura Integra, Honda Civic, Mazda MX-3, and Toyota Celica, which offer sportier styling, performance, and handling than their entry-level versions and are cheaper and more versatile to maintain than traditional sports cars; and muscle cars, which feature large engines and a few more creature comforts. The best deals in the latter category are the V8-equipped Ford Mustang and the GM Camaro or Firebird.

Other notable recommended sports models are the BMW Z3 (a looker that lacks the precise steering of a Miata), BMW Z4 (better steering and an upgraded suspension that equals the Porsche Boxster's), Mazda6 (plenty of horsepower, and with a stick shift not found on the Accord and the Camry), and the Mazda3.

There's a comprehensive forum at *www.sportscarforums.com* that goes into mind-numbing detail as to what makes a good sports car. Different cars are rated, service tips are given, and the age-old feud between Camaro/Firebird and Mustang owners is omnipresent and unresolved. There are also fewer contemptuous references to Asian "rice-burners" now that Toyota and other Asian automakers are successfully racing their cars at NASCAR-sanctioned tracks and building solid full-sized pickups.

Most sports cars, or "high-performance vehicles" as they're euphemistically named, don't offer the comfort or reliability of a Honda Civic, a Toyota Celica, or even a Hyundai Tiburon. Instead, they sacrifice reliability, interior space, and a comfortable suspension for speed, superior road handling, and attractive styling. They also need a whole slew of expensive high-performance packages, because many entry-level sports cars aren't very sporty in their basic form. Remember, too, that used sports cars often have serious accident damage that may not have been repaired properly, resulting in serious tracking problems if the chassis is bent.

Fully loaded used sports cars usually sell at a fraction of their original cost, and very few end up as collectibles. Most models that have been taken off the market—such as the Toyota Supra, Nissan 300ZX, and Chevrolet Corvette ZR1—aren't likely to become collectors' cars with soaring resale values. Even discontinued Japanese sports cars like the Nissan 1600, which are usually in high demand, haven't done nearly as well as some of the British roadsters that were taken off the market at about the same time.

Like early Mustangs, 2002 and earlier model-year GM Camaros and Firebirds can be fun cars to drive and can make you a tidy profit as well once they've been tricked out with some relatively inexpensive options. Not only are they reasonably reliable and cheap to maintain, but their resale prices are fairly stable and there's plenty of used stock to choose from. But don't expect them to appreciate in value any time soon (although the early muscle versions are now breaking away from the pack).

Horsepower Misrepresentation

Sports car buffs usually equate performance thrills with high horsepower ratings, even though there are many other handling features that need to be considered. Nevertheless, automakers are just as fixated on horsepower, and they aren't above falsifying the figures to get a marketing leg-up on the competition. In 1999, Ford suckered over 5,000 Mustang SVT Cobra owners with 270-hp Cobras that they claimed had 320 horses. Two years later, Ottawa's Competition Bureau found Hyundai had been boosting its ratings 4–9 percent on its entire lineup for over a decade, and that Hyundai-owned Kia's 2001–02 model figures were also suspect. Again in 2001, Mazda claimed that the Miata's horsepower had jumped from 140 to 155. When owners found that the 2001 version was no quicker than the 2000 model, Mazda quickly revised its numbers down to 142.

But Mazda is still playing with horsepower figures: Its 2004 RX-8 is less powerful than originally thought. First presented as having a 250-hp engine, the number was dropped slightly to 247. Then Mazda restated its horsepower rating to a still-optimistic 238 and offered customers $500 and free basic maintenance for 4 years/80,000 km (50,000 mi.).

SPORTS CAR RATINGS

Recommended

General Motors Camaro, Firebird,
    Trans Am (1997–2002)
Mazda Miata (1990–2006)

Porsche Boxster (1998–2006)*
Toyota Celica (1995–99; 2001–05)

Above Average

Ford Mustang (2006)
Hyundai Tiburon (1997–2006)*
Mitsubishi Eclipse (2005–06)*

Porsche 911 (1999–2006)*
Toyota Celica (1986–94; 2000)

Average

Ford Mustang (2001–04)
General Motors Camaro, Firebird,
    Trans Am (1994–96)

General Motors Corvette (1994–2006)

Below Average

DaimlerChrysler Crossfire (2004–06)*
Ford Mustang (1980–2000; 2005)

General Motors Camaro, Firebird,
    Trans Am (1992–93)

Not Recommended

Ford Cobra (1999–2004)
General Motors Camaro, Firebird,
    Trans Am (1982–91)

General Motors Corvette (1977–93)

*See Appendix I.

Ford

MUSTANG, COBRA ★★★★

RATING: *Mustang:* Above Average (2006)—the 2006 version worked out many of the 2005 redesign glitches, and incremental improvements reduced factory-related defects found on the pre-2005 models; Average (2001–04); Below Average (2005, 1980–2000)—2005 was the year of its last redesign. *Cobra:* Not Recommended (1999–2004). Here's the problem: Ford has alienated its parts suppliers and reduced reliability through unrealistic price-cutting and last-minute, poorly thought-out component changes. Mustangs that aren't equipped with traction control are treacherous on wet roadways, and they have had a frighteningly high number of safety-related mechanical failures (especially chronic stalling). Additionally, new crash data indicates the vehicles may be fire-prone following collisions at moderate speeds. GM's Camaro and Firebird are the Mustang's traditional competition as far as performance is concerned, and represent better buys even though they haven't been built since 2002. Ford has the price advantage, with a base Mustang costing a bit less than the cheapest Camaro, but it lags from a performance standpoint. In that area, the equivalent model-year Camaro and Firebird offer more sure-footed acceleration, crisper handling, standard ABS, a 6-speed transmission, and more comfortable rear seats. Fuel-savers beware: All 4-cylinder Mustangs should be shunned because they provide insufficient power, they aren't very durable, and the fuel savings are much less than you'd think. **"Real" city/highway fuel economy:** *Mustang 3.8L:* 11.8/7.4 L/100 km with a manual transmission or 12.0/8.0 L/100 km with an automatic. *Mustang 3.9L:* 11.7/7.4 L/100 km with a manual tranny or 12.3/8.2 L/100 km with an automatic. *Mustang 4.6L:* 14.0/8.7 L/100 km manual; 13.2/9.4 L/100 km automatic. *Mustang Mach 1:* 13.9/8.5 L/100 km manual; 13.8/9.5 L/100 km automatic. *Cobra:* 14.1/9.1 L/100 km. Fuel savings may be lower by about 20 percent on 4-cylinder models, 15 percent with 6-cylinders; and almost 25 percent with Mustangs equipped with an 8-cylinder version. **Maintenance/Repair costs:** Average, particularly because repairs can be done anywhere. **Parts:** Average costs, and parts are often sold for much less through independent suppliers. Some parts are continually back-ordered, particularly if involved in recall repairs. **Extended warranty:** A good idea for the powertrain. **Best alternatives:** Ford Probe, GM Camaro or Firebird, Hyundai Tiburon, Mazda Miata, and Toyota Celica. **Online help:** *forums.mustangworks.com, www.flamingfords.info, www.autosafety.org/autodefects. html, www.blueovalnews.com, www.tgrigsby.com/views/ford.htm* (The Anti-Ford Page), *www.antiauthority.com/cobra/service/#links,* and *www.flatratetech.com.*

Strengths and Weaknesses

This is definitely not a family car. A light rear end makes the car dangerously unstable on wet roads or when cornering at high speeds, unless equipped with traction control (optional on most models). But for those who want a sturdy and stylish second car, or who don't need room in the back or standard ABS, 2001–04 and 2006 Mustangs are a reasonably good sports car buy, thanks to their maxed-out depreciation, powertrain improvements, and fewer factory defects. Base models come equipped with a host of luxury and convenience items, which can be a real bargain once the base price has sufficiently depreciated—say, after the first three or four years.

1994–2006

Through the years, these models got more powerful engines, manumatic gearboxes with more gears, four-wheel disc brakes, additional airbags, and a more rigid chassis meant to reduce rattles and water leaks (which didn't work). Unfortunately, Ford's performance- and safety-related problems are carried over year after year (see "Safety Summary"). Engines and transmissions continue to be glitch-prone: Both the V6 and V8 have a propensity for chronic surging and stalling, and they experience blown engine intake manifold and head gaskets; failed motor mounts; ticking and rattling at 3000 rpm until the car shifts into Second gear; poorly shifting automatic transmissions, especially from First to Second gear; differential howling or whining (ring and pinion failures); dying on deceleration; fuel system malfunctions, highlighted by frequent fuel-injector replacement; faulty differential carrier bearings; and prematurely worn clutch pressure plates. Owners also frequently complain of electrical short circuits causing instrument panel shutdown; the early replacement of brake rotors, pads, and calipers; and unbelievably poor fit and finish highlighted by paint delamination and peeling, an easily pitted windshield, premature rusting, wind noise, water leaks, and various clunks and rattles. Other noises include engine ticking caused by bad lifters, steering creaks when turning, a clunking front suspension, tie-rod ends that "pop," and rear-end pinion gear whine. The Shaker 1000 stereo system constantly malfunctions, and fuel gauge readings are erratic, especially when the tank is less than half full.

Cobra

This is one mean snake.

Launched as a limited-production, high-performance 1993 sports car, the Cobra has garnered a reputation for mind-spinning depreciation, wallet-busting power-train defects, and mediocre performance and handling. The first models came with a 240-hp V8, a firm suspension, all-disc ABS, and unique styling. In subsequent years (there were no 2000 and 2002 models), Cobras got more powerful (yet unreliable) engines, a fully independent suspension, and hood and side scoops. The car's road performance remained seriously compromised by its loose rear end, which swings out when cornering under speed or on wet highways.

VEHICLE HISTORY: 1996—A 4.6L V8 with upgraded spark plugs, and the Cobra receives a 305-hp variant of the same powerplant. **1998**—GT gets a 10-hp performance boost. **1999**—Fresh styling and another horsepower boost. The V6 models also get suspension and steering gear upgrades. That year, Ford admitted that its 1999 SVT Cobra delivered up to 50 hp less than the 320 hp advertised. **2000**—Ford was forced to cancel the 2000 Cobra model year because no one believed in the horsepower claims. It took the company a year to fix the problem and get the Cobra back to dealer showrooms for 2001. Improved child safety seat anchoring. **2001**—GT models receive hood and side scoops and larger wheels. All models get an upgraded centre console, blacked-out headlights, and spoilers. **2002**—New 16-inch alloy wheels; sporty Cobra stays home again this year. **2003**—Three 4.6L V8 models: the GT with 260 hp, the new Mach 1 with 305 hp, and the 390-hp supercharged SVT Cobra. **2005**—Restyled, with more power, more features, and a 15 cm larger wheelbase. ABS and traction control are standard on the GT and optional on other models.

Safety Summary

All models/years: Regularly equipped Mustangs, like most rear-drive Fords, don't handle sharp curves or wet pavement very well. The rear end swings out suddenly, and the car tends to spin uncontrollably. Traction is easily lost, and braking is hardly reassuring. • Serious concerns have been raised about the Mustang's fuel system failing safety integrity standards and about the tendency of the convertible's doors to jam shut in a 57 km/h frontal collision. • Transmission allows vehicle to roll away when parked on an incline; emergency brake disengages. • Airbag fails to deploy; inadvertent airbag deployment. • Sudden acceleration because of a stuck throttle. • Brake failure, and premature replacement of the brake master cylinder. • Excessive vehicle vibration when accelerating. • Side windows fall off their tracks. **1994–98**—Brake-hose leaks. **1998–99**—Fuel-tank leaks. • Engine compartment fires. • Hood flies up unexpectedly while vehicle is underway. • Frequent stalling, hesitation, and power loss. • Airbag-induced injuries. • Parking brake doesn't hold (traced to a broken ratchet assembly). • Brake pedal goes to floor without braking. • Steering system failure. • Right ball joint fractured, causing wheel to turn inward. • Tire sidewall tread separation. • Seat belt continually tightens up. • Other repeats of previous problems: transmission, braking, and engine failures. • New problems: fire ignites in the centre console and dash areas; defective seat belt retractor, and poor design allows belt to slip out of guide; stalling caused by fuel pump or fuel relay cut-off switch failure; and original-equipment tire blowouts (the sidewall splits). **2000**—There are almost 400 safety complaints recorded by NHTSA for year 2000 models. • Fumes from airbag deployment make passengers ill and temporarily blind them. • Alternator melted battery wires; car caught fire. • Automatic transmission sticks in Reverse. • Convertible top unlatches and flips up while vehicle is underway. • Hood flies up. • Head restraints sit too low. • Many reports of rear axle failures. • Brake calipers and lines are replaced to correct brake fluid leakage. • Multiple function switch failure causes headlights to suddenly go out. **2001**—Safety-related complaints have trended downward dramatically; less than half the previous year's tally. • Fuel leaks from the fuel filler tube joint. • Lower control arm comes off. • Sudden brake lock-up. • Loose brake rotor responsible for collision. • ABS control module failures. • Foot hits fuse box when engaging clutch pedal. • In one incident, seat belt retracted unexpectedly, nearly choking the occupant, who had to be cut free. • Other incidences where the seat belt wouldn't retract into its holder, or became twisted. • Driver's seat rocks back when driving. • Headlights may not be bright enough, or may fog up from moisture. • Goodyear American Eagle GT tires fail due to dry rot. **2002**—Fire ignites in the wiring harness under dash area. • Chronic stalling when coasting or braking, or when clutch is depressed. • Serpentine belt comes off, causing loss of power steering and brakes. • Wheel lug nuts fall off. • Sudden acceleration. • Sudden loss of steering when making a left-hand turn. • In one incident, a car left on an incline with transmission in Park and motor shut off rolled down after 10 minutes and hit a tree. • Emergency brake ratchet assembly breaks, making mechanism inoperable. • Gas spills out of fuel tank because clamps not sufficiently tightened. • Left front wheel falls off when the lower control arm and ball joint become loose. • Defective transmission spider gear. • Stuck gas pedal. • Seat belt continually tightens up when worn. **2003**—Poorly designed speaker wires caused rear-seat fire. • Gas pedal is hooked by the carpet. • Sudden acceleration tied to the cruise control mechanism:

After cruise control was engaged, the vehicle suddenly accelerated. The vehicle reached speeds of 80 mph [130 km/h] and above. The contact tried depressing the brake pedal, shifting the vehicle into neutral and shutting off the engine. These attempts to deactivate the cruise control failed. The contact drove onto an on ramp to the interstate while still attempting to deactivate the cruise. The contact was able to dial 911 for assistance of the state police, who provided verbal instructions for stopping the vehicle safely. The contact placed both feet on the brakes and both hands on the emergency brake to get the engine to stall and the vehicle stopped.

• Chronic stalling when decelerating; computer reflash doesn't fix the problem. • Automatic transmission failures. • Loss of brakes. • Spark plug blows out of the passenger-side cylinder head:

This left me with a $4,463 repair cost to fix my car that I only owned for three months. While doing research on the Internet and asking questions in mechanic shops, it has been apparent that Ford engines have defective cylinder heads and a recall needs to be announced. There are many victims affected by this issue and Ford has done nothing about this problem. I drive a 2003 Ford Mustang Cobra. I have not repaired my car yet, because I'm still hoping for $4000 to fall from the sky.

• Serpentine belt often shreds, causing the brakes to fail and engine to overheat and stall. • Seat belt ratchets tighten. • Premature Goodyear Eagle ZR tire blow-outs, also reported on 2004 models. • Water leaks through side windows. • AC condensation drips onto the exhaust pipe, rusting it out prematurely. **2004**—A fuel smell permeates the interior. • Throttle sticks under the carpet:

The cause of this stuck throttle is a partial bending of the accelerator pedal, and the contact with and sticking under of the carpet by the pedal. A stuck wide open throttle in any car is very dangerous!!! A stuck wide open throttle in this particular car is insane!!! To correct the problem as soon as I arrived home I trimmed the carpet that was contacting the throttle when down so that it would no longer touch at all.

• Anti-theft device causes vehicle to stall or to be difficult to start. • Faulty rear differential; it whines and is wobbly when making turns. • Traction control and ABS failures. • Seatback collapsed from a rear-ender accident; seatback bolt broke while driving. • Head restraints don't adjust enough. • Steering locks up:

Power steering unit was excessively noisy and distracting... Locks up on hard turn. Dealer says nature of the beast, won't replace it. Complained 3 times, car just went out of warranty... Several hundred local police cruisers have had their power steering replaced by dealer after "negative publicity on TV...." Dealers attempt to make you out as stupid, and keep obfuscating [until] you just go away.

• Sharp tailpipe sticks out and can severely cut anyone brushing against it. • Rear window explodes for no reason:

When driver notified his insurance carrier, he was informed that their glass installer was aware of the spontaneous rear window explosions occurring in the 2002–2004 model year of Mustangs.

2005—Following Ford's redesign, almost a 150 safety-related incidents were reported to NHTSA. This is about a third more complaints than normal and equal to what the 2001 models have registered over seven model years. • Stuck accelerator pedal. • When slowing for a stop, engine hesitates, then surges, and the automatic transmission slams into gear. • When parking, car suddenly accelerates in Drive or in Reverse. • Faulty fuel pumps blamed for frequent stalling. • The manual transmission clutch engages abruptly. • Brake fluid leaks from the master cylinder. • Brakes suddenly lock up, and in some cases, catch fire:

> The parking brake calipers and pads freeze an will not release when temperature drops below 32 degrees [Fahrenheit] [zero degrees Celsius]—while the handle is fully released inside the vehicle. When in neutral and pushed car will not roll, and when in gear and given gas car barely budges. Taken twice to dealership—by tow truck—but when arrived temperature had risen above 32 degrees and pads etc. had released.

• The powertrain "tunnel" located down the centre of the car gets extremely hot while driving. • Steering locks while turning left. • Rear strut/shock absorber support brackets rust out. • Fuel spews out the filler pipe, and gas station pumps shut off before the fuel tank is full—a problem that's carried over to the 2006 models:

> Intermittently, will not allow a full fill-up on gas. Several different gas stations tested. Only allows for half tank fill-up. Seems to worsen when the weather is cold.

• Fuses may not be seated properly, resulting in dash gauges going dark. • When underway, flimsy hood vibrates and twists violently. • Dash panel cannot be read on a sunny day while wearing sunglasses. • Airbag warning light remains lit. • Newly designed tail lights look lit in daylight, confusing following drivers.

Secret Warranties/Internal Bulletins/Service Tips

All models/years: Paint delamination, peeling, or fading. • Ford's 7-year "goodwill" warranty extensions usually cover engine and transmission components. • Cold hesitation when accelerating, rough idle, long crank times, and stalling may all signal the need to clean out excessive intake valve deposits. • Excessive oil consumption is likely caused by leaking gaskets, poor sealing of the lower intake manifold, defective intake and exhaust valve stem seals, or worn piston rings; install new guide-mounted valve-stem seals for a better fit as well as new piston rings with improved oil control. • A buzz or rattle from the exhaust system may be caused by a loose heat shield. • A thumping or clacking heard from the front brakes signals the need to machine the front disc brake rotors. **All models: 1985– 2002**—Repeated heater core failures. **1994–2000**—Hood may be difficult to close. **1996–2001**—Manual transmission may stick in Reverse or pop out of Reverse. **1997–99**—Delayed or no 2–3 upshifts may be caused by a leaking accumulator seal. • Road noise or dust/water leaks in the luggage compartment can be fixed by sealing the wheelhouse flange. **1997–2000**—Automatic transmission fluid leaks at the radiator can be stopped by installing an O-ring on the transmission oil cooler fitting. **1997–2001**—7-year extended warranty for engine intake manifold gasket failure. **1998–99**—Tips for spotting abnormal ABS braking noises. **1998–2002**—Guidelines for replacing defective ignition lock cylinders. **1998–2006**—Troubleshooting tips for correcting a rough-running engine. **1999–2000**—An erratically operating front windshield wiper probably has a faulty multifunction switch. • Same thing goes for an inaccurate speedometer. **1999–2001**—Troubleshooting a downshift clunk and a driveline whine on coastdown. **1999–2004**—Manual transmission is hard to shift into Reverse or First. **2001–02**—Some vehicles equipped with a 4.6L engine may exhibit a Front End Accessory Drive (FEAD) belt jump-off toss. **2001–03**—Wind noise from the A-pillar area. **2001–04**—4.6L engine rattle. • AC panel vents rattle. **2002**—Air leaks in the intake manifold or engine. • Ford has found that engine cylinder heads often still leak after having been repaired. • Engine runs roughly after stopping. • In 4.6L engines, oil leaks from the head gasket area. • Oil pressure gauge shows low or no oil. • 3.8L engines may run roughly at idle; same engine may cause AM radio speaker interference. • Automatic transmission fluid leak near the radiator. • Manual transmission clashes or grinds. • Transmission ticking heard when First gear is engaged. • Rear whine heard during coastdown from 100 km/h. • Vehicles equipped with a 5-speed manual transmission may stumble or hesitate when cold. • Driveline vibration. • Electrical problems include erratic operation of turn signals, hard starting, and illuminated ABS warning light. • A shorted coil/open PCM fuse may result in no-starts or rough running. • Climate control stays in the defrost mode. • Inoperative door window because of faulty window regulator. • Defective ignition-switch lock cylinder. **2002–04**—Steering squeak, creak when turning. **2003–04**—Hard to shift, rattling manual transmission. • Ford will install four revised hood scoop insulators (#2L7Z-9P686-AA) to eliminate a rattle emanating from the hood of the vehicle. **2003–06**—Leaking, inoperative AC compressor. **2005**—Ford finally admits it has a fuel tank fill-up problem and offers to change the tank under warranty:

FUEL TANK DIFFICULT TO FILL

BULLETIN NO.: 05-15-12   **DATE: AUGUST 8, 2005**

2005 Mustang

ISSUE: Some 2005 Mustang vehicles built before 4/26/2005, may exhibit the fuel tank being slow or difficult to fill. The condition may be described as repeated rapid shut-offs of the filling station pump nozzle, or multiple nozzle shut-offs when attempting to fill the fuel tank. The condition may be due to the fuel tank vapor venting system inside the fuel tank.

ACTION: Install a new fuel tank. Refer to Section 310-01 of the Workshop Manual. The new fuel tank has a revised internal venting system to improve fuel filling.

For 2006s with a revised fuel tank already installed, Ford says no fix is available.

2005–06—Hesitation upon acceleration. • AC compressor clutch failure. • Erratic fuel gauge. • Parking brake cable freezes, rear brakes drag. • Rattling from the gearshift, dash area. • Rear axle hum, whine. • Paint blistering and early corrosion on aluminum body panels. • Abnormal convertible top wear; malfunction. *Cobra:* **2001–05**—Rear axle shudder, chatter. **2003**—Defective engine cylinder heads or valve guides (replacement cylinder head part number is 3R2Z-6049-GA). **2004**—Intermittent loss of power, no-starts. • Engine overheating. • Manual transmission gear whine and grind, and loss of Second gear. • Driveline clunk during gear changes or quick acceleration. • Squealing noise from the steering assembly. • Front suspension squeaking noise when vehicle passes over bumps. • Inoperative rear window defroster. • Thump noise when AC clutch engages. **2005–06**—AC compressor clutch failure. • Parking brake cable freezes, rear brakes drag. • Rattling from the gearshift, dash area. • Paint blistering and early corrosion on aluminum body panels.

MUSTANG, COBRA PROFILE

	1997	1998	1999	2000	2001	2002	2003	2004	2005
Cost Price ($)									
LX/Coupe	19,795	22,595	20,995	21,195	22,275	22,795	22,990	23,495	23,795
Cobra	33,795	36,095	36,995	—	38,495	—	41,995	50,650	—
Convertible	26,795	29,295	24,995	25,195	26,945	27,465	27,760	28,095	27,995
Used Values ($)									
LX/Coupe ▲	4,500	5,500	6,000	6,500	7,500	8,500	10,500	12,500	16,500
LX/Coupe ▼	4,000	4,500	5,500	6,000	6,500	7,500	9,000	11,000	14,500
Cobra ▲	7,000	7,500	8,500	—	15,500	—	18,500	22,000	—
Cobra ▼	6,000	7,000	7,500	—	12,000	—	17,000	20,000	—
Convertible ▲	7,000	7,500	8,000	9,000	10,000	12,000	13,500	16,500	27,000
Convertible ▼	6,000	7,000	7,500	8,500	9,000	10,500	11,500	14,500	25,000
Reliability	2	2	2	2	3	3	3	4	2
Crash Safety (F)	4	5	4	4	5	5	5	5	5
Convertible	5	—	—	—	—	—	—	—	—
Side	—	3	3	3	3	3	3	3	4
Convertible	—	—	—	—	2	2	2	2	—
Head Restraints (F)	1	—	1	—	1	1	3	3	—
Rear	—	—	—	—	—	—	1	1	—
Rollover Resistance	—	—	—	—	—	5	5	5	5

General Motors

CAMARO, FIREBIRD, TRANS AM ★★★★★

best buy

The 2000 Chevrolet Camaro.

RATING: Recommended (1997–2002); Average (1994–96); Below Average (1992–93); Not Recommended (1982–91). Camaro and Firebird were dropped for the 2003 model year. What a goofball decision! GM should have axed its money-losing Saturn and Saab divisions and kept Oldsmobile and the Camaro and Firebird. Fun to drive and easily repaired, these cars are more reliable than the Mustang, despite having elicited similar safety-related complaints such as airbag deployment injuries, sudden acceleration, brake failures, and steering loss. Be especially wary of brake rotor warpage, requiring rotor replacement every two years (about a $300 job). Bargain hunter alert: A V8-equipped Camaro convertible is the best choice for retained value a few years down the road. But you can do quite well with a used base coupe equipped with a high-performance handling package. **"Real" city/highway fuel economy:** *Camaro V6:* 11.3/6.9 L/100 km with a manual transmission or 12.2/7.0 L/100 km with an automatic. *Camaro V8:* 12.5/8.0 L/100 km with a manual tranny or 13.1/8.8 L/100 km with an automatic. Fuel savings will likely be lower by about 20 percent. **Maintenance/Repair costs**: Average, and repairs can be done by any independent garage. **Parts:** Reasonably priced and easy to find. **Extended warranty:** A waste of money; instead, spend an extra $100 getting the car checked out thoroughly *before* you buy it. **Best alternatives:** Ford Mustang or Probe, Hyundai Tiburon, Mazda Miata, and Toyota Celica. **Online help:** *www.autosafety.org/autodefects.html* and *www.sportscarforums.com.*

Strengths and Weaknesses

Camaros and Firebirds are reasonably priced rear-drive muscle cars that perform better than the Mustang and produce excellent crash protection scores and reasonable resale values. They also take the lead over the Mustang with their slightly better reliability record. Overall performance, however, varies a great deal depending on the engine, transmission, and suspension combination in each particular car. Base models equipped with the V6 powerplant accelerate reasonably well, but high-performance enthusiasts will find them slow for sporty cars. Like all rear-drive Detroit iron, handling is compromised by poor traction on wet roads, minimal comfort, and a suspension that's too soft for high-speed cornering and too bone-jarring for smooth cruising. The Z28, IROC-Z, and Trans Am provide smart acceleration and handling but at the expense of fuel economy—a small drawback, however, when you save thousands buying used. How many thousands? For example, a potent, head-turning 2002 Firebird Trans Am can be had for less than $15,000—the price of a new Toyota Yaris. A same-year Camaro will cost a few thousand less, and a 2002 convertible won't cost much over $17,000.

VEHICLE HISTORY: 1996—The 3.8L engine is used as the base powerplant, the 5.7L V8 gains 10 extra horses, and a new high-performance SS option is offered for the first time on the Z28. **1997**—GM offers a 30th birthday styling package for the Camaro and some interior upgrades, V6 engine dampening for smoother running at high speeds, optional Ram Air induction, and racier-looking, ground-effects body trim for the Firebird. **1998**—A minor facelift, and the Z28 and SS both receive a slight horsepower boost. **1999**—Electronic throttle control on V6-equipped versions, and a new Zexel Torsion differential used in the limited slip rear axle. **2000**—Camaros and Firebirds get alloy wheels and an improved throttle response for cars equipped with the manual transmission. **2001**—Z28 and SS models are given 5 more horses and restyled chrome wheels. **2002**—Improved ride quality and dashboard layout.

Much like Ford's embarrassing 4-banger, the puny and failure-prone 2.5L 4-cylinder powerplant was the standard engine up until 1986—part of the legacy of an earlier fuel crisis and the subsequent downsizing binge, which we are repeating today. The turbocharged V8 offered on some Trans Am models should be viewed with caution because of its poor durability and high repair costs. Body hardware is fragile, poor paint quality and application are common problems that lead to premature rusting, and squeaks and rattles are legion. Body integrity is especially poor on cars equipped with a T-roof. Areas particularly vulnerable to rusting are the windshield and rear-wheel openings, door bottoms, and rear quarter panels. The assorted add-on plastic body parts found on sporty versions promote corrosion by trapping moisture along with road salt and grime. Also note that the Camaro's flat seats don't offer as much support as the better-contoured Firebird seats.

These cars are also plagued by chronic fuel-system problems, especially on the Crossfire, and multi-port fuel-injection controls. Automatic transmissions, especially the 4-speed, aren't durable. The standard 5-speed manual gearbox has a stiff shifter and a heavy clutch. Clutches fail frequently and don't stand up to hard use. The 2.8L V6, used through 1989, suffers from leaky gaskets and seals and premature camshaft wear. The larger 3.1L 6-cylinder has fewer problems. However, malfunctioning dash gauges and electrical problems are common. Exhaust parts rust quickly and dual outlet exhaust systems used with V8 engines are especially expensive to replace. Front suspension components and shock absorbers wear out very quickly.

Stick with the 1996–2002 models for the best performance and price. They are much better overall performers than previous models, and additional standard safety features are a plus. These sporty convertibles and coupes are almost identical in their pricing and in the features they offer (the Firebird has pop-up headlights, a more pointed front end, a narrower middle, and a rear spoiler). All models got a complete make-over in 1995, making them more powerful and aerodynamic with less spine-jarring performance.

As one moves up the scale, overall performance improves considerably. The V8 engine gives these cars lots of sparkle and tire-spinning torque, but there's a fuel penalty to pay. A 4-speed automatic transmission is standard on the 5.7L-equipped Z28; other versions come with a standard 5-speed manual gearbox or an optional 6-speed. Many of these cars are likely to have been ordered with lots of extra performance and luxury options, including an attractive T-roof package guaranteed to include a full assortment of creaks and groans.

Not everything is perfect, however. Owners report premature automatic transmission failures, a noisy base engine, and excessive oil consumption with the larger engine. Fuel economy is unimpressive, the AC malfunctions, front brakes (rotors and pads, mostly) and MacPherson struts wear out quickly, servicing the fuel-injection system is an exercise in frustration, electrical problems are common, and gauges operate erratically. Body problems are frequent. These include door rattles, misaligned doors and hatches, T-roof water and air leaks, a sticking hatch power release, and poor fit and finish. Owners also complain that the steering wheel is positioned too close to the driver's chest, the low seats create a feeling of claustrophobia, visibility is limited by wide side pillars, and trunk space is sparse with a high liftover.

 ## Safety Summary

All models/years: Early brake rotor warpage and pad replacement. One dealer mechanic explains the problem this way:

> The rotors are not thick enough and have insufficient air to cool them. ASE-certified independent mechanics and dealership employees (unofficially) buy slotted "racing" rotors or use ceramic non-metal pads from other sources. This has apparently gone on since 1998 on both Firebirds and Camaros.

• Airbag malfunctions. • Engine seizures. • Sudden acceleration. • Seat belts fail to lock up. **All models: 1997–98**—Prematurely worn brake pads, warped or cracked rotors, and failure of the emergency brake to hold on an incline are all recurring problems. **1998**—Dash fires. • Axle seal, tie-rod, serpentine belt, fuel-pump, brake caliper bolt, AC blower motor, fuel gauge, and wiper failures. **1999**—Interestingly, both the Camaro and the Firebird have about one-third fewer safety-related complaints registered against them by NHTSA than does the same-year Ford Mustang. • Cracked fuel tank leaks fuel. • Accelerator pedal sticks. • Prematurely warped front brake rotors jerk to one side when brakes are applied and cause pulsation, excessive noise, and extended stopping distances. • Many incidents of clutch slippage at low mileage. • Frequent complaints that the stock shifter causes misshifts. • Electrical system shorts cause instrument panel and assorted gauges and lights to operate erratically. • Turn signal lights don't flash, headlights often dim to about 50 percent of their intended brightness, heater slows down, and power windows run slowly. **2000**—Frequent stalling. • Electrical wires melt. • Emergency brake fails to hold vehicle; comes off in driver's hand. • Rear brake lock-ups and chronic pad and rotor failures. • T-roof flies off vehicle. • Seat belt fails to retract in an emergency stop. • Headlights flicker or suddenly go out. • Horn collects water, which muffles sound. • Front end pulls to the right. • Headrests are set too low (same complaint heard from Mustang owners). • Replacement windshields are seriously distorted along the bottom edge. • Windows leak water. • Premature power-window motor failures. • Severe vibration when accelerating. **2001**—Engine management computer holds throttle open when foot is lifted off the accelerator. • Annoying and potentially engine-damaging piston slap:

> The original motor in this vehicle is defective. Poor design does not allow the outside cylinders to cool properly resulting in a scorching and breakdown of the piston, rings and cylinder walls. GM is well aware of the problem (and has been for some time) and it is large enough that GM is currently unable to provide enough replacement motors to customers.

• Premature automatic transmission failure. • Sudden complete brake failure. • Warped brake rotors and prematurely-worn pads. • T-roof flies off the Camaro while it is cruising on the highway. • The left side mirror often breaks for no reason. **2002**—Fire ignites in the window switch in the door panel. • Turn signal lights burn out and melt the socket wires. • Airbags fail to deploy. • Stalling due to a plugged catalytic converter or faulty fuel-pump and throttle body sensor. • Premature brake rotor warping and pad wear causes excessive shudder, vibration. • Design causes front windshield distortion. • Early headlight and power-window motor failures • Driver's seat belt doesn't retract.

Secret Warranties/Internal Bulletins/Service Tips

All models/years: Eliminate AC odours by applying an evaporator core cooling-coil coating. • A rotten-egg odour coming from the exhaust is probably the result of a malfunctioning catalytic converter, which may be covered by the emissions warranty on year 2000–02 models. • Paint delamination, peeling, or fading. • GM guidelines to dealers on troubleshooting exterior lamp condensation complaints. • Oil leaks between the intake manifold and engine block are most often caused by insufficient RTV bonding between the intake manifold and cylinder block. • Reverse servo cover seal leaks. **All models: 1993–2002**—GM has a special kit to prevent AC odours in warm weather. **1994–98**—GM guidelines for repairing front brake problems. **1997–2002**—Radio speaker buzz or rattle. **1998**—Tips on eliminating roof panel ticking. **1998–2000**—An engine that loses coolant or runs hot may simply need a new radiator cap or the radiator filler neck polished. • Install upgraded after-market disc pads to eliminate rear brake chirp or groan and front brake squeal when braking. • Silence accessory drivebelt chirping or squeaking by installing a double row idler pulley, generator bracket, and serpentine belt. **1998–2002**—Water runs out of front lower corners of rear hatch. • Engine-spark knock remedy. **1999–2001**—Excessive oil consumption. **1999–2002**—Poor transmission performance, slipping. **2000**—Repair tips for fixing an inoperative or erratically operating antenna. **2000–02**—Clogged injectors are the likely cause of poor engine performance. • Delayed shifting. **2001–02**—Tips for troubleshooting an engine that cranks but won't run. • Engine knocking or lifter noise. • Slipping or missing Second, Third, or Fourth gear. • Remedy for harsh upshifts. • Rear brake rattling. **2002**—Intermittent no-start caused by fuel pump and fuel gauge wiring harness short. • Harsh automatic transmission shifts. • Automatic transmission pump leaks. • Quarter trim panels pull away. • Troubleshooting guide for correcting wind noise and water leaks. • Exhaust ping. • Radiator cap may not hold sufficient vacuum. • Rattling door handles. • Noisy, faulty clutch pedal. *Models with 2.5L engines:* **All years:** Frequent stalling may require a new MAP sensor (TSB #90-142-8A). *Models with 3.8L V6 engines:* **1996–98**—These engines have a history of low oil pressure caused by a failure-prone oil pump. A temporary remedy is to avoid low-viscosity oils and use 10W-40 in the winter and 20W-50 for summer driving. **1998–2002**—Premature driveshaft wear.

CAMARO, FIREBIRD, TRANS AM PROFILE

	1995	1996	1997	1998	1999	2000	2001	2002
Cost Price ($)								
Camaro/RS	18,995	20,195	22,075	22,790	23,100	26,065	26,120	26,995
Z28	23,650	25,530	27,270	27,840	28,670	31,630	29,540	30,785
Convertible	26,045	28,365	29,080	29,795	30,105	38,270	38,585	39,225
Firebird	19,795	20,955	23,120	24,580	24,865	27,605	26,915	27,695
Trans Am	27,390	28,755	30,780	34,080	34,750	35,505	35,815	36,365
Used Values ($)								
Camaro/RS ▲	3,000	3,500	4,500	5,000	6,000	7,000	8,500	10,000
Camaro/RS ▼	2,500	3,000	3,500	4,500	5,500	6,000	8,000	8,500
Z28 ▲	4,000	4,500	5,000	6,000	7,000	8,000	9,000	12,500
Z28 ▼	3,000	4,000	4,500	5,500	6,000	7,000	8,000	11,000
Convertible ▲	5,500	6,500	7,500	9,000	10,000	12,000	14,500	17,000
Convertible ▼	5,000	6,000	7,000	8,000	9,000	11,000	13,000	15,500
Firebird ▲	4,000	4,500	5,000	5,500	6,500	8,000	9,500	11,000
Firebird ▼	3,500	4,000	4,500	5,000	6,000	7,000	8,500	10,000
Trans Am ▲	5,000	5,500	6,000	7,000	8,000	9,000	11,000	14,000
Trans Am ▼	4,500	5,000	5,500	6,000	7,500	8,000	9,500	12,500

Reliability	3	4	4	4	4	4	5	5
Crash Safety (F) (Camaro)	5	5	5	4	4	4	4	4
Side (Camaro)	—	—	3	3	3	3	3	3
Head Restraints	1	—	1	—	1	—	1	1

CORVETTE ★ ★ ★

RATING: Average (1994–2006); Not Recommended (1977–93). If you choose the 1997 model, try to get a second-series car that was made after April 1997. Keep in mind that premium fuel and astronomical insurance rates will further drive up your operating costs. And don't discount the serious safety-related problems you're likely to experience on all models. They run the gamut of sudden steering lock-ups when underway, electrical shorts causing vehicle shutdowns, non-functioning parking brakes, brake failures caused by premature rotor warpage (around 16,000 km), seat belts that jam in the retractor, and, on the 2005, the top suddenly flying off (a 2002 Ford Mustang trait, as well). The locked-up steering is particularly scary because it apparently has carried over to year 2001 models, and traffic accident investigators may simply conclude that a resulting accident was because of driver inexperience or unsafe driving. **"Real" city/highway fuel economy:** 12.3/7.7 L/100 km with a manual transmission or 13.2/7.9 L/100 km with an automatic. Fuel savings may actually be lower by more than 20 percent. **Maintenance/Repair costs:** Higher than average, although most repairs can be done by any independent garage. Long waits for recall repairs. **Parts:** Pricey, but easy to find. Surprisingly, it is often easier to find parts for older Corvettes through collectors' clubs than it is to find many of the high-tech components used today. **Extended warranty:** By all means—just saving the diagnostic fees will pay for the warranty. **Best alternatives:** Ford Mustang, GM Camaro or Firebird, Mazda Miata, and Toyota Celica or Supra. **Online help:** www.corvetteforum.com and www.carreview.com.

Strengths and Weaknesses

Corvettes made in the late '60s and early '70s are acceptable buys, mainly because of their value as collector cars and their uncomplicated repairs (though parts may be rare). Unfortunately, the Corvette's overall reliability and safety have declined over the past thirty years as its price and complexity have increased. GM has chosen to update its antiquated design with complicated high-tech add-ons rather than come up with something original. Consequently, the car has been gutted and then retuned using failure-prone electronic circuitry. Complicated emissions plumbing, braking, and suspension systems have also been added in an attempt to make the Corvette a fuel-efficient, user-friendly, high-performance vehicle—a goal that General Motors has missed by a wide margin.

The electronically controlled suspension systems have always been plagued by glitches. Servicing the different sophisticated fuel-injection systems is a nightmare—even (especially) for GM mechanics. The noisy 5.7L engine frequently hesitates and stalls, there's lots of transmission buzz and whine, the rear tires produce excessive noise, and wind whistles through the A- and C-pillars; these, and the all-too-familiar fibreglass body squeaks and paint delamination (yes, fibreglass delaminates), continue to be unwanted standard features throughout all model years. Also, the electronic dash never works quite right (speedometer lag is one example).

Ownership of more recent Corvette models does have its positive side. For example, the ABS vented disc brakes, available since 1986, are easy to modulate and fade-free. The standard European-made Bilstein FX-3 Selective Ride Control suspension can be pre-set for touring, sport, or performance. Under speed, an electronic module automatically varies the suspension setting, finally curing these cars of their earlier endemic oversteering, wheel spinning, breakaway rear ends, and other nasty surprises.

All used Corvettes are high-risk buys, but the 1977–93 models have been particularly troublesome. These models are notorious for complicated and failure-prone safety, emissions, and performance "innovations" that were routinely brought in one year and dropped shortly thereafter, making for difficult troubleshooting and hard-to-find parts. There's also a greater chance you'll get stuck with a turned-back odometer or an accident-damaged car, written off by the insurance company and then resold through wholesalers, auctions, body shops, or their employees. All these scams can be detected by running a Car Proof check online or by fax (see Part One).

Here's another precaution: Get a GM-backed supplementary warranty, or look for a recent model that has some of the original warranty left. The frequency of repairs and the high repair costs make maintenance outrageously expensive.

1997–2006

Owners admit the redesigned '97 models offer improved performance, better handling, and additional safety features, but they still find fault with the stiff ride, poor fuel economy, and excessive interior noise. From a reliability standpoint, these models are much more refined than earlier versions, but they are hell to diagnose and are knuckle-busters to service. And serious engine and transmission problems remain. You can expect chronic engine stalling and surging, excessive engine oil consumption, an oily black buildup on the exhaust tips, and catalytic converter failures within the first five years. A real hair-raiser is the tendency of steering columns on 1977 through 2001 models to suddenly lock while the vehicle is underway or parked. This continues to be a widespread hazard, despite a recall to fix the defect. Says the following Corvette owner:

> This item has failed on an estimated 3,000 Corvettes throughout the U.S. Please see Internet site *www.corvetteforum.com*. As a safety professional, I see this as a hazard that Chevrolet needs to address with more severity. The loss of steering control because the steering wheel locks can lead to property loss, as well as death.

The consumer's vehicle experienced the same problem as stated in NHTSA recall #04V060000 which states that on certain passenger vehicles equipped with electronic column lock systems (ED), when the ignition switch is turned to lock, the ED prevents turning of the steering system when the vehicle is started. The vehicle is designed so that if the column fails to unlock when the vehicle is started and the customer tries to drive, the fuel supply will be shut off so that the vehicle cannot move when the vehicle cannot be steered. The dealership indicated that the consumer's vehicle was not included in the recall.

Some performance deficiencies make these cars unsafe: The active handling system often malfunctions and makes the vehicle veer into traffic or spin out of control; faulty electronic and electrical systems cause it to abruptly shut down; the brake, suspension, and AC systems are unreliable; and body accessories and electronics suddenly short out.

Factory-related defects on the post-2000 models are commonplace: The engine is excessively noisy; the cabins overheat; the driver's seat moves while driving; the trunk door warps; seat belts twist easily and tend to pull down uncomfortably against the shoulder; the passenger seat belt jams and won't extend or retract; smelly exhaust fumes enter the cabin, causing watery eyes and dizziness; excessive heat buildup from catalytic converters deforms the rear bumper assembly and heats up the interior even more; the glass rear window limits vision; and front and rear wheel weights sometimes fly off the wheels.

Servicing the different sophisticated fuel-injection systems isn't easy, and this may be the primary reason why so many owners complain of having to take their Corvettes back to the shop repeatedly to correct poor engine and transmission performance.

The 2005–06 redesigned models have produced their own subset of problems, although not as extensive a list as prior models: engine stalling and transmission jerking, electrical short-circuits, lousy fit and finish, and squeaky, squealing brakes.

VEHICLE HISTORY: 1997—A substantial redesign was carried out in mid-1997. The transmission is moved back, creating a roomier cockpit; the interior is much more user-friendly; structural improvements reduce body flexing (a problem with most convertibles) and make for a more rigid hatchback; and a new aluminum 340-hp LSI V8 engine arrives on the scene. **1998**—Carryovers of the redesigned '97 that aren't worth a higher price. Debut of a high-performance hardtop. **2001**—A horsepower boost and an Active Handling performance upgrade, plus the addition of a high-performance Zo6 variant. **2002**—The Zo6 gets a 20-hp boost to 405 hp, enhanced rear shocks, aluminum front stabilizer bar links, high-performance brake pads, and new aluminum wheels. **2005**—GM saved its major changes for the 2005 model year. Dubbed the C6, to indicate the car's sixth redesign since

1953, Chevrolet's two-seat sportster received revised styling, more power, and new features. Available as a hatchback coupe with lift-off roof panel or as a convertible with a fabric soft top and heated glass rear window, its new power top was an instant success. Although the car's wheelbase is stretched by 3 cm over the 1997–2004 C5, overall length shrinks by 12.7 cm. The 400-hp 6.0L V8 replaces the C5's 5.7L V8 and adds 50 more horses for good measure. Standard performance safety features still include ABS and traction/anti-skid control. Cars sold with the Z51 package may fetch $1,000 more on the used market due to their firmer, nonadjustable suspension, larger brakes, and an automatic transmission built for sporty handling. Wheel diameter grows an inch to 18/19. Front side airbags remain standard on the convertible, but inexplicably optional on the coupe. Theft-magnet xenon headlights are newly standard, along with keyless access and ignition. Interestingly, original retail price for the upgraded 2005 was almost $2,500 less than the 2004's suggested retail price ($67,395 vs. $69,940). However, as used models, the 2005 sells at a $10,000 premium.

 ## Safety Summary

All models: 1997–98—Sudden loss of power, engine shuts down, and warning lights come on everywhere. • Defective throttle control module, parking brake, brake rotors and pads, seat belt retractors, fuel line clips, and Check Engine light. **1997–2001**—Over 350 complaints, 24 crashes, and 10 injuries related to steering column lock-ups have been reported to NHTSA; GM admits it processed 24,000 warranty claims and sent dealers three bulletins about the problem. **1998**—Fuel-tank leakage. • No airbag deployment. • Transmission failure, leaks. • Emergency brake won't hold. • Excessive vibrations when driving. • Poor headlight illumination. **1999**—Sudden, unintended acceleration. • Fuel tank leaks when gassing up; vehicle can catch fire as raw fuel is ignited by the catalytic converter. • Fuel pump failures. • Parking brake won't hold. • Chronic premature warpage of the brake rotors. • Front lapbelts jam in the retractor. • Electrical shorts cause headlights to stick open; rear-view mirror assembly melts; and a plethora of other electronic glitches lead to vehicle shutdown. • Engine serpentine belt and tensioner failures. • Poorly anchored driver's seat and warped trunk door. **2000–01**—Catalytic converter catches fire. • More reports that when the fuel tank is full, fuel leaks from the top of the vent. • More fuel leaks. This time owners report leaks from the fuel lines near the firewall inside the engine compartment. • Chronic stalling; fuel-injector failures cause vehicle to shudder and stall. • Engine dies while driving in the rain, and brakes don't work. • Early failure of the engine serpentine belt and tensioner. • If one wheel loses traction, the throttle closes, starving the engine. • Brakes drag and lock up; brake pedal doesn't spring back; overheated rotors are common. • Car is nearly uncontrollable at time of brake lock-up. • Seat belt doesn't retract properly when reeling it out and tightens up progressively when driving. • Driver's seat rocks. • Foot easily slips off clutch and brake pedals. **2002**—Sudden stalling on the highway accompanied by brake failure. • Erratic transmission performance (shifts to Fourth before entering Second gear; won't shift into Second when going uphill). • Horn is hard to access since it's just a small indentation on the steering wheel. **2003**—Very low number of complaints reported (28). •

Sudden engine surge while underway. • When accelerating from a stop, vehicle fails to shift from First to Second gear and stalls out. • Constant leaking and failure of rear differential and suspension system. • Leaking oil pan gasket. • Annoying dash reflection onto the windshield. • Inaccurate fuel gauge. • Driver's seat belt locks up. **2004**—Defective steering, despite recall:

> The so-called "fix" GM has for the 1997–2004 Corvette column lock problem does not fix the problem. It merely puts a band-aid on the problem to protect them from lawsuits. I do not understand how this can be allowed by law. I have had to resort to an aftermarket part to fix the problem and chose to ignore the recall.

•

> The contact stated while making a left hand turn out of a parking lot at 10 mph [16 km/h], the contact lost control of the vehicle. Although the steering wheel was manually adjusted to a straight position, it continued to move to the right. The vehicle then made a 270 degree turn to the left and hit another vehicle. There was no damage or police report taken. The vehicle was towed to the dealership and it was determined the steering linkage failed at the knuckle. A representative from the manufacturer read the black box and determined the failure was caused by the impact with the other vehicle. There is a NHTSA recall, # 04V27300, regarding the steering linkages. The vehicle has the same problems as indicated in the recall; however, it is not included in the recall due to the VIN.

• Fuel leaks found outside of the car at the fuel-tank, fuel-pump seal, and the interconnecting hoses. • Fuel leakage from the crossover pipe and other fuel lines:

> I smelled gas in my garage for approximately 1 week but found no leaks. While filling up at gas station I noticed a large puddle forming under the car and saw gas leaking from the tank. Dealer said gas leak was found in gas tank, crossover fuel line and two other fuel lines. Very dangerous situation. Dealer blamed a manufacturer defect in parts. Took 10 days to repair, as the first time tank was replaced there was no fuel pressure, and it had to be redone.

• Sudden stalling caused by faulty fuel pump. • Steering linkage failure at the steering knuckle. • Power seat pinned driver against the steering wheel. • Clutch won't disengage. • Shifter pops out of Reverse. • Parking brake won't hold car in Neutral on a hill. • Inoperative passenger window regulator. **2005**—Car often throws or shreds the serpentine belt, leading to steering/brake loss and engine overheating. Some owners have experienced the problem several times after it was first repaired. **2005–06**—Corvette also "throws" its top:

> Corvette has a removable roof top that has failed many times, local dealer does not want to replace with new part but wants to "squirt glue" into it to make right, which will not fix the problem. Have asked GM for new top, or glass top so I do not have to worry if I will kill someone with the top flying off! GM is no help or will [not] return my phone calls.

The contact stated the vehicle's roof had separated and flew off while driving 40 mph [65 km/h]. This was the second time the vehicle had problems with the roof. A NHTSA recall #06V181000 was performed in 05/06 regarding structure body: roof and pillars, however the recall did not remedy the problem. The dealership would not offer a second repair under the recall.

Secret Warranties/Internal Bulletins/Service Tips

All models/years: A rotten-egg odour coming from the exhaust is probably caused by a defective catalytic converter, which should be covered by the emissions warranty on 2002 and later models. • Clearcoat paint degradation, whitening, and chalking, long a problem with GM's other cars, is also a serious problem with the fibreglass-bodied Corvette, says TSB #331708. It too is covered by a secret warranty for up to six years. • Reverse servo cover seal leak. **All models: 1993–2002**—GM has a special kit to prevent AC odours in warm weather. **1995–2000**—Guidelines for repairing brake rotor warpage. **1997–98**—What to do when the Low Engine Coolant light comes on. • Silence a muffler insulator rumble noise by installing upgraded insulators. • Countermeasures to eliminate door-glass rattles and water leaks above the door glass. **1997–99**—A no-start condition can be corrected by reprogramming the power control module (PCM). • TSB #99-06-02-016 has the remedy for a Low Engine Coolant light that comes on at start-up. • Shift-boot squeaking can be silenced by installing a new shift-boot assembly. • Accessory drive squeaks can be corrected by installing a new idler pulley assembly. **1997–2000**—Repair tips for an inaccurate fuel gauge. **1997–2001**—Sound system speakers make the door panel rattle or buzz. **1997–2002**—Tips on correcting water leaks in various areas. • Loose driver's seat. **1997–2003**—Inoperative AC. **1997–2004**—Remedy for a leaking rear differential. **1998–2000**—Tips on correcting a faulty rear window defogger. • An inoperative or noisy window motor can be corrected by replacing the window regulator and motor assembly. **1998–2002**—Engine-spark knock remedy. **1999**—Rattling from the left fuel tank area can be silenced by installing a fuel-tank foam insulator pad. **1999–2000**—An engine that runs hot or loses coolant may simply need a new radiator cap or polishing of the radiator filler neck. **1999–2001**—Wind noise around the B-pillar. **1999–2002**—Poor transmission performance; SES light lit. • Excessive oil consumption. **2000**—Reducing exhaust boom. • Repair tips on fixing an inoperative or erratically operating antenna. • Left headlight door may not remain closed. **2000–06**—Delayed automatic transmission shifts. **2001**—Incomplete brake pedal return can be fixed by replacing the vacuum brake booster. **2001–02**—Slipping or missing Second, Third, or Fourth gear. **2001–03**—Engine knock or lifter noise. **2001–05**—Harsh upshifts. **2002**—Engine knock. • Erratic fuel gauge or radio operation. • False Service Engine light illumination. • Harsh transmission shifts; 2–4 band and 3–4 clutch damage; transmission pump leaks. • Light brake drag; brake light remains lit. • B-pillar wind noise. **2002–04**—Exhaust system jingle noise. **2003–06**—Oil leaks from engine's rear cover assembly. **2004**—Erratic idle, idle surge, rough running, and stalling. • Coolant leak from head cup plugs. • Transmission fluid leaks; inoperative Second, Third, and Fourth gears. • Rear axle side cover oil leak. • Poor automatic transmission shifting, slipping. • Transmission squawk, grunt, rattle, growl, or buzz noise. • Intermittent or inoperative fuel gauge addressed in TSB #01659, January 2004. • Wind noise or water leak at top of door glass. • Tire wander. • Seat belt won't release from retractor. • Blotches in all glass. • Inoperative Twilight Sentinel automatic headlight control. **2004–05**—Erratic fuel gauge readings. **2005–06**—Vibration or shudder at idle (replace power steering inlet pressure hose). • Vehicle's top flies off:

CAMPAIGN—POTENTIAL PAINTED ROOF SEPARATION

BULLETIN NO.: 05112D   **DATE: JUNE 23, 2006**

CUSTOMER SATISFACTION—PAINTED ROOF ADHESIVE SEPARATION

2005–06 CHEVROLET CORVETTE WITH PAINTED ROOF

This bulletin is being revised to include Z06 vehicles. A new procedure and labor time have been added. Discard all copies of bulletin 05112C, issued June 2006.

THIS PROGRAM IS IN EFFECT UNTIL MARCH 31, 2007.

CONDITION: On certain 2005–06 Chevrolet Corvette vehicles, the painted roof panel may separate from its frame in some areas if it is exposed to stresses along with high temperature and humidity. The occupants of the vehicle may notice one or more of these symptoms: a snapping noise when driving over bumps, wind noise, poor roof panel fit, roof panel movement/bounce when a door or hatch is closed, or a water leak in the headliner.

CORRECTION: Dealers are to apply adhesive foam to ensure proper adhesion, or in a small number of vehicles, replace the roof panel.

Ignore GM's cut-off date. The company is negligent and must pay all claims for as long as a provincial court judge decides is reasonable under the implied warranty.

CORVETTE PROFILE

	1997	1998	1999	2000	2001	2002	2003	2004	2005
Cost Price ($)									
Base	48,895	50,430	53,870	60,050	61,400	62,400	68,120	69,940	67,395
Convertible	—	58,430	60,850	66,965	68,315	69,665	74,120	75,940	79,495
Used Values ($)									
Base ▲	12,000	15,000	18,000	21,000	24,000	27,000	31,000	37,000	46,000
Base ▼	10,500	14,000	17,000	20,000	22,000	25,000	28,500	35,000	43,500
Convertible ▲	—	18,000	20,000	23,000	25,000	31,000	35,000	42,000	54,000
Convertible ▼	—	16,000	19,000	22,000	23,500	28,000	32,500	39,000	51,000
Reliability	2	3	3	3	3	3	3	3	3
Head Restraints (F)	—	—	3	—	3	3	3	3	—
Rear	—	—	—	—	2	2	2	2	—

Mazda

MIATA ★ ★ ★ ★ ★

RATING: Recommended (1990–2006). There was no 1998 model. For almost 16 years this has been an almost-perfect sports car, except for its poor braking performance on rain-slicked roadways. **"Real" city/highway fuel economy:** *5-speed:* 10.1/7.6 L/100 km with a manual transmission. *6-speed:* 10.2/7.7 L/100 km with a manual tranny or 10.6/7.8 L/100 km with an automatic. Owners say fuel savings may be lower than these estimates by about 10 percent. **Maintenance/Repair costs:** Below-average costs, and most repairs aren't dealer-dependent. **Parts:** Average costs, with good availability. **Extended warranty:** A waste of money. **Best alternatives:** Ford Mustang or Probe, GM Camaro or Firebird, Hyundai Tiburon, Nissan 200SX, and Toyota Celica. **Online help:** *www.miata.net*, *www. miataforum.com*, and *www.straight-six.com*.

Strengths and Weaknesses

The base engine delivers adequate power and accelerates smoothly. Acceleration from 0–100 km/h is in the high 8-second range. The 5-speed manual transmission shifts easily and has well-spaced gears; the 6-speed adds 27 kg (60 lb.) and isn't that impressive. The vehicle's lightness, precise steering, and 50/50 weight distribution make this an easy car for novice drivers to toss around corners.

VEHICLE HISTORY: 1996–98—The Miata changed very little. **1999**—Some handling upgrades and additional standard features. **2001**—A slight horsepower boost, a restyled interior and exterior, 15-inch wheels, seat belt pretensioners, improved ABS, and an emergency trunk release. **2003**—16-inch V-rated tires and strut-tower braces. **2004**—Debut of the MazdaSpeed, equipped with a 178-hp turbocharged engine, 6-speed manual transmission, sport suspension, and 17-inch wheels.

Owners' top performance gripes target the same characteristics that make other sports car enthusiasts swoon: inadequate cargo space, cramped interior for large adults, excessive interior noise, and limited low-end torque that makes for frequent shifting.

Owners also say that it's important to change the engine timing chain every 100,000 km. Other reported problems include crankshaft failures, leaky rear-end seals and valve cover gaskets, rear differential seal failures, leaking or squeaky clutches, hard starts and stalling, torn drive boots, transmission whining in upper gear ranges, engine and exhaust system rattles, electrical system glitches, brake pulsation, valvetrain clatter on start-up (changing oil may help), prematurely worn-out shock absorbers and catalytic converters, softtop covers that come off or break, and minor body and trim deficiencies. Early reports on the 2006s target rattling from the console area between the seats, convertible top leaks, and an interior leak that soaks the carpet from the driver's front area to underneath the seat.

Safety Summary

All models/years: Used Miatas will likely have some collision damage; make sure you run a Carfax check online or by fax (see Part One). **All models: 1999**—Airbags fail to deploy upon impact. • While passing another car on the highway, accelerator cable and the cable adjuster assembly disengaged from the horseshoe bracket that holds the cable. • Transmission suddenly failed, causing both rear wheels to seize. • Keizer aluminum wheel cracks, damaging brake caliper, rotor, and fender. • Performs poorly on wet roads. • At highway speeds, vehicle tends to wander all over the roadway. **2000**—In heavy rain, stepping on the brakes results in a 2-second delay before braking; must continually pump the brakes. • Airbags deployed two minutes after collision. • Convertible top latches may inadvertently open while vehicle is underway. • Hard shifting and stiff shifter at Neutral causes gear hunting, grinding, and rattling. • Gas pump shuts off before tank is full. **2001**—Vehicle rolled downhill despite being parked with emergency brake engaged. **2002**—Interior can heat up to 54°C (130°F) because exhaust system is mounted too close to the centre console. **2003**—When accelerating from a cold start, car lurches and then stalls. • Hard starts. • Wheel rims are easily bent. • Poor headlight illumination. **2004**—Hard starts despite changing the fuel pump. • Seat belt locks up during normal driving. **2006**—While complaints for other years have been non-existent or in the single digits, the 2006 models have logged 10 reports of safety-related failures. • Constant steering corrections are necessary due to the vehicle wandering all over the road. • In moderately cold temperatures, the power windows won't work. • It is easy to accidentally engage First gear when Reverse is required, or Reverse when First is needed:

To put the vehicle in reverse, slight downward pressure must be applied to first gear. Since the pressure is so slight, it is not possible to tell if the vehicle is in first gear or reverse until the accelerator pedal is depressed.

• The point where the manual transmission clutch catches keeps moving upward:

The clutch friction point (the location in pedal travel where the clutch begins to engage) moved from the bottom of the pedal (near the floor) to approximately one inch [2.5 cm] from the top (pedal normal position—not depressed). I'm assuming the pedal will have no effect whatsoever in about 500 miles [800 kilometres].

Secret Warranties/Internal Bulletins/Service Tips

All models/years: TSB #006/94 gives all of the possible causes and remedies for brake vibration. • TSB #N00198 addresses complaints that the steering wheel is off-centre. • Other bulletins address the issue of musty AC odours. **All models: 1990–99**—Paint damage caused by the trunk rubber cushions will be repaired under the base warranty. Ask for pro rata compensation if the warranty has expired. **1999**—A hard-to-start engine may have debris accumulated at the fuel pressure regulator valve area, causing the valve to stick open. • Engine rattling may be caused by premature wear of the engine thrust bearing or by the engine harness clips rubbing against the car's frame. • Muffler rattling may be silenced by installing an upgraded unit. **1999–2002**—Additional tips on reducing AC odours. **1999–2003**—Clutch chatter on cold start-up. **2000–06**—Troubleshooting body vibration and steering wheel shimmy. **2002**—Clutch chatter during cold takeoff on manual-transmission-equipped vehicles. • Fuelling difficulty caused by gas pump shutting off early. • The 6-speed manual transmission won't shift into Fifth gear or Reverse. **2004**—Door rattling. **2005**—Free replacement of the keyless entry fob.

MIATA PROFILE

	1996	1997	1999	2000	2001	2002	2003	2004	2005
Cost Price ($)									
Base	24,210	24,695	26,025	26,995	27,605	27,695	27,695	27,895	27,995
Used Values ($)									
Base ▲	5,500	6,000	7,500	9,000	10,500	13,000	15,000	18,500	21,000
Base ▼	5,000	5,500	6,500	8,000	9,000	11,500	13,500	17,000	19,500
Reliability	5	5	5	5	5	5	5	5	5
Crash Safety (F)	4	—	—	—	—	4	4	4	4
Side	—	—	—	—	—	3	3	3	3
Head Restraints (F)	1	—	1	—	3	3	3	3	—
Rear	—	—	—	—	2	2	2	—	—
Rollover Resistance	—	—	—	—	—	5	5	5

Toyota

CELICA ★★★★★

RATING: Recommended (2001–05, 1995–99); Above Average (2000, 1986–94). The reworked 2000 model has been downgraded because of its many factory-related deficiencies. Keep in mind that the 1989–96 GTS is far superior to the GT, with its 135-hp DOHC 2.0L engine, firmer suspension, better-equipped interior, ABS, and sportier feel. Nevertheless, all Celicas handle competently and provide the kind of sporting performance expected from a car of this class. The extra performance in the higher-line versions does come at a price, but this isn't a problem, given the high resale value and excellent reliability for which Celicas are known. There are few safety-related complaints or recalls. **"Real" city/highway fuel economy:** *5-speed:* 8.9/6.5 L/100 km with a manual transmission or 8.3/6.0 L/100 km with an automatic. *6-speed:* 9.6/6.6 L/100 km with a manual tranny or 9.4/7.0 L/100 km with an automatic. **Maintenance/Repair costs:** Average, and most repairs can be done at any garage. **Parts:** Reasonably priced and easy to find. **Extended warranty:** No, you'd be throwing your money away. **Best alternatives:** Ford Mustang, GM Camaro or Firebird, Hyundai Tiburon, and Mazda Miata. **Online help:** *www.toyotanation.com.*

Strengths and Weaknesses

Redesigned 1994 models are full of both show and go, with more aerodynamic styling, an enhanced 1.8L that gives more pickup than the ST's 1.6L, and better fuel economy. Among the upgraded models available, smart buyers should choose a used 1994 ST for its more reasonable price, smooth performance, quiet running, and high fuel economy.

Owner gripes target excessive engine noise, limited rear seatroom, and inadequate cargo space. Pre-1994 models get the most complaints regarding brakes, electrical problems, AC malfunctions, and premature exhaust wearout. The 1994 models may have a manual transmission that slips out of Second gear as well as hard starts caused by a faulty airflow meter (#22250-74200). Areas vulnerable to early rusting include rear wheel openings, suspension components, areas surrounding the fuel-filler cap, door bottoms, and trunk or hatchback lids.

VEHICLE HISTORY: 1996—Extra sound insulation and add-on skirts. **1997**—GT given 5 more horses and the notchback GT is axed. **1998**—ST dropped and GT given more standard features. **1999**—GT Sport Coupe is dropped. **2000**—Crisper handling, a new 180-hp engine, and a 6-speed gearbox (GT-S), plus lots of factory-related glitches. **2003**—Hatchback coupes are slightly restyled. **2005**—In the Celica's seventh generation makeover, the wheelbase gets larger, width is narrowed by 1 cm, and the coupe is shortened by almost 10 cm. The convertible is dropped, and the GT and GT-S get new trim.

All late-model Celicas offer decent reliability and durability, with three major exceptions: engine sludging; an engine-blowing, self-destructing 6-speed gearbox; and premature, costly replacement of brake calipers, pads, and rotors:

> Toyota has a big problem with their 6-speed in the new Celica. They even told me about it at Toyota. The malfunction is that when trying to shift from Third to Fourth gear, the transmission will slip into Second instead of Fourth. This then causes the engine to be blown.
>
> This is a very dangerous situation if trying to merge with traffic on interstate at around 70–75 mph [113–120 km/h] and suddenly your car decelerates instantly to around 50 mph [80 km/h]. They need to do something about it before someone gets seriously hurt....

Servicing and repairs are straightforward, and parts are easily found. The front-drive series performs very well and hasn't presented any major problems to owners. Prices are high for Celicas in good condition, but some bargains are available with the base ST model.

Some common problems over the years include engine failures caused by engine oil sludge (1997–2001 models), a problem covered by Toyota "goodwill" (see "Sienna" section); brake pulsations and pulling to one side; rear defroster terminals breaking on convertibles; sunroof leaks; erratic CD changer performance; and smelly AC emissions.

Another subset of problems shows up on the redesigned 2000 and later models. This includes engine failures while driving ("weak" valves blamed), not much power when the accelerator is floored, stalling after a cold start, engine knocking, excessive oil consumption, early replacement of the belt tensioner and airflow meter, the aforementioned failure-prone 6-speed transmission, insufficient AC cooling, lights dimming and heater lagging when shifted into idle, seat belt tabs that damage door panels, interior panels that separate, a driver's window that catches and doesn't go all the way up, a leaky convertible top and sun roof, drive-belt squeaks when turning, a squeaking gearshift lever, a grinding noise emanating from the front wheels and brakes, paint peeling, and limited rear visibility. The audible reverse alarm isn't Toyota's brightest idea: Audible only inside the vehicle, it adds a forklift cachet to your Celica.

Safety Summary

All models/years: Even if your vehicle has 4×4 capability, it's imperative to fit it with snow tires in order to avoid dangerous control problems on snow and ice. **All models: 1999**—Goodyear Eagle GT tire failure (tread separates). **2000**—A huge increase in safety-related complaints. • Fuel leak caused by a broken hose. • No airbag deployment. • Seat belts didn't hold driver in place in a frontal collision. • Cruise control suddenly slows car down without warning. • Constant stalling. • Won't shift into Overdrive. • Clutch and accelerator pedal stick to the floor. • Excessive steering-wheel play. • At 100 km/h, vehicle pulls to one side. • Passenger-side wheel suddenly locked up, causing an accident. • Shield protecting wires and fuel lines came off and caused extensive AC valve damage. • Spoiler fell off because of loose bolts. **2000–01**—Without a lockout on the 6-speed gearshift, car can be inadvertently shifted from Fifth to Second gear. **2001**—Engine failures due to weak valves, sludge, says one report. • Accessory belt tensioner squeaks, rattles, and the bolt breaks easily. • Steering over-corrects, causing the car to fishtail. **2001–02**—Airbags fail to deploy. • Hatch will not stay up:

> Rear hatch closes by itself. Dealer acknowledges problem but will not replace because it was not reported while still in warranty. The support arms are not strong enough to support the hatch. They have been discontinued and have been replaced with stronger ones. The hatch comes down without warning and could cause injury such as smash[ed] hands or fingers of children especially.

2002—Fuel tank easily punctured. • Gasoline spews out when refueling. • Total brake failure. • Poor wet roadway traction. **2003**—Hood latch failure. • Fuel leak because of defective valve clamp. • Fuel splashes out during fill-up, after recall fix:

> The same problem was encountered while attempting to put fuel in the vehicle. Fueling is now difficult and very time consuming. Only about one-tenth of a gallon [one-third of a litre] can be pumped before the fuel pump automatically shuts off. This appears to be caused by fuel backing up in the fuel inlet pipe and fuel splashing back out. Toyota has been contacted and a service appointment scheduled at a local dealership. However, I got the impression they are reluctant to remedy this free of charge since the problem was supposedly fixed 3 years ago.

• Inoperative cruise control. • Steering tends to over-correct. • Tire tread separates from the sidewall. **2004**—Premature wearout of the brake calipers and rotors.

Secret Warranties/Internal Bulletins/Service Tips

All models/years: Toyota TSB #TC002-01 confirms misshifts with the 6-speed tranny. • Troubleshooting updates for steering pulling complaints are found in TSB #ST005-01. • Older Toyotas with stalling problems should have the engine checked for excessive carbon buildup on the valves before any extensive repairs are authorized. • Owner feedback and dealer service managers (who wish to remain anonymous) confirm the existence of Toyota's secret warranty that will pay for replacing front disc brake components that wear out before 2 years/40,000 km. • To reduce front brake squeaks on ABS-equipped vehicles, ask the dealer to install new, upgraded rotors (#43517-32020). **All models: 1990–2000**—Toyota has put out a special grease to minimize brake clicking. **1991–2006**—Loose interior trim. **2000**—GT-S automatic transmission fluid leaks. • Loose outer door handle. • Sunshade improvements. • Cruise-control shock can be attenuated by replacing the ECU. • Moonroof creaking. • Squeak and rattle service tips. **2000–01**—Drivebelt and engine squealing. • Enhanced sunroof durability. **2000–02**—Insufficient rear hatch support. **2001–04**—Troubleshooting an inoperative AC. **2002–06**—Diagnosing and correcting vehicle pulling to one side. **2003**—Throttle body motor malfunctions. • Fuel-tank check valve Special Service Campaign. **2003–06**—Ticking noise at the upper and lower windshield areas. **2004–06**—Front seat squeaking.

CELICA PROFILE

	1997	1998	1999	2000	2001	2002	2003	2004	2005
Cost Price ($)									
Base	28,528	34,138	34,475	23,980	24,140	24,645	24,645	24,650	24,900
Used Values ($)									
Base ▲	5,000	6000	7,000	8,000	10,000	12,000	14,000	16,000	18,500
Base ▼	4,500	5,500	6,500	7,000	8,500	10,500	12,500	14,500	17,000
Reliability	5	5	5	5	5	5	5	5	5
Crash Safety (F)	—	—	—	—	4	4	4	4	4
Side	—	—	—	—	3	3	3	3	3
Head Restraints (F)	2	—	3	—	5	5	5	5	—
Rear	—	—	2	—	—	—	—	5	—
Rollover Resistance	—	—	—	—	—	—	5	5	5

All ratings on a numbered scale where 5 is good and 1 is bad. See pages 130–132 for a more detailed description.

MINIVANS

A Vanishing Breed

Now that Mazda, Ford, and GM have abandoned the minivan market, buyers have to be especially careful they don't buy a minivan that is an "orphan" in the making. The phase-out of Ford's Windstar/Freestar, Mazda's MPV, and GM's handful of front-drives, including the Venture, Montana, Relay, Terraza, Silhouette, and Outlander, has cleared the deck so that only the best have survived. Chrysler's minivans are still strong sellers despite stiff competition from Honda's Odyssey and Toyota's Sienna. However, with Chrysler sold to Cerberus, a group of equity investors, the Caravan et al. face an uncertain future. Hyundai and Kia (essentially the same firm) are coming on strong for 2007, offering their fully equipped Entourage and Sedona minivans for much less than the Odyssey and Sienna.

Minivans fall into two categories: upsized cars and downsized trucks. The upsized cars are "people-movers." They're mostly front-drives, they handle like cars, and they get great fuel economy. The Honda Odyssey and Toyota Sienna are the best examples of this kind of minivan. Following Toyota's 2004 Sienna upgrades and Honda's 2005 Odyssey improvements, their road performance, reliability, and retained value surpass that of the front- and rear-drive minivans built by DaimlerChrysler, Ford, and General Motors. Only Nissan is struggling with quality issues following its 2004 Quest redesign.

GM's Astro and Safari and Ford's Aerostar are downsized trucks that are dirt-cheap used choices. Using rear-drive, 6-cylinder engines, and heavier mechanical components, these minivans handle cargo and passengers equally well. On the negative side, their fuel economy is no match for the front-drives, their highway handling is more trucklike, and Aerostar parts are becoming hard to find. Overall, rear-drive GM minivans are much more reliable performers than the front-drive Ford Windstar/Freestar. As AWDs, though, they'll keep you in the repair bay for weeks.

Rear-drive vans are also better suited for towing trailers in the 1,600–2,950 kg (3,500–6,500 lb.) range. Most automakers say their front-drive minivans can pull up to 1,600 kg (3,500 lb.) with an optional towing package (often costing almost $1,000 extra), but don't you believe it. Owners report white-knuckle driving and premature powertrain failures caused by the extra load. It just stands to reason that Ford, Chrysler, and GM front-drives equipped with engines and transmissions that blow out at 60,000–100,000 km under normal driving conditions are going to meet their demise much earlier under a full load.

Declining Quality

Quality control has always been a more serious problem with minivans than with vans, trucks, or SUVs because owners want a vehicle that provides both transportation and "housing" in a relatively small, garageable vehicle—making minivans more complex and difficult to service. Plus, supplier cost-cutting and the addition of many new convenience, performance, and safety features have resulted in a steep decline in minivan reliability among the Detroit Big Three.

In the '60s, VW imported the first minivans to North America. They were unreliable, hard-to-diagnose, parts-challenged rustbuckets that spent more time in the service bay than they spent on the road. But the idea caught on when Chrysler repackaged the concept two decades later.

Chrysler

Chrysler churned out millions of units, paying scant attention to chronic 4-cylinder engine, automatic transmission, ABS, airbag control module, electrical system, and fit and finish deficiencies, and to rust-damaged steering and suspension systems. After all, thought Chrysler, the 7-year bumper-to-bumper warranty would fix the engine and transmission failures, and Daimler would be stuck with the rest.

Indeed, Chrysler minivans caught on from their debut in 1984, when they were seen as fairly reliable and efficient people-haulers; that is, until the comprehensive warranty expired, or was cut back post-2000. Nevertheless, these minivans have continued to dominate the market despite their well-known mechanical and body problems. In fact, it's amazing how little Chrysler's defect patterns have changed during the past two decades.

2005 CHRYSLER GRAND CARAVAN BULLETIN SUMMARY

NUMBER	DATE	TITLE
18-004-07	01/24/2007	Engine Controls—MIL ON/DTC P0480 Set
24-001-06A	11/10/2006	A/C—Water Leaks Under Passenger Side Carpet
08-045-06	10/17/2006	Body—Power Liftgate Does Not Open/Close Properly
05-001-06A	09/23/2006	Brakes—Rear Brake Drum Freezing/Water/Snow Ingestion
23-035-06	08/24/2006	Interior—Buzz/Rattle From Quarter Panel Speaker Area
24-006-06	08/10/2006	A/C—Musty Odors When Hot/Humid
23-012-06A	06/03/2006	Interior—Third Row Seat Front Leg Not Retracting
F10	06/01/2006	Recall—Wiper Motor Inspection/Replacement
23-019-06	05/10/2006	Interior—Adhesive Residue On Carpet
F06	04/01/2006	Campaign—Underbody Heater Hose Replacement
23-014-06	03/08/2006	Wipers/Washers—Wipers Smear or Streak Windshield
NHTSA06V067000	03/07/2006	Recall 06V067000: Wiper Motor Inspection/Replacement
21-004-06	03/01/2006	Engine Controls—MIL ON/DTC P1776 Set
24-001-06	02/23/2006	A/C—Water Leaks Under Passenger Side Carpet

NUMBER	DATE	TITLE
F01	02/01/2006	Campaign—Rear A/C/Heater Tube Corrosion
21-022-05	11/04/2005	Instruments—Speedometer Inaccurate by 6 mph Over 50 mph
18-037-05	10/20/2005	Engine Controls—Flash Programming Failure Recovery
08-055-05	10/19/2005	Audio System—Satellite Radio Static
23-047-05	10/07/2005	Body—Whistle Sound From Rear Quarter Glass
08-013-05A	10/01/2005	Cell Phone—UConnect® Hands Free Phone Inoperative
19-007-05A	09/30/2005	Interior—Rattle From Steering Wheel
24-015-05	08/18/2005	A/C—Condenser Stone/Road Debris Damage
19-006-05	08/04/2005	Steering—Low Speed Steering Shudder
23-035-05	07/26/2005	Body—Circular/Ring Marks on Glass
09-003-05	06/23/2005	Engine Compartment—Squeak Under Light Throttle
08-028-05	05/28/2005	Body Controls—MIL ON/Keyless Entry Inoperative/DTC Set
08-020-05	03/23/2005	Instruments—Parking Assist Tones Not Loud Enough
02-003-05	03/16/2005	Suspension—Front Suspension Rattle/Knocking Sound
18-010-05A	03/04/2005	Engine Controls—MIL ON/DTC P0135 Set
08-014-05	02/17/2005	Accessories—MOPAR® Remote Starter Inoperative
08-008-05	02/04/2005	Engine Controls—MIL ON/DTC P0135 (O$_2$ Sensor)
05-002-05	01/29/2005	Brakes—Vibration/Pulsation Felt in Steering Wheel
19-001-05	01/26/2005	Steering—Steering Wheel Tilt Mechanism Inoperative
23-002-05	01/14/2005	Body—Water Leaks To Interior From Roof Seam
08-040-04	12/09/2004	Electrical—Locks Inoperative/Liftgate Triggers Alarm
19-011-04	12/07/2004	Steering—Moaning Noise on Low Speed Turns
19-010-04	11/29/2004	Power Steering—Additive Prohibition
21-008-04A	10/16/2004	A/T—MIL ON/DTC P1776 Set
21-005-04A	10/09/2004	A/T—Coastdown Ticking Noise
19-008-04	10/05/2004	Steering—In and Out Steering Column Movement
08-027-04	07/30/2004	Safety Systems—Inadvertent Damage/Disabling
08-022-04	05/25/2004	Entertainment System—Crackling Noise From Headphones
18-018-04	04/27/2004	Engine Controls/Ignition—MIL ON/Misfire DTC's Set
18-016-04	04/13/2004	Engine Controls—Warm Engine Rough Idle
NHTSA04V047000	02/03/2004	Recall 04V047000: Seat Belt Retractor Defect
D04	02/01/2004	Recall—Right Front Seat Belt Retractor Inspection

Chrysler's first minivans were known to leak like a sieve when it rained—a recurring problem they have to this day.

Ford

Ford's minivans have gone from bad to worse. Its first minivan, the 1985–97 Aerostar, was fairly dependable, although it did have some recurring tranny, brake, and coil-spring problems. Collapsing coil springs have caused tire blowouts on all model years, although 1988–90 models are covered by a regional recall. Other years fall under a "goodwill" program, as this *Lemon-Aid* reader reports:

On vacation in Washington, our 1995 Aerostar blew a tire that was worn right through from the left rear coil spring (broken in two places). The right rear coil spring is broken, as well. I showed Dams Ford in Surrey, B.C., the broken spring and they have "graciously" offered to replace the tire or repair the right side at no cost to us.

Ford's quality decline continued with the mediocre front-drive Mercury Villager, a co-venture that also produced the Nissan Quest. Both vehicles were only so-so highway performers that often resided in dealer repair bays awaiting major engine, transmission, or electrical repairs. The Villager/Quest duo lasted through the 2000 model year. Quest continued on its own with minimal changes to its 2001–03 models. The 2004 Quest's redesign was both a conceptual and engineering disaster. First-year models were so glitch-prone and stylistically beyond the pale that Nissan sent over 200 engineers to North America to correct the defects and change the interior design. Sales have never recovered.

Then Ford brought out the 1995 Windstar—one of the poorest quality, most dangerous minivans ever built; the year 2000 model has logged 736 safety-related complaints at NHTSA. Renamed the Freestar in 2004, the vehicle's failure-prone powertrain, suspension (broken coil springs), electrical, fuel, and braking systems continue to put owners' wallets and lives at risk.

Ford has compounded the Windstar's failings with its hard-nosed attitude toward customer complaints and by refusing warranty coverage for what are clearly factory-induced defects. Fortunately, there's been a flood of Canadian small claims court decisions that have come to Ford owners' aid when Ford wouldn't. These Canadian courts say Ford and its dealers must pay for engine and transmission repairs, even if the original warranty has expired or the minivan was bought used (see page 105).

General Motors

GM's minivans are even less reliable than Ford's. To begin with, they have more serious powertrain problems than either Ford or Chrysler, other mechanical

components such as fuel gauges and brakes aren't dependable, and fit and finish is so bad that not even the roof can escape developing rust holes, as GM service bulletins confirm.

Asian Automakers

Asian competitors don't make perfect machines either, as a perusal of NHTSA-registered safety complaints, service bulletins, and online complaint forums will quickly confirm. Asian companies, looking to keep costs down, have also been bedevilled during the past decade by chronic engine and automatic transmission failures, sliding door malfunctions, catastrophic tire blowouts, and electrical glitches.

There is one big difference, though: Asian companies usually admit to their mistakes. The Detroit Big Three cover them up.

A word of warning about Nissan and Toyota. Yes, these importers have made fairly dependable vehicles—including minivans—for the past three decades. However, the newly redesigned Nissan Quest and Toyota Sienna minivans are less reliable than pre-2004 models.

Volkswagen

And, finally, we come back to where we started—Volkswagen. Its vans, including the 1979 Vanagon and 1993 EuroVan/Camper, have never been taken seriously since they came to North America in 1950 with the Transporter cargo van and the nine-seater, 21-window Microbus. A reputation for poor overall quality, puny engines, and insufficient parts and servicing support continues to drive buyers away.

The solution? VW has made a pact with Chrysler to sell 2008 Caravans under the VW logo. However, with Chrysler under new ownership, this pact is up for review.

Larger and Smaller Alternatives

Most minivans are overpriced for what is essentially an upgraded car or downsized truck. Motorists needing a vehicle with large cargo- and passenger-carrying capacities should consider a Chrysler, Ford, or GM full-sized van, even if it means sacrificing some fuel economy. You just can't beat the excellent forward vision and easy-to-customize interiors that these large vans provide. Furthermore, parts are easily found and are competitively priced because of the great number of independent suppliers.

On the other hand, a minivan may be too large for some shoppers who want the same versatility in a smaller package. For them, the new Mazda5 minivan/wagon (about $20,000) is a good place to start.

MINIVAN RATINGS

Recommended

Honda Odyssey (2006)

Above Average

DaimlerChrysler PT Cruiser (2001–06)   Kia Sedona (2006)
Honda Odyssey (2003–05)   Toyota Sienna (1998–2003; 2006)

Average

DaimlerChrysler Caravan, Voyager,
    Grand Caravan, Grand Voyager,
    Town & Country (2002–06)
Ford Villager/Nissan Quest
    (1997–2003)
General Motors Astro, Safari
    (1996–2005)

Honda Odyssey (1996–2002)
Kia Sedona (2002–05)
Mazda MPV (2002–06)
Toyota Previa (1991–97)
Toyota Sienna (2004–05)

Below Average

DaimlerChrysler Caravan, Voyager,
    Grand Caravan, Grand Voyager,
    Town & Country (1998–2001)
Ford Freestar (2004–06)
Ford Villager/Nissan Quest
    (1995–96)

General Motors Astro, Safari
    (1985–95)
Mazda MPV (1989–2001)
Nissan Quest (2004–06)

Not Recommended

DaimlerChrysler Caravan, Voyager,
    Grand Caravan, Grand Voyager,
    Town & Country (1984–97)
Ford Villager/Nissan Quest
    (1993–94)

Ford Windstar (1995–2003)
General Motors Montana, Montana SV6,
    Relay, Sihouette, Terraza, Trans Sport,
    Uplander, Venture (1990–2006)

DaimlerChrysler

CARAVAN, VOYAGER, GRAND CARAVAN, GRAND VOYAGER, TOWN & COUNTRY ★ ★ ★

RATING: Average (2002–06); Below Average (1998–2001); Not Recommended (1984–97). Chrysler's new owners, Cerberus, say they will keep the Caravan and its siblings around for some time, while GM and Ford phase out their models during the next year. Nevertheless, all three Detroit automakers' minivans are at the bottom of the heap as far as quality and dependability are concerned. Chrysler, however, is the best of the bad. Its minivans are fairly cheap and not as defect-ridden as what's offered by GM and Ford. True, failure-prone automatic transmissions are Chrysler's main weakness, but Ford and GM have serious transmission *and* engine problems. That's why the Chrysler lineup gets a higher rating than minivans sold by Detroit's other two manufacturers. **"Real" city/ highway fuel economy:** *Caravan 2.4L 4-cylinder:* 11.8/8.2 L/100 km. *Caravan 3.0L V6:* 12.7/8.3 L/100 km. *Caravan 3.3L V6:* 12.2/8.2 L/100 km. *Grand Caravan 3.3L V6:* 12.9/8.5 L/100 km. *Grand Caravan 3.8L V6:* 13.2/8.7 L/100 km. *Town & Country:* 13.6/9.1 L/100 km. *Town & Country AWD:* 13.6/9.1 L/100 km. Owners report fuel savings may undershoot the above estimates by 20 percent or more.

Maintenance/Repair costs: Maintenance and repair costs are average during the first three years, and then rise dramatically thereafter. **Parts:** Easy to find and reasonably priced when bought from and installed by independent suppliers. Independent garages offer cheaper parts, provide longer warranties, and will often give expert testimony when the replaced component is found to be poorly manufactured. This is especially important with transmission and ABS repairs, since an independent will furnish you with proof to get either a "goodwill" refund from Chrysler or a small claims court settlement. **Extended warranty:** The 7-year Chrysler powertrain warranty is ideal, but it was only a standard feature for a few years. If it's expired, opt for the same warranty sold through Chrysler, if possible. If you're buying the warranty from a dealer, bargain it down to about one-third of the $2,000 asking price. Forget the bumper-to-bumper extended warranty; it's simply too expensive. **Best alternatives:** Honda's Odyssey should be your first choice. Toyota's 2003 or earlier models are good second choices, inasmuch as the 2004 version is still working through its redesign glitches. The Mazda 2002 and 2003 MPV is also an acceptable alternative. GM and Ford front- and rear-drive minivans aren't credible alternatives because of their failure-prone powertrains; brake, suspension, and steering problems; electrical short-circuits; and subpar bodywork. Full-sized GM and Chrysler rear-drive cargo vans are more affordable and practical buys if you intend to haul a full passenger load or do some regular heavy hauling, if you are physically challenged, if you use lots of accessories, or if you take frequent motoring excursions. Don't splurge on 2003 or 2004 Chrysler luxury minivans like the Town & Country: They will cost up to $15,000 more than a base Caravan and only be worth a few thousand more after five years on the market. **Online help:** *www.geocities.com/plumraptor* (Caravan Sucks!), *www. autosafety.org/autodefects.html*, *www.datatown.com/chrysler*, *www.wam.umd.edu/ ~gluckman/Chrysler/index.html* (The Chrysler Products' Problem Web Page), and *www.daimlerchryslervehicleproblems.com* (The Truth Behind Chrysler).

Strengths and Weaknesses

Cheap and plentiful, these versatile minivans offer a wide array of standard and optional features that include AWD (dropped for 2005), anti-lock brakes, child safety seats that are integrated into the seatbacks, flush-design door handles, and front windshield wiper/washer controls located on the steering-column lever for easier use. Childproof locks are standard, and the front bucket seats incorporate vertically adjustable head restraints. The Town & Country, a luxury version of the Caravan, comes equipped with a 3.8L V6 and standard luxury features that make the vehicle more attractive to upscale buyers.

Chrysler's minivans continue to dominate the new- and used-minivan markets, though they're quickly losing steam because of the popularity of crossover wagons and better quality products from Japanese and South Korean automakers. Nevertheless, they offer pleasing styling and lots of convenience features at used prices that can be very attractive. They can carry up to seven passengers in comfort, and they ride and handle better than most truck-based minivans. The shorter-wheelbase minivans also offer better rear visibility and good ride quality, and are more nimble and easier to park than truck-based minivans and larger front-drive versions. Cargo hauling capability is more than adequate.

Caravans also give you a quiet and plush ride, excellent braking, lots of innovative convenience features, user-friendly instruments and controls, a driver-side sliding door, and plenty of interior room. Depreciation is much faster than with Japanese minivans.

Don't make the mistake of believing that Chrysler's Mercedes connection means you'll get a top-quality minivan. You won't. In fact, owner complaints and service bulletins tell me that the 2004–06 minivans will have similar powertrain, electrical system, brake, suspension, and body deficiencies as previous versions.

These minivans can pose maximum safety risks, as well. Owners report bizarre defects such as seat belts that may strangle children, airbags that deploy when the ignition is turned on, transmissions that jump out of gear, and sudden stalling and electrical short-circuits when within radar range of airports or military installations.

Recently launched minivans continue to exhibit an array of serious mechanical deficiencies that belie Chrysler's so-called commitment to quality improvement. Some of the most serious and common problems include the premature wearout of engine tensioner pulleys, automatic transmission speed sensors, engine head gaskets, motor mounts, starter motors, steering columns, front brake discs and pads (the brake pad material crumbles in your hands), front rotors and rear drums, brake master cylinders, suspension components, exhaust system components, ball joints, wheel bearings, water pumps, fuel pumps and pump wiring harnesses, radiators, heater cores, and AC units. Fuel injectors on all engines have been troublesome, the differential pin breaks through the automatic transmission casing, sliding doors malfunction, engine supports may be missing or not connected, tie-rods may suddenly break, oil pans crack, and the power-steering pump frequently leaks. Factory-installed Goodyear tires frequently fail prematurely at 40,000–65,000 km.

Since 1996, Chrysler's V6 engines have performed quite well—far better than the similar engines that equip Ford and GM minivans. Nevertheless, some owners have reported engine oil sludging and head gasket failures, hard starts, stalling, serpentine belt failures, and power-steering pump hose blowouts (which cause a loss of power steering).

Chrysler's A604, 41TE, and 42LE automatic transmissions, phased in with the 1991 models, are reliability nightmares that can have serious safety consequences. Imagine having to count to three in traffic before Drive or Reverse will engage, limping home in Second gear at 50 km/h, or suddenly losing all forward motion in traffic.

Catastrophic transmission failures through 2002 models are commonplace because of poor engineering, as the following reader discovered:

> My '99 Grand Voyager had a complete differential failure at 104,000 km. The retaining pin sheared off, which allowed the main differential pin to work its way out and smash the casing and torque converter.
>
> In our case this is what happened. The gear bit, the pin spun, shearing the retaining pin off. With the centrifugal force the main pin worked its way out of the housing and smashed a 2" × 4" [4 cm × 10 cm] hole through the bell housing and nearly punctured the torque converter. In my opinion this is a design flaw that should have been corrected 10 years ago. From my research I have determined that the transaxle identification number matches the original A604 transaxle. I was shocked that they would still use these in 1999.

Fit and finish has gotten worse over the past two decades. Body hardware and interior trim are fragile and tend to break, warp, or fall off (door handles are an example). Premature rust-out of major suspension and steering components is a critical safety and performance concern. Paint delamination often turns these solid-coloured minivans into two-tone models with chalky white stripes on the hood and roof. Chrysler knows about this problem and often tries to get claimants to pay half the cost of repainting (about $1,500 on a $3,000 job), but will eventually agree to pay the total cost if the owner stands fast or threatens small claims court action.

And as the minivan takes on its albino appearance, you can listen to a self-contained orchestra of clicks, clunks, rattles, squeaks, and squeals as you drive. Giving new meaning to the phrase "surround sound," these noises usually emanate from the brakes, suspension and steering assemblies, poorly anchored bench seats, and misaligned body panels.

VEHICLE HISTORY: 1996—Third generation models have more aerodynamic styling, a driver-side sliding door, roll-out centre and rear seats, a longer wheelbase, standard dual airbags and ABS (ABS later became optional on base models), and a more powerful 150-hp 2.4L 4-cylinder engine. **1998**—The 3.0L V6 engine is paired with a better-performing 4-speed automatic transmission, and the 3.8L V6 gets 14 additional horses (180). **2000**—A new AWD Sport model (it was a sales flop) and standard CD player and AC. **2001**—A small horsepower boost for the V6s, front side airbags, adjustable pedals, upgraded headlights, and a power-operated rear liftgate. **2002**—Fuel-tank assembly redesigned to prevent post-collision fuel leakage; a tire air-pressure monitor; a DVD entertainment system. **2003**—AutoStick transmission dropped; standard power liftgate on the Grand EX and ES models. **2004**—Not much new, except for a tire-pressure warning monitor, enhanced audio, and new keyless entry options. **2005**—Side curtain airbags and second- and third-row seats that fold flush with the floor; AWD dropped.

There's an abundance of used Chrysler minivans on the market selling at bargain prices. However, very few have any original warranty coverage left, "goodwill" repair refunds are spotty, and guidelines are vague. Don't even consider the 4-cylinder engine—it has no place in a minivan, especially when hooked to the inadequate 3-speed automatic transmission. It lacks an Overdrive and will shift back and forth as speed varies, and it's slower and noisier than the other choices. The 3.3L V6 is a better choice for most city-driving situations, but don't hesitate to get the 3.8L if you're planning lots of highway travel or carrying four or more passengers. Since its introduction, it's been relatively trouble-free, and it's more economical on the highway than the 3.3L, which strains to maintain speed. The sliding side doors make it easy to load and unload children, install a child safety seat in the middle, or remove the rear seat. On the downside, they run the risk of exposing kids to traffic, and they're a costly, failure-prone option. Child safety seats integrated into the rear seatbacks are convenient and reasonably priced, but Chrysler's versions have had a history of either tightening up excessively or not tightening enough, allowing the child to slip out. Try the seat with your child before buying it. You may wish to pass on the tinted windshields as well; they seriously reduce visibility. Be wary of models featuring all-wheel drive and ABS brakes: The powertrain isn't reliable and is horrendously expensive to repair, and Chrysler's large number of ABS failures is worrisome. Ditch the failure-prone Goodyear original-equipment tires and remember that a night drive is a prerequisite to check out headlight illumination, which many call inadequate.

Safety Summary

All models/years: Sudden, unintended acceleration; owners report that cruise-control units often malfunction, accelerating or decelerating the vehicle without any warning. • Airbag malfunctions:

> Get used to the term "clockspring." It's an expensive little component that controls some parts within the steering wheel and, when defective, can result in the airbag warning light coming on or cause the airbag, cruise control, or horn to fail. It has been a pain in the butt for Chrysler minivan owners since the 1996 model year. Chrysler has extended its warranty for 1996 through 2000 model year minivans in two separate recalls and replaced the clockspring at no charge. Apparently, the automaker has found that the part fails because it was wound too tight or short-circuited from corrosion.

• Defective engine head gaskets, rocker arm gaskets, and engine mounts. • Engine sag, hesitation, stumble, hard starts, or stalling. • No steering/lock-up. • Carbon monoxide comes through air vents. • Brakes wear out prematurely or fail completely. • Transmission fails, suddenly drops into low gear, won't go into Reverse, delays engagement, or jumps out of gear when running or parked. • One can move the automatic transmission shift lever without applying brakes. • Several incidents where ignition was turned and vehicle went into Reverse at full throttle, although transmission was set in Park. • ABS failure caused an accident. • Many complaints of front suspension-strut towers rusting then cracking at the weld seams; jig-positioning hole wasn't sealed at the factory. • Brakes activated by themselves while driving. • Prematurely warped rotors and worn-out pads cause excessive vibrations when stopping. • Seatbacks fall backward. • Rear windows fall out or shatter. • Power window and door lock failures. • Sliding door often opens while vehicle is underway or jams, trapping occupants. • Weak headlights. • Horn often doesn't work. • Several incidents where side windows exploded for no apparent reason. • Adults cannot sit in third-row seat without their heads smashing into the roof as the vehicle passes over bumps. **All models: 1996–2002**—Steering may emit a popping or ticking noise. **1998**—Engine overheating. • Right rear tail light caught fire. • Frequent replacement of the steering column and rack and pinion; in one incident, the steering wheel separated from the steering column. • Front suspension strut failure. • Many reports of defective liftgate gas shocks. • Many incidents reported of electrical short circuits and total electrical system failures. • Difficult to see through windshield in direct sunlight. • Defroster vent reflects onto the windshield, obscuring driver's vision. • Poor steering-wheel design blocks the view of instruments and indicators. • Rear-view mirror often falls off. • Horn hard to find on steering hub. **1999**—Instrument-panel fire. • Faulty speed sensors cause the automatic transmission to shift erratically and harshly. • A 5-year-old child was able to pull the shift lever out of Park and into Drive without engaging brakes. • Sudden tie-rod breakage, causing loss of vehicle control. • Chronic steering pump and rack failures. • Poor braking performance: brake pedal depressed to the floor with little or no effect; excessive vibrations or shuddering when braking. • Rusted-through front brake rotors and rear brake drums. • Power side windows fail to roll up. • Dash gauges all go dead intermittently. **2000**—Gas-tank rupture. • Engine camshaft failure. • Although the owner's manual says vehicle should have a transmission/brake interlock, the feature is lacking. • Cruise-control malfunctions. **2000–01**—Sudden loss of engine power, accompanied by fuel leakage from the engine compartment. • Emergency parking brake may not release because of premature corrosion. • Right front brake locks up while driving, causing the vehicle to suddenly turn 90 degrees to the right; same phenomenon when braking. • Transmission shift lever blocks the driver's right knee when braking. • Fifth-wheel assembly falls off while vehicle is underway. • Instruments are recessed too deep into the dash, making it hard to read the fuel gauge and speedometer, especially at night. **2001–02**—Engine camshafts may have an improperly machined oil groove. • Snow and water ingestion into rear brake drum. • Inaccurate fuel-tank gauge drops one-quarter to one-half while driving. • Faulty power seat adjuster. • Difficult to remove fuel cap (install a new seal); this free repair applies to the entire 2002 vehicle lineup. **2002**—Airbags deploy for no reason. • Middle rear seat belt unbuckles on its own. • Headlights come on and go off on their own. **2003**—Driver-side airbag deploys for no reason, injuring driver. • Fire ignites in the engine compartment while vehicle is idling with AC engaged. • Fuel-tank leak; not covered by previous recall. • Vehicle won't start:

> My 2003 Dodge Caravan will not start. Found the problem to be the ignition switch. The ignition switch destroyed the starter and relay and the ignition switch can only be purchased through the dealer.

• Exposed electrical wires under the front seats. • Frequent alternator replacement. • Lights and wipers suddenly shut off, despite new ignition switch and cluster module. • Engine Oil sensor light constantly comes on. • Transmission won't go into Reverse unless it is kept in Park for a few minutes. • Poor braking likely caused by warped rotors or a defective master cylinder. • Seat belts unlatch themselves; defective female clasp. • Steering locks up while driving. • Rack and pinion steering assembly and pump failures. • Steering wheel doesn't lock when the key is removed. • Early wearout of the tie-rod ends. • Missing suspension bolt causes the right side to collapse, and several reports of faulty front sway-bar link bushings. • Wiper blades stick together. • There is no key lock for the passenger-side door. **2004**—Fuel leakage while vehicle is parked. • Chronic stalling. • Airbag clock spring fails, causing cruise control to malfunction. • Seat belts don't latch properly. • Small pieces of fibreglass from the AC coil covering are blown out the dash. • Rusty rear brakes seize easily. **2005**—Stuck accelerator; loss of brakes. • Stuck throttle body. • Chronic stalling due to defective fuel-pump module. • Engine continually misfires. • 4-cylinder engine belts first squeal, then self-destruct. • Frequent transmission replacements. • Transmission won't go into Reverse; intermittently jumps out of gear. • Vehicle loses all power and steering while on the road. • Fluid leakage from power steering units will require the replacement of the rack and pinion steering assembly. • Front strut failure causes vehicle to go out of control. • Cold rain freezes the rear brake drum rock-solid. • Many complaints that the Airbag warning light is constantly lit due to a defective impact sensor:

> My airbag light is on all the time. I'm on my third sensor. For me, they last about six months before the problem returns. My mechanic says the airbag won't deploy if needed, others say it could deploy for no reason. The vehicle is beyond the original warranty and because the vehicle is beyond the original warranty, the dealer is not willing to cover the costs even though it is clearly a flaw with this vehicle. There is currently no recall that I am aware of.

• Chemical used in the preparation of the vehicle (Hexane) causes allergy flare-ups and respiratory distress for some. • Back window exploded while vehicle was being parked. • Inoperative sliding door remote control. • Power door locks often do not work. • When in gear, the rear sliding doors can't be opened. At first thought this seems like a good feature. However, if the vehicle is in an accident and remains in gear, how will passengers get out? • Overheated battery. • Headlight switch fails intermittently. • Tail light filled with water after a rainstorm; entire assembly had to be replaced. • Light cover panel falls off because excess heat melts the glue. • Invicta tires provide poor traction on wet roadways.

Secret Warranties/Internal Bulletins/Service Tips

All models/years: If pressed, Chrysler will replace the AC evaporator for free for up to seven years. Other AC component costs are negotiable. **All models: 1993–2002**—Paint delamination, peeling, or fading. • A rotten-egg odour coming from the exhaust may be the result of a malfunctioning catalytic converter, probably covered under the emissions warranty. **1995–98**—Possible causes of delayed transmission engagement (TSB #21-07-98). **1996–99**—A serpentine belt that slips off the idler pulley requires an upgraded bracket. • Upgraded engine head gasket. • Oil seepage from the cam position sensor. **1996–2000**—Strut tower corrosion. • Cruise control that won't hold the vehicle's speed when going uphill may have a faulty check valve. • Countermeasures detailed to correct a steering-column click or rattle. • Airbag warning light stays lit. **1996–2001**—AWD models must be equipped with identical tires; otherwise, the power transfer unit may self-destruct. • A suspension squawk or knock probably means the sway-bar link needs replacing under Chrysler's "goodwill" policy (5 years/100,000 km). **1996–2006**—Rusted, frozen rear brake drums:

REAR BRAKE DRUM FREEZING/WATER/SNOW INGESTION

BULLETIN NO.: 05-001-06 REV A   **DATE: SEPTEMBER 23, 2006**

This bulletin involves installing a revised rear drum brake support (backing) plate and possible replacement of the rear brake shoes and drums.

1996–2000 Town & Country/Caravan/Voyager; 1996-2000 Chrysler Voyager (International Markets); 2001–06 Town & Country/Voyager/Caravan

SYMPTOM/CONDITION: While driving through deep or blowing snow/water, the snow/water may enter the rear brake drums causing rust to develop on the rear brake drum and shoe friction surfaces. This condition can lead to temporary freezing of the rear brake linings to the drums. This symptom is experienced after the vehicle has been parked in below freezing temperatures long enough for the snow/water to freeze inside of the rear brake drums. When the parking brake has been applied the symptom is more likely to occur.

• Roof panel is wavy or has depressions. **1997–2000**—If the ignition key can't be turned or removed, TSB #23-23-00 proposes four possible corrections. **1997–2001**—Rear brake noise. **1998–2000**—Troubleshooting AC compressor failures. • Rusted out suspensions may cause vehicle to lose steering or suspension and go out of control. **2000**—Delayed shifts. **2000–01**—Poor starting. • Rear disc brake squeal. • AC compressor failure, loss of engine power when switching on the AC, serpentine belt chirping, and spark knocking can all be traced to a miscalibrated PCM. • No heat on front right side because of a defective blend air door. • AC compressor squeal. • Rear bench-seat rattle or groan. • Hood hinge rattle. • Inoperative overhead reading lamp and rear wiper. • Noisy roof rack and power-sliding door. **2001–02**—Engine surging at highway speeds. • Engine knocking. • Engine sag and hesitation caused by a faulty throttle position sensor (TPS). • Engine mount grinding or clicking. • Steering-wheel shudder; steering-column popping or ticking. • Poor rear AC performance. • AC leaks water onto passenger-side carpet. • Wind or water leaks at the rear quarter window. • High-pitched, belt-like squeal at high engine rpm. • Sliding door reverses direction. • Incorrect fuel-gauge indicator. • Loose tail light. • Flickering digital display. • Difficult to remove fuel cap (install a new seal); this free repair applies to all of the 2002 vehicle lineup. **2001–03**—Rear brake rubbing sound. • Oil filter leaks with 3.3L and 3.8L engines (confirmed in TSB #09-001-03):

> On February 25, 2003, my 2002 Grand Caravan lost almost all of its engine oil, which resulted in engine failure. At no time did the vehicle's warning sensors indicate any problem with the engine. The failure was the result of a leak in the filter gasket of the FE292 Mopar oil filter. Documentation from the oil filter manufacturer indicates that the oil filter gasket overhangs the inside diameter of the adapter head by .1 cm/side.

2001–04—AC water leaks. • Scratching noise from dash. • Front strut squeaking or squawking. **2001–05**—Rattle, knocking sound emanating from the front suspension (may require replacing the front sway bar bushings). • Low-speed steering shudder. **2001–06**—Water leaks under passenger-side carpet. • Tips on getting rid of musty odours in the interior. **2002**—Transmission slips in First or Reverse gear. • Airbags deploy for no reason. • Airbag warning light comes on randomly, and clock-spring defect disables the airbag. • Power-steering fluid leakage. • Middle rear seat belt unbuckles on its own. • Rear side vent window explodes while driving. • Headlights come on and go off on their own. • Noisy engine and transmission. **2002–03**—Sliding door or liftgate malfunctions. **2002–04**—Steering-column noise remedies. **2002–06**—Malfunctioning power liftgate. **2003**—Troubleshooting water leaks. • Three bulletins relating to automatic transmission malfunctions: delayed gear engagement, harsh 4–3 downshift, and excessive vibration and transfer gear whine. **2003–05**—Crack, split and/or water leak in the upper body-seam sealer at the B- or C-pillar. **2004**—Rough idle, hesitation, and hard starts. • Accessory drivebelt chirping. • Front suspension rattling. **2004–05**—Warm engine rough idle. • Transmission ticking. **2005**—Engine squeak under light throttle. • Inoperative steering wheel tilt. • Campaign for the free replacement of the rear AC heater tube if it is corroded; another campaign will replace at no charge the underbody heater hose. • Road debris damage to the AC condenser. • Brake vibration, pulsation. • Inaccurate speedometer. • Steering moan. **2005–06**—Rear quarter glass whistling. • Circular marks etched into the windshield. • Steering wheel rattling. • Third-row seat front leg may not retract. • Silencing a buzz/rattle coming from the rear quarter panel speaker area.

CARAVAN, VOYAGER, GRAND CARAVAN, GRAND VOYAGER, TOWN & COUNTRY PROFILE

	1997	1998	1999	2000	2001	2002	2003	2004	2005
Cost Price ($)									
Caravan	19,885	20,255	24,230	24,970	24,885	25,430	25,430	27,620	28,205
Grand Caravan	21,465	23,160	25,890	26,665	29,505	28,875	29,295	30,190	30,740
Town & Country	40,350	41,040	41,260	41,815	41,150	40,815	42,705	44,095	44,595
Used Values ($)									
Caravan ▲	2,500	3,500	4,000	4,500	5,500	7,500	9,500	10,000	14,000
Caravan ▼	2,200	3,000	3,500	4,000	4,500	6,500	8,000	8,500	12,500
Grand Caravan ▲	3,500	4,000	4,500	5,500	7,500	9,000	10,000	11,500	14,500
Grand Caravan ▼	3,000	3,500	4,000	5,000	6,000	8,000	9,000	10,500	13,000

| Town & Country ▲ | 5,000 | 6,000 | 6,500 | 7,500 | 9,000 | 11,000 | 15,000 | 19,000 | 24,000 |
Town & Country ▼	4,500	5,500	6,000	6,500	8,000	10,000	13,000	17,000	22,500
Reliability	1	2	2	2	2	3	3	3	3
Crash Safety (F)									
Caravan	4	3	—	4	4	4	4	4	4
Grand Caravan	3	3	4	4	4	4	4	4	—
Town & Country	4	3	—	—	—	—	4	4	4
Town & Country LX	3	3	4	4	4	4	4	4	—
Side									
Caravan	—	—	5	5	4	4	4	4	4
Grand Caravan	—	—	5	5	4	5	5	5	—
Town & Country LX	—	—	5	5	4	5	5	4	4
Offset (Grand Caravan)	2	2	2	2	1	3	3	3	3
Town & Country	2	2	2	2	1	3	3	3	3
Head Restraints (F)									
Town & Country	1	—	1	—	3	3	3	1	1
Town & Country LX	1	—	1	—	2	2	2	—	—
Rollover Resistance	—	—	—	—	3	3	3	—	—

Note: Voyager and Grand Voyager prices and ratings are almost identical to those of the Caravan and Grand Caravan.

PT CRUISER ★ ★ ★ ★

RATING: Above Average (2001–06). This mini-minivan has defied all of the odds and shown you can make a silk purse out of a sow's ear—or a reliable, good-quality car out of Neon parts. An improved powertrain and more refined components make a big difference in the Cruiser's rating. Nevertheless, despite its hot-rod flair, this Neon spin-off's popularity is waning. Similar hard times have hit other "nostalgia" cars such as the VW New Beetle and the resurrected Ford Thunderbird; only the Mini Cooper has defied the trend and remained quite popular. **"Real" city/highway fuel economy:** 9.8/7.5 L/100 km with a manual transmission or 11.0/8.1 L/100 km with an automatic. *Turbo:* 10.4/7.9 L/100 km with a manual tranny or 11.4/8.1 L/100 km with an automatic. **Maintenance/Repair costs:** Average until the 5-year mark, when first-year glitches and the warranty's expiration will likely hike maintenance and repair costs—another reason to buy a supplementary powertrain warranty or to choose a 2002 or later version protected by Chrysler's 7-year warranty. **Parts:** Reasonably priced, since many parts come from Neon's generic-parts bin. Body parts are another matter: Expect long delays and high costs. **Extended warranty:** A toss-up if the original 7-year warranty has expired. **Best alternatives:** Try Mazda's MPV minivan, the VW Jetta Wagon, or the Subaru Legacy Outback Limited. Sport-utilities worth considering are the Ford Escape, GM Tracker, Honda CR-V EX, Hyundai Santa Fe or Tucson, Jeep Liberty, Mazda Tribute, Subaru Forester, and Suzuki Grand Vitara. GM's Astro or Safari will do in a pinch if rear-drive brawn is needed. **Online help:** *www.ptcruiser.org,* *www.ptcruiserlinks.com*, *www.datatown.com/chrysler*, *www.wam.umd.edu/~gluckman/ Chrysler/index.html* (The Chrysler Products' Problem Web Page), *www.daimler chryslervehicleproblems.com* (The Truth Behind Chrysler), and *www.autosafety.org/ autodefects.html.*

Strengths and Weaknesses

Cobbled together with Neon parts and engineering, the PT Cruiser is essentially a fuel- and space-efficient small hatchback minivan. It's noted for excellent fuel economy (regular fuel), nimble handling around town, good braking, lots of inte-

PT Cruisers are mini-minivans that play the nostalgia card.

rior space, easy access, a versatile cargo area, many thoughtful interior amenities, slow depreciation, and unforgettable hot-rod styling.

Forget about hot-rod power with the base engine, though. The 150-hp 2.4L 4-cylinder powerplant is not very smooth running and, when matched with the automatic transmission, struggles when going uphill or merging with freeway traffic. This requires frequent downshifting and lots of patience—accelerating to 100 km/h takes

about 9 seconds. Costlier turbocharged models will give you plenty of power, but you risk some steep repair bills. The automatic transmission doesn't have much low-end torque either, forcing early kickdown shifting and deft manipulation of the accelerator pedal. High-speed handling is competent but not impressive; hard cornering produces an unsteady, wobbly ride because of the car's height. Count on a firm ride with lots of engine, wind, and road noise in the cabin area. ABS braking is acceptable—when the system functions as it should.

VEHICLE HISTORY: 2002—A CD player and underseat storage bin. **2003**—A new 215-hp turbocharged GT and 17-inch wheels. **2004**—A second optional turbo is unveiled with 40 fewer horses (180) than the 220-hp GT.

Reliability has been surprisingly good so far, although there have been some drivetrain complaints that include faulty valve cover gaskets causing oil burning, and automatic transmission failures and erratic shifting (forcing the drivetrain to gear down to "limp mode") caused by faulty powertrain control modules:

> I have had my transmission go out twice now. The first time the whole tranny had to be replaced, second time it just lost all its fluid. The 41TE transmission is one of the worst transmissions ever made. Go to any search engine and type in 41TE and all the websites talking about the problems with the tranny will come up. DC has known of the problems since 1989 and doesn't care.

Writes another owner of a 2001 PT Cruiser:

> Transmission control unit went out on the freeway in stop-and-go traffic. Tranny went
> into failsafe (Second gear) so I drove it to the dealership for repairs. Took one day
> (they had the part in stock). Two days later, my wife's Dodge Caravan had the same
> part go out on her.

Premature failure of the power-steering pump and the steering unit are also frequent problems that can result in costly repairs once the warranty expires.

Other owner complaints read like an anthology of common Chrysler defects: annoying wind noise when driving with the rear window or sunroof open, drivetrain whine, moisture between the clearcoat and paint that turns the hood a chalky colour, and water leaks through the passenger-side window.

Safety Summary

All models: 2001—Some side wind instability. • Tall drivers beware: The windshield is uncomfortably close, and its styling makes it difficult to see overhead traffic lights. • The three small and recessed instrument pods are difficult to read in the daylight. • Wide pillars obstruct one's view. • When parked, transmission slipped out of gear and vehicle rolled down driveway in one incident. • Hot exhaust may melt the rear bumper. • Oil blows through tailpipe. • Engine suddenly shuts down when vehicle passes through a large puddle. • Sudden loss of all electrical power. • Chronic stalling caused by a faulty ignition coil. • Defective powertrain control module (PCM). • Steering wheel loosens on its shaft. • Excessive vibration caused by out-of-round tires or a loose suspension. • Head restraints won't stay in position; they tend to drift up. • Headlights flicker from bright to dim. • Low-beam headlight may suddenly go out. • Only part of the headlight beam illuminates the roadway. **2002**—Sudden, unintended acceleration. • Gas pedal goes to the floor with no acceleration. • Airbags deploy for no reason. • Suddenly shifts into First gear while cruising. • Sudden brake lock-up. • Headrests are too high and block vision. • Optima battery leaks acid. • White powder leaks from airbag. • Hard-to-read speedometer. **2002–05:** Airbags fail to deploy:

> Vehicle was in an accident. It flipped into a phone pole, upon impact the air bags
> failed to deploy, killing the driver.

2003—Chronic engine overheating. • In one incident, sudden front axle/bearing seizure threw car out of control and caused $7,000 damage to the drivetrain. • Other automatic transmission failures while car is underway. • Premature failure of the clutch assembly. • Headlights flicker when braking. • Sudden, unintended acceleration while stopped at a traffic light or when braking. • Self-activating door locks and seat heater. • Goodyear Eagle tire sidewall blows out. **2004**—Electrical fires. • Check Engine light stays lit. • Vehicle is prone to stalling. • Front axle breaks while vehicle is underway. • Premature failure of the manual transmission's clutch and bearing. • Steering locks up. • Severe vibration at high speeds. • Doors lock and unlock on their own. • Electrical short causes all dash lights and gauges to cease functioning. • Dash gauges are not adequately lit. **2005**—Stalling complaints continue:

The car randomly stalls or dies when approaching a stop. Also, did this when turning a sharp corner. The car is in the shop now for this problem. Mechanic does not know what is wrong, but has had the same problem. Chrysler knows about this problem, but they do not have a fix for this problem. Other cars of the same year and make are having the same problem; also, some newer models are having the same problems according to the dealers that [the] caller spoke too.

• Front axle breaks while vehicle is underway. • All instrument panel functions shut down. • Power windows can strangle a child due to the location of the button:

We were parked in a parking lot with the car running talking to another group when my 6 year old stuck her head out the window to join the discussion. When she did, she accidentally kicked the power window button with her foot. The button was located near the floor in the backseat on the middle console. She rolled the window up on her own head and was stuck in the window. She only lived through the event because 1) her head was tilted at the time so the window rolled up on the side of her neck and not on her trachea; and 2) her 8 year old sister in the back seat with her heard her screams and got her foot off the button and rolled the window back down. It was terrifying and painful and totally preventable. The button should be in a different place where it cannot be kicked or bumped so easily, and there should be a mechanism that allows the window to roll back down if it meets resistance.

• Steering stiffens; in one incident, caused vehicle to hit a pole. • Electrical shorts cause engine and dash lights to shut off. • Instrument panel is hard to read. • Sunlight reflects off the silver-painted airbag, blinding the driver. • Doors lock by themselves after the vehicle has been washed.

Secret Warranties/Internal Bulletins/Service Tips

All models: 2001—Hard starting caused by a faulty fuel-pump module. • Hard starting in cold weather because of the 5-volt regulator failure in the SBEC PCM. • A faulty transmission control module (TCM) may cause harsh shifting. • MIL comes on because of a faulty TCM harness connector or a defective evaporator purge flow monitor. • Poor acceleration and spark knock. • Because of a delamination problem, the accessory drivebelt for the power-steering pump and AC compressor may need replacement. • Left or right floor latch on rear seat won't release. • Fuel gauge won't indicate full. • Missing or loose roof luggage rack stanchion. • Airbag pads fall off. • Airbag rattles. • Ticking noise caused by faulty rear body exhauster. • Discoloured B- and C-pillar door appliqués. • Wind buffeting with the windows and/or sunroof open or partially open. • The front door water dam may contact the speaker and create a buzzing or humming noise. **2001–02**—Highway speed surge. **2001–03**—Alarm sounds for no reason. • Transmission slips in Reverse or First gears. • High-speed engine surging. **2001–06**—Moisture accumulation in headlights. **2002–03**—Steering-column clicking. **2003**—Turbo engine hesitation, loss of boost, and screeching. • Delayed gear engagement. • Harsh 4–3 downshifts. • Rear windshield-washer nozzle leak. • Warning lights come on for no reason. • Warped rear bumper. **2005–06**—Driveability improvements.

PT CRUISER PROFILE

	2001	2002	2003	2004	2005
Cost Price ($)					
Base	23,665	23,850	22,500	24,360	21,270
Limited	27,180	27,305	27,420	28,800	26,755
Turbo	—	—	27,700	31,350	31,665
Used Values ($)					
Base ▲	6,500	7,500	9,000	10,000	11,500
Base ▼	5,000	6,500	7,500	9,000	10,000
Limited ▲	7,500	9,000	10,000	11,000	13,500
Limited ▼	6000	8,000	9,000	10,000	12,000
Turbo ▲	—	—	11,000	13,000	15,500
Turbo ▼	—	—	9,500	12,000	14,000
Reliability	4	4	4	4	4
Crash Safety (F)	2	4	4	4	4
Side	4	4	4	—	—
Head Restraints	5	5	5	5	—
Rollover Resistance	4	4	4	—	—

Ford

FREESTAR, WINDSTAR ★ ★

RATING: *Freestar:* Below Average (2004–06). Freestar is a warmed-over Windstar with its own serious quality control problems. Windstars have similar transmission, brake, and AC failures to the Chrysler and GM competition, and their engines aren't very reliable. *Windstar:* Not Recommended (1995–2003). Infamous for atrocious quality control, stonewalled owner complaints, and life-threatening defects. **"Real" city/highway fuel economy:** 11.0/7.1 L/100 km. Owners report fuel savings may undershoot this estimate by at least 15 percent. **Maintenance/ Repair costs:** Average while under warranty; outrageously higher than average thereafter, primarily because powertrain breakdowns aren't covered by warranty or are insufficiently covered by parsimonious "goodwill" gestures. **Parts:** Reasonably priced parts are easy to find. Independent suppliers are lured by attractive profits sustained by parts that apparently have high failure rates, such as automatic transmissions, brake master cylinders, and speedometers. Digital speedometers are often defective and can cost almost $1,000 to repair. **Extended warranty:** Definitely, and don't leave home without it. A Saint Christopher medallion would also help. **Best alternatives:** You still can't beat the Japanese for minivan reliability and performance. Honda's Odyssey and the 2003 or earlier Toyota Sienna are the best choices if you don't mind spending a few thousand dollars more. You can cut costs and get acceptable reliability from recent Mazda MPVs and GM's Astro or Safari. Some full-sized GM (Chevy Van and Vandura) or Chrysler rear-drive cargo vans might be more affordable and practical buys. Even an older Ford Aerostar rear-drive minivan may fit the bill if the automatic transmission, electrical system, and brakes check out okay. **Online help:** *www.tgrigsby. com/views/ford.htm* (The Anti-Ford Page), *ca.geocities.com/windstarwoes* (1996 Windstar Head Gasket Issues), and *www.autosafety.org/autodefects.html.*

Strengths and Weaknesses

Ford can call it the Windstar or the Freestar; the fact remains that owners call it garbage.

Sure, the Windstar combines an impressive five-star crash safety rating, plenty of raw power, an exceptional ride, and impressive cargo capacity. But these minivans have failure-prone engines, self-destructing automatic transmissions, "do I feel lucky?" brakes, and unreliable electrical systems. Particularly scary is Ford's admission that Windstar's suspension includes poor-quality coil springs that frequently break, blow out the front tire, and make the minivan uncontrollable. As solace, Ford says it will pay for coil breakage up to 10 years on vehicles registered in rust-prone regions.

And, as another counterpoint to Ford's Windstar crashworthiness boasting, there's a frightening archive of Windstar safety-related failures compiled by the U.S. Department of Transportation's NHTSA. Besides the many coil-spring failures already noted (these have affected almost all of Ford's vehicles for practically a decade), owners report sudden acceleration, stalling, steering loss, exploding windows, horn failures, wheels falling off, sliding doors that open and close on their own, and vehicles rolling away while parked.

Other safety-related deficiencies include the lack of head restraints for all seats on early Windstars and a digital dash that's often confusing, failure-prone, and expensive to replace. Optional adjustable pedals help protect drivers from airbag injuries. Be careful, though; some drivers have found that these pedals are set too close together and seem loose. Drivers must also contend with mediocre handling, restricted side and rear visibility, and an abundance of clunks, rattles, and wind and road noise.

VEHICLE HISTORY: 1996—There are 45 more horses added to the 3.8L engine (200); a smaller 3.0L V6 powers the GL; and seat belts have been upgraded. A tilt-slide driver-side seat improves rear-seat access. **1998**—A wider driver-side door, easier rear-seat access, and new front styling. **1999**—A bit more interior space, and the third-row bench gets built-in rollers. Improved steering and brakes are compromised by rear drums. An anti-theft system, ABS, new side panels, a new liftgate, larger headlights and tail lights, and a revised instrument panel. **2001**—The base

3.0L V6 is gone; the Windstar gets an upgraded automatic transmission, a low-tire-pressure warning system, "smart" airbags, new airbag sensors, and a slight restyling. **2002**—Dual sliding doors. **2003**—An optional anti-skid system. **2004**—Freestar arrives and flops.

Freestar: Too little, too late

In 2004, the Windstar was reincarnated and renamed the Freestar. Sales almost immediately nosedived about 22 percent from the Windstar's poor 2003 sales figures as shoppers saw through the masquerade and fled.

Built on a modified Taurus platform, Freestar gives you the same uninspired, though predictable, carlike handling characteristics of Ford's mid-size family sedans. You'll encounter many of the horrific engine, automatic transmission, electrical, suspension, and brake system problems experienced by Taurus and Sable owners.

Freestar does feature some upgrades in safety, interior design, steering, ride, and performance, but it still lags far behind the Japanese competition for overall performance and dependability. Entry-level LX models come with a 200-hp 3.9L V6 based on the Windstar's 3.8L engine. Uplevel SE and top-line limited models get a new 201-hp 4.2L V6, also derived from the 3.8L. Freestar comes with larger four-wheel disc brakes and an optional "safety canopy" side curtain airbag system that offers protection in side-impact collisions and rollovers for all three rows of seating. There's also better access to the third-row seat, which folds flat into the floor.

Engine and transmission failures

Engine and transmission failures are commonplace. The 3.0L engine is overwhelmed by the Windstar's heft and struggles to keep up, but opting for the 3.8L V6 may get you into worse trouble. Even when it's running properly, the 3.8L knocks loudly when under load and pings at other times. Far more serious is the high failure rate of 3.8L engine head gaskets shortly after the 60,000 km mark. Owners may have to pay from $1,000 to $3,000 for an engine rebuild, depending upon how much the engine has overheated. Transmission repairs seldom cost less than $3,000.

Early warning signs are few and benign: The engine may lose some power or over-heat, and the transmission pauses before downshifting or shifts roughly into a higher gear. Owners may also hear a transmission whining or groaning sound accompanied by driveline vibrations. There are no other prior warnings before the transmission breaks down completely and the minivan comes to a sudden banging, clanging halt:

> Phil, I just want to thank you for saving us at least $1,500. The transmission in our '98 Windstar went bang with only 47,300 miles [75,700 kilometres]. After reading about Ford's goodwill adjustment, we were told by our local Ford dealer that owner

participation would be $495. We received a new rebuilt Ford unit installed. Believe
it or not, I am a fairly good mechanic myself and this came with no warning! We even
serviced the transmission at 42,000 miles [67,200 kilometres] and found no debris
or evidence of a problem.

Ford admits automatic transmission glitches may afflict its 2001 Taurus, Sable, Windstar, and Continental. In a March 2001 Special Service Instruction (SSI) #01T01, Ford authorized its dealers to replace all defective transaxles listed in its TSB, which describes the defect in the following manner:

> The driver may initially experience a transaxle "slip" or "Neutral" condition during a 2–3 shift event. Extended driving may result in loss of Third gear function and ultimately loss of Second gear function. The driver will still be able to operate the vehicle, but at a reduced level of performance.

Ford's memo states that owners weren't to be notified of the potential problem (they obviously didn't count on *Lemon-Aid* getting a copy of their memo).

Brakes are another Windstar worry. They aren't reliable, and calipers, rotors, and the master cylinder often need replacing. Other frequent Windstar problems concern no-starts and chronic stalling, believed to be caused by a faulty fuel pump or powertrain control module (PCM); electrical system power-steering failures; hard steering at slow speeds; excessive steering-wheel vibrations; sudden tire-tread separation and premature tread wear; advanced coil-spring corrosion, leading to spring collapse and puncturing of the front tire (only 1997–98 models were recalled); rear shock failures at 110 km/h; left-side axle breakage while underway; exploding rear windshields; power-sliding door malfunctions; and failure-prone digital speedometers that are horrendously expensive to replace. There have also been many complaints concerning faulty computer modules, engine oil leaks, AC failures, and the early replacement of engine camshafts, tie-rods, and brake rotors and calipers.

Getting compensation

Since 1997, I've lobbied Ford to stop playing *Let's Make a Deal* with its customers and set up a formal 7-year/160,000 km engine and transmission warranty similar to its 1994–95 model 3.8L engine extended warranty and emission warranty guidelines. I warned the company that failure to protect owners would result in huge sales losses by Ford as the word spread that its vehicles are lemons.

In the ensuing three years, under the capable leadership of Ms. Bobbie Gaunt, president of Ford Canada, hundreds of engine and transmission claims were amicably settled using my suggested benchmark.

But it didn't last. Ford USA got wind of it and squashed the Canadian initiative. Interestingly, the three top Ford Canada executives who pleaded the Canadian case have since left the company. And Jac Nasser, Ford USA's CEO who rejected additional protection for owners, was fired shortly thereafter when he tried a similar move with Firestone claimants. (No, Nasser isn't one of my favourite auto executives.)

As I predicted, Ford's sales have plummeted, small claims court judgments are pummelling the company, and owners are vowing to never again buy any Ford product:

> Hi Phil: I just wanted to let you know that I did have to go to small claims court to nudge Ford into action. In pretrial settlement proceedings, the Ford representative at first gave me an offer of $980 for my troubles. I countered with the actual cost of $2,190 to replace my '96 Windstar's transmission. He did not like that idea, and we went back into the court setting. After instruction from the judge, I began to copy my 200+ pages (for the judge as evidence) of documentation for why this is a recurring problem with Ford transmissions (thank you, by the way, for all the great info).
>
> I think it made him a little scared, so I asked if he would settle for $1,600 (a middle ground of our original proposals) to which he accepted. My transmission costs were $2,190, so I basically paid about $600 for a new transmission (not a Ford replacement, either).
>
> Anyway, I figured a guaranteed $1,600 was better than not knowing what would happen in court. Thanks for your help!

Ford's denial of owner claims has been blasted in small claims court judgments across Canada over the past few years. Judges have ruled that engines and transmissions (and power-sliding doors) must be reasonably durable long after the warranty expires, whether the vehicle was bought new or used, notwithstanding that it was repaired by an independent or that it had the same problem repaired earlier for free. The three most recent engine judgments supporting Ford owners are *Dufour v. Ford Canada Ltd, Schaffler v. Ford Motor Company Limited and Embrun Ford Sales Ltd.*, and *John R. Reid and Laurie M. McCall v. Ford Motor Company of Canada* (see Part Two).

Automatic transmission lawsuits have also been quite successful. They are often settled out of court because Ford frequently offers 50–75 percent refunds if the lawsuit is dropped. For one *Lemon-Aid* reader's tips on beating Ford, see pages 103–104.

Dangerous doors

We noted previously that the courts have slammed Ford for allowing dangerously defective sliding doors to go uncorrected year after year. Typical scenarios reported by owners include the following: a sliding door slammed shut on a child's head while the vehicle was parked on an incline; passengers are often pinned by the door; the door reopens as it is closing; the door often pops open while the vehicle is underway; a driver's finger was broken when closing a manual sliding door; and the handle is too close to the door jam, which is a hazard that has been reported on the Internet since 1999. Owners also report that the 2003 Windstar's automatic sliding door opens by itself, or the door will not power open, and the door lock assembly freezes:

> I am writing about our 2003 Ford Windstar. Our passenger automatic sliding door frequently pops open after it appears to have latched shut. It has opened by itself on three occasions while the van was in drive. Recently my three-year-old daughter almost fell out of the van headfirst onto concrete because the door popped back open as soon as it "latched" shut. The van has been in to repair this problem seven times without success. We first started having problems with both doors within the first 2 weeks of purchase. The times the door has popped back open are way too numerous to count.

•

> The door has opened [by] itself while the vehicle is in motion—very scary and dangerous for my children. This is a problem Ford has known about but have not been proactive about fixing (see Ford TSB article 03-6-8).

Mental distress (door failures)

In *Sharman v. Formula Ford Sales Limited, Ford Credit Limited, and Ford Motor Company of Canada Limited,* Ontario Superior Court of Justice (Oakville), No. 17419/02SR, 2003/10/07, Justice Sheppard awarded the owner of a 2000 Windstar $7,500 for mental distress resulting from the breach of the implied warranty of fitness plus $7,207 for breach of contract and breach of warranty. The problem—the Windstar's sliding door wasn't secure and leaked air and water after many attempts to repair it. Interestingly, the judge cited the *Wharton* decision, among other decisions, as support for his award for mental distress (see page 116).

 ## Safety Summary

All models: 1995–98—The following is a short summary of problems carried over year after year; I don't have the space to list the many other reported defects. Nevertheless, you can easily access NHTSA's website (see Appendix III) for the details of thousands of other Windstar complaints. • Severe injuries caused by airbag deployment. • Control arm and inner tie-rod failures cause the wheel to fall off. • Sudden steering lock-up or loss of steering ability. • Engine head gasket failures. • Loose or missing front brake bolts could cause the wheels to lock up or the vehicle to lose control. • Chronic ABS failures. • Transmission and axle separation. • Faulty fuel pump, sensor, and gauge. • Built-in child safety seat is easy to get out of, but the securing seat belts are too tight; in one incident, a child was almost strangled. • Faulty rear liftgate latches; trunk lid can fall on one's head. **1995–99**—Airbag fails to deploy. • Frequent transmission failures, including noisy engagement, inability to engage Forward or Reverse, and slipping or jerking into gear. • Many reports that the vehicle jumps out of Park and rolls away when on an incline or slips into Reverse with the engine idling; in one incident, vehicle jumped into Reverse and pinned driver against tree (similar transmission problems have affected Ford vehicles for almost three decades). **1995–2000**—Horn button "sweet spot" is too small and takes too much pressure to activate; one owner says, "Horn doesn't work unless you hit it with a sledgehammer." • Chronic stalling caused by fuel-vapour lock or faulty fuel pump; engine shuts down when turning. • While parked, cruising, turning on the ignition, or applying brakes, vehicle suddenly accelerates. **1999**—Stuck accelerator causes unintended acceleration. • Check Engine light constantly comes on because of a faulty gas cap or over-sensitive warning system. • Sudden loss of power steering, chronic leakage of fluid, and early replacement of steering components such as the pump and hoses. • Excessive brake fade after successive stops. • When brake pedal is depressed, it sinks below the accelerator pedal level, causing the accelerator to be pressed as well—particularly annoying for drivers with large feet. • ABS module wire burns out. • Complete electrical failure during rainstorm. • Sliding door opens and closes on its own, sticks open or closed, or suddenly slams shut on a downgrade. • Door locks don't stay locked; in one incident, passenger-side door opened when turning, causing a passenger to fall out. • Rear defogger isn't operable (lower part of windshield isn't clear) in inclement weather when windshield wipers are activated. • Windshield wipers fail to clear windshield. • Water pours from dash onto front-passenger floor. • Floor cupholder trips passengers. • Large A-pillar (where windshield attaches to door) seriously impairs forward visibility, hiding pedestrians. • Seat belts aren't automatically retractable, as described in the owner's manual. • Two incidents where flames shot up out of fuel-tank filler spout when gassing up. **1999–2000**—Front passenger-side wheel falls off when turning; in one reported incident, dealer found that five lug nuts had broken in half. • Rear side windows, liftgate window, and windshield often explode suddenly. **2000**—Vehicle caught on fire while parked. • Sudden, unintended acceleration while stopped. • Sometimes cruise control won't engage or engages on its own. • One Ingersoll, Ontario, owner of a 2000 Windstar recounts the following harrowing experience:

> Last week, as my wife was running errands, the support arm that goes from the rear crossmember (not an axle anymore) up under the floor broke in half. The dealer replaced the whole rear end as it is one welded assembly. If she had been on the highway going 80 km/h she would probably have been in a bad accident.

• Driver heard a banging noise, and Windstar suddenly went into a tailspin; dealer blamed pins that "fell out of spindle." • Transmission jumped out of gear while on highway. • Many reports of premature transmission replacements. • Transmission lever can be shifted without depressing brake pedal (unsafe for children). • After several dealer visits, brakes still spongy, pedal goes to floor without braking, and emergency brake has almost no effect. • When braking, foot also contacts the accelerator pedal. • Emergency brake is inadequate to hold the vehicle. • Dealers acknowledge that brake master cylinders are problematic. • Joints aren't connected under quarter-wheel weld; one weld is missing and three aren't properly connected. • Passenger door opened when vehicle hit a pothole. • While underway, right-side sliding door opens on its own and won't close (see "mental distress" judgment on page 116). In one incident, when vehicle was parked on an incline, sliding door released and came crashing down on a child. • Hood suddenly flies up on the freeway. • Steering fails multiple times. • Steering wheel is noisy and hard to turn. • When the interior rear-view mirror is set for night vision, images become distorted and hard to see. • Second-row driver-side seat belt buckle won't latch. **2000–01**—Harsh 3–2 shifting when coasting then accelerating. • Transmission fluid leaks from the main control cover area. • Power steering whines, grunts, shudders, and lurches; leaks fluid. • Faulty self-activating wipers and door, trunk, and ignition locks. **2001**—Airbag may suddenly deploy when the engine is started. • Transmission shudder during 3–4 shifts. • Power-steering grunt or notchy feel when turning; leaks. • Drifting or pulling while driving. • Rear drum brakes drag or fail to release properly. • Fogging of the front and side windows. • Twisted seatback frame. **2002**—Sudden automatic transmission failure. • Back door won't open or close properly. • Both sliding doors won't retract. • Child can shift transmission without touching brake pedal. **2002–03**—Airbags fail to deploy. • Brake and gas pedals are mounted too close together. **2003**—Wheel suddenly breaks away. • Sudden, unintended acceleration when braking. • Engine surging. • Chronic stalling from blown fuel-pump fuses. • Coolant leak from the timing-cover gasket. • Advanced tracking system engages on its own, causing vehicle to shake violently. • Automatic transmission suddenly seizes. • Steering wheel locks up. • Interior windows are always fogged up because of inadequate defrosting. • Gas-pedal arm pivot causes the pedal to flip almost horizontally, exaggerating any pedal pressure. • Body seams not sealed; water intrudes into floor seat anchors. • Driver's seat poorly anchored. • Dashboard glare onto the windshield. • Check Tire warning light comes on for no reason. • Tire jack collapses. *Freestar:* **2004**—Sudden, unintended acceleration. • Loss of steering. • Airbag warning light stays on; airbags may not deploy. • A-frame drops out of the tie-rod collar. • Front axle suddenly breaks while underway. • Automatic transmission failure. • Left inner brake pad falls apart and locks up brake. • Sliding door closed on a child in one incident, causing slight injuries; in another incident it crushed an adult's leg:

> We just purchased a 2004 Ford Freestar. I am 67 and went to get out of the back door and the driver accidentally pushed the button to close the door. It crushed my leg, as there is no way to stop the door. There are no safety switches. Everyone in the car tried to help, and the door would not go back. This would have killed a child or my 89-year-old mother. There needs to be a recall. My husband has size 14 shoes, and when he tried to get out the same door, his knee almost hit the door closing button...and he was watching out for the problem.

• Thumb trimmed by seatback release mechanism:

> I was cleaning my 2005 Ford Freestar and pulled the lever that releases the back of the bench seat directly behind the drivers seat. The back of the seat came down so hard that it cut the end of my thumb off....

• Plastic running board broke, blocking sliding door operation and locking occupants inside the vehicle. • Headliner-mounted DVD screen blocks rear-view mirror.

Secret Warranties/Internal Bulletins/Service Tips

All models/years: An exhaust buzz or rattle may be caused by a loose catalyst or heat shield. • Sliding door malfunctions. • Buzzing noise in speakers caused by fuel pump. • A MIL lit for no reason may simply mean that the gas cap is loose. • If the power-sliding door won't close, replace the door controller; if it pops or disengages when fully closed, adjust the door and rear striker to reduce closing resistance. • Front wipers that operate when switched off need a revised multifunction switch (covered under service program and recall). • Engine oil mixed with coolant or loss of coolant signals the need for revised engine lower intake manifold side gaskets and/or front cover gaskets. Ford's benchmark for refunding repair costs for this problem: 7 years or 160,000 km. **All models: 1995–98**—Silencing instrument panel buzzing, rattling, squeaking, chirping, and ticking. • The front end accessory drive belt (FEAD) slips in wet weather, causing a reduction in steering power assist. • Water leakage onto carpet or headliner in rear cargo area is a factory-related defect covered in TSB #98-5-5. **1995–99**—Tips for correcting excessive noise, vibration, and harshness while driving; side-door wind noise; and windshield water leaks. **1995–2000**—Diagnostic tips on brake vibration, inspection, and friction material replacement. **1995–2002**—Silencing suspension noise. **1996–2003**—Tips on troubleshooting faulty automatic transmission torque converters. **1997–98**—A rattling or clunking noise coming from the front of the vehicle may be caused by a loose front tension strut bushing retainer. **1998**—Lack of AC cooling may be caused by refrigerant leak at the P-nut fitting. **1999–2003**—Inoperative rear window defroster. **2000–03**—Erratic automatic transmission fluid readings; leak at the dipstick tube. **2001**—Ford admits automatic transmission defects (slippage, delayed shifts) in Special Service Instruction #01T01. **2001–02**—Service tips for reports of premature engine failures. • Vacuum or air leaks in the intake manifold or engine system causing warning lights to illuminate. • Concerns with oil in the cooling system. • Engine cylinder heads that have been repaired may still leak coolant or oil from the gasket area. • Hard starts; rough running engines. • Shudder while in Reverse or during 3–4 shift. • Transmission fluid leakage. • Power-steering fluid leaks. • Brake roughness and pulsation. • Rear brake drum drag in cold weather. • Fogging of the front and side windows. • False low-tire warning. • Repeated heater core failures. • Troubleshooting malfunction indicator light. **2001–03**—Remedy for a slow-to-fill fuel tank. **2002**—Automatic transmission fluid leaking at the quick connect for the transmission cooler lines. • MIL comes on; vehicle shifts poorly or won't start. • Buzz, groan, or vibration when gear selector lever is in Park. • Some vehicles may run roughly on the highway or just after stopping. • Defective ignition-switch lock cylinders. • Anti-theft system operates on its own. • Battery may go dead after extended parking time. • Sliding doors rattle and squeak. • Steering system whistle/whine. • Loose rear wiper arm. **2003**—Front-end grinding, popping noise when passing over bumps or making turns. • Airbag warning light stays lit. •

Inoperative rear window defroster. *Freestar:* **2004**—Transmission has no 1–2 upshift (TSB #04-15-12). • False activation of parking assist. • Bulletin No. 04-2-3, published 02/09/04, lists ways to find and fix the sliding doors' many failures. • Loose rear door trim. **2004–05**—Accelerated rear brake pad wear. • Front brake squeal or squawk. • Excessive vibration. • Faulty, inoperative power door and liftgate. **2004–06**—Seat belts are slow to retract.

FREESTAR, WINDSTAR PROFILE

	1997	1998	1999	2000	2001	2002	2003	2004	2005
Cost Price ($)									
Freestar/Base	—	—	—	—	—	—	—	27,295	27,995
SE	—	—	—	—	—	—	—	29,695	29,695
SEL	—	—	—	—	—	—	—	37,695	37,020
Windstar/Base	24,495	24,295	—	—	—	—	—	—	—
LX	28,995	28,995	28,195	25,995	26,750	25,995	26,195	—	—
SEL	—	—	36,195	36,195	33,190	33,685	37,015	—	—
Used Values ($)									
Freestar/Base ▲	—	—	—	—	—	—	—	10,500	12,500
Freestar/Base ▼	—	—	—	—	—	—	—	9,000	11,000
SE ▲	—	—	—	—	—	—	—	11,500	13,500
SE ▼	—	—	—	—	—	—	—	10,000	12,000
SEL ▲	—	—	—	—	—	—	—	14,000	17,500
SEL ▼	—	—	—	—	—	—	—	12,500	16,000
Windstar/Base ▲	2,000	2,500	3,000	—	—	—	—	—	—
Windstar/Base ▼	1,500	2,000	2,500	—	—	—	—	—	—
LX ▲	3,000	3,500	4,000	5,000	6,000	7,500	9,500	—	—
LX ▼	2,500	3,000	3,500	4,500	4,500	6,000	8,000	—	—
SEL ▲	—	—	5,000	5,500	6,500	8,500	11,000	—	—
SEL ▼	—	—	4,500	5,000	5,500	7,000	9,500	—	—
Reliability	1	1	1	2	2	2	3	3	3
Crash Safety (F)	5	5	5	5	5	5	5	5	5
Side	—	—	5	4	5	4	4	4	4
Offset	5	5	3	3	3	3	3	5	5
Head Restraints (F)	1	—	3	—	5	5	5	5	5
Rear	—	—	1	—	3	3	3	5	—
Rollover Resistance	—	—	—	—	4	4	4	4	4

Ford/Nissan

RATING: *Quest:* Below Average (2004–06). Even though it's larger, more powerful, and better-appointed than the old Villager, the 2004's redesign was badly done. Engineering goofs and poor-quality body and electrical components are everywhere. On top of that, Nissan servicing and warranty support has soured. *Villager and Quest:* Average (1997–2003); Below Average (1995–96); Not Recommended (1993–94). **"Real" city/highway fuel economy:** *3.0L:* 13.4/9.3 L/100 km. *3.3L:* 13.9/9.0 L/100 km. *3.5L:* 12.4/8.2 L/100 km. Owners report fuel savings may undershoot the above estimates by at least 20 percent if the vehicle is equipped with poorly performing Goodyear LS2 tires. **Maintenance/Repair costs:** Higher than average. Costs can be kept down by frequenting independent repair agencies, but the 2004–05 models are highly dealer dependent. **Parts:** Both Ford and Nissan dealers carry reasonably priced parts for early models. The exceptions to this rule are broken engine exhaust manifold studs (a frequent problem through 1996), AC, and electrical components. **Extended warranty:** A good idea. **Best alternatives:** Other minivans worth considering are the Chrysler Caravan and its off-shoots, Honda's Odyssey, and 2003 or earlier Toyota Siennas (Toyota's 2004 reworked model has quality bugs similar to the Quest's). **Online help:** *www.mycarstats.com/auto_complaints/MERCURY_complaints.asp* and *www.autosafety.org/autodefects.html.*

Strengths and Weaknesses

Smaller and more carlike than most minivans, the pre-2004 Villager and Quest are sized comfortably between the regular and extended Chrysler minivans. These minivans' strongest assets are a 170-hp 3.3L V6 engine that gives them carlike handling, ride, and cornering; modular seating; and reliable mechanical components. Nissan borrowed the powertrain, suspension, and steering assembly from the Maxima, mixed in some creative sheet metal, and left the job of outfitting the sound system, climate control, dashboard, steering column, and wheels to Ford.

These fuel-thirsty minivans are quite heavy, though, and the 3.0L and 3.3L engines have to go all out to carry the extra weight. GM's 2.8L engines produce more torque, and the Villager/Quest powertrain set-up trails the Odyssey in acceleration and passing. Other minuses: The interior looks cheap, the control layout can be a bit confusing, suspension is too soft, and rear-seat access can be difficult.

VEHICLE HISTORY: 1996—Annoying motorized shoulder belts were dropped, a passenger-side airbag was added, and the dash and exterior were slightly restyled. **1999**—The Pathfinder's 3.3L V6 debuts, giving the Villager and Quest an additional 19 horses. *Villager:* **1999**—The Villager gains a fourth door, more interior room, a revised instrument panel that's easier to reach, restyled front and rear ends, and improved shifting, acceleration, and braking. The suspension has been retuned to give a more carlike ride and handling, and the old climate control system has been ditched for a more sophisticated version with air filtration. Mercury's top-of-the-line model, the Nautica, is dropped. **2002**—The Villager's last year. *Quest:* **1999**—A larger platform, standard ABS brakes, a driver-side sliding rear door, upgraded headlights, and rear leaf springs. The second row of seats can be removed, and the third row is set on tracks. **2000**—An improved child safety seat anchoring system; an entertainment centre with a larger screen is standard on all Quest models; a stabilizer bar on the GLE. **2001**—A slightly restyled exterior and upgraded dashboard. **2002**—Restyled wheels. **2004**—Totally redesigned—and made less reliable. **2005**—A new base model called the 3.5 is added to the Nissan lineup.

1994–2003 problems

Most owner-reported problems involve excessive brake noise and premature brake wear, door lock malfunctions, interior noise, and driveline vibrations. There have also been many reports of engine exhaust manifold and crankshaft failures that cost up to $7,000 to repair. Other problems include electrical shorts; brake failures because of vibration, binding, or overheating; premature wear of the front discs, rotors, and pads; chronic stalling, possibly because of faulty fuel pumps or a shorted electrical system; and loose steering and veering at highway speeds. Other common problems include film buildup on windshield and interior glass; a sulfur smell from the exhaust system; poor AC performance or compressor failures accompanied by musty, mildew-type AC odours; and recurring fuel pump buzzing heard through the radio speakers.

Body integrity has been subpar and disappointing up to and including the 2006 models. Owners complain of doors opening and closing on their own and poorly fitted panels that produce a cacophony of wind noise, squeaks, and rattles as well as water leaks. Paint defects are legion, and there have been some reports of premature rusting on the inside sliding door track.

2004–06 Quest

A totally different minivan than its predecessor, the 2004–06 Quest is one of the largest and priciest minivans on the road. Based on the Altima/Murano platform, it offers a more powerful engine and all the standard high-tech safety, performance, and convenience features one could want. Its long wheelbase allows for the widest-opening sliding doors among front-drive minivans, rear-seat access is a breeze, and a capacious interior allows for flexible cargo and passenger configurations that can easily accommodate 4' × 8' objects with the liftgate closed. Standard fold-flat third-row seats and fold-to-the-floor centre-row seats allow owners to increase storage space without worrying about where to store the extra seats, although third-row headrests must be removed before the seats can be folded away.

Although it feels a bit heavy in the city, the revamped Quest is still very carlike when it's driven on the highway. Ride and handling are enhanced by a new four-wheel independent suspension, front and rear stabilizer bars, and upgraded anti-lock brakes.

Safety features include standard head curtain supplemental airbags for outboard passengers in all three rows, supplemental front-seat side-impact airbags, standard traction control, and ABS brakes with brake assist.

2004–06 problems

Fit and finish deficiencies are still the number one complaint and have become even more common than in previous models:

> The windows go down completely on their own with vehicle turned off. The passenger sliding door opens randomly on its own. The tire alarm goes off when tire pressure is fine. Air vents fly off and lights fall out of the ceiling.

In its Customer Satisfaction Initiative Bulletin #BT04-014, Nissan pledged to fix a number of mechanical and body defects for free to eliminate squeaks and rattles and to improve window and door operation. Skyroof leaks and dangerous sliding doors are quite common. Owners also complain of malfunctioning engines, transmissions, and brakes. Goodyear tires are notorious for premature wear and poor performance on these minivans, as this complaint logged by *www.tirerack.com* (The Tire Rack) confirms:

> This tire is the worst out there. For the amount they cost they should be great.... Goodyear can charge...[top dollar] for this crap cause they think that its the only tire that Quest owners could put on the vehicles. Wrong again. I'm going with the Kumno Ecsta Asx 235/60/16 price[d] $66 on Tire Rack. Talked with various tire pros and they told me that this size is no problem for the Quest. Bye, bye GOODYEAR.

Safety Summary

All models: 1993–2003—Airbags fail to deploy. • Inadvertent airbag deployment. • Vehicle suddenly accelerates forward. • Sudden stalling caused by faulty fuel pump. • Steering wander and excessive vibration. • Chronic ABS failures; brake pads and rotors need replacing every 5,000 km. • Brake failures (extended stopping distance, noisy when applied). • Brake and accelerator pedals are the same height, so driver's foot can easily slip and step on both at the same time. • Cycling or self-activating front door lock failures; occupants have been trapped in their vehicles. **1997–99**—Gas fumes leak into the interior. • Gas pedal sticks. **2000**—Vehicle tends to lurch forward when the AC is first engaged. • Weak tailgate hydraulic cylinders. • Instrument panel's white face is hard to read during daylight hours. **2000–01**—Missing seat belt latch plate stopper button. • Shift indicator may be misaligned because the shift-lock cable plate is broken. • 22-month-old child was able to pull the clasp apart on integrated child safety seat. • Seat belts don't retract properly. • Rear window on liftgate door shattered for unknown reason (replaced under warranty). • Power-steering fluid leakage caused by O-ring at rack gear splitting. **2002**—Stuck accelerator pedal. • Excessive vibration at highway speeds. • Leaking front and rear struts degrade handling. • Steering wheel may be off-centre to the left. **2004**—Sudden, unintended acceleration. • Sliding door traps occupants, or continually pops open. • Reflection of dash onto windshield. • Automatic transmission won't downshift. • Dome light fuse blows continually. • Faulty tire valve stems. • Excessive tire wear (Goodyear Eagle LS2 224/60/17), and it may be hard to find replacement tires (see *www.tirerack.com/tires/surveyresults/index.jsp*):

> If you go to the optional OEM size 225/65/16 you will worsen the already questionable fuel efficiency of this Quest vehicle line. Goodyear laughs at customers like me when bringing my "sooner than expected" tire wear out conditions and they openly admit that they have no idea why Nissan required these Eagle LS2 to be OEM equipment.

Secret Warranties/Internal Bulletins/Service Tips

All models: 1993–2002—Paint delamination, peeling, or fading. • Repeat heater core failures are a common Ford problem for over a decade. **1996–2002**—Power door locks that intermittently self-activate are a common occurrence that's covered in TSB #98-22-5. **1999–2004**—Troubleshooting abnormal shifting. • Cooling system leaks/overheating. • Side windows pop open. **2004**—No-start, hard start remedies. • Silencing a ticking engine/exhaust noise. • Tips on correcting an abnormal shifting of the automatic transmission. • Harsh 1–2 shifts. • AC blows out warm air from floor vents. • Guidelines on troubleshooting brake complaints. **2004–05**—Low power, stays in Third gear. • Insufficient AC cooling. • Sliding door squeaks and rattles and is hard to latch. **2004–06**—Skyroof water leaks.

VILLAGER, QUEST PROFILE

	1997	1998	1999	2000	2001	2002	2004	2005
Cost Price ($)								
Villager GS	24,295	24,595	24,595	24,595	—	—	—	—
Villager LS	29,195	29,495	29,495	29,495	—	—	—	—
Quest GXE/S	30,898	30,898	27,798	30,498	30,498	30,698	32,900	31,698
Quest GXE/SL	25,598	25,598	32,498	33,498	35,198	35,198	36,600	36,100
Used Values ($)								
Villager GS ▲	3,500	4,000	5,000	6,000	—	—	—	—
Villager GS ▼	3,000	3,500	4,500	5,000	—	—	—	—
Villager LS ▲	4,500	5,500	6,000	7,000	—	—	—	—
Villager LS ▼	4,000	4,500	5,500	6,000	—	—	—	—
Quest GXE/S ▲	4,000	5,000	6,000	7,000	9,000	12,000	18,000	22,000
Quest GXE/S ▼	3,500	4,500	5,000	6,000	7,500	10,500	16,000	20,000
Quest XE/SL ▲	5,000	6,000	6,500	8,500	10,500	13,500	15,000	24,000
Quest XE/SL ▼	4,000	5,500	6,000	7,500	9,500	12,500	14,000	22,000

Reliability	3	3	3	3	3	3	2	2
Crash Safety (F)	4	4	—	—	4	5	5	5
Side	—	—	—	—	5	5	5	5
Offset	2	2	1	1	1	1	5	5
Head Restraints (F)	2	2	—	2	—	1	1	2
Rear	2	2	—	1	—	1	1	2
Rollover Resistance	—	—	—	—	—	4	4	4

General Motors

ASTRO, SAFARI ★★★

RATING: Average (1996–2005); Below Average (1985–95). These run-of-the-mill rear-drive minivans are beginning to look quite good when compared to the problem-plagued GM and Ford front-drive minivans and the overpriced Asian competition. They have fewer safety-related problems reported to the government, are easy to repair, and cost little to acquire. Stay away from the unreliable all-wheel-drive models; they're expensive to repair and not very durable. **"Real" city/highway fuel economy:** *Cargo:* 15.0/10.7 L/100 km. *Base:* 16.6/11.9 L/100 km. *AWD:* 17.3/12.6 L/100 km. Owners report fuel savings may undershoot the above estimates by more than 20 percent (especially in regard to the AWD model). **Maintenance/Repair costs:** Average. Any garage can repair these rear-drive minivans. **Parts:** Good supply of cheap parts. A large contingent of independent parts suppliers keeps repair costs down. Parts are less expensive than they are for other vehicles in this class. **Extended warranty:** A powertrain-only warranty is all you'll need. Most repairs will be surprisingly cheap, but one rebuilt automatic transmission can set you back $3,000. **Best alternatives:** The classified ads are jam-packed with sellers wanting to unload their Astros and Safaris simply because their vehicles have high mileage or burn too much fuel, or because their businesses need larger vans. Whatever the reason, you can find some real bargains if you're patient. Otherwise, Chrysler's minivans should be your first choice; you will pay about $10,000 for a 3-year-old model and will likely have some of the original warranty left. Nissan and Toyota minivans have better handling and are more reliable and economical people-movers, but they are way over-priced and lack the Astro's considerable grunt, essential for cargo hauling and trailer towing. **Online help:** *www.autosafety.org/autodefects.html.*

Strengths and Weaknesses

More a utility truck than a comfortable minivan, these boxy rear-drives are built on a reworked S-10 pickup chassis. As such, they offer uninspiring handling, average-quality mechanical and body components, and relatively high fuel consumption. Both the Astro and Safari come in a choice of either cargo or passenger vans. The cargo van is used either commercially or as an inexpensive starting point for a fully customized vehicle. The Safari is identical to the Astro, except for a slightly higher base price.

With the right options, the Astro and Safari have the advantage of being versatile cargo-haulers when equipped with heavy-duty suspensions. In fact, Astro's 2,500 kg (5,500 lb.) trailer-towing capability is 900 kg (2,000 lb.) more than that of the front-drive Venture. The base 4.3L V6 gives acceptable acceleration, but the High Output variant of the same engine (first available in the 1991 model) is a far better choice, particularly when it's mated to a manual gearbox. The full-time AWD versions aren't very refined, have a high failure rate, and are expensive to diagnose and repair.

VEHICLE HISTORY: 1998—An improved automatic transmission. **1999**—A reworked AWD system doesn't improve reliability. **2000**—Only seven- and eight-passenger models available; engine made quieter and smoother, while the automatic transmission has been toughened up to shift more efficiently when pulling heavy loads; a larger fuel tank has been installed. **2001**—Tilt steering wheel; cruise control; CD player; remote keyless entry; power windows, mirrors, and locks. **2002**—A rear heater on cargo models. **2003**—Upgraded four-wheel disc brakes.

The 1985–95 versions suffer from failure-prone automatic transmissions and AC compressors, poor braking systems, and fragile steering components. The early base V6 provides ample power, but also produces lots of noise, consumes excessive amounts of fuel, and tends to have leaking head gaskets and failure-prone oxygen sensors. These computer-related problems often rob the engine of sufficient power to keep up in traffic. While the 5-speed manual transmission shifts fairly easily, the automatic takes forever to downshift on the highway. Handling isn't particularly agile on these minivans, and the power steering doesn't provide the driver with enough road feel. Unloaded, the Astro provides very poor traction, the ride isn't comfortable on poor road surfaces, and interior noise is rampant. Many drivers find the driving position awkward (no left legroom) and the heating/defrosting system inadequate. Many engine components are hidden under the dashboard, making repair or maintenance unwieldy. Even on more recent models, highway performance and overall reliability aren't impressive.

Owners report that the front suspension, steering components, computer modules, and catalytic converter can wear out within as little as 60,000 km. There have also been lots of complaints about electrical, exhaust, cooling, and fuel system bugs; inadequate heating/defrosting; failure-prone wiper motors; and axle seals wearing out every 12–18 months.

Body hardware is fragile, and fit and finish is the pits. Water leaks from windows and doors are common but hard to diagnose. Squeaks and rattles are legion and hard to locate. Sliding-door handles often break off, and the sliding door frequently jams in cold temperatures. The hatch release for the Dutch doors occasionally doesn't work, and the driver-side vinyl seat lining tears apart. Premature paint peeling, delamination, and surface rust are fairly common.

The 1996–99 models have problems carried over from earlier years, with stalling, hard starts, and expensive and frequent automatic transmission, power-steering, wheel bearing, brake pad, caliper, and rotor repairs heading the list.

Year 2000–05 models are a bit more reliable and better performing, inasmuch as they underwent considerable upgrading by GM. Nevertheless, buyers should pay extra attention to the following areas: excessive vibration transmitted through the AWD; automatic transmission clunk; poor braking performance (brake pedal hardens and brakes don't work after going over bumps or rough roads) and expensive brake maintenance; electronic computer module and fuel system glitches that cause the Check Engine light to remain lit; hard starts, no-starts, or chronic stalling, especially when going downhill; heating and AC performance hampered by poor air distribution; electrical system shorts; and sliding door misalignment and broken hinges.

Safety Summary

All models/years: NHTSA has recorded numerous complaints of dashboard fires. • The power steering locks up or fails unexpectedly, components wear out quickly, and steering may bind when turning. • Seat belt complaints are also common: They tighten up unexpectedly, cannot be adjusted, or have nowhere to latch. **All models: 1999**—Very few safety-related complaints, compared with most other minivans. Many of the 1999 model problems have been reported by owners of earlier model years. • Hard shifting between First and Second gear; transmission slippage. • Delayed shifting or stalling when passing from Drive to Reverse. • Leaking axle seals. • Rear cargo door hinge and latch slip off, and door opens 180 degrees. • Floor mat moves under brake and accelerator pedals. • Brake pedal set too close to the accelerator. • Fuel-gauge failure caused by faulty sending unit. **2000**—Brake and gas pedals are too close together. • When brakes are applied, rear wheels tend to lock up, while front wheels continue to turn. • Vehicle stalls when accelerating or turning. • Astro rolls back when stopped on an incline in Drive. • Sliding door slams shut on an incline, or hinges break. • Extensive damage caused to bumper and undercarriage by driving over gravel roads. **2001**—Sudden acceleration. • Chronic stalling. • Sudden total electrical failure, especially when going into Reverse. • Brake pedal set too high. • Differential in transfer case locks up while driving; defective axle seals. • Vehicle rolls backward on an incline while in Drive. • Fuel-gauge failure. • Faulty AC vents. • Water can be trapped inside the wheels and then freeze, causing the wheels to be out of balance. **2002**—Airbag fails to deploy. • Sticking gas pedal. • Brake pedal goes to floor without braking. • Seat belts in rear are too long; don't fit children or child safety seats. • Driver-side window failures. • Sliding-door window blows out. **2003**—Automatic transmission failure. • Harsh, delayed shifting. • ABS engages erratically on dry pavement at slow speeds and increases stopping distance considerably (probable cause is corrosion buildup within the ABS sensors):

There is a GM recall (#05068) for other like models of GM cars but not mine. So my problem is the dealer can't fix the ABS without a recall and GM won't issue a recall because there hasn't been enough complaints.

• Excessive steering vibration. • Painful harmonic roar from the rear of the vehicle. • On a slight incline, sliding door will unlatch and slam shut. • Intermittent windshield wiper failure. • Rapid wearout of Bridgestone tires. **2004**—Cruise control suddenly shuts off. • Rear driver-side window explodes. **2005**—Airbags fail to deploy.

Secret Warranties/Internal Bulletins/Service Tips

All models: 1993–99—Tips on getting rid of AC odours. • Defective catalytic converters. **1993–2005**—GM says that a chronic driveline clunk can't be silenced and is a normal characteristic of its vehicles. • Paint delamination, peeling, or fading. **1995–2000**—Dealer guidelines for brake servicing under warranty. **1995–2004**—Booming interior noise at highway speeds. **1996–2000**—Hard start, no-start, backfire, and kickback when starting may be corrected by replacing the crankshaft position sensor. • A rough idle after start and/or a Service Engine light that stays lit may mean you have a stuck injector poppet-valve ball that needs cleaning. **1996–2001**—Poor heat distribution in driver's area of vehicle (install new heat ducts). • Exhaust rattle noise. **1996–2004**—Silence a booming noise heard during engine warm-up by installing an exhaust dampener assembly (TSB #00-06-05-001A). **1999–2000**—If the engine runs hot, overheats, or loses coolant, try polishing the radiator filler neck or replacing the radiator cap before letting any mechanic convince you that more expensive repairs are needed. • A popping or snapping sound may emanate from the right front-door window area. **1999–2004**—Automatic transmission malfunctions may be caused by debris in the transmission (Bulletin No. 01-07-30-038B). **2000–04**—Automatic transmission delayed shifts. **2001**—Harsh automatic transmission shifts. • 2–4 band and 3–4 clutch damage. • Steering shudder felt when making low-speed turns. • Excessive brake squeal. • Wet carpet/odour in passenger footwell area (repair evaporator case drain to cowl seal/open evaporator case drain). • Delayed shifts, slips, flares, or extended shifts during cold operation (replace shift solenoid valve assembly). **2002**—Automatic transmission slips, incorrect shifts, and poor engine performance. • Service Engine light comes on, no Third or Fourth gears, and loss of Drive. • Slipping or missing Second, Third, or Fourth gears. • Inadequate heating. • Roof panel has a wavy or rippled appearance. • Water leak in the windshield area. **2002–03**—Engine runs rough or Service Engine warning light comes on. • Sliding door difficult to open. **2003**—Hard starts, rough idle, and intermittent misfiring. • Transfer case shudder. • Right rear-door handle breakage. **2004**—Measures to silence a suspension pop or sliding-door squeak.

	1997	1998	1999	2000	2001	2002	2003	2004	2005
Cost Price ($)									
Cargo	25,110	25,110	23,290	24,015	24,465	—	—	26,390	26,875
CS/base	26,920	26,920	23,839	25,675	26,440	27,255	27,600	27,615	28,895
Used Values ($)									
Cargo ▲	2,500	3,000	3,500	4,000	5,000	—	—	12,000	15,000
Cargo ▼	2,000	2,,500	3,000	3,500	4,000	—	—	10,500	13,500
CS/base ▲	3,000	3,500	4,000	5, 000	6,500	8,000	10,500	13,000	16,000
CS/base ▼	2,500	3,000	3,500	4,500	5,500	7,000	9,000	11,500	14,500
Reliability	2	3	3	3	4	4	4	4	4
Crash Safety (F)	3	3	3	3	3	3	3	3	3
Side	—	—	—	—	—	—	5	5	5
Offset	1	1	1	1	1	1	1	1	1
Head Restraints (F)	2	—	2	—	2	2	1	1	1
Rear	2	—	—	—	—	—	—	—	—
Rollover Resistance	—	—	—	—	3	3	3	—	—

MONTANA, MONTANA SV6, RELAY, SILHOUETTE, TERRAZA, TRANS SPORT, UPLANDER, VENTURE ★

bad buy

RATING: Not Recommended (1990–2006). With these minivans scheduled to be phased out by year's end, GM has given up on them. You should too. *Lemon-Aid's* low rating continues for the above models for the following reasons: serious automatic transmission and engine head gasket/intake manifold gasket failures, deteriorating reliability combined with an inadequate warranty, and safety defects such as sliding doors that crush and injure children. These minivans are almost as bad as Ford's Windstar/Freestar and actually make Chrysler's mediocre minivans look good. **"Real" city/highway fuel economy:** *3.4L:* 12.0/7.8 L/100 km. *3.4L AWD:* 13.7/9.6 L/100 km. Owners report fuel savings may undershoot the above estimates by at least 15 percent. **Maintenance/Repair costs:** Average costs, except for powertrain glitches where GM dealers force $3,000 engine and tranny repairs on customers in order to be eligible for GM "goodwill" refunds. Engine intake manifold gaskets, automatic transmissions, ABS, and the electrical system are all high-maintenance items with an equally high failure rate occurring at around the fifth year of ownership. **Parts:** The same parts are used on many other GM models, so they're reasonably priced and not hard to find. Body parts are likely to be more problematic and costly. **Extended warranty:** Definitely needed for both the engine and automatic transmission. **Best alternatives:** Chrysler minivans, the Honda Odyssey, or Toyota's pre-2004 Sienna. **Online help:** *www.cartrackers.com/Forums/live/YourLemon/231.html* and *www.autosafety.org/autodefects.html.* An excellent law article relative to successfully framing your engine intake manifold claim can be found online at *www.rosnerandmansfield.com/press_main.*

html (John W. Hanson, "New Guidance for *Consumers Legal Remedies Act* Claims," *Trial Bar News*, February 2006, 7–8). Click on the headline "AFLC Attorney John Hanson weighs in on landmark *Chamberlain v. Ford* Decision" at the bottom of the page.

Strengths and Weaknesses

These minivans have more carlike handling than GM's Astro and Safari. Seating is limited to five adults in the standard models (two up front, and three on a removable bench seat), but this can be increased to seven if you find a vehicle equipped with optional modular seats. Seats can be folded down flat, creating additional storage space.

As with most minivans, be wary of vehicles equipped with a power-assisted passenger-side sliding door—it's both convenient and dangerous. Despite an override circuit that should prevent the door from closing when it's blocked, a number of injuries have been reported. Furthermore, the doors frequently open when they shouldn't and can be difficult to close securely.

All models and years have had serious reliability problems—notably engine head gasket and intake manifold defects; electronic module (PROM) and starter failures; premature front brake component wear, brake fluid leakage, and noisy braking; short circuits that burn out alternators, batteries, power door lock activators, and the blower motor; AC evaporator core failures; premature wearout of the inner and outer tie-rods; automatic transmission breakdowns; abysmal fit and finish; chronic sliding door malfunctions; and faulty rear-seat latches. Other problems include a fuel-thirsty and poorly performing 3-speed automatic transmission; a badly mounted sliding door; side-door glass that pops open; squeaks, rattles, and clunks in the instrument panel cluster area and suspension; and wind buffeting noise around the front doors. The large dent- and rust-resistant plastic panels are robot-bonded to the frame, and they absorb engine and road noise very well in addition to having an impressive record for durability.

VEHICLE HISTORY: 1996—3.4L V6 debuts, and the Lumina is replaced by the Venture at the end of the model year. **1997**—Dual airbags and ABS. **1998**—The sliding driver-side door is available on more models. **1999**—A 5-hp boost to the base V6 engine (185), de-powered airbags, an upgraded automatic transmission, a rear-window defogger, and heated rear-view mirrors. **2000**—Dual sliding rear side doors. **2001**—Slightly restyled with a fold-flat third-row seat, a driver-side power door, and a six-disc CD player. The cargo version is dropped. **2002**—Nothing major. Optional AWD and DVD entertainment centre. **2003**—Optional ABS and front side airbags. **2005**—Renamed and slightly redesigned.

By the way, don't trust the towing limit listed in GM's owner's manual. Automakers publish tow ratings that are on the optimistic side—and sometimes they even lie. Also, don't be surprised to find that the base 3.1L engine doesn't handle a full load of passengers and cargo, especially when mated with the 3-speed automatic transmission. The ideal powertrain combo would be the 4-speed automatic coupled to the optional 3800 V6 (first used on the 1996 versions). These minivans use a quiet-running V6 powerplant similar to Chrysler's top-of-the-line 3.8L 6-cylinder, providing good mid-range and top-end power. Less torque hampers the GM engine, however, making for less grunt when accelerating and frequent downshifting out of Overdrive when climbing moderate grades. The 1996–2005 models also have chronic powertrain problems highlighted by engine manifold, head gasket, and camshaft failures along with frequent automatic transmission breakdowns and clunky shifting (covered by a 6-year/100,000 km secret warranty).

The 1996 and later models are less rattle-prone because they have a more rigid body structure than that of their predecessors. However, fit and finish quality is still wanting. Body panels corrode easily and paint is prone to blister or delaminate. The front windshield is particularly prone to leak water from the top portion into the dash instrument cluster (a problem also affecting rear-drive vans and covered by a secret warranty):

> Our 2002 Venture has a poorly fitted windshield and a misaligned dash and hood, as well as quarter panels, front doors, and the sliding rear door on the passenger side. I have inspected other 2002 and 2003 Chevrolet Ventures and have seen the same windshield fit errors.

Other trouble spots include EGR valve failures; electrical glitches; excessive front brake noise and frequent repairs (rotors and pads); early wheel bearing failures; assorted body deficiencies, including peeling and blistering paint; blurry front windshields; air being constantly blown through the centre vent; failure-prone AC condensers; and eccentric wipers:

> My wife and I have had these wipers reset twice and the motor replaced once already. Seems every time there is snow in the wiper seat, they will not rest in their designated resting position and end up resting in the upright position, requiring service or motor replacement.

Safety Summary

All models/years: Fire may ignite around the fuel-filler nozzle or within the ignition switch. • Tie-rod failures may cause loss of steering control. • Sudden steering loss in rainy weather or when passing through a puddle (serpentine belt slippage). • Chronic brake failures or excessive brake fade. • Airbags malfunction. • Sliding doors suddenly open or close, come off their tracks, jam shut, stick open, injure children, and rattle during highway driving. • Transmission failures; slips from Drive into Neutral; won't hold gear on a grade. • Some front door-mounted seat belts cross uncomfortably at the neck, and there's a nasty blind spot on the driver's side that requires a small stick-on convex mirror to correct. **All models: 1995–99**—Headlight assembly collects moisture, burns bulb, or falls out. • Seatback suddenly collapses. • Windshield wipers fail intermittently. • Accelerator and brake pedals are too close together. • Fuel slosh/clunk when vehicle stops or accelerates (replacement tank is useless). • Self-activating door locks lock occupants outside or inside. • Door handles break inside the door assembly. • Horn is hard to access. • Window-latch failures. **2000–2001**—Fire ignited under driver's seat. • Windshield suddenly exploded outward while driving with wipers activated. • Faulty fuel pump causes chronic stalling, no-starts, surging, and sudden acceleration. • Rear control arm snaps:

> In May we were driving our 2002 Pontiac Montana with 6 adults inside (luckily), on a small two-lane road, doing about 50 or 60 km/h. Suddenly, the right rear control arm snapped and the rear axle rattled and shook.
>
> Our mechanic said in 28 years he had never seen such a thing happen. If we'd been going 120 on a 400 highway we'd be dead.
>
> The dealer we bought it from paid all the costs for a used part to be installed, even though there was no warranty, but our mechanic suggested we photograph the parts he had removed. He was surprised at the thinness of the metal of the control arm. Also that the control arm is welded to the axle, so it can't be replaced without replacing the entire component. New, they are $2000!
>
> KITCHENER, ONTARIO

• Steering idler arm falls off because of missing bolt. • Brakes activate on their own, making it feel as if the van is pulling a load. • Loose fuel tank because of loose bolts/bracket. • In one incident, the fuel tank cracked when passing over a tree branch. • Plastic tube within heating system falls off and wedges behind the accelerator pedal. • Bracket weld pin that secures the rear split seat shears off. • Centre-rear lap seat belt isn't long enough to secure a rear-facing child safety seat. • Children can slide out of the integrated child safety seat. • Electrical harness failures result in complete electrical shutdown. • Headlights, interior lights, gauges, and instruments fail intermittently (electrical cluster module is the prime suspect). • Excess padding around horn makes it difficult to depress horn button in an emergency. • Weak-sounding horn. • Frequent windshield wiper motor failures. • Heater doesn't warm up vehicle sufficiently. • Antifreeze smell intrudes into interior. • Premature failure of the transmission's Fourth clutch. • Delayed or extended shifts, slips, or flares in cold weather. • Poorly performing rear AC. • Flickering interior and exterior lights. • Airbag warning light stays lit. • Windshield glass distortion. **2002**—Rear hatch handle breaks, cutting driver's hand. • Vehicle jumps out of Park and rolls downhill. • Vehicle suddenly shuts off in traffic. • Windshield water leaks short out dash gauges. **2003**—Rear seat belts fail to release. • Weld holding the lift wheel pin is not adequate to support weight of trailer. **2004**—Engine surging, stalling. • Loss of coolant, engine overheating. • Broken rear sway bar. • Firestone tire blowout. • Frequent brake failures blamed on faulty brake master cylinder. • Tail lights fail intermittently. • Power-sliding door opens and closes on its own while vehicle is underway. • Two childrens' wrists were fractured after their elbows and hands were caught between the seat and the sliding door handle. • Door doesn't lock into position; slides shut and crushes objects in its path:

We are very concerned that another child, or adult, is going to be injured in this van's automatic sliding door. We were curious just how far the 2004 Venture's door would go before it would bounce back open so we put a stuffed animal in the door and hit the auto door close button. I have to say, the stuffed animal did not fare well. We also put a large carrot and a banana in the door, in an attempt to simulate a small child's arm. The carrot was sliced right in half, and the banana was smashed and oozing out of its peel. I will never purchase a Chevrolet Venture after our experience with the van.

2005—Sudden transmission failure. • When underway, vehicle suddenly veers to one side. • Excessive steering effort. Windshield wiper actuating bar cuts into wiring harness. • Flickering interior lights and headlights. • Traction control comes on at the wrong time, forcing vehicle to limp home. • Early failure of the sliding door motor. • Power-sliding door opened on its own. • Child crushed by the power-sliding door:

My daughter was crushed by the automatic door in our Chevy Uplander. She was getting into the vehicle and the door suddenly closed on her. Luckily she only had serious bruising. It turns out that the automatic doors on the Uplander are not equipped with safety features, such as a sensor that would stop the door from closing if someone was still in the doorway. My daughter is 10; what would have happened if it were a younger child?

• Excessive swaying and poor handling. • No armrests on the second-row seats. • Vehicle stalls if gas tank is half full. • Dash lights are too dim for bright days. • Blower fan motor slows down and the headlights dim when the vehicle comes to a stop. • Windshield chips easily. • Windshield wipers freeze in cold weather:

The windshield wipers on the vehicle were hidden under the hood. When the temperature dropped to freezing the windshield wipers froze. Had to open the hood and chip away the ice to get the windshield wipers out from under the hood.

Secret Warranties/Internal Bulletins/Service Tips

All models: 1993–2000—GM says that a chronic driveline clunk can't be silenced and is a normal characteristic of its vehicles. • Paint delamination, peeling, or fading. **1996–2001**—Poor heat distribution in driver's area of vehicle (install new heat ducts). **1996–2004**—Engine intake manifold/head gasket failures are covered by a secret warranty up to 6 years/100,000 km (see Part Two, pages 77–79). The GM 3800 Series engines leak around the upper composite intake where the EGR heat riser tube (stovepipe) from the lower aluminum intake joins the upper intake (see GM TSB #01-06-01-007A). Motormite/Dorman makes a redesigned composite upper plenum for these engines as well as for the Ford 4.6L and 5.4L engines. They are less expensive than GM replacements and use a better design and stronger composite. **1997–98**—A fuel tank thud or clunk noise may require new fuel-tank straps and insulators. • Loose-lumber noises coming from the rear of the vehicle when it passes over bumps mean upgraded rear shock absorbers are required. **1997–2002**—Psst! GM minivans may show premature body panel corrosion and paint blistering/delamination. A dealer whistle-blower tells me that dealers have been authorized to repair the hoods free of charge (refinish and repaint) up to six years under a GM "goodwill" program. • Mildew odour; water leaks. • Wind noise at base of windshield. **1997–2003**—Rust holes in the roof. **1997–2004**—Second-row seat belt won't release. • Windshield wind noise. **1999**—Diagnostic tips for an automatic transmission that slips, produces harsh upshifts and garage shifts (shifting between Reverse and Forward when parking), or causes acceleration shudders. **1999–2000**—If the engine runs hot, overheats, or loses coolant, try polishing the radiator-filler neck or replacing the radiator cap before considering more expensive repairs. • Before taking on more expensive repairs to correct hard starts or no-starts, check the fuel pump. • An automatic transmission that whines in Park or Neutral or a Service Engine light that stays on may signal the need for a new drive-sprocket support bearing. **1999–2002**—Transmission noise/no movement. **1999–2003**—Incorrect fuel-gauge readings caused by a contaminated fuel-tank sensor/sender. If a fuel cleaner doesn't work, GM says it will adjust or replace the sensor/sender for free on a case-by-case basis (*Toronto Star*, June 13 and 14 and December 20, 2003). This failure afflicts GM's entire lineup and could cost up to $800 to repair. **2000–02**—Service Engine light comes on, and automatic transmission is harsh shifting. • Hard start, no-start, stall, and inoperative fuel gauge. **2000–04**—Tail light/brake light and circuit board burns out from water intrusion. Repair cost covered by a "goodwill" policy (TSB #03-08-42-007A) up to five years. **2000–06**—Delayed shifts. **2001**—Customer Satisfaction Program (secret warranty) to correct the rear HVAC control switch. **2001–02**—Poor engine and automatic transmission operation. • Slipping automatic transmission. **2003**—Shudder, chuggle (bad surge because of combustion instability), and hard shifting, plus transmission won't downshift. **2003–04**—Power-sliding door binding. • Windshield whistle. **2004–06**—Noisy steering can be silenced by replacing the inner tie-rod boot, says TSB #06-02-32-005. **2005**—Inoperative turn signals and tail lights. • Lumpy seats may require a new cushion. **2005–06**—A defective harmonic balancer may cause severe engine damage. GM will retorque the balancer bolt free of charge. • Hard/no start, stalling, inoperative gauges. • Excessive effort to sound horn. • Silencing sliding door rattles. • Steering may need to be fixed by replacing the inner tie-rod boot. • Inaccurate temperature and fuel readings. • Poor AC performance (see bulletin on following page). This is a strange bulletin that excludes Canadians, tells Americans the problem exists but the cause is unknown, and estimates it will take over two hours to investigate. Smart owners will go to the dealer and ask for a fix under warranty. If refused, get an independent mechanic to replace the system and then use the above bulletin to get a refund.

A/C TEMPERATURE WON'T CHANGE/POOR PERFORMANCE

BULLETIN NO.: 06-01-39-004A

DATE: APRIL 25, 2006

2005–06 Montana SV6, Relay, Terraza and Uplander

ATTENTION: THIS IS NOT A RECALL. "GM of Canada" dealers are not authorized to use this bulletin. This bulletin ONLY applies to vehicles in which the customer has commented about this concern AND the EI number shows in GMVIS. All others should disregard this bulletin and proceed with diagnostics found in published service information.

CONDITION: IMPORTANT: If the customer did not bring their vehicle in for this issue, DO NOT proceed with this bulletin.

Some customers may comment that they are unable to change the HVAC mode and/or temperature. Customers may also comment that the A/C may be inoperative or have poor performance.

CORRECTION: GM Engineering is attempting to determine the root cause of this condition. GM has a need to obtain information first hand BEFORE any repairs are made.

WARRANTY INFORMATION:

Labor Operation	Description	Labor Time
D9719*	HVAC — Engineering Investigation	1.0 hr
Add	Recover and Recharge A/C System WITH Rear A/C	0.7 hr
Add	Recover and Recharge A/C System WITHOUT Rear A/C	0.5 hr

*This labor operation is for bulletin use only. It will not be published in the Labor Time Guide.

531

MONTANA, MONTANA SV6, RELAY, SILHOUETTE, TERRAZA, TRANS SPORT, UPLANDER, VENTURE PROFILE

Cost Price ($)	1997	1998	1999	2000	2001	2002	2003	2004	2005
Montana	—	—	25,130	26,625	26,755	27,870	28,520	29,380	32,840
Montana SV6	—	—	—	—	—	—	—	—	26,620
Relay	—	—	—	—	—	—	—	—	27,995
Silhouette	—	29,410	29,955	30,630	31,105	33,060	35,695	36,290	—
Terraza	—	—	—	—	—	—	—	—	33,745
Trans Sport/SE	23,690	24,650	—	—	—	—	—	—	—
Uplander	—	—	—	—	—	—	—	—	25,405
Venture	23,185	24,145	24,725	24,895	25,230	25,195	25,865	26,680	30,590
Used Values ($)									
Montana ▲	—	—	3,500	4,500	5,500	7,500	10,000	12,000	15,000
Montana ▼	—	—	3,000	4,000	4,500	6,000	8,000	10,500	13,500
Montana SV6 ▲	—	—	—	—	—	—	—	—	16,000
Montana SV6 ▼	—	—	—	—	—	—	—	—	14,500
Relay ▲	—	—	—	—	—	—	—	—	15,000
Relay ▼	—	—	—	—	—	—	—	—	13,500
Silhouette ▲	—	3,500	4,000	4,500	6,000	8,000	10,500	13,000	—
Silhouette ▼	—	3,000	3,500	4,000	4,500	6,500	9,000	11,500	—
Terraza ▲	—	—	—	—	—	—	—	—	17,000
Terraza ▼	—	—	—	—	—	—	—	—	15,500
Trans Sport/SE ▲	2,000	3,000	—	—	—	—	—	—	—
Trans Sport/SE ▼	1,500	2,500	—	—	—	—	—	—	—

Uplander ▲	—	—	—	—	—	—	—	—	13,500
Uplander ▼	—	—	—	—	—	—	—	—	12,000
Venture ▲	2,500	3,000	3,500	4,000	5,500	7,500	9,000	11,000	14,000
Venture ▼	2,000	2,500	3,000	3,500	5,000	6,000	8,000	9,500	12,500
Reliability	2	2	2	2	2	2	2	2	2
Crash Safety (F)	4	4	4	4	4	4	4	4	4
Side	—	—	5	5	5	5	5	5	5
Offset (Venture)	1	1	1	1	1	1	1	1	1
Montana/Trans Sport	—	—	—	—	—	—	—	—	5
Montana SV6	—	—	—	—	—	—	—	—	5
Relay	—	—	—	—	—	—	—	—	5
Terraza	—	—	—	—	—	—	—	—	5
Uplander	—	—	—	—	—	—	—	—	5
Head Restraints (F)	2	—	2	—	5	5	3	3	—
Rear	—	—	1	—	3	3	2	2	—
Rollover Resistance	—	—	—	—	3	3	3	—	—

Honda

best buy

ODYSSEY ★★★★★

RATING: Recommended (2006); Above Average (2003–05); Average (1996–2002). Odyssey redesigns don't engender as steep a decline in quality as we have seen with Mazda, Nissan, and Toyota redesigns. The upgraded 2005 Odyssey surpassed the Sienna in safety, performance, and convenience features. Nevertheless, there have been frequent reports of safety- and performance-related failures, hence that model year's downgrade. Of particular concern are complaints of run-flat Pax tire problems, airbag malfunctions, automatic sliding door failures, damaged AC condensers, transmission breakdowns with erratic shifting, and sudden brake loss. **"Real" city/highway fuel economy:** *2.2L:* 11.9/9.2 L/100 km. *2.3L:* 10.9/

8.3 L/100 km. *3.5L:* 13.2/8.5 L/100 km. Owners report fuel savings may undershoot these estimates by about 10 percent. Fuel economy drops dramatically if the rear AC is engaged. **Maintenance/Repair costs:** Average; any garage can repair these minivans. **Parts:** Moderately priced, and availability is better than average because the Odyssey uses many generic Accord parts. **Extended warranty:** Not needed; save your money. **Best alternatives:** If you want something cheap and reasonably reliable, consider a three-year-old Chrysler minivan, a 1997–2002 Quest, or a 2006 Kia Sedona. If you want handling and dependability, look to Toyota's early Sienna. Sadly, GM's front-drive minivans aren't in the running because of their self-destructing engines and malfunctioning automatic transmissions. GM's Astro, Safari, or full-sized van are much more reliable and provide additional towing muscle. **Online help:** *consumeraffairs.com/automotive/honda_van.html, www.mycarstats.com/auto_complaints/HONDA_complaints.asp,* and *www.autosafety.org/autodefects.html.*

Strengths and Weaknesses

When it was first launched in 1995, the Odyssey was a sales dud. Canadians and *Lemon-Aid* saw through Honda's attempt to pass off an underpowered, mid-sized, four-door station wagon with a raised roof as a minivan. In 1999, however, the Odyssey was redesigned, and it now represents one of the better minivans on the Canadian market.

It's easy to see what makes the Odyssey so popular: strong engine performance, carlike ride and handling, easy entry/exit, a second driver-side door, and a quiet interior. Most controls and displays are easy to reach and read, there's a lot of passenger and cargo room and an extensive list of standard equipment, and Honda is willing to compensate owners for production snafus.

This minivan does have its drawbacks, though. A high resale price makes bargains rare, front-seat passenger legroom is marginal because of the restricted seat travel, and third-row seating is suitable only for children. Additionally, power-sliding doors are slow to retract, there's some tire rumbling and rattling and body drumming at highway speeds, premium fuel is required for optimum performance, and rear-seat head restraints impede side and rear visibility.

One can sum up the strengths and weaknesses of the 1996–98 Odyssey (and the Isuzu Oasis, its American twin through the 1998 model) in three words: performance, performance, and performance. You get carlike performance and handling, responsive steering, and a comfortable ride offset by a raucous engine, slow-as-molasses acceleration with a full load, and limited passenger/cargo space because of the narrow body.

VEHICLE HISTORY: 1997—Small improvements. **1998**—A new 2.3L engine adds 10 horses (not enough!), and a restyled grille and instrument panel debut. **1999**—A new, more powerful engine and increased size make this second-generation Odyssey a more versatile highway performer; still, steering requires fully extended arms, and power-sliding doors operate slowly. **2001**—User-friendly child safety seat tether anchors, upgraded stereo speakers, and an intermittent rear-window wiper. **2002**—A slight restyling, 30 additional horses, disc brakes on all four wheels, standard side airbags, and additional support for front seats. **2003**—Changes included an auto up/down driver-side window, plus new-style keys that Honda says are harder to duplicate. **2005**—Honda updated its minivan for 2005, revising the styling and adding additional safety features. The '05 Odyssey continues with a 255-hp 3.5L V6 and a 5-speed automatic transmission. EX-L and Touring models come with a Variable Cylinder Management system. To save fuel, it deactivates three cylinders when cruising or decelerating, and so far has not generated many owner complaints. Standard safety features include anti-lock four-wheel disc brakes, traction control, an anti-skid system, front side airbags, and side curtain airbags for all three seating rows. Most models (except the LX) have power-sliding side doors. 2005s also have a storage compartment in the floor and side windows that power partly down into the sliding doors.

1999–2005 models

The upgraded 1999 models have powerful 6-cylinder engines and a larger interior, wiping out most of the previous models' deficiencies.

Reliability for the above models is much better than average, but Honda still has a few safety- and performance-related problems to work out. Three examples: failure-prone sliding doors; troublesome, expensive-to-replace Pax run-flat tires; and easily damaged AC condensers. The sliding doors open when they shouldn't, won't close when they should, catch fingers and arms, get stuck open or closed, are noisy, and frequently require expensive servicing. The Check Engine light may stay lit because of a defective fuel-filler neck. There's a fuel sloshing noise when accelerating or coming to a stop, and the transmission clunks or bangs when backing uphill or when shifting into Reverse. There are also reports of rattling and chattering when the minivan is in Forward gear. Owners note a loud wind noise and vibration from the left side of the front windshield along with a constant vibration felt through the steering assembly and front wheels. Passenger doors may also require excessive force to open. And owners have complained of severe static electricity shocks when exiting.

Other problems include transmission breakdowns; near engine stalling, while producing a noise like valve clattering when shifting into Fourth gear; and transmission gear whine at 90 km/h or when in Fourth gear (the transmission can be replaced under a new "goodwill" warranty). One owner reported the following noisy annoyances with his 2000 model year Odyssey:

> At 10,000 miles [16,000 km] I complained to the dealer about the torque converter rattle and was told it was not there. I have since taken it in four times to make sure it's documented and I was told last week that Honda is aware of the annoying rattle but is not willing to make any repairs at this time. As you know, Honda is experiencing other transmission "concerns" and has extended its warranty on certain transmissions....

Front-end clunking is caused by welding breaks in the front subframe; the exhaust rattles or buzzes; fuel splashes loudly in the fuel tank when coming to a stop; the vehicle pulls to the right when underway; the front brakes wear prematurely and are excessively noisy; the sliding side door frequently malfunctions; there are electrical glitches and defective remote audio controls; the leather seats split, crack, or discolour; and accessory items come loose, break away, or won't work. Plastic interior panels have rough edges and are often misaligned.

The comprehensive base warranty has lots of wiggle room that the service manager can use to apply "goodwill" adjustments for post-warranty problems. However, dealer servicing and after-warranty assistance have met with a great deal of criticism from *Lemon-Aid* readers. Owners complain that "goodwill" refunds aren't extended to all model years with the same defect, recall repairs take an eternity to perform, and dealers exhibit an arrogant, uncaring "take it or leave it" attitude.

Safety Summary

All models/years: Passenger seatbacks collapsed when vehicle was rear-ended. • Airbag malfunctions. • Sudden, unintended acceleration when slowing for a stop sign or when in Drive with AC turned on. • Stuck accelerator. • Automatic transmission failures. • Transmission doesn't hold when stopped or parked on an incline; gas or brakes have to be constantly applied. • Power-sliding doors are a constant danger. **All models: 1999**—Fire ignited in the electrical harness. • Plastic gas tank cracks, leaks fuel. • Gasoline smell when transmission is put into Reverse. • Side window explodes while vehicle is underway. • Check Engine light comes on, and vehicle loses all power. • When driving, all the instrument-panel lights will suddenly go out (faulty multiplex controller suspected). • Complete loss of power steering because of a pinhole in the power-steering return hose. • Poor power-steering performance in cold weather. • Power doors lock and unlock on their own. • Design of the gear shifter interferes with the radio controls. • Seat belt buckle locks up. • Faulty fuel gauge. **1999–2001**—During fuelling, fuel tank burst into flames. **2000**—458 safety complaints recorded by NHTSA. • Many incidents where driver-side sliding door opens onto fuel hose while fuelling, damaging gas-flap hinge and tank. • Catastrophic failure of the right-side suspension, causing wheel to buckle. • Vehicle continually pulls to the right; dealers unable to correct problem. • Excessive steering-wheel vibration at 105 km/h or more. • Electric doors often inoperative. • Chronic automatic transmission problems: It won't shift into lower gears and suddenly loses power, the torque converter fails, and it makes a loud popping sound when put into Reverse. • Two incidents where vehicle was rear-ended because of transmission malfunction. • Dash lights don't adequately illuminate the dash panel. • Protruding bolts in the door assembly are hazardous. • Seat belt buckle fails to latch. • Driver-side mirror breaks away; mirror glass falls out because of poor design. • Easily broken sliding-door handles. **2000–01**—On cold days, accelerator pedal is hard to depress. • Rear seat belt tightened up so much that occupant had to be cut free. • Driver's seatback suddenly reclined, hitting rear passenger's legs, even though power switch was off. • **2001**—In a frontal collision, van caught fire because of a cracked brake-fluid reservoir. • Chronic stalling. • Many reports of sudden transmission and torque converter failures. • Cracked wheel rims. • Check Engine light constantly on (suspect faulty fuel-filler neck). • Entire vehicle shakes excessively at highway speeds and pulls to the right. • Passenger-side door window suddenly exploded while driving on the highway. • Driver's seatback collapsed from rear-end collision. • Too much play in rear lapbelts, which won't tighten adequately, making it difficult to install a child safety seat securely. • Inoperative driver's seat belt buckle. • Faulty speedometer and tachometer. • Remote wouldn't open or lock vehicle. • Frequent static electricity shocks. • Many owners report that the rear head restraints seriously hamper rear and forward visibility and that it's difficult to see vehicles coming from the right side. **2002**—Owners say many engines have faulty timing chains. • Loose strut bolt almost caused wheel to fall off. • Axle-bearing wheel failure caused driver-side wheel to fall off. • Left to right veering, and excessive drivetrain vibration. • Many complaints that the brake pedal goes to the floor with no braking capability. • Sticking sliding door. • Head restraints are set too low for tall occupants. • Rear windshield shatters from area where the wiper is mounted. • Rear seat belt unlatches during emergency braking. • Brake line freezes up in cold weather. • Abrupt downshift upon deceleration. • Driver-side door came off while using remote control. • Dashboard lights come on and go off intermittently. • Passenger window exploded. • Airbag light comes on for no reason. **2003**—Fire ignited in the CD player. • In one incident, a child was injured from a side collision when the second-row seat belt failed to hold her in because of gap caused by door attachment. • Rear seat belts lock for no reason. • Defective speed sensor caused vehicle to suddenly lose power when merging into traffic. • Vehicle suddenly shut down in traffic. • Hard starts and engine misfiring. • Faulty steering causes wander. • Sudden brake failure. • Driver often electrically shocked when touching door handle. • Fuel spits out when refuelling. • Inaccurate fuel gauge readings. • Sliding door closes on driver's hand. **2004**—Front airbags fail to deploy. • Passenger-side airbag is often inoperative. • Chronic stalling even after recall; repairs to the fuel-pump relay to correct the problem. • Gas pedal will not work due to a broken throttle cable. • Interior lights flicker on and off. • Sliding door crushes arms and legs. • Right-hand fingers can get caught in the gap on the steering wheel between the cruise-control buttons and the airbag area. • Second-row seat dislodges and tips forward. • If vehicle is started and left in idle, the doors lock automatically. This could lock the driver out after a 10-second delay. **2005**—Sudden acceleration while cruising. • Excessive steering wheel vibration. • Defective power steering pump and fuel pump. • Windshield noise remedy. • Front and rear AC temperature varies. • AC condenser easily damaged by road debris. • Snow and ice accumulated under the spoiler, causing it to fall off along with the brake light. • Child's hand was crushed in one incident by rear power-sliding door. • Run-flat tire problems:

My wife and I purchased a new Honda Odyssey van in 2005 which was equipped with Pax run-flat tires. At the time, we were told that the tires would wear like regular non run-flat tires, and would be 10–15% more expensive to replace. We were also told that all Honda dealers would have the necessary equipment to service these special tires. None of these statements has proven to be true. The tires are all worn out at

31K miles [50,000 kilometres], and we were quoted a price of $1300 plus tax to have them replaced. Worse yet, our nearest dealer (Flagstaff Honda) does not have the necessary equipment to service them 2 years after their release. To make things worse, we now have a flat and getting it fixed will require us to drive 50 mph [80 km/h] on a busy interstate.

•

Pax tires fall apart and the dealer did not service them well. Tread failure 1 to 2 inches [2.5 to 5 centimetres] of rubber fell off, down to threads. Dealer claimed that running into a curb could cause this to happen. Tires failed before 30 thousand miles [48,000 kilometres]. Cost approximately $100 more than normal tires. Honda provided no other options to tire problem, monopoly on the manufacturer of tire, Michelin. Monopoly on service to vehicle where little other [independents] are available to replace tire. Discount Tire is the only other provider. Honda does not recognize any other optional tires for use on their Odyssey. Discount Tire proposes a replacement with a 18 inch Z rated tire that might leave vehicle with a dash warning that can't be turned off or disarmed. Tire pressure system also is not accurate or reliable.... Weather changes set off the tire pressure alarm that can only be reset by dealer. One of the Pax features was to replace a spare because of weight. A Pax tire is 25 lbs [11 kg] more per tire than a normal tire thus nullifying any benefits. Cost is a hundred dollars more per tire and reliability is less. Service ability is less. A dealer this last time was unable to break the bead on the tire. Before that they had to replace tire and rim, 2 to 3 weeks to get it done.

Secret Warranties/Internal Bulletins/Service Tips

All models/years: Most of Honda's TSBs allow for special warranty consideration on a "goodwill" basis by the company's District Service Manager or Zone Office, even after the warranty has expired or the vehicle has changed hands. Referring to this euphemism will increase your chances of getting some kind of refund for repairs that are obviously factory defects. • There's an incredibly large number of sliding door problems covered by a recall and a plethora of service bulletins too numerous to print here. Ask Honda politely for the bulletins or "goodwill" assistance. If refused, subpoena the documents through small claims court, using NHTSA's summary as your shopping list. **1999**—Poor engine performance may require a new rear intake manifold end plate and gasket, PCV hose, and the intake manifold cover. **1999–2001**—Extended warranty coverage on Odysseys with defective 4- and 5-speed automatic transmissions to 7 years/160,000 km to fix erratic or slow shifting. **1999–2003**—Engine oil leaks will be corrected under a "goodwill" policy. • Deformed windshield moulding. **1999–2006**—Troubleshooting vehicle pull or drift to one side. **2000–01**—Third-row seat won't unlatch. • Clunk or bang when engaging Reverse. • Bulletin confirms Honda USA has investigated complaints of pulling or drifting (Service Bulletin Number: 99165, Bulletin Sequence Number: 802, Date of Bulletin: 99/09, NHTSA Item Number: SB608030). • Excessive front brake noise. • Dash ticking or clicking. **2002**—Hesitation when accelerating. • Diagnosing automatic transmission problems. • No-starts; hard starts in cold weather. • Driver's seat heater may not work. • Thump at cold start. • Loose rear wiper arm. • AC can't be turned off while in defog setting. **2002–03**—Free replacement of the engine timing belt auto-tensioner and water pump under both a recall and "product update" campaign. **2002–04**—Free tranny repair or replacement for insufficient lubrication that can lead to heat buildup and broken gears. **2002–06**—Warranty mileage limitation extended by 5 percent to compensate for defective odometers:

VEHICLE WARRANTY EXTENSION CAMPAIGN

BULLETIN NO.: 06-085   DATE: NOVEMBER 21, 2006

BACKGROUND: On November 7, 2006, a federal court preliminarily approved the settlement of a class action lawsuit that alleged the odometers on certain 2002 through 2006 Honda models, and some 2007 Fit models, were overstating mileage. As part of the settlement, American Honda has proposed extending the mileage based coverage period of all warranties and Honda Care Service Contracts by five percent (5%).

• Transmission noise will signal if there is gear breakage; transmission may also lock up. • Rear brake noise. **2003**—Engine cranks but won't start. • ABS problems. • Power-steering pump noise. • Warning lights blink on and off. • Exhaust rattling. • Leather seat defects. • HomeLink remote system range is too short, hard to program. • Factory security system won't arm. • Faulty charging system; electrical shorts. • Front door howls in strong crosswind. • Squealing from rear quarter windows and motors. • Fuel tank leak. • Front damper noise. • Steering wheel bent off-centre. • Manual sliding door is difficult to open. **2005**—Excessive steering wheel vibration. • Windshield noise remedy. • Front and rear AC temperature varies. • Correction for middle-row seat that won't unlatch. **2005–06**—Power steering pump noise. • Front brake drone. • Front wheel bearing noise. • Windshield wind noise. • Noisy power sliding door operation. • Exhaust system moan and drone.

ODYSSEY PROFILE

	1997	1998	1999	2000	2001	2002	2003	2004	2005
Cost Price ($)									
LX	28,995	29,800	30,600	30,600	30,800	31,900	32,200	32,400	32,700
EX	—	—	33,600	33,600	33,800	34,900	35,200	35,400	35,900
Used Values ($)									
LX ▲	6,000	8,000	10,500	13,000	15,000	18,500	21,500	24,000	28,000
LX ▼	5,500	7,000	9,500	11,000	13,500	16,500	20,000	22,000	26,000
EX ▲	—	—	12,500	14,500	17,000	20,500	23,000	26,000	30,500
EX ▼	—	—	11,500	13,000	15,000	18,500	21,500	24,000	28,000
Reliability	3	3	4	5	5	5	5	5	5
Crash Safety (F)	4	—	5	5	5	5	5	5	5
Side	—	—	—	5	5	5	5	5	5

All ratings on a numbered scale where **5** is good and **1** is bad. See pages 130–132 for a more detailed description.

Side (IIHS)	—	—	—	—	—	2	2	2	5
Offset	2	2	2	2	2	5	5	5	5
Head Restraints (F)	2	—	2	—	2	2	2	2	1
Rear	—	—	1	—	—	—	—	—	—
Rollover Resistance	—	—	—	—	4	4	4	—	4

Kia

SEDONA ★ ★ ★ ★

RATING: Above Average (2006); Average (2002–05). Sedona is a very user-friendly, roomy, versatile, and comfortable mid-sized minivan that comes with a comprehensive base warranty. Too bad the early models are so unreliable. **"Real" city/highway fuel economy:** 15.4/10.9 L/100 km. Owners report fuel consumption may be even worse than this estimate by about 20 percent. **Maintenance/Repair costs:** Average. **Parts:** Likely to be back-ordered and cost more than average. Safety recall repairs are often delayed because parts are unavailable. **Extended warranty:** Yes, until these minivans have proved themselves on a long-term basis. **Best alternatives:** Hyundai's version of the 2006 Sedona, the 2007 Entourage; Honda's Odyssey; and a pre-2004 Toyota Sienna. **Online help:** *www.kia-forums.com* and *www.autosafety.org/autodefects.html*.

Strengths and Weaknesses

Used Sedonas cost several thousand dollars less than comparable Detroit-built minivans. Embodying typically bland minivan styling, the front-drive, seven-passenger Sedona is 18 cm shorter than a Honda Odyssey and 11 cm longer than a Dodge Caravan. It comes with a good selection of standard features, including a 195-hp 3.5L V6 engine hooked to an automatic 5-speed transmission, a low step-in height, and a commanding view of the road. For convenience, there are two sliding rear side doors; folding, removable second- and third-row seats; a flip-up hatchback; standard front/rear air conditioning; and a large cargo bay. Other standard amenities are 15-inch tires; AM/FM/CD stereo; power steering, windows, door locks, and heated mirrors; tilt steering; a rear defroster and wiper; dual airbags; and six adjustable head restraints.

On the plus side, Sedonas are reasonably priced and appointed. The transmission shifts smoothly and quietly, and the low ground clearance enhances passenger access and cargo loading. The Sedona also provides a comfortable ride; a convenient "walk-through" space between the front seats; well laid out, user-friendly instruments and controls; lots of storage areas; good visibility; and minimal engine and road noise. Fit and finish is acceptable, though quality is uneven.

From a safety perspective, braking is efficient and predictable, with little brake fade after successive stops, and crashworthiness scores are quite impressive.

Engine power is drained by the Sedona's heft, giving it a 10–20 percent higher fuel-consumption rate than the V6-equipped Dodge Caravan and Toyota Sienna. The upgraded 2006 V6 engine, however, provides much more power while posting fuel economy numbers that are similar to those of the competition. Handling is compromised by vague steering and a wallowing suspension, owners' ears are assailed by excessive engine and wind noise, braking is mediocre, and overall fit and finish is embarrassingly bad.

Poor quality control may be too much for the base warranty to handle, making reliability the Sedona's weakest link, especially with its small dealer network. So far, the areas of most concern have been the engine (head gasket leaks), seat belts, fuel and electrical systems, brake pads and rotors, AC compressor, windows, and overall body construction.

VEHICLE HISTORY: 2003—All minivans get new tail lights; the LX adds a standard AM/FM/CD player, central door-lock button, and remote fuel-door release, while the EX version gets additional stereo speakers and a second remote for the keyless entry. **2004**—A new grille, and the LX's centre tray table become a standard feature. **2006**—Kia's first major redesign is a winner that allows it and partner Hyundai to leapfrog over the Asian competition, while keeping base prices under $30,000. The new feature-laden Sedona offers larger dimensions, more power, and standard side curtain airbags, all housed in a single body that is more than 7.5 cm longer in wheelbase and almost 20 cm longer overall than its predecessor. A more powerful 244-hp 3.8L V6 hooked to a 5-speed manumatic is an important 50-horsepower boost. Comfort and convenience are enhanced through seven-passenger seating, second-row removable bucket seats that slide fore and aft, a third-row bench that splits 60/40 and folds into the floor, and sliding side-door power windows. Standard anti-lock four-wheel disc brakes and traction/anti-skid control are two new standard safety features that distinguish these models from the rest of the pack. Additionally, all Sedonas have front side airbags and side curtain airbags that cover all three seating rows.

 Safety Summary

All models: 2002—Only about 100 safety-related complaints reported so far on the 2002 model, which is about normal for such a low-volume seller. • Fuel-tank design could cause fuel to spray onto hot muffler in a collision. • Oil leaks onto the hot catalytic converter. • Fuel leaks from the bottom of the vehicle. • Loose fuel-line-to-fuel-pump clamp. • Fuel tank filler hose vulnerable to road debris. • Fuel spits back out when refuelling. • Vehicle continues to accelerate when brakes are applied. • Intermittent stalling. • Brake failure; pedal simply sinks to the floor. • Excessive brake shudder when slowing going downhill. • ABS brake light comes on randomly. • Power-steering pulley breaks. • Windshield may suddenly shatter for no apparent reason. • Windshields have distortion at eye level. • Second- and third-row seats don't latch as easily as touted. • Electrical shorts cause lights, windows, and door locks to fail. • Sliding doors won't retract if an object is in their way. • Stuck rear hatch door. • Child safety seat can't be belted in securely. • Child-door safety lock failure. • Inoperative rear seat belts. • Seat belt holding child in booster seat tightened progressively, trapping child. **2003**—Under-hood fire ignites while car is underway. • Airbags fail to deploy. • Sudden, unintended acceleration. • Stuck accelerator pedal. • Brakes fail because of air in the brake lines. • Fuel odour in cabin. • Broken window regulator. • Rear-seat removal instructions can throw your back out. • Tires peel off the rims. • While reclined, passenger seatback releases upright and slams occupant forward. • AC condenser vulnerable to puncture from road debris. • Electrical shorts cause door lock malfunctions. **2004**—Fire ignites in the under-hood wiring. • Airbags don't work properly. • Chronic stalling. • Transmission and TCM replaced because vehicle loses power and gears down constantly. • Loose left rear wheel and suspension struts. • Rear brake assembly and wheel fall off. • Excessive brake rotor wear. • Parking brake doesn't hold vehicle on an incline. • Windshield has a cloudy haze. • Multiple electrical shorts; electrical system continually blows fuses. • Dash lights fail repeatedly; replacing the instrument-cluster board is only a temporary solution. • Weak rear hatch struts. • Seat belts fail to lock upon impact. • Low-beam headlights burn out repeatedly. **2005**—Many complaints relate to the unavailability of parts to carry out recall campaigns. • Sudden, unintended acceleration. • Chronic stalling. • Poor braking performance due to warped brake rotors and prematurely worn brake calipers and pads. • Airbags fail to deploy.

Secret Warranties/Internal Bulletins/Service Tips

All models: 2002—Correction for engine hesitation after cold starts. • Free replacement of seat belt buckle anchor bolts. **2002–03**—Changes to improve alternator output to prevent hard starts or battery drain. **2002–05**—Harsh, delayed shifts. • Insufficient AC cooling and excessive AC noise. • Sliding door is hard to open. **2004**—Engine head gasket leak.

SEDONA PROFILE

	2002	2003	2004	2005
Cost Price ($)				
LX	24,595	24,995	25,595	26,995
EX	27,595	28,295	28,995	29,495
Used Values ($)				
LX ▲	8,000	11,000	13,000	15,000
LX ▼	6,500	9,500	11,500	13,500
EX ▲	8,500	12,000	14,000	16,000
EX ▼	7,500	10,500	12,500	14,500
Reliability	3	3	3	3
Crash Safety (F)	5	5	5	5
Side	5	5	5	5

Offset	3	3	3	3
Head Restraints (F)	5	5	5	—
Rear	3	3	3	—
Rollover Resistance	4	4	—	4

Mazda

MPV ★ ★ ★

RATING: Average (2002–06); Below Average (1989–2001). Too bad Mazda has thrown in the towel and scheduled the MPV for extinction after the 2006 model year. The company accomplished an amazing turnaround five years ago when it made the 2002 MPV sportier and more nimble than its more space- and comfort-oriented counterparts. Previous models were underpowered, lumbering, undersized, and overpriced. **"Real" city/highway fuel economy:** 15.6/10.9 L/100 km. Owners report fuel savings may undershoot this estimate by at least 15 percent. **Maintenance/Repair costs:** Average; independent garages can service these minivans more cheaply than Mazda dealers. **Parts:** Likely to be back-ordered and cost more than average—two problems that will get worse now that the MPV has been axed. **Extended warranty:** An extended warranty is worth having, particularly since powertrain problems plague these vehicles after the first three years of use. **Best alternatives:** The MPV is still best suited for owners who don't want the biggest family-hauler on the block, for those who prefer sporty handling, and for those who don't mind spending less to get less. When the MPV is compared with Honda's Odyssey, the value equation gets a little murkier. With the price reduction, the base MPV LX gains a competitive advantage over the base Odyssey. When compared with the more feature-laden Odysseys, the savings don't make up for the MPV's smaller size and less powerful engine. And the Odyssey is already available with a DVD entertainment system. Go for a cheaper 2002 MPV, but make sure it's a second-series version to keep factory-induced glitches to a minimum. There are plenty of reasonably priced 4- and 5-year-old MPVs on the market that have come off lease. Other models to consider are GM's Astro or Safari, Honda's Odyssey, and pre-2004 Toyota Siennas. **Online help:** *townhall-talk.edmunds.com/direct/view/.ee93de8* (Mazda MPV: Problems and Solutions), *forums.mazdaworld.org/index.php?showforum=35*, and *www.autosafety. org/autodefects.html.*

Strengths and Weaknesses

This small minivan offers a number of innovative features such as "theatre" seating (the rear passenger seat is slightly higher) and a third seat that pivots to become a rear-facing bench seat or folds into the floor for picnics or tailgate parties. Another feature unique among minivans is Mazda's Side-by-Slide removable second-row seats, which move fore and aft as well as side to side while a passenger is seated.

Sliding-door crank windows are standard on the entry-level model, and power-assisted windows are standard on the LX and ES versions.

Mazda's only minivan quickly became a bestseller when it first came on the market in 1989, but its popularity fell just as quickly when larger, more powerful competitors arrived. Mazda sales have bounced back recently as a result of price-cutting and the popularity of the automaker's small cars and pickups. This infusion of cash allowed the company (34 percent of which is owned by Ford) to put additional money into its 2002 redesign, thus ending a sales slump that has plagued Mazda for over a decade. Early MPVs embodied many of the mistakes made by Honda's first Odyssey: Its 170 horses weren't adequate for people-hauling, and it was expensive for what was essentially a smaller van than buyers expected—30 cm shorter than the Ford Windstar and 15 cm shorter than the Toyota Sienna and the Nissan Quest.

VEHICLE HISTORY: 1996—A passenger-side airbag, four-wheel ABS, and four doors. **2000**—A new model with front-drive and sliding side doors. **2002**—A 200-hp V6 and 5-speed automatic transmission, power-sliding side doors, revised suspension settings, and 17-inch wheels. **2003**—More standard features (LX) that include power-sliding rear side doors, 16-inch wheels, a flip-up side table, and a doormat. **2004**—Refreshed interior and exterior styling of no real consequence, except for the additional lumbar support for the driver's seat.

The MPV presently uses the Taurus 200-hp 3.0L Duratec V6. Some refinements produce a lower torque peak—3000 rpm versus 4400 rpm—giving the Mazda engine better pulling power at lower speeds. Making good use of that power is a smooth-shifting 5-speed automatic transmission, which should cut fuel consumption a bit. One immediate benefit—the 3.0L is able to climb hills without continually downshifting, and Mazda's "slope control" system automatically shifts to a lower gear when hills get very steep.

Torque is still less than with the Odyssey's 3.5L or with the 3.8L engine in top-of-the-line Chryslers, though it's comparable to lesser Chrysler products and GM's Venture and Montana. The suspension has been firmed up to decrease body roll, enhancing cornering ability and producing a sportier ride than with other minivans. This firmness may be too much for some, however.

I've been tougher on the MPV than *Consumer Reports* and others have been because of price-gouging, poor servicing, small size, underpowered drivetrain, and reliability problems (all too common on pre-2000 models). It now looks like most of these concerns have been addressed, although I'm still worried that the 3.0L Duratec may not hold up.

On more recent models, engine overheating and head gasket failures are commonplace with the 4-banger, and the temperature gauge warns you only when it's too late. Some cases of chronic engine knocking in cold weather with the 3.0L have been fixed by installing tighter-fitting, Teflon-coated pistons. Valve lifter problems are also common with this engine. Winter driving is compromised by the MPV's light rear end and mediocre traction, and low ground clearance means that off-road excursions shouldn't be too adventurous. Vehicles from the last couple of model years are much improved; nevertheless, expect some transmission glitches, ABS malfunctions, rotten-egg exhaust smells, stalling and surging, and oil leakage. Owners report that the electronic computer module (ECU), automatic transmission driveshaft, upper shock mounts, front 4×4 drive axles and lash adjusters, AC core, and radiator fail within the first three years. Cold temperatures tend to fry the automatic window motor, and the paint is easily chipped and flakes off early, especially around the hood, tailgate, and front fenders. Premature brake caliper and rotor wear and excessive vibration/pulsation are chronic problem areas (repairs are needed about every 12,000 km). Premature paint peeling commonly afflicts white MPVs.

Safety Summary

All models: 1998—Rear anti-sway bar brackets snap off from rear axle housing. • ABS brake failure. • Defective gas cap causes the false activation of the Check Engine light. **2000**—Fixed seat belt anchors and buckle placement prevent the safe installation of child safety seats. • Vehicle windshield and side glass suddenly shattered while parked. • Rear hatch door flew open when rear-ended. **2000–01**—Engine valve failure. • Cupholders will spill drink when making a sharp turn; holders were redesigned in 2002. **2000–03**—Airbags fail to deploy. **2001**—Engine surging. • Malfunctioning #1 spark plug causes chronic engine hesitation. • Tranny lever can be shifted out of Park without key in ignition; sometimes it won't shift out of Park when you want it to. • Brake failure. • Brake caliper bolt fell off, causing vehicle to skid. • Sliding doors don't lock in place. • Rear visibility obstructed by high seatbacks. **2002–03**—Engine oil leakage. • Sudden stalling. • Shifter obscures dash and is easily knocked about. **2003**—Child's neck easily tangled in seat belt. **2003–04**—Rotten-egg exhaust smell. **2004**—Engine seizes when connecting rod fails. • Transmission failure caused by worn shaft solenoid. • Blown tire sidewall. • Tread separation on Dunlop tires. **2005**—Seat belt failed to hold front-seat occupants when the vehicle was rear-ended. • Transmission slippage, then failure. • Rear window shattered when the defroster was turned on.

Secret Warranties/Internal Bulletins/Service Tips

All models/years: TSB #006-94 looks into all the causes and remedies for excessive brake vibrations, and TSB #11-14-95 gives an excellent diagnostic flow chart for troubleshooting excessive engine noise. • Serious paint peeling and delamination will be fully covered for up to six years under a Mazda secret warranty, say owners. • Troubleshooting tips for correcting wind noise around doors. • Tips for eliminating a musty, mildew-type AC odour. **All models: 1996–98**—Tips for correcting water leaks from the sliding sunroof. • Brake pulsation repair tips. • Front power-window noise. • Wind noise around doors. • Steering wheel may be a bit off-centre. **2000–01**—Hard starts caused by inadequate fuel-system pressure are because of a fuel-pressure regulator that's stuck open. • Front brake clunking can be silenced by replacing the eight brake guide plates (TSB #04-003/00). • Insufficient airflow at bi-level setting. • Door key difficult to insert or rotate. **2000–03**—A corroded rear heater pipe may leak coolant (see TSB #07-004/03). **2000–04**—A-pillar clicking on rough roads. • Second-row seat rattling. **2000–05**—Rust on door sash areas. **2000–06**—More tips on silencing front brake clunk. • Countermeasures for excessive body vibration. **2001**—Rear brake popping, squealing, or clicking. **2002**—Engine tappet noise. **2002–03**—Cargo net hooks detach. **2002–06**—Camshaft ticking noise. • Key won't pull out of the ignition lock. • Power sliding door opens after closing. **2003–04**—Remedies for shift shock (transmission slams into gear). • No warm air from heater. **2005–06**—Idle RPM drop, stalling, rough idle, or hesitation.

MPV PROFILE

	1996	1997	1998	2000	2001	2002	2003	2004	2005
Cost Price ($)									
Base	27,330	—	—	—	—	—	—	—	—
DX/GX	—	—	—	25,505	25,095	25,975	26,090	26,600	27,595
LX/GS	30,900	27,845	25,199	29,450	29,450	29,150	29,090	29,995	30,295
Used Values ($)									
Base ▲	2,500	—	—	—	—	—	—	—	—
Base ▼	2,000	—	—	—	—	—	—	—	—
DX/GX ▲	—	—	—	6,000	7,500	10,000	12,500	14,500	17,500
DX/GX ▼	—	—	—	5,000	6,500	8,500	11,000	13,000	16,000
LX/GS ▲	3,500	4,500	6,000	7,500	9,500	11,500	13,500	16,500	19,500
LX/GS ▼	3,000	4,000	5,000	6,500	8,500	10,000	12,000	15,000	18,000
Reliability	3	3	3	4	4	4	4	4	4
Crash Safety (F)	4	4	4	4	4	5	5	5	5
Side	2	2	—	5	5	5	5	5	5
Side (IIHS)	—	—	—	1	1	1	1	1	1
Offset	2	2	2	3	3	3	3	3	3
Head Restraints (F)	1	—	—	3	2	2	2	1	1
Rear	—	—	—	—	1	1	1	—	—
Rollover Resistance	—	—	—	—	3	3	3	—	—

Toyota

SIENNA, PREVIA ★ ★ ★ ★

RATING: *Sienna:* Above Average (2006, 1998–2003); Average (2004–05). A resurgence of safety-related defects carried over to the 2005 model following the 2004 Sienna's redesign. *Previa:* Average (1991–97). The Previa has reasonable reliability, mediocre road performance, and limited interior amenities. Nevertheless, it's far better than any of Toyota's earlier LE minivans. **"Real" city/highway fuel economy:** *Previa 2.4L:* 13.3/10.0 L/100 km. *Previa 2.4L 4×4:* 14.1/10.7 L/100 km. *Sienna 3.0L:* 12.4/8.8 L/100 km. *Sienna 3.3L:* 12.2/8.1 L/100 km. *Sienna 3.3L AWD:* 13.1/9.0 L/100 km. Owners report fuel savings may undershoot these estimates by about 10 percent. **Maintenance/Repair costs:** Like the Camry, Sienna's costs are much lower than average. The only exception is engine sludge, requiring expensive repairs. Previas aren't afflicted with the sludge problem, but their maintenance costs are still higher than average. Only Toyota dealers can repair these minivans, particularly when it comes to troubleshooting the supercharged 2.4L engine and All Trac. **Parts:** There's an excellent supply of reasonably priced Sienna parts taken from the Camry parts bin. Previa parts are in limited supply, but they're reasonably priced. Automatic transmission torque converters on 1998–2000 models are frequently back-ordered because of their poor reliability. **Extended warranty:** Yes, for the more problematic 2004 and 2005 models. **Best alternatives:** Mazda minivans are catching up to Honda and Toyota in performance and reliability, while the less reliable and low-tech Ford and GM models are hardly in the running. Chrysler's extensive 7-year powertrain warranty, generous rebates, and innovative styling have kept its minivans on life-support for the past several years. Earlier Toyotas are outclassed by the brawnier, more innovative Odyssey. Be wary of the power-sliding door. As with the Odyssey and Ford and GM minivans, these doors can injure children and pose unnecessary risks to other occupants. **Online help:** *www.autosafety.org/autodefects.html, yotarepair.com/Sludge_Zone.html,* and *www.cartrackers.com/Forums/live/MiniVansEnthusiastDiscussionGroup/page8.html.* Also, see *www.1010tires.com* for owner reports on poorly performing Goodyear/Dunlop tires and *www.lawyersand settlements.com/case/toyota_dunlop_tire_classaction* for a copy of a class action filed in New York.

Strengths and Weaknesses

The completely redesigned 2004 Sienna provides lots more interior room than previous models (accommodating up to eight passengers), handles much better, rides more comfortably, and uses a more powerful, fuel-efficient engine. Standard four-wheel disc brakes and all-wheel drive are offered for the first time.

A new 230-hp 3.3L V6 turns in respectable acceleration times under 9 seconds—almost as good as the Odyssey's. Handling is completely carlike, there's less vulnerability to wind buffeting, and there's minimal road noise.

Sienna's interior and exterior have been gently restyled. The third-row seats split and fold away, head restraints don't have to be removed when the seats are stored, and second-row bucket seats are easily converted to bench seats.

The Sienna is Toyota's Camry-based front-drive minivan. It replaced the Previa for the 1998 model year and abandoned the Previa's futuristic look in favour of a more conservative Chevrolet Venture styling. The Sienna seats seven and offers dual power-sliding doors with optional remote controls and a V6 powerplant. It's built in the same Kentucky assembly plant as the Camry and comes with lots of safety and convenience features, including side airbags, anti-lock brakes, and a low-tire-pressure warning system.

Some of the Sienna's strong points are standard ABS and side airbags (LE, XLE); a smooth-running V6 engine and a transmission that's a bit more refined and capable than what the Odyssey offers; a comfortable, stable ride; a fourth door; a quiet interior; easy entry/exit; and better-than-average fit and finish and reliability. Its weak areas: V6 performance is compromised by the AC and the automatic transmission powertrain, and it lacks the trailer-towing brawn of rear-drive minivans:

> Imagine our surprise when we discovered within the owner's manual a "Caution" stating that one must not exceed 72 km/hr while towing a trailer…. This limit is not stated in the promotional literature we were provided, or on the *Toyota.ca* website, or in any trailer towing rating guide. This limit was also not mentioned at any time during our purchase negotiations. Alarmingly, Toyota defines a "Caution" as a "warning against anything which may cause injury to people if the warning is ignored." As it turns out, the dealer was not aware of this speed limit….

Although the rear seats fold flat to accommodate the width of a 4' × 8' board, the tailgate won't close, the heavy seats are difficult to reinstall (it's a two-person job, and the centre seat barely fits through the door), and the middle roof pillars and rear head restraints obstruct rear visibility. Also, there's no traction control, the rear drum brakes are less efficient, fuel economy is mediocre (using premium fuel), the low-mounted radio is hard to reach, and third-row seats lack a fore/aft adjustment to increase cargo space.

Reliability is still problematic on 1997–2005 models, with a cluster of redesign-related deficiencies around the 2004–05 model years. There has been a disturbing increase in factory-related defects reported by owners during the past few years. The most serious reliability problems concern self-destructing, sludge-prone engines (1997–2002 models) and defective automatic transmissions (1998–2005 Siennas). Many other failure-prone mechanical and body components, like collapsing rear hatch struts and faulty power-sliding doors, continue to compromise the Sienna's safety and drive up ownership costs.

Toyota Canada advises owners who notice the telltale signs of engine sludge formation to take their vehicle to their local dealer to have the engine inspected.

These signs may include the emission of blue smoke from the tailpipe and/or excessive oil consumption, which may cause overheating and rough running or the Check Engine light to come on.

Other recent model problems reported by owners include automatic transmission failures; a clunk or banging in the driveline; the car jolting or creeping forward when at a stop, forcing you to keep your foot firmly on the brake; stalling when the AC engages; electrical shorts; premature brake wear and excessive brake noise (mostly screeching); a chronic rotten-egg smell; distracting windshield reflections and distorted windshields; sliding door defects; the window suddenly shattering; easily chipped paint; and various other body glitches, including a hard-to-pull-out rear seat, water leaks, and excessive creaks and rattles (seat belt, sun visor).

VEHICLE HISTORY: 1996—The supercharged engine is the only powerplant offered. **1997**—Extra soundproofing. **1998**—Introduction of the Sienna; no more Previa. **2001**—A rear defroster, some additional horsepower and torque, and a driver-side sliding door. **2004**—Completely redesigned with new styling, larger dimensions, more power, more safety options, and about 90 extra kilograms. Optional AWD adds more weight as well and includes problematic run-flat tires. The new 230-hp 3.3L V6 and 5-speed automatic transmission add 20 more horses, which raises the question: Why bother? Kia's 2006 Sedona and Hyundai's Entourage upped the ante by 50 and provide more safety, performance, and convenience features as standard rather than optional items. Power windows for the sliding rear side doors are newly standard on the Sienna, however. CEs and LEs can carry eight with a removable second-row bench seat. The new hideaway third-row bench seat folds into a floorwell, as on the Honda Odyssey minivan, but the Sienna's 60/40 split adds to its functionality. **2005**—Standard dual front power seats for both the driver and passenger.

Previa

The redesigned 1991 Previa's performance and reliability were so much improved over its LE predecessor that it almost seemed like a different vehicle. Roomier and rendered more stable thanks to its longer wheelbase, equipped with a 2.4L engine (supercharged as of the 1994 model year), and loaded with standard safety and convenience features, 1991–97 Previas are almost as driver-friendly as the Chrysler and Mazda competition, and a 1997 model won't cost more than a few thousand dollars. Still, they can't match Ford, GM, or Chrysler front-drive minivans for responsive handling and a comfortable ride, and Toyota's small engine is overworked and doesn't hesitate to tell you so. Previa owners have learned to live with engine noise, poor fuel economy, premature front brake wear, excessive brake vibration and pulsation, electrical glitches, AC malfunctions, and fit and finish blemishes. The 4×4 models with automatic transmissions steal lots of power from the 4-cylinder powerplant, though they have fewer reliability problems than similar drivetrains found on competitors, especially Chryslers.

 **Safety Summary**

All models/years: A multiplicity of sliding door defects covered by internal bulletins. • Windshield distortion. • Reflection of the dashboard on the windshield impairs visibility. **All models: 1999**—Wheel lug nuts broke and allowed wheel to fall off. • Window exploded while idling. • Rear brake drums may overheat and warp. • Faulty fuel cap causes the Check Engine light to come on. **2000**—Chronic transmission failure because of faulty torque converter. • Wheel lug nuts shear off. • Driver's seat belt anchor bolt on door pillar unscrewed and fell to the floor. • Premature tire blowouts (Dunlop and Firestone). • Right rear passenger window suddenly exploded. • Annoying dash/windshield reflection also impairs visibility (very bad with black and beige colours). **2000–01**—Sudden, unintended acceleration. • Defective transmission torque converter causes the engine warning light to come on. **2001**—Sudden stalling when the AC is turned on. • Automatic transmission suddenly went into Neutral while on the highway. • Vehicle rolled down a hill with shifter in Park and ignition shut off. • Rear seat belts can't be adjusted. • Centre rear seat belt doesn't tighten sufficiently around children. • Slope of the windshield makes it hard to gauge where the front end stops. • Rear window exploded as front door was closed. • Sunroof flew off when opened while Sienna was underway. **2002**—Several electrical fires in the engine compartment. • Neither front nor side airbag deployed in a collision. • Defective power steering. • Loss of steering. **2003**—Unsafe transmission Overdrive design. • Child safety seat second-row tethering is poorly designed. • Vehicle jerks to one side when accelerating or stopping. **2004**—Engine surging with minimal pedal pressure. • When proceeding from a rolling stop, acceleration is delayed for about two seconds.

> While parking, accelerating no more than 5 mph [8 km/h] vehicle surged forward. Although I was applying the brake, the car would not stop until it ran into a tree trunk.

• Child can knock gearshift lever into Drive from Park without key in the ignition. • Difficulty shifting into a higher gear. • Sluggish transmission downshift; vehicle sometimes seems to slip out of gear when decelerating. • Skid control system lockup. • Fuel tank leakage after recall repairs; leaking fuel line. • Complete loss of brakes. • Rapid brake degradation (glazed and warped rotors). • Sliding door catches passenger's arm or leg; manual door doesn't latch properly (particularly when windows are open); door opens when turning, jams, or closes when vehicle is parked on an incline:

> Our two-year-old son pulled on the sliding door handle, and the door began to open (we thought the child locks were on, but this was not the case). He was surprised and was afraid of falling out of the van, so he just held onto the handle. As the door was opening, his head then was dragged between the sliding door and the side of the van. But the van door did not stop opening. It just continued opening, exerting even more force on our son's head. Fortunately we were able to grab the door and forcefully pull it back closed before our son was horribly injured.

• Second-row seat belt locks up; faulty seat belt bracket in rear passenger seat. • Seat belts won't retract. • Battery-saver device doesn't work, particularly if interior lights are left on (they don't turn off as advertised). • Small brake lights inadequate. • Foot gets stuck between pedals. • Rotten-egg smell. • Daytime running lights blind oncoming drivers (2004 Highlander has the same problem). • Long delay for fuel tank recall campaign parts. **2005**—NHTSA has logged almost 150 safety-related complaints; about double what would be deemed normal. • Sudden acceleration when parking or shifting to Reverse. • Many reports that the front and side airbags fail to deploy. • Airbag deployed for no reason while vehicle was underway. • Airbag is disabled when passenger seat is occupied. • Hesitation when accelerating, then sudden acceleration. • Laser-controlled cruise control jerks back to former speed when the way seems clear. • Gear shift lever can be accidently knocked from Fourth gear to Reverse. • Vehicle Stability Control (VSC) engages when it shouldn't:

> I was driving my 2005 Toyota Sienna on a dry, straight road at about 30 mph [48 km/h] and for no reason the Vehicle Stability Control (VSC) engaged and brought the car to a violent stop. The nose of the car came down and I could feel the rear of the van begin to lift off of the ground. If I was traveling on a highway at a higher rate of speed, I have no doubt this van would have flipped over. I had to drive to the dealer when this occurred at least ten times while not driving over 10 mph [16 km/h]. My dealer said they have never heard of this problem but I have found numerous owners online who have experienced this issue.

• Brake pedal stiffens intermittently. • Premature brake rotor wear leads to longer stopping distance and increased braking noise. • Run-flat tires don't signal driver when they are damaged; may catch fire:

> 2005 Toyota Sienna has Bridgestone run flat tires and the back right passenger tire went flat, then smoked and caught fire.

• When the rear windows are down, the door will not stay open. • Sliding doors fail to latch when they are opened. • Power-sliding door continues closing even if something is in its way (similar to complaints on previous model-year Siennas). • Rear hatch may fall:

> The liftgate on a power liftgate 2005 Toyota Sienna will not stay open. It has come down and wacked my wife and I on the head many times. I found out the replacement is $450.

• Automatic interior light shut-off fails intermittently, draining the battery. • Rear heater core leaks coolant. • Front heater airflow is inadequate.

Secret Warranties/Internal Bulletins/Service Tips

All models/years: Sliding door hazards, malfunctions, and noise are a veritable plague affecting all model years and generating a ton of service bulletins. • Owner feedback confirms that front brake pads and discs will be replaced under Toyota's "goodwill" policy if they wear out before 2 years/40,000 km. • Loose, poorly fitted trim panels (TSB # BO017-03, revised September 9, 2003). • Rusting at the base of the two front doors will be repaired at no cost, usually with a courtesy car included. According to *www.siennaclub.org*, the proper fix is: Repaint inside of doors (presumably after removing paint and rust), cover with 3M film, and replace and coat inside seals with silicone grease. **1997–2002**—Free engine overhaul or replacement because of engine sludge buildup. The program includes 1997 through 2002 Toyota and Lexus vehicles with 3.0L V6 or 2.2L 4-cylinder engines. There is no mileage limitation, and tell Toyota to shove it if they give a song and dance about proof of oil changes. **1998**—Upgraded brake pads and rotors should reduce brake groan and squeak noises. **1998–2000**—An 8-year/160,000 km warranty extension for automatic transmission failure. Says Toyota:

> We have recently become aware that a small number of Sienna owners have experienced a mechanical failure in the automatic transaxle, drive pinion bearing. This failure could result in slippage, noise, or a complete lack of movement.
>
> To ensure the continued satisfaction and reliability of your Sienna, Toyota has decided to implement a Special Policy Adjustment affecting certain 1998–2000 Sienna models.... This Special Policy will extend the warranty coverage of the automatic transaxle to 8 years or 160,000 km, whichever occurs first, from the original warranty registration date.

• Outline of various diagnostic procedures and fixes to correct vehicle pulling to one side. • Power steering squeaks can be silenced by installing a countermeasure steering rack end under warranty. • Power steering feel can be improved by replacing the steering rack guide. • False activation of the security alarm can be fixed by modifying the hood latch switch. • Power window rattles can be corrected by installing a revised lower window frame mounting bracket. **1998–2003**—A new rear brake drum has been developed to reduce rear brake noise. • An upgraded alternator will improve charging (see TSB #EL013-03) and is also subject to "goodwill" treatment. **1999–2001**—Tips on fixing power seat motor cable to prevent a loose seat or inoperative seat adjustment. • Power-sliding door transmitter improvements. **2000**—Toyota has field fixes to correct washer fluid leakage from the rear washer nozzle and to eliminate moisture and odours permeating the vehicle interior. • Correction for an inoperative spare-tire lift. • Speedometer or tachometer troubleshooting. **2001**—False activation of the security alarm. • Power windows rattling. • Entertainment system hum. • Faulty speedometer and tachometer. • Inoperative third-row sliding seat. • Special service campaign to inspect or replace the front subframe assembly on 2001 models. • Water leaking into the trunk area. • Troubleshooting interior moisture or odours. • Loose sun visor. • Front wheel bearing ticking. **2002**—Troubleshooting complaints that vehicle pulls to one side. **2002–03**—Steering angle sensor calibration. • Loose sun visor remedy. **2003–05**—No start in extreme cold. **2003–06**—Upper, lower windshield ticking noise. **2004**—VSC activates intermittently when it is not needed. • New ECM calibration for a poor shifting transmission (TSB #TC007-03). •

Premature front brake pad wear is corrected with upgraded brake pads. • Rear disc brake groan (TSB #BR002-04). • Intermediate steering shaft noise on turns. • Steering column pop, squeak, and click. • Front door area wind noise (TSB #NV009-03). • Power-sliding door inoperative, rattles (the saga continues). • Back door shudder and water leaks. • Charging improvement at idle (TSB #RL013-03). • Seat heaters only operate on high. **2004–05**—Remedy for hard starts in cold weather. • Transmission lag, gear hunting. • Premature brake pad wear. • Fuel-injector ticking. • Inoperative AC light flashing. • AC blower or compressor noise; seized compressor. • Poor rear wiper performance. • Exhaust system squeak or creak. **2004–06**—Silencing engine ping, knock. • Power hatch door shudder and leakage. • Power-sliding door rattles. • Excessive steering effort in high road-salt areas:

INCREASED STEERING EFFORT

BULLETIN NO.: ST001-07   **DATE: JANUARY 19, 2007**

2004–06 Sienna

In areas where road salt is used during winter months, some customers may experience a slight increase in steering effort, which may gradually become more noticeable over time. The steering intermediate shaft has been modified to help address this condition.

APPLICABLE WARRANTY: This repair is covered under the Toyota Comprehensive Warranty. This warranty is in effect for 36 months or 36,000 miles [68,000 km], whichever occurs first, from the vehicle's in-service date. Warranty application is limited to correction of a problem based upon a customer's specific complaint.

• Front seat squeak. • Upgraded brake pads will extend durability:

FRONT BRAKE PAD WEAR

BULLETIN NO.: BR009-04   **DATE: DECEMBER 23, 2006**

2004–07 model year Sienna vehicles.

INTRODUCTION: A new brake pad kit has been developed to address brake pad wear complaints on vehicles operated under severe conditions. Continue to use the original service part for all other vehicles.

NOTE: Use of this pad kit may increase brake noise under certain conditions.

SIENNA, PREVIA PROFILE

	1997	1998	1999	2000	2001	2002	2003	2004	2005
Cost Price ($)									
Previa	36,998	—	—	—	—	—	—	—	—
Sienna Cargo 3d	—	24,438	24,570	24,570	—	—	—	—	—
Sienna CE 4d	—	26,808	26,940	27,770	29,535	29,335	29,060	30,000	30,000
Sienna LE 4d	—	29,558	29,980	30,705	31,900	32,985	31,925	35,000	35,420

Used Values ($)

Previa ▲	3,500	—	—	—	—	—	—	—	—
Previa ▼	3,000	—	—	—	—	—	—	—	—
Sienna Cargo 3d ▲	—	4,500	6,000	7,000	—	—	—	—	—
Sienna Cargo 3d ▼	—	3,500	5,000	6,000	—	—	—	—	—
Sienna CE 4d ▲	—	6,000	7,500	8,500	10,500	12,500	15,000	18,000	21,000
Sienna CE 4d ▼	—	5,000	7,000	7,000	9,000	11,000	13,500	17,000	19,500
Sienna LE 4d ▲	—	6,000	7,500	9,000	11,500	14,000	16,500	19,500	23,000
Sienna LE 4d ▼	—	5,000	6,500	8,000	10,000	13,000	15,000	18,500	21,000

Reliability	3	4	4	4	4	4	4	3	4
Crash Safety (F)	4	5	5	5	5	5	5	5	4
Side	—	—	4	4	4	4	4	5	5
Offset	1	5	5	5	5	5	5	5	5
Head Restraints (F)	—	1	1	—	2	2	2	5	1
Rear	—	—	—	—	—	—	—	3	—
Rollover Resistance	—	—	—	—	4	4	4	4	4

BEGINNERS, BARGAINS, AND "BEATERS"

"Beginners" are recent automobile models that haven't generated enough owner feedback or manufacturer service bulletins to be rated fairly. There are also many cars and minivans that are no longer built or are sold in small numbers that don't merit extensive consideration either. Nevertheless, we have prepared the following thumbnail sketches for some of the vehicles passed over in Part Three.

Acura's **CSX** is an Above Average buy that came on the scene as the 2006 model replacement for the entry-level EL, a successful Honda spin-off that was made in Canada (except for the engines, which were shipped from Japan) for Canadians. The EL debuted in 1997 with the Acura 1.6 EL and, later, the 1.7 EL. Selling for about $20,000 used, the 2006 CSX Touring is essentially a restyled, more powerful luxury version of the Honda Civic sedan. The base and Type S engines are lifted from the Acura RSX and Honda Si, respectively.

CSX is powered by Honda's 155-hp 2.0L DOHC iVTEC engine, which burns regular gas and is hooked to a 5-speed manual or automatic transmission. Wheel-mounted paddle shifters, seldom found in this price range, are standard with the 5-speed automatic, as are electronic stability control, anti-lock brakes, side airbags and side curtain airbags, heated mirrors with integrated turn signals, steering-wheel audio controls, a CD/MP3 player, automatic climate control, cruise control, auto up/down windows, and a 60/40 folding rear seat.

Unfortunately, there's no independent crashworthiness data available specific to these models because the Canada-exclusive CSX hasn't been crash-tested by U.S. safety agencies. Nevertheless, since it does share the Civic's platform, it would be reasonable to extrapolate the CSX's crashworthiness by using the Civic's scores: five-star frontal collision occupant protection, four-star front-passenger protection five-star rear-seat occupant protection in side collisions, and four stars for the car's rollover resistance.

This small luxury compact does have some distinctive features that set it apart from the Civic. For example, it comes with a more powerful base engine that is currently found in the Acura RSX; handling is enhanced by a sportier suspension;

and the front bumper, fenders, and hood are exclusive to the CSX, making it a bit longer than the Civic.

Undoubtedly, the CSX is a well-balanced car that is both practical and fun to drive in much the same way as we remember the Acura Type R Integra and Toyota Celica being. It has more than enough power; handling is superb; interior room is adequate, with lots of thoughtful storage areas; controls are a breeze to decipher and access; visibility is fairly good; outstanding workmanship and top-quality materials are evident everywhere (Ontario auto plants are renowned for high quality control, regardless of the automaker); and its resale value is extraordinarily high. On the other hand, the high-tech two-tiered dash might not be to all tastes, and the thick front side pillars obstruct forward visibility.

Acura's **RSX** is an Average buy that was first launched as a 2002 coupe hatchback with a $24,000 base price (a Type S cost $7,000 more). Used, an entry-level 2003 is reasonably priced at $11,000–$13,000; a 2005 should fetch between $16,000 and $17,500.

The RSX is built on the Civic platform and is powered by a base 170-hp 2.0L twin-cam iVTEC 4-banger or a torquier 200-hp variant used by the high-performance Type S. Three transmissions are available: a 5-speed manual and a 4-speed automatic offered with base models, and a 6-speed manual found on the Type S. Both engines are torquier than the powerplants they replaced; however, the base engine has more useful commuting low-end torque than the so-called sportier Type S engine.

The RSX appeals to drivers who want to shift fast and often and don't mind a firm ride. The car is well appointed; has good acceleration and handling above 3000 rpm; provides user-friendly gauges and controls; brakes well, especially with the Type S; gives good fuel economy (first tune-up at 160,000 km); depreciates slowly; has garnered a five-star frontal crash rating for both the driver and front-seat passenger and a four-star front side-impact rating; and has head restraints rated "Good" up front and "Average" in the rear by IIHS. The car has high-quality construction, except for transmission components and electronic glitches.

On the downside, the car exhibits so-so acceleration in lower gears; overall acceleration that's compromised by the automatic transmission; heavy steering that's a bit vague; limited front and rear headroom; cramped rear seating, with barely adequate knee and foot space; difficult rear access; high rear-hatch liftover that complicates loading; excessive road and engine noise; and rearward visibility that's obstructed by small side windows, thick roof pillars, and a tall rear deck. There have also been many manual and automatic transmission complaints (see *forums. clubrsx.com*).

All components are of above-average quality except the airbag sensors and the manual and automatic transmissions, which are quite problematic on Acura's entire vehicle lineup. Owner reports target defective airbag sensors that disable the passenger-side airbag; engine hesitation upon acceleration, with excessive exhaust noise; Second to Third gear shifting glitches and grinding; automatic transmission leaks; a faulty half-shaft shield causing a buzzy exhaust, and the plastic cover over the cylinder head/valve cover buzzes a bit, too; heater blower motor overheating; rough shifting; premature brake and rear strut wear; an airbag warning light that remains lit; a rear bumper cover that may fall off, is often misaligned, or comes loose; and chipped paint. Original-equipment tires are poor performers in snow; however, reducing front-tire pressure to 31 psi (approximately 214 kPa) improves performance. In very cold weather, flip-up wipers freeze at the joint.

Other cars worth considering are early Acura Integras (see page 251), the Mazda Miata, and Toyota Celica GT or GT-S. An extended warranty isn't needed. Fuel economy is fairly decent: The base engine burns 8.6/7.1 L/100 km with a manual transmission or 9.8/7.1 L/100 km with an automatic gearbox; the Type S gets 9.8/7.6 L/100 km.

The 2002–06 **BMW Mini Cooper** is also an Average buy. The model was launched in 1959 as a minuscule front-engine/front-drive subcompact that retailed for $786 and became a cult favourite during the '60s. BMW subsequently bought the make as part of its money-losing purchase of Rover in the 1990s and introduced the Mini Cooper to North America in 2002. It's distinctively styled, depreciates

slowly, and has been given "Good" offset crash protection and head-restraint effectiveness ratings by IIHS. On one hand, NHTSA says that the little tyke merits a four-star rating for its resistance to rollovers. On the other hand, these little urban guerillas aren't cheap, and they provide a mediocre ride and so-so handling along with limited front visibility, glitch-prone mechanical components, and body problems (cracked windshields caused by body panel flexing, for example).

The 2007 BMW Mini Cooper.

A 2002 base Mini is a bargain at $10,500 (add $2,000 more for the S model), much less than its original $25,200 retail price; the 2003 and 2004 models sell for about $13,500 to $14,500; and a $23,500 2005 version is now worth $17,000. Other cars you may wish to consider are the Mazda Miata and Porsche Boxster.

Although not as small as the original Austin Cooper, the Mini is less than 4 metres long, with a 239-cm wheelbase, a width of 1.9 metres, and a height of only 1.4 metres (smaller than GM's Geo Metro). The 115-hp 1.6L 4-banger can be teamed with a 5-speed manual or automatic transmission, and it turns in a 0–100 km/h time of a leisurely 9.2 seconds. The Cooper S uses a 163-hp supercharged version of the same 1.6L motor (with more robust components set on a sturdier frame) and a standard 6-speed manual transmission.

Minis do have some major drawbacks, however. The forward-mounted windshield makes it next to impossible to see traffic lights when stopped at a corner. Take away the retro styling, and you get an undersized, under-performing, and untried British import thrust into a market where many proven competitors do more for less money. When compared with the Mercedes C230, the Subaru WRX, and the VW New Beetle, the Cooper S seems relatively overpriced for a car with such a small interior and cargo area. And it's built in England, which guarantees a plethora of quality bugs. Said *The Christian Science Monitor* in an early review:

> Quality is suspect in both [models]. Thrumming wheel bearings, whining steering, loose and missing interior parts marred two weeks of driving.

Most owner safety complaints concern inaccurate speedometers and jammed passenger-side seat belt shoulder retractors. Other deficiencies mostly relate to poor ergonomics, a surprising oversight for a German-engineered car. For example, inside door handles are located too far back on the doors, getting the spare tire from under the vehicle is a chore, and shoulder belts are uncomfortable. Service bulletins target engine idle fluctuations and poor acceleration; AC whistling, sunroof squeaking, and rear hatch/door window rattling; seat heaters that run too hot or not warm enough; windshield stress cracks; and inoperative interior lights. See *www.mini.ca* and *www.mini2.com/forum* for good overviews of ownership pros and cons.

Chrysler's 2004–06 **Crossfire** is an expensive, low-volume luxury sports coupe that gets a Below Average rating. This low-slung, sleekly styled two-door two-passenger coupe offers a cramped interior, high windowsills, and a low roofline that combine to create a claustrophobic cabin. Service bulletins and owner feedback indicate serious reliability problems during the car's first year on the market. Depreciation has also been brutal: A $47,745 base 2004 model is now worth only $22,500—a good price for a bad car.

Crashworthiness for the 2004–06 is quite good, with five stars given for frontal occupant protection, side protection, and rollover resistance. Furthermore, very few owner complaints have surfaced relative to the 2005–06 Crossfire; nevertheless, many safety-related incidents logged by NHTSA are particularly frightening:

> Lack of power when at a stop, even though you might be mashing in the gas pedal (pedal to the metal). So if you fear for your life when you're in the middle of an intersection and your car won't move, don't worry because it's normal? I believe I have a major safety issue with this car because multiple times I have been stopped on the road and then unable to move because my car does not register that I'm pushing down on the pedal. This past week-end it happened and I had a truck coming at me but the car would not move! Thankfully the driver swerved around my car with a lot [of] honking and such. But because [DaimlerChrysler could] not replicate that problem, they say it's fine. I'm concerned that this will happen again and I won't be lucky enough to get out of the way.

Apart from lack of power when accelerating from a stop, owners also complain of sudden acceleration when the brakes are applied, high-performance tires and a low-slung body that impair safe handling in inclement weather, airbags that fail to deploy, chronic stalling, transmission breakdowns, a manual transmission that abruptly slips out of First gear into Neutral, defective wheel bolts that lead to the wheel separating from the car, a short circuit in the dash wiring harness that poses a fire risk, and original-equipment Continental tires with weak sidewalls:

> The tires are low-profile and can't seem to take the impact of potholes without blowing out the sidewall.

Other concerns: $400 wheel rims that are easily bent in normal driving, front and rear strut failures, headlights that don't adequately illuminate the road, lights that dim at stoplights and at idle, and erratic voltage (faulty voltage regulator?):

> The car's electrical system can't regulate its voltage properly. You would think that Daimler would have the electrical system built as tough as nails...seeing that the car's life support is all dependent upon pulse power. So my complaint is [due] to the car's failure to regulate its power, it cooked my transmission's drive plate located internally on top of the valve body...then surged back to the transmission control module and fried that. And somehow, and I can't figure out why this occurred, but the internal gears inside my throttle body got fused together. This is strange to me seeing that the gears are made out of a composite. So with all that has occurred it has left the car lifeless for over 90 days.

Additionally, owners report that condensation forms inside the headlight casing, the radio display screen is too dim and can't be adjusted for brightness, the spoiler jams in the "up" position, and the dash clock doesn't tell the right time.

Chrysler's audacious high-performance rear-drive 2006 **Charger** and **SRT8** are Average buys that are spin-offs of the mediocre Chrysler 300 and Magnum. The cars' strong points are horsepower, a rear-drive cachet, distinctive muscular styling, five-star frontal crash protection, and four-star side protection and rollover resistance. On the minus side, owners report terrible gas mileage, even with the cylinder deactivation feature; a stiff, jarring ride; poor handling; optional stability control; overly assisted steering that requires constant correction; and marginal rear headroom. Charger has also been rated "Poor" for offset crash protection (without optional side airbags) by the Insurance Institute for Highway Safety. Also, head-restraint protection was rated "Marginal" by IIHS.

The 2006 Charger SE and SXT are equipped with Chrysler's 3.5L V6 and sell at a starting price of $27,635 and $31,525, respectively. Used values are about $10,000 less. In Canada, the base model Charger has a 2.7L V6, which produces 190 hp and 190 lb.-ft. of torque. The 3.5L V6 produces 250 hp and 250 lb.-ft. of torque. R/T versions use the 5.7L Hemi V8 and sell for $40,745 new and almost $10,000 less used. This engine produces 340 hp and 390 lb.-ft. of torque. The SRT8 model comes with a 6.1L Hemi V8 and has a base price of $44,790, which can also be bought for $10,000 less as a used car. The 6.1L Hemi produces 425 hp and 420 lb.-ft. of torque. Other cars using it are the Chrysler 300, the Dodge Magnum, and some Dodge trucks. Best alternatives: The Dodge 300/Magnum, Ford Five Hundred or Mustang, and Mazda Miata. Look for a high-performance Challenger clone as soon as late 2007, designed to do battle with the new Ford Mustang and Chevy's resurrected Camaro.

Safety-related complaints logged by NHTSA include one about the heater core leaking hot coolant onto a driver's right leg:

> I work for a Chrysler-Dodge auto dealership in Texas. We are currently repairing a 2006 Dodge Charger heater core leak. The heater core leaked hot antifreeze onto the gas pedal and onto the leg of one of our salesmen.... The heater core is a very poor design and should be recalled before someone gets burned while driving down the road. The heater core tubes are held on to the core by a small cheesy clamp that comes off very easy. Even the new heater core we received from Chrysler [had] tubes [that] were halfway off of the heater core.

There are also complaints about airbag, ABS, and AC compressor failures; gas tank leaks; passenger-side tire separation from the wheel; chronic stalling; front brake squealing, vibration, rotor warping, and premature deterioration (see *www.chargerforums.com/forums/showthread.php?t=23835*); and an accident that was caused by prematurely worn brake rotors.

Although this car may be fun to drive and buys you entry into the high-performance crowd, it is destined to be a loser. High fuel, insurance, and depreciation costs will quickly thin out your wallet, and the absence of a comprehensive powertrain warranty and the recent sale of Chrysler to equity investor Cerberus means owning this car is like performing a high-wire act without a net. The Charger, like Ford's resurrected Thunderbird, will likely have a short shelf life, judging by the number of 300s and Magnums piling up on dealers' lots. Chrysler revived the Hemi name in 2002 with a 5.7L Hemi V8 engine used in its pickups, and then extended it to the 300 Ram Wagon sedan—a winning combination that revived lagging pickup, sedan, and wagon sales. But that was when fuel was relatively cheap. With the Charger and SRT8, bigger is definitely not better.

Bland but solid looking, the spacious 2005–06 **Ford Five Hundred** and **Freestyle** (an SUV wagon clone) have not captured buyers' hearts due to a combination of high gas prices and early reports of poor-quality components. Both models are rated Below Average buys and are priced similarly. Although originally priced at $29,295, used 2005 versions are going for $15,000 less; 2006 versions sell for about $11,000 less. A spin-off of the Volvo S80, the Five Hundred will eventually replace the Crown Victoria to become Ford's flagship sedan. It uses a modified Volvo XC90 SUV and S80 wagon/sedan platform capable of giving the car some SUV advantages such as higher seating, increased interior space, and optional four-wheel or all-wheel drive. There is more interior space and trunk capacity than in the full-sized Crown Victoria. Additionally, crash test scores are impressive: Frontal and side crash protection are rated at five stars, and rollover resistance scored four stars.

Owners will find plenty of shortcomings with this large car, though. For example, the 203-hp V6 isn't powerful enough for a 1,860 kg (4,100 lb.) vehicle; it has a very limited towing capability of approximately 907 kg (2,000 lb.); the self-levelling shocks are unproven; the optional all-wheel-drive system is part Volvo, part Ford (not the best combination for trouble-free performance); front occupants will want more legroom; and the 18-inch tires make for a stiff, choppy ride.

Owners are most unhappy about a number of serious factory-related defects affecting primarily the automatic transmission, fuel supply, and ignition (hard starts, stalling, and dieseling). They report that the transmission jumps out of Park into Reverse, has no intermediate or second gear for descending mountains, and often hunts for the right gear:

> Vehicle constantly shifting. "Searches" for correct gear. Had computer replaced and a week later reoccurred. Reprogrammed computer again and reoccurred. Ford unable to repair. Losing 6–8 mpg [29–39 L/100 km].

Owners also point out that battery acid may eat away the plastic transmission cable; the engine loses power when accelerating; various rear brake and suspension problems crop up; there's insufficient dash lighting, and the dash reflects onto the windshield; the fuel gauge gives incorrect readings; rear seat belts cross at childrens' necks; doors leak water into the interior; and Continental tires may fail prematurely.

Ford's 2000–06 **Jaguar S-Type** is a Not Recommended buy primarily because of its persistent factory-related and design deficiencies compounded by a small dealer network and chaotic Ford mismanagement. Jaguar, Land Rover, Volvo, and Saab will likely be the next auto marques to be dumped by Ford and General Motors.

The car itself is an attractively styled, small rear-drive luxury sedan that shares its platform with the Lincoln LS. Resale prices reflect a stunningly high depreciation rate. A 2000 model originally selling for $62,795 is now worth barely $11,000; the $61,950 2004 version costs almost three times as much at $28,000. The S-Type's

V8 engine provides plenty of power, and the car handles well. Nevertheless, this car is a terrible buy due to its clunky, failure-prone automatic transmission; limited cargo room; unreliable engine and electronics and fuel delivery systems; and frequently needed brake repairs. The 3.0L V6 is derived from a Ford design, while the 4.0L V8 is Jaguar-bred. Both engines are mated to a Ford/Jaguar 5-speed automatic transmission, which explains their overall poor performance.

An Average buy, **GM**'s 2005–06 **Allure** (called the **LaCrosse** in the United States) is a substantially upgraded and stiffened version of the Century and Regal, resulting in improved ride and handling qualities. The rack-and-pinion steering is revised for better response, and the four-wheel disc braking system is completely new. Nevertheless, the Allure isn't that much different from the cars it replaces, and it has been selling poorly, with 2005 and 2006 models selling between $13,000 and $17,000, respectively. The car has a full complement of standard safety features, along with optional Ultrasonic Rear Parking Assist (of doubtful value) and a factory-installed remote starting system. Crash test scores have been acceptable, with frontal crash protection rated at five stars, side protection given three stars, and rollover resistance earning four stars.

Another Average Buy: The 2005–06 **STS**, with its $55,995 price tag for the 255-hp 3.6L V6 (coupled to a 5-speed automatic transmission) and $68,725 for the 320-hp 4.6L V8 (AWD). Bargain hunters can pick up a used entry-level 2005 STS for about $26,000; a used V8 goes for about $31,000. Whopping depreciation aside, this rear-drive/AWD Seville replacement has plenty of power and versatility. The V6 engine is more powerful than the BMW 5 Series' and Mercedes E-Class' 6-cylinders, while the V8 produces slightly less horsepower than the comparable BMW but more than the Mercedes or Lexus. Without question, Cadillac's switch to rear- or all-wheel drive improves the STS's balance, handling, and overall performance considerably. Shoppers will have to decide if the car's elegant interior and vastly superior performance make up for the loss of a little rear seatroom (it still has at least a couple centimetres more than its closest competitors, and it's close to 7.5 cm larger than the problematic Mercedes E-Class), unproven mechanical components, mediocre fit and finish, and untested crashworthiness.

Although there have been fewer than average complaints relative to STS reliability, owners do report a number of serious safety-related failures. For example, the passenger side airbag sensor fails to detect the seat is occupied and leaves the system disabled:

> The dealership tried for over a week to solve the problem, but would only say that the procedure to activate the sensor requires the passenger to enter and sit in the vehicle in a certain convoluted way that is basically unnatural and impossible for certain passengers to achieve.

Acceleration is erratic, the car suddenly loses power when passing another vehicle, the rear differential may suddenly lock up, and the car has poor traction in snow:

The contact stated that the 2006 STS fails to operate properly while driving in snow. The vehicle slides and causes crashes because there is no traction. The contact was involved in a crash, but no police report was filed. The manufacturer stated that nothing could be done and suggested the contact purchase new tires to accommodate the weather conditions.

Owners report that eye-watering, throat-burning emissions emanate from the interior, principally the trunk area; the sun roof may blow out from excessive interior air pressure; the voice recognition feature executes different commands than what it is given, and prior commands can't be countermanded; the wiring harness and module under the front seat may melt; and electrical shorts play havoc with lights, gauges, and accessory systems. There have also been some complaints that the differential leaks fluid, brake pads quickly wear out and brake rotors warp prematurely, the air dam shield falls down and drags on the pavement, windshields shatter for no reason, headlamps have stress cracks, and the battery dies if the car isn't started for several days.

And if all of the above-listed failures aren't embarrassing enough, owners also report that their front seat makes a "noxious" noise:

Front car seats are making a farting noise. I have had [the] car in the dealership three times and each time they said they fixed the problem. They have not.

The 2005–06 GM **Cobalt** and **Pursuit** are Average buys that replace the Cavalier and Sunfire with what GM calls a "premium" small car, though there is little that merits that designation. For example, all-important side curtain airbags and traction control are optional, while many automakers list them as standard features. Set on the Saturn Ion Delta platform for increased body rigidity, structural integrity, and crashworthiness, the Cobalt Sedan is about 5 cm shorter in length, about the same width, and has a slightly shorter wheelbase than the Cavalier it replaces. A trio of 4-cylinder engines provide power: a 140-hp 2.2L, a 170-hp 2.4L, and a 205-hp 2.0L supercharged version. These small cars offer good handling and a handful of standard amenities. The 2005's $15,495 base price has been reduced to about $8,500 for a used version; a new LS sedan that first sold for $19,795 now costs $11,000 used; an LT sedan that first sold for $22,995 now sells used for $13,000; and the supercharged SS coupe, once priced at $24,995, has lost $10,000 in value and now can be bought used for $15,000. Crash test scores are mixed for the 2005s and 2006s—frontal crash protection and rollover resistance are rated at four stars and side protection is given between two and four stars.

Owner complaints have targeted the premature wearout of the front brakes, poor fit and finish, assorted powertrain glitches, and electrical and fuel system malfunctions.

GM's 2006 **Lucerne** is another also-ran that gets only a Below Average rating. It's a competent front-drive family car that replaced the venerable LeSabre. Two engines were offered with this new 2006 model: a 197-hp 3.8L V6 and a 275-hp V8. With a list price of $30,995, the base model is barely worth $21,000 today.

Smart used-car shoppers may wish to consider a 2007 Lucerne a few years down the road to escape first-series 2006 model glitches (over 110 reported so far), like: no airbag deployment; sudden acceleration when the cruise control is engaged; light steering that allows the car to wander, pulling to the right once underway; dash gauges that can't be read in daylight; a trunk lid that closes too easily on one's head; a driver's mirror that cannot be adjusted to compensate for the rear blind spot and often fogs up; and a fuel gauge that gives incorrect readings (such as indicating "Full" when the tank isn't).

GM's 2005–06 **G6** is also rated as a Below Average used-car buy. It sells for $24,670 new and about $14,000 used ($16,000, for a 2006). It's a mid-sized replacement for the Grand Am and is built on GM's new front-drive Epsilon platform, used on the Saab 9-3 and the 2004 Chevrolet Malibu. The G6 comes with a weak 3.5L V6 engine, which is rated at 200 horsepower—much less power than with most of the family-sedan competition. Crash test scores are acceptable: Frontal and side crash protection are rated at five and three stars, and rollover resistance scored between four and five stars.

These cars have major reliability problems that put both your life and your wallet in danger. Foremost of these is the steering system, which can suddenly lock up, throwing your car out of control:

> This has happened in cold weather and mainly in low speed situations immediately after starting my vehicle. The failure prevents you from turning the wheel at all and you are unable to steer the vehicle for a limited amount of time.

Additionally, the ABS module can overheat and catch fire; brake pads and rotors are in constant need of replacement, and an intense, painful noise occurs if the car is driven with the rear window open:

> Open rear window or windows at speed of 40 mph [64 km/h] and above creates a safety problem as the noise from the rear of the car becomes so intense that you either have to close the window or stop the car. The noise sounds like a [rotor] on a helicopter and the faster you go over 40 the louder it becomes and your hearing becomes so bad you must stop or put [the] window back up.

Another owner reported that, when pulling into a sloped driveway, the chassis was bent back due to the I-beam structure catching the concrete driveway slope. This caused the entire engine cradle to shift, requiring thousands of dollars in repairs. Other concerns include brake lights that remain lit, automatic transmissions that shift erratically, an instrument panel that can be hard to read in daylight, a sun visor that shorts out, a windshield that chips easily, and dash rattles and noisy struts. And, as if that wasn't enough to worry about, how about staining your clothes? Yep, when the seat material is wet, it transfers its colour to any other material that it contacts…ugh.

Hyundai's 1997–2006 Above Average **Tiburon** is a steal for buyers who want some high-performance features without spending much money. Essentially a sportier variant of the Elantra, this is a fun-to-drive budget sport coupe with a good overall reliability record. Since dealer maintenance and repair costs can be a bit higher than average, owners usually get inspections and repairs done cheaply by independent garages. Used prices vary from $3,500–$15,000 for 1997–2006 models. On early models, the base 16-valve 1.8L 4-cylinder engine is smooth, efficient, and adequate when mated to the 5-speed manual transmission. Put in an automatic transmission and performance suffers somewhat, plus engine noise increases proportionally. Overall handling is crisp and predictable. The 1998 versions use a stronger 145-hp 2.0L engine, and the $12,000 2003 GT is powered by a sizzling 2.7L V6.

Crashworthiness and rollover resistance as tested on the 2004 model have been outstanding: five stars for frontal and side occupant protection and four stars for rollover resistance. Head restraints have been judged "Poor" up to 2001 models but "Above Average" thereafter. Standard brakes are adequate, though sometimes difficult to modulate. As with most sporty cars, interior room is cramped for average-sized occupants. Although no serious defects have been reported, be on the lookout for body deficiencies (fit, finish, and assembly), harsh shifting, slipping with the automatic transmission, clutch failures, oil leaks, and brake glitches (premature front brake wear and excessive brake noise).

Confidential service bulletins address the following Tiburon problems: **1997–99**—Poor automatic transmission performance (TSB #97-40-031). • Automatic transmission drain-hole oil leak, and fluid leak behind the torque converter. • Delayed engagement into Drive or Reverse (TSB #99-40-006). **1997–2001**—Correction for an erratically shifting or slipping automatic transmission that often flares or sticks in gear. **1999**—Tips on dealing with a hard-to-fill fuel tank. **1999–2003**—Erratic-shifting remedies. **2000**—Timing-belt noise may be caused by the belt rubbing against the front dust cover. **2002**—Malfunctioning automatic transaxle solenoid. • Malfunction indicator light (MIL) troubleshooting guide. **2003**—Differential seal oil leaks. • Sunroof leaks. **2003–04**—Free fuel pump and filter sub-assembly replacement for a rough-running engine (Service Campaign #T13, found in Bulletin No. 04-01-003, published March 2004). **2004–06**—Firm, abrupt 2–3 shifts.

Another newcomer from the 2006 model year, the **Mazda5** is an Above Average buy. It's mostly a compact mini-wagon that's based broadly on the Mazda3 and carries six passengers in three rows of seats. Used mostly for urban errands and light commuting, the "5" employs a peppy, though fuel-frugal, 153-hp 2.3L 4-cylinder engine (the same engine that produces three more horses in the Mazda3 and Mazda6) hooked to a standard 5-speed manual transmission or a 4-speed automatic. So far, that engine has had few problems during the past two years the

Mazda5 has run in Canada. In its favour, it has all the advantages of a small minivan without the handling or fuel penalties. Furthermore, it's reasonably priced used at $14,500 to $16,000, is powered by a competent 2.3L engine, and provides a comfortable ride and relatively quiet interior (except for omnipresent road noise—a common trait with small wagons). There are a few minuses, however. The small 4-cylinder engine doesn't have much torque ("grunt," or pulling power) for heavy loads or hill climbing, and towing isn't recommended. There isn't much room for two

Mazda's 2006 Mazda5 mini-minivan.

passengers in the third-row seat. There's also a history of automatic transmission malfunctions (but much fewer than with Honda or Toyota), prematurely worn-out brake rotors and pads, and fit-and-finish deficiencies:

> I've had it in the shop 6 times with the same problem. When my Mazda5 shifts from 1st to 2nd or 3rd it sometimes hesitates and [has] stalled a handful of times. Mazda still has not [fixed] and/or found a solution for my problem.

So far, only 13 complaints have been reported to NHTSA concerning transmission malfunctions, steering lockup, the vehicle rolling downhill with the parking brake engaged, poor wet-road traction, and premature tire wear. Neither IIHS nor NHTSA have crash-tested the car. In the past, some Mazda dealers have been caught overcharging for scheduled maintenance.

The 2005–06 **Mercedes-Benz Smart Fortwo** Coupe and Cabriolet are Below Average buys because cheaper Asian micro-cars like the Honda Fit, Nissan Versa, and Toyota Yaris are almost as economical to drive, more refined, and easier to service and repair. Daimler has lost billions on the Smart since its 1998 European debut, and the company is leery of expanding the brand into the States before 2008. Without that American expansion, Canadian Smart owners may be limited to Canadian roads if they're at all worried about servicing. Even if they stay home, parts supply and servicing will eventually become a huge problem. Here's what Mercedes says on its Smart Canada website at *www.thesmart.ca/index.cfm?id=4904*:

Can I drive or import a Smart Fortwo to the U.S.?

Yes, you can drive your Canadian Smart Fortwo into the U.S. However, our Smart Fortwo is currently certified for the Canadian market only will therefore **not** comply for export. American residents who have purchased a Smart in Canada for use in Canada who wish to take their vehicle across the border on occasion should contact U.S. Customs directly regarding this issue.

The Smart *is* fuel-frugal, depreciates slowly, is distinctively styled, and is sold in most of Canada's Mercedes-Benz dealerships. On the other hand, understand you will pay a maxi price for a mini car that has lethargic acceleration, highly dealer-dependent servicing (trips must be planned carefully for servicing accessibility), no long-term reliability figures, and no NHTSA crashworthiness data. It is not a "green" car, as many pretend, since diesel emissions contain particulates that exacerbate lung disorders. Furthermore, micro cars just arriving from Honda (Fit) and Nissan (Versa) are cheaper by a few thousand dollars, much more refined, and all-around better performers.

Sold new for $16,500, a used 2005 Smart now goes for about $11,500; a new $22,200 2005 "Passion" convertible (Cabriolet) now sells for almost $16,000. Smarts are powered by an 800-cubic centimetre, 3-cylinder turbo diesel motor that produces 41 hp—nowhere near the 108 horses offered by Toyota's smallest car, the $13,725 (new) Yaris. Furthermore, the car is only 2.5 metres long and weighs in at only 730 kg, which is very light when compared to the Toyota Echo or Yaris. These factors combine to give the Smart an estimated 4.4 L/100 km rating, much better than the Toyota Echo's estimated city/highway fuel economy of 6.7/5.2 L/100 km, and much more frugal than the outrageously inaccurate fuel-savings claims bandied about by Honda and Toyota when they hype their hybrids.

Like Fiat, Lada, Peugeot, and Renault—four automakers that abandoned Canada after failing to expand into the States—Smart owners may be left high and dry if Mercedes decides Smart cannot compete successfully against the existing and forthcoming Asian economy cars. And Mercedes wouldn't hesitate to "flip the switch," as it did by dumping Chrysler in May 2007. In fact, you have to admit that Mercedes hasn't had a great record with small entry-level models. Remember the "Baby Benz" models, such as the 190 model that was introduced over a decade ago and quickly abandoned, or the C-Class hatchback that was recently dropped? This wouldn't be much of a problem if Smarts were conventional small cars backed by an extensive dealer network and a large parts inventory. But that's not the case. Furthermore, unlike old MGs and Triumphs, there isn't a body of independent repairers and part suppliers who can step into the breach.

Mitsubishi sold the following 2005–06 models in Canada: the compact **Lancer ES** ($15,998); the mid-sized **Galant DE** ($23,998); and the **Eclipse GS** ($25,498), **GT** ($32,998), and **Spyder** ($34,998). Plus, there are the Montero Limited ($48,598), Endeavour ($34,298), and Outlander LS ($23,998) sport-utilities.

There's not much to dislike with the Lancer, and that's why we give it an Above Average rating. You get spirited acceleration with the OZ Rally's turbocharged engine, excellent frontal and offset crashworthiness scores, and good overall quality. The only drawbacks—the base engine is a bit horsepower-challenged, especially with the automatic transmission; you can expect some parts delays; and front side crashworthiness is below average.

These entry-level front-drive econocars have been sold in Canada through Chrysler dealers since 2003 and offer an incredible choice of vehicles that run the gamut from the cheap and mundane ES to the high-performance street racer called the

OZ Rally. Yes, Mitsus depreciate faster than most Japanese vehicles, but if you are shopping for used models, that's an important advantage. For example, a 2003 base Lancer that retailed originally for $15,998 is now worth $6,000, a 2004 sells for $7,500, and a 2005 goes for $9,000. And don't forget that Mitsubishis are just as reliable as other Asian makes and can be serviced practically anywhere.

The Mitsubishi Eclipse.

Crash test scores are both good and bad: Frontal crash protection and rollover resistance got four stars, and side protection earned two stars. The few owner complaints received by NHTSA deal with engine stalling and stumbling; automatic transmissions that lurch, jerk, and slip; clutch failures; broken axles; windshield creaking; frequent paint defects that include swirls, scratches, and peeling; and rear bumper-support rusting.

The Galant is another Above Average offering from Mitsubishi. It's reasonably priced, carries competent 4- and 6-cylinder powerplants, handles very well, enjoys good crashworthiness scores, and is fairly reliable, as was its Colt predecessor over a decade ago. Depreciation is rather steep: A $23,097 2003 model now sells for $9,000, a $23,498 2004 is now worth $11,000, and a $23,948 2005 now goes for $14,000.

On the downside, some model years don't have a manual transmission to make full use of the car's spirited engine, and rear-seat entry and exit can take some acrobatics. Surprisingly, first-year glitches haven't plagued the redesigned 2004 models, which came out with more powerful engines, handling enhancements, larger interiors, and sleeker styling.

Crash test scores are better than average on the 2004 and 2005 versions: Frontal and side crash protection are given five stars, and rollover resistance scored four stars. Overall quality control is impressive, generating few owner complaints. Some of the problems that have been mentioned, though, are engine hesitation; transmission and brake malfunctions; noisy, squeaking front brakes; AC that may not provide an even flow of cool air through the lower vents; and a loose driver's seat. Technical service bulletins cover rear suspension rattling, seat adjustments, window glass freezing to the moulding, and tips on reducing brake noise.

The Eclipse is an Above Average, beautifully styled, and reasonably priced sporty coupe whose on-road performance lags behind its looks. As with other Mitsubishis, early models quickly lose their value, making the car a bargain if bought used. A $23,857 2003 model sells for $9,500, a $23,998 2004 is now worth $11,500, and a $35,148 2005 Spyder (the cheapest model available) is now worth almost $22,000.

There are two engine choices available: a 162-hp 2.4L 4-banger and a 263-hp V6. A manual 5-speed is standard, but the optional automatic 5-speed and the 6-speed manual are better performers. A convertible version will return this year as a 2007 model. Both engines have plenty of grunt throughout their power range when mated to a manual gearbox, but much less when hooked to an automatic transmission. Handling is exceptionally good on all models, but the sportier GT and Spyder are better than the rest. Front-seat occupants get a firm, comfortable ride with fairly supportive seats and adequate room.

Crash test scores are mixed: Frontal crash protection is rated at four stars, side protection gets three stars, and rollover resistance garners four stars. Some of the Eclipse's deficiencies include an automatic transmission that doesn't have the quickness needed for confident highway merging; frequent shifting with the manual transmission; real-world fuel economy that's much less than promised with the automatic tranny; the V6 engine's thirst for premium fuel; so-so steering with the base sedan; a larger-than-expected turning radius for the coupe; considerable "torque steer" (a pulling to the side upon acceleration) felt with the GT; brakes that are overly aggressive; excessive engine, tire, and wind noise; difficult rear entry and exit; and rear seating adequate only for children or small adults.

Porsche's 1999–2006 **911** Carrera Coupe and Turbo are Above Average buys. The 911 was redesigned in 1999, gaining additional length and width and 8 cm to the wheelbase. The 3.4L engine switched from air-cooling to water-cooling and produced 296 horsepower—more than the previous 3.6L powerplant. A 6-speed manual transmission, side airbags, and ABS were standard. Although originally sold for $96,020, a year 2000 911 Carrera is now worth about one third of that amount, or $32,000–$35,000. The 2000 models got four more horses; 2001 models came with a 415-hp 3.6L twin-turbo engine; and 2002 models adopted the 320-hp 3.6L engine and upgraded the 5-speed automatic transmission. These cars are famous for high-performance acceleration and handling, impressive braking, and excellent fit and finish. As with most sports cars, you can expect lots of engine and road noise, acrobatic entry and exit, cramped rear seating, and limited storage space. Although *Consumer Reports* shows a higher-than-average number of factory-related problems, Canadian Porsche owners have been relatively quiet.

The 1998–2006 rear-drive **Boxster** is a Recommended roadster that competes with the Mercedes-Benz SLK, the BMW Z3, and the Mazda Miata. It is powered by a 201-hp 2.5L dual-overhead-cam 6-cylinder engine coupled to either a 5-speed manual or an optional 5-speed automatic gearbox. The car offers all of the same advantages and disadvantages as the more refined 911. A 1998 Boxster sells for about $21,000; a 2004 commands almost $47,000.

Rated an Above Average buy, **Toyota**'s 2006 **Yaris** is an entry-level, five-passenger econocar that replaced the 2005 Echo. It is larger and more refined than the Echo, gives impressive fuel economy without sacrificing performance, and can be purchased used for about $10,500. Yaris has a more modern look than the Echo, and its interior improvements—like large windows, additional legroom, and high-quality trim and seats—give it the allure of a much more expensive car. Yaris is powered by a 106-hp 1.5L DOHC 4-cylinder engine featuring Variable Valve Timing (VVT) cylinder head technology. It's the same design used by Lexus to combine power and fuel economy in a low-emissions vehicle. An engine this small would provide wimpy acceleration for most cars, but thanks to the car's light weight, acceleration is more than adequate with a manual gearbox and is acceptable with the automatic. Standard safety features are dual airbags, anti-whiplash seats, a collapsible steering column, and ABS on RS models (optional on CE three-door and LE five-door models).

Yaris is remarkably well-built for an entry-level subcompact and hasn't been the object of a single complaint received by NHTSA. Nevertheless, the car's tall profile and light weight make it vulnerable to side-wind buffeting, base tires provide poor wet traction, there is excessive torque steer (sudden pulling to one side when accelerating), some wind noise is heard from the base of the windshield, the steering wheel is mounted too far away for some drivers, and crashworthiness scores could be much better. NHTSA gives the 2007 Yaris a four-star rating for frontal impact crashworthiness and rollover resistance and only a three-star rating for side-impact protection. IIHS rates only the 2007 and gives it a "Good" rating for offset crash protection, a "Poor" score for side-impact occupant protection without side airbags, and a "Marginal" rating for head-restraint effectiveness.

Phil's "Beater" Beat

I refuse to throw my money away. That's why I stay away from new-car dealers.

I won't pay the $31,045 average price for a new vehicle ($25,056 for a car or $37,855 for a truck) quoted by Toronto auto analyst Dennis DesRosiers. And that's just the beginning. DesRosiers says taxes add another 21–23 percent to the suggested retail prices listed above. On top of that, fuel and insurance costs are scary, with gas prices setting record levels and insurance premiums soaring despite huge increases in insurance profits.

Yet millions of Canadians believe a new car is their only choice. They want a vehicle that's safe, cheap to buy and run, reliable, and capable of taking them to work, school, or the shopping mall without breaking down or putting their lives in danger (two factors that are particularly important to new drivers, who usually don't have much experience with highway emergencies). Young drivers also want vehicles that they can easily repair and customize and that will still project a "cool" cachet to their peers.

So, they figure, new is worry-free. New is safe. New is "cool."

Actually, new is dumb. There are plenty of cheap, reliable used cars and minivans out there that will suit your driving needs and budget. In the 1970s, the average car was junked after around seven years or 160,000 km; two decades later, the average car was driven for almost eight years or 240,000 km before it was discarded. Industry experts now say that the 2005 models will easily last 10 years or 300,000 km before they need to be "recycled." This means you can get good high-mileage vehicles for less than one-quarter to one-half of their original price and expect to drive them for five years or more.

Depreciation Quirks

Depreciation varies considerably among different vehicle types and models. For example, minivans depreciate a bit more slowly than cars, and diesel cars and trucks hold their value better than do gas-powered vehicles.

Generally, those vehicles sold with the highest rebates depreciate the fastest. Detroit spent about $4,000 per vehicle last year, European makers spent $2,500, Nissan spent $2,100, and Honda and Toyota paid out $700 and $850, respectively.

Gas-electric hybrids, which have been on the market since 1999, apparently lose their value at about the same rate as conventional cars. Undoubtedly this is because used-car buyers are afraid to replace the costly high-tech components (imagine paying $8,000 for a replacement battery once the 8-year warranty has expired).

Ten "Beater" Rules

1. First, try to buy a vehicle that's presently being used by one of your family members. Although you may risk a family squabble somewhere down the road, you'll likely get a good buy for next to nothing, you will have a good idea of how it was driven and maintained, and you can use the same repair facilities that have been repairing your family's vehicles for years. Don't worry if a vehicle is almost 10 years old—that's becoming the norm for Canadian ownership, particularly the farther west you go.
2. Buy from a private seller—prices are usually much cheaper and sales scams less frequent.
3. Cut insurance and fuel costs. Use the Internet (*www.insurancehotline.com*) to compile a list of models that are the cheapest to insure. Be wary of diesel-equipped or hybrid cars that may require more expensive dealer servicing and thus wipe out any fuel consumption savings. Also, pay attention to the quality and performance of your fuel-efficient choice: A fuel-sipping Ford Focus will likely have higher repair bills than gas bills, and a 4-cylinder minivan, though cheap to run, can make highway merging a white-knuckle affair.
4. Find out the vehicle's history through a franchised dealer, CarProof, or provincial licensing authorities and then have an independent garage (preferably CAA-affiliated) check out the body and mechanical components.
5. Look for high-mileage vehicles sold by rental agencies like Budget Rent A Car—a company that offers money-back guarantees and reasonably priced extended warranties.
6. Refuse all preparation or "administration" fees and 50/50 warranties where the repair charges are submitted by the seller.
7. Stay away from vehicles or components known for having a high failure

rate. American front-drives, for example, have more frequent failures and costlier repairs than rear-drives. "Orphaned" American models like the Ford Contour/Mystique or Cadillac Catera are also poor choices because of low-quality components and inadequate servicing support from dealers who wish these cars were never made. Other sinkholes—any vehicle equipped with a turbocharger or supercharger, a CVT transmission (Audi, Ford, Honda, Mini, Nissan, Saturn, Subaru, and Toyota), multiple computers (BMW's 7 Series, for example), ABS brakes, or motorized seat belts; minivans equipped with four-wheel drive; Cadillacs with 4.1L engines and/or front-drive; and Chryslers with sludge-prone 2.7L engines or 4-speed automatic transmissions. If the engine has a timing chain instead of a belt, you will save a fortune. Timing chains frequently survive the lifespan of the engine, whereas timing belts must be replaced every 70,000–100,000 km.

8. Steer clear of European models. They are often money pits. Parts and competent, reasonably priced servicing will likely be hard to find, and quality control has declined considerably over the past decade.

9. Buy 3-year-old Hyundais, and stay away from Excels, early Sonatas, and all Kias and Daewoos. Also look for 5- to 10-year-old single-owner Japanese models.

10. Shop for used rear-drive full-sized wagons or vans instead of front-drive American minivans.

"Beaters" You Will Love

Acura—The 5-cylinder **Vigor**, a 1992–94 Honda Accord sedan spin-off, sells for $4,000–$5,000. This compact has power to spare, handles well, and has an impressive reliability/durability record. Problem areas: excessive brake noise and premature brake wear in addition to fit and finish deficiencies. The 1992 Vigor turned in below-average crash test scores.

The **Legend** is an above average $3,000–$3,500 buy (1989–95), although the 1986–88 model years aren't recommended. Resale value is high on all Legend models, and especially so on the coupe. Shop for a cheaper 1989 or later base Legend with the coupe's upgraded features and fewer reports of unintended sudden acceleration. Pre-1990 Legends were upscale, enlarged Accords that were unimpressive performers with either of the two 6-cylinder powerplants. The 3.2L V6 that appeared in 1991 is by far a better performer.

Chrysler—**Dart**, **Valiant**, **Duster**, **Scamp**, **Diplomat**, **Caravelle**, **Newport**, rear-drive **New Yorker Fifth Avenue**, and **Gran Fury**. Problem areas— electrical system, suspension, brakes, body and frame rust, and constant stalling when humidity is high. The Caravelle, Diplomat, and New Yorker Fifth Avenue are reasonably reliable and simple-to-repair throwbacks to a time when rear-drive land yachts ruled the highways. Powered with 6- and 8-cylinder engines, they will run practically forever with minimal care. The fuel-efficient "slant 6" powerplant was too small for this type of car and was changed to a gas-guzzling but smooth and reliable V8 after 1983. Handling is vague and sloppy, though, and emergency braking is often accompanied by rear-wheel lock-up. Still, what do you want for a

$500–$1,000 1984–89 "retro rocket?" Other problem areas include the carburetor (don't ask what that is; your dad knows), ignition, electrical system, brakes, and suspension (premature idler-arm wear). It's a good idea to adjust the torsion bars frequently for better suspension performance. Doors, windshield pillars, the bottoms of both front and rear fenders, and the trunk lid rust through more quickly than average.

Chrysler's 1991–93 **2000 GTX** is an above average buy that may cost $1,500–$2,000. It's a reliable Japanese-built sedan that was discontinued in 1994. It has a competitive price, modern styling, and high-performance options that put it on par with such benchmark cars as the Honda Accord and Toyota Camry. The major problem area is the front brakes, which need more attention than average. This car was never crash-tested.

The **Stealth** is a serious, reasonably priced sports car that's as much go as show. Although 1995 was its last model year in Canada, it was still sold in the United States as the Mitsubishi 3000GT. Prices range from $2,500–$3,500 for the 1991–93 base or ES model. A '95 high-performance R/T will go for about $4,500—not a bad price for an "orphaned" sports car, eh? Problem areas are engine, transmission, front brake, and electrical failures. The 1993 model excelled in crash tests.

Chrysler's 1999–2001 **Prowler** is a recommended fast, sporty rear-drive coupe that handles well and is attractively styled to resemble a hot-rod roadster from the '50s. On the minus side, it has little interior room, entry and exit is a chiropractor's delight, and overall visibility is less than ideal. Its 253-hp 3.5L V6 was borrowed from Chrysler's 300M and LHS. A 1999 Prowler costs about $20,000, or a third of the car's original selling price; the 2001 model is worth about $29,000.

Ford—Maverick, Comet, Fairmont, Zephyr, Tracer, Cougar, Thunderbird V6, Torino, Marquis, Grand Marquis, LTD, and LTD Crown Victoria. Problem areas are trunk, wheelwell, and rocker panel rusting and brake, steering, and electrical system failures. The 1993 **Festiva** is marginally acceptable for city use as long as you check out the brakes, exhaust system, and body panels for rust. The 1990–97 **Probe** is essentially a Mazda MX-6 sporty two-door coupe in Ford garb. It's quite reliable and gives better-than-average highway performance. Problem areas are AC, CV joints, and electrical and body glitches. Good crash-worthiness ratings. Prices range from $1,000 to $3,000.

General Motors—Chevette and **Acadian** are inexpensive rear-drive city runabouts. Problem areas are steering system defects and brakes that you have to stand on to make the car stop. Rear-drive **Nova, Ventura, Skylark,** and **Phoenix** problem areas are undercarriage, steering system, and suspension rust-outs. Front-drive **Nova, Spectrum, Camaro, Firebird, Malibu, LeMans, Century, Regal, Cutlass, Monte Carlo,** and **Grand Prix** problem areas are rear brake backing-plate rust-outs and steering failures. With the **Bel Air, Laurentian, Catalina, Parisienne, LeSabre, Bonneville,** and **Delta 88,** be wary of undercarriage, suspension component, and rear brake backing-plate rust-outs.

GM's 1982–96 **Caprice**, **Impala SS**, and **Roadmaster** are better-than-average, comfortable, and easy-to-maintain large cars that have been off the market since the 1996 model year. Overall handling is acceptable, but expect a queasy ride from the too-soft suspension. The trunk is spacious, but gas mileage is particularly poor. Despite the many generic deficiencies inherent in these rear-drives, they still score higher than GM's front-drives for overall reliability and durability. The Impala SS is basically a Caprice with a 260-hp Corvette engine and high-performance suspension. Good, cheap cars for first-time buyers, the 1991–93 models can be bought for $700–$1,000, while later models will cost $1,500–$2,500. Maintenance is inexpensive and easy to perform, and any corner garage can do repairs. Average parts costs can be cut further by shopping at independent suppliers, who are generally well stocked.

The 1991–96 models have shown the following deficiencies: AC glitches; prematurely worn brake (lots of corrosion damage), steering, and suspension components, especially shock absorbers and rear springs; serious electrical problems; and poor-quality body and trim items. Body assembly is not impressive, but paint quality and durability is fairly good considering the delamination one usually finds with GM's other models. Wagons often have excessive rust around cargo-area side windows and wheelwells, and hubcaps on later models tend to fly off.

The Geo **Storm**, GM's Japanese-made small car, only lasted two model years in Canada (1992–93). Owners report serious body hardware deficiencies (not paint or rust, however) in addition to brake, exhaust, electrical, and ignition problems. Prices vary between $1,000 and $2,000, depending on the model chosen.

GM's 1984–96 rear-drive Cadillac **Brougham** and **Fleetwood** are above average luxury "land yacht" buys. Originally front-drives, these big sedans adopted the rear-drive stretched platform used by the Buick Roadmaster and Chevrolet Caprice in 1993. Equipped with a 185-hp V8 mated to a 4-speed automatic transmission, all models came with standard traction control and anti-lock brakes. The rear-drive configuration is easy to repair and not hard to diagnose, unlike the cars' front-drive brethren. Other cars worth considering are Cadillac's DeVille and a fully loaded Ford Crown Victoria or Mercury Grand Marquis. The most serious problem areas are the fuel-injection system, which frequently malfunctions and costs an arm and a leg to repair; engine head gasket failures; automatic transmissions that shift erratically; a weak suspension; computer module glitches; brakes that constantly need rotor and pad replacement; poor body assembly; and paint defects. From a reliability/durability standpoint, the rear-drives are much better made than their front-drive counterparts.

Pontiac's 1991–95 **Sunbird** was GM's smallest American-built car, along with its twin, the Chevrolet **Cavalier**. Sunbirds were available as two-door coupes, four-door sedans, and two-door convertibles. Nearly all Sunbirds were powered by a wimpy 96-hp 2.0L 4-cylinder engine as standard equipment, mated to a clunky, performance-sapping, fuel-wasting 3-speed automatic tranny. GT models featured a 165-hp turbocharged version of the same engine. Both engines weren't very dependable. A better-quality optional 140-hp 3.1L V6 came on the scene in 1991. In 1992, ABS became a standard feature, increasing the complexity and cost of brake maintenance for years to come. The 2.0L engine gained 14 more horses.

Several joint ventures between GM and Suzuki from 1987 to 2001 produced four fairly reliable subcompact economy cars called the Chevrolet and Geo **Metro**, the Pontiac **Firefly**, the Suzuki **Sprint**, and the Suzuki **Swift**. These minicars are rated above average (1998–2001), average (1995–97), and below average (1987–94). They are most reliable when bought unadorned; stay away from AC-equipped versions unless you want to invest in an AC repair facility. Look at the redesigned 1998 version for better quality, a new body style, standard dual airbags, and a peppier 4-cylinder engine. Convertibles pack plenty of fun and performance into a reasonably priced subcompact body. The Suzuki Swift carried on alone after the 2000 model year. Used prices vary, however; 1998–2001 models cost between $2,000 and $3,000. Maintenance costs are average, but powertrain parts are drying up and can be hard to find. Body components are often back-ordered several weeks. Some better cars worth considering are the Honda Civic LX, Hyundai Accent, Suzuki Esteem, and Toyota Tercel. They all perform well and offer better quality.

Cheap to buy and run and providing better-than-average quality control and crashworthiness, these tiny 3- and 4-cylinder front-drive hatchbacks offer good performance and impressive economy for urban dwellers. The turbocharged convertible model is an excellent choice for high-performance thrills in an easy-to-handle ragtop. The redesigned 1995s were built with more care.

On the downside, owners will face an anemic, noisy engine that makes these cars the antithesis of "swift;" a harsh, choppy ride; lots of interior noise; a spartan interior; poorly performing original-equipment tires; and inadequate braking. Remaining problems on the 1995–2001 models have been premature front brake wear, electrical system and AC malfunctions, and subpar body assembly, highlighted by paint peeling and discoloration, early rusting, and poorly fitted body panels leading to rattles and air and water leaks.

Honda's 1984–91 **CRX** is a highly recommended and seriously quick two-seater sports car—a Honda Civic spin-off that was replaced in 1991 by the less sporty and much less popular Honda del Sol. Prized by high-performance "tuners," a well-maintained CRX is worth between $2,000 and $3,000.

The 1985–2001 **Preludes** are an above average buy. They are unimpressive as high-performance sports cars, but instead deliver a stylish exterior, legendary reliability, and excellent resale value. Preludes are, nevertheless, a bit overpriced and over-hyped; cheaper, well-performing makes such as the Ford Mustang or Probe, GM Camaro or Firebird, Mazda Miata, and Toyota Celica should be checked out first. Prelude repair costs are average, though some dealer-dependent repairs to the steering assembly and transmission can be quite expensive.

The year for big Prelude changes was 1997, while 1998–2001 models just coasted along with minor improvements (their prices vary from $4,500 to $11,500, while earlier models run about $3,000 to $4,500). The '97 was restyled, re-powered, and given handling upgrades that make it a better-performing, more comfortably riding sports coupe. There is no crashworthiness data, though head-restraint protection has been given a "Below Average" designation. On these more recent models, owners report that the engine tends to leak oil and crank bolts often loosen (causing major engine damage). AC condensers frequently fail after a few years and often need cleaning to eliminate disagreeable odours. Most corner mechanics are poorly equipped to service these cars, and the Automatic Torque Transfer System (ATTS) won't make their job any easier. Owners also report that a poorly designed clutch disc causes harsh shifting, and there have been clutch-spring failures. Internal service bulletins confirm that the 2000 and 2001 models are covered by an automatic transmission warranty extension up to 7 years/160,000 km (Bulletin No.: 02-062, published May 28, 2004).

Mazda—Sports car thrills, minus the bills: The 1992–96 **MX-3**'s base 1.6L engine supplies plenty of power for most driving situations, and it's reasonably priced at $2,000–$2,500. When equipped with the optional 1.8L V6 powerplant (the smallest V6 on the market at the time) and high-performance options, the car transforms itself into a 130-hp pocket rocket. In fact, the MX-3 GS easily outperforms the Honda del Sol, Toyota Paseo, and Geo Storm on comfort and high-performance acumen. It does fall a bit short of the Saturn SC because of its limited low-end torque, and fuel economy is disappointing. Reverse gear is sometimes hard to engage, and brake and wheel bearing problems are commonplace. Most of the MX-3's parts are used on other Mazda cars, so their overall reliability should be outstanding. Crash safety ratings have been average. Also consider the **MX-6** (see Ford Probe, page 572).

The keyword for the 1988–95 **929** is understatement: The engine is unobtrusive, the exterior is anonymous, and the interior is far from flashy. In spite of its lack of pizzazz and its imprecise power steering, the 929 will accelerate and handle curves as well as the best large European sedans, and it has proven to be fairly reliable. For these advantages, you can expect to pay $2,500–$3,000 for a 1988–93 model. The '94s and '95s are priced in the $4,000–$5,000 range. Owners report some problems with electronic shock-absorber durability (particularly with the 1989–91 models), premature disc brake wear, electrical glitches, exhaust system rust-out, and fit and finish deficiencies. The only real safety negative is the consistently poor crash test scores the 929 has earned since the '88 model was first tested.

Selling for $2,500–$3,000 for a base 1988–91 model, the Mazda **RX-7** is an impressive performer with a ride that can be painful on bad roads, primarily because of the car's stiff suspension. The GSL and Turbo models are very well equipped and luxuriously finished. Except for some oil-burning problems, apex seal failures, and leaking engine O-rings, the RX-7 has served to dispel any doubts concerning the durability of rotary engines. Nevertheless, careful maintenance is in order, since contaminated oil or overheating will easily damage the engine. Clutches wear quickly if used hard. Disc brakes need frequent attention paid to the calipers and rotors. The MacPherson struts get soft more quickly than average. Fuel and exhaust system, electrical, and AC malfunctions are also common. Be wary of leaky sunroofs. Radiators have a short lifespan. Rocker panels and body seams are prone to serious rusting. The underbody on older cars should also be inspected carefully for corrosion damage. Fuel economy has never been this car's strong suit, and crash test scores were below average.

Nissan—The **Micra** is a $300–$500 subcompact commuter car that was sold from 1985 to 1991. It uses generic Nissan parts that are fairly reliable and not difficult to find. Electrical shorts, premature front brake wear, and body rusting along the door rocker panels and wheelwells are the more common deficiencies.

The 1990–92 **Stanzas** are roomy, reasonably priced ($1,000–$1,500) four-passenger compacts that offer peppy performance, responsive steering, nimble handling, and good fuel economy. Overall reliability has been fairly good over the years. Except for some road noise, suspension thumps, starting difficulties, transmission malfunctions, and a biodegradable exhaust system, no major problems have been reported.

Toyota—All late '80s and early '90s models are above average buys, except the **LE Van**, which has a history of chronic brake, chassis, and body rusting problems. Chassis rusting and V6 engine head gasket failures are common problems with the 1988–95 sport-utilities and pickups (Toyota has paid for the engine repairs up to eight years). **Celicas** are an especially fine buy, combining smooth engine performance and bulletproof reliability with sports car thrills.

Selling for $3,000 to $3,500, the 1987–93 **MR2** is a mid-engine, rear-drive, 4-cylinder sports car that's both reliable and fun to drive. On the downside, you have to put up with a cramped interior, quirky turbo handling, inflated insurance premiums, and undetermined crashworthiness. In order of frequency, the most common complaints on all MR2s are brake, transmission, electrical glitches, and fit and finish deficiencies.

The **Cressida** ages well and offers an excellent combination of dependable, no-surprise rear-drive performance, plus comfort and luxury. All this comes with a price range from $3,000 to $3,500 for a 1985–92 model. There is little to fault when it comes to overall reliability, and the engine is a model of smooth power. The 1990–93 models are more crashworthy, reliable, and trouble-free than earlier versions, but they're also much more expensive. Complaints heard throughout the years are engine head gasket failures, premature front brake wear and excessive brake pulsation/vibration, AC glitches, electrical short circuits, and a quirky Panasonic sound system.

From its humble beginnings in 1979, the **Supra** became Toyota's flagship sports car by 1986 and took on its own unique personality—with the help of a powerful

3.0L DOHC V6 powerplant. Supra prices range from a low of $6,000 for a '90 model up to $20,000 for a '97. It's an attractively styled high-performance sports car that had been quite reliable up until it caught the Corvette/Nissan 300ZX malady in 1993. Early models (pre-'93) are more reasonably priced and are practically trouble-free, except for some premature front brake wear and vibrations. On later models, owners report major turbocharger problems; frequent rear differential replacements; electrical short circuits; AC malfunctions; and premature brake, suspension, and exhaust system wear. The 3.0L engine is an oil-burner at times, and cornering is often accompanied by a rear-end growl. Seat belt guides and the power antenna are failure-prone. Body deficiencies are common.

Toyota's 1991–99 **Tercel** and **Paseo** models are above average buys, while the 1987–90 Tercel remains a good average pick. Prices vary little: A 1992–1995 Tercel will cost from $1,000 to $2,000, while the 1996–99 versions sell for $3,000 to $3,500. Paseos will fetch about $500 more. These economy cars are dirt cheap to maintain and repair, inexpensive parts are everywhere, and repairs can be done by almost anybody. Tercels are extraordinarily reliable, and the first-generation improvements provided livelier and smoother acceleration and made the interior space feel much larger than it was. Owners report these early models had hard-shifting automatic transmissions, premature brake and suspension component wearout, brake pulsation, leaking radiators, windshield whistling, and myriad squeaks and rattles. Be careful with very early models (1985–90). Updated 1995–99 Tercels are noted for sporadic brake, electrical system, suspension, and body/accessory problems. Frontal crashworthiness was rated two stars on the 1992 Tercel, four stars on the 1993–94, and three stars on the 1995–97. Head restraints were always rated "Poor."

The 1996–99 Paseo is a baby Tercel. Its main advantages are a peppy 1.5L 4-cylinder engine, a smooth 5-speed manual transmission, good handling, a supple ride, great fuel economy, and above-average reliability. This light little sportster is quite vulnerable to side winds; there's lots of body lean in turns; there's plenty of engine, exhaust, and road noise; front headroom and legroom are limited; and there is very little rear-seat space. Generally, safety problems and defects affecting the Tercel are also likely to affect the Paseo.

"Beaters" You Will Hate

These cars will keep you eternally poor and healthy from your daily walks, and they'll quickly teach you humility—and mechanics.

Audi—Fox, **4000**, and **5000**. Engine, transmission, and fuel system problems; a combination of sudden acceleration and no acceleration.

British Leyland—Austin Marina, **MG**, **MGB**, and **Triumph**. Electrical system, engine, transmission, and clutch problems; chassis rusting.

Chrysler—Cricket, Omni/Horizon, and **Volaré/Aspen**. Engine, brakes, and steering problems; chassis rusting. **Charger, Cordoba,** and **Mirada**. Brake, body, and electrical system problems. The 1985–89 **Lancer** and **LeBaron GTS** may only cost $500–$700, but they're no bargain. In fact, they suffer from many of the same problems as the Aries and Reliant K cars and their 1989 replacements, the Spirit and Acclaim. Poor reliability causes maintenance costs to mount quickly. Turbo models are especially risky buys. Head gaskets are prone to leaks on all engines. Shock absorbers, MacPherson struts, and brakes wear out quickly. Front brake rotors are prone to rusting and warping. Crash test scores are below average.

Although they don't cost much—$300–$700, depending on the year—steer clear of 1983–89 **Aries** and **Reliants**. Uncomplicated mechanical components and roomy interiors made these cars attractive buys when new, but they quickly deteriorated once in service. Both cars use dirt-cheap, low-tech components that tend to break down frequently. They have also performed poorly in crash tests. Serious corrosion generally starts along the trunk line, the edges of the rear wheelwells, and the front fenders.

The 1990–98 **Laser** and **Talon** are not recommended. Maintenance and repair costs are much higher than average, mainly because of a scarcity of parts and a failure-prone and complicated-to-repair powertrain and emissions system.

Datsun/Nissan—210, 310, 510, 810, F-10, and **240Z,** Electrical system and brake problems; rusting. Not worth buying at any price.

Eagle—Medallion, Monaco, and **Premier**. These bargain-priced French imports—$500 for the Medallion and $1,000 for the Premier—had a 1988–92 model run. Sold through Chrysler's Renault connection, they are some of the most failure-prone imports to ever hit our shores.

Fiat—"Fix it again, Tony." All Fiat models and years are known for temperamental fuel and electrical systems and disintegrating bodies. **Alfa Romeos** have similar problems.

Ford—Cortina, Pinto, Festiva, Fiesta, Bobcat, and **Mustang II**. These 3-decade-old cars are disasters. Watch out for electrical system, engine, and chassis rusting—fire-prone Pintos and Bobcats are mobile Molotov cocktails. The German import Fiesta and the South Korean–built Festiva are two small imports that only survived a few years in Canada. Parts are practically unobtainable for both vehicles.

The 1994–97 Korean-built **Aspire**'s size, engine, and drivetrain limitations restrict it to an urban environment, and its low quality control restricts it to the driveway. Be wary of brake, electrical, and fuel system failures. Parts are also hard to find. That said, you can pick up an Aspire dirt cheap for less than $1,500. In its favour, the car has consistently posted higher-than-average crash-test scores.

Stay away from the **Contour** and the **Mystique** (1995–99); they are two of the most failure-prone, hazardous vehicles you can buy—industry insiders call the Mystique the "Mistake." The reason these cars are an even worse buy than the Taurus and Sable is that they've been taken off the market—drying up a minuscule parts supply and driving up parts prices (try $700 for an alternator). Resale values vary between $1,500 and $3,000.

General Motors—**Vega**, **Astre**, **Monza**, and **Firenza**. Engine, transmission, body, and brake problems. Cadillac **Cimarron**, **Allanté**, and **Catera**. All gone; all bad. Overpriced, with poor-quality components, and all front-drives suffer engine, automatic transmission, electronic module, steering, and brake problems, not to mention rust/paint peeling. **Citation**, **Skylark**, **Omega**, and **Phoenix**. Engine, brake, and electronic module problems; severe rust canker.

The Pontiac **Fiero**, sold from 1984 to 1988, snares lots of unsuspecting first-time buyers with its attractive sports-car styling, high-performance pretensions, and $500–$1,000 price. However, one quickly learns to both fear and hate the Fiero as it shows off its fiery disposition (several safety recalls for engine compartment fires) and its "I'll start when I want to" character.

Hyundai—**Pony** and **Stellar**. Two of the worst South Korean small cars ever imported into Canada. Their most serious problems involve electrical and fuel-system failures that cause fires, no-starts, stalling, and chronic engine hesitation. Stellars have irreparable suspension, steering, and brake deficiencies that make them dangerous to drive. Cost: from $300–$500. The **Excel** is a low-tech and low-quality economy car that was orphaned in 1995. Resale prices are low ($300 for an '88; $1,000 for a '94). Likely problem areas are defective constant velocity joints, water pumps, oil-pan gaskets, oil pressure switches, and front struts and leaking engine head gaskets. An Excel cross-dressing as a sports car, the 1991–95 **Scoupe** (for $2,000–$2,500) is essentially a cute coupe with an engine more suited to high gas mileage than hard driving.

Mercedes-Benz—Worth between $1,500 and $2,000, the 1990–93 **190E** "Baby Benz" was a flop from the very beginning. It was the company's smallest and cheapest sedan, powered by a 158-hp 2.6L 6-cylinder gasoline engine borrowed from the midsize 260E sedan. A 5-speed manual transmission was standard, but most models were bought with the optional 4-speed automatic. A less powerful 130-hp 2.3L 4-cylinder engine was added to the 1991 model. Standard safety features were a driver-side airbag and ABS. Owners found the car to be both unreliable (automatic transmission, electrical and fuel system, and brake problems) and hard to service. Now that it has been dropped, parts are almost impossible to find and mechanics run away when one pulls into their service bay.

Merkur's 1985–89 **XR4Ti** was a decently performing European import based on the European Ford Sierra; the Merkur **Scorpio** was a Euro Ford Granada spin-off. Either car can be bought for $1,500 to $2,000. Poor-quality components, American emissions regulations, and a poorly supported dealer network killed the car after only five model years. Lesson learned? If you can't pronounce the name, don't buy the product.

Nissan—The 1989–96 **300ZX**, Nissan's answer to the Corvette, has everything: high-performance capability, a heavy chassis, complicated electronics, and average depreciation, resulting in a price range of $4,000–$5,000. Turbocharged 1990 and later models are much faster than previous versions and better overall buys. This weighty rear-drive offers a high degree of luxury equipment along with a potent 300-hp engine. Traction is poor on slippery surfaces, though, and the rear suspension hits hard when going over speed bumps. Crashworthiness scores have been average. The complexity of all the bells and whistles on the 300ZX translates into a lot more problems than you'd experience with either a Mustang or a Camaro—two cars that have had their own reliability problems but are far easier and less costly to repair. The best example of this is the electrical system, long a source of recurring, hard-to-diagnose shorts. Fuel injectors are a constant problem and guarantee sustained poor engine performance. The manual transmission has been failure-prone, clutches don't last long, front and rear brakes are noisy and wear out quickly, and the aluminum wheels are easily damaged by corrosion and road hazards. The exhaust system is practically biodegradable. The weird spongy/stiff variable shock absorbers and the glitzy digital dash with three odometers are more gimmicky than practical. Body assembly is mediocre.

Pulsar and **NX** models are below average small-car buys ($1,000–$1,500, depending upon the year) as long as you stay away from failure-prone and expensive-to-repair turbo models. The Pulsar was replaced by the 1991 NX, a similar small car that also shares Sentra components. For 1983–86 models, overall reliability is poor to very poor. As with other discontinued Nissans, the 1987–93 models showed remarkable performance improvement and better quality control. Crash test scores were below average for the 1990 and earlier models, while the 1991 and later versions scored quite well. All Pulsars are prone to AC malfunctions and premature wearout of front brakes and suspension components, and their exhaust systems don't last very long (two years, tops).

Saab—**900**, **9000**, **9-3**, and **9-5** models sold from 1985 to 2003 are very poor buys. Maintenance and repair costs can be quite high and must be done by a GM or Saab dealer. The 1996–2003 used prices range from $3,000–$15,000. The 900 and 9000 series have similar deficiencies affecting the engine, cooling (disintegrating water pumps) and electrical systems, brakes, automatic transmission (clutch O-rings), and body hardware. Interestingly, the upscale 9000 series isn't as crashworthy as the cheaper 900 versions, nor is it more reliable, exhibiting similar generic deficiencies to its entry-level brother. The 9-5 models have garnered a five-star crash protection rating. On more recent models, chronic stalling can make these vehicles extremely dangerous to drive. Short circuits are legion and run the gamut from minor annoyances to fire hazards. Electrical glitches in the traction control system's relay module shuts the engine down, and engine sludging affects 9-3 and 9-5 models (covered by a "goodwill" warranty). Turbo-equipped models should be approached with caution because owner abuse or poor maintenance can make them wallet busters. Air conditioners and exhaust system parts have a short lifespan, and leaky seals and gaskets are common. Rust perforations tend to develop along door bottoms and the rocker panels.

Subaru—Sold from 1988 to 1995, the $1,000–$1,200 four-wheel drive **Justy** pairs smooth and nimble handling with precise and predictable steering. The Justy's reliability record has been below average, with pre-1991 models having the most problems. Parts and servicing are hard to find. Owners complain about poor engine idling, cold-weather stalling, manual and automatic transmission malfunctions, premature exhaust system rust-outs, catalytic converter failures, and paint peeling. Servicing and troubleshooting the CVT is a mechanic's nightmare. Not as hard to service but only so-so performers, Subaru's 1991–94 front-drive **Loyale** models came on the scene as underpowered Japanese-built small cars that offered optional 4×4, either on demand or permanently engaged. The noisy 90-hp 1.8L 4-cylinder engine and 115-hp turbo variant both perform better when hooked to a manual transmission; the 3-speed automatic is harsh shifting and not very economical. Although overall reliability is about average, powertrain and emissions components are scarce. Loyale models are below average buys, even though many sell for less than $1,000.

Volkswagen—The original **Beetle** was cheap to own but deadly to drive. Its main deficiencies—poorly anchored, unsafe front seats; a heater that never worked (fortunately, we were young and hot-blooded enough in those days to generate our own heat); fuel-tank placement that was dangerous in collisions; and poorly designed wheels and seat tracks. The **Camper** minivan was safer but less reliable, with engine, transmission, fuel-system, and heater failings. VW's 1987–93 **Fox** was the company's cheapest small car, combining good fuel economy with above-average road handling. An upgraded 5-speed manual transmission was added to the 1993 model year. This Brazilian-made front-drive never caught on because of its notoriously unreliable engine and transmission; quirky electronics; excessive road, wind, and body noise; atrocious fit and finish; and a cramped interior in the sedan. Parts are especially hard to find. Crashworthiness is way below average. Priced between $300 and $500, these cars are more skunk than fox.

VW's **Scirocco** is fun to drive but risky to own. Chronic breakdowns, parts short-ages, and poor crashworthiness are just the beginning. Electrical short circuits, chronic fuel supply problems, premature front brake wear, and fragile body parts are common owner complaints. Expect to pay $1,000. Selling for $2,000 to $3,000, the 1990–95 **Corrado** gives good all-around performance, with the accent on smooth acceleration, a firm but not harsh ride, and excellent handling with little body roll. So why is it not recommended? Poor reliability, hard-to-find parts, limited servicing outlets, and undetermined crashworthiness.

Volvo—The 1989–93 **240 Series** is a below average buy, costing approximately $2,000. Avoid the turbocharged 4-cylinder engine and failure-prone air conditioning system. Diesels suffer from cooling system breakdowns and leaky cylinder head gaskets. The brakes on all model years need frequent and expensive servicing, and exhaust systems are notorious for their short lifespan.

When a '79 Volvo 240 was crash-tested, researchers concluded that both the driver and passenger would have sustained severe head traumas. The 1992–93 models, however, received excellent NHTSA crashworthiness scores.

Selling for $2,000 to $3,000, the 1986–92 **700 Series** models are more spacious, luxurious, and complicated to service than the entry-level 240. The standard engine and transmission perform well but aren't as refined as the 850's. The 700 Series suffers from some brake, electrical, engine cooling, air conditioning, and body deficiencies. Brakes tend to wear rapidly and can require expensive servicing. The 1988 model performed poorly in crash tests, while the 1991–92 versions did quite well.

LEMON-PROOFING AND COST-CUTTING

Examine What You've Bought

Now that you've chosen a vehicle that's priced right and seems to meet your needs, run the registration through a CarProof check at *www.carproof.com* (the price varies between $25 and $45) if it wasn't done before the purchase. Then decide if any misrepresentations are important enough to claim compensation through small claims court.

As previously discussed in Part Two, Canadian federal and provincial laws provide the means to impose harsh penalties against new- and used-car dealers who hide or embellish important facts. Ontario's *Consumer Protection Act* (*www.e-laws.gov. on.ca/DBLaws/Statutes/English/02c30_e.htm*), for example, lets consumers cancel a contract within one year of entering into an agreement if a dealer makes a false, misleading, deceptive, or unconscionable representation. This includes failing to state a material fact, or using exaggeration, innuendo, or ambiguity regarding a material fact, with the intention of deceiving a buyer.

Just keep in mind the following points:

- Dealers are *presumed* to know the history, quality, and true performance of what they sell.
- Even details like fuel economy can lead to a contract's cancellation if the dealer gives a higher than actual figure. In *Sidney v. 1011067 Ontario Inc. (c.o.b. Southside Motors)*, the plaintiff was awarded $11,424.51 plus prejudgment interest because of a false representation made by the defendant regarding fuel efficiency. The plaintiff claimed that the defendant advised him the vehicle had a fuel efficiency of 800–900 km per tank of fuel when, in fact, the vehicle's maximum efficiency was only 500 km per tank.

Now, let's assume you are dealing with an honest seller and that you've chosen a vehicle that's priced right and seems to meet your needs. Take some time to assess its interior, exterior, and highway performance with the checklists below. If you're buying from a dealer, ask to take the vehicle home overnight in order to drive it over the same roads you use during your daily activities. Of course, if you're buying privately, it's doubtful you will get the vehicle for an overnight test—you may have to rent a similar one from a dealer or rental agency.

Safety Check

1. Is the vehicle equipped with electronic stability control (recommended) that works properly?
2. Do the side airbags protect both the head and torso (recommended)?
3. Are the front airbags de-powered?
4. Does the front seat have sufficient rearward travel to put you at a safe distance from the airbag's deployment (about 30 cm) and still allow you to reach the brake and accelerator pedals? Are the brake and accelerator pedals adjustable and spaced far enough apart?
5. Is outward visibility good in all directions?
6. Are there large blind spots (such as side pillars) impeding vision?
7. Are the mirrors large enough for good side and rear views; do they block your view?
8. Are all instrument displays clearly visible (not washed out in sunlight), is there daytime or nighttime driving dash glare on the windshield or side mirrors, and are the controls easily reached?
9. Are the handbrake and hood release easy to reach and use?
10. Will the car roll backward or forward when stopped or parked on an incline?
11. Are the head restraints adjustable or non-adjustable? (The latter is better if you often forget to set them.)
12. Are the head restraints designed to permit rear visibility? (Some are annoyingly obtrusive.)
13. Are there rear three-point shoulder belts similar to those on the front seats?
14. Is the seat belt latch plate easy to find and reach?
15. Does the seat belt fit comfortably across your chest?
16. Does the seat belt release easily, retract smoothly, and use pretensioners for maximum effectiveness?
17. Are there user-friendly child seat anchorage locations?
18. Are there automatic door locks controlled by the driver, or are there child-proof rear door locks? Does the automatic side sliding door latch securely and immediately stop when encountering an object as it opens or closes?
19. Do the power windows have the power to kill? Look for a child protection feature to prevent children from being strangled if they inadvertently stick their head through the window while touching or standing upon the window Up control.
20. Do the rear windows roll only halfway down? When they are down, are your ears assailed by the wind "boom," or does the vehicle vibrate excessively?

Note: Dashboard reflection onto the windshield is a common problem with all light-coloured vehicles. Ford's Explorer, Edge, Five Hundred, and Fusion are particularly bad, however:

> I have had my Edge for one week. I test drove it on a cloudy day. One week later the sun came out. The glare is BRUTAL. I have contacted Ford, however, they are not going to do anything (not enough complaints). It is a safety hazard. I have pictures where you can't even see out of the bottom third of the windshield the glare [is] so bad. I just found an article that said Ford gave out polarized sunglasses to the media test drivers...

Fortunately, the reflection can be reduced by wearing polarized glasses, or eliminated by putting a dashmat on the front or rear dash shelf (available on the Internet at *www.mysimon.com/9000-10940_8-0.html?sdcq=dnatrs-dashmat/dfllTrail-Dashmat*) or, in Ford's case, by covering the decorative chrome strip around the instrument cluster with some blackout tape. Yes, the tape does look like crap.

Exterior Check

Rust

A serious problem with the roofs of GM vans for more than two decades, "rust" is a four-letter word that means trouble. Don't buy any used vehicle with extensive corrosion around the roof-rails, rear hatch, wheelwells, door bottoms, or rocker panels. Bodywork in these areas is usually only a temporary solution.

Cosmetic rusting (rear hatch, exhaust system, front hood) is acceptable and can even help push the price way down, as long as the chassis and other major structural members aren't affected. Bumps, bubbles, or ripples under the paint may be due to repairs resulting from an accident or caused by premature corrosion. Don't dismiss this as a mere cosmetic problem; the entire vehicle will have to be stripped down, re-primed, and re-painted. GM has a secret warranty covering these hood repairs that can be extrapolated to other models and different body panels (see Part Two, page 82, and look at the GM minivan section in Part Three).

Knock gently on the front fenders, door bottoms, rear wheelwells, and rear doors—places where rust usually occurs first. Even if these areas have been repaired with plastic, lead, metal plates, or fibreglass, once rusting starts, it's difficult to stop. Use a small magnet to check which body panels have been repaired with non-metallic body fillers. Use a flashlight to check for exhaust system and suspension component rust-out. Make sure the catalytic converter is present. In the past, many drivers removed this pollution-control device in the mistaken belief that it would improve fuel economy. Police can fine you for not having the converter and can force you to buy one ($400 or more) before your vehicle can be certified.

Tires

Be wary of tire makes that have a poor durability record. Stay away from Firestone/Bridgestone makes for just that reason. Don't be concerned if the tires are worn, since retreads are inexpensive and easy to find. Look at tire wear for clues that the vehicle is out of alignment, needs suspension repairs, or has serious chassis problems. An alignment and new shocks and springs are part of routine maintenance and are relatively inexpensive in the aftermarket. However, if it's a 4×4 or the MacPherson struts have to be replaced, you're looking at a $1,000 repair bill. Expect to pay several thousand dollars more if your vehicle is equipped with run-flat tires. Owners report premature wearout, poor highway performance, and expensive replacement costs of over $1,000—if a replacement can be found.

Accident damage

Accident repairs require a further inspection by an independent body shop in order to determine if the frame is aligned and the vehicle is tracking correctly. Frameless minivans need extensive and expensive work to straighten them out, and proper frame and body repairs can often cost more than the vehicle is worth. In British Columbia, all accidents involving more than $2,000 in repairs must be reported to subsequent buyers. Here are some tips on what you can do to avoid buying a damaged vehicle. First, ask the following questions about the vehicle's accident history:

- Has it ever been in an accident?
- If so, what was the damage and who fixed it?
- Is the auto body shop that repaired the vehicle registered with the provincial government?
- Is there any warranty outstanding? Can you have a copy of the work order?
- Has the vehicle's certificate of title been labelled "salvage?" (Salvage means an expert has determined that the cost to properly repair the vehicle is more than its value. This usually happens after the vehicle has been in a serious accident.)

If the vehicle has been in an accident, you should either walk away from the sale or have the car checked by a qualified auto body expert. Remember, not all salvage vehicles are bad—properly repaired ones can be a safe and sound investment if the price is low enough.

Interior Check

The number of kilometres on the odometer isn't as important as how well the vehicle was driven and maintained. Still, high-mileage vehicles depreciate rapidly because most people consider them to be risky buys. Calculate 20,000 kilometres per year as an average and then take off about $200 for each additional 10,000 kilometres above this average. Be suspicious of the odometer reading. Confirm it by checking the vehicle's maintenance records. The condition of the interior will often give you an idea of how the vehicle was used and maintained. For example, sagging rear seats and a front passenger seat that's in pristine condition indicate that your minivan may have been used as a "minibus." Delivery vans will have the paint on the driver's doorsill rubbed down to the metal while the passenger's doorsill will look new.

What to look for

1. Watch for excessive wear of the seats, dash, accelerator, brake pedal, armrests, and roof lining.
2. Check the dash and roof lining for radio or cell phone mounting holes (suggesting it was a police car, taxi, or delivery vehicle). Is the radio tuned to local stations?
3. Turn the steering wheel—listen for unusual noises and watch for excessive play (more than a couple centimetres).
4. Test the emergency brake with the vehicle parked on a hill.
5. Inspect the seat belts. Is the webbing in good condition? Do the belts retract easily?
6. Make sure that door latches and locks are in good working order. If rear doors have no handles or locks, or if they've just been installed, your minivan may have been used to transport prisoners.
7. Can the seats be moved into all of the positions intended by the manufacturer? Look under them to make sure that the runners are functioning as they should.
8. Can head supports be easily adjusted?
9. Peel the rugs back and check the metal floor for signs of rust or dampness.

Road Test

1. Start the vehicle and listen for unusual noises. Shift automatics into Park and manuals into Neutral with the handbrake engaged. Open the hood to check for fluid leaks. This test should be done with the engine running and should be repeated 10 minutes after the engine has been shut down following the completion of the test-drive.
2. With the motor running, check out all dashboard controls: windshield wipers, heater and defroster, and radio.
3. If the engine stalls or races at idle, a simple adjustment may fix the trouble. Loud clanks or low oil pressure could mean potentially expensive repairs.
4. Check all ventilation systems. Do the rear side windows roll down? Are there excessive air leaks around the door handles?
5. While in Neutral, push down on the accelerator abruptly. Black exhaust smoke may require only a minor engine adjustment; blue smoke may signal major engine repairs.
6. Shift an automatic into Drive with the motor still idling. The vehicle should creep forward slowly without stalling or speeding. Listen for unusual noises when the transmission is engaged. Manual transmissions should engage as soon as the clutch is released. Slipping or stalling could require a new clutch. While driving, make absolutely sure that four-wheel drive can be engaged without unusual noises or hesitation.

7. Shift an automatic transmission into Drive. While the motor is idling, apply the emergency brake. If the motor isn't racing and the brake is in good condition, the vehicle should stop.

8. Accelerate to 50 km/h while slowly moving through all gears. Listen for transmission noises. Step lightly on the brakes; the response should be immediate and equal for all wheels.

9. In a deserted parking lot, test the vehicle's steering and suspension by driving in figure eights at low speeds.

10. Make sure the road is clear of traffic and pedestrians. Drive at 30 km/h and take both hands off the steering wheel to see whether the vehicle veers from one side to the other. If it does, the alignment or suspension could be defective, or the vehicle could have been in an accident.

11. Test the suspension by driving over some rough terrain.

12. Stop at the foot of a small hill and then see if the vehicle can climb it without difficulty.

13. On an expressway, it should take no longer than 20 seconds for most cars and minivans to accelerate from a standing start to 100 km/h.

14. Drive through a tunnel with the windows open. Try to detect any unusual motor, exhaust, or suspension sounds.

15. After the test-drive, verify the performance of the automatic transmission by shifting from Drive to Neutral to Reverse. Listen for clunking sounds during transmission engagement.

Many of these tests will undoubtedly turn up some defects, which may be major or minor (even new vehicles have an average of half a dozen major and minor defects). Ask an independent mechanic for an estimate and try to convince the seller to pay part of the repair bill if you buy the vehicle. Keep in mind that many 3- to 5-year-old vehicles with 60,000–100,000 km run the risk of an engine timing belt or timing chain failure that can call for several thousand dollars' worth of repairs. If the timing belt or chain hasn't been replaced, plan to do it and deduct about $300 from the purchase price for the repair.

It's important to eliminate as many duds as possible through your own cursory check since you'll later invest two hours and about $100 for a thorough inspection by a mechanic of your choice. Garages approved by the Automobile Protection Association (APA) or members of the Canadian Automobile Association (CAA) usually do a good job. CAA inspections run from $100 to $150 for non-members, depending upon their complexity. Remember, if you get a bum steer from an independent testing agency, you can get the inspection fee refunded and hold the garage responsible for your subsequent repairs and consequential damages, such as towing, missed work, or a ruined vacation. That little-known but highly useful court decision is found in Part Two.

Cutting Driving Costs

Used is a good start

Deciding to buy a used vehicle already cuts your acquisition costs in half. It's also likely that you will continue to save money during the sixth to the 10th year. After 10 years, some major repairs may be needed; however, you will still have saved a bundle of money.

Lower insurance rates

Insurance costs can average between $700 and $2,500 per year depending on where you live, the type of vehicle you own, your personal statistics and driving habits, and whether you can obtain coverage under your family policy. In fact, the ideal situation would be to buy a relative's car and add an insurance rider to the family policy, assuming everyone lives under the same roof. Although it seems unfair, your parents' premiums may be hiked automatically if you are a licensed driver living at home, whether you have your own car or not.

The Ontario-based InsuranceHotline.com (*www.insurancehotline.com*) has found that it pays to shop around for cheap auto insurance rates. In February of 2003, the group discovered that the same insurance policy could vary in cost by a whopping 400 percent. We are told the price gap is still just as wide in 2007.

A good insurance broker will offer you a variety of insurance discounts depending upon the type of car you drive, your driving record, and the number of vehicles insured. For example, some insurers will cut your rate by as much as 10 percent if a child on your policy is away at college (and not driving) or has an A or B average. Insurers also offer discounts to carpoolers and drivers who insure more than one car, have been accident-free for three years, are over 55 years old, are longtime customers, take defensive driving courses, or insure both their auto and home with the same insurer. Vehicles equipped with an anti-theft system also get discounted rates.

High deductible—Take a chance only with what you are willing and able to lose. A common collision deductible is $500. Raise it to $1,000, and your premium savings could jump to 40 percent. If it's an older car, you may want to drop collision altogether.

Low-risk vehicles—The Canadian Loss Experience Automobile Rating (CLEAR) assesses lower premiums for vehicles that experience fewer and smaller losses. Set up by the non-profit Vehicle Information Centre of Canada (VICC), CLEAR publishes a free pamphlet called *How Cars Measure Up*. Checking a vehicle's rating in the pamphlet before you buy could mean substantial insurance premium savings. See *www.ibc.ca/en/Need_More_Info/Car_Insurance_Publications.asp* (Insurance Bureau of Canada).

Keep in mind that all sizes of minivans, vans, pickups, and SUVs can be prohibitively expensive, while small economy cars will cost much less to insure. Also, vehicles five years or older will cost much less to insure for collision and comprehensive because they have already depreciated almost half their value.

Low mileage—Usually less than 20,000 km annually.

Driver education—Despite many independent health and safety studies that conclude driving education can give young drivers a false sense of security and lead to an increase in deaths and injuries by allowing them on the road before their sense of judgment is fully developed, insurers continue to give this discount. It applies no matter whether you take your course from a private or public agency or whether you're a young driver or a senior citizen.

Good driver—This means no moving violations or accidents over the past three to five years.

Accident settlements

Don't settle if it's not your fault; don't settle for less than you lost; and don't settle for the loss of your deductible.

If the accident was caused by a safety-related failure of the vehicle or by other external factors beyond your control, insist that the insurance company hold the guilty party responsible. There are thousands of lawsuits each year where automakers, municipalities, and provinces pay out millions in settlements for their negligence. Send a letter to the insurer stating you deny all liability and will *not* accept a rate increase for the accident.

Don't let the repairer put used or off-brand parts in your car. The U.S. Supreme Court has ruled that insurers must replace damaged parts with original-equipment parts sold by the auto manufacturer (*Avery v. State Farm* (1999) *www.state.il.us/court/Opinions/AppellateCourt/2001/5thDistrict/April/Html/5990830.htm*), and an Ontario class action lawsuit seeking similar relief was settled on January 31, 2006, in *Albert Hague and Terrance O'Brien v. Liberty Mutual Insurance Company*, Ontario Superior Court, Case No. 01-CV-204787CP, June 14, 2004.

The Ontario class action settlement isn't just for Liberty Mutual policyholders: *Lemon-Aid* readers throughout Canada may use the settlement as a bargaining chip with any insurer to get OEM parts put in their vehicles or to get a refund of the cost difference for non-OEM parts already installed (see *www.deloitte.com/dtt/cda/doc/content/Liberty%20Notice%20of%20Approval.pdf*).

Now we'll discuss how you can get the most out of your claim. If the vehicle is declared a "total loss," make sure you get its highest appraised value from either the *Canadian Red Book* or the *Black Book*. Better yet, visit a used-car lot and ask the sales agent what a car like yours would normally fetch. Give him or her a few dollars to write the estimate on a business card. This gives you an expert in your pocket who most insurers won't contest. Once the appraised amount has been agreed upon, insist that the insurer add the federal and provincial sales taxes you would owe on the appraised amount if you were to purchase an identical vehicle to the one you just lost (*restitutio in integrum*).

Most insurers will pay your deductible if the accident is clearly not your fault. If you are told it's your responsibility, file suit in small claims court against your insurer and the other party to recover your deductible.

Finally, when the repairs have been carried out, ask that the insurance adjuster approve the final job and then ask for a copy of the work order and any warranties that may apply to the repair. If there are any subsequent failures related to the repair, don't hesitate to bring the agent back to confront the repairer as your representative. This is particularly effective if the insurer chose the garage.

Fuel savings

Buy the cheapest brand of fuel available and use *www.gasbuddy.com* to take advantage of the 7–10 cent-per-litre price spread among gas stations. Sure, the oil company names and logos are different, but they mostly buy and sell the same gas from each other. So although you feel your car runs best on Shell, that last Shell fill-up may have been gas from elsewhere. Don't buy premium fuel unless it is required by the manufacturer: It can cause damage to your emissions system that will cost hundreds of dollars to rectify.

Cheap repairs

Watch out for "service advisors." They are there to sell check-ups and repairs, and they get a commission on each sale. In most garages, just opening a work order means they must charge you $50 to meet their costs. Therefore, know which small repairs and maintenance chores you can do yourself to save money, such as minor rust repairs, paint touch-ups, replacing wiper blades and headlight bulbs, and changing the air filter. Generally, independent garages that specialize in a particular service and offer extensive warranties on specific parts carry out the cheapest and most competent repairs.

Find a mechanic you can trust

Ask friends and neighbours for recommendations and then "test-drive" the garage by taking in your car for a few small jobs, such as an oil change, a tune-up, or a brake repair. It's a good idea to frequent repair agencies approved by a national motorist group like the non-profit Automobile Protection Association (APA), Canadian Automobile Association (CAA), the Alberta Motorist Association (AMA), or the Automobile Consumer Coalition. Canadian auto clubs are quite effective in steering owners toward good garages. When they make a mistake, they correct it, sometimes paying the claim themselves. They have work standards and complaint procedures that affiliated garages must follow, and they have a joint responsibility to ensure that your complaint is settled promptly and fairly. Be a bit of a pest. Try to find a garage that doesn't bar vehicle owners from interacting with the mechanics for "insurance reasons."

Trim scheduled maintenance costs

There are two ways to cut the cost of scheduled maintenance check-ups prescribed in the owners manual: Shop around and compare dealer prices (CBC TV's *Marketplace* found prices varied among Mazda dealers by hundreds of dollars), or get the check-up done by an independent garage (potential savings of about 30–50 percent). Contrary to what dealers will suggest, warranty repairs and after-warranty "goodwill" cannot be denied simply because the vehicle was checked out or repaired by an independent repair agency. Third-party oil changes, tune-ups, and other inspections are accepted by all automakers and have nothing to do with your warranty coverage. Just keep copies of your detailed work orders.

Making your car last

Here are some little things you can do: Clean corroded battery terminals with a stiff brush after pouring cola on the terminals to remove built-up deposits; wash your car weekly, and wax it at least twice a year; and keep your vehicle out of heated garages in snowbelt regions with heavy highway salt use.

INTERNET SLEUTHING

There are many important money-saving facts automakers and sellers don't want you to know, like realistic fuel-economy figures, their "bottom-line" price, lawsuits they have lost, whether other car owners have collected refunds for the exact same problem you have experienced, and the existence of secret warranties and internal technical service bulletins (TSBs).

All this information is updated annually in *Lemon-Aid*.

However, you can be your own *Lemon-Aid* expert on your vehicle if you have the time and knowledge to research websites that provide the most accurate and current data. Understand, you will find an abundance of information about used cars and minivans on the Internet, but much of it is distorted, misleading, or simply untrue. Automobile companies have helpful—though self-serving—websites featuring detailed sections on history, research, and development, and all sorts of information of interest to auto enthusiasts. Some automakers, such as Toyota, will even give you an online appraisal of your trade-in, although you can get a more realistic idea from the latest edition of *Lemon-Aid Used Cars and Minivans*. You can easily access manufacturers through a search engine like Google by typing in the automaker's name. For extra fun and a more balanced presentation, type in the vehicle model or manufacturer's name, followed by "lemon."

Auto Safety, Costs, Servicing, and Reviews

ALLDATA Service Bulletins (*www.alldata.com/recalls/index.html*)
This website gives you free summaries of automotive recalls and technical service bulletins. Detailed summaries will cost only $25 (U.S.) for hundreds of bulletins applicable to your vehicle dating back almost 30 years. This is a wise investment only if your car is a few years old, if there are quite a few accumulated bulletins, and if the base warranty has expired.

Use the service bulletins to prove that your vehicle's failure is caused by a manufacturing defect and shouldn't cost you a penny to fix, even if the expressed warranty is no longer in effect. Bulletins are highly useful as bargaining chips leading up to pre-trial mediation and small claims court hearings, especially if you threaten to present the bulletin in court and have it authenticated by the dealer's service manager or the car company's customer assistance rep.

Autoblog (*www.autoblog.com*)

All things automotive are found on this site. Despite numerous ads from the auto industry, Autoblog manages to be refreshingly independent in the news stories and articles it publishes. Information is always current, pictures are used effectively, and news sources are worldwide.

Automobile Consumer Coalition (*www.carhelpcanada.com*)

Founded by the former director of the Toronto Automobile Protection Association, Mohamed Bouchama, the ACC's Car Help Canada website provides many of the same services as the APA; however, it is especially effective in Ontario and Alberta.

Automobile Protection Association (*www.apa.ca*)

This Montreal-based consumer group fights for safer vehicles and has exposed many scams associated with new-vehicle sales, leasing, and repairs. For a small fee, it will send you the invoice price for most new vehicles.

Blue Oval News (*www.blueovalnews.com*)

This is a fiercely independent web site devoted to news, commentary, and speculation about the Ford Motor Company. It is the premier place to go for insider info on Ford's quality problems, administrative chaos, and future models. It was started in 1998 by Warner Robert, who posted Ford internal documents to prove that the 1999 Mustang Cobra had less horsepower than was hyped, forcing Ford to recall the model the following year. Ford lawyers were apoplectic and sued to have the information removed. The suit against Blue Oval News was filed in U.S. Federal court. It claimed illegal dissemination of trade secrets and copyright infringement and asked that the website be shut down. On September 7, 1999, Judge Nancy Edmunds ruled in favour of Blue Oval News on the basis of First Amendment rights to free speech (*www.blueovalnews.com/lawsuit_ford*):

> This case represents just one part of one skirmish—a clash between our commitment to the freedom of speech and the press, and our dedication to the protection of commercial innovation and intellectual property...in this case the First Amendment wins.
>
> U.S. FEDERAL JUDGE NANCY EDMUNDS

> Judge Edmund's order should be considered a precedent that underscores the fact that the First Amendment, which protects traditional media like print and television, also covers speech in cyberspace.
>
> WALL STREET JOURNAL

Canadian Automobile Association (*www.caa.ca*)

A non-profit, bilingual motorists' association that will save you tons of money if you use an affiliated garage to check out the vehicle you plan to purchase. The CAA's inspection reports are so credible that car sellers often negotiate the selling price downward to encompass repairs suggested by the CAA (called AMA in Alberta). CAA advisors are fairly knowledgeable about industry practices and scams in Canada's different regions. Approved garages are also obligated to let the Association mediate member and non-member sales or repair disputes. CAA has a handy checklist for "Keeping Track of Your Own Vehicle Costs" in their *Driving Costs* pamphlet found at *www.caa.ca/pdf/2007-04-27%20DrivingCostsBrochure 2007.pdf*.

CanadianDriver (*www.canadiandriver.com*)

An exceptionally well-structured and current Canadian website for new- and used-vehicle reviews, MSRPs, and consumer reports. Other auto magazine websites are *Automotive News* (*www.autonews.com*), *Car and Driver* (*www.caranddriver.com*), *Motor Trend* (*www.motortrend.com*), and *Road & Track* (*www.roadandtrack.com*).

CarProof (*www.carproof.com*)

CarProof (Email: *info@CarProof.com*; Tel: 519-675-1415) will tell you if a vehicle has been "scrapped," had flood or accident damage, been stolen, been paid for, or had its mileage turned back. There's a $25 (CDN) fee for an initial report; $45 (CDN) for an in-depth investigation.

CarTrackers (*www.cartrackers.com*)

Used vehicles, consumer advice, and environmental issues are all well covered in this site, which also features a terrific auto image gallery and an excellent automotive glossary.

CBC TV *Marketplace* (*www.cbc.ca/consumers/market/files/cars/index.html*)

An impressive array of auto consumer info based on investigative reports and other sources. The site features well-researched, useful Canadian information on used vehicles and safety-related issues.

Center for Auto Safety (*www.autosafety.org*)

A Ralph Nader–founded agency that provides free online info on safety- and performance-related defects for each vehicle model. Free vehicle reports based on owner complaints, but service bulletins are sometimes dated. Still, it's a good starting place for defect listings.

Chrysler Products' Problem Web Page (*www.wam.umd.edu/~gluckman/Chrysler*)
This is a great site for technical info and tips on getting action from DaimlerChrysler.

Consumer Guide, **Edmunds**, and **Kelley Blue Book** (*www.consumerguide.com, www.edmunds.com, www.kbb.com*)
In-depth reviews and owner critiques of almost every vehicle sold in North America, plus an informative readers' forum.

Consumer Reports and Consumers Union (*www.consumerreports.org*)
It costs $4.95 (U.S.) per month to subscribe online, but *CR*'s database is chock full of comparison tests and in-depth stories on products and services, including a "Cars for Teen Drivers" special feature. Download info like crazy during the first month of your subscription and then wait until the need arises to buy another month's worth of info.

Crashtest.com (*www.crashtest.com/netindex.htm*)
A website where crash tests from around the world can be analyzed and compared. A very helpful site if you are buying an older European vehicle that's never been crash-tested by NHTSA or IIHS.

VOLKSWAGEN CRASH-TEST RESULTS

	US front	US side (F)	EU front	EU side	Weight class	Overall rating
Beetle (1998–2006)	4	5	4	5	3	3
Golf (1999–2006 4 door)	5	4	4	5	3	5
Jetta (2005–06)	4	5	—	—	3	5

Source: Crashtest.com

Lawyers and Settlements (*www.lawyersandsettlements.com*)
This is a useful site for using a company's class action woes in U.S. jurisdictions as leverage in settling your own Canadian claim out of court. Plus, if you decide to go the Canadian class action route, most of the legal legwork will have been done for you. Suits regarding Lexus transmissions; Chrysler engine head gaskets; poorly performing, faulty Dunlop tires on Toyota Sienna minivans; Carfax deception; and the high sulfur content in Shell oil ruining GM gas gauges are among the many listed.

Lemon-Aid (*www.lemonaidcars.com*)
The official website of the *Lemon-Aid* annual consumer car guides. It is frequently updated with follow-up stories and comments from regional correspondents.

National Highway Traffic Safety Administration (www.nhtsa.dot.gov/cars/problems)
This American site has a comprehensive free database covering owner complaints, recall campaigns, crashworthiness and rollover ratings, defect investigations, service bulletin summaries, and safety research papers. Use with ALLDATA to compare service bulletins and owner complaints.

Online metric conversion (*www.sciencemadesimple.net/conversions.html*)
A great place to instantly convert gallons to litres, miles to kilometres, etc. An excellent website for converting fuel economy figures is *www.pege.org/fuel/convert.htm* (Planetary Engineering Group Earth).

OnTheHoist (*www.onthehoist.com*)
Kurt Binnie is a Canadian auto enthusiast who set up this website to give auto owners and shoppers balanced information relating to all aspects of the car industry. His reports are tough but fair. Kurt is especially knowledgeable about European cars and automotive pricing.

The Tire Rack (*www.tirerack.com*)
What, a tire retailer that puts out information stating that some new tires are trash? Yep, since 1997, The Tire Rack has published independent consumer surveys to help drivers know which are the best and worst tires on the market.

***Top Gear* road tests and buyer's guides** (*www.topgear.com*)
Britain's *Top Gear* blows the whistle on the best and worst European-sold vehicles, auto products, and industry practices.

Finally, here are a number of other websites that may be helpful:

General Auto Sites

everythingfordrivers.com/carforums.html
forum.freeadvice.com
www.all-lemons.com
www.autowarrantyreviews.org
www.baileycar.com
www.canadianwarrantycorp.com/news_tips.htm
www.carforums.com/forums
www.cartrackers.com/forums
www.mycarsucks.com
www.straight-six.com
www.which.net and *www.60millions-mag.com/page/common.accueil.* (British and French car ratings)
www.womanmotorist.com/index.php/welcome

Automakers

AUDI: *www.audiworld.com*

BMW: *www.bimmerfest.com/forums*
www.bmwboard.com
www.e38.org
www.mwerks.com

CHRYSLER: *dodgestories.blogspot.com*
www.flinksnorph.com/chrysler.html
intrepidhorrorstories.blogspot.com
www.angelfire.com/pa5/mspaul/autohome.html
www.daimlerchryslervehicleproblems.com
www.datatown.com/chrysler
www.donotbuydodge.ca
www.dontbuyone.org
www.mydodgesucks.org
www.ptcruiserclub.org
www.ptcruiserlinks.com
www.ptcruiserproblems.com

FORD: *forums.focaljet.com*
www.autosafety.org/article.php?scid=&did=309
www.consumeraffairs.com/automotive/ford_spark.html
www.consumeraffairs.com/automotive/ford_transmissions.htm
www.focusfanatics.com
www.ford-trucks.com/forums
www.v8sho.com/SHO/autoweek_online_cam_story.htm
www.v8sho.com/SHO/CamFailureClassActionSuitFiled.htm

GM: *www.mygmlink.com*
www.gminsidenews.com/forums
www.cadillacforums.com/forums
agmlemon.freeservers.com/index.html

LAND ROVER: *www.freelanderliving.com*
www.amug.org/~jthomas/for.html

LEXUS: *us.lexusownersclub.com*

MERCEDES-BENZ: *www.benzworld.org*
www.mercedesproblems.com
www.nagele.co.uk/ml320

MINI: *www.mini2.com/forum*

MITSUBISHI: *www.mitsubishisucks.com*

SAAB: *www.saabclub.co.uk*

TOYOTA: *www.siennaclub.org*

VW: *myvwlemon.com*
www.tdiclub.com
www.thesamba.com/vw
www.vwvortex.com

Help for Consumers

Government and non-government associations

Canadian Competition Bureau (*www.competitionbureau.gc.ca*)
The Competition Bureau is responsible for administration and enforcement of the *Competition Act*, the *Consumer Packaging and Labelling Act*, the *Textile Labelling Act*, and the *Precious Metals Marking Act*. Its role is to promote and maintain fair competition so that Canadians can benefit from lower prices, increased product choice, and quality services.

Most auto-related complaints submitted to the Bureau concern price-fixing and misleading advertising. The $2.3-million Toyota settlement announced a few years ago followed the Bureau's investigation into charges that the automaker rigged new car prices. Complaints can be filed online at *www.competitionbureau.gc.ca/internet/index.cfm?itemID=19&lg=e*.

Protégez-Vous (Protect Yourself) (*www.protegez-vous.qc.ca*)
Quebec's French-language monthly consumer protection magazine and website is a hard-hitting critic of the auto industry. It contains dozens of test-drive results and articles relating to a broad range of products and services sold in Canada.

See also: *www.consumeraffairs.com*
www.epa.gov/otaq/consumer/warr95fs.txt

Insurance

www.autoinsurancetips.com
www.insurance-canada.ca/consquotes/onlineauto.php
www.insurancehotline.com

Judgments

Canadian court decisions (*www.canlii.org* and *www.legalresearch.org/docs/internet3.html*)
Be your own legal researcher and save big bucks. Scan these websites to find court judgments from every province and territory, all the way up to the Supreme Court of Canada.

Supreme Court of Canada (*www.lexum.umontreal.ca/csc-scc/en/rec/index.html*)
It's not enough to have a solid claim against a company or the government. Supporting your position with a Supreme Court decision also helps. Four pro-consumer judgments rendered during the past four years are particularly useful:

- *Prebushewski v. Dodge City Auto (1985) Ltd. and Chrysler Canada Ltd.* Punitive damages are rarely awarded in Canadian courts and are almost never charged against automakers. When they are given out, it's usually for sums less than $100,000. In *Prebushewski*, the plaintiff got $25,000 in a judgment confirmed by the Supreme Court of Canada on May 19, 2005. It followed testimony from Chrysler's expert witness that the company was aware of many cases where daytime running lights shorted and caused 1996 Ram pickups to catch fire. The plaintiff's truck had burned to the ground, and Chrysler had refused the owner's claim, in spite of its knowledge that fires were commonplace.
- *Bannon v. The Corporation of the City of Thunder Bay.* An injured resident missed the deadline to file a claim against Thunder Bay; however, the Supreme Court maintained that extenuating factors, such as being under the effects of medication, extended her time to file. A good case to remember next time your vehicle is damaged by a pothole or you are injured by a municipality's negligence.
- *R. v. Guinard.* An insured posted a sign on his barn claiming the Commerce Insurance Company was unfairly refusing his claim. The municipality of Saint-Hyacinthe, Quebec, told him to take the sign down. He refused, maintaining that he had the right to state his opinion. The Supreme Court agreed.
  This judgment is the Canadian equivalent of the previously mentioned American judgment of *Ford v. Blue Oval News*. *Guinard* states that consumer protests, signs, and websites that criticize the actions of corporations cannot be silenced or pulled down simply because they say unpleasant things.
- *Whiten v. Pilot Insurance Co.* The insured's home burned down, and the insurance company refused to pay the claim. The jury was outraged and ordered the company to pay the $345,000 claim, plus $320,000 for legal costs and $1 million in punitive damages, making it the largest punitive damage award in Canadian history. The Supreme Court maintained the jury's decision, calling Pilot "the insurer from hell." This judgment scares the dickens out of insurers, who fear that they face huge punitive damage awards if they don't pay promptly.

See also: *classactionsincanada.blogspot.com*
www.cs.cornell.edu/Info/People/kreitz/Jeep/main.html
www.sshwlaw.com
www.vehicle-injuries.com/suv-safety-news.htm